TEACHING READING IN HIGH SCHOOL
Selected Articles

TEACHING READING

IN HIGH SCHOOL
Selected Articles

ROBERT KARLIN
Queens College of the City University of New York

The Bobbs-Merrill Company, Inc.
A Subsidiary of Howard W. Sams & Co., Inc.
Indianapolis • New York

TO EDITH

PREFACE

This anthology of high school readings is intended to serve as a companion book to *Teaching Reading in High School,* written by the author. It may be used also as a textbook on high school reading or as supplementary reading with other reading textbooks.

Such a book of readings serves several purposes. It enables the student of high school reading instruction to become acquainted with a number of viewpoints. It serves to give him a broad as well as a deep perspective on various aspects of teaching reading at the junior and senior high school levels. It makes it possible for him to become familiar with latest trends and developments. Finally, it makes available to him materials which he might not otherwise be able to enjoy.

The book is divided into fourteen chapters and three parts which parallel the organization of *Teaching Reading in High School.* The selections, most of which have been published since 1960, have been drawn from periodicals, monographs and bulletins which serve as primary sources in reading. Outstanding scholars and authorities in the field of reading as well as reading practitioners are represented in this collection of superior articles. Some of the selections are theoretical in nature; others represent research activities; still others are of the "how to" or practical type. The collection gives the student the opportunity to sample the best of the literature in high school reading and obtain a thorough understanding of problems and their solutions.

The author wishes to express his appreciation to all the publishers and authors who gave him permission to reprint the articles.

Robert Karlin

Sea Cliff, New York, 1968

CONTENTS

PART 2   THE READING SKILLS

1
Some Aspects of the Reading Problem in High School

Introduction

The importance of teaching reading in high school has not lessened. In fact, the need for providing a well-conceived reading program has grown, what with the increase in secondary schools' populations and the recognition that their curricula must be comprehensive.

Nevertheless, high schools as a rule have not provided for reading as they have for the physical and social sciences, mathematics, home economics, shop, art and music, and physical education. Investigators find that high school teachers and administrators believe in the importance of teaching reading but that comparatively few schools translate this belief into positive reading programs.

In this chapter Burton raises some serious questions about the status of reading instruction and reading, and he offers a challenge to those who would assume responsibility for change and innovation. Penty demonstrates the importance of teaching reading in high school and the relationship of a reading program to successful school performances. Carter and McGinnis underscore gaps in high school reading and suggest responsibilities of teachers and administrations.

The challenge is great. Are we ready to accept it?

HEADS OUT OF THE SAND:
Secondary Schools Face the Challenge of Reading
Dwight L. Burton

"The last American who sat down to read died in about the days of Henry Clay," remarked the humorist Stephen Leacock.[1] Leacock had in mind a certain kind of reading, but he was not serious and he certainly was not correct. In the days of Henry Clay,

Reprinted from *The Educational Forum*, XXIV (March 1960), 285–293, with permission of the author and © Kappa Delta Pi honor society.

[1] Stephen Leacock, "L'Evoi in Praise of Americans," *Laugh Parade* (New York: Dodd, Mead and Co., 1940), pp. 324–326.

reading, the gift of the few, was of small importance in the life of the average man, while today the American citizen cannot avoid reading (though he may not sit down when he does it!) even if he wanted to. Never before has the printed word assumed such importance as it does in American life today. The citizen, whether still in school or rather frighteningly out of it with his neat diploma, must shoulder a considerable burden of reading to get along independently.

Speaking of books, T. V. Smith says: "They tell us how to live alone and like it, or how to be happy though married. They teach us to grow thin if fat, fat if thin. They tell us how to keep accounts, repair machines, build houses, make love, bury our dead, till our soil, and lose our wrinkles."[2] Some facts reported by Dora V. Smith[3] show that this statement is not all facetious: (a) *The Pocket Book of Baby and Child Care* had sold 2,270,000 copies by 1949, surpassing all other information books in that series. (b) The Pittsburgh Plate Glass Company had received over a million requests each year for its booklet entitled *Color Dynamics in the Home*. (c) The Price Fireplace, Heater, and Tank Corporation had received sixty thousand requests for a set of instructions for making outdoor and indoor fireplaces. (d) The American Rose Society had more than 10,000 members who grew roses from printed directions in a handbook. (e) Star Kist Tuna's bulletin of favorite recipes of Hollywood stars went out at a rate of three thousand copies per week. (f) Over 800,000 people have studied music from printed directions sent out by the United States School of Music. (g) Within one week

[2] T. V. Smith, "Our Reading Heritage," in Alfred Stefferud, ed. *The Wonderful World of Books* (New York: New American Library, 1952), p. 19.

[3] Dora V. Smith, unpublished material partially reported in William S. Gray, ed. *Keeping Reading Programs Abreast of the Times* (Chicago: University of Chicago Press, 1950), pp. 3–8.

Country Gentleman magazine had fifteen hundred requests for a travel booklet on where to go and what to see on one's vacation. (h) Within one year, over 70,000 Girl Scouts learned to knit from the American Woolen Council's pamphlet, *Wool Around the World*. Americans read for assistance in the vital concerns of everyday life—and much of this reading is not easy.

I

Preparation for effective citizenship is a major aim of the secondary school program. All three of the traditional "R's" have always been closely linked to this aim, but the role of reading in effective citizenship today especially needs careful analysis by everyone associated with teaching in the junior and senior high school. For many students, graduation from high school marks the end of formal education and their induction into adult life. A question with which every high school teacher and administrator must reckon is "What does the high school diploma mean in terms of reading capacities for citizenship?"

The communication scene in contemporary American life presents a paradox. With the development of radio, motion picture, and television, this is an age of mass communication. A subject of much study has been the relationship of reading to these mass media. On the one hand, radio, motion pictures, and especially television compete with reading for the attention of people. The rather marked decline in the reading of fiction since World War II has been attributed, in part, to the development of television. The studies of televiewing habits reported by Paul Witty reveal the rather astonishing lien that TV has on the time of children and adults.

Yet, on the other hand, the mass media supplement and promote reading, too. Studies have shown, for example, that movie and

TV dramatizations of well-known books greatly accelerate the reading of those books, and radio commentary on important events and issues stimulates the reading of newspaper coverage of the same matters. Teachers of literature have found it helpful to refer to movies and television programs in discussing such points as credibility of plot, effective characterization, and theme in fiction. The paradox in the modern communication and entertainment scene lies in the fact that reading becomes more and more, rather than less and less, important with the constant expansion of other modes of communication and resultant vicarious experience. Preston identifies six unique functions of reading in an age of mass communication.[4]

(1) To supply a semblance of balance to the content of vicarious experience. Mass media entertainment tends to overstress certain elements in human experience.

(2) To provide a needed check upon the authenticity of the content of motion pictures and radio.

(3) To augment the individual's self-respect. Mass media tend to suggest that "the common man is indifferent to thought."

(4) To foster substantial human and social values. Radio and motion pictures "underplay elements essential in artistic living which are independent of wealth."

(5) To facilitate the exercise of language analysis without which comprehension of verbal communication remains incomplete. Re-reading, underscoring, checking, leisurely reflection are possible only with the printed page.

(6) To preserve mental health. Reading provides essential private experience in an "age of noise."

In another analysis, Nila B. Smith finds four advantages of reading over motion pictures and radio:[5]

(1) Reading embraces a greater range and variety of material.

(2) Reading material is more accessible at the time it is needed.

(3) Reading is more economical of time for the efficient reader. For example, a five-minute reading of the newspaper may be worth a fifteen-minute newscast on the radio.

(4) The reading process is more adjustable to individual purposes and interests.

That reading and the mass media are complementary has been emphasized by David Riesman, who points out that the mass media tend to bring people together while ". . . the book, like an invisible monitor, helps liberate the reader from his group and its emotions, and allows the contemplation of alternative responses and the trying on of new emotions."[6] Riesman points out that modern communication creates important new groupings—readers and non-readers and listeners and non-listeners—who may belong to the same economic and social groupings, "yet they have different values, different tastes, different turns of mind."[7] Teachers, then, can be less inhibited, perhaps, by concern for "socio-economic" level. Of course, Riesman reminds us, neither television nor books, of themselves, will necessarily proliferate nor alleviate the evils of the modern world, and Dan Lacy rejoices that George Orwell's gloomy prediction about the effect of mass media (*Nineteen Eighty-Four*) has not so far come true: "What speaks to us from the television screen is . . . only ourselves in our bland and blended average."[8]

[4] Ralph Preston, "The Changed Role of Reading," *Reading in an Age of Mass Communication* (Chicago: National Council of Teachers of English, 1949), pp. 1–18.

[5] Nila B. Smith, "Can Reading Withstand the Competition?" *Education*, 68 (June 1948), 616–620.

[6] David Riesman, *The Oral Tradition, The Written Word, and The Screen Image* (Yellow Springs, Ohio: Antioch Press, 1956), p. 13.

[7] *Ibid.*, p. 39.

[8] Dan Lacy, *Books and The Future: A Speculation* (New York: New York Public Library, 1956), p. 26.

Statements such as these stress reading's personal values at a time when other modes of communication and entertainment may seem to take over some of its functions. Reading for personal fulfillment remains a prominent activity of the mature citizen who realizes that the printed page is a major resource in the cradle-to-grave search for the "I," about which David Riesman was speaking when he said: "In place of the vision quest which led the Plains Indian youngster to face the desert alone, to discover his totem and his identity, I am suggesting that we substitute the solitary vision quest in the library."[9] This quest demands that the individual, adolescent or adult, occasionally through the pall of routine hold up his own inner vision of himself to comparison with others who, when circumstances demanded, were able to call up the necessary reserves of courage and resourcefulness, and that he test his own normality or lack of it against that of others. This he can do in reading where a theoretical and stereotyped average is not necessarily the measure of all things.

A hallmark of personal fulfillment, of maturity of mind itself, is an awareness of the complexity of human nature and an understanding of human motivation. The TV and movie screen ignores, in the main, this awareness, and presents a far more narrow range of motivation than does the printed page. Through reading, whether of fiction like *The Man in the Grey Flannel Suit* or non-fiction like *Annapurna*, the individual can probe the spirit that impels men, linking his own destiny to that of the entire human community and approach nearer that amorphous goal which we call wisdom.

Because, of course, effective living involves not only one's personal life and needs but also one's relations to the group and to the rest of the environment. The citizen who would be informed of the events, problems, and people of his society must, of necessity,

read. He has need of information that was of little importance in the past. For example, responsibilities of citizenship, as we define them today, extend beyond our national borders. World vision was demanded abruptly of the American people by a World War II which found Americans dying in lands they could not spell nor locate on a map, and by a subsequent "cold war" of ideas which embraces the globe. Foreign lands and people occupy a more prominent place today than ever before in American newspapers, magazines, and books. The role of reading in world understanding is defined clearly in a recent book:

> With the close of the war came the effort to establish a permanent peace. It was evident at once that this goal could not be achieved without a clear understanding of the conditions that existed in different parts of the world and of the characteristics, modes of life, ideals, and aspirations of various racial and nationality groups. In response to this need, much material has been published recently which aims to promote a penetrating grasp of current world problems. Its chief purpose is to make clear the conditions under which different peoples of the world can proceed with security and confidence in their efforts to attain common goals and aspirations. This purpose can be achieved only if the reader acquires an intellectual grasp and an emotional appreciation of world conditions and needs.[10]

Mere consumption of information in printed form is not enough, however. Critical reading is the all-important need in a society where a free marketplace of ideas is a cherished tradition. Americans of today are among the minority of the world's people who are not under some form of government censorship of reading material. But this means that in print the crooked and the inflammatory is marketed along with the straight and judicious. In his oft-quoted *Pref-*

[9] Riesman, *The Oral Tradition*, p. 27.

[10] William S. Gray and Bernice Rogers, *Maturity in Reading: Its Nature and Appraisal* (Chicago: University of Chicago Press, 1956), p. 6.

ace to Critical Reading, Richard Altick states that "because the use and misuse and abuse of words determine how people make up their minds, in a very real sense words are constantly shaping our destiny."[11] Altick goes on to challenge teachers to provide our democracy with "citizens who will use their dispassionate intelligence in weighing and acting upon the appeals which are directed to them from every source of social and political pressure."[12] And Dora V. Smith declares that "students must be alert to the techniques of the propagandist, to the slanted news story, and to the dangers of false inferences, of unsubstantiated generalization, and of the hidden implications and motives of the writer. Ability to analyze the source of the data and the purposes of the communication is a major need of today's readers."[13]

Although the American public, as a whole, has made steady progress toward greater literacy, studies of the reading habits of our people continue to produce some jarring results. In towns which have public libraries, card-holders comprise a small percentage of the population, and in many communities, especially in the Southeastern region, library facilities are meager or nil. Many schools and municipalities are tolerating depression-level libraries in a time of unparalleled prosperity. Mr. Dan Lacy poses this challenge:

> We have seen that the regular use of books as a principal source of ideas and inspiration and delight has been the practice of a quite small minority of the population who are participants in a highly literate cultural tradition. The future of books hangs really from two questions. One is whether we shall be able, as we hope, by a revolutionary extension of higher education to enlarge that minority. The other is whether the frequent use of books can be extended beyond that small minority to the many tens

of millions of adults who now rarely read a book.[14]

The results of a Gallup Poll in 1956 tended to show that the minority who habitually read books was "quite small" indeed. At the time of the poll only seventeen percent of the people sampled were reading books. The study by Gray and Rogers concluded that

> . . . not more than 10 per cent of adults voluntarily seek serious, challenging reading material; that half or more of the adult population read little more than the daily newspaper, a few periodicals of mediocre value, and an occasional mystery book; that another 30-40 percent limit their reading largely to immediate-reward reading, including low-grade fiction, in preference to serious reading that promises only delayed rewards.[15]

It is easy and quite customary to become doleful about the intellectual attainments of "the average man." Yet statements such as those just cited make complacency impossible. Undoubtedly the main influence on the reading habits of the public will continue to be the high school course of study.

II

Though the high school student is a citizen in his own right and is nearing full adult responsibilities of citizenship, one of his major concerns, shared by his teachers, is success in his school work. The junior and senior high school curriculum remains a reading curriculum to a large extent, and the student who cannot keep the pace in reading is destined for trouble. Consider the case of Frank, a seventh grader, whom the author followed through four classes one morning. In the social studies class the first period, Frank and his classmates were asked to read from the textbook a chapter entitled "This Is the City" and to be ready to discuss the questions at

[11] Richard Altick, *Preface to Critical Reading* (New York: Henry Holt and Company, 1946), p. xv.
[12] *Ibid.*, p. 7.
[13] Dora V. Smith, in Gray, *Keeping Reading Programs Abreast*, p. 5.

[14] Dan Lacy, *Books and the Future*, p. 20.
[15] Gray and Rogers, *Maturity in Reading*, p. 45.

the end. The chapter presented an enumeration of different ways of thinking of a city, definitions of the terms *urban* and *rural*, and a discussion of how towns and cities grow. A map depicting the steps in the growth of Baltimore was included along with a world map of urban areas of various sizes. The questions on the chapter were: (1) If you had your choice, would you prefer to live in a rural or urban area? List your reasons. (2) Tell how the Industrial Revolution helped cities grow. (3) Explain how a village in the United States might grow into a town and then a city.

Next Frank went to his class in mathematics where the students considered discount as a part of their study of percent. The class was given several problems to solve in which the regular price of an article and the rate of discount were given; the students were to find the amount saved on the article and the net price. In English the third period, the class read and discussed a short story. The students were asked to "characterize" one of the people in the story, to tell in what part of the country the story took place, and to select words by which the author let the reader know that the weather was hot. Next came the science class. Frank and the other students were assigned a chapter on water and asked to find out the following: (1) What are the sources of water? (2) How does pollution take place and how is water purified? (3) What is the water cycle?

It is obvious from this brief account of Frank's experience that reading is the common denominator in his work. Essential to his success in doing his various assignments is his ability to bring into play a number of reading skills, skills which differ from class to class and which represent a more complex level than those he needed in the elementary school. It is not surprising, then, that research shows a high relationship between reading ability and success in high school

work. A study by Aukerman[16] which concluded that general reading ability was the most significant differentiating factor between good and poor eleventh-grade students is characteristic. Reading ability is linked importantly with the holding power of the high school, too, since the student having difficulty with his work is the potential dropout.

The wide range in reading ability among junior and senior high school students presents secondary school teachers with one of their most vexing problems. Though Mr. Jones' students, for example, are all classified as seventh graders, there may be boys and girls who are the equal of tenth or eleventh graders. Some of Miss Smith's twelfth graders may be fifth or sixth graders in reading ability while others are at the level of college seniors. Classes above the sixth grade commonly present ranges of at least eight school years in ability to read. The challenge to adjust methods and materials of teaching to these ranges of ability is a stern one.

Complicating the problem is the extent of retardation in reading among secondary school students, the causes of which are various. Up to twenty percent of all junior and senior school students may be in need of small group or individual remedial work to correct specific reading disabilities. Reading abilities vary greatly not only from student to student but from school to school. In one area, an entire school may fall two or three years, on the average, behind national norms, while a school a few blocks away may be far above the average. Teachers in secondary schools must face the fact that grade labels may mean nothing in terms of reading ability.

[16] R. C. Aukerman, "Differences in Reading Status of Good and Poor Eleventh-Grade Students," *Journal of Educational Research*, 41 (March 1948), 498–515.

III

Planning a reading program in the high school will require before anything else a taking stock of the faculty's thinking. Certain relatively widespread assumptions among high school teachers have tended to impede progress. One of these is that the teaching of reading is a concern only of the elementary school. The genesis of the idea that a young-ster, at the completion of the sixth grade, should have mastered the complex process of reading remains one of the darkest mysteries of educational life. The plaints that "I could teach these kids something if they learned to read in the elementary school as they should" have been resounding for years.

Another of these assumptions is that teach-ing reading is separate and distinct from teaching subject matter. One irate science teacher remarked recently, "This about teach-ing reading is all very well, but I have too much science to teach to spend time fooling with reading." Yet the teaching of reading and study skills is an integral part of teach-ing any subject in which reading is a tool of learning. The efforts of teachers to teach reading in the various content fields are basic to the success of any junior or senior high school reading program.

Common, too, is the idea that the reading problem in the secondary school can be solved through remedial work alone. In at-tacking the reading problem, some secondary school faculties have failed to make an essen-tial distinction between "developmental" or general reading, which aims to meet the needs of all students, and "remedial" reading, which provides specific assistance to the small minority of retarded readers. Of course, the retarded reader needs attention, but the read-ing needs of all students must be the first concern. As general reading instruction be-comes increasingly effective, the need for remedial reading diminishes accordingly.

Another widely-held opinion is that the reading specialist or the English teacher should be responsible for the teaching of reading. Many teachers feel that only a read-ing specialist is qualified to do anything about reading at the secondary level. The specialist, which of course many schools do not have, can be highly important, since he usually acts as co-ordinator and resource person on read-ing and instructs the seriously-retarded read-ers, but his efforts are negligible if the class-room teachers take no responsibility for teaching reading.

Frequently, too, there is a feeling that English classes should take care of whatever reading instruction is needed. It is logical that the English teachers should spearhead the reading program; often they have greater background and interest in the field. But reading is no more important as a tool for learning in the English class than in most others, and responsibility for teaching read-ing cannot be delegated solely to English teachers any more than to teachers of social studies or science.

A final assumption is that the teaching of reading and the teaching of literature are one and the same. The unfortunate tendency to consider "reading" and "literature" as synonymous words has been given added impetus by the publication recently of "an-thology-readers," particularly for the junior high school. Such textbooks purport to be literature anthologies with handy reading programs built in. This is commercial bally-hoo. Reading skills are important means to ends in the study of literature, as in any other content. But it is farcical to reduce the study of literature, even in the junior high school, to the reading of stories followed by vocabu-lary drills, exercises in finding details or "main ideas," and drills designed to improve eye movements. It is treacherous, too, to as-sume that one is improving his general read-ing ability through practice only with selec-tions of literature.

In spite of these assumptions, the idea of all teachers teaching reading in junior and senior high schools is not a novel one. A number of successful programs are being carried on throughout the country, and reports of them furnish a basis for some conclusions about the steps necessary for a school to mobilize for the improvement of the students' reading. First, of course, someone, usually a person with over-all supervisory or administrative responsibility, has to initiate action. However, a committee of teachers, preferably representing various subject fields, may be set up to make other teachers aware of the problem and to enlist their support. Distribution of material showing the relationship between reading ability and achievement in various subjects is effective in arousing interest, since teachers naturally are interested in improving achievement in their subjects.

Since most high school teachers have had little or no training in the teaching of reading in their professional preparation, some faculty study of reading may be a necessary step. Misconceptions like those discussed earlier arise mainly from lack of insight into the nature of the reading process. Faculty meetings, seminars, or conferences may be organized at which professional materials and consultants are available.

An effective preliminary step, too, may be for teachers to study the reading demands of their subjects to discover what reading skills are particularly important in various subjects and what special difficulties in reading the various subjects pose. For example, in Rockford, Illinois, teachers in five areas—English, social studies, science, mathematics, and home economics—made an analysis of the reading skills necessary to do the assignments in their classes. The results of the analysis were summarized and made available to all teachers.[17]

[17] Lois Dilley, "All Teachers Teach Reading," School Review, 52 (December 1944), 597–605.

An essential step is the appraisal of the reading abilities and habits of the students. "Where do our students stand in reading now?" is a question that must be answered before definite plans for improvement can be made. This question can be answered through the use of standardized tests, teacher-made tests, and inventories of interests and habits.

With these things done, the time comes for definite action in which adjustments are made in courses of study and in materials and methods of teaching used in the classroom. This is the point at which the teacher makes a definite attack on those skills important in his subject, attempts to meet ranges of ability, and exploits the possibilities of his subject for developing the reading skills and habits important for effective citizenship. In short, as the cliche has it, each teacher becomes a teacher of reading within his subject.

It will be necessary, too, for the school to make some provision for corrective or remedial reading, to deal with specific reading disabilities of students whose reading achievement lags behind their intellectual potential. Many books and articles about procedures and material for such a program are available.

Although the all-school attack on reading is the hallmark of an effective program, experience in many colleges and high schools has proved the value, too, of direct attention to basic reading skills outside the framework of any particular subject.

Most commonly in high schools, basic reading instruction—involving attention to vocabulary and word attack skills, comprehension, and speed—has been centered in the English classes. Some excellent results have been reported, but it seems questionable to make general reading instruction the exclusive responsibility of English teachers. Already the English curriculum is overcrowded, and English teachers complain, with some justification, that everything that needs doing is "dumped" into the English course merely because it is the only one required at all grades.

A more satisfactory solution is found in the separate reading improvement course which is required or offered as an elective in a number of schools. If the course is elective, it is important that students who really need the work be guided into it. It is highly important, too, that the stigma of a "dummy" class not be attached to the reading improvement course and that it not become the dumping ground for discipline problems and slow learners.

Apparently, the developmental reading program prospers most when an all-school attack on reading is supplemented with general, basic reading instruction. With a curriculum that demands a high level of reading proficiency and a way of life in which effective citizenship is thwarted and personal fulfillment stunted without reading skill and interest, the high schools of the land cannot afford to keep their heads in the sand.

READING ABILITY AND HIGH SCHOOL DROP-OUTS
Ruth C. Penty

As director of counseling in the Battle Creek High School, I had opportunity to talk with boys and girls about both their scholastic difficulties and personal problems. I also had opportunity to talk with teachers and parents about the problems of young people. In addition, I had access to the mental maturity and reading scores as well as to the cumulative records of the boys and girls enrolled in our high school.

All of these contacts seemed to point to trouble with reading as one of the basic difficulties in connection with academic problems. Trouble with reading also appeared to be related to some personal problems. Therefore, while I was continuing my work in the guidance area, I also took some courses in secondary school reading so that I could better assist these young people who were having difficulties with reading and so that I

Reprinted from the *Journal of the Association of Women Deans and Counselors*, XXIII (Oct. 1959), 42–48, with permission of the author and National Association of Women Deans and Counselors.

could better assist teachers in helping them.

Reading test scores showed that many of our incoming sophomore students were reading far below grade level, and corresponding mental maturity scores pointed to the fact that these students had potential for growth in reading. At the other end of the scale, our Principal-Freshman Conferences were informing us that some of our freshmen college students were not doing well in their content areas or were staying up until one or two o'clock in the morning in an attempt to prepare their assignments, as they read so slowly, did not comprehend or know how to comprehend what they read.

In 1951, we therefore started a reading improvement program in our high school, concentrating our help on our sophomore and senior students. We encouraged all teachers to assume responsibility for the development of vocabulary in their respective subject areas, to help students enrolled in their classes to read and study the content involved, and to organize that material through notetaking, outlining, answering of questions, or some other method appropriate to the subject. We also encouraged all classroom teachers to adjust textbooks and other reading materials to the reading level of students. The tenth- and twelfth-grade English teachers assumed responsibility for many aspects of the reading program: (1) the diagnosing of individual difficulties, (2) helping with techniques of finding main thought and important detail, (3) improving speed of comprehension and several other skills needed by the boys and girls in their classes. Special reading groups were also organized to assist those students who were very retarded in reading and who needed help with basic vocabulary and the development of word attack skills. For these students, very easy reading material had to be provided.

As you who work in public schools would predict, not all teachers became enthusiastic participants in this reading improvement effort, either because they felt that the high school was assuming an elementary school task, because they actually believed that high school students should be able to read and study their assignments if they applied themselves, or because they felt insecure about giving help because of lack of training.

At this time, our high school administration became very interested, as did administrators across the nation, in the number of boys and girls who were dropping out of school before high school graduation. We therefore increased our extracurricular program, set up a Basic Living Course requirement for all sophomore students, and prepared an Exit Interview Sheet for the use of all counselors so that we could gather together some data based on reasons why young people leave school. We had a hunch that reading ability might be an important factor connected with the school leaving of boys and girls. However, we did not have valid evidence. The reasons most frequently given on our Exit Sheets were (1) work too

difficult, (2) lack of interest, (3) work not suited to the abilities of students, (4) desire to get a full-time job.

Here was a doctoral research problem in which I was really interested—a study of reading ability and high school drop-out. I felt that it might give impetus to our reading program and that the findings might add to the literature on early school leaving. In searching the literature, I found only four very brief studies of reading ability as a factor in school drop-out. None of these was a concentrated study of the specific problem.

In addition to the reading and mental maturity testing data on sophomore students for a four-year period, for those who left school and for those graduated, and Exit Interview Sheets for drop-outs, we decided to interview the poor readers enrolled in the current senior class in the high school, the poor readers who had graduated in the three-year period, and all of the poor readers who had dropped out of school. Interviewing was done after school, evenings, week ends, and during the summer in the homes of former students or in a private office in the local YWCA.

The order of presentation of data was then prepared. It was planned to study (1) reading achievement of the group studied, (2) proportion of drop-outs and graduates among poor readers and good readers, then to make (3) a more intensive study of the poor readers with the questions in mind: (a) What percentage dropped out of school? (b) What percentage remained to graduate? (c) At what time did students drop out of school? (d) How did the drop-outs and graduates among poor readers compare in intelligence test scores? (e) What was the reading growth potential of the poor readers who dropped out and those who graduated? (f) How did a sampling of these two groups feel about themselves and their school subjects? (g) What was their attitude toward reading and toward teachers? (h) What were their relations with other students? and (i) What reasons did they give for leaving school or for graduating?

The interviews held with both drop-outs and graduates were very interesting in themselves and they also yielded highly significant data. The free response questions asked of the school leavers were these:

1. Please think back to the time you left school. What reasons did you give for leaving school?
2. As you think back now, what would you you say were your *real* reasons for leaving school?

The free response question asked of the graduates was: What do you think are the main reasons why you remained in school until graduation?

The structured question included:

1. Those related to subjects liked and disliked
2. Types of reading troubles encountered when reading was mentioned as a source of difficulty
3. The amount of time spent in preparation of subjects
4. Frequency of participation in class discussions
5. Feelings of students toward themselves, toward other students, and toward teachers
6. Participation in extraclass activities
7. Help obtained in the reading area

In very few cases were reasons given on the Exit Sheet by students at time of school leaving like the reasons given by these young people from one to six years afterwards. Only 5 percent of the students who dropped out of school gave the same reason at the time of school leaving that they gave later in their interview. The type of answer given at exit was in most cases one which was acceptable and which permitted easy escape. In the later conference, reasons given seemed more nearly like basic reasons. The following are selected from reasons given by dropouts who were far below grade in reading:

> I was discouraged. I was not getting any place in school. I thought the Marines was a better place to be. I had difficulty in reading. I couldn't remember what I read. I was often embarrassed in class.
>
> I didn't like school too well. I wanted to get married. I couldn't remember what I read. I didn't like to go to classes and be around other kids who seemed to learn more easily than I did.
>
> I left school because I had to help support my mother and I was under the impression that I was inferior to the rest of the kids. I had trouble with reading, too. I couldn't keep my mind on it. I was afraid of being laughed at if I didn't know the answers. I would like to read better and still would.
>
> I was nervous at school. I felt all right when I started to work outside. I had trouble in getting the ideas from my reading. The words bothered me, too. I didn't like to recite in class. I would rather write my answers than give them before the class.
>
> We were always quarreling at home. I wasn't getting along in some subjects at school either. I wanted to get married. I think now that marriage isn't always rosy. It is better for kids to finish school first. I understand what I read if I am interested. English and history were hard for me. I didn't know some of the words so I couldn't understand them.

These statements made by poor readers during the interviews emphasize the multiplicity of reasons why boys and girls leave school before graduation. They also point to the influence which reading difficulty has in causing young people to make a decision to leave school when that difficulty causes them to fail subjects, to receive low grades, and to feel that they are inadequate and not able to learn through reading.

In response to the interview question, "What do you think are the main reasons why you continued in school until graduation even though you had some difficulty with reading?" these were some of the answers given:

> Because I realized that you couldn't get much of a job if you did not graduate.
> My parents encouraged me.
> It was taken for granted that I would. My parents finished high school.
> My dad and my counselor encouraged me.
> I liked the classes, especially the discussions. I also liked band and physical education.
> I had a deep desire to graduate. I am the only one in my family who did.
> My mother and dad wanted me to. I liked the kids.

Strong personal desire to graduate, encouragement of family, family expectation, interest in specific subjects, interest in sports and other extracurricular subjects, desire for a better job, help from counselors and teachers, and liking to be with other young people were among the reasons why these students who had trouble in reading continued through school until graduation.

The following is a summary of findings,[1] followed by conclusions and implications for education.

More than three times as many poor readers as good readers dropped out of school before graduation; the peak of the school leaving among the drop-outs was during the tenth grade.

There was no significant difference in average reading scores at the tenth-grade level of the poor readers who dropped out of school before graduation and of the poor readers who remained in school until graduation.

The interview data emphasized that difficulty in reading played a very important role in the school leaving of boys and girls, especially when certain other problems and pressures were present.

It was evident from the data that the poor readers who remained in school also had difficulty in reading. However, the better emotional and social adjustment of the graduates, probably the result of home security, interest, and economic status superior to that of the boys and girls who dropped out of school, and also of more fortunate school experiences, permitted them to be less burdened by a multiplicity of problems among which the reading problem was one. Among the poor readers who graduated were some who felt that people expected them to graduate: they had always expected to graduate from high school; their parents encouraged them; their teachers and counselors helped them; they had "made up their minds" to graduate and had set this as their goal. A few thought a high school education would help them get a better job. Last, but not least, they were getting some real satisfactions from school: they enjoyed the school dances, athletics, and other extraclass activities, were interested in doing well in one or more subjects, and "liked the kids" in their school. These seemed to be some of the reasons why pupils of low reading ability persisted in school until they graduated. To prevent a high percentage of drop-outs, more attention should be given to these favorable conditions.

A study of the disparity between reading ages and mental ages of the poor readers who dropped out of school and of the poor readers who remained in school but who experienced difficulty in reading, revealed that a very large percentage of the young people in both groups had potential in reading ability. With proper help, these students could have shown marked improvement in reading ability, which would probably have contributed to better scholastic achievement and personality adjustment.

[1] For more detail see Ruth Penty, *Reading Ability and High School Drop-Outs* (New York: Bureau of Publications, Teachers College, Columbia University, 1956).

SOME SUGGESTIONS GROWING OUT OF AN EVALUATION OF READING INSTRUCTION BY SECONDARY TEACHERS AND THEIR STUDENTS

Homer L. J. Carter and Dorothy J. McGinnis

A study (7)* made at Western Michigan University in 1958 shows that secondary teachers in Michigan recognized the reading deficiencies of their students and pointed out frankly that they, in general, were not assuming responsibility for the teaching of reading and were not adequately prepared to do so. It is the purpose of this presentation to show some of the needs of reading instruction at the high school level and several of the factors involved. Sporadic attempts now being made to meet the reading needs of pre-college students are briefly summarized. Four types of reading instruction and means of implementation are set forth.

REPORTED NEED OF READING INSTRUCTION

In the study by McGinnis each of 570 secondary teachers was asked to estimate the percent of his students possessing reading skills essential to the work required. The mean percent was 67. It is obvious, then, that approximately one-third of the students being taught by these teachers did not read well enough to do the work expected in high

Reprinted from *New Concepts in College-Adult Reading, Thirteenth Yearbook of the National Reading Conference* (1964), 43–50, with permission of the authors and National Reading Conference, Inc.
[*Numbers in parentheses refer to Bibliography at the end of this article.]

school classes. The responses of 1,029 college freshmen provide further evidence to substantiate the need of reading instruction at the high school level. When asked, "Did your high school teachers show you how to improve your ability and skill in reading?" 61 percent answered "No." Furthermore, 83 percent said that "a high school course in the improvement of reading would have been beneficial to them." Upon entering college 30 percent of these students reported that they were not reading well enough to do satisfactory college work. Some specific reading skills recognized by these young people as essential to their academic progress are:

1. Vocabulary development
2. Word study and spelling
3. Chapter reading
4. Concentration upon reading
5. Problem solving
6. Critical evaluation of writer's bias and preconceived ideas
7. Identification, interpretation and evaluation of ideas
8. Adjustment of rate to purpose and difficulty of material

It is obvious from a consideration of these skills identified by the students that the high school program in reading should be designed to develop at least these minimal essentials.

RESPONSIBILITIES AND EDUCATIONAL BACKGROUND OF SECONDARY TEACHERS

In the study reported by McGinnis approximately 70 percent of the high school teachers responding to the questionnaire stated that they were not expected to assume responsibility for providing instruction in reading. Furthermore, 90 percent of the teachers indicated that while in college they did not receive any instruction on how to teach reading to high school students. In answering, however, the question, "Should prospective secondary teachers be taught how to develop on the part of their students fundamental reading skills?" ninety percent of the 570 teachers gave an affirmative answer. From 56 percent to 80 percent of the secondary teachers did not receive instruction while in college or university on the subject of how to:

1. Develop vocabularies of their students
2. Teach chapter reading
3. Teach students to concentrate
4. Develop problem-solving skills in field of specialization
5. Teach students to read critically and evaluate a writer's bias and use of preconceived ideas
6. Show students how to identify, interpret and evaluate organization and relative importance of facts, data, and information
7. Adjust materials to the interest and reading levels of their students

In view of these facts, it is obvious that the majority of high school teachers are not expected to assume responsibility for providing instruction in reading, and it is apparent that they believe that they are not prepared to do so. An analysis of the responses of 570 secondary teachers and of 1,029 college freshmen shows that the latter point out their lack of reading skills in the identical areas in which high school teachers proclaim their lack of instruction.

SOME ATTEMPTS TO DEVELOP BETTER READERS

Investigations (1, 10) show that teachers in the content fields are assuming increased responsibility for teaching reading and study skills. Teachers in some high schools are devoting specified amounts of time to such instruction. Reading teachers serve as consultants as well as teachers of developmental reading. Faculties cooperate systematically in providing developmental instruction for all students and individualized instruction for those in need of specialized help.

Some high schools devote one day a week to teaching reading and study skills in connection with assignments in the content areas. Other schools have reading laboratories to which classes are assigned throughout the year. Some high schools have courses in reading, the content of which provides half of the year's required work in English. In other schools developmental instruction in reading is provided by English teachers as a part of the language arts program. In some high schools classes in reading are scheduled for periods generally spent by students in the study hall. Consequently, no time is taken from other classes and instruction is provided in a reading laboratory adequately equipped. In general, local conditions and the educational philosophy of the staff determine the choice of plans for providing developmental and clinical approaches to the teaching of reading. It is significant that in some communities something is being done.

KNOWLEDGE OF STUDENT BACKGROUND, A FACTOR

Teachers, in general, are fairly well acquainted with some of the psychological and educational differences of their students. They are aware of the great range of abilities and interests found within their classes. They understand the loyalty of adolescents for members of the group. Most teachers appreciate the sensitivity and insecurity experienced by their boys and girls and how overcompensating behavior is a natural consequence. Few secondary teachers, however, recognize the extent to which home environment and experiential background affect the vocabularies and reading skills of their students. Parr (8), in his study of students who were poor readers, found a lack of reading material in the home, lack of interest in reading, and little or no recreational reading during childhood. Jackson (5) found socio-economic status, family size, and parental education level to be distinguishing factors between retarded and non-retarded readers. A more recent study by Sheldon and Carrillo (9) shows that retarded readers generally come from large families of lower socio-economic status, have fewer books available, and have parents who left school earlier than the parents of advanced readers. A study by McGinnis (6) in 1963 shows that the parents of superior readers and the parents of inferior readers differ significantly in their attitudes toward certain child rearing practices, the importance of reading, the value of language development, and the importance of experiential background. These differences in attitudes suggest differences in kind and degree of mental content which children have an opportunity to acquire. Most parents prepare their children physically for a trip to the mountains by providing them with adequate shoes and warm clothing suitable for changes in temperature. Some parents also prepare their children educationally and psychologically for these new experiences by stimulating interest and by encouraging questions such as:

How and when were mountains formed?
Why are some rocks in layers?
Why do the trees differ from those in the valleys?
Why does it rain so frequently in the mountains and so seldom in the desert?

Family discussions can stimulate a desire for more information and can lead to an effective use of reference materials. Some parents are aware of the fact that if their children are to learn, they must have adequate background and mental content for they realize that new experiences are interpreted in terms of the old. The secondary teacher should understand that mental content is of the utmost importance because each student must bring to the printed page even more than he is able to take away. Mental content will affect his thinking, his doing, and his feeling. To a large degree the school must provide not only a place where mental content is acquired but, more important, a source of stimulation for greater accumulation and integration of content essential to thinking, doing, and feeling. This is a requirement for effective reading.

FOUR TYPES OF READING INSTRUCTION

If high school students are to grow in reading efficiency, the administration should maintain four kinds of reading instruction. 1) Basic instruction can develop the student's ability to identify, interpret, and evaluate ideas. 2) Corrective and individualized instruction can be provided for students who are reading below the sixth grade level. 3) Instruction can be designed to integrate basic skills in order to meet the requirements of the content subjects. 4) Instruction utilizing reading materials of various types can be helpful in developing mental content, extending interests, and improving literary tastes. In order to make it possible for high school students to have these experiences, it may be advisable to organize a course in developmental reading and establish a reading laboratory for diagnosis and individualized instruction.

A course, for example, known as Effective Reading can be taught to high school students so as to provide basic instruction in reading and also to show how these basic skills may be integrated in order to meet the requirements of the content subjects. This use of textbooks has been demonstrated by Carter and McGinnis in their work with college students (2, 3, 4). In other words, students can improve their reading as they do their regular academic work. Furthermore, in this course students can be encouraged to read materials of various kinds of degrees of difficulty so as to develop mental content, develop latent interests, and improve literary tastes. Flexible grouping of students makes it possible for those studying the same texts or subjects to work and receive aid at the same time. In group discussion, mental content can be "pooled" so that each individual can profit from the experiential background of his associates. It is obvious, then, that such a course can utilize three of the four types of reading instruction previously suggested.

In every secondary school, however, there are students reading at the fifth grade level and below who are in need of diagnostic and individualized instruction. In dealing with these students one is concerned with the individual, his physical and psychological background, his home environment, his personality, and his immediate and ultimate goals. An emphasis is placed upon why the student is having difficulty and upon selection and organization of treatment. This approach is primarily clinical in nature.

In addition, classroom teachers should assume responsibility for developmental reading in their subject matter fields. These teachers can teach chapter reading, develop vocabularies, and adjust reading materials to the interest and reading levels of their students. Is it not possible for teachers of English, social studies, science, and mathematics to set forth and demonstrate reading procedures and thinking skills which are especially related to these subject matter areas?

Surely, they can if they are adequately prepared.

PREPARATION OF TEACHERS

Data presented in this paper show that individuals should be made available for the teaching of reading at the secondary level. Suitable courses and laboratory experiences must be provided in colleges and universities at both the undergraduate and graduate levels which will adequately prepare these teachers for their classes in Effective Reading. They, as well as subject matter specialists, should be ready to show their students how to read a chapter effectively and well. They should be acquainted with the various ways of developing the vocabularies of their students. They should be familiar with the steps in problem solving and the different factors to be considered in doing critical reading. They should be able to teach their students how to concentrate, how to identify, interpret and evaluate ideas, and how to adjust rate of reading to the purpose of the reader and the difficulty of material. On the other hand, clinical work in reading for high school students achieving at the fifth grade level and below should be done under the direction of a special teacher with background not only in education but psychology, sociology, and medicine. Teaching and intern experiences under careful supervision are necessary prerequisites. This individual should be certified by the state board of education as a competent and well trained reading clinician.

SUMMARY

In general, teachers recognize the need of developmental reading at the secondary level. The majority, however, are not required to assume the responsibility of providing reading instruction nor are they prepared to do so. Some high school teachers are developing basic reading skills and are showing how these may be integrated while the student does his regular academic work. In this paper four kinds of reading instruction have been set forth, and two procedures have been outlined showing how they may be facilitated. A knowledge of the student's background and the importance of his mental content have been stressed. Suggestions for the preparation of high school teachers who are to provide specific instruction in reading have been briefly outlined. Cooperative effort and integration of educational philosophy on the part of teachers and administrators are essential if young people at the pre-college level are to be taught to read effectively.

BIBLIOGRAPHY

1. BOND, GUY L., and KEGLER, STANLEY B., "Reading in Senior High School," in N. B. Henry, ed. *Development in and through Reading.* Chicago: University of Chicago Press, 1961, Ch. 18.
2. CARTER, HOMER L. J., "Effective Use of Textbooks in the Reading Program," in O. S. CAUSEY and W. ELLER, eds. *Eighth Yearbook of the National Reading Conference.* Fort Worth: Texas Christian University Press, 1959, pp. 155–163.
3. CARTER, HOMER L. J., "Improving Reading in the Subject Matter Areas," in O. S. CAUSEY and E. P. BLIESMER, eds. *Ninth Yearbook of the National Reading Conference.* Fort Worth: Texas Christian University Press, 1960, pp. 67–71.
4. CARTER, HOMER L. J., and McGINNIS, DOROTHY J., *Effective Reading for College Students.* New York: The Dryden Press, 1957.
5. JACKSON, JOSEPH, "A Survey of Psychological, Social, and Environmental Differences Between Advanced and Retarded Readers," *Pedagogical Seminary and Journal of Genetic Psychology,* 65:113–131, 1944.
6. McGINNIS, DOROTHY J., *A Comparative Study of the Attitudes of Parents of Superior and Inferior Readers Toward Certain Child Rearing Practices, the Value of Reading, and the Development of Language Skills and Experiential Background Related to Reading.* (Unpublished doctoral dissertation, Michigan State University, 1963.)
7. McGINNIS, DOROTHY J., "The Preparation and Responsibility of Secondary Teachers in the Field of Reading," *The Reading Teacher,* 15:92–97, November, 1961.
8. PARR, FRANK W., "Factors Associated with Poor Reading Ability of Adults," *School and Society,* 35:626, May 7, 1932.
9. SHELDON, WILLIAM D., and CARRILLO, LAWRENCE W., "Relation of Parents, Home, and Certain Developmental Characteristics to Children's Reading Ability," *Elementary School Journal,* 52:262–270, January, 1952.
10. STRANG, RUTH, and BRACKEN, DOROTHY KENDALL, *Making Better Readers.* Boston: D. C. Heath and Company, 1957, Ch. 4.

PART 1
BACKGROUND TO READING

Introduction

This section consists of three chapters: Causes of Reading Difficulties, Psychology of Reading and Learning, and Measurement and Evaluation of Reading Achievement. They provide the background and bases for understanding the nature of reading and the reading-learning process and for developing strategies that translate present knowledge into dynamic teaching plans.

In Chapter 2 Johnson offers a comprehensive summary of the research into the causes of reading failures. Barbe takes the position that some reading problems are caused by instructional failures. Strang supports a guidance approach to overcoming reading difficulties since she found that most serious reading problems involve emotional difficulties.

Chapter 3 contains several models for explaining the nature of the reading process although Weaver takes the position that there is no adequate theory of reading. Holmes suggests the dimensions of reading ability and cites the results of studies to support them. Warfel discusses the science of linguistics and its relationship to the study of reading. Social factors that influence reading growth are discussed by Havighurst. Ausubel describes known learning principles that suggest teaching strategies for culturally different pupils. Lastly, Karlin raises questions regarding reading research and the reading process and offers some suggestions for dealing with current areas of concern.

The importance of measurement and evaluation of reading ability in providing meaningful teaching programs is reflected in Chapter 4. Strang offers procedures classroom teachers can use to discover each student's strengths and weaknesses. Davis offers several cautions in selecting and administering standardized reading tests and interpreting their results. Bliesmer explores formal and informal assessment of vocabulary and word-attack skills and provides guidelines for assessing these skills. McDonald challenges present practices and suggests meaningful ways to measure flexibility in reading.

Together, these three chapters serve as foundation stones upon which schools can build reading programs. They offer some rationale for establishing unique reading programs that possess common as well as different features. Thus, indiscriminate efforts are avoided and students receive the benefits of superior reading plans.

2
Causes of Reading Difficulties

FACTORS RELATED TO DISABILITY IN READING
Marjorie Seddon Johnson

INTRODUCTORY STATEMENT

One of the pressing problems facing educators and psychologists in recent years has been that of the child who fails to acquire facility in the processes of reading and writing. Some of the pupils do not achieve in written language on a level with others of their age because they do not have the general capacity for achievement in any area. Others who lag considerably behind the average for the age group are alert in areas which do not require dealing with printed and written language symbols.

For those pupils who are mentally retarded, various plans for education have been evolved. Considerable attention has been devoted to them in the professional literature (95)* as well as in the teachers' meetings of most schools. Special classes have been set up. Attempts have been made to provide these people with whatever kind of help will enable them to lead most nearly normal and self-directing lives. The futility of attempt-

Reprinted from the *Journal of Experimental Education*, XXVI (September 1957), 1–26, with permission of the author and Dembar Educational Research Services.

[*Numbers in parentheses refer to Bibliography at the end of this article.]

ing to teach them information and processes beyond their capacity has been fairly widely recognized. Instead of many "reteachings" of matter beyond their grasp, adjustments have been made in the programs which they follow.

Unfortunately, equivalent steps have not been taken to care for those who "fail" in reading but are otherwise alert. Too often the child who fails, not because of limited general capacity, but for other reasons, has been neglected. In many cases he has been labeled as of low level capacity and, therefore, not expected to achieve. He has been placed with children of limited intelligence and provided the same type program as they. At other times he has been considered lazy and negativistic to learning. Parents and teachers alike may have recognized that he is not unintelligent. He speaks and acts intelligently about things that interest him. He does well in out-of-school activities that obviously require an alert mind. Hence, they reach the conclusion that the explanation can only be that he does not try to do well in school. They are certain that all it would take for him to achieve is a bit of determined effort. For these reasons the child of this type has frequently not been promoted in school, partially as punishment for his "laziness" and partially in an honest effort to make him learn. In addition, he has been goaded and threatened at home, kept in at night to do extra work, drilled on work assigned for the next day—all with the principal result of frustration for both parent and child.

Gradually it has been recognized that normal intellectual capacity does not guarantee success in any particular field of learning. An individual's mental capacity as measured by accepted intelligence tests may be normal or superior and yet he may be failing in certain intellectual pursuits. When the specific difficulty which is causing his failure is an observable physical handicap, blindness for example, the problem is recognized and an attempt made to do something about it. When the difficulty does not show on the surface, the person is not likely to be so aided.

Many investigations have been made in an attempt to determine some of the causes for and to study factors related to failure among those of high mental capacity. Attention will be focused here only on those which specifically relate to failure in reading. The consensus among those who have carried on studies of reading disability occurring in cases of adequate capacity is that rarely is there a single causal factor which can be identified. Rather, a constellation of related factors is usually found. The prospect for correction of the inadequacies is good, however, if the contributing factors are identified and the instructional program adjusted in terms of them.

Gates (62:15) has summarized this viewpoint:

> In brief, reading disabilities result from failure to identify all possible handicaps and to arrange instruction in such a way that they are directly or indirectly surmounted. The causes of reading disability

are many; the remedies lie in improved, especially highly individualized instruction.

That many factors may be involved in a specific reading disability and that there is considerable difficulty in identifying causative factors has been pointed out by many investigators. Gates and Bennett (64) felt that acquired techniques, rather than any inherent or basic brain organization, were probably responsible for defeats in acquisition of reading skills. They emphasized that the contributing factors were many, and gave a rather extensive list of possible causes, including basic physical defects and the results of training. In addition, they cautioned against assuming that correlation of certain factors with reading disability necessarily implied causation.

Monroe (107) was careful to point out that even the occurrence of particular errors in reading might not indicate that the same causative factors were operating. She summarized with these ideas on the causes of reading disability:

1. Although certain factors (e.g., auditory discrimination, or left-eye and right-hand preference) were statistically significant in distinguishing groups of achieving readers and disability cases.
   a. these factors also appeared in certain cases in the achieving group.
   b. there was no one factor which was operative in all of the disability cases.
2. Although some factors (e.g., illnesses or accidents, visual acuity) were not statistically significant in distinguishing between achieving and retarded readers, they might still be factors which impeded the progress of certain individuals in learning to read.
3. The special defect in acquiring skill in dealing with visual symbols was probably attributable to a constellation of factors rather than to any single one.
4. Specific difficulty with reading is probably a result of the fact that the number and severity of the negative factors exceeds the number and strength of the positive ones.

ORIGIN OF SPECIFIC READING DISABILITY

The first identification of cases of disability in reading not accompanied by general mental retardation or serious visual deficiency appears to have been in England. In 1896 Morgan (112) noted the similarity between children experiencing a specific difficulty in learning to read and adults who had lost the ability to read after damage to the brain. It was he who first used the term congenital word-blindness, the use of the label being predicated upon the theory of neurological involvement.

Twenty-five years later Hinshelwood (84), likewise, interpreted his observations of cases to mean that the disability in dealing with visual symbols was attributable to malfunctioning of certain brain areas. He assigned the causes of the disability to destruction or improper development of the visual memory center, the gyrus angularis and gyrus supramarginalis of the left hemisphere of the brain. He suggested the classification of reading disability cases into three groups and the use of three different terms to describe them:

1. Congenital word-blindness—pure defect of the visual memory for words and letters.
2. Congenital dyslexia—slighter degrees of defect, but characterized by much greater difficulty with learning to read than is encountered by the average child.
3. Congenital alexia—defect of the visual memory center as only one part of general cerebral deterioration.

Another English investigator, Rutherford (138), wrote in 1909 that he considered specific reading disability one of the many biological variations which could be expected in the total population and felt that it would be distributed on the normal curve. He felt that the occurrence of these cases represented a reversion in the species caused by the loss of certain specialized determinants in the germ plasm. This theory of origin would lead to the implication that remedial work with these cases would probably be unprofitable.

Ranschburg (124) agreed with others that the visual memory center for words was at the root of specific reading disability. However, he explained the malfunctioning of the center not in terms of structure but in terms of blood supply to the area. He felt that the brain was not structurally imperfect, but was under supplied with blood and, therefore, unable to perform adequately.

Another theory of the origin of specific reading disability which centered in functioning of the brain rather than on structure was that of Orton (115, 116, 117, 118). He disagreed with the possibility advanced by earlier writers, such as Hinshelwood, that there was congenital maldevelopment of the angular gyrus. He based his lack of acceptance of this theory on the fact that post-mortem examinations did not show defects of structure with nearly the frequency of reading disability. He also pointed out the fact that if the theory of one hemisphere's taking over the functions was accepted, such disabilities would have to involve the same portion of both sides of the brain, an exceedingly rare occurrence.

Orton agreed that the disturbance was one of defect of visual memory. He explained it in terms of inability to retain a visual picture which would lead to recognition of the form when it was again encountered. He held to the earlier idea of actual records stored in the brain. He saw this process as a function of both hemispheres of the brain, each forming its own record of the word form which was seen. One side of the brain was dominant and the records, or "engrams," in that hemisphere were retained for interpretation of the word form when it was again encountered. The engrams formed in the non-dominant hemisphere, oppositely oriented, were elided under normal conditions. When the dominance in the brain was not clearly established, he felt that these reversed engrams interfered with proper identification of previously contacted forms.

Orton's opinion that specific reading disability is a functional disorder rather than a result of structural defects of the brain is well founded. However, the idea that actual visual patterns are stored in the brain is untenable. He developed this theory in an attempt to explain certain symptoms of difficulty with reading. There is no support in neurological and psychological findings for such a theory.

Other theories of causation which involve the idea of lateral dominance have been advanced. The influence of this factor on reading disabilities will be discussed further in the section on Dominance.

More recently, the possible influence of birth injuries as causative factors in reading disability has been pointed out. Anderson and Kelley (2) included it in their list of possible causes. Gesell and Amatruda (69) expressed the opinion that many injuries so slight as to escape detection undoubtedly occur at birth or during the first three years of life. They felt that these relatively mild neurological disturbances might account for the lack of clear cut dominance and result in reading or speech disabilities as well as poor muscular coordination.

Jensen (90) agreed with the theory set forth by Gesell. He felt that these neurological injuries might also account for some faulty coordination of the eyes and unsatisfactory auditory discrimination. He noted that, in the cases he studied, there was frequently a history of difficult birth.

Harris (78:221, 222), in discussing signs of neurological difficulties, indicated that he would agree with the opinions expressed above:

Symptoms which may lead a psychologist or teacher to recommend a neurological examination include the following: a his-

tory of difficult birth, with prolonged labor, instrumental delivery, marked deformity of the head, difficulty in getting breathing started, difficulty in sucking and swallowing, etc.; poor equilibrium and general awkwardness; convulsive seizures; and signs of organic helplessness on certain psychological tests such as the Rorschach and the Kohs Block-Design Tests.

ACQUIRED AND CONGENITAL DISABILITY IN READING

Although much has been learned from the study of cases in which ability to read was lost after brain injury (70, 72, 80, 166, 169), the acquired and congenital difficulties are not entirely similar. Many of the theories of causation discussed above had their basis in the idea that the two types of inability to read were almost identical. Actually the manifestations of difficulty may be very closely related. However, certain differences in the cases must be kept in mind. Head (80), Weisenburg and McBride (166), Goldstein (70), Granich (72), and Wepman (169) all discuss cases in which the functions of language were disturbed. In their consideration of the training of these cases, however, they are dealing with functions which previously had been intact. The problem of learning to read when the function had been disturbed was one of retraining rather than one of first learnings.

Wepman (169:121, 122) indicated this essential distinction in the type of cases:

Aphasia re-education is not a matter of teaching a new vocabulary, new reading, new spelling, etc., but rather reopening of the pathways leading to previous learning of the individual. What is expected is recall of previously learned material, physiologically repressed by trauma to the neurological system.

The complexity of the language disturbances occurring seems to be similar in both acquired and congenital cases of reading disability. Orton (*115, 116*) pointed out that the various facets of language—reading, writing, and speech—are so closely linked that there is rarely a disturbance in one without accompanying defects in the others. In his discussions of children who encounter unusually severe problems in dealing with written language, he refers to frequent instances of "degradation of speech." He found that spelling was almost always impossible for these cases. In other words, the difficulty with reading was not a "pure" defect in the sense that all other language functions were undisturbed. Rather it was the most strikingly severe of a number of disturbances.

Because language abilities develop in an orderly sequence and are dependent on each other, disturbance in one facet of language would not be expected without accompanying disturbances in other facets. Difficulties in speech, for instance, might easily result in problems with reading and spelling. Difficulties in various facets of language might cause difficulties in others, or might arise from common causes.

This same complexity of disturbance has been pointed out by investigators of alexia traceable to specific brain injury after the ability to deal with written language had been acquired. Weisenburg and McBride (*166*:66), after reviewing various accounts of "pure" alexia, stated:

> Actually the well-studied and fully reported cases in the literature are not pure in the sense of being uncomplicated by other language disturbances.

Goldstein (*70*:121) summarizes the complex symptoms which were evidenced in one of the cases studied. He felt that the primary difficulty with this case might lie in the "impairment of abstraction." Head (*80*:312-317) shows the variations in reading disability which occur with the four different aphasias—verbal, syntactical, nominal and semantic. He gives certain basic character-istics of each of these disturbances of language function. In verbal aphasia there is an inability to find the exact word forms or word combinations needed for speech or writing. In syntactical aphasia, the rhythmic and syntactical patterns of speech and writing are disturbed, speech is apt to be overly rapid and incoherent with most connectives omitted. In nominal aphasia, the ability to find appropriate words to label objects, situations, etc., is lacking in spite of the subject's large stock of words. In semantic aphasia the primary disturbance is of the ability to interpret the significance of language except on a very superficial and immediate basis. In each case, the disability in reading is closely tied to the manifestations of the difficulty in other facets of language.

Fernald (*57*:164), having reviewed the literature on the reading disabilities caused by brain damage, found that her subjects manifested much the same pattern of symptoms:

> The resemblance of our cases of extreme reading disability to those of alexia caused by brain lesion or injury seems to suggest the possibility that the former are due to certain variations in the integrated brain functioning involving the same region as that in which the lesion is found in acquired alexia.

In summary, in all cases of disturbed language functions, more than one facet of language will probably be affected. The program of correction of disturbances of language must be planned with this fact in mind and with full consideration to the interrelationships among language functions. In the normal developmental sequence, ability to interpret language precedes ability to reproduce it. Ability to deal with oral language precedes ability to deal with visual language symbols. Hence, the order of development is understanding of spoken language, speaking, understanding of printed symbols (reading), reproduction of visual language symbols (writing). Unless success had been achieved in one of these areas, attempts to go on to the next will be futile.

RELATIONSHIPS OF SELECTED FACTORS TO READING DISABILITY

In an attempt to arrive at the identification of possible causative or contributing factors in reading difficulty, many investigators have studied the relationships between selected factors (e.g., intelligence, visual difficulties, emotional status, dominance, etc.,) and ability to read. Certain weaknesses are evident in many of these studies. There has frequently been no adequate definition of achieving and retarded readers in terms of general capacity (e.g., 10, 28, 87, 177). In some cases, only subjective judgment was used to determine rankings in reading achievement (e.g., 176). In others, interest in one factor or viewpoint has seemed to prejudice the population, the design, or the results of the study (e.g., 42, 60). Within these and other limitations, however, the investigations suggest possible relationships between the factors studied and reading disability.

Because the interest in this study is focused on the child of normal or superior intelligence who has difficulty with interpreting and reproducing visual language symbols, investigations of intelligence and reading ability will not be considered. The results of investigations of the relationship of other factors of ability in reading will be reviewed.

VISUAL FUNCTIONING

Obvious cases of extremely limited vision have usually been taken care of through training in sight saving classes or with adjustments of the program to eliminate the need for reading when it was visually impossible. Many cases of undetected malfunctioning of the eyes, causing trouble with reading,

have unfortunately been missed and the child's failure blamed on such factors as lack of intelligence or failure to try (111). Conversely, there have, in all probability, been cases in which a visual difficulty was thought to be the causative factor in lack of achievement, whereas actually some other factor or group of factors existed. The relationship between reading and visual performance has consequently been rather widely investigated.

After a thorough review of the results of many studies, Robinson (133) pointed out the lack of agreement as to the importance of visual difficulties in reading disability. Reports of the amount of association between problems of seeing and achievement in reading have varied greatly. Selzer (142) found that 85 percent of the reading disability cases he studied had some visual problem. At the other extreme, Witty and Kopel (174) found that the reading disability cases in their population had higher visual acuity than did the good readers. Edson et al., (51) found no evidence that poor vision limited the reading achievement of the fourth graders they studied.

The particular populations studied and the types of visual screening may be responsible for the apparent disagreement in the findings. Reading disability has not always been defined in the same way. Some investigators have used populations of college students while others have used pupils in the primary grade. For some studies, vision specialists have made complete examinations; for others, the only criterion of good or poor vision was whether or not the subject wore glasses.

Of those who studied visual acuity and the presence of refractive errors, the majority have reported negative results. Eames (49), Monroe (107), and Witty and Kopel (175) all reported that findings in these areas did not distinguish the low and the high achievers, except that Eames did not find excessive exophoria associated with the group of low achievers. Fendrick (55), on the other hand, found visual acuity to be a differentiating factor between the two groups. All of the investigators emphasize the fact that very serious difficulties of this type would, of course, be detrimental to the development of adequate reading ability.

When the coordinate functioning of the two eyes was studied, the results seemed to be somewhat more consistent. In general, there appears to be agreement that eye muscle imbalance and faulty fusion are found more frequently among reading disability cases than among the groups of normal achievers. Betts (15), Eames (49), and Witty and Kopel (173) all report positive findings on the presence of a low level of coordinate functioning of the two eyes. The problem appears to be one of lack of comfort and efficiency in normal, two-eyed performance.

Robinson (133) observed that although visual defects frequently could be detected in cases of reading disability, not all of them appeared to be contributing factors in the difficulty. Originally, there were visual problems found in 73% of the cases she studied. In the final consideration of the cases, the visual difficulties were listed among the contributing causes in only 50%.

Betts and Austin (18:74), in summarizing the results of a thorough study of the visual status of a fifth-grade population, said:

> There appears to be no significant relationship between achievement in reading, in terms of mental capacity for achievement, and the summation of visual factors appraised in this study. However, this should not be interpreted as meaning that ocular comfort and efficiency are not desirable prerequisites for sustained reading activities.

The preponderance of evidence appears to lead to three conclusions. First, visual functioning and reading achievement are not significantly related. Second, visual difficulties may be contributing factors in reading disability. Third, detection and correction of visual difficulties may enhance comfort and efficiency in reading.

AUDITORY FUNCTIONING

The relationships between reading achievement and two facets of hearing have been investigated in most studies in this area. Tests of auditory acuity and auditory discrimination have been employed. In general, rather inconclusive results have been obtained on the possible relationship between acuity and reading disability. Kennedy (94) found that there was some tendency for poor hearing to be associated with low achievement in reading, but the relationship between auditory acuity and reading was not significant. She and Henry (81) both found that high frequency losses seemed to be more important than those in the lower ranges. Kennedy (94:250), although she used too few cases to consider significant, states that the high frequency loss cases "tended to become very good and more often poor readers." These losses seemed to separate the ends of the distribution of reading achievement from the middle of the group. She did not state the specific frequencies which seemed crucial. Henry (81) made no mention of particular high achievers with high frequency losses, but said that this type of loss was related, in her group, to deficiency in reading. Betts (16) reported more hearing impairments among those below average on the standardized reading test he administered than among those above average. He noted a striking similarity in the audiograms of the six below-average readers who had hearing losses. Whereas the three above-average readers had their maximum loss at 512, the below-average had losses at higher frequencies.

Only one important study seems to indicate a positive relationship between auditory acuity and reading disability. Bond (28) reported a significant difference between the reading disability cases and the controls in acuity, with the difference in favor of the control group. Ewers (*54*), Henry (*81*), Kennedy (*94*), and Robinson (*133*) found no conclusive evidence on this point. Kennedy, however, does state (*94*:250) that "there is a somewhat greater tendency for good hearers to become good readers and for those somewhat handicapped in hearing to read less well."

All the above mentioned investigators, with the exception of Henry, who did not investigate the area, seem to agree that the most direct relationships found were between auditory discrimination, the ability to detect likenesses and differences in sounds, and reading ability. Bond (*28*), Ewers (*54*), Kennedy (*94*), Monroe (*107*), and Rutherford (*138*) all found positive relationships between ability in auditory discrimination and reading ability. Monroe emphasized the point that poor discrimination of sequence of sounds as well as of individual sounds was an important factor. She lists these difficulties among the possible causative factors in reading disability. Whether the relationship is a causative one is difficult to determine, but her control group did make consistently fewer errors in auditory discrimination than did her reading defect cases. Robinson (*133*) concurs on the fact that auditory discrimination difficulty appeared to be a cause of reading difficulty, and emphasized the fact that tests in this area are still not entirely adequate.

Discrimination of both speech sounds and pure tones has been investigated. Bond (*28*) emphasized, as did Monroe (*107*), the significance of the difficulty encountered by the poorer readers with the discrimination of speech sounds. Ewers (*54*) and Kennedy (*94*) both found the ability to discriminate pure tones of different frequencies to be similarly related to achievement in reading. Jones (*92*) included "training in auditory perception, especially sound discrimination," in the special lessons he gave his experimental group of "average third-grade pupils." Those who received these speech lessons made significantly higher gains on a standardized test of silent reading ability than did the matched members of the control group.

In summary, it would appear that there is no convincing evidence that auditory acuity and reading achievement are closely related. Poor auditory discrimination appears to be rather definitely linked to, and possibly a causative factor in, reading disability.

SPEECH AND LANGUAGE DEVELOPMENT

Gaines (*59*), who reviewed the literature and presented possibly the best bibliography available to 1942, made it clear that only rather tentative conclusions on the relationship of speech problems to reading disability can be drawn. She states (*59*:109):

> That some relationship exists between speech defects and reading disability can be reasonably suspected from these various outstanding but by no means complete studies.

She attributed some of the difficulty in the area to the loose ratings of performance in speech. A second point to be considered is that in most of these studies groups of "good" and "poor" readers were selected on the basis of comparative rank on standardized tests of reading achievement. Actual amount of retardation in terms of capacity for achievement varied greatly within the groups. Even on the incidence of peculiarities and defects of speech there appears to be no general agreement, however.

Bond (*28*) found no more speech defects among low achievers in reading than among high achievers. Anderson and Kelley (*2*) recognized the tendency for more speech defects to occur among the reading disability cases. Monroe (*107*) and Bennett (*10*) found peculiarities of speech a positive factor in differentiating groups of low and high achievers. Rutherford (*138*) and Yedinack

(*177*) found articulatory defects and difficulty with reproduction of sounds to be associated with low achievement in reading. Yedinack's study was concerned with second-grade children. She stated (*177*:57):

> Children with functional articulation defects are significantly inferior in both oral and silent reading to children with normal speaking ability. Furthermore, children with reading disability frequently have articulation defects. . . . Strong relationship between these two handicaps shows that either they result from a common cause or that articulatory defectiveness had a deleterious effect upon the development of normal reading ability.

Differences in interpretations of the relationships depend somewhat on whether oral or silent reading or both served as a criterion of reading performance. Bond (*28*) pointed out that in his group 35 percent of those who achieved decidedly lower ratings on tests of oral reading ability than on tests of silent reading ability had speech defects. Those who rated low in both oral and silent reading showed no significant incidence of speech problems. Obviously, difficulty with speech would be reflected in poor oral reading performance. However, Jones (*92*) found that speech training also brought significant gains in silent reading achievement.

Both Monroe (*107*) and Robinson (*133*) emphasize the point that speech and reading difficulties may be symptoms of a common cause of difficulty. Artley (*4*) points out, in addition, that difficulties in one area may cause difficulty in the other. Growth in one area is likely to bring growth in the other (*5*).

In view of the sequential development of language abilities, it would seem likely that retardation in general language development and retardation in reading might be related. Van Riper (*158*) describes three kinds of retardation in speech development. Speech may be delayed (fail to develop), interrupted, or incomprehensible. He points out

that both intrinsic factors (e.g., low intelligence, poor hearing, birth injury, diseases affecting the central nervous system and disturbing perceptual processes, paralysis, deficiencies in coordination, prolonged illness) and environmental influences (e.g., lack of motivation for talking, emotional conflicts, negativism, inadequate teaching of speech by parents, inadequate speech environment) can result in retarded speech development. Beckey (*8*) likewise found many of these same factors to be related to retardation in speech. One or more of these factors, in themselves, or because they led to an inadequate foundation in oral language facility, could produce retardation in reading. Bennett (*10*) pointed out that children with a history of retarded language development or speech defect, even if it was not currently in evidence, appeared to be more liable to failure in reading than those whose oral language had developed normally.

In a recent summary, Eames (*50*:53–54) has concluded:

> However, certain broad generalizations can be drawn.
> 1. Neurological lesions in the language centers or their interconnections may impair speech and reading.
> 2. Failure or inadequacy of auditory association and discrimination may predispose to either speech or reading trouble.
> 3. Speech defects occur in a certain proportion of reading failure and vice versa.
> 4. Emotional reactions to speech difficulties may impair reading.
> 5. Oral reading is more difficult for a person with a speech defect.
>
> Both speech and reading troubles are likely to stem from the same basic defect. Essentially the problem is neurological with psychological overtones.

The factors seem important in the relationships of speech and language development to reading disability. First, problems in either or both of the areas may be indicative of some more basic problem of which the speech and reading disabilities are symptoms. Certainly it has been concluded that disturbances of language functions do not occur without other accompanying disturbances of behavior and mental functions (70, 86). Second, deficiencies in speech and interpretation of oral language may interfere in the normal development of reading ability because of the sequence in which language develops.

DOMINANCE

Two phases of patterns of lateral dominance have been extensively studied: dominance of areas in one hemisphere of the brain over comparable areas in the other hemisphere, referred to as "central" dominance; and preference for the use of one eye, hand, or foot over the other in certain designated activities, referred to as peripheral dominance. The relationship of all facets of achievement in reading and specific reading disability has been considered.

"Central" Dominance—Although disagreement still exists on specific localization of functions in certain areas, clinical observation of cases of acquired disabilities has led to some general conclusions. Head (79), Weisenburg and McBride (166), Goldstein (70), and Smith (146), for example, have all reviewed the various theories expounded since the early 19th century. The tendency, at present, appears to be consideration of language activity from a dynamic viewpoint. The position of the lesions found in cases in which reading had been disturbed, however, indicated that many of them occurred in the area designated by Hinshelwood (84).

Morgan and Stellar (110:505) stated:

> There is no doubt that in some functions, particularly language, one side of the cortex is frequently the major side while the other is the minor.

They observed that injury to the minor side did little to disturb reading; to the major side, sometimes caused complete inability to read.

Nielson (114) stated that there was a special area for coordination of language functions and that it was dominant in one hemisphere of the brain. When the major side did not function, language was greatly disturbed, but the area in the non-dominant side could take over in time.

Chesher (38), in a study of 157 patients with lesions in the language area of one hemisphere, found evidence which supported the view that there was a dominant hemisphere for language functions. This was the side opposed to that of the preferred hand. He pointed out, however, that great individual differences occurred and that for some patients, injury in either hemisphere could disturb language.

Weisenberg (165) found similar evidence of localization of lesions and of handedness as a criterion of the dominant brain hemisphere. He and McBride (166:452) reported evidence that handedness was a reliable index of "central" dominance in approximately 95 percent of their cases. On the specific difficulty of "word-blindness" they said (166: 68):

> The purest cases coming to autopsy have shown a lesion in the tissue of the lingual gyrus.

Accepting the opinion of other investigators, as well as his own observations, Goldstein (70:51) says:

> There is no doubt that defects of the higher mental performances, and hence particularly of language, occur in lesion in one—the 'leading'—hemisphere. Thus, we are almost always correct if we localize the lesion of a right-handed aphasic patient in the left hemisphere, and vice versa. That we are sometimes mistaken, e.g., that the lesion in a right-handed aphasic is found in the right hemisphere, can have various causes. It may be the effect of a lack of conclusiveness of the methods to determine the 'handedness' and the prevalence of the hemisphere.

Van Riper (*159, 160*), in his tests of "central" dominance, assumed that the dominant hand and brain area were opposed. The patterns drawn by the non-dominant hand were reversed at certain critical angles (*159*). He stated (*160*:294) that reversal of patterns with the hand normally preferred was indicative of confusion in lateral dominance. He found that those who were ambidextrous tended either to reverse with both hands or not to reverse at all.

Smith (*146*:58), in summarizing her review of literature on central dominance says:

> Word blindness can be caused by injury to appropriate areas in only one hemisphere. . . . Eleven subdivisions of the cerebral hemisphere comprise the functional area for association. These subdivisions are in pairs. The degree to which laterality has been developed varies from pair to pair. The extent and degree of dominance varies within the individual.

Smith (*146*) attempted to determine whether or not "central" dominance characteristics differentiated pupils achieving at their capacity levels from those whose reading achievement was significantly below their capacity levels. To measure central dominance, she used the Van Riper Form Board. She found that severely retarded readers made significantly more reversals with the right hand than with the left at 360°. This was true in spite of the fact that there was a higher percentage of right-handed among the retarded readers than among the achieving readers. No other evidence exists of the frequency with which apparent confusion of "central" dominance is associated with reading disability. This indication of higher incidence of confusion in "central" dominance, however, may have clinical significance in the analysis of cases of specific reading disability.

The implication appears to be that reading can be disturbed by malfunction of certain areas of the brain. The areas are usually dominant in one hemisphere of the brain and the malfunctioning in that side alone can cause language disorders.

The dominant side is usually, but not always, that opposed to the dominant hand. Confusion in "central" dominance appears to be related to specific disability with reading.

Peripheral Dominance—Peripheral dominance has been determined by testing hand, eye, and foot performance for activities of different types. Handedness and eyedness, particularly, have been studied in relation to reading disability. Widely varying viewpoints have been presented on the relationship of lateral preference in peripheral areas to reading achievement. In general, most of the proportions of right, left, and mixed preference found among reading disability cases do not fall outside the limits of the proportions to be found in a normal, unselected population. Dearborn's (*42*) figures deviate significantly. From his observations of children having difficulty with reading, he felt that the peripheral dominance factor might be significant as a cause of specific reading disability. The fact that he was known to be interested in problems of dominance probably led to his seeing an unusually large number of cases with peculiar hand and eye preference patterns.

Three manifestations of lateral preference in the peripheral areas have been considered as possibly important in relation to reading achievement. These are hand preference, eye preference, and the relationships between the two. Bennett (*10*) found the reported incidence of left-handedness from 4 percent to 11 percent; of left-eyedness, 22 percent to 44 percent; of unilateral preference for hand and eye, 54 percent to 85 percent; of preference for one hand and the opposite eye, 15 percent to 48 percent with a median of 20 percent; and of confused or indeterminant preference, 0 percent to 10 percent. Smith (*146*:16–17) gives a summary of the results of the studies of incidence of left-handedness and enumerates various factors which may influence the determination of such data. In this study only certain investigations which have considered dominance patterns as related to reading achievement will be discussed.

1. Hand Preference. The majority of investigators reported that there was no pattern of peripheral dominance, as indicated by hand preference, which distinguished reading disability cases from the normal population. Anderson and Kelley (*2*), Bennett (*10*), Fendrick (*55*), Gates (*62*), Gates and Bond (*66*), Gates and Bennett (*64*), Haefner (*75*), Harris (*77*), Robinson (*133*), Smith (*146*), and Woody and Phillips (*176*) all reported that handedness of low achievers in reading did not differ significantly from that of the achieving readers. No particular handedness could be found with greater frequency among the retarded readers than among other groups. Spadino (*147*) found this to be true of speech disability cases also.

Certain other investigators reported dissimilar evidence on the relationship of handedness to achievement in reading. Lord, Carmichael and Dearborn (*100*) reported greater incidence of left-handedness and felt that the sinistrad tendency would tend to conflict with the conventional dextrad pattern of reading and writing. Monroe (*107*) found that there had been more changes of handedness in the reading disability cases she contacted than among the normal group. She also reported greater incidence of left-handedness among the members of the families of the reading disability cases. Smith (*146*) found, in her population, no significant differences between retarded and achieving readers in changes of handedness or incidence of left-handedness in the families. Selzer (*142*) found what he considered a disproportionate number of cases of left-handedness among the reading disability cases. However, he pointed out that much depended on the criteria of handedness. Some investigators used the hand preferred for

writing as the only criterion of handedness. Others have used a variety of one- and two-hand performances and found the hand used most commonly.

Downey (*46*), likewise, emphasized the inaccuracies which were almost unavoidable in labeling handedness patterns of individuals. She presented evidence in support of her contention that handedness was definitely not a true dichotomy. She found that 60 percent of the "right-handed" preferred the left hand in some or all bimanual activities and that 70 percent of the "left-handed" made similar use of the right hand.

The overwhelming evidence seems to be on one side of the question of the relationships between handedness and achievement in reading. Left-handedness or confusion in handedness alone does not appear to be a significant factor in reading disability.

2. Eye Preference. Like hand preference, eye preference can be determined in many ways. Means of determining the preferred eye have varied from acceptance of the eye with the highest acuity as the preferred one to acceptance of the one used most consistently in a series of activities involving sighting, following objects, and other similar activities as the preferred one.

Bennett (*10*), Fendrick (*55*), Gates and Bond (*66*), Robinson (*133*), Smith (*146*), and Woody and Phillips (*176*) all reported negative findings. In the groups which they studied, patterns of eye preference did not appear to be a factor which helped to differentiate between achieving and retarded readers. They found no evidence of unusually frequent left or mixed eye preference among the low achievers in their groups.

Other investigators have revealed some positive findings or tendencies toward the significance of eye preference in reading disabilities. Gates and Bennett (*64*) felt that left-eye preference might be a real source of difficulty in reading. They found that as many as 10 percent of the left-eyed children they studied were likely to develop difficulty. Monroe (*107*) and Selzer (*142*) also stated that there was a greater incidence of left-eyedness among reading disability cases than in the normal population and that the left-eye preference might be a significant factor in reading disability. Harris (*77*), in his summary of the findings of various studies including his own, stated that right-eyedness was less frequent and left- and mixed-eyedness more frequent among the reading disability cases than in the normal population.

In spite of the variations in eye preference, one conclusion seems valid. Eye dominance alone is unreliable as an index to reading achievement.

3. Relationships Between Hand and Eye Preference. Although the consensus appears to be that neither handedness nor eye preference alone is a significant factor in reading achievement, another possible source of difficulty exists in the relationships between the two. Again, opinion is widely diverse.

Fendrick (*55*), Fernald (*57*), Gates and Bond (*66*), and Smith (*146*) all report that preference for one hand and the opposite eye did not occur with significantly greater frequency among the reading disability cases than among the achieving readers. Even though the greatest difference, in peripheral dominance, between the reading achievers and the retarded readers in her population occurred in the left-eyed, right-handed group —34 percent retarded, 24 percent achieving—Smith stated (*146*:141):

> On the basis of all the tests of hand and eye preference given, very small differences were found between retarded readers and reading achievers.

Dearborn (*42*) felt that preference for the use of one hand and the opposite eye was a real source of difficulty, especially because of the directional problems involved. Orton (*118*) pointed out as one of the characteristics of the group of specific reading disability cases the presence of a large number of children who showed mixed or crossed peripheral dominance patterns. Monroe (*107*), although she found more consistently right dominant cases among the disability cases than any other type, found more left-eyed, right-handed cases among the disability cases than among the controls.

Bennett (*10*) felt that preference for one hand and the opposite eye appeared to occur with undue frequency among the disability cases. He assumed that unilateral dominance in peripheral areas was the normal development and that deviation from it arose from confusion in "central" dominance. He expressed the view that crossed dominance, in itself, probably was considered a causative factor when actually it should be traced back to its source and more fundamental factors discovered. He also stated that the presence of crossed dominance had sometimes been considered responsible for difficulty when possibly other unrelated factors were more likely operating as causes of reading disability.

Harris (*77*) reviewed various data on peripheral dominance findings. Some of the populations included were heavily weighted with cases of unusual dominance patterns. From the combined data, he reached certain conclusions relative to mixed dominance. He found that generally, the reading disability cases showed more deviations from the normal than did the reading achievers. Right-hand, left-eye preference was the most common pattern, apart from consistent right-sidedness, among the reading disability cases.

In summary, the evidence available on the significance of the relationships between hand and eye preference and reading disability is inconclusive. Greater incidence of lack of clearcut lateral preference in these areas among low achievers in reading than among high achievers has been reported by some investigators. However, some doubt may be cast on the evidence from these studies: 1) achieving and retarded readers were not adequately defined; 2) a disproportionately high number of cases with unusual dominance patterns may have been studied by some of the investigators because of their special interest in such cases. Finally, the possibility exists that unusual patterns of peripheral dominance may be symptomatic of more basic difficulties rather than causal factors in reading disability.

REVERSAL TENDENCY

The relationship of the occurrence of reversals in reading and writing to achievement in reading has been thoroughly investigated. In some instances it has been considered a cause of difficulty and, in others, a symptom of the specific disability. The latter is probably much closer to the facts.

Mirror reading and writing represent the complete reversal of the word forms. Blom (26), Orton (117), and Tinker (155) have pointed out the tendency for children or adults who evidence this kind of difficulty to have trouble with achievement in reading and writing. Orton (117) also stated that those who have specific reading disability had greater facility in mirror reading than did the normal population. Tinker (155), however, found great individual differences in achievement in mirror reading when he taught it to a group of adults in an attempt to study perceptual processes.

Both Fildes (58) and Orton (118) pointed out that confusion in direction of spatial orientation of similar words was outstanding as a characteristic of the reading disability group. Gates and Bennett (64), Hildreth (82), Monroe (107), Smith (146), Witty and Kopel (175) all agreed that more reversals were made by poor than by good readers.

Several points must be considered in evaluating the fact that reversal errors are more common among low achievers than among high. Most important, of course, is the fact

that the same is true of any other type of error. The "good" readers make fewer errors of all kinds than do the "poor" readers. Hildreth (82) mentions that there are no more errors of a reversal type than of any other.

The matters of maturity and training may also influence the frequency of occurrence of reversal errors. Teegarden (153) found that children with kindergarden experience showed less tendency to reverse than did those whose first school experience was in first grade. The tests were made by having children match script or printed forms, or write from memory or by copying. Davidson (40, 41), in her studies of children's reactions to letters confusing because of direction and of reversal errors in attempts to discriminate between certain forms and words, found that as many as 60 percent of children entering school make reversals in dealing with printed symbols. She pointed out that the number of reversals tended to decrease with age. Witty and Kopel (175), reported that the number of reversal errors occurring among poor readers tended to decrease with advancing grade level of the subjects.

Dearborn (42) felt that the dominance patterns were influential in determining the tendency toward reversal. He stated that marked peculiarities of dominance, marked incidence of reversals, and the presence of reading disability were apt to be found together. Gates and Bennett (64) found that the percentage of left-eyed making reversals was greater than the percentage of right-eyed making such errors. However, no real agreement appears to exist on the question of dominance and reversals. Gates and Bennett (64), Hildreth (82), and Witty and Kopel (175) all reported that handedness was not related to number of reversal errors. Woody and Phillips (176) even found their left-handed group made fewer reversals than did their right-handed group. For purposes of observation of reversal errors, Fildes (58) and Ranschburg (124) both found numbers somewhat more satisfactory material than letters or words. This would seem to be true because, with these materials, the problem becomes one of form discrimination rather than a meaningful activity such as reading. The presence of meaning in the process would tend to lessen the chance of reversal errors.

The following conclusions seem valid:

1. Reversals in visual perception appear to be directly related to immaturity, occurring frequently among children just entering school.

2. Poor readers make more reversal errors than do good readers. This is particularly true because poor readers are frequently forced to try to deal with materials too difficult for them. They are unable to derive meaning from the materials. Thus, errors of all types are very frequent. The reversals, per se, do not destroy the meaning, but may result, at least partially, from a lack of meaning.

3. The reversal errors are, in all probability, not any more common than any other kind of error.

4. The relationship of particular dominance patterns to the tendency to make reversal errors is not entirely clear.

MEMORY SPAN

In order to be successful in reading, an individual must be able to deal with oral and printed language symbols. His auditory and visual perception must be adequate to assure his associating meaning with these symbols. In addition he must be able to recall these associations and thus recognize the language symbols. This means that memory and memory span must be considered in relation to reading. Measures of memory span are, in part, measures of attention and concentration (164). Personality deviations which disturb or make impossible concentrated attention, therefore, would tend to decrease the measurable memory span. Relationships between memory span and reading

ability, therefore, must be considered in the light of many other factors such as visual and auditory perception and emotional status.

General research on memory and the various measures of memory span has been excellently summarized by Blankenship (25), and Raymond (126). That deficiencies of memory span have a deleterious effect on achievement in reading is a conclusion which appears to be supported by most of the investigations which have been completed in the area. Gray and other (74) have reported that poor auditory memory span frequently leads to difficulty with the confusion in reading. Harris (78:204) has said:

> Poor memory for sequence of letters, numbers, or words may be found in children of otherwise normal mental ability. If a child's memory span is very short— for instance, if he can keep in mind a sequence of only three or four letters—he may have difficulty in remembering larger words. This difficulty is especially likely to happen if a sound-blending method of teaching is used. Children with short memory spans usually do better with methods that teach words as units than with letter-by-letter methods.

Monroe and Backus (109) also list lack of success on auditory memory span as indicative of possible difficulty with reading.

Various approaches have been made to investigation of the possible influence of memory span on reading ability. In certain studies the developmental viewpoint has been taken. In others, the relationships between performance on tests of memory span and achievement in reading have been studied. In the third kind of investigation, the interrelationships among the performances on various memory span tests have been investigated.

Saunders (139) worked from the developmental angle. She pointed out that children with short auditory memory span tend to talk at a late age, have speech peculiarities, have difficulty acquiring facility with language, confuse oral directions, encounter difficulty in learning to read, tend to be poor spellers, and to be generally slow in all school progress. She found children with these difficulties to be shy and unassertive, preferring to play alone and tending to become behavior problems, and to evidence immaturity and lack of self-reliance. Saunders concluded that although inadequate auditory memory span is not associated with all disabilities in reading, it invariably leads to difficulty with reading and spelling.

Betts (*13*) has pointed out, also from the developmental viewpoint, that memory span is a significant factor in readiness for beginning reading. A short auditory memory span is reflected in inability to master word recognition techniques. An adequate memory span is essential to reading success.

Rizzo (*131*) used the technique of comparing the achievement on tests of memory span in the case of good and poor readers. He found the correlation between scores in reading and the results of the memory span tests "significant at a low level of relationship." (*131*:234) He also stated:

> When the comparison between good and poor readers was made in terms of group mean scores on the memory span tests, the scores of the former for all measures exceeded the scores obtained for the latter.

Bond (*28*), using digits as the material to measure auditory memory span, found significant differences between low and high achievers in reading in memory span for them. Both Anderson (*3*) and Robinson (*133*) used isolated speech sounds for the materials to measure memory span. Robinson found that those who had inadequate memory spans for these materials made less progress during the instructional period than did those with satisfactory spans. Anderson did not correlate the results of his tests with those measuring success in reading, but did find success in the tests to be positively related to success in learning foreign languages.

Lichtenstein (*98*) found that among low achievers in reading the auditory memory span for related materials was usually definitely inferior to the general learning ability. However, he did not compare achievement on other measures.

These studies comparing good and poor readers contained no attempt to compare the memory spans for various types of materials or determine the effects of various modes of presentation. Implications were drawn in most cases on the basis of one test. However, Achilles (*1*:74) concluded:

> A person who recalls one material well may or may not recall another material well. There is a tendency for the correlation to be positive rather than negative.

Thus the possiblity had to be investigated that there might be a significant relationship among findings with tests of memory span employing different types of materials and different modes of presentation.

Brener (*30*), using many different types of materials, found no significant difference in performance when the presentation was visual and when it was oral. He did, however, find that materials for testing memory span varied in difficulty. In his experiments, digits proved easier to handle and sentences most difficult.

Betts (*12*:44), as a result of observation of severely retarded readers, found differences where Brener had found none:

> The relationships between memory span findings are being studied as factors in reading disabilities. From the available evidence (admittedly inadequate), it appears that individuals tending toward dyslexia achieve higher scores on auditory span tests of related syllables (i.e., sentences) than they do on visual tests of unrelated letters.

Further investigation of the interrelationships among the results of various tests of memory span was completed by Stauffer (*148*). He found several significant relationships among test findings for the retarded readers he studied (149:449):

a. Retarded readers achieve significantly higher scores on non-verbal measures of visual memory span than on verbal measures of auditory memory span.
b. Retarded readers tend to achieve higher scores with related items than with unrelated items on verbal measures of memory span.
c. Retarded readers achieve significantly higher scores with non-verbal than with verbal measures of visual memory span.
d. Retarded readers achieve significantly higher scores on forward span tests than on reverse span tests when digits are used to measure auditory memory span.
e. Retarded readers tend to make relatively low scores when related materials are presented arhythmically as measures of memory span.

Investigation of the relationships among memory span findings on achieving readers was completed by Raymond (126). Her population consisted of boys each of whom had an average reading score on a standardized test at least two years higher than his mental age expectancy. She found that they scored significantly higher when the presentation was visual than when it was auditory, when the materials were related than when they were unrelated, when digits were to be repeated forward than when they were to be repeated in reverse. The achieving readers did not do better with non-verbal than with verbal materials when both types were used as visual stimuli. They made relatively high scores on related materials presented arhythmically. These data would appear to indicate that certain significant differences between memory span findings on achieving readers and those on retarded readers were revealed by Stauffer (148) and Raymond (126). However, the two groups were not directly comparable.

It would appear, from the available evidence, that inadequate memory span, in itself, can be a causative factor in reading

disability or a symptom of some attention defect such as an emotional disturbance. In addition, severely retarded readers are characterized by a tendency toward certain patterns of relative achievement on tests of memory span with varying test materials and modes of presentation. Whether such relationships might exist also among other groups has not been adequately investigated.

ASSOCIATIVE LEARNING ABILITY

In her study of memory span Achilles (1) found that, for both recall and recognition, the material richest in associations was remembered most easily, but that with few or no associations was poorly remembered. Richness of association is, then, a factor of importance in the kind of retention necessary for reading. More basically, however, the acts of visual perception involved in reading demand that associations exist between meanings derived from experience and word forms. Reading is actually reconstructing the ideas which the word symbols represent. Identification of word forms as symbols of the intended meaning is a process of perception or recognition, forming a new link between symbols and meaning, or recalling a previous association. Acquisition of reading ability, therefore, is impossible if the individual is not able to form percepts, make and retain associations between experience and printed symbols (134).

Both Bronner (31) and Schmitt (140) point out the fact that among otherwise normal children there may be deficiencies in ability to make associations. Betts (12) lists inability to make associations, in spite of adequate general capacity, as one of the primary characteristics of a dyslexia. If there is an associative disorder, if few or no associations are made with printed symbols, the process of perception stimulated by word forms cannot reach its final stage, emergence of meaning. Instead, it is arrested at the stage of awareness of a visual pattern for which meaning must be sought.

Level of operation in perception or ability to form and retain associations must be considered not as an isolated factor which may be related to reading ability but as a factor closely related to others. Relationships between association and memory span have already been indicated. Either may be affected negatively by emotional disturbances which make attention and concentration difficult or impossible. Rapaport (125:168) has said:

> Attention is considered here an effortless, passive unhampered contact with outside reality—a free receptivity. This free receptivity appears to be hampered if the subject's affects and anxieties are not well-controlled and get out of balance. . . . In contrast to attention, concentration may be characterized as an *active* relationship to outside reality. When one finds himself unable to take in freely what the flow of a book, a lecture, or a conversation brings to him, he may exert conscious effort to keep out of consciousness all material that is not directly pertinent. This focusing of consciousness upon the current topic, by exclusion of other emotional or thought content, we shall designate as concentration.

Thus, when emotional aberrations are such that content extraneous to the learning situation cannot be kept out of focus, the ability to make necessary associations or to arrive at the necessary percept will be disturbed. Likewise, inadequate vision or hearing might make the forming of associations between word symbols and meaning difficult or impossible. Doll (48) pointed out that brain lesions or anomalies may bring about the same kind of perceptual disorders.

Disturbances of the ability to make associations may affect reading ability in other ways than in the connection of meaning with a specific word form. Trow (156) pointed out that all reading skills—comprehension, organization, rate of reading, etc.—are either the result of pure associative learning or of associative learning combined with sensorimotor skills. Garrett and Schneck (61) emphasize the fact that the most important test in reading, the comprehension check, is actually a controlled association test.

Gates (62) was aware of the fact that great individual differences exist in associative learning ability. He considered deficiency in this ability a factor in reading disability, and, consequently, felt that there should be means to measure performance in the area. He stated, p. 105:

> Children will differ in their ability to learn by associating a visual stimulus, such as a printed word, with a meaning given orally.

Of the test he devised he said:

> It is not a measure of 'word blindness' but rather of a complex of factors involved in 'associative' or 'associational' learning of the general type involved in reading.

Stauffer (148) investigated the relationship between various sets of findings on associative learning tests and tests of general capacity. He concluded (149:448–49):

1. Significant relationships exist between different associative learning test findings on retarded readers.
   a. Retarded readers tend to achieve significantly higher scores by a visual-auditory mode of presentation than by a visual-visual.
   b. Retarded readers achieve significantly higher scores on geometric test targets than on word-like test targets.
   c. Retarded readers tend to achieve significantly higher scores on tests involving the use of visual, auditory, and voco-motor associations.
   d. Retarded readers tend to achieve significantly higher scores on a verbal test of intelligence than on an oral vocabulary test (verbal opposites).

Raymond's study of achieving readers (126) revealed that they, too, achieved significantly higher scores with visual-auditory presentation than with visual-visual and with geometric figures than with word-like figures. However, the achieving readers made scores on verbal opposites test which were equal to their mental age scores as determined by the Stanford-Binet.

These findings would seem to indicate that the child with a specific reading disability may have difficulty in learning to associate meaning with visual symbols and, particularly, with word forms. A second implication is that although addition of auditory clues facilitates learning somewhat, the visual-auditory clues given in teaching the average child to read may not be sufficient for the child with a specific reading disability. That the introduction of voco-motor clues tends to improve performance in associative learning appears to support this idea. Dr. Grace Fernald (47) apparently recognized this need for additional cues for the establishment and retention of associations when she recommended the use of a word-learning technique which involved visual, auditory, kinaesthetic, and tactile stimulation.

Several conclusions can be drawn from the literature on associative learning. First, ability to form percepts or, specifically, to make associations between experience and visual symbols is a basic factor in learning to read. Second, certain patterns of deficiency in associative learning tend to characterize severely retarded readers. Whether such patterns might exist in normally achieving readers has not been conclusively demonstrated. Third, ability in this area may be disturbed by defects of vision, hearing, or memory, or by emotional aberrations.

SOCIAL AND EMOTIONAL ADJUSTMENT

The possible influences of disturbances of attention and concentration on acquisition of reading ability have already been discussed.

There are various researches which indicate the deleterious effects on all learning of negative emotional states. Bird (21) found, in a study of children from four to six years of age, that such states were fairly common. Thirty percent of those she studied had personality handicaps that interfered with learning. The children with the least adequate adjustment took twice as many trials for learning as did those with the best adjustment. Fear reactions were especially potent in inhibiting learning. Children in whom such difficulties were present needed as many as three times the trials required for the best adjusted. Carter (35) found that retention was affected by the emotional tone of the learning situation. Castner (36) pointed out that certain negative traits, especially an unstable and excitable personality, tended to predispose to failure in reading, largely through fluctuation of attention. Page (119), likewise, emphasized that the presence of strong emotions prevented the kind of attention necessary for learning to read.

Both Prescott (121) and Lund (101) indicated that the basic needs and satisfactions of the child must be considered. Difficulties may arise when his achievement is in poor relationship to his desires. McClusky (103) stated that the learning of any subject must be considered in terms of the total personality and that this is particularly evident in the research on reading disabilities. Knowing the child for whom remediation of reading disability is being planned does not mean knowing merely the skills or deficiencies in his handling of various language areas. His feelings affect his ability to learn and, consequently, must be investigated. Bell (9) recommends the use of story telling, creative drama, art work, and the like for gaining understanding of the child. Having gained insight into the child's basic personality structure through tests and observations and into his reactions to various situations, the clinician is in a better position to understand his specific difficulties and plan for his wholesome growth.

Increasing attention has been given to the relationships between reading and emotional status. Various authors have summarized the opinions expressed on the significance of these relationships (63, 136, 171, 172, 179). The need for further research, especially that of a controlled nature, is great (7, 63). However, there appears to be at least one point of general agreement. As Stewart (150:415) expresses it:

> Personality disturbances may be causal, concomitant or consequent to reading disability.

Emotional Disorders in the Etiology of Reading Disability—One means which has been used in the attempts to determine the relationship of emotional status to reading disability is the comparison of achieving and retarded readers. Are emotional problems characteristic of retarded readers? Is emotional status a differentiating factor between groups of children succeeding in reading and those having difficulty? Unfortunately, there are certain weaknesses in many of these studies which make it impossible to present conclusive evidence from them. In particular, attention must be given to these points:

First, a clear differentiation was not always made between achieving and retarded readers. Instead, the groups were divided by deciding on a crucial score on a standardized reading test without reference to the level of achievement this represented in terms of capacity. For example, Bennett (10) used teacher report of achievement and standardized tests as criteria of level of reading ability. There was no attempt to get exceptionally good readers. The "achieving readers" were ones whose scores on standardized tests were at or above the grade level. The "poor readers" were, generally speaking, about a year below the grade level. There was no guarantee that some of these poor readers were not

actually doing as well as could be expected in terms of their capacities. Likewise, some of the "good readers" may actually have been retarded in view of the fact that they were capable of considerably more. Others, in their studies, used similarly inadequate means of setting up their groups on the basis of reading achievement (60, 97, 133).

Second, variability within the groups was not always adequately treated and compared with the inter-group variability. Gann (60), for example, gave no concentrated attention to the different patterns which she found within her "good" and "poor" reader groups. Instead, she emphasized the differences found between the groups.

Third, certain investigators approached the studies with a definite set for education problems (10, 63, 97), and others with a set for psychological and emotional problems (24, 60). This question of set appeared to lead them to overemphasize the factors of particular interest to them and exclude adequate attention to others.

Fourth, in some cases, only very superficial evaluations of personal adjustment were made (10, 97, 135).

Fifth, there has been no study reported of groups equated on the basis of emotional patterns with an attempt to find whether or not there were similar or different effects of these patterns on achievement in reading.

With these differences in approach to the study of the relationships between emotional adjustment and reading ability, it is natural that quite contradictory results have sometimes been obtained. Bennett (10) found that behavioral or adjustment status did not distinguish between his "good" and "poor" readers. On the other hand, Gann (60) reported that the best differentiating factor she found was personal adjustment. She found that the group of retarded readers even felt that their teachers were less friendly to them than to the achieving group. It is possible that her experimental design rather logically dictated this conclusion of a real difference between the groups. Ladd (97) found that the "good" readers she studied seemed to surpass the "poor" readers in their general feeling of happiness and success in school, in their persistence and self-control, and in ability to get along with others without quarreling. Sheldon and Carrillo (143) found a general dislike of school among the poor readers. Jackson (87:125) concluded:

> Among retarded readers one may expect a larger than chance number of individuals who possess personality traits that deviate considerably below average.

Analysis of the various maladjustments found among the poorer readers studied has led some writers to conclude that certain types of emotional problems may be ones which are basic to failure in reading. Monroe and Backus (109) listed these as emotional factors which probably would be causal in reading difficulty: general immaturity, excessive timidity, prejudice against reading and fear of its difficulty, and predeliction against all school activities. All of these should, more rightly, be considered as symptoms of maladjustment. Challman (37) similarly listed overprotection and consequent immaturity, and insecurity. Jameson (88) emphasized the fact that when the child has already recognized his lack of success, his feelings of inadequacy and insecurity are exaggerated by the intense concern shown by adults about his lack of achievement.

Emotional instability has been considered a causal factor in reading disability (22, 85, 102, 106). This again appears to be labeling without defining the specific emotional difficulty which is present. Hollingworth (85) emphasized the fact that achievement in reading requires close cooperation and concentration, ability to follow directions, and ability to sustain attention. The child who is unstable, excitable, timid, or dreamy has difficulty in exerting effort in the necessary areas. Both Zirbes (178) and Vorhaus (161,

162) also felt that personal maladjustments were major factors in the reading disability cases they considered.

Tulchin (157) pointed out that emotional reactions to reading, predisposing to lack of achievement in that area, may be determined by conditions present in the child's environment before reading was attempted. She felt that reading might be identified by the child as a symbol of growing to fit an accepted pattern, one which he could not bring himself to fall into under the circumstances.

Stewart (150), Vorhaus (161), and Blanchard (24), similarly state that the failure to achieve in reading may, in some cases, be an expression of hostility or guilt, or a means of drawing closer to the parents through anxiety accompanying lack of success in academic work. Blanchard's theory of guilt is expressed thus (24:410):

> In many instances, the reading disability is a disguised expression of hidden motives, satisfying the need for punishment and relieving guilt by exposing the child to a situation of failure in school and of criticism.

Such manifestations as these would be signs of deep-seated emotional conflicts, and, as Tulchin (157) points out, would lead to difficulties in other areas as well as in reading.

On the other hand, the majority of investigators seem to feel that, although personal maladjustments may be causal factors in reading disability in some cases, the emotional problems may also be a direct result of the failure to achieve in reading. Especially in the earlier considerations of the relationship of personal adjustment to reading disability, the majority opinion appeared to be that failure to achieve in reading was responsible for more of the emotional disturbances observed in the disability cases (37, 65, 89, 113, 118). Wilking (171), in summary of the research to 1940, concluded that the preponderance of cases of disability in reading responded to a direct educational approach with no real need for psychotherapy. He found a minimum of personal maladjustment and felt that its role as either a causative or contributing factor was far from definitely determined. Gates (63) also felt that clear-cut cases of emotional disturbance as primary causal factors in reading disability were exceedingly rare. Fernald (57) presented as evidence that emotional disturbances were most frequently symptomatic of the difficulty in reading the fact that only four of her seventy-eight cases had shown emotional instability before the time they entered school. However, several investigators have concluded that there are frequently emotional problems which are not evident at the time of the original analysis of the cases (24, 85, 144). In such situations they found that it was only after remedial work had been initiated that the subject was able to bring to the fore the personal maladjustment so that the need for psychotherapy became clear. In some cases, the lack of response to the remedial situation was a clear indication of emotional maladjustment and the need for treatment (24).

Sherman (144, 145), Strang (151), Fenton (56), Ridenour (130), and Robinson (132) all pointed out the effects that the frustrations of lack of achievement had on the personal adjustment of pupils. Lack of motivation, resistance to help, excessive fatigue in a reading situation, and other attempts to escape from a disturbing task were evident after pupils had encountered difficulty with reading.

Monroe and Backus (109) felt that certain emotional factors were ones which resulted from reading disability and acted to further retard progress in the area. They listed aggressive opposition, withdrawal, compensating mechanisms, defeatism, and hypertension as characteristic difficulties arising from failure in reading.

Blanchard (24) has expressed an opinion with which others seem to concur. In addition to the evidence that emotional disturbances can either cause or result from reading disability, there is evidence that both may arise from a common cause. In many cases, determination of causal relationships is extremely difficult.

Influence of Home Life—Robinson (133) considered one of the unique contributions of her study to be the evidence given of the overwhelming influence of the home on achievement in reading. She stated (113: 222):

> Maladjusted homes or poor interfamily relationships were found to be contributing causes in 54.5% of the cases studied.

The insecurity, fears, and worries which accompanied poor home relationships seemed to militate against success in reading.

Difficulties arising in the home are not always recognized at first in the consideration of a child's problem with reading. Once suspected, they may be difficult to attack. Blanchard (24:396) pointed out factors which may be responsible for this situation:

> The unconscious wish of the parent to see a child's difficulty with reading as primarily educational rather than emotional is not hard to understand. The former implies a problem in the child's relationship to the school; the latter may lead to the parent's beginning to question his own relationship to the child and to the need to do something about it.

Ephron (53) has suggested that frequently it is possible to get help for the child, in the emotional area, only by bringing in psychotherapists to the staffs of reading clinics. The parents, she feels, will bring the children for help in reading even when they cannot face the fact that psychological or psychiatric help may be needed.

The evidence rather definitely, however, points to the fact that the influence of the home is strong in determining a child's ability to succeed in reading. Gann (60), Hincks (83), Missildine (106), Preston (122, 123), Stewart (150), and Witty (172) all stress the importance of parent-child and of sibling relationships. Hincks (83) found that where the emotional problems were deeply imbedded in the family life, they tended to persist even when some improvement in reading was effected. Preston (122) stressed the injustice of placing blame on the child, making disagreeable comparisons, removing privileges, and evoking physical punishment for failure. She pointed out that the great concern and tenseness of the parents, combined with these other unfortunate reactions, were extremely destructive of the child's security. Missildine (106) found similar reactions among the parents of the boys she studied.

Emotional Status and Remedial Work— Depending on the particular emotional difficulty will be the decision as to whether specific therapy may be necessary before or concurrent with the remedial work in reading (24, 57, 83, 87, 152, 178). There have been differences of opinion on the need for special therapy and its effect on reading ability. Axline (6), in an investigation of thirty-seven below average readers in the second grade, found that play therapy with no remedial work in reading was effective in bringing gains in both personal adjustment and reading. The significance of these gains was not adequately determined. Damereau (39) studied twenty-two cases of reading disability, all of them having personality problems. She did not find that alleviation of one problem necessarily helped materially with the alleviation of the other. Hincks (83) found that, except in certain cases in which the emotional problems were especially deep-seated, improvement in behavior accompanied improved reading ability. The majority opinion appears to be that when gains are achieved in one area, they also occur in the other. Really effective treatment must be planned in terms of the child's personal adjustment. Through the treatment, alleviation of both the personal maladjustments and the specific difficulties in reading must be sought. When treatment in

the two areas is being given by separate individuals, cooperation between them must be close (170). As Ellis has stated (52:61):

> It was concluded that both educational factors seem to be of vital importance in the etiology of reading disabilities, and that the most effective attack upon them must be made on a concerted educational-emotional basis.

Sherman has stated (144:134) that the first step in the planning of the remedial program must be a thorough understanding of the child's emotional status:

> No therapeutic plan can be formulated without first reorganizing a child emotionally and, second, . . . consistent motivation for improvement cannot be introduced if the child is distracted by personal problems. The eagerness of the therapist to institute a direct remedial program often retards rather than accelerates the progress.

As Hardwick (86) and others have concluded, if the personality problem is basic to reading failure, it must be treated before real gains can be expected. On the other hand, if the personal maladjustment has resulted from frustrations in learning to read, some success must be achieved before the emotional disorders will be alleviated. Burfield (33), Robinson (132), and Hollingworth (85) pointed out that, as the severity of emotional problems increases, the necessity for individual rather than group instruction becomes stronger.

Gellerman (67) stressed another point of importance in the matter of emotions and the remedial process. The longer the difficulties are allowed to continue without correction the more serious they become. Orton (118) felt that a child with good intelligence and normal development aside from the reading problem should not be allowed to go into his second year of schooling without at least examination to determine the advisability of special treatment. He felt that this kind of attention would help to guard against the accumulation of problems, emotional and academic.

Challman (37) has listed these as essential points in treating any remedial case, but especially in dealing with the emotionally maladjusted: a good start, in a pleasant and brief first session; the arousal of interest; placing of work in the sphere of play; emphasis on success to rebuild confidence; a leisurely pace and plenty of time; the enlistment of cooperation from the parents. Practices to be avoided are these: having remedial work replace a favorite activity; employing after school time; exerting pressure for achievement; using books designated for certain levels; causing embarrassment or stigma to be attached to the work. Schubert (141) makes similar recommendations.

Conclusions—Studies of the relationships between emotional adjustment and reading disability have been made by many individuals. Certain weaknesses of these studies, considered at the beginning of the section, make it impossible to state definitely the part which emotions play in reading disability and the effect of reading disability on the personality organization. Certain general conclusions, however, seem sound.

First, there is no single personality trait or combination of traits which is invariably associated with either success or failure in reading. Variability of personality structure, according to the existing evidence, will probably be great within groups of either achieving or retarded readers.

Second, personal maladjustments which lead to inability to attend and concentrate will, in all probability, have a negative effect on the development of reading ability.

Third, the presence of many or very serious symptoms of personal maladjustment is more frequently associated with failure in reading than with success in reading.

Fourth, emotional problems and reading disability, when they occur together, are apt to aggravate each other. Both must be con-

sidered in the alleviation of the total problem.

Fifth, the influence of home conditions is strong in determining both the personal adjustment and achievement in reading.

Sixth, the more basic and severe the emotional problem, the greater is the likelihood that individual instruction will be necessary and that psychotherapy will have to either precede or accompany remedial instruction.

SUMMARY

In choosing studies and opinions to be reviewed, those designed to determine the relationships between intelligence and reading ability were omitted because this study was concerned only with children in at least the normal range of the general American population in general capacity. An attempt was made to find literature related to factors which might cause or contribute to reading disability among those not held back by inadequate general capacity.

Certain weaknesses limit the data obtained from the studies reviewed. First, in many cases, there was no adequate definition of "good" and "poor" readers with consideration given to level of general capacity. Second, the methods of rating or measuring specific factors studied was not always adequate. Third, in many studies no attempt was made to study comparative intra-group and inter-group variability. Fourth, emphasis was sometimes placed on one factor or viewpoint to the virtual exclusion of others. Fifth, there are insufficient data available, in some areas, on the normal population to allow evaluation of the significance of results obtained on retarded readers.

Definition of "good" and "poor" readers in the groups to be studied varied considerably and, therefore, results are not directly comparable. In most of the studies reviewed, comparison was not actually made of retarded and achieving readers and their status in certain areas. The relative rank in the group was more often a criterion of placement than was the relationship between the child's present achievement level and his capacity for achievement. Group, verbal-type tests of intelligence were sometimes used as the only measure of capacity. Thus the actual capacity of some of the pupils may never have been determined adequately for comparison with the present achievement level.

Lack of specificity in measuring or rating can be illustrated from several studies. In one instance (176), measurement of reading ability was by teacher rankings on a five-point scale, "often with the aid of standardized tests." In another (64), some conclusions on vision were drawn merely on the basis of whether or not the children were wearing corrections. Gaines (59) evaluated studies on the relationships between speech and reading and concluded that ratings of speech functioning were inadequate. In studying social and emotional adjustment, in some cases (e.g., 97) very superficial subjective judgments based on observation were the only criteria. Conclusions drawn in individual studies, therefore, must be considered only very tentatively and cannot, with any degree of confidence, be compared with those drawn from other apparently related investigations.

Emphasis has too often been placed on apparent differences between groups without adequate investigation of the variability with the groups. Thus, conclusions which are drawn imply closer association of certain factors with reading disability than is actually indicated by the results. Indications of certain personal maladjustments, for example, were present in the "good" as well as "poor" reader (60), but the tendencies toward differences in the groups were emphasized and these variations within the groups not emphasized.

Special interests of investigators have, in many cases, led to study of one factor or manifestation of difficulty without adequate attention to others. Emphasis on problems of dominance (42), certain personality characteristics (60), or vision (49) has led, in certain studies, to overemphasis on the influence of these factors and to almost a "one-factor type" theory of causation.

After data have been obtained on the status of disability of cases in a particular area, it has been impossible at times to determine whether or not they were different from the normal population or from groups of achieving readers. There is a great need for normative data for use as a standard of comparison in certain areas. For example, in the area of speech, emotional status, memory span, association, or "central" dominance certain data have been obtained on reading disability cases. However, similar data have not been obtained on large or carefully selected and stratified samples of nondisability cases. Conclusions, therefore, about the relationships of these factors to reading disability must still be very tentative.

Within these limitations, however, certain conclusions can be drawn about the relationship of some factors to reading disability. At present a multiple-factor theory of causation, in which the specific factors studied might have a part, seems most logical.

In the past, specific disabilities have been considered traceable to destruction or maldevelopment of brain tissue (84, 112), to loss of certain specialized determinants in the germ plasm (138), to malfunction of certain brain areas (57, 118, 123), and to results of birth injuries (2, 69, 78, 90). Many of these theories arose from comparison with cases of acquired reading disability. Although there are similarities in the two types of cases in that the reading disability seems always to be accompanied by disturbances in other language functions (57, 70, 72, 79, 80, 118, 169), no one of the theories advanced appears adequate to account for all cases of reading disability. Hence, investigators have sought to determine the relationships between the factors which follow and reading disability.

VISUAL FUNCTIONING

Because of differences in definition of reading disability and in the measurement of adequacy of visual functioning, widely varying results have been obtained on the possible importance of vision as a causal or contributing factor in reading disability. With the limitations thus placed on the combined data, only a few conclusions seem tenable. First, many visual problems existing in cases of reading disability cannot be considered factors which cause or contribute directly to the difficulty (*49, 107, 133, 173*). Second, although visual acuity or the presence of refractive errors is probably not directly related to reading ability (*49, 107, 173*), lack of adequate coordination in the functioning of the two eyes probably contributes to reading disability (*15, 49, 173*). Third, although visual functioning and reading achievement are not directly related, the detection and correction of visual difficulties may enhance comfort and efficiency in reading (*18*).

AUDITORY FUNCTIONING

Inadequate discrimination between retarded and achieving readers again limits the conclusiveness of the results. However, it can tentatively be concluded that no direct, significant relationship exists between auditory acuity and reading achievement (*54, 81, 94, 133*) except that high frequency losses and low achievement in reading appear to be rather directly related (*16, 81, 96*). Second, poor auditory discrimination, inadequate ability to detect likenesses and differences in sounds, appears to be rather definitely related to and possibly a causative factor in reading disability (*28, 54, 92, 94, 107, 133, 138*).

SPEECH AND LANGUAGE DEVELOPMENT

Loose ratings of speech performance and failure to consider general capacity in evaluating adequacy of reading achievement levels limit the results of studies of the relationships between the two. In view of this fact, only two points seem conclusively supported at this time. First, speech disabilities and reading disability may result from a common cause (*4, 50, 77, 107, 133, 158*). Second, because of the sequence of language development, difficulty in oral language development may affect adversely the development of reading ability (*4, 8, 10, 50, 59, 70, 86, 158*).

DOMINANCE

"Central" Dominance—There appears to be adequate evidence that language functions can be disturbed by malfunctioning of certain areas of the brain in the dominant hemisphere, usually the side opposed to the dominant hand (*38, 70, 110, 114, 146, 166*). Present inadequate evidence, using tests which involve bimanual production of certain patterns (*159*), suggests that there may be a positive relationship between confusion in "central" dominance and specific reading disability (*146*).

Peripheral Dominance—Ratings of lateral preference in peripheral activities have not always been adequate nor have the investigator's ratings of achievement in reading given adequate attention to level of general capacity. In addition, this factor has sometimes been emphasized unduly because of special interests of the investigators. Only two conclusions seem reliable in view of the limitations of the studies. First, neither hand nor eye preference appears to be, in itself, a significant factor in reading disability (*2, 10, 55, 62, 64, 65, 133, 146, 176*). Second, preference for one hand and the opposite eye is probably not a significant factor in itself (*55, 57, 65, 146*), but may be indicative of some more basic problem.

REVERSAL TENDENCY

The presence or absence of reversal errors has been investigated in such a way that its relationship to low achievement rather than retardation and to maturity has been demonstrated. Several conclusions from the studies seem perfectly reliable. First, although the number of reversal errors is closely related to difficulty in reading (*26, 42, 58, 64, 82, 107, 115, 116, 118, 146, 155, 173*), they are no more common than errors of any other type (*82*). When reading material is above a suitable level, meaning is destroyed and errors of all kinds become numerous. Second, reversals in visual perception appear to be directly related to immaturity, occurring frequently among children just entering school (*40, 41, 153, 175*). Third, in spite of conflicting evidence, there appears to be no direct relationship between lateral preference in peripheral activities and frequency of reversal errors (*64, 82, 175, 176*).

MEMORY SPAN

Conclusions on the relationship of memory span to acquisition of reading ability have, in many studies, been made without adequate attention to type of material or mode of presentation used in the tests. In two studies (*126, 148*) relationships among memory span findings, with attention to these factors, were investigated. From the available evidence, two major conclusions seem tenable. First, deficiencies in memory span, in themselves or as symptoms of difficulties such as deficiencies in attention, have a deleterious effect on learning generally and acquisition of reading ability in particular (*13, 28, 74, 78, 109, 131, 133, 139*). Second,

children with specific reading disabilities are characterized by certain patterns of relative achievement in memory span. Based on present evidence, the following appear to be characteristic of severely retarded readers: visual span for non-verbal materials superior to auditory span for verbal materials; auditory span for related materials superior to auditory span for unrelated materials; visual span for non-verbal materials superior to visual span for verbal materials; ability to repeat digits forward superior to ability to repeat digits in reverse order; relatively short auditory span for verbal materials presented arhythmically (*12, 148*).

ASSOCIATIVE LEARNING ABILITY

In order for the process of perception stimulated by word forms to reach its conclusion in the emergence of meaning, associations between meaning and the visual form must be made and retained. Investigation of this associative learning ability has not been extensive. However, from the literature in the field, certain conclusions can be drawn. First, deficiencies in associative learning may exist in individuals who are otherwise normal, and may lead to difficulty with reading (*12, 31, 62, 140*). Second, certain relationships among results of associative learning tests appear to be characteristic of severely retarded readers. The following are characteristic of these cases: achievement with a visual-auditory presentation superior to achievement with a strictly visual presentation; greater difficulty with forming associations with word-like figures than with geometric figures; improvement in ability to make associations when voco-motor clues are added to the visual and auditory; achievement on a verbal opposites test below the mental age level established by a verbal test of intelligence (*12, 148, 149*). Certain of these same characteristics appear in achieving readers, however (*126*). Third, disturbance of attention and concentration may affect ability in this area.

SOCIAL AND EMOTIONAL ADJUSTMENT

In studies of the relationships between personal adjustment and reading disability, certain weaknesses have limited the validity of the results. The inadequate measurement of reading achievement and of emotional status, the failure to consider the similarities in as well as differences between groups of different levels of adequacy in reading, and the poor experimental design of some of the studies makes it impossible to state definitely the part which emotions play in reading disability and the effect of reading disability on personality organization. Six general conclusions seem sound, however.

First, there is no single personality trait or combination of traits which is invariably associated with either success or failure in reading. Variability of personality structure, according to the existing evidence, will probably be great within groups of either achieving or retarded readers (*10, 63, 136, 149*).

Second, personal maladjustments which lead to inability to attend and concentrate will, in all probability, have a negative effect on the development of reading ability (*21, 35, 36, 119, 125*).

Third, the presence of many or very serious symptoms of personal maladjustment is more frequently associated with failure in reading than with success in reading (*22, 63, 87, 178*).

Fourth, emotional problems and reading disability, when they occur together, are apt to aggravate each other. Both must be considered in the alleviation of the total problem (*22, 24, 52, 57, 67, 83, 87, 152, 170, 178*).

Fifth, the influence of home conditions is strong in determining both the personal adjustment and achievement in reading (*60, 83, 96, 106, 122, 123, 133, 149, 172*).

Sixth, the more basic and severe the emotional problem, the greater is the likelihood that individual instruction will be necessary and that psychotherapy will have to either precede or accompany remedial instruction (*23, 24, 33, 85, 132, 144*).

BIBLIOGRAPHY

1. ACHILLES, EDITH MULHALE. "Experimental Studies in Recall and Recognition," reprinted from *Archives of Psychology,* No. 44. Lancaster, Pa.: New Era Printing Co., 1920.
2. ANDERSON, M., and KELLEY, M. "An Inquiry into Traits Associated with Reading Disability," *Smith College Studies in Social Work,* II (1931–32), 46–63.
3. ANDERSON, V. A., "Auditory Memory Span as Tested by Speech Sounds," *American Journal of Psychology,* LII (January 1939), 95–99.
4. ARTLEY, A. STERL. "A Study of Certain Factors Presumed to be Associated with Reading and Speech Difficulties," *Journal of Speech and Hearing Disorders,* XIII (December 1948), 351–60.
5. ———. "Oral Language Growth and Reading Ability," *Elementary School Journal,* LIII (February 1953), 321–28.
6. AXLINE, VIRGINIA M. "Nondirective Therapy for Poor Readers," *Journal of Consulting Psychology,* XI (March-April 1947), 61–69.
7. ———. "Treatment of Emotional Problems of Poor Readers by Nondirective Therapy," in *Clinical Studies in Reading I,* Supplementary Educational Monograph, No. 68. Chicago: University of Chicago Press, 1949, pp. 141–53.
8. BECKEY, RUTH E. "A Study of Certain Factors Related to Retardation of Speech," *Journal of Speech Disorders,* VII (September 1942), 223–49.
9. BELL, J. E. "Emotional Factors in the Treatment of Reading Difficulties," *Journal of Consulting Psychology,* IX (May-June 1945), 128–31.
10. BENNETT, CHESTER C. *An Inquiry into the Genesis of Poor Reading,* Contributions to Education, No. 755. New York: Bureau of

Publications, Teachers College, Columbia University, 1938.

11. BEST, C. H., and TAYLOR, N. B. *The Physiological Basis of Medical Practice*. Baltimore: Williams and Wilkins Co., 1945.

12. BETTS, EMMETT A. "Classification of Reading Disabilities," *Visual Digest*, IX (Summer 1945), 36–44.

13. ———. *Foundations of Reading Instruction*. New York: American Book Co., 1950.

14. ———. "Inter-relationship of Reading and Spelling," *Elementary English Review*, XXII (January 1945), 13–23.

15. ———. "A Physiological Approach to the Analysis of Reading Disabilities," *Educational Research Bulletin*, XIII (September and October 1934), 135–40; 163–74.

16. ———. "Reading Problems at the Intermediate Grade Levels," *Elementary School Journal*, XL (June 1940), 737–46.

17. ———. *Spelling Vocabulary Study*. New York: American Book Co., 1940.

18. ———, and AUSTIN, A. S. "Visual Problems of School Children," reprinted from *Optometric Weekly*. Chicago: Professional Press, 1940–41.

19. BILLS, ROBERT E. "Nondirective Play Therapy with Retarded Readers," *Journal of Consulting Psychology*, XIV (April 1950), 140–49.

20. ———. "Play Therapy with Well-Adjusted Retarded Readers," *Journal of Consulting Psychology*, XIV (August 1950), 246–49.

21. BIRD, GRACE E. "Personality Factors in Learning," *Personnel Journal*, VI (June 1927), 56–59.

22. BLANCHARD, PHYLLIS. "Psychoanalytic Contributions to the Problems of Reading Disabilities," *Psychoanalytic Study of the Child*, II (1946), 163–87.

23. ———. "Psychogenic Factors in Some Cases of Reading Disability," *American Journal of Orthopsychiatry*, V (October 1935), 361–74.

24. ———. "Reading Disabilities in Relation to Difficulties of Personality and Emotional Development," *Mental Hygiene*, XX (July 1936), 384–413.

25. BLANKENSHIP, ALBERT B. "Memory Span: A Review of the Literature," *Psychological Bulletin*, XXXV (January 1938), 1–25.

26. BLOM, E. C. "Mirror Writing," *Psychological Bulletin*, XXV (1928), 582–94.

27. BOLAND, JOHN L., JR. "Type of Birth as Related to Stuttering," *Journal of Speech and Hearing Disorders*, XVI (March 1951), 40–43.

28. BOND, GUY L. *The Auditory and Speech Characteristics of Poor Readers*, Contributions to Education, No. 657. New York: Bureau of Publications, Teachers College, Columbia University, 1935.

29. BORISH, IRVING M. *Clinical Refraction*. Chicago: Professional Press, 1949.

30. BRENER, ROY. *An Experimental Investigation of Memory Span*, private edition reprinted from *Journal of Experimental Psychology*, XXVI, May 1940. Chicago: University of Chicago Libraries.

31. BRONNER, AUGUSTA. *The Psychology of Special Abilities and Disabilities*. Boston: Little, Brown, and Co., 1917.

32. BROWN, FRED. *Manual, Brown Personality Inventory for Children*. New York: Psychological Corporation.

33. BURFIELD, LEONE M. "Emotional Problems of Poor Readers Among College Students," in *Clinical Studies in Reading I*, Supplementary Educational Monograph, No. 68. Chicago: University of Chicago Press, 1949.

34. BURT, C. *Mental and Scholastic Tests*. London: P. S. King and Son, 1921, pp. 269–95.

35. CARTER, HAROLD D. "Emotional Correlates of Errors in Learning," *Journal of Educational Psychology*, XXVII (January 1936), 55–67.

36. CASTNER, B. M. "Prediction of Reading Disability Prior to First Grade Entrance," *American Journal of Orthopsychiatry*, V (October 1935), 375–87.

37. CHALLMAN, R. "Personality Maladjustment and Remedial Reading," *Journal of Exceptional Children*, VI (October 1929), 9–10.

38. CHESHER, E. C. "Some Observations Concerning the Relation of Handedness to the Language Mechanism," *Bulletin of the Neurological Institute of New York*, IV (1936), 556–62.

39. Damereau, Ruth. "Influence of Treatment on the Reading Ability and Behavior Disorders of Reading Disability Cases," *Smith College Studies in Social Work*, V (December 1934), 160–83.

40. DAVIDSON, HELEN P. "A Preliminary Study to Determine the Extent to Which Unselected Young Children Make Reversal

Errors," *Journal of Genetic Psychology*, XLV (December 1934), 452–64.

41. ———. "A Study of the Confusing Letters B, D, P, and Q," *Journal of Genetic Psychology*, XLVII (1935), 458–68.

42. DEARBORN, WALTER F. "Structural Factors Which Condition Special Disability in Reading," in *Proceedings and Addresses of the Fifty-Seventh Annual Session of the American Association on Mental Deficiency* (May-June 1933), 268–286.

43. DILLER, JULIET C. "The Sex Factor in Enuresis," *Journal of Child Psychiatry*, II (1951), 194–204.

44. DOLL, EDGAR A. *Manual for the Vineland Social Maturity Scale.* New York: Educational Test Bureau, 1953.

45. ———. "Varieties of Slow Learners," *Exceptional Child*, XX (November 1953), 61–64, 86.

46. DOWNEY, JUNE E. "Types of Dextrality and Their Implications," *American Journal of Psychology*, XXXVIII (June 1927), 317–67.

47. DUKE-ELDER, SIR STEWART. *The Practice of Refraction.* Philadelphia: P. Blakiston's Sons and Co., 1938.

48. DVORINE, ISRAEL. *Theory and Practice of Analytical Refraction and Orthophis.* Baltimore: Franch-Bray Printing Co., 1948.

49. EAMES, THOMAS H. "A Comparison of Ocular Characteristics of Unselected and Reading Disability Cases," *Journal of Educational Research*, XXV (March 1932), 211–15.

50. ———. "The Relationship of Reading and Speech Difficulties," *Journal of Educational Psychology*, XLI (January 1950), 51–55.

51. EDSON, WILLIAM H., and others. "Relationships Between Visual Characteristics and Specific Silent Reading Abilities," *Journal of Educational Research*, XLVI (February 1953), 451–57.

52. ELLIS, ALBERT. "Results of a Mental Hygiene Approach to Reading Disability Problems," *Journal of Consulting Psychology*, XIII (February 1949), 56–61.

53. EPHRON, BEULAH KANTER. *Emotional Difficulties in Reading.* New York: Julian Press, 1953.

54. EWERS, DOROTHEA W. F. "Relations Between Auditory Abilities and Reading Abilities: A Problem in Psychometrics," *Journal of Experimental Education*, XVIII (March 1950), 239–62.

55. FENDRICK, PAUL. *Visual Characteristics of Poor Readers*, Contributions to Education, No. 656. New York: Bureau of Publications, Teachers College, Columbia University, 1935.

56. FENTON, NORMAN. *Mental Hygiene in School Practice.* Stanford, California: Stanford University Press, 1943.

57. FERNALD, GRACE M. *Remedial Techniques in Basic School Subjects.* New York: McGraw-Hill Book Co., 1943.

58. FILDES, L. G. "A Psychological Inquiry into the Nature of the Condition Known as Congenital Word-Blindness," *Brain*, XLIV (1921–22), 286–307.

59. GAINES, F. P. "Interrelations of Speech and Reading Disabilities," *Quarterly Journal of Speech*, XXVII (1941), 104–10.

60. GANN, EDITH. *Reading Difficulty and Personality Organization.* New York: King's Crown Press, 1945.

61. GARRETT, H. E., and SCHNECK, M. R. *Psychological Tests, Methods and Results.* New York: Harper and Brothers, 1933.

62. GATES, A. L. *Improvement of Reading,* revised. New York: Macmillan Co., 1947.

63. ———. "The Role of Personality Maladjustment in Reading Disability," *Journal of Genetic Psychology*, LIX (September 1941), 77–83.

64. ———, and BENNETT, C. C. *Reversal Tendencies in Reading.* New York: Bureau of Publications, Teachers College, Columbia University, 1933.

65. ———, and BOND, GUY L. "Failure in Reading and Social Maladjustment," *Journal of the National Education Association*, XXV (October 1936), 205–6.

66. ———, "Relation of Handedness, Eye-Sightedness and Acuity Dominance to Reading and Social Maladjustment," *Jourogy*, XXVII (1936), 450–56.

67. GELLERMAN, SAUL W. "Causal Factors in the Reading Difficulties of Elementary-School Children," *Elementary School Journal*, XLIX (May-June 1949), 523–30,

68. GENS, GEORGE W., and BIBEY, M. LOIS. "Congenital Aphasis: A Case Report," *Journal of Speech and Hearing Disorders*, XVII (March 1952), 32–8.

69. GESELL, ARNOLD, and AMATRUDA, CATHERINE S. *Developmental Diagnosis: Normal*

and Abnormal Child Development. New York: Paul B. Hoeber, Inc., 1947.

70. GOLDSTEIN, KURT. *Languages and Language Disturbances.* New York: Grune and Stratton, 1948.

71. GOODENOUGH, FLORENCE. *The Measurement of Intelligence by Drawing.* Yonkers-on-Hudson, N.Y.: World Book Co., 1926.

71ª. GRAHAM, E. ELLIS. "Wechsler-Bellevue and Wisc Scattergrams of Unsuccessful Readers," *Journal of Consulting Psychology,* XVI (August 1952), 268–271.

72. GRANICH, LOUIS. *Aphasia, A Guide to Retraining.* New York: Grune and Stratton, 1947.

73. GRAY, WILLIAM S. *Summary of Investigations Relating to Reading,* Supplementary Educational Monographs, No. 28. Chicago: University of Chicago Press, 1925.

74. ———, et al. *Remedial Cases in Reading: Their Diagnosis and Treatment,* Supplementary Educational Monographs, No. 22. Chicago: University of Chicago Press, 1922.

75. HAEFNER, RALPH. *The Educational Significance of Left-Handedness,* Contributions to Education, No. 360. New York: Bureau of Publications, Teachers College, Columbia University, 1929.

76. Hardwick, Rose S. "Types of Reading Disability," *Childhood Education,* VIII (April 1932), 423–27.

77. HARRIS, ALBERT J. *Harris Tests of Lateral Dominance, Manual of Directions for Administration and Interpretation.* New York: The Psychological Corporation, 1947.

78. ———. *How to Increase Reading Ability,* revised. New York: Longmans, Green and Co., 1948.

79. HEAD, HENRY. "Aphasis: An Historical Review," *Brain* (1920), 87–165.

80. HENRY, SYBIL. "Children's Audiograms in Relation to Reading Attainment," *Journal of Genetic Psychology,* LXX (1947), 211–31.

81. ———. *Aphasia and Kindred Disorders of Speech,* Vol. I. Cambridge, Mass.: Harvard University Press, 1926.

82. HILDRETH, GERTRUDE. "Reversals in Reading and Writing," *Psychological Bulletin,* XXX (1933), 670–671.

83. HINCKS, E. *Disability in Reading in Relation to Personality,* Harvard Monographs in Education, No. 7, Series 1, Vol. II. Cambridge, Mass.: Harvard University Press, 1926.

84. HINSHELWOOD, J. *Congenital Word-Blindness.* London: H. K. Lewis and Co., Ltd., 1917.

85. HOLLINGWORTH, LETA S. "Reading," in *Special Talents and Defects.* New York: Macmillan Co., 1923, Ch. IV.

86. HUBER, MARY. "Re-education of Aphasics," *Journal of Speech Disorders,* VII (December 1942), 289–93.

87. JACKSON, JOSEPH. "A Survey of Psychological, Social, and Environmental Differences Between Advanced and Retarded Readers," *Pedagogical Seminary and Journal of Genetic Psychology,* LXV, first half (September 1944), 113–31.

88. JAMESON, AUGUSTA. "Methods and Devices for Remedial Reading," in W. S. GRAY, ed. *Recent Trends in Reading,* Supplementary Educational Monographs, No. 49. Chicago: University of Chicago Press, 1939, pp. 170–78.

89. JASTAK, JOSEPH. "Interferences in Reading," *Psychological Bulletin,* XXXI (April 1934), 244–272.

90. JENSEN, M. B. "Reading Deficiency as Related to Cerebral Injury and to Neurotic Behavior," *Journal of Applied Psychology,* XXVII (1943), 535–45.

91. JOHNSTON, PHILIP W. *The Relation of Certain Anomalies of Vision and Lateral Dominance to Reading Disability,* Monograph of the Society for Research on Child Development, VII, No. 2. Washington, D.C.: Society for Research in Child Development, National Research Council, 1942.

92. JONES, MORRIS VAL. "The Effect of Speech Training on Silent Reading Achievement," *Journal of Speech and Hearing Disorders,* XVI (September 1951), 258–63.

93. JONES, W. FRANKLIN. *A Study of Handedness.* Los Angeles: University of Southern California, 1918.

94. KENNEDY, HELEN. "A Study of Children's Hearing as it Relates to Reading," *Journal of Experimental Education,* X (June 1942), 238–51.

95. KIRK, SAMUEL A., and KOLSTOE, OLIVER P. "The Mentally Retarded," in *Review of Educational Research,* XXIII (December 1953), Ch. II.

96. KUNST, MARY S. "Psychological Treatment

in Reading Disability," in *Clinical Studies in Reading I,* Supplementary Educational Monograph, No. 68. Chicago: University of Chicago Press, 1949, pp. 133.

97. LADD, MARGARET R. *The Relation of Social, Economic and Personal Characteristics to Reading Ability,* Contributions to Education, No. 582. New York: Bureau of Publications, Teachers College, Columbia University, 1933.

98. LICHTENSTEIN, ARTHUR. "An Investigation of Reading Retardation," *Journal of Genetic Psychology,* LII (1938), 407–23.

99. LODGE, WILLIAM J. "Developmental Characteristics of Childhood Related to Language Arts Curriculum," *Elementary English,* XXX (February 1953), 106–115, 122.

100. LORD, E. E., and others. *Special Disabilities in Learning to Read and Write,* Harvard Monograph in Education, Series I, Vol. II, No. 1. Cambridge, Mass.: Graduate School of Education, Harvard University, 1925.

101. LUND, FREDERICK H. *Emotions.* New York: Roland Press, 1939.

102. MCCALLISTER, JAMES M. "Character and Causes of Retardation in Reading Among Pupils of the Seventh and Eighth Grades," *Elementary School Journal,* XXXI (September 1930), 35–43.

103. MCCLUSKY, HOWARD Y. "Mental Health in School and Colleges," *Review of Educational Research,* XIX (December 1949), 405–412.

104. MALONE, ANTHONY J., and MASSLER, MAURY. "Index of Nail-Biting in Children," *Journal of Abnormal and Social Psychology,* XLVII (April 1952), 193–202.

105. MAY, CHARLES H. *Manual of the Diseases of the Eye.* Baltimore: William Wood and Co., 1934.

106. MISSILDINE, W. H. "The Emotional Background of Thirty Children with Reading Disability with Emphasis on Its Coercive Elements," *The Nervous Child,* V (July 1946), 263–72.

107. MONROE, MARIAN. *Children Who Cannot Read.* Chicago: University of Chicago Press, 1932.

108. ———. "Methods for Diagnosis and Treatment of Cases of Reading Disability," *Genetic Psychological Monographs,* IV (1928), 335–456.

109. ———, and BACKUS, BERTIE. *Remedial Reading.* Boston: Houghton Mifflin Co., 1937.

110. MORGAN, C. T., and STELLAR, E. *Physiological Psychology.* New York: McGraw-Hill Book Co., 1950.

111. MORGAN, JOHN. "Disorders of Sensation," in *The Psychology of Abnormal People.* New York: Longmans, Green and Co., 1928, Ch. II.

112. MORGAN, W. PRINGLE. "A Case of Congenital Word-Blindness," *British Medical Journal,* II (November 1896), 1612.

113. NEWELL, NANCY. "For Non-Readers in Distress," *Elementary School Journal,* XXXII (March 1931), 183–95.

114. NIELSON, J. M. *Agnosia, Apraxia, Aphasia, Their Value in Cerebral Localization,* revised. New York: Hoeber, 1946.

115. ORTON, S. T. "Certain Failures in the Acquisition of Written Language: Their Bearing on the Problem of Cerebral Dominance," *Archives of Neurology and Psychiatry,* XXII (1929), 841–50.

116. ———. "An Impediment to Learning to Read, A Neurological Explanation of the Reading Disability," *School and Society,* XXVIII (1928), 286–90.

117. ———. "A Physiological Theory of Reading Disability and Stuttering in Children," *New England Journal of Medicine,* CXCIX (1928), 1046–52.

118. ———. *Reading, Writing and Speech Problems in Children.* New York: W. W. Norton and Co., 1937.

119. PAGE, JAMES D. "Emotional Factors in Reading Disabilities," *Education,* LXXII (May 1952), 590–95.

120. PHILLIPS, A. "Six Cases of Dyslexia," *Psychological Clinic,* XIX (1930–31), 185–200.

121. PRESCOTT, DANIEL A. *Emotion and the Educative Process.* Washington, D.C.: American Council on Education, 1938.

122. PRESTON, MARY I. "The Reaction of Parents to Reading Failure," *Child Development,* X (September 1939), 173–79.

123. ———. "Reading Failure and the Child's Security," *American Journal of Orthopsychiatry,* X (April 1940), 239–52.

124. RANSCHBURG, P. *Die Lese-und Schreibstoringen des Kindesalters.* Halle a S.: Marhold, 1928.

125. RAPAPORT, DAVID. *Diagnostic Psychological Testing,* Vol. I. Chicago: Year Book Publishers, Inc., 1946.

126. RAYMOND, DOROTHY MACLEAN. *Performance of Reading Achievers on Memory Span and Associative Learning Tests*, unpublished doctoral dissertation, Temple University, Philadelphia, 1952.

127. REYNOLDS, M. C. "A Study of the Relationships Between Auditory Characteristics and Specific Silent Reading Abilities," *Journal of Educational Research*, XLVI (February 1953), 439–49.

128. RICHARDS, T. W. "A Case of Reading Disability Due to Deficient Visual Imagery," *Psychological Clinic*, XX (1931–32), 120–24.

129. ———. "A Clinical Study of a Severe Case of Reading Disability in a Left-Handed Child Who was Taught to Read by a Combined Grapho-Motor and Voco-Motor Method," *Psychological Clinic*, XIX (1930–31), 285–90.

130. RIDENOUR, NINA. "The Treatment of Reading Disability," *Mental Hygiene*, XIX (1935), 387–97.

131. RIZZO, N. D. "Studies in Visual and Auditory Memory Span with Special References to Reading Disability," *Journal of Experimental Education*, VIII (December 1939), 208–44.

132. ROBINSON, HELEN M. "Emotional Problems Exhibited by Poor Readers, Manifestations of Emotional Maladjustment," in *Clinical Studies in Reading I*, Supplementary Educational Monograph, No. 68. Chicago: University of Chicago Press, 1949.

133. ———. *Why Pupils Fail in Reading*. Chicago: University of Chicago Press, 1946.

134. RUSSELL, DAVID H. "Development of Thinking Processes," in *Review of Educational Research*, XXIII (April 1953), Ch. IV.

135. ———. "Interrelationships of the Language Arts and Personality," *Elementary English*, XXX (March 1953), 167–80.

136. ———. "Research on Reading Disabilities and Personality Adjustment," in *Improving Educational Research*, Official Report. Washington, D.C.: American Educational Research Association, NEA 1948, pp. 10–13.

137. ———. "Reading Disabilities and Mental Health," *Understanding the Child*, XVI (January 1947), 24–32.

138. RUTHERFORD, W. J. "The Aetiology of Congenital Word-Blindness; with an Example," *British Journal Child. Dis.*, VI (1909), 484–88.

139. SAUNDERS, MARY JANE. "The Short Auditory Span Disability," *Childhood Education*, VIII (October 1931), 59–65.

140. SCHMITT, C. "Developmental Alexia: Congenital Wordblindness, or the Inability to Learn to Read," *Elementary School Journal*, XVIII (1917–18), 680–700, 757–69.

141. SCHUBERT, DELWYN C. "Emotional and Personality Problems of Retarded Readers," *Exceptional Children*, XX (February 1954), 226–28.

142. SELZER, CHARLES A. *Lateral Dominance and Visual Function, Their Application to Difficulties in Reading, Writing, Spelling and Speech*, Harvard Monographs in Education, No. 12. Boston: Harvard University Press, 1933.

143. SHELDON, WILLIAM D., and CARRILLO, LAWRENCE. "Relation of Parents, Home, and Certain Developmental Characteristics to Children's Reading Ability," *Elementary School Journal*, LII (January 1952), 262–70.

144. SHERMAN, MANDEL. "Emotional Disturbances and Reading Disability," in GRAY, W. S., ed. *Recent Trends in Readings*, Supplementary Educational Monographs, No. 49. Chicago: University of Chicago Press, 1939, pp. 126–34.

145. ———. "Psychiatric Insights into Reading Problems," in GRAY, W. S., ed. *Clinical Studies in Reading I*, Supplementary Monographs, No. 68. Chicago: University of Chicago Press, June 1949.

146. SMITH, LINDA C. *A Study of Laterality Characteristics of Retarded Readers and Reading Achievers*, unpublished doctoral dissertation, Temple University, 1949.

147. SPADINO, E. J. *Writing and Laterality Characteristics of Stuttering Children*, Contributions to Education, No. 837. New York: Bureau of Publications, Teachers College, Columbia University, 1941.

148. STAUFFER, RUSSELL G. *Certain Psychological Manifestations of Retarded Readers*, unpublished doctoral dissertation, Temple University, 1947.

149. ———. "Certain Psychological Manifestations of Retarded Readers," *Journal of Educational Research*, XLI (February 1948), 436–52.

150. STEWART, ROBERT S. "Personality Maladjustment and Reading Achievement,"

American Journal of Orthopsychiatry, XX (April 1950), 410–17.

151. STRANG, RUTH. *Problems in the Improvement of Reading in High School and College*. Lancaster, Pa.: Science Press, 1938.

152. SYLVESTER, EMMY, and KUNST, MARY S. "Psychodynamic Aspects of the Reading Problem," *American Journal of Orthopsychiatry*, XIII (January 1943), 69–76.

153. TEEGARDEN, L. "Tests for the Tendency to Reversal in Reading," *Journal of Educational Research*, XXVII (1933), 81–97.

154. TERMAN, LEWIS M., and MERRILL, MAUD A. *Measuring Intelligence*. Boston: Houghton Mifflin Co., 1937.

155. TINKER, MILES A., and GOODENOUGH, FLORENCE L. "Mirror Reading as a Method of Analyzing Factors Involved in Word Perception," *Journal of Educational Psychology*, XXII (1931), 493–502.

156. TROW, WILLIAM CLARK. *Educational Psychology*. Boston: Houghton Mifflin Co., 1931.

157. TULCHIN, SIMON H. "Emotional Factors in Reading Disabilities in School Children," *Journal of Educational Psychology*, XXVI (1935), 443–454.

158. VAN RIPER, CHARLES. "Children Who Are Slow in Learning Speech (Speech Retardation)," in W. JOHNSON, ed. *Speech Problems of Children*. New York: Grune and Stratton, 1950, Ch. V.

159. ———. "The Quantitative Measure of Laterality," *Journal of Experimental Psychology*, XVIII (June 1935), 372–82.

160. ———. *Speech Correction, Principles and Methods*. New York: Prentice-Hall, 1947.

161. VORHAUS, PAULINE G. "Non-Reading as an Expression of Resistance," *Rorschach Research Exchange*, X (June 1946), 60–69.

162. ———. "Rorschach Configurations Associated with Reading Disability," *Journal of Projective Techniques*, XVI (March 1952), 3–41.

163. WARREN, HOWARD C., and CARMICHAEL, LEONARD. *Elements of Human Psychology*. Boston: Houghton Mifflin Co., 1930.

164. WECHSLER, DAVID. *The Measurement of Adult Intelligence*. Baltimore: Williams and Wilkins Co., 1944.

165. WEISENBURG, T. H. "A Study of Aphasia," *Archives of Neurology and Psychiatry*, XXXI (1934), 1–33.

166. ———, and MCBRIDE, F. *Aphasia*. New York: The Commonwealth Fund, 1935.

167. WELLS, F. L. *Mental Tests in Clinical Practice*. Yonkers-on-Hudson: World Book Co., 1927.

168. ———, and RUESCH, J. *Mental Examiners' Handbook*. New York: The Psychological Corporation, 1942.

169. WEPMAN, JOSEPH M. *Recovery from Aphasia*. New York: Ronald Press, 1951.

170. WIKSELL, WESLEY. "The Relationship Between Reading Difficulties and Psychological Adjustment," *Journal of Educational Research*, XLI (March 1948), 557–58.

171. WILKING, S. VINCENT. "Personality Maladjustment as a Causative Factor in Reading Disability," *Elementary School Journal*, XLII (December 1941), 268–79.

172. WITTY, PAUL A. "Reading Success and Emotional Adjustment," *Elementary English*, XXVII (May 1950), 281–96.

173. ———, and KOPEL, DAVID. "Causation and Diagnosis of Reading Disability," *Journal of Psychology*, II (1936), 161–91.

174. ———. "Factors Associated with the Etiology of Reading Disability," *Journal of Educational Research*, XXIX (February 1936), 448–59.

175. ———. "Sinistral and Mixed Manual-Ocular Behavior in Reading Disability," *Journal of Educational Psychology*, XXVII (February 1936), 119–34.

176. WOODY, CLIFFORD, and PHILLIPS, ALBERT J. "The Effects of Handedness on Reversals in Reading," *Journal of Educational Research*, XXVII (May 1934), 651–62.

177. YEDINACK, JEANETTE G. "A Study of the Linguistic Functioning of Children with Articulation and Reading Disabilities," *Journal of Genetic Psychology*, LXXIV (1949), 23–59.

178. ZIRBES, LAURA. "Some Character and Personality Problems of Remedial Cases in Reading," *Childhood Education*, V (December 1928), 171–76.

179. ZOLKOS, HELENA H. "What Research Says About Emotional Factors in Retardation in Reading," *Elementary School Journal*, LI (May 1951), 512–18.

INSTRUCTIONAL CAUSES OF POOR READING
Walter B. Barbe

There are, of course, many causes of a child's difficulty in learning to read. To single out any one cause, regardless of how important it may be, tends to create the impression that it is *the* cause. Early research in the field of reading reflected the attitude that particular factors were the cause of all reading problems. But as one author attempted to show that poor reading was due to one factor, another author attempted to lay the blame elsewhere.

An examination of current research in the field of reading disability clearly indicates that the multiple-causation belief is most prevalent today. This means that not only are there many various factors which cause reading problems, but within each case itself there is possibly more than one cause. The very combination of causes sometimes creates a problem, although the single causative factor may not have been important enough alone actually to cause a reading problem of any serious nature.

The reason for so much attention to the cause of reading problems is twofold. First of all, if the reason for the reading difficulty can be determined, the cure is more readily achieved. The second reason, however, has more far-reaching effects. It has to do with preventing additional problems from occurring. By understanding what has caused reading problems, there is more likelihood of

Reprinted from *Education*, LXXVII (May 1957), 534–540, with permission of the author and Bobbs-Merrill Company, Inc.

preventing future problems from developing. It is in this phase of any remedial reading program that the greatest value actually exists. To be continually correcting problems is a never ending task, involving the expense of far more money per pupil than any school system can justify. If the expense of both time and money on these particular children results in a better reading program so that future problems are avoided, then there can be no complaint against the diagnostic and remedial reading program.

The most commonly mentioned causes of reading difficulties are physical factors. Poor vision and hearing, generally poor health and low intelligence are all mentioned as being the underlying cause of reading problems. Emotional factors have, of late, come to receive their full share of attention as causes of reading problems. But less frequently mentioned, and certainly as important, are reading difficulties due to instructional problems.

Children having difficulties in reading due to an instructional cause are in a peculiar position. With any of the other causes of reading problems, there can be little actual blame. It is no one's fault that a child could not see well enough to learn to read, even though it could perhaps have been avoided if early and proper diagnosis had taken place. But in any event, there are no guilt feelings attached to a child's failure to learn to read because of a physical problem. Exactly the opposite is true with respect to instructional causes. The very mention that the child's problem may be due to something within the school and not within the child threatens us as teachers. It is perhaps for this reason that we have not examined carefully enough those reading problems which have as their origin flaws in the instructional program.

It seems likely that the child who is having reading problems as a result of nothing within himself, but something within the school program, falls into one of two categories. Either the child has received (1) *inadequate instruction* or (2) *improper instruction*. At first reading they may be one and the same thing; but they are definitely separate and distinct instructional causes of reading problems.

INADEQUATE INSTRUCTION

Critics attacking the public schools have directed far too much attention to inadequate instruction as a cause of reading problems. While it is true that many reading problems are caused because of this, it is not true that this is the single reason for reading problems. As teachers, we are all trying to improve, and the ability to recognize that we are making mistakes and want to do something about them is the hope that fewer and fewer reading problems will develop as a result of inadequate instruction.

Lack of Skill Instruction

In considering inadequate instruction, it is necessary to realize that some children have not been taught to read. This may be because the teacher does not believe in teaching the skills, or it may be that her program has failed to reach particular children. Overcrowded classrooms would be one explanation of this, and too wide a range of ability in a single room would be another explanation. Frequent changing of teachers or schools interrupts the program and may cause problems. The reason which most teachers would be first to mention, however, would be the cutting down of time in which they can teach by needless interruptions and special activities.

The most important question to be asked when inadequate instruction is mentioned is, "Has the child been taught to read, or has he been left to learn on his own?" Now it is a fact that many children will learn to read with or without the help of the teacher. Some children actually reach a certain level of maturation when the ability to read comes as naturally as did the ability to walk and talk. But with the majority of children, this almost miraculous stage is never reached if it is left to maturation alone. The teacher, or the parent, must give the maturation process a helping hand. If this is not done, many children will not learn to read well.

Merely placing books in front of some children will so stimulate them to want to read that they will learn in spite of our instructional method, certainly not because of it. This is a fine method for those children with whom it works. It is a deplorable method for all the others.

Is reading a subject or a skill? Perhaps it would be more nearly correct to say that it is a skill after it has been learned; but until that time of mastery, it can be little more than a subject. As a subject, there are certain skills that have to be learned. Too many children are not learning these skills, and are unable to read.

Incidental teaching has been highly praised, but the teacher who believes that incidental teaching means to teach those things when and if she stumbles on to them is not in the group that deserves the praise. Incidental teaching means teaching all the basic skills of reading as the need arises. The skillful teacher sees that the need does arise for all the necessary skills. The teacher who confuses incidental teaching with accidental teaching fails to give the children certain basic skills in reading that they will need when they progress to a high level of reading material.

Children must be taught to read. They learn to read as a result of this teaching. They cannot be expected to learn to read without the benefit of guidance from the teacher. The few children who are exceptions to this are better off for having been exposed to the skills, for later on they may need to use these skills even if they do not at the particular moment see the need. An inadequate coverage of the basic skills in reading is a major cause of reading problems.

INFLEXIBLE PROGRAM

The teacher may teach the skills necessary for reading, but not reach all of the children. In a classroom in which there are too many students, some children are victims of inadequate instruction. There are just too many children for the teacher to reach every child. Classrooms of thirty, forty and sometimes even fifty are not unheard of. In such instances, it is a certainty that some reading problems are being developed because the instruction is inadequate for some of the children. They simply need more teaching than they can possibly get under such circumstances. It is no fault of the teacher that all such children are not taught, but is instead an administrative fault brought about by the unfortunate notion that large classes are economical.

Even within a class with a normal pupil load, it is still possible that the range of abilities is so great that the teacher is unable to give adequate instruction to all levels. It is not uncommon for a class to contain children reading on as many as eight different reading levels. Actually, the higher in school the children go, the greater is this spread. It is little wonder that teachers do not provide instruction when they are expected to teach skills to children who range in reading ability from the first through the twelfth grades, all within

the same room and expected to learn at approximately the same rate.

CHANGING TEACHERS

Another reason why a child may have a reading problem due to inadequate instruction is the change in teachers. Probably even one year with a particular teacher of reading is not enough, but certainly less than one year is too short a time. The teacher must devote too much time learning the particular child, to have him leave at less than a year. The learning about the child which the teacher has done is the child's best hope for success. When this is wasted by either the teacher's leaving, or the child's moving, instruction cannot be as effective.

In this period of learning the child, the teacher is following a program of presenting the skills. She is establishing channels by which she can teach the child. She is developing attitudes which will make the child receptive to her particular type of teaching. Only in rare instances, therefore, should the program be interrupted. This stresses the need for requiring teachers to respect their contracts to teach throughout the year, in all but the most urgent circumstances. By the same standard, signing a contract without intending to complete the school year is nothing less than fraud and should not be treated lightly for the children suffer as a result of such action.

Even one move may put a child into the position that he learns little of the actual content material of a particular grade. The three and four shifts, which are not uncommon even within a single city, doom the child to inadequate background of skills. Where it is at all possible, the child should be transported to the school in which he was originally registered, rather than transferred to the new school which may be closer.

This may appear as undue concern about what teacher a child may have, but it actually is more important today than ever before. Schools of some years ago followed rigid curriculum guides, and it made relatively little difference into which room the child might go. Changing from one teacher to another meant probably little more than a difference in personality of the teacher. But today, when strict adherence to a curriculum guide is recognized as ineffective teaching for all children, a change in teachers may well mean a completely different approach with different stressing of skills. While it would not be desirable to return to the rigidity of earlier days, it might nevertheless be wise to have flexible curriculum guides, particularly in areas in which there is a mobile school population.

INTERRUPTIONS IN PROGRAM

Interruptions in the class period may well account for many children failing to learn to read. Children are scheduled to spend approximately six hours a day in school, or approximately thirty hours a week. When lunch periods and recesses are subtracted from this, there is probably from twenty to twenty-four hours left for instruction each week. (This is the same amount of time that researchers are reporting that children watch T.V. each week.) Classroom routine, such as calling the roll, collecting money, and many other expected tasks, takes more of this time. If a teacher is not careful, there will be no time left for instructional purposes. It is a certainty that many reading problems exist for no other reason than that the children have just never been taught. In spite of the value of the many enrichment activities being carried on in the modern school, when they take on more importance than the regular instructional program they need to be curtailed.

These are certainly not all of the reasons for inadequate instruction, but they are the more important ones. The hope that can be seen in this situation is that none of them are things which must continue.

IMPROPER INSTRUCTION

It sometimes hurts us to recognize that in this day of better trained teachers, more adequate psychological services and more and better methods and materials for teaching reading, that there can still be reading problems. There are these problems, however, and some of them are due to improper instruction.

Of importance to all people concerned with helping children is the number of children who are reading problems because of improper instruction. This cause of reading problems may be due either to the teacher or the parent. It may be because the teacher simply has not been taught how to teach reading, or because she isn't interested enough in teaching to use what she knows. It may be that the teacher is too rigid to adapt the program to each particular child. If none of these, improper instruction may be caused by either a wrong diagnosis of the child's difficulty, or no diagnosis at all.

UNTRAINED TEACHERS

Because of the tremendous increase in the birth rate in the past fifteen years, the schools are now packed to capacity with eager youngsters who want to learn to read. But along with this desire to read, is also a desire to watch T.V. and look at the comics. If the learning process is too difficult, the child will forego the pleasure of learning how to read and turn to other less difficult media of communication for gaining information.

Along with the sudden upswing in the birth rate a sudden upswing in the enrollment in teachers' colleges did not come. While the enrollment in colleges has gone up, the number entering teaching has been alarmingly low. As a result of this, schools which have had hordes of children descend upon them must find someone to teach these children. Ideally, the schools would like to raise the standards of their teachers. But when no one applies for the vacancy, the school can hardly demand that any standards be met, much less that higher than ever standards be reached.

Recognizing this problem, many states have lowered their standards to those of a generation ago. No longer is the four year degree a requirement to teach. In some states only two years' college work is required for a certificate, and in special instances there are beginning teachers with only a high school diploma. It is hardly a solution to bring untrained people into the classroom for, even though many may actually make a good teacher, there will be many who actually harm the children by not knowing what they are trying to teach nor how to go about teaching it.

Teaching reading is not just a matter of having the children read page after page, but this is the technique that is being used by many untrained teachers. Unlike the medical profession that has constantly raised its standards, even though there have not been enough doctors available, the teaching profession has been forced to lower the standards required for teachers. It is certainly questionable whether this is a wise move, for it has resulted in lower prestige for teachers. This, in turn, has resulted in more capable students turning to other professions in alarmingly large numbers.

Teaching children to read by the wrong method is the beginning of a problem which will be a costly one if it is to be corrected. The hiring of substandard teachers, who do not know how to teach reading, is no solution to the teacher shortage but is instead only adding to the problems of education.

No Systematic Program

The need for systematic reading instruction must not be minimized. Instruction in the skill of reading in a haphazard, hit and miss fashion results in far too many reading failures for it to be considered an effective method. There are certain sequences which should be followed in teaching the skills in-volved in learning to read. These sequences are as important as the more obvious sequences involved in learning to use arithmetic. Just as the child cannot be expected to be able to multiply before he can add, neither should the child be expected to read new words before he has been taught the skills of word attack. And by the same measure, the child who cannot read second grade material in his reader, certainly should not be expected to read fourth or fifth grade material in the content areas.

The skills involved in learning to read, while not rigidly set as they are in some areas, are logical. Research studies show, for example, that teaching initial consonant sounds before initial vowel sounds is a better practice. But if the danger is that neither will be taught, then the teacher should be allowed to teach either first. The tragedy is that trained teachers know these things; untrained teachers do not know them. Is it fair to the pupils that they must try to learn the difficult task of reading from an untrained, unskilled person?

Single Method of Instruction

The great danger of a so-called "new" method of teaching reading is that so much attention is directed to this single method that the teacher may fail to recognize that no one method will work for all children. It is going from one extreme to the other that has characterized educational philosophy as an indefinite, always uncertain field. Actually, every teacher can do a better job of teaching reading, and it is the constantly changing program that insures the child the best possible education. But there needs to be caution exercised against going from one extreme to the other because not all children learn by one particular method. Not all children will learn by any one method, and the teacher who tries to teach all children by exactly the same method is doomed to failure before she starts.

Some children learn to read most easily by a phonic approach. They hear sounds clearly, can distinguish between sounds without difficulty, and enjoy the developing of words out of sounds. Phonics help them so much that this is the method by which they should be taught. But within the very same classroom there will be children who not only can't hear the sounds, but can't seem to learn them. In the school or class in which the teacher is convinced that she has discovered *the* way to teach reading, these individuals will fail. It is true that in some select communities, special single-method programs appear to be successful. But the question arises whether these same children would not have been just as successful with any program in which the teacher put so much faith.

Other children learn by a sight method far better than by a phonic approach. These children need to be taught by the method with which they have the greatest success. But even those children who have one particular way in which it is easiest for them to learn, under some circumstances an appeal to another sense will aid in the learning. Some children, and they are usually the ones who have the greatest difficulty in learning to read, can be reached by neither a visual nor an auditory approach. With them the teacher must use the kinesthetic or tactile sense.

In identifying children who have reading difficulties because of a single approach in their teaching, it is frequently necessary to know something about the school in which the child is enrolled and the teacher he has. The symptom of such improper instruction is usually total failure in reading, with the knowledge of some skills which can be recited but which cannot be used in the reading situation.

Inadequate Undertaking of Child

Before an adequate reading program can be carried on, the child needs to be understood by the teacher. Certainly not all children will need diagnosis of a more highly specialized nature than the teacher can provide but those who do should receive the best possible. No diagnosis of the child's problems can lead to a much more severe reading problem as well as to other types of personal and social maladjustment. An inadequate or incorrect diagnosis can have the same effect.

Frequently specialists in reading see so many cases of poor reading due to a particular cause that they are inclined to believe that they have found the cause of all reading problems. About the time that this happens, the specialist is in danger of then making the case fit what he already believes, instead of finding out what the problem actually is. There are, of course, many symptoms which are quite common in reading disability cases. But these symptoms are only symptoms, and should not be considered causes of the problem itself.

Until the teacher knows what the problem is, there is little chance of success in treating the problem. Therefore, adequate diagnosis is essential for a successful reading instruction.

There can be little doubt that some reading problems are actually caused by some phase of the instructional program. Because as teachers we have the responsibility of doing as much as possible to improve reading instruction, it is necessary for us to examine ourselves and our procedures in order that we will profit by our mistakes. There has been too much of this by the journalist, eager to produce sensational material. But there has perhaps been too little by teachers, who are not concerned with the profits to be made by sensational exposé. This discussion of where we as teachers have failed is intended only to make us more aware of how we can improve our reading programs, and is not meant to be an attack on those who are doing a better job of educating all children than ever before in the history of American education.

INTERRELATIONS OF GUIDANCE
AND READING PROBLEMS
Ruth Strang

Some emotional disturbance accompanies most serious reading difficulties. The retarded or reluctant reader often feels inadequate and inferior to his classmates. His failure to read may disturb his relationships with his parents, increase sibling rivalry, and evoke criticism from his teachers. These secondary emotional factors may interfere more seriously with his learning to read than the immediate causes of the reading difficulty.

Accordingly, reading teachers should be aware of these emotional difficulties in reading. By providing tasks in which the individual can succeed, by focusing attention on his potential for positive growth, by helping parents to take a more hopeful attitude toward the child, and by helping him to build realistic expectations of success, the teacher of reading will provide conditions in which optimum learning will take place.

The teacher of reading, however, will not focus his attention on these emotional aspects; he will deal primarily with the individual's reading development and difficulty. He will diagnose the individual's present reading status and difficulties and provide instruction and practice that will help him overcome the difficulties and move ahead on his true developmental reading trend. This procedure itself often reduces emotional distur-

Reprinted from *Education*, LXXV (March 1955), 456–461, with the permission of the author and Bobbs-Merrill Company, Inc.

bance; it may have considerable therapeutic influence.

When the individual is not accessible to reading instruction because of emotional disturbance, he should be treated by someone who is expert in psychotherapy. The referral itself may have therapeutic value insofar as it helps the individual to see his problem more clearly and recognize the kind of treatment that may, at the time, be most beneficial. After resolving some of the emotional conflicts that have been preventing him from concentrating and putting forth the necessary effort, he will be ready for instruction and practice in reading skills. Thus the teaching of reading and guidance are intertwined.

"Guidance in learning" is a familiar idea. "Guidance in reading" is a familiar aspect of guidance in learning. It is less widely recognized that there is a reciprocal relation between reading and guidance.

A READING PROBLEM MAY TURN INTO A GUIDANCE PROBLEM

One day when the teacher called on a fifth-grade boy to read aloud, he began reading, "And then Christopher Columbus . . ." and finished the sentence by saying, "ran round and round the barn." The other children laughed and the teacher told him to sit down. After class she said kindly, putting her hand on his shoulder, "Why do you do things like that, Jimmy?" He pushed her hand away and said angrily, "Everyone is always picking on me."

The teacher sought the help of the school social worker who asked for more details about Jimmy's behavior in class. "What is your explanation?" she asked. "Perhaps, he's misunderstood at home," the teacher said, "and perhaps in school he's ashamed to have the other children know he can't read. So he says silly things when he comes to words he cannot understand."

When the school social worker visited the home, she found the parents favored the older brother, Ted. When something was needed at the store, Ted would speak up: "I'll go, Pop; I know just what you want." When the family were planning a picnic Jimmy was not expected to have any ideas. His lack of progress in school, and especially in reading, was of great concern to his parents, and they were constantly critical of him. As they talked, the school social worker was able to offer the parents a few interpretations: "When his parents are constantly critical of him, a child sometimes feels that they do not love him as much as they love their other children"; "Even children in the same family may be so very different—we cannot compare one child with another"; and "A child's unhappiness at home often makes it impossible for him to pay attention in school." When the father remarked that they could include Jimmy more often in their family plans, the school social worker said, "That's a fine idea."

In her next interview with the teacher, the school social worker began by saying, "You were right, Miss Brown. Jimmy is not a bad boy; he's a misunderstood boy." Together they planned ways to help Jimmy gain approval by making contributions to the class rather than by resorting to clowning, and to give him special instruction in reading. Since the teacher felt that she could not give him as much time as he needed to learn the basic reading skills, she referred him to the read-ing teacher who served the school. The reading teacher began with the instruction he had missed through illness and change of residence in the early grades. For the first time he was able to see progress. This success made it easier for the parents to be less critical and more approving. It took time. But at the end of the year Jimmy said, "I guess I'm not such a headache to everybody any more—or to myself either."

In this case, as in so many others, reading and personal relations are interwoven. Jimmy's failure to learn to read at the age when other children did disturbed his parents. Reading seemed very important to them. Their way of coping with the situation was to criticize Jimmy and to hold up his brother as a model. Both of these responses made the situation worse. The criticism made Jimmy feel still more inadequate and he interpreted the praise of the brother as a withdrawal of parental love. Added to these home conditions was the teacher's criticism of his poor reading. His desire to be accepted by his classmates led to his evading the reading situation by clowning.

Since so much of this behavior problem stemmed from the boy's inability to read the kinds of material expected of him in the grade, the teacher was wise to begin with the instruction he needed in reading. The help with reading was augmented by more sympathetic understanding on the part of parents and teacher. Thus guidance and skillful reading instruction combined forces in the process of removing the cause of the boy's feeling of inferiority and one source of criticism. It helped him, as well as his parents and teacher, to take a more positive, accepting attitude.

GENESIS OF SOME READING PROBLEMS

Guidance workers are even more concerned with "developmental guidance," and with creating conditions that help to prevent serious problems from arising. Here is where an understanding of the multiple causation and varied treatment of reading difficulties is essential.

Reading problems may be created by a curriculum that has no meaning, use, or purpose for the student; by dull, poorly written books; by methods of instruction that do not provide for individual differences and needs. The intrapersonal relations in the classroom may stimulate or discourage a child from realizing his potentialities. Poor medical service may permit physical impairments to go uncorrected. In many ways the guidance worker, through his policy-making function and community contact, may help to prevent reading problems at their source.

READING PROBLEMS OFTEN TURN INTO GUIDANCE PROBLEMS

A common sequence is: inability to comprehend the reading assignments in one's grade; failure in subjects requiring a good deal of reading; dissatisfaction with school and either truancy or behavior problems in class.

In the last stages of this sequence, the student is often referred to the counselor. By that time the complexity of the problem has usually increased so much that the initial cause may not be recognized, except by a counselor who is aware of the possible ramifications of a reading difficulty.

A GUIDANCE PROBLEM TURNS INTO A READING PROBLEM

A high school boy came into the counselor's office and announced that he was leaving school. The counselor, knowing the boy's background and that his family were financially able to keep him in school, said, "Why, Don, you don't have to leave school to go to work. Your family would be glad to have

you stay and graduate." Finally, Don admitted that his real reason for wanting to leave school was his difficulty with reading. "The kids laugh when the teacher makes me read out loud, and the books I have to read don't make sense to me," he told her.

"That would discourage anyone," the counselor said. "But it is possible to improve your reading. Lots of students in high school have learned to read better."

Fortunately, this counselor, who had such a good relationship with Don, had taken some work in reading. First, she tried to find out more definitely what his reading potentialities were. On the Bellevue-Wechsler individual intelligence test he obtained an IQ of 115 on the quantitative tests and an IQ of 90 on the verbal part. These results indicated potential ability to read high school material. The auditory comprehension test of Diagnostic Reading Committee battery showed much higher ability to comprehend what he heard than to comprehend a similar selection which he read silently. This, too, pointed to potentiality for improvement.

Having established Don's potentiality to read better, the second step was to learn more about his reading level and the difficulties he was encountering. To obtain a general idea of his reading level, the counselor looked through Don's cumulative record folder for results of a recent reading test. She found an Iowa Silent Reading Test given the previous year. Don's score corresponded to a fifth-grade level.

Although some diagnostic information could be obtained from the standardized test, the counselor wanted more specific information about Don's reading difficulties. To obtain this, she asked him to read some fifth-grade selections. Standardized tests do not always indicate the level on which the student is actually reading books and articles of various kinds. Don stumbled over third-grade material that embarrassed him by being childish in content and read more difficult material in which he was keenly interested.

The third step combined diagnosis and instruction; its purpose was to alleviate his immediate distress in trying to get his studying done. The counselor sat beside him as he began to read his day's assignment in history. Thus she not only learned about his approach to reading, but also taught him a better approach—to recall what he knew about the subject and raise questions before beginning to read. She not only learned about his difficulties in word recognition and meaning and in comprehension, but also gave him immediate instruction in the reading skills which he needed to improve.

The counselor's fourth step was to give the further practice and instruction specifically indicated by her informal diagnostic procedure. While thus helping him to meet his immediate problems, she also encouraged wide reading of interesting books and articles on his present reading level. This helped to increase his fluency, and change his attitude toward reading and toward himself as a boy who could not read.

Helping Don took considerable of the counselor's time, especially at the beginning. Later, by working with his teachers, the counselor helped them acquire methods of helping other students improve their reading in their respective subjects. Was this use of counselor's time justified in a school having no reading specialist? It most certainly was. Not only did the counselor help an individual pupil develop his learning potentialities and prepare himself better for life; she also helped a number of teachers to deal more adequately with one of the most serious problems in high school today—failure in academic subjects from ineffective reading and study habits.

EMOTIONAL DISTURBANCE MAY BE ALLEVIATED BY INSTRUCTION IN READING

A freshman college girl in the middle of the spring semester was becoming so emotionally disturbed that she was referred to the mental hygiene center at the college. The psychiatrist, in the initial interview, recognized the girl's intense fear of flunking out of college. Her father was a noted professional man; the girl was very fond of him and felt that her dismissal from college would be a disgrace to the family. She studied late at night, could not sleep, became more and more depressed. Recognizing that her inability to keep up with the academic requirements was a basic cause of her trouble, the psychiatrist referred her to the reading specialist on his staff.

For the first two interviews, the student talked about her fears and difficulties. In the presence of a sympathetic, understanding person, her anxieties became less. In the following periods they worked more intensively on analyzing the purpose of each assignment, recognizing what the instructor expected, listening to lectures, taking effective notes, building a vocabulary in each field, getting the main ideas, varying rate and method of reading with the kind of material and one's purpose in reading it, improving concentration and memory, preparing for and taking examinations.

This combination of a supporting relationship plus specific instruction in methods of reading daily assignments enabled this girl to complete her freshman year. She was permitted to return to college the next fall and eventually graduated from college with a satisfactory record.

In schools and colleges having high academic standards and stressing competitive examinations, mental health problems are likely to arise. In some cases the student is attempting the impossible, and some adjustment of his program should be made. In other cases, able students have "got by" on lower educational levels without learning efficient reading and study methods. Worse yet, they have formed indolent, inefficient habits and attitudes that are hard to break. When they come to college they are not able to meet the academic demands. This is a new and often frightening experience. However, with some help in reading, they are helped to make a good adjustment to college.

It is not only these special cases that need help in reading. It is much better, whenever possible, to prevent failure and its attendant nervous wear and tear. To this end, a course in reading should be an intrinsic part of the program of all freshmen. Every student can increase his reading efficiency. Such a course, in both high school and college, is a way of preventing many problems that would have to be referred to the guidance worker.

SUMMARY OF INTERRELATIONSHIPS

The three cases cited illustrate some of the interrelations of guidance and reading problems on all educational levels. These may now be supplemented and summarized.

The theory underlying both guidance and reading problems is essentially the same. In the literature of both fields, one finds the same principles: respect for the individual, recognition of the resources he has within himself for solving his own problems, the need for understanding causes instead of treating surface behavior, and the influence of the group on individual development.

Most serious reading problems involve emotional difficulties. Some reading problems stem from ineffective or premature instruction in reading. The child's failure to acquire a culturally important skill disturbs the parents, and their concern often affects the child's concept of himself and his relationship with his parents. Thus emotional difficulties gather around what was initially only a reading problem. Sometimes an emotionally disturbed child is not able to put forth the effort to keep his mind on reading. He is inaccessible to reading instruction until the emotional conflicts are resolved.

However, the fact that there is a relation between emotional difficulty and reading does not mean that only psychotherapy is needed. Reading instruction may have therapeutic value. The acquiring of needed skills may relieve some of the individual's immediate distress in the classroom; success in reading builds self-confidence which may spread to other areas; the pupil's improvement in reading may lead his parents and teachers to take a more favorable attitude toward him.

If the problem is primarily emotional, individual counseling may be required. This means that the reading teacher should be aware of indications of serious emotional disturbances, such as extreme withdrawal, depression, and shifts of mood.

There is an advantage, however, in avoiding transferring a student from one specialist to another. If the guidance person has some background in reading, and the reading specialist has become skillful in counseling, it is possible for the client to capitalize on the good relationship he has established with the first person who interviewed him.

More and more, counseling and reading programs are being fused administratively. Some guidance and personnel departments have reading specialists on their staffs. Even if they are in separate departments, they may still work together closely in the prevention and treatment of reading problems.

3
Psychology of Reading and Learning

ON THE PSYCHOLOGY OF READING

Wendell W. Weaver

In the Eleventh Yearbook, Kingston (*8*, p. 20)* defined reading as "a process of communication by which a message is transmitted graphically between individuals." The treating of language processes as parts of a communication system analogous to a mechanical system is an outgrowth of advances in communications engineering. These concepts of communications theory, especially their mathematical elaboration, do not always fit well the psychological situations but the implications of the ideas are so intriguing and seem to have such potential for explanation that many psychologists have not been able to leave them alone.

The most common classification of communications systems involves five components—a source, a transmitter, a channel, a receiver, and a destination. Here, I refer to the operations of the source and the trans-

Reprinted from *New Concepts in College-Adult Reading, Thirteenth Yearbook of the National Reading Conference* (1964), 67–74, with permission of the author and National Reading Conference, Inc. [*Numbers in parentheses refer to Bibliography at the end of this article.]

mitter as encoding and to the operations of the receiver and the destination as decoding. Our system of graphic symbols encoded into and decoded out of the neurophysiological code of the organism is the coding operation. The graphic symbols themselves are the external display, and the figure and ground, in the case of reading, is the channel. By the psychology of reading I mean the scientific study of graphical decoding operations in the human organism.

Such a scientific psychology of reading is difficult to come by. Not the least of the problems of the psychological thinker is the pervasive idea that reading is a human sort of thing of such a nature that it is unpredictable, unmechanical, even unmeasureable. This attitude is expressed in many ways, some subtle, some not so subtle as the following:

> I think that I shall never see
> A calculator made like me.
> A me that likes Martinis dry
> And on the rocks a little rye.
> A me that looks at girls and such,
> But mostly girls, and very much.
> A me that wears an overcoat
> And likes a risky anecdote.

A me that taps a foot and grins
Whenever Dixieland begins.
They make computers for a fee,
But only moms can make a me.

(*10*, p. 111)[1]

A cognition involving not only a psychological but also a biological half-truth. Such sentiments are not at all proper for a psychologist studying reading, for here the search is explicitly for the predictable, the mechanical, the measurable. Other considerations are for philosophy or for art. As psychologist one does not concern himself with the whole person, but only with that part of the person which with simplification can be shown to exhibit lawful behavior.

Not only must the psychologist ignore popular assumptions that the reading process is scientifically unanalyzable but he must overcome biases in his own training. Reading processes are largely covert. Since the introspectionists, psychologists have not been comfortable with covert processes.

The psychologist does not feel uncomfortable in dealing with the auditory display, which we call speech, for he treats the display as an overt behavior directly related to the source. Thus Skinner (*11*) labels speech, and other overt acts, as verbal behavior but excludes listening from this category. If we consider carefully however, we see that speech and writing are but the *end* products of an encoding operation; they are not complete displays of that operation. They are only the part of the encoding operation which has potential for subsequent decoding operations. There is no reason to assume that we can learn more about the total speech or writing act from the external display of speech or writing than we can learn about reading or listening from the same external display. In studying any part of the language process the psychologist has been restricted largely to the message in transit from one organism to an-

other. There seems no virtue in considering these messages in transit as outputs only. As elements in the channel of communication these messages are at once both output and input. It seems valid to look either way along the channel of communication, back to the source of the message, or forward to the destination of the message. In either case, the primary interest of the psychologist is not in the message in transit, but in the originator and destination of the message.

Whatever inferences psychologists make from the vantage point of the channel of communication, the inferences are directed toward those "black boxes" we call human organisms. The "black box" is another term originating in engineering. It describes a problem situation which contains an unknown "machine" with input and output connections. The problem solver may vary the characteristics of the input and measure the effects on the output. He cannot open the box. From his knowledge of what went in and his measurement of what comes out he is to deduce the internal operations performed in the box.

The psychologist dealing with his problem cannot be sure of the operations that are "really" performed in the box. He can only be sure that he has an analogue. Although he is in contact with the covert only by inferences he is able to draw from the overt, certain assumptions must be maintained if the psychologist is to remain scientific. How easy it is to stray from these assumptions is illustrated by this quotation from Wendell Garner's otherwise insightful book *Uncertainty and Structure as Psychological Concepts*.

> The significance of a word is the actual identifying relation, and it cannot exist in lesser or greater degree. It is simply a statement of the nature of a relation and while the nature of the relation can be changed, this change is qualitative and cannot be quantified. To a child, the signification of the word *honesty* may be very simple, while

to an adult it may be very complex. But this change is not one of quantity of signification, but rather of quality. (6, p. 142)

Now whatever the signification of a word is, as psychologist we should assume it is a state of the organism and as such must be a physical state, in principal reducible to quantity or form, or to sequences of quantity or form. That is, in the broadest sense it must be quantifiable unless extra-scientific assumptions are made.

Because the obvious approach to all language study is along the channel of communication with its "public" content, the psychologist studying reading shares an interest in language in transit with several other disciplines. Discoveries in these related fields while providing many analyses suggestive to psychological thinking, may also distort the proper psychological approach to reading. The linguists for example share several concerns with the psychologist. There is a basic difference however in the direction of the effort exerted. The linguist is not ordinarily interested in the question, "What does this language sample imply about the source or the destination of the message?" He asks rather, "What does this language sample imply about language samples in general?" The linguist ordinarily assumes that his task is accomplished when he demonstrated the lawfulness of the language display itself.

A recent examination of reading from the linguistic point of view while appearing to contribute to reading instruction could misdirect the psychologist. In his book *Linguistics and Reading*, (4), C. C. Fries develops the position that reading is a substitution of a printed display for the previously learned sounds of the language. The assumption is that, organismically, graphic symbols encode verbal symbols. As the sounds have been related previously to semantic structures the semantic structures already learned are transferred directly to the written cues. The thesis implies that anyone who can talk can read

and those who talk but do not read are the victims of inadequate instruction in transferring graphic symbols into sound symbols. For all I know this is an acceptable hypothesis, but the point here is that Fries gives the impression he is dealing with linguistic fact while he is actually stating an untested neurophysiological hypothesis. Accepting the hypothesis is tantamount to saying the psychology of reading is the psychology of speech once the word is matched with the sound it represents.

Fries goes on to draw the implication that the teacher of reading is not concerned with "meaning" as such. Perhaps it would be fairer to say Fries believes the "meaning" is already there, as a result of previous verbal experiences, so the reading teacher does not need to be concerned. Whether this absence of concern for meaning is proper for the teacher of reading or not, the psychologist interested in decoding operations of the organism is concerned. He assumes meaning must be represented in organic tissue or be a result of states of the organism. Just as the structures which make reading possible are coded organic structures, the structures which make meaning possible are coded organic structures. The reading process is not completed until the organism has determined if the message has meaning, I use this phraseology advisedly.

Meaning, as I think of the term, is the result of the application of prior codings of the organism to the present decoding task. The prior codings of the organism do not seem entirely dependent on input sources external to the organism. That is, the internal system seems to be productive of new input to the system. External inputs into the system are interpreted by previous external inputs plus internal reorganizations which have occurred.

A message is communicated as the coding of the message approaches relevant coded structures within the organism. Communication by reading depends upon equivalent states in source and destination. Under certain circumstances a message may be meaningful without communicating. The written display may activate structures in the receiver not congruent with structures the same coding activates in the source. These activated structures are under the control of the internal organization of the destination rather than under the control of the organization of the source of the message. The popular terms for this condition are "misreadings" or "variant readings."

There is no theory of language worthy of the name. Until there is, of course, there will be no adequate theory of reading. As one looks at reading research for aid in framing such a theory he gets the impression of intense interest and activity but little consistency of direction. Traditional approaches have been barren as far as theory is concerned; current approaches are "far out" and who can tell what will become of them. The approach I prefer is based on a result that keeps cropping up in many studies, in many disciplines.

Language, on the one hand, is highly redundant. By developmental criteria, the structure of language is easily learned. The redundancy of a third reader is about the redundancy of a simple adult text. The redundancy of a fifth reader approaches the redundancy in average adult texts (1). The three-year-old fashions many structurally correct sentences. Certain language elements are tied down early, and these elements tend to remain invariant. They seem to function in some fashion as a frame on which to hang other elements carrying lexical information.

On the other hand, abundant stores of lexical information take much longer to acquire. The lexical unit is many times unique to a context but the most infrequently used item of information once learned can be made to appear at the appropriate time though kept under cover for years.

This sort of dichotomy of language elements has been widely noted. Colin Cherry views language as a set of constraints and theorizes that these constraints may be categorized as operating at two levels of redundancy—syntactic and semantic (2). Researchers in the field of the mechanical translation of language usually refer to the dichotomy as grammatical and nongrammatical (e.g. 9). John Chotlos (3) examining distributions in the light of Zipf's harmonic equation concludes, using a mathematical argument, that the words of a language should be divided into two categories, structural words which form the core or framework of the language, and content and action words that have directly or indirectly an extensional reference. The linguist, Fries (5), uses the terms I adopted for this paper, structural and lexical, and considers it possible to study each in isolation.

In attempting research in this area a few assumptions about how decoding processes operate have had to serve as my theory. When there is no king in Israel every man does as he desires. I assume that language elements in a neurophysiological code entering the central nervous system perform different functions. One of these functions is a control function involving relating incoming elements to elements already present in the internal environment of the organism. This control function seems to be a property of the structure of the language.

I imagine the structural part of language to be in a different system from the lexical elements of language. One bit of evidence here is that structural units are not stored with lexical units, at least, we have great difficulty in repeating intact long language sequences in the exact order in which they were presented.

I have operated with the view that language codes for the organism a progression from points of high redundancy to points of low redundancy. Points of high redundancy are points of control (i.e., these points provide directions for reorganizing and storing lexical elements). The points of high redundancy may be a few nouns for the beginning decoder—function words, punctuation, word order, and position of language element in context for the sophisticated decoder. The points of low redundancy are points of lexical information—the content or the semantic focus of the message. The analogy to the computer program is obvious. The program controlling the operation must be determined at any point in time, yet flexibility can be built into the system, even to the point of having the program alter itself. Not that the organism performs as the computer, but that the computer performs, under certain conditions, as a very insensitive and rigid, but logical organism. We can determine more accurately the nature of this simpler operation. Such a dialectic between organism and computer seems to hold much promise both for the formulation of theory and for the testing of hypotheses.

I am not recommending these assumptions to others. To date all of us have apparently missed the mark so widely that more searching among alternative formulations seems appropriate. The psychology of reading is in part beneficiary, in part victim, of the utilitarian background of the research effort: beneficiary in having a large number of people who care, who would like to see something accomplished; victim because practicality is not a prolific breeder of the imaginative. William Blake once said, "What is now proved was once only imagined." Reading theory exemplifies lack of imagination, of looking beyond what "is" to what "might be." Imagination in science must eventually be criticized by experiment, but without imagination experiment cannot come into being. We have many models and we have many investigations, but no model plus extensive fitting of the data to the model.

A scientific psychology of reading can only come into being from people with a point of view who research the point of view long enough to determine its explanatory efficiency.

BIBLIOGRAPHY

1. CARTERETTE, EDWARD C. and JONES, MARGARET HUBBARD. "Redundancy in Children's Texts," *Science*. 140: 1309-1311, June 21, 1963.
2. CHERRY, COLIN. *On Human Communication*. New York: The Technology Press of Massachusetts Institute of Technology and John Wiley & Sons, 1957.
3. Chotlos, John W. "A Statistical and Comparative Analysis of Individual Written Language Samples," *Psychological Monographs*, Vol. 56, No. 244, 1944.
4. FRIES, CHARLES C. *Linguistics and Reading*. New York: Holt, Rinehart and Winston, Inc., 1962.
5. ———. *The Structure of English*. New York: Harcourt, Brace and Company, 1952.
6. GARNER, WENDELL R. *Uncertainty and Structure as Psychological Concepts*. New York: John Wiley and Sons, Inc., 1962.
7. GLANZER, MURRAY. "Grammatical Category: A rote learning and word association analysis," *Journal of Learning and Verbal Behavior*, 1: 31–41, 1962.
8. KINGSTON, ALBERT J. "Some Thoughts on Reading Comprehension," in EMERY P. BLIESMER and RALPH C. STAIGER, eds., *Eleventh Yearbook of the National Reading Conference*. Milwaukee: National Reading Conference, 1962, 20–23.
9. REIFLER, EDWIN. "The Mechanical Determination of Meaning," in WILLIAM N. LOCKE and A. DONALD BOOTH, eds., *Machine Translation of Languages*. New York: The Technology Press of the Massachusetts Institute of Technology and John Wiley & Sons, Inc., 1955, 136–164.
10. SCHENCK, H. JR. *"Me," The Best from Fantasy and Science Fiction*: Ninth Series. New York: Doubleday. Copyright 1959 by Mercury Press, Inc. Reprinted from *The Magazine of Fantasy and Science Fiction*.
11. SKINNER, B. F. *Verbal Behavior*. New York: Appleton-Century-Crofts, 1957.

SPEED, COMPREHENSION AND POWER IN READING*
Jack A. Holmes

INTRODUCTION

Speeded reading is demanded by the tempo of the times, but the keen appreciation of crucial ideas, the understanding of those great concepts which have taken the human race thousands of years to evolve, need not, indeed cannot, be fully grasped as one's speed approaches its limit.

The secret of good reading lies in the ability to know when and how to change pace. The mundane material concerning the commerce of life may well be read quickly; but when one comes to the crux of the message, or when one fortuitously encounters one of those fountainhead concepts from which ideas flow, then one must deliberately drink the delightful draught until the full meaning has been drained. Even then such passages are well-springs that may be read again and again, each time affording the reader a little deeper insight, a greater understanding, a new zest for life!

Indeed, the deepest satisfactions come not

Reprinted from *Problems, Programs and Projects in College-Adult Reading, Eleventh Yearbook* of the National Conference (1962), 6–14, with permission of the author and National Reading Conference, Inc.

* This paper draws heavily upon a research study done by the writer and Dr. Harry Singer, "The Substrata Factor Theory: Substrata Differences Underlying Reading Ability in Known Groups." This study was a Cooperative Research Project supported by the University of California, the United States Office of Education, and the Carnegie Foundation of New York.

when one is able to read a book in 30 minutes flat (the goal stressed by some teachers today), but rather when one chances upon a beautifully written passage carrying so much meaning, sparkle, and conviction that it verily sings—as when great poetry clarifies the meaning of life and causes one to bring his value system into closer harmony with the realities of the universe.

My first point, then, is this: If one *already knows* how to read, his *rate of comprehension* of the printed page can be increased enormously by persistent practice on easy material over an extended period of time. This is all to the good. Nevertheless, as one pushes his speed above the four to eight *hundred* words per minute mark into the next higher order of magnitude, say two to eight *thousand* words per minute, the reader simply rides in on the crest of the wave. As his eyes race down the page it is true that he may learn to catch the gist of the story; but the beauty of the syntax, the style, the sting, the twinkle, the music in the well-turned phrase, the technical explanation, or logic of a philosophical discussion cannot be truly pondered, grasped, and appreciated. One may gain a knowledge of a subject by speeded reading, but he cannot gain a *working knowledge* of it. To achieve such a working knowledge, i.e., technical mastery of scientific material, or high appreciation for the music and sense of great literature, one must read not for comprehension alone, but for *power*—and it is just this *power of reading* that I wish to discuss with you in my next go-around. That is, what *is* it that makes for power in reading; and what exactly is meant by the word "power" when used in this context?

THE THEORY

It was my intent, a moment ago, to imply that theory and fact can be brought together to explain just what it is that makes one student differ from another in his ability to read with what I term "power." To this end, then, I will first outline the basic essentials of the Substrata-Factor Theory and, second, report some of the findings of an experiment we have recently completed in our labs at the University of California.

Fig. 1 presents a diagrammatic model of a working-system for power of reading. The large ball at the apex represents power of reading, the lines-of-support umbellating out from it represent psychoeducational associations between power of reading and the substrata factors at Level I.

Holding to the same logic, the Theory hypothesizes that underlying each of the subabilities discovered at Level I, we may expect to find even more fundamental ones at Level II. Below such secondary abilities, we might further expect to find a set of tertiary elements.

The Substrata-Factor Theory of Reading is concerned with the way the mind *mobilizes* sets of *subabilities* (which we will refer to as elements) into an ordered arrangement or hierarchy. In varying degrees, according to their existing strengths, the elements of this hierarchy simultaneously stimulate and reinforce each other. They compare and contrast incoming information with existing knowledge leading to a new conception, a new working knowledge, gained from the reading material. This complex ability, with its various elements, we have sought to measure and have termed it "power of reading."

The Theory holds that the auditory, visual, and kinesthetic components of incoming information are ordered and stored in localized cell-assemblies in the brain. Individuals differ in the degree to which they tend to use one of these input channels over others. At the high school level approximately two-thirds of the students are predominantly visually minded; somewhat *less* than one-third will learn better through their auditory senses, and a small percentage (mostly boys) must rely heavily upon the proprioceptive or kinesthetic senses as their most efficient input channel. This part of the Theory gives us the key as to why the majority of a class learn quickly and easily by the Look and Say method, why some children appear to thrive under a system that stresses phonics, and why still others who fail to learn by either of these methods are, in fact, able to learn to read by Fernald's tracing method.

In the brain, sets of these cell-assemblies form centers, each with its distinctive function. Oversimplified:

1. The function of one center is to store the memory traces from visual impulses which arise when viewing a concrete object.
2. The function of a second visual center is to store *symbolic representations* of the *ideas about* concrete objects, relationships, or other ideational abstractions. Here, then, is where words are perceived, registered, categorized, and filed for future reference and recall.
3. A third center stores auditory impulses which carry information conveyed by *spoken* language.
4. A fourth center stores kinesthetic impressions from tactile and muscle sensations. The location of these centers in the brain is a long-established anatomical fact.

COMPREHENSION

According to the Substrata-Factory Theory, as a result of the on-going cerebral activity during the act of perception (as in

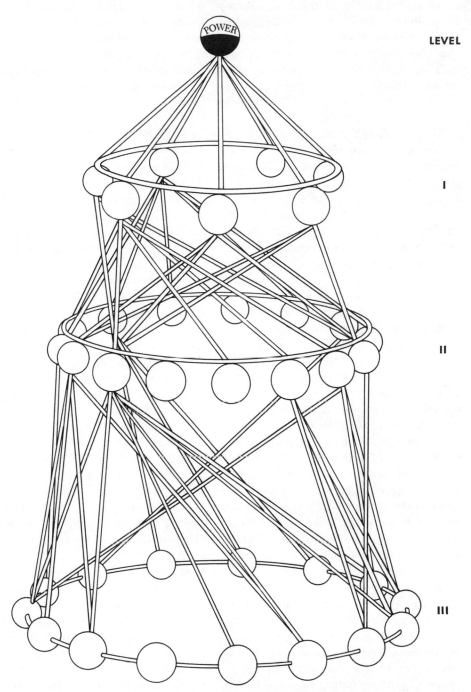

Figure 1. Ping-Pong Model of Working System

reading), the details deposited in the separate centers are now reassociated as faithfully coded representations of the objects themselves. In other words, during reading coded audio-visual and kinesthetic impressions derived from the descriptions of concrete objects are reassembled in the mind—this is comprehension.

POWER

However, simultaneously with the foregoing process, as a result of the heightened cerebral activity engendered by increased concentration, conceptual abstractions are wrought by the process of comparing and contrasting the incoming information with relevant information already stored from past experiences—this is power of reading.

It is important to understand that the input channel predominant in sensory perception need *not* coincide with the modality used in imagination and thinking. In fact, it would seem that the highest reasoning tends toward not the conjuring up of visual, auditory, or kinesthetic images, but of abstract conceptualization mediated either as (a) subarticulated verbalizations, or (b) vague generalizations unattached to words or coded representations of concrete details.

Substrata factors, then, are psychoeducational subsets of information stored in neurological subsystems of cell-assemblies. Such substrata factors stand ready to be *mobilized* into a *working-system* in accordance with the purposes of the reader. When connected into such a working-system, each substrata factor exerts an influence on all other information centers. Hence, the more efficient and the greater the number of associations among the substrata factors, the higher the *interfacilitation* of the total working-system. The explanation of how speeded reading is accomplished rests, therefore, not in the persistent practice of reading easy material, but in persistent pressure forcing the individual to increase the number of the interfacilitating associations. This, in turn, results in a heightened activity of perception, integration, abstraction, and generalization.

This being the Theory, the task of the experiment was to find whether such a model could, in fact, be statistically constructed; and, if so, what abilities would be found making up such substrata levels.

THE EXPERIMENT

In the experiment, 400 students were given some 56 separate tests, including such diverse elements as primary mental abilities, linguistic abilities, perceptual abilities, study methods skills and attitudes, and such interest factors as are recorded by the Kuder interest inventory. A host of psycho-sociological problem areas were also assessed with respect to their ability to explain individual differences in the criteria, Speed and Power of Reading. These variables were analyzed by the Substrata-Factor Analysis. Time does not allow us to go into the statistical details or methodology. Suffice it to say that when this was done, a very interesting set of abilities were indicated as substrata factors underlying Power of Reading.

Fig. 2 presents the results diagrammatically, and it will be seen that under Power of Reading we were able to account for 75 per cent of the variance as indicated distributed among the seven following variables: Vocabulary in Context, 16%; Mechanical Interest, 1%; Study Planning and Deliberation, 1%; Visual Verbal Meaning, 6%; Verbal Analogies, 16%; Auding Ability, 16%; Tone Intensity, 3%; and Vocabulary in Isolation, 16%, at Level I.

It is strikingly apparent that Power of Reading is greatly dependent upon a knowledge of words and the concepts that they symbolize. Notice that Vocabulary in Isolation, Vocabulary in Context, and Visual Verbal Meaning are all different phases of the vocabulary domain. Verbal Analogies it-

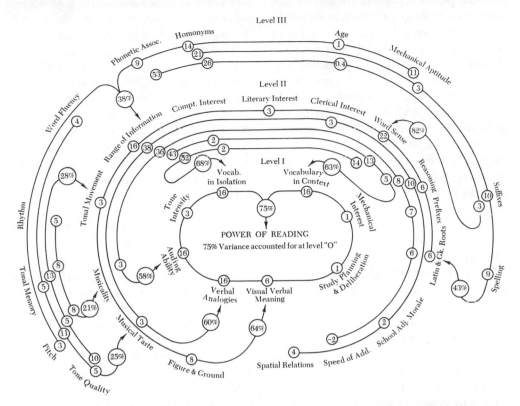

Figure 2. Power of Reading Concentric Flowchart for Total Sample of 400 High School Students. (Concentric rings from target center represent hierarchial organization of substrata factors at Levels I, II, III in the working system for power of reading. The discs give per cent of variance accounted for in each substrata factor's line of support. *Holmes 1961*)

self is reasoning through the manipulation of verbal concepts. Auding ability has to do with listening comprehension of human speech. So it is definite that at the first level the most essential element of Power of Reading is a knowledge of the meaning of words and the ability to manipulate the concepts behind these auditorily and visually perceived verbal symbols on the printed page. (This point favors the Look-Say method.)

As shown by Fig. 2 at Level II, underlying the various forms of vocabulary are a host of other factors such as Range of Information, Computational, Literary, and Clerical Interest, Word Sense, Reasoning, Prefixes, Latin and Greek Roots, School Adjustment, Speed

of Addition, Spatial Relations, Figure and Ground, Musical Taste, Musicality, and Tonal Movement.

As shown by Fig. 2, Pitch, Phonetic Association, Homonyms, Age, and Mechanical Aptitude all combine to account for 38% of Range of Information at Level III. Now I think this is an important result because, of all the elements, Range of Information is the most ubiquitous. Like Reasoning, it underlies the basic verbal elements that enter into Power of Reading at Level I. For instance, it accounts for over half, 52%, of Vocabulary in Isolation; 43% of Vocabulary in Context; 36% of Auding Ability, 38% of Verbal Analogies, and 16% of Visual Verbal Meaning. And yet, we are able to account for only about 38% of Range of Information itself by the more fundamental factors in our matrix. This would lead us to believe that the information represented by this particular substrata factor is information of a specific sort and goes way beyond the mechanics of the language itself. And, if I might say so, this gives us definite proof that those who have criticized our basal readers of the last thirty years have some justification. That is to say, there has been very little real information given to the student in most of our primary readers up to the present time.

IMPLICATIONS

Most of the basal readers have been a Dick and Jane, a Bob and Barbara type of chit-chat, centered on exercises which will increase vocabulary. But that vocabulary has been of a very low order and tied to the everyday concepts the child has already learned around the house. What I am saying is that these concepts do not give the child a chance to stretch his mind. He knows nothing more in terms of information, of new knowledge, after having read through a set of primary and elementary textbooks in *reading* than he did before he started, except that he now knows how to read a certain high-frequency list of words with some fluency. This in itself is good, but the fact that he does not get those basic concepts, or ideas, or information which will help him expand his mind when he begins to read in order to learn is a valid criticism of this type of reader.

Perhaps here we can stress the difference between learning to read and reading to learn. I think that we are prolonging the initial period of learning to read beyond the time that is profitable. Learning to read must also, sooner or later, begin to take on the concepts of reading to learn, because later reading depends upon prior learning, and that prior learning is not only a matter of the right pro-

nunciation or visual identification of words, but also (and more important) the mental manipulation of abstractions and an increased store of pertinent information.

If we were to return, as many people are now suggesting, to the McGuffey type of reader, we would not be much better off. There is so much in the McGuffey Readers that would be unacceptable to most moderns. For instance, a class system is definitely implied. There is the Horatio Alger type of story told over and over again, which is really not applicable today. While we admire the fortitude of the person in the story, teachers know better than to suggest that hard work on the job is a substitute for education. We know very well that times have changed and that many of the concepts expounded in the McGuffey Readers are no longer practical or tenable. Furthermore, while its code of ethics is unassailable, the manner of its presentation is effusively sentimental.

A hope for the future, in answer to this dilemma, is to introduce into our programs reading textbooks that have not only a graded list of words, but a graded list of *concepts*. And these concepts must become deeper, more difficult and more complex than we have previously thought possible for children to learn. I maintain, I think with some justification, that children are more capable than many educators would have us believe. For as they begin to understand more, as the reading material becomes more meaningful, their interest and power of reading will increase.

One bright spot in the developmental reading in the modern curriculum is the introduction of science and modern geography, history, and social studies into the elementary school classrooms. We must have, I think, more of these subjects in our *reading* textbooks; that is, we need the technical words that will carry over into the so-called solid disciplines, keyed to the major concepts that the child must know in order to read in these fields. And the reading teacher is in a strategic position to help the child expand and consolidate those substrata elements involved in power of reading, of which the most important is Range of Information.

BIBLIOGRAPHY

HOLMES, JACK A. "The Substrata-Factor Theory of Reading: Some Experimental Evidence," in J. ALLEN FIGUREL, ed. New Frontiers in Reading, International Reading Association Conference Proceedings, Volume 5 (1960). New York: Scholastic Magazine, 1960, pp. 115–121.

HOLMES, JACK, and SINGER, HARRY. The Substrata-Factor Theory: Substrata Factor Differences Underlying Reading Ability in Known-Groups at the High School Level. United States Office of Education Monograph Series, 1962 (in press). (Based upon final experimental reports covering Contracts No. 538, SAE-8176, and No. 538A, SAE-8660, U.S. Dept. of Health, Education, and Welfare, 1961.)

READING IN THE LIGHT OF MAJOR FORMS AND OBJECTIVES
Harry R. Warfel

The latest discoveries about the nature of language have important implications for reading instruction. The new insights direct attention to language as the instrument whereby ideas are transmitted from one mind to another. Hitherto, primary emphasis has been on perceptual problems and vocabulary in the reading process, but there has been no adequate theory of the relationship that exists between these two elements—the human body mechanisms and the areas of knowledge. I should like, therefore, to take a step beyond the conclusions which I reached in *Language: A Science of Human Behavior* and propose a context in which all elements of the reading process can be viewed as parts of a single integrated performance. Particularly I wish to demonstrate that the language system is the chief, though usually the disregarded, element in the reading process.

Language is a physical manifestation—a set of sounds emitted from the mouth or, as a substitute therefor, a set of graphic marks placed in homogeneous relationships on a durable substance The origin of the process is in the human body; the purpose of the action is to transmit a vocal or written message to one or more other human bodies. This process is possible because all human bodies have identical working parts that engage in identical integrated operations for identical purposes. The sender's nervous system originates and controls the language-coding process (the sounds or marks which the sender makes), and similar receiving nervous systems decode the messages which have been transmitted. On the level of human physiology, granted that the communications suffer neither lack nor loss of brain or organ, there would seem to be no mechanical reason why complete identity in giving and receiving messages is not possible. But our experience proves otherwise. Despite the mechanical

Reprinted from *Challenge and Experiment in Reading*, Proceedings of the International Reading Association Annual Convention, Vol. 7 (1962), 253–256, with permission of the author and International Reading Association.

equivalence of sender and receiver, an inequality shows up. The usual explanation has been that the factor of intelligence causes communication weakness or failure. In view of the fact that mongoloids, despite brain lack, can carry forward intelligible communication, serious doubt arises whether intelligence is the major factor in the language process. The production and reception of language are habit patterns and must be so viewed.

Reading is a mechanical, habitual process that must proceed in harmonious relationship with the speech-producing process. (In the earliest stages, reading requires talking.) Again granted that there is no lack or loss of brain or organ, the reading process should go forward with the perfection inherent in the human-body mechanisms. Again it must be admitted that there is a breakdown: excellent speakers sometimes are poor readers, and some halting speakers are superb readers. These apparent inequalities of performance certainly are not traceable to intelligence. There must be another factor of essential significance.

When the language process is examined behavioristically, it is apparent that three distinct elements or systems combine to make oral and written communication possible. The first is the human body. The second is the language code. The third is the area of knowledge about which the human body frames or receives a message in a specific code. Each of these elements exists independently of the other. Although all human beings are organically alike, each person possesses and uses only one or a few of the three thousand different language codes. Languages do not exist a priori in the mind. They exist apart from our awareness of them. Similarly the areas of knowledge, whether of nuclear science, or of calculus, or of plant pathology, do not depend for their survival upon their presence in your mind or mine. Of course, every individual language and every knowledge area need users for their preservation, but each exists as a separate entity that can be viewed as objectively as the human body.

It is true that the language process is an internalization within the human body and that the code and the area of knowledge, or at least a part of each, must be in the human mind before they can be put to use. Thus if I want to ask the question, "Do you speak English?" I can say *"Sprechen Sie Englisch?" "Parlais vous anglais?" "Parla inglese?"* or *"Habla usted inglés?"* only if this much of the code of these tongues is known to me. Similarly if I say "Ontogeny repeats phylogeny," the intelligibility of my sentence depends not upon your body mechanism alone or upon your capacity to use the English language but upon your familiarity with these vocabulary items in the area of knowledge called biology.

Each of these three elements has its own methods and logic of operation. Since language depends upon physiology, it is doubtless true that the human nervous system imposes analogous principles upon the operation of language and of subject matter; for example, the successive, linear, discrete sensory messages that enter the human body when one eats an apple are somehow combined into a single complex in accordance with principles of order, unity, and form. Because every language code is a product of the human nervous system, the same principles must exist in each one. But a language code has its own methods of operation, as with the *s* in English that forms the possessives and plurals of nouns, or *ed* that forms the past tense of regular verbs. Each language code has its own way of making statements, as with English "I am cold" and French *"J'ai froid"* (that is, I have cold"). Each area of knowledge has its own mode of procedure that is independent of the nervous system and of the language code. For example, Euclidean geometry proceeds with a set of postulates that include the axiom that the sum of the angles of a triangle is 180 degrees, but non-Euclidean geometry postulates that the sum may be either more or less than 180 degrees. Algebra has different principles from arithmetic, and calculus has still other principles. The procedures or the logics of the different areas are unique; though language can carry each of these, the language system does not impose its principles upon those of calculus or oceanography. Thus three wholly different systems of operation and logic lie imbedded in any simple statement which is uttered by language.

The systems of the human body and of a language code are permanent, finite, and fixed. The human body and a language code are like finite-state machines. But an area of knowledge is alway changing, and the logical procedures may change. Thus astronomy (but not the universe) underwent a tremendous change when the center of our universe was shifted from the earth to the sun. Political science changed successively as the logic of the divine right of kings gave way to a theory of popular control, and then in the last century the logic of democracy was challenged by those of fascism and communism. A dialectic belongs to the area of knowledge; though originated in the human brain and expressed by language, a dialectic has no necessary connection with the nervous system or the code of a language. The meanings of words change as they are taken over into new areas of knowledge or as new dialectical or logical systems are created for the handling of ideas. I repeat that the nervous system and the language code do not change to accommodate these ideational changes that are accomplished through vocabulary.

The reading process thus involves the interaction of the human body, the language code, and the vocabulary manipulations of an area of knowledge. The body takes in and acts upon stimuli that come primarily through the eye. These stimuli are the graphic marks of a language code. This code is a mediate instrument between the human body of the sender who prepared the stimuli and the human body of the receiver who is seeking to comprehend the message delivered by the code. Comprehension can occur only when the code is present within the reader's mind and when the area of knowledge is, at least, of interest to him. That is, the reader must have some desire and an adequate cognitive experience to take into the nervous system the ideational materials which are being presented.

Great literature is achieved through the artistic use of language. I now wish, therefore, to indicate the structures implicit in superb dramas, poems, prose fiction, and essays. When extended discourse is presented in one of the literary forms, additional modes of structure are necessarily present; these devices for shaping expression are found in literary criticism in haphazard rather than systematic form. In an analysis of the reading process a full explanation of them is desirable. In this short paper I can merely name them and briefly illustrate their presence in a familiar but little understood poem. These language structures are related to:

1. The idea or the area of knowledge being discussed and its vocabulary.
2. The literary genre.
3. The rhetorical organization.
4. The language code and its syntax.
5. The image system.
6. The musical patterning.

A speaker or writer must first have an idea which he wishes to communicate. Thus Sidney Lanier in "The Marshes of Glynn" desired to show that a mystic vision is possible when the tidal action of the sea is examined in relation to the marshes. His statement must be made in accordance with the structuring, logic, and vocabulary belonging to the theory that man while in the flesh can commune directly with God. Traditionally the steps in this process involve purgation, meditation upon holy thoughts, contemplation of the divine person, illumination or the shining of a great light into the mind, the disembodiment of the soul at the vision of God, the union with God, and the ecstasy associated with this experience. Lanier put these steps of the mystical process in the poem.

Second, a particular form of discourse must be chosen. Lanier might have selected music or painting, a drama or prose fiction as readily as poetry. He happened to choose lyric poetry; therefore, his composition must follow those rules of structure which apply to poetry and to lyric poetry in particular.

Third, the rhetorical organization of the idea had to be determined. Lanier might have used the inductive method, the deductive method, the method of comparison and contrast. He happened to choose to organize his materials into a time sequence of three pictures: noon, twilight, and night.

Fourth, the particular language code had to be selected; in this case it was English. It might have been any other language. Having selected English, Lanier was required to follow the structural procedures of English. One may note in passing that the first independent clause runs to 20 lines containing 161 words, and that the complete sentence extends through 36 lines with a total of 339 words (counting compounds as one word). The intricacy of this long sentence was possible only because each element conformed to the patterning operations of the English language.

Fifth, Lanier chose to employ the metaphor system of language to make the physical facts of the marsh (with its trees and grasses), the sea, and the movement of the sun in bringing night correspond to the spiritual events which constitute the mystic vision. The structuring of the images necessarily required selectivity in accordance with the original idea.

Sixth, the rhythms and melodies which play through the composition—all discourse has its musical accompaniment—must be unified and in harmony with the author's purpose. The alternation of long and short rhythmic passages and their melodic differences are apparent to an ear sensitive to the music inherent in language. But this music is a structured addition; it is not in the idea, the genre, the rhetoric, the code, or the image system any more than each of these is in any of the others.

The implication for the reading process of this statement is that the reading of any extended discourse must involve, first, the human body for the rules of perception and the physiological processes; second, the idea and its mode of structuring; and, third, those areas of language which operate as structured systems: genre, rhetoric, syntax, images, and music. Further, the implication is that each of these structuring systems must be lifted to a reader's awareness at the moment when he is capable of understanding its procedures. Only partial solutions to reader's problems have been given by phonics, sight-reading, and ideational reading. The whole language process must be examined. Extensive research in all areas is necessary, both as they operate individually and as a systematic and unified complex. Reading is a performance like playing the piano, and superior performance can be achieved only when all the language elements are fully understood and exploited.

SOCIAL FACTORS THAT INFLUENCE LEARNING AND READING
Robert J. Havighurst

There are two views or theories of learning, both of which have some truth. One is that the environment stimulates and causes learning; the other is that the individual actively strives to learn.

The environmental theory rests on the well-known Laws of Exercise and of Effect. This view of learning has great usefulness, and has served as a basis for the planning and organizing of education by many educators. It tacitly assumes that the human being is formed by his society. Society, through the family and school, *socializes* the child, by the skillful use of rewards and punishments. The child gradually expands his ability to be rewarded or punished. Experiences which at first have no reward value, such as the mother's smile and the father's praise, become strong rewards. Other experiences become punishments, such as the expression used by parents or teachers, "You are a naughty boy," and "That was a stupid thing to do." But still these are externally-imposed rewards and punishments.

The other view of human nature and of the nature of human learning sees the human being as an active, out-reaching, exploring individual who has an inner drive to learn. According to this view, learning can be its own reward. The child and the adult can find pleasure in learning for its own sake.

Reprinted from the *Journal of The Reading Specialist*, V (October 1965), 18–25, with permission of the author and Journal of the Reading Specialist.

There is abundant evidence of this phenomenon, if we look for it. And the principle that learning can be its own reward underlies much of the recent revolutionary work on the school curriculum. In mathematics and science and geography and other "hard" subjects, skillful teachers are presenting the subject matter so that it is a pleasure for children to learn it.

The children not only learn the basic facts of arithmetic or science, which they would also do under the traditional methods; what is more important, they learn to enjoy their study, and thus they become autonomous learners.

IS THERE A HUMAN DRIVE TO LEARN?

There is evidence that children have a kind of drive to learn, as they eagerly explore their world and take its measure with their minds. Some students of human nature believe they find in human nature a drive to expand one's interests and activities through childhood, adolescence, young adulthood, and middle age, if not into old age. They believe that this drive is often blocked, but that it can sometimes be uncovered and set free again, even in adults who have not shown it for years.

It is doubtful that human infants have an *instinctive* drive to learn. Rather, this drive is acquired. It has to be learned. Jerome Bruner and the other psychologists who have been responsible for bringing the concept of learning for its own sake into our active thinking about the school curriculum do not believe that the human child has an inborn drive to learn. They believe that he acquires this drive as a result of being raised in a propitious environment.

How does one acquire the drive to learn? Is it a long slow process which starts with being rewarded for learning language and concepts and continues through being rewarded for a series of learning tasks, such as reading, writing, arithmetic in sequences of complexity? Is it, therefore, simply the result of successful learning which is rewarded and begets more successful learning?

Or is the drive to learn acquired during some crucial period when the organism is ripe and the situation is right? If this is so, then the rearing of children should be organized so as to give all children a maximum opportunity to achieve this developmental task of learning for its own sake.

There is some evidence that the drive to learn is the result of a slow, cumulative process. We know that children, and adults as well, become interested in what they become good at. A young boy learns to identify a few makes of automobiles. As he develops this skill he becomes more interested in it and works harder at it, thus acquiring more and more knowledge. Or a girl may start simple sewing, and find that she has some talent for sewing; then she may work harder at it, and enjoy it more and more.

Also, it seems probable that children learn to love learning through the process of *modelling*. They associate with parents, teachers, club leaders, and coaches who know things and do things that mark them in the eyes of the children as models of competence. The children learn through unconscious imitation of these models, and they learn to enjoy learning if these model persons set an example of learning.

On the other hand, there is support for the theory that the drive to learn for its own sake is best acquired at one or more crucial periods in the life of the child. For example, consider a child of 3 or 4 who is beginning to try to understand the world about him and attempts to get this understanding by asking questions of his mother and father and other people. What? and Why? become a standard part of his vocabulary.

At this particular age the child is just ready to become an autonomous learner. If he is encouraged to use his mind as a learning instrument he will form habits of inquiry and of observation. His mind is ready for a crucial step.

Different families treat children differently at this time. Consider the following examples of two mothers riding with their 4-year-old children on a bus. The mothers want to teach their children to sit properly on a bus seat, while the bus starts and stops suddenly.

CASE A

MOTHER: Hold on tight to your seat.
CHILD: Why?
MOTHER: Hold on tight.
CHILD: Why?
MOTHER: You'll fall.
CHILD: Why?
MOTHER: I told you to hold on tight, didn't I?

CASE B

MOTHER: Hold on tightly, darling.
CHILD: Why?
MOTHER: If you don't you will be thrown forward and then you'll fall.
CHILD: Why?
MOTHER: Because if the bus stops suddenly you'll jerk forward and bump against the seat in front.
CHILD: Why?
MOTHER: Now hold on tightly, darling, and don't make such a fuss.

The first thing that strikes the observer of these two cases is that the mother in case A does not try to explain to the child. Thus the child does not have an opportunity to learn the "Why" of things, and if this kind of situation occurs again and again, the child may lose the habit of asking why? The next thing is that the vocabulary in case A is more restricted than in case B. Thus the child does not get practice in extending his vocabulary. Perhaps the next thing that will be noticed is that there is a difference in the *relation* between child and mother in the two situations. In case A the mother asserts her authority through categorical statements. She does not really try to explain why the child should hold on tight, but *orders* the child to do so. The mother's *authority* is invoked almost at once, with the result that the natural curiosity of the child is pushed back, and the child is learning *not* to think for himself. In case B the mother attempts to satisfy the child's curiosity with explanations. Although she finally resorts to her authority, she has first given the child a chance to learn about the world in a relationship which permits him to challenge authority with his questions.

The child who experiences language and social relations of case A during his early years is likely to develop a different kind of mind than the child who experiences language and social relations of case B.

The differences between these two children will lie partly in the way their minds work. Child A will not have an inquiring mind, while Child B will be an inquirer. The two children will have different attitudes toward learning.

HOW DOES LEARNING DEPEND ON THE ENVIRONMENT?

The foregoing example helps us to see how learning depends on the environment of the child. The child's mind grows upon the language he hears. If the language is barren, his mind is stunted. If the language is rich, and if it includes the child as an active per-

son, his mind is stimulated to grow. The following example from Dr. Robert Hess illustrates the difference between two kinds of language environment.[1]

"Assume that the emotional climate of two homes is approximately the same—the significant difference between them is in style of communication employed. A child is playing noisily in the kitchen with an assortment of pots and pans when the telephone rings. In one home the mother says, "Be quiet," or "Shut up," or any one of several short, peremptory commands, and she answers the phone while the child sits still on the floor. In the other home the mother says, "Would you keep quiet while I answer the phone." The question our study poses is this: what inner response is elicited in the child, what is the effect upon his developing cognitive network of concepts and meaning in each of these two situations. In one instance, the child is asked for a simple mental response. He is asked to attend to an uncomplicated message, and to make a conditioned response (to comply); he is not called upon to reflect or to make mental discriminations. In the other example, the child is required to follow two or three ideas. He is asked to relate his behavior to a time dimension; he must think of his behavior in relation to its effect upon another person. He must perform a more complicated task to follow the communication of his mother in that his relationship to her is mediated in part through concepts and shared ideas; his mind is stimulated or exercised (in an elementary fashion) by a more elaborate and complex verbal communication initiated by the mother. As objects of these two divergent communication styles, repeated in various ways, in similar situations and circumstances during the preschool years, these two imaginary children would be expected to develop significantly different verbal facility and cognitive equipment by the time they enter the public school system . . ."

Every child's mind must feed on the lan-

[1] Robert D. Hess, "Educability and Rehabilitation: The Future of the Welfare Class." Paper presented at the Thirtieth Groves Conference on Marriage and the Family, April 15, 1965.

guage provided in the home. If families differ systematically in the nature of the language they use, their children's minds must differ systematically. There is now substantial evidence that families do differ in this respect, and that the better-educated parents, with higher socio-economic status, provide a more elaborate language environment. The sociologist, Basil Bernstein,[2] has analyzed family language patterns, and has distinguished two forms or styles of language: *restricted* and *elaborate*. The restricted form is found most frequently in working-class families and in rural families. It tends to use short sentences, often unfinished; there are few adjectives and adverbs and few subordinate clauses; much of the meaning is implied rather than specified; the language cannot be used to state precise and differentiated meanings. It limits the range and detail of concepts.

An elaborate form of language is generally found in middle-class urban families, though such families often use a restricted language a part of the time. An elaborate language uses more exact words to fit a particular situation. It has more adjectives and adverbs and subordinate clauses. It permits the speaker to express complex thoughts clearly. It is the language of the school.

A child who has learned a *restricted* language at home is likely to have difficulty in school, where an *elaborate* language is used and taught by the teacher; and the difficulty of the child is likely to increase as he goes further in school, unless he learns the elaborate language that is expected in the school. On the other hand, the child who has had experience with an elaborate language from his earliest years has a relatively easy time in school, because he must simply go on developing the kind of language and related thinking which he has already started.

Bernstein has studied the language usage of boys aged 15–18, from middle-class and working-class families. The groups studied by Bernstein showed clear social class differences in language usage *even with IQ the same*. The boys were placed in small groups of 4 or 5 and asked to discuss the abolition of capital punishment.

The middle-class groups used a higher proportion of: subordinatives, complex verbal stems, passive voice, total adjectives, uncommon adjectives, uncommon adverbs, uncommon conjunctions, and "I think" expressions.

The working-class groups used a higher proportion of "you" and "they" personal pronouns, and of expressions of the type "isn't it," "you know," "wouldn't he," which indicate that the speaker requires assurance that his message has been received. Bernstein found these differences in the *quality* of language between different social-class groups which were equal in measured IQ. He also found little difference between social class groups in the *quantity* of language. He concludes that the tendency to use an elaborate as contrasted with a restricted language system is not a matter of intelligence, but depends on the *social relationships* a person has experienced.

Bernstein's two forms of language are believed by him to arise from the social interactions in two different kinds of families. He distinguishes between the *status-oriented family* and the *person-oriented family*.

The status-oriented family is one in which each person has a definite status which is associated with *power to make decisions*. The father's position is generally one of high power, and he generally makes decisions arbitrarily, without discussing them with others, and especially without discussing them with the children. The mother has her definite status with corresponding power. The children have low status and low power. In this kind of family system there is very little "feed-back." That is, there is very little discussion of the pros and cons of a decision made by a person in power, and very little discussion of the consequences of the deci-

[2] Basil Bernstein, "Elaborated and Restricted Codes." Unpublished paper. Committee on Human Development, The University of Chicago, 1964.

sion. Children may make decisions within their own domains, and their decisions are insulated from their parents; the children's decisions are likely to be influenced by the peer group, in which there is a considerable amount of interaction and of feed-back in the making of decisions, since the children tend to be of equal status and power in their peer group.

In this kind of family, one would expect the language to be limited to commands and categorical statements, and to include many non-verbal gestures which can reenforce or take the place of simple verbal statements. This kind of family uses a *restricted* language system, and the child's mind develops in a very limited way in such a language environment. Such families are found in all parts of society, but more frequently in rural and lower working-class areas, where people are dealing with things rather than ideas, and a simple language is likely to be adequate for everyday business.

The contrasting family type is *person-oriented*. Here, the influence of each member of the family is determined by his personal characteristics rather than by his status. Each person has a say in the making of most decisions, and there is a maximum of "feed-back" or discussion of the consequences of a decision. It is true that the senior members of the family have greater power, but this is exerted through discussion and persuasion, and only applied directly as a last resort. In this kind of family the decisions made by children are not insulated from the decisions made by adults. The children discuss their problems and the decisions of their peer groups with their elders. This kind of family spends much time considering alternatives, and trying to understand the points of view of the various members, before coming to a decision.

It is clear that the language environment of such a family will be quite different from the language environment of a status-oriented family. An *elaborate* language system will de-velop, in which members of the family *explain* things to each other, *explore* alternatives, use many qualifying verbal expressions, and try to put themselves in the position of others. The child's developing self is differentiated through continuous adjustment to the verbally differentiated interactions and interests of others.

This kind of family is likely to teach its children a wider vocabulary, but the most important difference between its elaborate language system and the simple language system of a status-oriented family is one of *quality* rather than *quantity* of language.

Since middle class urban life needs an elaborate language system, and since the school in an urban society tends to use an elaborate language system, the children of person-oriented families have a great advantage in school and in adult life. There is a strong statistical tendency for the middle classes to have more person-oriented families than the working classes.

There are also many *transitional families*, whose role-structures fall in between these two broad types just described. Many working-class families are transitional, and give their children some but not all of the intellectual and personal characteristics of a person-oriented family.

If a child grows up in a family with a restricted language, and plays with children of similar families, and goes to school with such children, he is likely to find the elaborate language of the school to be strange and confusing, and he is likely to have difficulty in learning the school's language, unless he has an unusually gifted teacher who knows how to teach such children.

HOW LEARNING AND READING DEPEND ON THE CHILD'S EXPERIENCE WITH THE REAL WORLD

Another aspect of the environment which is important for mental growth is the variety of objects and events which the child experiences through his senses. The child must get acquainted with things in the real world by seeing, smelling, hearing, and feeling them. Thus he acquires a supply of *images.* Later he learns the names for these images. The reverse process is not likely to work with young children or even with children in middle childhood. They cannot readily learn a word or a name, and then search out what it refers to. This kind of learning comes later, and is important, but it is not useful in the early stages of mental growth.

There is reason to believe that, after about the age of 2, children of low-income families *on the average* get less experience of the world's variety through their senses than do children of high income families. They are not as likely to be taken by the parents or older children to see things beyond their immediate neighborhood. Their toys have less variety. Indeed, their mothers do not consider toys as important in their education. Bernstein asked a sample of London mothers what toys were good for in a child's life. His middle-class mothers nearly always said that toys were good for the education of children, but his working-class mothers seldom said this. They generally said that toys kept a child satisfied, so that he did not bother his mother or others in the family.

The genius of the Montessori method is that it systematically builds the child's sensory experience, through giving him a series of playthings that expand his experience of seeing, feeling, and hearing. Thus his mind grows so that, according to Madame Montessori, her orphan children in Rome began to read of their own accord at the age of 5 or 6.

HOW TO BUILD UP THE CHILD'S DRIVE TO LEARN

These illustrations show how the child's social environment—the persons who bring him up—can encourage or discourage his mind to grow. They also can help him develop a desire or a drive to learn. Good teachers know how to do this with children, but they sometimes are lost with children who come to school without such a drive. Perhaps they could work better with disadvantaged children if they knew more about the ways mothers teach or do not teach their children to learn. Professor Hess has been exploring this matter with mothers of various socio-economic levels. He finds a great deal of difference from one mother to the next, with a tendency for middle-class mothers to behave more like the first of the following examples, and working-class mothers to behave more like the third of these examples. The mother is asked to teach her child how to group or sort a number of small toys, which consist of animals, motor cars, furniture, of various colors and sizes.

The first mother outlines the task for the child, gives sufficient help and explanation to permit the child to proceed on her own. She says:

"All right, Susan, this board is the place where we put the little toys; first of all you're supposed to learn how to place them according to color. Can you do that? The things that are all the same color you put in one section; in the second section you put another group of colors and in the third section you put the last group of colors. Can you do that? Or would you like to see me do it first?"

CHILD: "I want to do it."

This mother has given explicit information about the task and what is expected of the child; she has offered support and help of various kinds: and she has made it clear that she impelled the child to perform. A second mother's style is not quite so easily grasped by the child. She says in introducing the same task:

"Now, I'll take them off the board; now you put them all back on the board. What are these?"

CHILD: "A truck."

"All right, just put that right here; put the other one right here; all right, put the other one there."

This mother relies more on physical signs and non-verbal communication in her commands; she does not define the task for the child; the child is not provided with ideas or information that she can grasp in attempting to solve the problem; neither is she told what to expect or what the task is, even in general terms.

A third mother is even less explicit. She introduces the task as follows:

"I've got some chairs and cars, do you want to play the game?"

Child does not respond. She continues:

"O.K. What's this?"

CHILD: "A wagon?"

MOTHER: "HM?"

CHILD: "A wagon?"

MOTHER: "This is a wagon, what's this?"

The conversation continues with this sort of exchange for several pages. Here again, the child is not provided with the essential information he needs to solve or to understand the problem. There is clearly some impelling on the part of the mother for the child to perform, but the child has not been told what he is to do.

We think of the consequences of this sort of exchange as affecting both the cognitive ability of the child, the motivation for achievement and the child's sense of self-confidence.

READINESS TO LEARN

It is clear that we have been discussing *readiness*, a state in which the child is prepared to learn and wants to learn. Readiness consists of a drive to learn plus experience necessary to learn the things that are to be taught—reading, arithmetic, etc.

We are learning that a considerable subgroup of children come to school without sufficient readiness for the learning that is ordinarily expected in the first grade. And they will not acquire this readiness from the usual curriculum of the first grade, or by repeating the usual first grade. For them the school must find ways of compensating for their lack of previous experience and lack of mental growth.

This may possibly be done through preschool classes which are skillfully conducted to make up for what the child does not get in the home. It may also be done through a kindergarten or first grade curriculum aimed at building readiness.

It is less clear how the school should work with disadvantaged children after they have reached the age of 9 or 10, when they have a pattern of school failure and have accommodated themselves to it in one way or another.

THE AVERAGE AND ABOVE-AVERAGE CHILD

The child who is average or above in his readiness for school work already has a desire to learn which can be cultivated by the school, as it does the following:

a. Gives him experience in exploring and explaining the unfamiliar, both in the physical world and in social relations;

b. Gives him experience with increasingly complex social relationships, in areas of history, economics, geography, government, etc.;

c. Expands his control of language and meanings, expressed in speech;

d. Rewards him for autonomous learning by giving him more opportunity and more interesting opportunities.

CONCLUSIONS

The social environment influences learning by creating a language environment and an experience environment which stimulate the mind to grow, and by systematically rewarding a child for learning. We see now more clearly than before that in the preschool years there are critical periods for mental development. When families do not meet the child's need for mental growth at these periods, the school may have to compensate the child through pre-school classes or through a modified kindergarten-first grade curriculum.

For children of school age the school is a place where a stimulating environment meets an individual with a drive to learn. Things can be done both to make the environment more stimulating and to increase the drive to learn.

A TEACHING STRATEGY FOR CULTURALLY DEPRIVED PUPILS: COGNITIVE AND MOTIVATIONAL CONSIDERATIONS
David P. Ausubel

The possibility of arresting and reversing the course of intellectual retardation in the culturally deprived pupil depends largely on providing him with an optimal learning environment as early as possible in the course of his educational career. If the limiting effects of prolonged cultural deprivation on the development of verbal intelligence and on the acquisition of verbal knowledge are to be at least partially overcome, better-than-average strategies of teaching are obviously necessary in terms of both general effectiveness and specific appropriateness for his particular learning situation. Yet precisely the opposite state of affairs typically prevails: the learning environment of the culturally deprived child is both generally inferior and specifically inappropriate. His cumulative intellectual deficit, therefore, almost invariably reflects, in part, the cumulative impact of a continuing and consistently deficient learning

Reprinted from the *School Review*, LXXI (Winter 1963), 454–463, with permission of The University of Chicago Press. Copyright 1963 by The University of Chicago.

environment, as well as his emotional and motivational reaction to this environment. Thus, much of the lower-class child's alienation from the school is not so much a reflection of discriminatory or rejecting attitudes on the part of teachers and other school personnel—although the importance of this factor should not be underestimated; it is in greater measure a reflection of the cumulative effects of a curriculum that is too demanding of him, and of the resulting load of frustration, confusion, demoralization, resentment, and impaired self-confidence that he must bear.

An effective and appropriate teaching strategy for the culturally deprived child must therefore emphasize these three considerations: (a) the selection of initial learning material geared to the learner's existing state of readiness; (b) mastery and consolidation of all on-going learning tasks before new tasks are introduced, so as to provide the necessary foundation for successful sequential learning and to prevent unreadiness for future learning tasks; and (c) the use of structured learning materials optimally organized to facilitate efficient sequential learning. Attention to these three factors can go a long way toward insuring effective learning for the first time, and toward restoring the child's educational morale and confidence in his ability to learn. Later possible consequences are partial restoration of both intrinsic and extrinsic motivation for academic achievement, diminution of anti-intellectualism, and decreased alienation from the school to the point where his studies make sense and he sees some purpose in learning. In my opinion, of all the available teaching strategies, programmed instruction, minus the teaching-machine format, has the greatest potentialities for meeting the aforementioned three criteria of an effective and appropriate approach to the teaching of culturally deprived pupils.

Readiness—A curriculum that takes the readiness of the culturally deprived child into account always takes as its starting point his existing knowledge and sophistication in the various subject-matter areas and intellectual skills, no matter how far down the scale this happens to be. This policy demands rigid elimination of all subject matter that he cannot economically assimilate on the basis of his current level of cognitive sophistication. It presupposes emphasis on his acquisition of the basic intellectual skills before any attempt is made to teach him algebra, geometry, literature, and foreign languages. However, in many urban high schools and junior high schools today, pupils who cannot read at a third-grade level and who cannot speak or write grammatically or perform simple arithmetical computations are subjected to irregular French verbs, Shakespearean drama, and geometrical theorems. Nothing more educationally futile or better calculated to destroy educational morale could be imagined!

In the terms of readiness for a given level of school work, a child is no less ready because of a history of cultural deprivation, chronic academic failure, and exposure to an unsuitable curriculum than because of deficient intellectual endowment. Hence, realistic recognition of this fact is not undemocratic, reactionary, or evidence of social class bias, of intellectual snobbery, of a "soft," patronizing approach, or a belief in the inherent uneducability of lower-class children. Neither is it indicative of a desire to surrender to the culturally deprived child's current intellectual level, to perpetuate the status quo, or to institute a double, class-oriented standard of education. It is merely a necessary first step in preparing him to cope with more advanced subject matter, and hence in eventually reducing existing social class differentials in academic achievement. To set the same *initial* standards and expectations for the academically retarded culturally deprived child as for the non-retarded middle- or lower-class child is automatically to insure the former's failure and to widen prevailing discrepancies between social class groups.

Consolidation—By insisting on consolidation or mastery of on-going lessons before new material is introduced, we make sure of continued readiness and success in sequentially organized learning. Abundant experimental research has confirmed the proposition that prior learnings are not transferable to new learning tasks unless they are first overlearned.[1] Overlearning, in turn, requires an adequate number of adequately spaced repetitions and reviews, sufficient intratask repetitiveness prior to intra- and intertask di-

[1] See R. W. Bruce, "Conditions of Transfer of Training," *Journal of Experimental Psychology*, XVI (1933), 343–61; C. P. Duncan, "Transfer in Motor Learning as a Function of Degree of First-task Learning and Inter-task Similarity," *Journal of Experimental Psychology*, XLV (1953), 1–11, and his "Transfer after Training with Single versus Multiple Tasks," *Journal of Experimental Psychology*, LV (1958), 63–72; L. Morrisett and C. I. Hovland, "A Comparison of Three Varieties of Training in Human Problem Solving," *Journal of Experimental Psychology*, LV (1958), 52–55; and J. M. Sassenrath, "Learning without Awareness and Transfer of Learning Sets," *Journal of Educational Psychology*, L (1959), 202–12.

versification,[2] and opportunity for differential practice of the more difficult components of a task. Frequent testing and provision of feedback, especially with test items demanding fine discrimination among alternatives varying in degrees of correctness, also enhance consolidation by confirming, clarifying, and correcting previous learnings. Lastly, in view of the fact that the culturally deprived child tends to learn more slowly than his non-deprived peers, self-pacing helps to facilitate consolidation.

Structured, sequential materials—The principal advantage of programmed instruction, apart from the fact that it furthers consolidation, is its careful sequential arrangement and gradation of difficulty which insures that each attained increment in learning serves as an appropriate foundation and anchoring post for the learning and retention of subsequent items in the ordered sequence.[3] Adequate programming of materials also presupposes maximum attention to such matters as lucidity, organization, and the explanatory and integrative power of substantive content. It is helpful, for example, if sequential materials are so organized that they become progressively more differentiated in terms of generality and inclusiveness, and if similarities and differences between the current learning task and previous learnings are explicitly delineated.[4] Both of these aims can

be accomplished by using an advance organizer or brief introductory passage before each new unit of material, which both makes available relevant explanatory principles at a high level of abstraction and increases discriminability. Programmed instruction can also be especially adapted to meet the greater needs of culturally deprived pupils for concrete-empirical props in learning relational propositions.

Although programmed instruction in general is particularly well suited to the needs of the culturally deprived child, I cannot recommend the small-frame format characteristic of teaching-machine programs and most programmed textbooks. In terms of both the logical requirements of meaningful learning and the actual size of the task that can be conveniently accommodated by the learner, the frame length typically used by teaching machines is artificially and unnecessarily abbreviated. It tends to fragment the ideas presented in the program so that their interrelationships are obscured and their logical structure is destroyed.[5] Hence it is relatively easy for less able students to master each granulated step of a given program without understanding the logical relationships and development of the concepts presented.[6] In my opinion, therefore, the traditional textbook format or oral didactic exposition that follows the programming principles outlined above, supplemented by frequent self-scoring and feedback-giving tests, is far superior to the teaching-machine approach for the actual presentation of subject-matter content.[7]

[2] See Duncan, "Transfer after Training with Single versus Multiple Tasks," *ibid.*; Morrisett and Hovland, *ibid.*; and Sassenrath, *ibid.*

[3] D. P. Ausubel and D. Fitzgerald, "Organizer, General Background, and Antecedent Learning Variables in Sequential Verbal Learning," *Journal of Educational Psychology,* LIII (1962), 243–49.

[4] D. P. Ausubel, "The Use of Advance Organizers in the Learning and Retention of Meaningful Verbal Learning," *Journal of Educational Psychology,* LI (1960), 267–72; D. P. Ausubel and D. Fitzgerald, "The Role of Discriminability in Meaningful Verbal Learning and Retention," *Journal of Educational Psychology,* LII (1961), 266–74, and their "Organizer, General Background, and Antecedent Learning Variables in Sequential Verbal Learning."

[5] S. L. Pressey, "Basic Unresolved Teaching-Machine Problems," *Theory into Practice,* I (1962), 30–37.

[6] D. G. Beane, "A Comparison of Linear and Branching Techniques of Programed Instruction in Plane Geometry" ("Technical Report," No. 1 [Urbana: Training Research Laboratory, University of Illinois, July 1962]).

[7] Pressey, "Basic Unresolved Teaching-Machine Problems."

MOTIVATIONAL CONSIDERATIONS

Thus far I have considered various environmental factors that induce retardation in the culturally deprived child's intellectual growth, as well as different cognitive techniques of counteracting and reversing such retardation. These factors and techniques, however, do not operate in a motivational vacuum. Although it is possible separately to consider cognitive and motivational aspects of learning for purposes of theoretical analysis, they are nonetheless inseparably intertwined in any real-life learning situation. For example, school failure and loss of confidence resulting from an inappropriate curriculum further depress the culturally deprived pupil's motivation to learn and thereby increase his existing learning and intellectual deficit. Similarly, although a number of practice and task variables are potentially important for effective learning in a programmed instruction context, appropriate manipulation of these variables can, in the final analysis, only insure successful long-term learning of subject matter provided that the individual is adequately motivated.

Doing without being interested in what one is doing results in relatively little permanent learning, since it is reasonable to suppose that only those materials can be meaningfully incorporated on a long-term basis into an individual's structure of knowledge that are relevant to areas of concern in his psychological field. Learners who have little need to know and understand quite naturally expend little learning effort; manifest an insufficiently meaningful learning set; fail to develop precise meanings, to reconcile new ideas with existing concepts, and to formulate new propositions in their own words; and do not devote enough time and energy to practice and review. Material is therefore never sufficiently consolidated to form an adequate foundation for sequential learning.

The problem of reversibility exists in regard to the motivational as well as in regard to the cognitive status of the culturally deprived pupil, inasmuch as his environment typically stunts not only his intellectual development, but also the development of appropriate motivations for academic achievement. Motivations for learning, like cognitive abilities, are only potential rather than inherent or endogenous capacities in human beings; their actual development is invariably dependent upon adequate environmental stimulation. Cognitive drive or intrinsic motivation to learn, for example, is probably derived in a very general sense from curiosity tendencies and from related predispositions to explore, manipulate, and cope with the environment; but these tendencies and predispositions are only actualized as a result of successful exercise and the anticipation of future satisfying consequences from further exercise and as a result of internalization of the values of those significant persons in the family and subcultural community with whom the child identifies.

Intrinsic motivation—The development of cognitive drive or of intrinsic motivation for learning, that is, the acquisition of knowledge as an end in itself or for its own sake, is, in my opinion, the most promising motivational strategy which we can adopt in relation to the culturally deprived child. It is true, of course, in view of the anti-intellectualism and pragmatic attitude toward education that is characteristic of lower-class ideology,[8] that a superficially better case can be made for the alternative strategy of appealing to the incentives to job acquisition, retention, and advancement that now apply so saliently to continuing education because of the rapid rate of technological change. Actually, however, intrinsic motivation for learning is more potent, relevant, durable, and easier to arouse

[8] F. Riessman, *The Culturally Deprived Child* (New York: Harper & Bros., 1962).

than its extrinsic counterpart. Meaningful school learning, in contrast to most kinds of laboratory learning, requires relatively little effort or extrinsic incentive, and, when successful, furnishes its own reward. In most instances of school learning, cognitive drive is also the only immediately relevant motivation, since the greater part of school learning cannot be rationalized as necessary for meeting the demands of daily living. Furthermore, it does not lose its relevance or potency in later adult life when utilitarian and career advancement considerations are no longer applicable. Lastly, as we know from the high dropout rate among culturally deprived high-school youth, appeals to extrinsic motivation are not very effective. Among other reasons, the latter situation reflects a limited time perspective focused primarily on the present; a character structure that is oriented more to immediate than delayed gratification of needs; the lack of strong internalized needs for and anxiety about high academic and vocational achievement, as part of the prevailing family, peer group, and community ideology;[9] and the seeming unreality and impossibility of attaining the rewards of prolonged striving and self-denial in view of current living conditions and family circumstances, previous lack of school success, and the discriminatory attitudes of middle-class society.[10]

If we wish to develop the cognitive drive so that it remains viable during the school years and in adult life, it is necessary to move still further away from the educational doctrine of gearing the curriculum to the spontaneously expressed interests, current concerns, and life-adjustment problems of pupils. Although it is undoubtedly unrealistic and even undesirable in our culture to eschew entirely the utilitarian, ego-enhancement, and anxiety-reduction motivations for learning, we must place increasingly greater emphasis upon the value of knowing and understanding as goals in their own right, quite apart from any practical benefits they may confer. Instead of denigrating subject-matter knowledge, we must discover more efficient methods of fostering the long-term acquisition or meaningful and usable bodies of knowledge, and of developing appropriate intrinsic motivations for such learning.

It must be conceded at the outset that culturally deprived children typically manifest little intrinsic motivation to learn. They come from family and cultural environments in which the veneration of learning for its own sake is not a conspicuous value, and in which there is little or no tradition of scholarship. Moreover, they have not been notably successful in their previous learning efforts in school. Nevertheless we need not necessarily despair of motivating them to learn for intrinsic reasons. Psychologists have been emphasizing the motivation-learning and the interest-activity sequences of cause and effect for so long that they tend to overlook their reciprocal aspects. Since motivation is not an indispensable condition for short-term and limited-quantity learning, it is not necessary to postpone learning activities until appropriate interests and motivations have been developed. Frequently the best way of motivating an unmotivated pupil is to ignore his motivational state for the time being and concentrate on teaching him as effectively as possible. Much to his surprise and to his teacher's, he will learn despite his lack of motivation; and from the satisfaction of learning he will characteristically develop the motivation to learn more.

Paradoxically, therefore, we may discover that the most effective method of developing intrinsic motivation to learn is to focus on the cognitive rather than on the motivational aspects of learning, and to rely on the moti-

[9] A. Davis, "Child Training and Social Class," *Child Behavior and Development*, eds. R. G. Barker, J. S. Kounin, and H. F. Wright (New York: McGraw-Hill Book Co., 1963), 607–20.
[10] *Ibid.*

vation that is developed retroactively from successful educational achievement. This is particularly true when a teacher is able to generate contagious excitement and enthusiasm about the subject he teaches, and when he is the kind of person with whom culturally deprived children can identify. Recruiting more men teachers and dramatizing the lives and exploits of cultural, intellectual, and scientific heroes can also enhance the process of identification. At the same time, of course, we can attempt to combat the anti-intellectualism and lack of cultural tradition in the home through programs of adult education and cultural enrichment.

Extrinsic motivation—The emphasis I have placed on intrinsic motivation for learning should not be interpreted to mean that I deny the importance of developing extrinsic motivations. The need for ego enhancement, status, and prestige through achievement, the internalization of long-term vocational aspirations, and the development of such implementing traits as responsibility, initiative, self-denial, frustration tolerance, impulse control, and the ability to postpone immediate hedonistic gratification are, after all, traditional hallmarks of personality maturation in our culture; and educational aspirations and achievement are both necessary prerequisites for, and way-station prototypes of, their vocational counterparts. Hence, in addition to encouraging intrinsic motivation for learning, it is also necessary to foster ego-enhancement and career-advancement motivations for academic achievement.

As previously pointed out, however, the current situation with respect to developing adequate motivations for higher academic and vocational achievement among culturally deprived children is not very encouraging. But just as in the case of cognitive drive,

much extrinsic motivation for academic success can be generated retroactively from the experience of current success in schoolwork. Intensive counseling can also compensate greatly for the absence of appropriate home, community, and peer-group support and expectations for the development of long-term vocational ambitions. In a sense counselors must be prepared to act *in loco parentis* in this situation. By identifying with a mature, stable, striving, and successful male adult figure, culturally deprived boys can be encouraged to internalize long-term and realistic aspirations, as well as to develop the mature personality traits necessary for their implementation. Hence, as a result of achieving current ego enhancement in the school setting, obtaining positive encouragement and practical guidance in the counseling relationship, and experiencing less rejection and discrimination at the hands of school personnel, higher vocational aspirations appear to lie more realistically within their grasp. Further encouragement to strive for more ambitious academic and vocational goals can be provided by making available abundant scholarship aid to universities, to community colleges, and to technical institutes; by eliminating the color, ethnic, and class bar in housing, education, and employment; by acquainting culturally deprived youth with examples of successful professional persons originating from their own racial, ethnic, and class backgrounds; and by involving parents sympathetically in the newly fostered ambitions of their children. The success of the Higher Horizons project indicates that an energetic program organized along the lines outlined above can do much to reverse the effects of cultural deprivation on the development of extrinsic motivations for academic and vocational achievement.

VIEWS ON READING RESEARCH
Robert Karlin

In a recent Review of Educational Research on Language Arts and Fine Arts, Holmes and Singer wrote that "all signs indicate that the psychology of reading is on the threshold of . . . a forward thrust and that both stimulating and disturbing days lie immediately ahead. In this new atmosphere, cherished ideas are bound to be challenged, and new ones will contend for their places when the old ones fall."[1] They based these promising views on three trends: attempts at developing theories of reading, improved research designs and statistics, and new instruments and techniques. Other reporters of reading research were much more guarded in expressing hopeful views for the future. It is not unlikely that they had cause to be less effusive.

STATUS OF READING RESEARCH

I am not familiar with any efforts to determine how much research has been conducted in the field of reading. It is my guess that a list covering reading research since 1930 would be exceedingly long. All you need do is consult the bibliographical sources to realize reading is an area that has attracted re-

Adapted from a paper presented at the Annual Reading Research Forum of The Council on Experimental Research in Reading, University of Bridgeport, March 26, 1966.

[1] Jack A. Holmes and Harry Singer, "Theoretical Models and Trends Toward More Basic Research in Reading," *Language Arts and Fine Arts, Review of Educational Research*, XXXIV, No. 2 (April 1964), 150.

searchers. There is no doubt that a challenge to creative minds exists, for a definitive explanation of the process of reading has eluded our best efforts. I suspect that this basic failure to explain the process has prevented us from finding answers to other questions with which we are involved. There are some researchers who have turned their attention to process but not unlike their earlier counterparts have not succeeded in shedding much new light on the issue. More about this later.

It is difficult to separate the quantity of reading research from its quality. Considering the basic limitation with which the reading researcher has to work—the human being —one can appreciate the advances apparent in the research designs and statistics of many of our studies. Researchers in the social sciences have tried to meet the challenge which pure scientists have established. That the former have been unable to match efforts is predictable. Some observers believe that human behavior just can't be studied in the same ways that physicists experiment with natural phenomena, and that precise explanations of human behavior (which means also ability to predict behavior) are unlikely unless dramatic changes occur in our ability to design new instruments and procedures. My own guess on this question is that a breakthrough in our lifetime is unlikely but that we might look forward to some progress in our efforts to chart the process of learning.

I believe the nature of the bulk of reading research reflects the problem to which I have just referred. Most reading research is of the status variety. By status variety I mean the evaluation of the existing state of affairs without any efforts to manipulate the environment. Among examples of such research are studies that seek to determine relationships between beginning reading readiness (whatever that is) and success in learning to read, or intelligence and reading ability, or personality correlates and reading problems and so on. These types of studies are quite different from those in which the investigator controls the environment. (I hasten to add that we should not assume that experimental studies, by their very nature, are superior to status studies.) But we have drawn too many unwarranted conclusions from the results of status studies. Too many of us have interpreted results which indicate a *statistical* relationship to mean a *causal* relationship. A correlation coefficient might suggest a connection between two variables, but it does *not* suggest that one is the result of the other and that a change in one will bring about a change in the other. I can't help but look back to the results of some of the studies with which I had been associated. When the findings of one were published, they were interpreted by some as though there were justification to regard the results as conclusive proof that skeletal growth determines reading growth. One school I know of began to x-ray children's wristbones inasmuch as a significant relationship between carpal age and first-grade reading appeared to exist. This in spite of the fact that the coefficient was small. This school and some other reporters never considered the possibility that carpal growth merely reflects other conditions which might be more closely tied to reading. Had we taken those children who were low achievers in both growth and reading and somehow stimulated their growth and at the same time observed changes in their reading behavior, perhaps then a less tenuous conclusion about the two might have been drawn!

Experimental research in reading has had its share of problems too. Here I'm thinking about efforts some of us have made to ascertain whether one method of teaching reading is better than another method. The results of such studies could have an impact upon what we do in the classroom. What do the results of such research say? Either that there are no significant differences between the methodologies or that one methodology appears to be superior to the other. In the latter instance it is not very difficult to cite one or more studies which produced opposite findings or questionable findings. This state of affairs, as well as the other in which no differences are obtained, has caused some of us to look critically at these investigations. What some of us have found points up some real weaknesses in many investigations. One almost might have predicted results by knowing these weaknesses.

One of our problems in conducting research involving comparisons of methods is the common practice of using standardized tests to measure changes in behavior. With very few exceptions standardized reading tests are gross measures of skills. And a very limited number of skills at that. Reading tests intended for young readers generally contain a section in which children are asked to select from a group of words one which is related to a picture. This exercise aims to determine a child's ability to recognize words in isolation. A second section usually consists of short paragraphs followed by simple questions whose answers are found in the paragraph. A few tests contain paragraphs with missing words which the children must select from groups of words. Suppose you were comparing a teaching program which was heavily letter-sound oriented with one which provided a balanced approach to word identification. Within a given period of time children in the former program would have covered more phonic elements and in an intensive way. These children would be expected to obtain higher scores on this phase of the test than children in the latter group as a natural outcome of the nature of their instruction and the nature of the test. Here we obtain differences in favor of one method over another when in reality these differences could be spurious because the instrument used to measure change does not adequately provide opportunities for each group to show what it really can or cannot do.

As far as the comprehension section of the test is concerned, its inherent limitations in measuring deeper understandings—and higher level tests suffer from similar weaknesses—favor children who are actually quite inferior in their ability to probe beneath the surface. Thus, even though one group of children has made great strides in ability to infer meanings as a result of a superior instructional program and a second group has not developed such skills in the same way, both appear equal to the task of understanding what they read. Since the results do not vary significantly we conclude that method A is not superior to method B. True, it is possible that A is not better than B, but our instrument is not sensitive enough to measure finer differences were they to exist.

All too often research which has been concerned with the superiority of one program over another has failed to ascertain the extent to which the results continue to hold. If I were to establish a pure, individualized reading program in a given grade and match its outcomes at the end of the year with the outcomes of other programs, what assurance would I have of obtaining similar results over subsequent years? Expediency has often dictated research designs of short duration. I'm referring particularly to doctoral research which is motivated by an understandable desire to complete one's requirements with the least amount of difficulties and in the shortest time possible. Government-sponsored research—the 27 first-year studies for example —have made little provision for the collection of data over extended periods of time, although some investigators, realizing the futility of basing conclusions on results obtained over short periods of time, have requested and obtained funds to extend their investigations into a second year.

The problem of the teacher variable is infrequently mentioned in reporting reading research. However, evidence is beginning to accumulate that programs might not be as important as the teachers who administer them. You undoubtedly have heard off-the-cuff comments about the superior teacher being able to obtain good results with any type of program. A study which has not yet been reported in the literature did not seek to verify this belief but rather the effect of the teacher's implementation of a reading method on different groups of children and on the components of reading. This study sought to gauge the teacher's perception and understanding of a reading program in order to see possible relationships between implementation and pupils' reading achievement. One of the investigators informed me that the teacher appears to be a significant variable in pupil progress.

There are other teacher variables that few investigators are willing to examine seriously. One is the consistency with which teachers follow a prescribed program. I recently discussed this factor with the person responsible for a government-sponsored project. She candidly admitted that even though teachers were cautioned about the importance of not polluting the results by varying teaching procedures, there was no real way of preventing such from occurring short of stationing a full-time observer in all the classrooms of which there were a large number. Unannounced periodic visits revealed that some teachers were actually engaging in activities reserved for other groups. Under these conditions, to what elements do we ascribe outcomes? Unfortunately, this particular but not unusual circumstance will be disregarded when the results are in and reported!

Then there is the common practice of giving teachers who will be responsible for introducing a new and different approach special training while at the same time ignoring the teachers who will be operating under conditions of "business as usual." What kind of logic suggests that the teachers who carry on their usual programs are equal, *ipso facto*, to the teachers of experimental groups after the latter have had the benefit of guidance? I suppose we have assumed that our experimental teachers are at a disadvantage until we provide them with help. Is it possible some investigators have relied too long on factors such as years of experience and professional preparation to equate teachers? Is it not also conceivable that personality, chronological age, sex, intelligence, creativity, appearance, enthusiasm and attitude as well as other characteristics are factors with which we should reckon? Is it inconceivable that one combination will favor a set of conditions and cause negative reactions under another? I'm thinking of such possibilities in dealing with unique populations—the disadvantaged or pre-school populations, for example. And even with typical ones too. To whom do you react more positively—a cheerful, pleasant-looking teacher with a sense of humor or a highly critical, severe-appearing boor? Why should we assume children are not affected and their responses do not reflect positive or negative feelings?

What I'm suggesting in all this is a reluctance on the part of some investigators to consider variables that might have influenced their results. There is a tendency to ignore that for which the design has not provided.

This brings me to a related matter—the overly-enthusiastic investigator. And we have our fair share of them. Do we expect the reading researcher to be a completely disinterested observer? Of course not. Although some reading research may have had its origins in mere curiosity, I suspect a substantial number was the product of hunches or beliefs based upon educated guesses, prior research and knowledge of the moment. Any research that I have conducted was based upon views that I felt were valid but needed support. What I'm saying is that even though we follow the route of the disinterested observer by stating hypotheses in a negative way—the null approach—we really are anticipating outcomes favorable to our beliefs. I doubt very much that the majority of reading research would have ever seen daylight were its investigators not anticipating confirmation of their beliefs. Perhaps this is as it should be but excessive enthusiasm frequently interferes with rational evaluation of data. How many reports in which nonsignificant differences were obtained, but interpreted nevertheless as important, have you read? I have been aware of too many that reported no significant differences at five percent levels of confidence (not at one percent levels) but which proclaimed such differences as evidences of trends in favor of one direction over another.

"What I should have done" is the name I give to that section of a report reserved for discussion of the findings and implications of the research. Here the investigator who obtained results other than those he expected suggests how he might have been more successful. He often lays negative results at the door of his design and instrumentation. It seems to me that these kinds of explanations serve only to highlight weakness inherent in the researcher. Even if we were to assume the validity of the comments, wouldn't it be better to leave them unsaid and do the study again?

But who has the time for such luxuries? Unlike researchers in the pure sciences, we who conduct reading research rarely devote our full-time efforts to seeking truths. We sandwich our research among teaching, writing and "jaunting." We just can't afford to allow time to go down the drain. So we make the most of it. How many reading studies of short or long duration have been replicated by the same investigator? How many times have you seen reported in the literature finding which a year or more later were repudiated by the same person? Few if any.

There is another matter involving researchers that few of us appear willing to discuss. It is the question of the researcher's vested interests in outcomes. I suspect there are more questionable practices in certain activities than in others, few of which we even hear about. Each of us is familiar with cases in which a drug was certified by its manufacturer as having been carefully researched as to value, side effects and so on, when in reality no such conditions had been met. The practice of withholding data has not been uncommon. We may draw our own conclusions explaining the motivation for unethical and dangerous evasions. Is there any danger of similar occurrences in the conduct of reading research? I don't know the answer to this question, but I suggest that when the stakes are high the possibility, however remote, exists. For public agencies to support and publish research under the aegis of persons with commercial interests in the activity, I find difficult to comprehend. Lest there be any misunderstanding, I want to make it perfectly clear that I know of no case in which we might doubt the accuracy with which information has been reported or note any deliberate efforts to mislead. What I am saying is simply this: lest there be any doubts cast upon our motivation, I would suggest a divorce between the persons who are in an advantageous position commercially and any efforts to study the values of what they are promoting. Surely if the question to be researched is of sufficient importance, we shall find others to undertake its study.

THE PROCESS OF READING

There have been other problems associated with reading research: samples not representative of the population, statistics based upon tenuous assumptions, conclusions inappropriately drawn, Hawthorne influences, and so on. We might address ourselves to these; instead, let us turn briefly to the process of reading, which most reading research ignores.

Early reading investigations seeking to understand the process of reading concentrated upon physical aspects, eye movements and visual perception with slight attention paid to the thinking aspects. Experiments in these areas and others continue. Answers to questions related to word recognition ability might be extremely useful for offering a teaching program that would reduce the numbers of reading failures due to weaknesses in decoding words. Two models—one chemical and the other neurological—to explain the mechanics of word recognition—have been suggested by Smith and Carrigan and Delacato, respectively. Smith and his coworker theorized that a balance maintained at the neural junctions controlled one's ability to recognize words. On the basis of traits common to boys with reading problems (reversals, difficulty with small words, etc.), which he interpreted as symptoms of neurological dysfunction, Delacato suggested the strengthening of unilaterality and omission of tonality.

Both models have been examined. You may be familiar with Harris' review of Smith and Carrigan's report in which he raised serious questions regarding faulty assumptions, unwarranted conclusions, and weaknesses in the use of tests, statistics and procedures. Delacato's theoretical model has been subject to severe criticism too: insufficient data, lack of cause-effect relationships, etc. I tend to agree with the critics. However, we need to entertain more theoretical models and subject them to dispassionate evaluation.

A third model which seeks to explain the thought process in reading through an analysis of abilities required in reading has been advanced by Holmes and Singer. By using statistical treatments involving correlation and factor analysis, the investigators claim to account for a hierarchy of variables that influence power and speed in reading. Plessas has taken the model to task on several grounds. Among them is the failure to establish cause-effect relationships between dependent and independent variables and inability to study variables other than those included in the matrix. He also pointed out the fact that test performance does not reveal how responses are reached. I too have had reservations about the model as I've heard it explained by the investigators. But it should be clear that we are not likely to do better than we have done in the past, unless we are willing to encourage the pursuit of ideas however tenuous they might seem. Surely there is ample evidence in other disciplines to warrant encouragement of reading research which raises eyebrows. Such practice does not preclude careful scrutiny, however. We need more people who are willing to expose themselves to review. Let us hope that the new research journal of IRA will promote just such attitudes—a process in which other disciplines have engaged profitably.

THE FUTURE

One reviewer of reading research summarized his report in this way: "Research in reading continues to create an interesting mosaic of conflict, consensus, and contribution. During the past six or seven years a steady stream of articles and reports have added to our fund of knowledge . . . while at the same time raising more questions than have been settled."[2]

How might we find more answers and raise fewer questions? I will suggest a few steps we might take to help us achieve such a goal:

1. Promote a core of professional reading researchers whose full-time efforts are supplemented by adequately trained part-time specialists. Endowed chairs at universities, as well as laboratories financed by public and private funds, might be channels through which the program is supported. It is conceivable a government agency such as the U.S. Office of Education would bring together personnel under its roof and provide the wherewithal for research activity as do some other government agencies. In addition to conducting research, these agencies could support programs for training reading reseachers.

2. Coordinate research programs through cooperative planning and activity. We have seen such an effort in the 27 first-year reading studies.

3. Publish complete reports of research so that other investigators might be able to evaluate them and replicate those which seem promising.

4. Integrate multi-discipline research in long-term investigations. We are now able to utilize modern technology to study countless variables from prenatal periods through birth and beyond. Data gathering after the fact can be and should be avoided.

5. Establish truly experimental schools where laboratory findings can be tested in typical environments. Results obtained under a given set of conditions might not hold under others.

Yes, "stimulating and disturbing days" can lie ahead. It might no longer be possible to defend and practice those things which we now hold dear. We must support the search for truth. Otherwise, we will continue to dredge up ideas that once held promise but later were found wanting. We must reach for the stars; perhaps we will achieve the moon.

[2] Harold G. Shane and June Grant Mulry, *Improving Language Arts Instruction Through Research*. Washington Association For Supervision And Curriculum Development, 1963, p. 34.

4
Measurement and Evaluation of Reading Achievement

DIAGNOSTIC TEACHING OF READING IN HIGH SCHOOL
Ruth Strang

What is the diagnostic teaching of reading? It is teaching that is based on an understanding of individual students and of the class as a whole. It is a process of identifying, appraising, diagnosing, and evaluating. It goes on continuously during the school years. In this process the teacher learns how each student reads—what his strengths and weaknesses are; what the student reads; why he reads—what his purposes in reading are; and what conditions facilitate or hinder his reading development.

The teacher makes immediate use of much of the understanding thus obtained. He interweaves diagnosis with instruction, and, in fact, with the total educational process. The entire school staff uses this information about students in building the curriculum and in selecting the texts, other instructional materials, and even the specific stories, poems, novels, or articles to be read by a given class. In every reading lesson, the teacher uses his

Reprinted from the *Journal of Reading,* VIII (January 1965), 147–154, with permission of the author and International Reading Association.

knowledge of the students in setting up the objectives, orienting the students, giving instruction, guiding their thinking, and testing and evaluating the knowledge and the reading skills that they have gained from their learning experiences.

COMPLEXITIES OF DIAGNOSTIC TEACHING

The diagnostic teaching of reading in high school is as complex as it is necessary. Students may range in ability from nonreaders to college preparatory students who want to increase their reading efficiency. In high schools today there are many students who lack word recognition skills and a working knowledge of the basic elements of a sentence. There are others who understand the relation between subject, verb, and object in a sentence, but are unable to see relationships among the ideas in a paragraph. There are others who lack the necessary experience with life and literature to interpret the words and literary passages they are expected to comprehend.

Moreover, departmental organization offers the teacher less opportunity for observation and personal contact than does the self-contained classroom. And the larger majority of high school teachers have had little or no preparation for the teaching of higher-level reading skills—recognizing the author's intent, mood, and purpose; interpreting character and motivation; tracing sequences in thought; and reading critically and creatively.

Diagnosis of the reading proficiency of high school students is further complicated by social and emotional factors. Some students seem to feel no need to improve their reading; their daily activities require a minimum of reading. Only when they are confronted with the need to get a driver's license, fill out an application blank, pass the army classification test, or get training for skilled work do they become aware that they need more reading ability.

It is even more difficult to understand and help the student who feels no responsibility for developing his potentialities or for contributing to the work of the world. Others have become apathetic, have cultivated an aloofness from the realities of life, or have developed feelings of worthlessness and hopelessness. Some have never had successful reading experiences or been in an environment in which people enjoy and profit by reading. Still others have not been helped to take advantage of crucial periods of learning readiness in early childhood, and have consequently not developed a love of learning. At first glance it seems impossible for high school teachers to diagnose the multiple factors that are involved in reading development and reading difficulties.

However, if we view the diagnostic-teaching process as a continuum, we see that one end comprises many tasks that every teacher can do; at the other end there may be a need for expert clinical, psychological, or psychiatric service.

SCHOOL AND CLASS RECORDS

It takes time to study every student's cumulative record. If a teacher were to spend only ten minutes on each record, it would take twenty-five hours to examine the records of 150 students—the average high school teacher's load. It is unrealistic to expect every teacher to spend as much time as this.

However, the teacher may ask each student to prepare a personal data card. If this card is introduced as an opportunity for self-appraisal, students are likely to fill it out fairly accurately and frankly.

This record includes blanks for the student's name, age, and address; the subjects he likes best and least; his educational and vocational plans; his special interests and hobbies; the titles of the books and articles he has read during the past month and the past year; and other information that the teacher thinks is particularly pertinent. Having these cards filled out not only lightens the teacher's clerical work, but also gives each student a certain perspective on his educational plans and progress. The "Reading Autobiography"[1] accomplishes this purpose still more effectively.

To the information supplied by the pupil the teacher may add, in all or only in certain cases, test results and other significant information from cumulative records. By spending a short time reading these cards, the teacher will get an idea of the make-up of the class as a whole, and some understanding of the individual pupils. This information he can use immediately in selecting books and in planning instruction.

UNDERSTANDING GAINED THROUGH ORAL RESPONSES

In an oral English period, at the beginning of the school year, each student may be asked

[1] Thomas Boning and Richard Boning, "I'd Rather Read than . . . ," *The Reading Teacher*, X (April 1957), 196–200.

to tell about his vacation. The film, "Helping Teachers Understand Pupils" (McGraw-Hill) shows how this practice gives the teacher some understanding of each student and of the class as a whole. The teacher notes indications of the individual's interests and of his social attitudes and relationships. He appraises pronunciation, speaking vocabulary, sentence patterns, and organization of ideas. He can quickly identify adolescents from culturally deprived homes or homes where no English is spoken; these youngsters need special practice and instruction in speech and functional English grammar. The glimpses he gets of the student's personal relationships aid him in forming congenial groups whose members will be mutually helpful.

In other subjects, a period of oral reporting enables the teacher to learn something about each student's background and special interests in the subject. The teacher is often amazed by the quantity of knowledge some individuals have gained from radio, television, and other out-of-school sources. Such information enables the teacher to gear his classroom instruction to outside interests and experience, and to supply the experience background which some of them lack.

UNDERSTANDING GAINED WHILE TEACHING

Diagnostic teaching should be an intrinsic part of the teacher's day-by-day instruction. The skillful teacher is always gaining insights that he uses in meeting individual needs; he guides as he teaches. The following excerpts are examples of diagnostic teaching that occurred in an English lesson on a short story:

TEACHER: "The first question I want to ask you is, 'How did you like my choice of story?'"
HELEN: "I liked it."
TEACHER: "Why?"
HELEN: "Well, I liked the style—the way she wrote it."
TEACHER: "Any other reasons?"

PATTY: "I don't know. You usually give us something where we have to dig for the meaning, but in this story the meaning was right on the surface."
DONALD: "I didn't like it."
TEACHER: "Why?"
DONALD: "I thought the story and the plot and everything was too simple to have all those big words and mythological references."
TEACHER: "That's an interesting statement."

Here the teacher elicited differing appraisals of a piece of writing. Donald was skillful in recognizing a *phony* story and in pointing out its wordy, inappropriate images. Others were not so discriminating. They either did not recognize the poor quality of the story, or were not morally courageous enough to mention it because this author's books had been highly recommended.

The teacher also noted wide differences in the students' ability to express themselves clearly, as in the following excerpt:

TEACHER: "Does 'Boy Meets Girl' accurately describe the plot?"
CHARLES: "No."
TEACHER: "Why not?"
CHARLES: "Because the girls, except one, have already met him and they are chasing *him*."
TEACHER: "You don't see this as a simple boy-meets-girl plot?"
CHARLES: "No."
TEACHER: "What are the boy's characteristics?"
CLAIRE: "Well, first of all, why, he has a mechanics job; he is always greasy."
TEACHER: "Is that unrealistic?"
CLAIRE: "Well, I mean for a mechanic, it isn't, no, but I mean, it's the greasy character that, you know, most girls—if he has grease on his hands you know or all slouched up, that puts a bad impression into the girl's mind."

Charles tends to speak thoughtfully and to the point. Claire is fuzzy in her thinking and incoherent in her oral expression.

This technique may also bring out a student's creativity. In the same story the author thus described the main character: "At the stroke of twelve his work-a-day garments dropped from him magically as though he were a male and reverse Cinderella." One student interpreted this figure of speech as follows: "Cinderella at twelve o'clock became grubby again, but at twelve o'clock *he* became ungrubbier."

The teacher can usually tell whether a class has the readiness for reading a given assignment by asking them a few preliminary questions. In teaching the story of Casey Jones, one teacher assumed much more knowledge about railroads than the modern boy or girl possesses. He found that the students were unable to make inferences about who was to blame or how the accident could have been prevented because they understood so little about trains. They consulted the dictionary for words such as "switch" and "Pullman," but came up with inappropriate meanings. This experience taught the teacher to check the students' backgrounds before reading other stories.

In dictionary study, a teacher discovered that though the students knew the alphabet and knew how to use the guide words, they would accept the first meaning given after the entry word. They needed to recognize that a word may have multiple meanings; they needed practice in selecting the meaning that is appropriate to the context. The teacher encouraged them first to apply their knowledge of structural analysis and guess the meaning of the word in its context, and then use the dictionary to see whether they were right. They began with simple words in a context where the meaning was clear. Later they went on to more difficult exercises.

During a silent reading period the teacher observed the way each student approached the material: Does he appear to enjoy it? Is he absorbed in his reading? Does he consult other sources? Is he enthusiastic in his discussion of what he has read? If the answers to any of these questions are negative, the teacher reevaluates his teaching: Did he pro-

vide sufficient motivation, instructions, and background? Was the material too hard or too easy? Did the student clearly perceive the purpose of reading the selection? Would it be helpful to have a personal interview with the student, or could the problem be handled better in a group situation?

The diagnostic information that the teacher may gain while teaching is not limited to the reading process. In compositions in which they are free to express their own thoughts and feelings, students often reveal previous experiences that are having an important bearing on their present attitudes and behavior. For example, a sophomore revealed that she had an illegitimate child and that her cousin was making it possible for her to attend school in another town. By means of several conferences, the teacher helped this girl overcome her indifference toward school, and to accept it as an opportunity to make the most of herself.

The student who is making progress in reading gains a sense of acceptance and personal worth if his progress is noticed and praised by the teacher or by his classmates. Opportunity to express one's opinion, especially if it is a divergent point of view, encourages students to take initiative and to become independent in their thinking about what they read. If the class reading periods are enjoyable and rewarding, adolescents are likely to continue reading when they leave school.

DIAGNOSTIC VALUE OF INFORMAL TESTS

The quickest and best way of assessing each student's ability to comprehend and communicate what he reads is to give him an informal test on a selection from a book he will soon be expected to read. The selection should be long enough—500 to 1,000 words—to test his ability to grasp the structure of the passage. He reads the selection in his usual way and, without looking back, answers two types of questions. The first is unstructured—"What did the author say?" or "What did you get out of the selection you just read?" The second comprises a series of short-answer, multiple-choice, or other objective questions that are designed to ascertain his ability to recognize and remember the main ideas and important details, to interpret and generalize, to draw inferences and conclusions, and to determine the meanings of key words in a given context.

As the students finish the selection, they record how long it took them, and begin to answer the questions. Later the teacher then shows them how to rate the free response and how to score the objective-type questions and answers. A student may want to know *why* his answer is not the best answer. This discussion will motivate him to learn to read more accurately the next time. Instruction follows immediately. In two or three weeks the teacher will give a similar informal test. The students will again go through the process of reading the selection and scoring, recording, and discussing their responses. This informal diagnostic-testing-teaching process continues throughout the school year. After the second try, many begin to see that they are making progress.[2] In some classes, the first informal test may show clearly that the grade text in a given subject is far too difficult for some of the students. Further diagnosis of their reading is indicated.

If the teacher has time for conferences with individuals during a free period or while the class as a whole is reading or studying independently, he can learn more about the problems of retarded readers. If he finds that they cannot quickly recognize the basic sight vocabulary of 220 frequently recurring words, he will give them practice with the

Dolch games (Garrard Press) or other practice material. If an individual tachistoscope such as the Flash-X (EDL) is available, he will let them use it to develop instantaneous recognition of these 220 words. If the problem seems to be difficulty in pronouncing unfamiliar words, the teacher may use the Phono-Visual charts for diagnosis and practice. If the student does not know the meanings of words even when he can pronounce them, he may be encouraged to read more widely and to build up a vocabulary file of key words.

If the student knows the separate words but has not acquired the ability to comprehend the meaning of sentences, he needs instruction and practice in the comprehension of sentences, paragraphs, and longer passages. The customary practice of testing students exclusively or principally on the literal meaning of reading material has left many of them weak in interpreting meaning, making inferences and generalizations, and drawing conclusions. These students may need extra instruction, individually or in small groups, in addition to the practice that is regularly given in class.

Although most standardized reading tests are of the survey type, some diagnostic value can be extracted from them. Teacher and student can go over the completed tests together, noting the total score and the subtest scores, noting errors, trying to determine the causes of these errors, and discussing ways of correcting them. This use of standardized tests for instructional purposes is now sanctioned by experts in the field of testing. Of course this procedure would not be used with tests that have been given for research purposes or to measure pupil progress.

THE INCOMPLETE
SENTENCE TECHNIQUE

If there is a mutual relationship of trust and respect between students and teacher, the incomplete-sentence technique will reveal students' attitudes toward themselves and to-

[2] For more detail on this procedure, see Amelia Melnik, "The Improvement of Reading Through Self-Appraisal," *A Procedure for Teaching Reading in Junior High School Social Studies* (unpublished doctoral dissertation, Teachers College, Columbia University, New York, 1960).

ward reading.[3] For this purpose items such as the following are pertinent:

I like to read about . . .
Comic books . . .
When I have reading to do, I . . .
When I read math . . .
I like to read when . . .
For me, studying . . .
Reading science . . .
I'd read more if . . .
I'd rather read than . . .
When I read aloud . . .
To me books . . .
I wish my parents knew . . .
I wish teachers . . .
I can't understand why . . .
I wish . . .
Today I feel . . .

The teacher interprets the replies, which are always to be given voluntarily, as he would interpret any other observed behavior, and checks his interpretation against his daily observation.

REFERRAL OF COMPLICATED CASES

There will be individuals who do not respond to any "reading first aid" that the teacher can give. These adolescents have dif-

[3] Ruth Strang, *Diagnostic Teaching of Reading* (New York: McGraw-Hill, 1964), pp. 76–85.

ficulties that need deeper diagnosis. The reading specialist explores deficiencies in visual and auditory acuity and discrimination, and in conceptualization. He measures different kinds of mental ability such as those assessed by the Wechsler Intelligence Tests.

It may be that the student has emotional difficulties or a negative self-concept that limits his functioning in reading. If so, the teacher may refer him to the school counselor who, in turn, may refer him to psychologist, psychiatrist, or neurologist for deeper diagnosis.

Without departing from the area of his competence, any high school teacher, whatever his subject, may help his students to improve their reading. As they see progress and experience success, they become more self-confident and put forth more effort. "Nothing succeeds like observed success." The distance between a low self-concept and a high level of aspiration can thus be reduced. Students who know they are making progress in reading have less need to cover up their failures by resorting to attention-getting devices. They no longer feel hostility toward the teacher or the school. As they become more competent in reading, they are likely to elicit a more favorable response from their parents, teachers, and classmates. If this process of diagnostic teaching were to be adopted in every subject, it might well have an enormous effect on the personal growth and reading development of every student.

THE ASSESSMENT OF CHANGE
Frederick B. Davis

Reprinted from *Phases of College and Other Adult Reading Programs, Tenth Yearbook of the National Reading Conference* (1961), pp. 86–99, with permission of the author and National Reading Conference, Inc.

To assess a pupil's current level of proficiency in any skill, ability, or subject-matter field, it is first necessary to define carefully and explicitly the variable being measured.

Second, a test of the variable, or as close an approximation to it as can be secured, must be administered under conditions that assure a high degree of cooperation on the part of the pupil. Third, a pupil's obtained score must be compared with suitable norms, such as percentile ranks in his own age or grade group. Fourth, the possibility that the pupil's obtained score represents a sizable deviation from his true score must be considered. To do so, the standard error of measurement of the pupil's obtained score must be used to construct an appropriate confidence interval.[1] For practical purposes, the 15-percent confidence interval is often satisfactory and forms a basis for asserting that the chances are 85 out of 100 that the range of scores so designated includes the pupil's true score.

These four steps may seem unduly elaborate to many teachers and supervisors, but the task of assessing the pupil's *improvement* in any skill, ability, or subject-matter field may be even more complicated. This assessment is, however, of great practical importance to pupils and their parents as well as to teachers, school administrators, and supervisors. After all, the primary purpose of teaching is to produce improvement in the learner. Procedures that may be used in assessing improvement in learning will be discussed under the four main headings indicated.

OBTAINING APPROPRIATE MEASURING INSTRUMENTS

Test Validity—The first consideration in selecting an instrument for estimating improvement is the validity of the instrument for measuring what the examiner wants to measure. Teachers and administrators should give careful thought to the appropriateness of their measuring instruments prior to the beginning of the instructional period and select for detailed study tests that appear to measure the most relevant combination of skills, abilities, and knowledges. Ordinarily, a teacher interested in measuring the improvement of a pupil during all or part of a school year wants to know how well the pupil has learned certain specific skills that he has been practicing and how much effect his specific practice and his general maturation have had on his over-all proficiency. For example, to measure reading ability it is usually fairly easy to select tests of specific skills (such as oral reading, word recognition, or use of an index), but it is more difficult to decide which test of over-all reading ability measures the most appropriately weighted combination of skills. The total scores of tests of comprehension in reading commonly used in American secondary schools constitute measures of rather different combinations of skills and abilities. The *Iowa Silent Reading Tests* (4)* include measures of study skills and rate of reading in the total scores; the *Nelson-Denny Reading Test* (9) consists of rather highly speeded tests of word knowledge and paragraph comprehension; and the *Cooperative Reading Comprehension Test* (2) includes in its total score an essentially unspeeded test of word knowledge and both speeded and unspeeded measures of paragraph comprehension. It tends to have a more literary flavor than the two tests mentioned previously. The *Davis Reading Test* (3) yields two scores, the first an unspeeded measure of comprehension and the second a speed-of-comprehension score.

A source of unwanted and invalid variance in scores on aptitude and achievement tests that is often unrecognized even by sophisti-

[*Numbers in parentheses refer to Bibliography at the end of this article.]

---

[1] In practice, the standard error of measurement precisely applicable to a given pupil's obtained score is rarely obtainable. If standard errors of measurement for several levels of score value are available, the one for the value closest to that of the pupil's score should be used. If not, the overall standard error of measurement for the pupil's age or grade group may be employed.

cated examiners is the practice of guessing on the part of many examinees. The effect of this practice is particularly troublesome when tests are used to measure *improvement* because, over a period of time, pupils are apt to change their rates of work or methods of approach to the task set by the test. If tests are scored with an appropriate correction for chance success, the directions of administration can legitimately discourage guessing and can reduce the effect of such guessing as nonetheless takes place. For these reasons, among others, the writer strongly recommends that only tests scored with correction for chance success be employed to estimate improvement resulting from learning. This is especially important in measuring growth in comprehension in reading because many courses designed to improve reading stress speed of reading as well as depth of comprehension. Improvement in both objectives of instruction should, therefore, be measured separately. Unless the test of comprehension is scored with correction for chance success, it is, in practice, likely to become partly a measure of the examinee's tendency to mark answers to items even when he does not understand the material on which they are based. Since many teachers, psychologists, and school administrators are not familiar with the way guessing on the part of the examinee can impair the validity of test scores, illustrations will be provided here to show how it can spuriously increase or decrease the observed change in a pupil's score.

In 1949, Murphy and Davis administered Form B of the *Nelson-Denny Reading Test* to 393 eleventh- and twelfth-grade pupils in Nashville, Tennessee. (8) The 47 pupils who obtained the lowest scores were called in for retesting. They were encouraged to do better and to mark an answer to every item even if they did not know the answer. These instructions changed their mental sets toward the task and their methods of work. Their average score rose from 25.53 on Form B to 46.32 on Form A. Part of this increase was the result of regression to the group mean, but most of it resulted from the fact that pupils marked answers to a greater number of test items than they had at first. Since the scores on the test are not corrected for chance success, a pupil is likely to increase his score simply by marking answers to more items. After correction for chance success, the average score of the same pupils rose only from 13.62 to 15.62, a difference largely accounted for by regression to the group mean. Correction for chance success removed the spurious *inflation* of the observed gain in the average reading-test scores of the 47 pupils.

Another example will illustrate how correction for chance success can remove a spurious *reduction* of the observed change between testings. A ninth-grade pupil, markedly retarded in recognition vocabulary, was given the vocabulary section of Form B of the *Nelson-Denny Reading Test* at the beginning of the school year in September. Finding that he had great difficulty in reading the words, he moved rapidly along, marking every item and hoping to get a few of them correct on the basis of what he could read. Since he actually did know the answers to some of the items, his score was better than could most reasonably have been expected on the basis of chance alone; he got a score of 23. The published norms indicated that this corresponded to a grade score of 11.0. After 9 months of school, including special tutorial work in reading with emphasis on word-recognition skills, he was given Form A of the same test. This time he approached the test differently because he could read the words more readily. He tried each item seriously and was able to read 34 of them in the time limit. Of the 34 he tried, he marked 14 correctly. The published norms indicated that this corresponded to a grade score below the beginning of grade 9. These scores might lead one to conclude that the boy had retrogressed markedly in recognition of words during the course of the school year. But we can easily show that this conclusion is unjustified. After correction for chance, the boy's score on Form B in September was 4; on Form A in June it was 9. Thus, correction for chance success removed the spurious *reduction* of the amount of improvement that the boy had actually made and showed that, in fact, he had increased his score.

Availability of Parallel Forms. Since the estimation of *improvement* demands testing at two different times, the availability of parallel forms is important. Thus, a teacher might prefer to use the *Neal Analysis of Reading Test*, of which several parallel forms are available, rather than the *Gray Oral Paragraphs Test*, of which only one form is available.* It is undesirable to use the same form of a test more than once because a pupil may remember part of it or even look up some of the material in it during the interim between testings.

Accuracy of Measurement. Because the amount of improvement that can be shown to be statistically significant at any given level of confidence varies with the accuracy of the measuring instruments employed, it is desirable to use, among tests of equal validity and availability, those with the smallest standard errors of measurement at the score levels obtained by the pupils for whom improvement is to be established. In practice, it is often impossible to make comparisons among tests on this basis because few test publishers provide standard errors of measurement at several score levels. If reliability coefficients are compared, it is important that they shall have been obtained by similar methods on reasonably similar groups, such as pupils in a given age or grade group. Whenever a test is appreciably speeded, reliability coefficients computed by split-half or Kuder-Richardson techniques are spuriously high in comparison with those computed by parallel-forms techniques.

* More than one form is available now.—Ed.

SECURING CONSISTENT RAPPORT WITH THE EXAMINER

It is important that the degree of cooperation and motivation shown by the examinee be as nearly the same as possible during all testing sessions. Otherwise, differences between the resulting scores cannot properly be ascribed to changes in the pupil's level of skill or ability. For the same reason, the approach of the examinee to the mechanics of testing should be consistent at all testing sessions. This does not mean that the mental set of the pupils should not change; after successful training in reading, for example, it is to be expected that pupils will anticipate and work on a reading test with greater confidence than they did before. Changes of this kind in mental set are a natural concomitant of the successful teaching of reading. What is meant is that mere familiarity with the format of items and answer sheet should not serve to increase a pupil's score. To minimize these irrelevant influences and, at the same time, to minimize the effect of regression to the group mean on the difference between test scores, two equivalent forms of a test may be administered to a class or grade group. Scores for the first of the two forms may be used to identify pupils for remedial instruction before the second set of test papers has been scored. Scores from the latter may be obtained and used for comparison with those obtained from a third parallel form given at the end of the period of remedial work.

Teachers and others may be surprised to find that considerable improvement in test scores ordinarily takes place between the first and second testings—improvement that would erroneously be ascribed to the effects of the remedial teaching if the second test had not been given prior to the training period.

One of the most important factors in keeping constant the pupil's approach to the mechanics of testing is the type of directions used. These should be clear-cut, understandable, unambiguous, and honest. If standardized tests are used, the directions given by the publisher must be followed precisely; otherwise, the norms may not be applicable. Therefore, when tests are selected, consideration should be given to the adequacy of the directions. These should provide at least a brief explanation of how the scoring is to be done. Directions for tests corrected for chance success can, and ordinarily do, state this. The following phraseology has been found satisfactory for secondary-school pupils: "You should mark answers to items even when you are not sure that your answers are correct, but it is better to omit an item than to guess *wildly* because each one of your incorrect answers results in a small subtraction from the number of your correct answers."

SELECTING TESTS THAT HAVE APPROPRIATE STANDARDS OR NORMS

Tests used to measure a pupil's improvement should have norms appropriate for representative groups at the pupil's grade level even though the pupil's score may be equivalent to the mean scores of pupils in grades considerably higher or lower. Say, for example, that a pupil entering the ninth grade is scheduled to take the *Stanford Reading Test* in September along with his class. Even though his reading ability is known to be low, it is best to administer the Advanced reading test, which has norms appropriate to Grade 9 and is intended for pupils having the backgrounds and experiences of ninth graders. The change in this pupil's reading ability can then be estimated by one of the methods described in the next section of this paper. If the pupil answers no items correctly in September, the Advanced test will have been shown to be unusable and one of the lower-level tests in the same series should be administered to him. In fact, if the pupil's September grade score were below

40 (the lowest grade score on the Profile Chart of the *Stanford Reading Test*, Advanced) the inaccuracy of measurement would be sufficiently great to warrant the use of a lower-level test—say, the Intermediate test if his grade score were 30–39; the Elementary test if it were 20–29; or the Primary test if it were below 20. To measure progress the June test should be an equivalent form of the level of test given in September.

ESTIMATING THE AMOUNT OF CHANGE

There are many ways of estimating the true amount of improvement (or retrogression) of an individual or of a group. In Table I, five methods for estimating the change in an individual and three methods for estimating the change in the average of a group are provided.[2] These range from crude to sophisticated estimates. Choice among them is determined by the data available and by the use to be made of the data. A classroom teacher might have available only the data and time required for using Method 1 for individuals or Method 6 for groups. An experimenter, conducting a study to determine the gains by certain individuals or groups, should make plans to obtain and use the data required by Method 5 for individuals or Method 8 for groups.

To illustrate the application of several of the methods presented in Table 1 to practical data, information about the scores of the 200 pupils in a public high school has been used. These data are shown in Table III. The pupils were tested in September with Form A of the *Davis Reading Test* and in June with Form B of the same test. Only the Speed-of-Comprehension scores of the pupils are considered for illustrative purposes. From the group of 200 pupils, one named Hazel Brown was selected at random prior to the first testing and was also given Form C in September

[2] Tables I, II, III, and IV are presented at the end of this paper.

and Form D in June. Her scores are denoted in Table III as A, B, C, and D. Averages of the scores on Forms A and B in the entire group are indicated by placement of a bar over the form letter.

Various estimates of Hazel's true gain in Speed of Comprehension are shown in Table IV. As noted in Table I, Methods 1, 2, and 3 should be used only if an individual pupil has been selected for retesting at random from an age or grade group. Even then, they provide no more than crude estimates unless the number of equivalent forms used in Method 3 is fairly large. In practice, a sufficient number of equivalent forms is not likely to be available for published tests. Hence, it is ordinarily best to plan to use either Method 4 or Method 5 if the requisite data and computing time can be obtained. Method 1 is the simplest and by far the most commonly used estimate of a pupil's gain. It consists simply of getting the difference between his initial and final scores. For Hazel, the difference (d_1) is shown in Table IV to be 5 scaled-score points. When the appropriate expression for D_1 in Table II is employed to find the smallest difference obtained by Method 1 that is significantly different from zero at the 15-percent level, Hazel's gain of 5 points is not established as significant. Hence, we cannot conclude that she has made any real gain in speed of comprehension in reading. It should be noted that the 15-percent level is not a stringent requirement for significance.

Let us see what our conclusion would be if we were to use the data from both Form A and C (given in September) and Form B and D (given in June). If we employ Method 2, as indicated in Table I, and find the difference between the average of these two pairs of scores, we obtain an estimated gain of 5 points, as before. Use of the appropriate equation from Table II to compute the smallest difference obtained by Method 2 that is significantly different from zero at the 15-percent level yields 4.3, as shown in table 4. Hazel's gain of 5 points is larger; hence we

may conclude that this gain is significant. Increased accuracy of measurement provided by the use of averages of pairs of scores permits the 5-point gain to be regarded as significant.

Method 3 is presented in Table I to show how the average of any number of equivalent forms at either the initial or final testings may be employed. The corresponding test of significance for the 15-percent level is shown in Table II.

Methods 4 and 5 for estimating change may be employed even in the case of an individual pupil who was selected for retesting because he had an unusually high or unusually low score in the initial test. In practice, pupils are often assigned to remedial work in reading if their scores on a suitable test, administered at the beginning of the school year, are low. Then they are retested in June to find the extent of their gains, if any. Such gains should be estimated by Method 4 or 5. Let us say that Hazel's September score of 59 was one of the lowest in her grade and that she was one of the lowest-scoring 20 pupils assigned to remedial work. For her, Method 4, as specified in Table I, yields an estimated gain of 4.6 scaled-score points. Since a gain of less than 4.9 points, computed by Method 4, cannot be considered significant at the 15-percent level, as shown in Table IV, we cannot conclude that she has made a real gain.

It should be noted that use of Method 4 requires that the initial and final tests be administered to the entire group of 200 pupils in Hazel's grade group. Their scores provide the means, $\overline{A}$ and $\overline{B}$, and are used to estimate reliability coefficients, r_{aA} and r_{bB}, as follows:

$$r_{aA} = 1 - \frac{s^2_{meas_p}}{s_A{}^2}, \text{ and } r_{bB} = 1 - \frac{s^2_{meas_p}}{s_B{}^2},$$

where s_{meas_p} is the standard error of measurement given by the publisher for a sample of twelfth-grade pupils reasonably similar to the 200 in Hazel's grade group.

In addition to the data required for Method 4, Method 5 demands that the correlation of scores of the 200 pupils on the initial and final tests, r_{AB}, be computed. If Method 5 is used to estimate Hazel's change, a gain of 4.2 points is found. However, the increased accuracy of estimation provided by taking into account the correlation of September and June scores among the 200 pupils in Hazel's grade group permits establishment of the significance of this gain at better than the 15-percent level. The clear implication of this illustration for psychologists, teachers, and remedial workers is to make provision in advance for obtaining the data required for use of Method 5 whenever the effects of remedial or other special treatment are to be evaluated.

Estimates of change for a group of pupils chosen at random from an age or grade group can be made by Methods 6, 7, and 8 presented in Table I. If the members of the group have been chosen on the basis of their initial test scores, Method 6 should not be used for this purpose. As shown by the data in Table IV, an average gain of 1.3 points would be significant at the 15-percent level for a group of 20 pupils chosen *at random* from the 200 in Hazel's grade group. The amount of change in the group of 20 pupils selected from the group because of low initial test scores should be estimated by either Method 7 or 8. The former yields an estimate of 5.5 points and the latter 4.9 points. Both estimated gains are highly significant statistically since they both greatly exceed the smallest differences of 1.1 and .8, respectively, required to establish significance at the 15-percent level.

A word of caution may be in order with respect to the tests of significance of the estimates of mean gain obtained by Methods 6, 7, and 8. These should be used as a basis for drawing inferences about the gain (or loss) estimated for any given group. They should *not* be used as a basis for drawing inferences about the gains (or losses) that could be expected in *other* comparable samples drawn at random from the same population and exposed to the same influences between tests. The bases for inference of the latter kind are the conventional appropriate standard errors of differences between means.

BIBLIOGRAPHY

1. DAVIS, F. B. "Interpretation of Differences Among Averages and Individual Test Scores," *Journal of Educational Psychology*, 50:162–170, 1959.
2. ———, et al., *Cooperative Reading Comprehension Test*, Forms Q-Z. Princeton, New Jersey: Educational Testing Service, 1940–53.
3. ———, and DAVIS, C. C. *Davis Reading Test*. New York: Psychological Corporation, 1958.
4. GREENE, H. A., JORGENSEN, A. N., and KELLEY, V. H. *Iowa Silent Reading Tests* (New Edition, Revised), Advanced Test. Yonkers: World Book Company, 1943.
5. KELLEY, T. L. *Fundamentals of Statistics.* Cambridge: Harvard University Press, 1947.
6. LORD, F. M. "Measurement of Growth," *Educational and Psychological Measurement*, 16:421–437, 1956.
7. McNEMAR, Q. "On Growth Measurement," *Educational and Psychological Measurement*, 18:47–55, 1958.
8. MURPHY, H. D., and DAVIS, F. B. "A Note on the Measurement of Progress in Remedial Reading," *Peabody Journal of Education*, 27:108–111, 1949.
9. NELSON, M. J., and DENNY, E. C. *Nelson-Denny Reading Test.* Boston: Houghton Mifflin Company, 1938.

TABLE I
METHODS OF ESTIMATING TRUE CHANGE OF IMPROVEMENT

Estimate of Change (d) for an Individual Pupil

Chosen at Random from an Age or Grade Group
Difference Between Equivalent Obtained Scores

1. $B - A = d_1$

2. $\dfrac{B + D}{2} - \dfrac{A + C}{2} = d_2$

3. $\dfrac{\overset{m}{\Sigma}Y}{m} - \dfrac{\overset{n}{\Sigma}X}{n} = d_3$

Chosen on the Basis of Initial Test Scores
Difference Between Regressed Obtained Equivalent Scores

4. $r_{bB}B - r_{aA}A + (\overline{B} - \overline{A} + r_{aA}\overline{A} - r_{bB}\overline{B}) = d_4$

Difference Between True Scores on Tests That Yield Equivalent Scores

5. $W_B B + W_A A + (\overline{B} - \overline{A} - W_B\overline{B} - W_A\overline{A}) = d_5$

Estimate of Change (d) for a Group of Pupils

Chosen at Random From an Age or Grade Group
Difference Between Averages on Tests That Yield Equivalent Scores

6. $B_g - A_g = d_6$

Chosen on the Basis of Initial Test Scores
Difference Between Averages of Regressed Obtained Equivalent Scores

7. $r_{bB}\overline{B}_g - r_{aA}\overline{A}_g + (\overline{B} - \overline{A} + r_{aA}\overline{A} - r_{bB}\overline{B}) = d_7$

Difference Between True Group Averages on Tests That Yield Equivalent Scores

8. $W_B\overline{B}_g + W_A\overline{A}_g + (\overline{B} - \overline{A} - W_B\overline{B} - W_A\overline{A}) = d_8$

Explanation of Symbols Used

A, B, C, D represent individual obtained scores on equivalent forms of the same test (1:164);

X, Y represent individual obtained scores on any equivalent form of the same test;

m, n represent the numbers of equivalent forms administered to one individual;

N represents the number of pupils in an age or grade group;

N_g represents the number of pupils in a subgroup of the N pupils;

$\overline{A}, \overline{B}$ represent arithmetic averages of individual obtained scores of N pupils on equivalent forms of the same test;

TABLE I—*Continued*

$\overline{A}_g, \overline{B}_g$ represent arithmetic averages of individual obtained scores of N_g pupils on equivalent forms of the same test;

s_{meas} represents the standard error of measurement in the group of N pupils;

r_{aA}, r_{bB} represent the reliability coefficients of Forms A and B in the group of N pupils;

$$W_A = \frac{s_B r_{AB}(1 - r_{bB}) - s_A(r_{aA} - r_{AB}^2)}{s_A(1 - r_{AB}^2)};$$

$$W_B = \frac{s_B(r_{bB} - r_{AB}^2) - s_A r_{AB}(1 - r_{aA})}{s_B(1 - r_{AB}^2)};$$

$$s_{meas d_5} = s_{d_5}\sqrt{1 - r_{d_5 d'_5}};$$

$$s_{d_5} = \sqrt{W_A^2 s_A^2 + W_B^2 s_B^2 + 2W_A W_B s_A s_B r_{AB}};$$

$$r_{d_5 d'_5} = \frac{(s_B r_{AB} - s_A r_{aA})^2 + (s_B r_{bB} - s_A r_{AB})^2 - 2r_{AB}(s_B r_{AB} - s_A r_{aA})(s_B r_{bB} - s_A r_{AB})}{(1 - r_{AB}^2)(s_A^2 r_{aA} + s_B^2 r_{bB} - 2s_A s_B r_{AB})}$$

TABLE II

SMALLEST CHANGE (D) SIGNIFI-CANT AT THE 15-PERCENT LEVEL*

1. $D_1 = 2s_{meas A}$

2. $D_2 = 1.44 s_{meas A}$

3. $D_3 = 1.44 \sqrt{\dfrac{s^2 meas_A}{m} + \dfrac{s^2 meas_B}{n}}$

4. $D_4 = 1.44 s_{meas A}\sqrt{r_{aA}^2 + r_{bB}^2}$

5. $D_5 = 1.44 s_{meas d_5}$

6. $D_6 = \dfrac{2s_{meas A}}{\sqrt{N_g}}$

7. $D_7 = \dfrac{1.44 s_{meas A}}{\sqrt{N_g}}\sqrt{r_{aA}^2 + r_{bB}^2}$

8. $D_8 = \dfrac{1.44 s_{meas d_5}}{\sqrt{N_g}}$

* *Changes significant at any other level can be identified by appropriate changes in the equations. For example, if the expression on the right-hand side in each of equations 1 through 8 is multiplied by 1.36, the 5-percent level is provided; if each is multiplied by 1.79, the 1-percent level is provided.*

TABLE III

DATA PERTAINING TO DAVIS READING TEST SCORES
IN A TWELFTH-GRADE CLASS

	Scaled Score		Scaled Score
A_i	59.0	r_{aA}	.84
B_i	64.0	r_{bB}	.87
C_i	61.0	r_{AB}	.65
D_i	66.0	W_A	$-.57$
$\overline{A}$	70.3	W_B	.61
$\overline{B}$	74.5	s_{d_5}	3.79
$\overline{A}_g$	60.1	$r_{d_5 d'_5}$	.60
$\overline{B}_g$	66.1		Number
s_A	7.3	N	200
s_B	8.0	N_g	20
s_{meas}	2.9		

TABLE IV

ESTIMATED CHANGES (d) AND SMALLEST CHANGES
SIGNIFICANT AT THE 15-PERCENT LEVEL (D) FOR
PUPIL i AND GROUP g

	Estimated Change (Scaled Score)	Smallest Change Significant at 15% Level
d_1	5.0	5.8
d_2	5.0	4.2
d_3	$6.0 \left(\dfrac{B+D}{2} - A \right)$	5.1 $\left(\begin{array}{l} \text{average of two tests} \\ \textit{versus } \text{one test} \end{array} \right)$
d_4	4.6	4.9
d_5	4.2	3.4
d_6	6.0	1.3
d_7	5.5	1.1
d_8	4.9	0.8

ASSESSING VOCABULARY AND WORD-ATTACK SKILLS
Emery P. Bliesmer

When assessing vocabulary and word-attack skills, or attempting to determine the status of children with respect to such, we as teachers are concerned basically with several matters. One of our concerns is the extent of the sight vocabulary possessed by the individual child. More will be said or brought out later about the role or function of a sight vocabulary. There is concern also with the extent to which various word-attack skills are possessed by the child. The concern here is chiefly with phonics skill and skill with respect to structural analysis. We wish to ascertain just how far a child has progressed in the relatively sequential development of certain skills; we wish to know what elements have or have not been mastered. A third concern is with the actual effectiveness of the word-attack skills possessed by the individual. Specifically, we wish to determine how well a child is really able to apply the skills he has in actually figuring out strange or unknown words. We need to keep in mind that this, after all, is the main purpose or objective with regard to word-attack skill development.

In our assessing or evaluating efforts we need to keep sight of the aforementioned items and of our overall or ultimate goals or aims with respect to the word attack skills

Reprinted from the *University of Pittsburgh Conference Proceedings*, No. 18 (1962), 121–130, with permission of the author and University of Pittsburgh Conference Proceedings.

program. Observation of practice would seem to indicate that it is very easy for us as teachers to lose sight of this and to become somewhat vague with respect to our purposes for teaching word-attack skills, that is, to lose sight of our ultimate aims in the midst of our day by day teaching of pieces of word-attack skills. We need to keep reminding ourselves what all of this is for.

In assessing or evaluating vocabulary and word-attack skills, both formal and informal methods are used. The formal methods which are or might be employed involve tests which have been more or less standardized. Results obtained with different standardized tests can give most important and useful information, and much can be learned from such tests. However, informal methods play an equally, if not more, important role and are apt to be, or need to be, utilized more frequently.

FORMAL ASSESSMENT PROCEDURES

A number of standardized tests useful in evaluating word-attack skills is available. Among these are such as the following (with the publisher of each test being indicated parenthetically): the *Roswell-Chall Diagnostic Reading Test* (Essay Press); the *Durrell Analysis of Reading Difficulty* (Harcourt, Brace and World); the *Gates Reading Diagnostic Tests* (Bureau of Publications, Teachers College, Columbia University);

the *McKee Inventory of Phonetic Skill* (Houghton Mifflin Company); the Bond-Clymer-Hoyt *Silent Reading Diagnostic Tests* (Lyons and Carnahan); the *Dolch Basic Sight Vocabulary Test* (Garrard Press); the *Botel Reading Inventory* (Follett Publishing Company); the *Leavell Analytical Oral Reading Test* (Educational Test Bureau); and the *Gray Standardized Oral Reading Paragraphs* (Public School Publishing Company). Parts of some of the tests developed and provided by some publishers for their particular basal reading series might also be used at times.

It will be noted that the tests listed above tend to be diagnostic reading tests rather than reading achievement tests. It should also be pointed out that, while a number of tests have been listed, the list is by no means an exhaustive one. The fact that most of the tests listed are diagnostic ones is not accidental. When serious or sustained efforts to evaluate word-attack skills of an individual pupil are made, the purpose is usually a diagnostic one rather than one of determining specific achievement level. Rather than determining the general status level of the individual child's particular skill, the purpose is one of determining more specifically just what is keeping the child from performing or achieving as well as he might.

Assessment of a number of items or specifics with respect to word-attack skills is afforded through administration of tests. Among the various skills and abilities evaluated are to be included such as the following: locating or recognizing root words in variant or derivative forms of words, extent of sight vocabulary, freedom from reversal tendencies, ability to divide words into syllables, ability to blend or to synthesize sounds or sound elements into words, recognizing sounds of elements in various parts of words (marking the proper visual form after hearing the oral element or giving the visual form orally), recognizing whether a vowel sound is long or short (or recognizing other variations of vowel sounds), determining the number of syllables heard in a word, indicating accented syllables, and the like.

There are various ways in which specific tests are administered and the pupil is required or expected to respond. On some tests the teacher or examiner reads words, or combinations of words, or makes certain noises, and the pupil marks or records answers on the basis of what he hears the examiner saying. Among the situations involving this type of administration and responding would be such as the following:

1. Marking the word in a group of words which is the same as the word spoken by the teacher.
2. Marking the word in a group of given words which has the same sound (represented by a letter or a combination of letters) in a given place as a spoken word.
3. Marking whether a vowel sound in a word is long or short, or marking the word among a group of words or letter combinations which contains the vowel sound spoken by the teacher or examiner.
4. Marking the letter(s) which represent(s) the word or sound spoken by the teacher.
5. Marking the letter, or combination of letters, heard at the beginning, or in other parts, of a word.

On some other tests the pupil does the entire test silently, that is, he reads the test to and by himself. Among the various skills measured by this procedure are such as the following, and in the manners indicated:

1. Sight vocabulary is measured by having the pupil mark the word among a group of given words which goes with a specific picture.
2. Skill in the use of context clues is measured by having the pupil mark the right word to go in a blank among a group of words or sentences, with perhaps a beginning or ending letter clue being given.

3. A type of syllabication skill is measured by having the pupil mark or indicate where the syllabic divisions in words would occur.
4. Skill in determining proper structural elements might be evaluated by having the pupil pick out the proper variant ending form to go with a given root word in a given context.

In still other tests the pupil is required to read portions of the test aloud. These are almost always diagnostic reading tests and need to be done individually. Among skills assessed through this procedure are such as the following:

1. Sight vocabulary.
2. Knowledge of sounds of various phonetic elements (beginning, ending, or other parts of words—and single letters or a combination of letters).
3. Knowledge of basic elements such as common variant endings or affixes.
4. Recognition of sounds of given syllables.
5. Ability to blend single sounds into words.
6. Ability to blend syllables into words.

The concern at this time and at this point, in this paper, is not with presenting further detailed information with respect to any particular standardized test or tests. However, it is strongly urged that teachers become familiar with a number of different tests, such as those listed earlier, and study those in some detail and with some care. Such study should have definite benefits in the way of carryover or transfer values with respect to informal evaluation or assessment.

INFORMAL ASSESSMENT PROCEDURES

As was indicated earlier, informal assessing is the type of evaluation which will need to be done, and should be done, most frequently. Informal assessment should be a regular day by day procedure as teachers work with youngsters. Methods of informal assessment are, to a considerable extent, adaptations or less formal imitations of methods used in connection with more or less standardized tests. While much informal assessing or evaluating will be done intentionally or with the purpose of assessing definitely in mind, it needs to be realized that every time a teacher works with a child in a situation which relates to reading, the situation can also be a diagnostic or assessing situation; and advantage needs to be taken of such opportunities.

A type of evaluation which is actually a relatively old one but which has remained, and is becoming increasingly more popular is one which is usually designated, in general, as "an informal inventory." With this procedure, a number of short reading selections, graded in difficulty and covering a range of difficulty levels, is presented to a child. Usually the selections in such an inventory are taken from a series of basal readers. In fact, the readers themselves with the books opened to given pages are frequently used. A child is asked to read each of several portions or selections; and a written record is made of his performance while he reads. Some teachers have found it helpful to record a child's reading performance with a tape recorder. This has the obvious advantage of permitting a repeat of a performance exactly as it was given the first time, which repetition is desirable when it is not possible to make a record of all of an individual's performance the first time. Among points, relevant to word-attack skills, to be noted as a child reads are such as the following:

1. Words he fails to know instantly, or the words which are not yet a part of his sight vocabulary.
2. Words the child mispronounces.
3. Words on which help needs to be given.
4. Omissions of, or errors in various parts of words.

Some sort of organized listing and study of the various errors on words which the child has made is then done; and some type of diagnosis or judgment is made, on the basis of the errors, as to where the child has, in a manner of speaking, "missed the boat" with respect to word attack skills.

Similar sorts of analyses or assessments might also be made, although in a less complete and systematic way, whenever a youngster has occasion to read something aloud within the hearing of the teacher. Further additions to the picture yielded by informal evaluation may be made by noting or studying words for or on which the child asks for help. Further information is also yielded through study of spelling errors in written words, including spelling lessons. (However, it needs to be kept in mind, insofar as follow up procedures are concerned, that phonics skill in spelling involves, in a sense, the inverse of what is involved in phonics skill in reading.)

POINTS TO CONSIDER
IN ASSESSING SKILLS

The remaining portion of this paper will be devoted to a number of points relative to various aspects of measuring vocabulary and word attack skills which need to be kept in mind while evaluating such skills. The first of the several points to be made relate to the area of sight vocabulary. A number of available tests include, or consist mainly of, a sight vocabulary test (for example, the *Dolch Basic Sight Word Test*, the *Botel Reading Inventory*, the *Durrell Analysis of Reading Difficulty*, and the *Gates Reading Diagnostic Tests*). While these tests may be highly desirable and useful in individual situations where careful and extensive diagnosis is desired, the most frequently used procedure for assessing sight vocabulary will perhaps be an informal one in which the teacher utilizes some given list of words, usually a list of words found in the reader the child is using.

1. *Importance of sight vocabulary.* It should be pointed out here that stressing acquisition of a sight vocabulary is not synonymous with stressing use of a sight word approach as the only or major approach to teaching beginning reading. Regardless of the initial approach used (and it would be rather difficult to find an example of that often maligned and condemned straw man, the sight-word approach advocate), an individual needs to acquire an extensive sight vocabulary if he is to read effectively. While most of the words an individual learns in reading are not learned initially as sight words, most of the words he reads will eventually need to become sight words. (Or perhaps we should say that the individual needs to develop almost instant powers of word attack as well as an extensive sight vocabulary.) While it is rather common practice in a number of circles to condemn or decry an emphasis on sight vocabulary, and a common procedure for getting a laugh from an audience easily is to imitate a child reading something in which vocabulary control and repetition has been employed, most of those who work closely with children who have difficulty in reading, repeatedly see youngsters becoming bogged down because they do not recognize enough words quickly enough ever to get "a running start." There is some question as to just when vocabulary control, which plays a relatively important role in the acquisition of a sight vocabulary, should stop. And, as intimated previously, there are some who would question or maintain that it should ever be begun. It would perhaps be wise for teachers in general to consider the strong possibility that if the matter of extent of sight vocabulary is still a matter of major concern beyond a third grade level, or perhaps a second grade level, the concern should probably be more with acquisition of word-attack skills than extension of sight vocabulary, at least at that particular time.

2. *Criterion for "sight word."* A further point to be made with respect to sight vocabulary relates to the criterion for determining whether or not a word is actually a sight word. If a word is a sight word, it will be known quickly or instantly. While various authorities may attempt to define "instantly" in terms of fractional portions of seconds, it is quite likely that "instant" will vary with individuals. At any rate, if a child tends to hesitate noticeably on a number of words but gets those words correctly after this noticeable hesitation, he probably does not quite have those words in his sight vocabulary. What the child is most likely doing is analyzing rather quickly those words of which he is still rather unsure. It should be encouraging to a teacher to find that a child has developed word analysis or word attack skills to this point of effectiveness; but it should also be kept in mind that a word for which noticeable hesitation is required is really not yet a sight word.

3. *Sight vocabulary pertinent to specific material.* Still another point with respect to sight vocabulary assessment is that a sight vocabulary is pertinent to the materials which the child will be reading, particularly at beginning and lower grade levels. Therefore, the words involved in the assessment should be ones which are found regularly in the material used with the child for his reading instruction, or should be ones which will eventually appear in such materials.

4. *Need for keeping purposes of word-attack skills in mind.* Another point to consider when evaluating or assessing vocabulary and word-attack skills is one which is made, in a fashion, earlier. This is what the teacher needs to keep in mind just what the various word-attack skills and the skill-teaching sessions are really for. Actually, this point or admonition is a rather pervading one and it is involved with practically all the other points.

5. *Need for ability to apply skills function-*
ally. As well as finding out what specific pieces or parts of skills have been mastered, it is also very necessary to know how well a child can put these various pieces or parts together. For example, people in reading clinics and in other reading centers and many teachers in classrooms frequently see children who supposedly "ain't had no phonics." Further study or diagnosis of many of these children will indicate that many, perhaps most of them, have had considerable phonics instruction of a sort. They have mastered many pieces, or at least some have; but they are unable to put these pieces together so that the phonics skills they have mastered will help them in getting words. Checking or previous knowledge of actual classroom situations from which many of these youngsters come will also indicate that many have had the same instruction in phonics which many of their classmates have had; but such instruction "didn't take," or for them it was a matter of phonics being "taught at them." The point of this is to bring out the obvious fact that for phonics skills to be really adequate a child needs to be able to blend or to synthesize his knowledge of sounds or separate elements of words. He needs to be able to make successful functional application of such skills before he has really mastered those adequately. Knowing sounds of letters is no guarantee that he will be able to apply such skill in analyzing unknown words successfully or that he will be a good reader. The need to apply skills successfully in a functional situation is applicable with respect to other word attack skills also.

6. *Auditory discrimination basic to phonics skill.* A further point to make is that auditory discrimination skill is basic to phonics skill. The importance of auditory discrimination skill is usually recognized insofar as lip service recognition is concerned, but at times our practice in the classroom is not consistent with our lip service. Phonetic analysis skill is basically a matter of generalizing about

sounds in words we know and of applying these generalizations about sounds to help us in figuring out new words successfully. Generalizations are made with respect to visual-auditory associations. That is, we associate a visual symbol (a letter or a combination of letters) with an auditory symbol (a sound). Before a child can make adequate visual-auditory associations, he will need to be able to make visual associations and auditory associations or discriminations separately first. Close checking of children in the primary grades who have difficulty in learning to read will most likely reveal that a great many of them are lacking, relatively, in auditory discrimination skill. The same will probably be found in the case of youngsters at higher grade levels who are reading at a low primary grade level. Before a youngster is able to benefit from, or to make effective use of, phonics instruction given in the primary grades, he will need to develop auditory discrimination skill (skill in hearing likenesses and differences in spoken speech, particularly his own).

7. *Syllabication basically a hearing matter.* Still another point to be made is that syllabication skill is basically a hearing matter. Examination of much of the practice given to youngsters in middle grades (where most of the syllabication work is supposedly done) and in levels beyond will reveal that much of the so-called syllabication activity is essentially visual discrimination work. Children are asked or required to divide words into syllables, usually on the basis of visual clues for syllabic division. It is quite possible for youngsters to divide ten or twenty words into proper syllables—and not know a single one of the words! The point to be made here is that we need to consider the purpose of syllabication. If one's skill in dividing words into syllables does not enable him to tell what a difficult or strange word is, just what is the purpose? It should be kept in mind that a syllable is basically a sound unit; before we

ask youngsters then, to do a lot of visual discrimination work with syllables, we need to make certain that they can actually "hear" syllables.

8. *Visual discrimination often only skill possessed and applied.* A further point, and one related to several of the previous points, is that the poor reader, especially one without much phonics skill (And what poor reader does this not apply to?) is apt to have only visual discrimination skill to rely or fall back upon. Therefore, we should be on the lookout for occasions when we might be misled into thinking responses are made on some other basis than on the basis of visual discrimination. It was pointed out previously that it was possible for youngsters to divide words into syllables without knowing what the words, or the sound values of the syllables, are. Similarly, it is quite possible for a youngster to give a teacher words he knows which begin with the same sound as a group of words given by the teacher without the youngster actually hearing that the words he gives are alike in sound at the beginning. Careful observation and recall of experience on the part of those who have not given this particular thought previously will no doubt aid in convincing a number at this point. Such observation and analysis will indicate that when some poor readers are asked to give words which begin with the same sound as some given words they will tend to associate a given letter with the beginning sound they hear; and they will then try to recall visually words they can remember which begin with that same letter. Clues to this behavior are frequently yielded by the squinting and the screwing up of the forehead exhibited by a youngster as he tries to recall words visually or by his asking, "What letter does that begin with?" or "You mean begin with a 'b'?"

9. *Consistency in reversal tendencies.* The "reversal case" is another type commonly referred to remedial or clinic centers. It should

be kept in mind that one should spot more than errors on "no" and "saw" before a child is diagnosed as an extreme reversal case. If a child has a strong tendency to reverse, he should show this by reversing on more than words where reversals are very easily possible. If reversal tendencies are actually there, they should be reflected by the writing errors of the youngster also.

10. *Finding little words in big words.* Caution also needs to be exercised with respect to the very common or popular activity of "finding the little word in the big word." It is quite possible that a youngster might stand a good chance of winning contests involving the finding of little words in big words; but if he is not able to use this skill in getting the "big word," he is lacking in word attack skill. It should further be recognized that words used for assessing this type of skill and, especially, words used for providing practice in this kind of skill, should be ones in which the "little words" to be detected are ones which actually function either as words or as sound units in the big words or larger units.

11. *Use of context clues.* A final point to be made relates to the matter of assessing skill in the use of context clues. The "guessing" which many critics claim poor readers do and the seemingly irrelevant words which some youngsters read on a given page frequently actually give evidence of the youngster's use of context clues. It should be kept in mind, however, that if a youngster does not know some of the words in the context surrounding a given word, he stands a rather poor chance of getting or determining a given word.

An attempt has been made in the latter half of this paper to list and present a rationale for a number of important or pertinent points which should be kept in mind when assessing or making judgments concerning the vocabulary and word attack skills of pupils. In summary, these points have been as follows: (1) A sight vocabulary plays an important role in effective reading and in the acquisition of word attack skills. (2) One needs to know or recognize a word quickly or instantly before it can be considered a sight word. (3) Words and lists used for determining extent of sight vocabulary should be ones pertinent to specific materials the child uses for reading instruction. (4) The real or actual purposes for word-attack skill need to be kept in mind. (5) Word-attack skills are not possessed adequately until or unless those can be applied successfully in functional situations. (6) Auditory discrimination skill is a very important prerequisite for phonetic analysis skill. (7) Syllabication skill is basically or fundamentally a hearing matter. (8) Visual discrimination skill is often the only skill possessed and, consequently, applied by poor readers; and we need to avoid being misled by this. (9) Evidences of consistent tendencies to make reversal errors need to be looked for and found before making strong or definite diagnoses of "reversal cases." (10) "Little words" found in big words need to function as sound units or words in the big words; and skill in finding "little words" needs to function successfully in attack on big words. (11) To make effective use of context clues, the words of the context need to be known or recognized.

TESTING READING FLEXIBILITY
Arthur S. McDonald

Research dealing with reading tests reflects the lack of agreement on methods of measuring reading rate and comprehension. Researchers disagree as well on the relationship of speed and comprehension in the reading process. Conflicting methods of computing reading test scores involving diverse combinations of rate and comprehension have been proposed. Much doubt, however, exists about the meaning of these different measures.

We suggest that much of this confusion is the result of considering "rate" (i.e., the number of words over which a reader moves his eyes in a set time) and "comprehension" (the number of questions about a given reading selection answered correctly) as independent or co-equal entities. The concept of reading rate as an independent factor in reading is patently illogical. What is the advantage of "taking in" visually thousands of words in however brief a time if the chief outcome is an accumulation of misunderstandings? Similarly, treating comprehension as an independent factor introduces a host of complex variables, many of which are only distantly related to the reading process, however much a part of the behaviorial process of the person involved they may be. Furthermore, what is the benefit of achieving perfect comprehension on a piece of writing

Reprinted from *Changing Concepts of Reading Instruction*, Proceedings of the International Reading Association Annual Convention, Vol. 6 (1961), 228–230, with permission of the author and International Reading Association.

when the reading situation calls for a lesser degree of understanding of only one or two points?

Modern linguistic studies have shown that reading (as one of the means of human communication) is a set of cultural associations taking place in a structured social situation. The naive assumption that words are important repositories of meaning (which Malinowski termed the "bucket theory" of magic meaning) is no longer held by any serious student of language. Rather, research studies indicate that reading is a psycho-physiological structured mode of interaction depending on the reader's knowledge of a common, many-leveled, complex, integrated package of cultural norms and values of varying difficulty.

If one accepts this view, then it will be apparent that test measures of speed of reading and accuracy of understanding are only estimates of the reader's efficiency in completing the communication process. Just as the results of a well designed intelligence test permit inferences about the intellectual capacity of the person tested (provided that certain assumptions basic to the test have been met); so a well designed reading test will likewise permit *inferences* of reading efficiency (subject also to certain important limitations). A test of reading flexibility, for instance, would be inappropriate with handicapped readers who had not mastered the fundamentals of reading demanded by the test. Although the results of the test would provide some indications of basic weaknesses, use of another type of test would still be necessary.

Leading authorities in the reading field have repeatedly pointed out the importance of reading flexibility. A good reader possesses those reading skills, techniques, and methods of attack which enable him to achieve as complete an understanding of the author's meaning as is dictated by the reader's purpose. He also has a psychological set toward the reading process which leads him to differentiate his reading approach to suit the difficulty of the article's content and style, the amount of background knowledge he possesses, as well as the urgency of his need to satisfy his purpose through reading the article. This kind of reader understands that the language used by the writer did not completely state his meanings because of linguistic and cultural limitations, and that he, the reader, faces the same limitations.

Despite this widespread recognition of the importance of reading flexibility, relatively little has been done to develop materials and tests designed to measure and develop this reading characteristic. Important pioneering work, including the construction of diagnostic instruments, has been carried out by Letson,[1] Sheldon and Carillo,[2] and Spache.[3] In the main, however, teachers have at their disposal only standardized instruments which yield one or two rate or rate-of-comprehension scores based on a few limited reading situations.

In order to develop reading flexibility, students and teachers need to see evidence of weaknesses which may exist. They can benefit from experience with a diagnostic instrument which offers them selections differing in difficulty of content, style of writing, and

[1] Charles T. Letson, *The Construction and Evaluation of a Test to Measure the Flexibility of Reading Rate*, unpublished doctoral thesis, Boston University, 1956.
[2] W. D. Sheldon and L. W. Carillo, "The Flexibility of Reading Rate," *Journal of Educational Psychology*, 43 (May 1952), 299–305.
[3] George D. Spache, "Diagnostic Tools" in *Fifth Yearbook* of the Southwest Reading Conference, 1955.

in purpose set for reading. Students should see evidence of the extent to which they actually are able to take account of these factors in their reading. Teachers of reading need to establish the present level of proficiency of their students so that instruction may be adapted to individual deficiencies.

Instruments for this purpose have been developed and standardized at Marquette University. One, designated *Inventory of Reading Versatility*, is intended for use with students reading at the 11th grade level or higher. Another, termed *Reading Versatility Test*, is designed to be used with pupils in the 5th through 9th grades who possess 5th grade fundamental reading skills (a short pre-test accompanies this instrument to eliminate those students who lack this level of reading ability).

These instruments both consist of three reading selections, each requiring a different reading approach. The student is set a different purpose for reading each selection. He is asked to read in accord with that stated purpose. It is recognized, of course, that students may modify the stated purpose, consciously or unconsciously, in accord with their individual needs or learned reading strategies. Modification in the wrong direction, however, will result in the choice of an inappropriate reading approach. The three specific purposes stated in the directions tell the student to read one section carefully and thoroughly, one section for its main points only, and to skim (scan) one section. Our research with 1,500 high school students, 2,500 college students, and 1,000 adults has shown that a flexible reader will read each succeeding section of the Inventory 1.5 to 2 times faster than the preceding one. In contrast, an inflexible reader will tend to have a nearly uniform rate throughout. These findings are basically in accord with the researches cited above.

The reading of each section is timed. The amount-time or power method is used. Students are allowed to finish the whole reading selection. We have investigated the questions raised about possible differential effects of time-limit and power reading tests in a number of reading situations. This research has indicated that contrary to the commonly accepted hypothesis, either time-limit or amount-limit tests may be used to measure reading performance with comparable results provided, of course, that the tests are equivalent in other respects.[4] A number of multiple-choice questions follow sections 1 and 2 of these instruments. These questions require answers in accordance with the directions preceding the reading selections. Rate of reading is computed in words per minute.

The reading selections in each of the Inventories have been adapted from different sources. In the higher level Inventory the first selection is an adaptation from De Tocqueville concerning judicial power. Its readability level according to the Flesch formula is 45; high tenth grade according to the Dale-Chall formula.

For this selection the student's purpose for reading is given as follows:

> Your purpose for reading is to determine the author's views of the nature and characteristics of judicial power in the United States. Adapt the method of reading which will enable you to achieve maximum comprehension. After reading, you will be questioned on the arguments, supporting statements, important details, and inferences which can be logically drawn from this selection. Read carefully. In answering the questions do not refer to the selection.

Note that *nothing* is said about reading the selection only once. The answering of the questions is untimed.

The second section of the Inventory is a selection of general fiction adapted from Ambrose Bierce. Approximately equal in length

to the first selection, its Flesch readability level is 72; Dale-Chall level, 8th grade. For this selection the student is given directions as follows:

> Your purpose is to read as rapidly as you can to understand the main points of the story. Read this story only once. The questions will test your comprehension of the main events of the story. In answering the questions which follow do not refer to the story.

In this section, also, the answering of the questions is untimed.

The third section of the Inventory requires skimming to find answers to three questions which may be answered with specific information. The students are given ample opportunity to familiarize themselves with the questions. Timing of the section covers the entire period from the beginning of skimming to the completion of answering the questions.

The format of the lower level Versatility Test is similar to that described above with, of course, necessary modifications in the wording of the instructions to suit the different age range covered.

Equivalent parallel forms of both the Inventory of Reading Versatility and the Versatility Test have been developed. The corresponding reading selections of the two forms of each deal with similar subject material and have been adapted so that readability and content level are equivalent. Testing of all questions on the four forms used with large representative samples of persons at various age ranges who did not read the selections indicates that correct answers due to background knowledge will occur with statistically and educationally insignificant frequency.

The existence of two equivalent forms of these tests of this type offers the teacher an opportunity to observe the results of instruction which she has carried on over a period of time with the aim of developing reading flexibility in her students.

[4] Arthur S. McDonald, "Factors Affecting Reading Test Performance," *Ninth Yearbook* of the National Reading Conference, TCU Press, 1960, 28–35.

PART 2
THE READING SKILLS

Introduction

It is not enough to know *what* to teach; *how* to teach is equally important. The main objective of Part II of this book is to offer a series of strategies for teaching reading to high school students—strategies which reflect the results of research and consensus. It is a well-established fact that there is no royal road to reading improvement. No single method or approach can insure success. However, teachers are more likely to gain the goals they seek if their methods are compatible with ways to which students are apt to respond.

Included in this section are two articles on word identification. Although the better high school reader typically does not require intensive instruction in how to attack words, there might be some among them who have failed to master one or more aspects of this basic reading skill. And included among most high school populations are students with serious reading difficulties. They are not able to apply word-identification skills singly or in combination to identify many words they fail to recognize. Gagon summarizes some of the more recent research findings on word perception and ways to develop it. Sartain explains the characteristics that materials used for teaching these skills should possess and describes the features of some representative sets.

Chapters 6 and 7 deal with meanings and study skills—areas with which all high school students are concerned. It is in these areas that teachers can make significant contributions to improving their students' reading ability. Stauffer sets the stage by stressing the importance of reading *quality* over reading quantity. O'Donnell reports on a study which examined the relationship between reading comprehension and knowledge of grammar. Cooper explains how semantic principles can be applied to reading in order to increase understanding. A provocative article by McDonald raises questions about present practices in vocabulary development. Niles details a series of strategies for helping students to discern patterns of writing and improve their comprehension. Ennis describes the major aspects of critical thinking and gives examples that will suggest teaching ideas.

A. Robinson offers a step-by-step plan to teach students to recognize key ideas. F. P. Robinson explains how his SQ3R method of study operates. Finally, Catterson describes successful study skills and meanings programs which might serve as models for new ones.

Chapter 8, Reading for Appreciation, contains a message especially directed toward English teachers. It is this: students must be taught how to read literature, just as they must be taught how to read other types of materials. Carlin describes one pattern for teaching literature that has proved successful. Broening suggests ways to foster the development of appreciation for and taste in literature. Smiley addresses herself to the difficult task of providing a meaningful literature and reading program for culturally different students and makes observations based upon her work with that population.

Chapter 9 places the role of speed in reading in proper perspective. Bliesmer reviews the research on rate and comprehension, eye movements, and the use of machines. Stauffer emphasizes the importance of flexibility in reading rate and its relation to comprehension. Shores reports the results of an investigation that studied the relationship between reading speed and comprehension.

Chapters 10 and 11 examine the adolescent and his world, show how reading can help meet his needs, and describe ways teachers can promote independent reading. Calitri studies the culturally different youth. Jungeblut and Coleman report the reading interests and informational needs of typical high school students. Russell suggests the hypothesis that reading can change our students' attitudes and values.

How can I get my students to read more? Answers to this question are found in using paperbacks (Fishco), reading aloud to students (Farrell), and giving books "that hit him where he lives" (Spiegler).

Part II, then, contains information about the basic reading skills and ways in which high school teachers can help their students to develop them. In addition, the importance of reading as one leisure-time activity—a major goal of reading instruction—is underscored.

5
Word Recognition

MODERN RESEACH AND WORD PERCEPTION

Glen S. Gagon

Gray, in defining word perception as one of the four components in the reading process, indicates that it consists of the analysis of the elements of the word form to identify or recognize its probable pronunciation, and its use or meaning (*1*).* For purposes of this article our definition will be restricted to the analysis of the word form to identify its probable pronunciation.

WORD IDENTIFICATION AND RECOGNITION

Many of the early studies by Huey (*2*), Hamilton (*3*), and Vernon (*4*) on perception related to single words or phrases and were primarily concerned with the problem of whether we perceive by total word form or by going from parts to the whole. While these studies have significance for the area of perception, they have little direct relationship to the reading process.

The studies of eye fixations in reading con-

Reprinted from *Education*, LXXXVI (April 1966), 464–472, with permission of the author and Bobbs-Merrill Company, Inc.
[*Numbers in parentheses refer to Bibliography at the end of this article.]

nected discourse have implications for resolution of the issues raised in early research. Taylor, in compiling norms for the components of the fundamental reading skills, has determined that the average first-grade child reading material of the 1.8 grade level of difficulty with at least 70 percent comprehension made an average of two hundred twenty-four fixations per running one hundred words as compared to ninety fixations per running one hundred words for the average college student (*5*). The marked and consistent decrease in number of fixations from grade one to the college level is suggestive that the perceptual act may vary according to the efficiency of the reader on a given reading selection.

In the initial process of learning to read the student fixates on the component parts of the word in the process of identifying the word. With repeated exposures to the word he arrives at the recognition stage of perceiving the word as wholes. The perceptual act in word identification differs from the perceptual act in word recognition because of the degree to which analysis is made of word form. In efficient, rapid word perception the reader relies almost wholly on context clues and total word form or the recognition skill (4), while in the identification process he may use varying amounts of phonetic, structural, or dictionary skills in conjunction with context to figure out the pronunciation of a strange word.

HOW MUCH WORD ANALYSIS IS NEEDED?

While considerable effort has been put forth to determine which method yields better results in teaching word attack skills, little has been done to determine just how much word attack is necessary for a child to know to be independent. Much of the research indicates that we are attempting to develop a perfection of the means which is resulting in a confusion of the ends; or one might say that we have lost sight of our goals in word attack and have redoubled our efforts to reach them.

In the absence of good research to indicate what skills are necessary in word attack we have reverted to the opinions of experts and the analysis of our language. But the experts do not agree. McKee states ". . . you can learn to read if all you have in the way of phonic clues are the associations of the consonant letters with the sounds they stand for. You can get along without the vowels. Furthermore, no one can give you any reliable key to the sounds that are to be associated with English vowels. If, in our reading we use context and consonant clues, the vowels take care of themselves" (6, pp. 23–24).

McKee further states that the child knows how to speak the language, and by using context and consonant clues he can identify most words contained in beginning reading. The child knows the sound value of the vowels in most words because the words are in his speaking vocabulary and he already knows how to pronounce them.

Under this approach if the word is not in the speaking vocabulary of the child the only sure way of figuring out its pronunciation is to consult the dictionary. In the use of phonic and structural analysis the speaking vocabulary of the child is a check against his analysis procedures. English is too unreliable to accept the pronunciation figured out through word analysis procedures if the word is not in the speaking vocabulary of the child (6, p. 24).

In conducting research with over 600 first-grade children who were taught only letter sound associations on the consonant sound in first grade, McKee has determined that the average first-grade child after one year of instruction has taught himself seventeen of twenty-four vowel associations which his test measured (6, personal report on research conducted in 1964–65, in Denver and Greeley Public Schools).

Other reading authorities indicate that much knowledge about vowel sounds is necessary for the child to be independent in figuring out the pronunciation of strange words. Most basal readers include principles of syllabication and accent to be taught to assist the child in figuring out the sound of the various vowel symbols. Once these principles are taught the child is supposed to be able to use them deductively to figure out the pronunciation of new words with which he comes in contact.

Linguists are saying that little or no formal instruction on word analysis is necessary except for word form changes. They feel that if only regular phonemic words are presented to the child in the initial reading vocabulary the child will acquire the alphabetic principle inductively without formal instruction on letter-sound association.

LeFevre states, "It remains to be established precisely how much analysis of sound-letter relationships within words is required in reading and in reading instruction, or in composition, for that matter. The patternless reading of many pupils at all levels suggests that we have paid too much attention to the alphabetical principle, to words singled out of their normal structures. This is one fatal flaw in most phonics methods; another is unsound and false information about sound spelling relationship" (7).

While the issues in the amount of word attack needed are beginning to be raised and brought into focus, there is little empirical evidence at the present time on the amount of word analysis needed in learning to identify strange printed words. Two basic questions seem to result from the issues mentioned.

First, how consistent or inconsistent is the phonetic structure of written English. Is it reliable enough to teach basic concepts about vowel sounds; and is the child able to apply these generalizations once they have been taught to him. And second, should the child be left to himself in arriving at the alphabetic principles through restricting word introduction to regular phonetic words until this alphabetical principle is established.

STRUCTURE OF WRITTEN ENGLISH

In the early studies on structure of the language by Vogel (8), Washburne (9), Osburn (10), Cordts (11), Atkins (12), Denny (13), Stone (14), Catey (15), and many others, emphasis was placed on the frequency of occurrence of letter sounds and phonograms in the words in the various vocabulary lists. Later research by Cordts (16), Spache (17), Denny (13), and Brown (18) placed emphasis on the syllable rather than the phonograms as the pronunciation units in words. Rules for determining the long and short sound were suggested, but the literature does not contain a consensus on the value of vowel "rules" or generalizations.

In 1952 Oaks investigated the incidence of each vowel situation at each reader level and the incidence of each vowel principle used in figuring out the pronunciation of words in the primary grades. From her analy-sis of the data collected, she concluded that there was a relatively large number of different vowel situations embraced in the vocabularies of primary readers and that the highest percentage of these different situations were introduced at the primer level. She found that five types of vowel situations accounted for 70 percent of the different situations in the selected vocabulary and 80 percent of the total situations. Oaks identified eight vowel principles which were applicable in approximately 50 percent of the total vowel situations (19).

A report in a recent journal brings to light evidence which suggests that some of the vowel principles presently taught in phonics programs may not have utility sufficiently high to justify teaching them. Clymer's analysis of the generalizations contained in four basal readers at the primary grade levels indicated that only eighteen of forty-five generalizations related to more than twenty words and were at least 75 percent consistent. Of the forty-five generalizations, twenty-four related to vowel principles of which only six met his criteria of consistency. Clymer concludes from his findings that confusion exists as to the value of phonic generalizations and that it seems quite clear that many generalizations commonly taught are of limited value (20).

While confusion exists it seems logical to raise certain questions about research on word structure conducted up to this time. Some of these questions are as follows:

1. Does a generalization have to be 75 percent consistent to be of value to a student? Petty and Burns indicate that perhaps 50 percent consistency might be considered adequate (21).
2. Is research done on primary grade reading vocabularies applicable to that at the intermediate grade level or in adult reading where the child has more opportunity to apply principles of word structure?

3. Does a child have to be able to pronounce the word before figuring out whether a syllable is stressed as Clymer indicates or are their visual clues such as those described by Gray (1) which assist the child in figuring out where the stress is to be given before pronouncing the word?

Findings from Oak's research suggest the importance of clarifying at least four conditions regarding the vowel situation in the word before the sound associated with it can be determined. These conditions involve the position of the vowel letter in the syllable, its relation to other letters in the syllable, the number of vowel letters used to indicate the vowel sound, and the type of syllable in which it appears whether it be stressed or unstressed (19). In view of these questions it seems that much of the research done up to this time is very incomplete, confusing, and misleading when judged according to the above questions.

LINGUISTICS IN WORD RECOGNITION

The linguistic approaches raise the question whether vocabulary control in beginning reading should be based upon the theory of social utility, as is used in most basal readers, or on a logical pattern of organization going from words which are phonetically regular to the irregular words after the alphabetic principle is established.

There is limited research in current literature concerning this problem. Arthur Heilman at the IRA conference in Detroit indicated that informal examination of the primary reading vocabulary indicates only 35 percent of the words as being phonetic (22). If this is true, it would appear that the number of phonetically regular words might stilt the type of reading matter which is developed in that it doesn't approximate the oral

conversation commonly used by the child. If printed symbols are just printed talk, then these symbols should represent normal conversation which uses irregular words as well as regular words.

In the logical pattern of organization the alphabetic principle can be acquired inductively without formal instruction. McKee, in research done in one first grade, has determined that most first-grade children teach themselves about two-thirds of the vowel generalizations without the teacher ever referring to them (6). While a child may teach himself something about the alphabetic principle, it would seem that the whole thesis of the school's existence is that we as teachers can assist the child in being more efficient in learning than to leave him to self-discovery or trial-and-error learning. If the child is teaching himself something about the alphabetic principle or vowel sounds, what assurance do we have that he isn't teaching himself other concepts which are not valid?

LETTERS AND WORDS OR TECHNIQUE?

Research studies over the past several years have raised questions concerning the desirability of building an initial sight vocabulary of seventy-five or more words before teaching letter-sound association. Linehan, in experimenting with 614 first-grade children to determine the effect of teaching letter forms, names, sounds in words in early first grade, determined that the differences were statistically significant in favor of the experimental group in oral reading, paragraph meaning, and in all tests of phonic ability (23). Similar findings have been reported by Hudek and Wentzel (24), Sparks and Fay (25), Henderson (26), Zajac and Alger (27), Bliesmer and Yarborough (28), and Olson (29).

McKee has determined in the Denver experiment that kindergarten children, when taught letter-sound association and the use of oral context in the pre-reading program as a technique of attacking strange words, read more independently by the end of grade one than those children taught the same program at the beginning of grade one, that they not only read more difficult materials but read more on their own than in the regular program (6).

Anderson has also determined that all levels of intelligence during the kindergarten pre-reading program profit from instruction on the development of a technique of attacking a strange word using letter-sound association and the use of oral context; and that letter-sound association by itself was more difficult than when combined with the use of oral context (30).

Some linguistic and phonic programs advocate teaching vowels before consonants, but little research has been done to determine the superiority of either procedure. Inasmuch as both vowels and consonants are used in the initial vocabulary, it may be that both need to be taught concurrently. Research indicates that a child learns a certain amount of knowledge about vowel sounds even though they are not taught in the instructional program presented by the teacher in grade one.

MODALITIES USED IN WORD PERCEPTION

Visual Perception. Few if any reading authorities suggest the exclusive use of one mode in the teaching of reading but do suggest that varying amounts of visual, auditory, and kinesthetics be employed according to the situation.

Considerable research on the development of visual perception of the child has been reported in research summaries by Anderson and Dearborn (31), Vernon (32), and Morris (33). From these summaries it is concluded that visual perception is learned;

therefore, teachers can assist pupils in learning such perception. Research studies show a high correlation between visual discrimination on geometric forms and gross objects and reading, but few if any show a cause and effect relationship (34). This is interpreted to mean that it might profit the child more to have visual discrimination exercises on the letters and word forms which he meets rather than to expect the transfer to take place after being taught on geometric forms and gross objects.

Auditory Perception. A number of excellent evaluations of research are available on the relationship between reading and listening. Findings from summaries by Witty and Sizemore (35) and Berg (36) agree that reading and listening ability are closely related in the first year or two of reading but begin decreasing thereafter (37).

Postman and Rosenzweig concluded that prior training improves for both visual and auditory perception, but that the transfer effects from visual training to auditory recognition are more pronounced than the converse. This may indicate that auditory discrimination may be present as part of the visual discrimination (38).

Duggins (39) has hypothesized that auditory perception must precede visual perception for visual images interfere with formation of clear auditory images. While this seems reasonable from observed experience, little or no research was found which supports this position.

Taylor, in reviewing research on span of word recognition, indicates that findings from over one hundred studies on eye movement show that the training to widen span of recognition has not resulted in the ability to "see" phrases during continuous reading. The span of recognition appears to be much smaller in reading connected discourse than in flashed exercises through tachistoscopic training (5). (Concerning the value of tachistoscopic training, little or no research was found showing the value of transfer of tachistoscopic training in the functional reading situation.) Feinberg's study suggests that the physiological limitations of the eye will probably prevent readers from ever perceiving words by phrases in continuous reading (40).

Kinesthetic Perception. Historically, kinesthetic perception in the teaching of reading has been defined as learning resulting from movement of the arms or hands in writing or drawing. In recent years some researchers have included aspects of vocalization as part of kinesthetics. Gagolewski, in her experiment with 280 first-grade children, determined there were no significant differences in the effectiveness of using speech correction methods for improving ability to distinguish separate sounds in spoken words over traditional methods of teaching auditory perception (41).

Some researchers have attempted to identify the dominant mode by a given child. Mills gave his *Learning Methods Test* to students in grades two through four; the test employs using a visual, phonic, kinesthetic, and a combination of all three methods. He concluded from his findings that students vary in the dominant method they use in learning to identify words, and that teachers should determine the method or methods used by a given child (42). However, research is not clear whether the child is consistent from day to day in the dominant mode which he might use.

Roberts and Coleman, using a visual and visual-kinesthetic presentation with remedial students and normal readers, determined that remedial readers are significantly lower than normal readers in visual perception acuity and they are less efficient when taught by visual methods alone, and that normal readers do not get help from kinesthetic experience (43).

Rivikind reported that with five different teachers working for a school year with 183 pupils using the visual, phonic, kinesthetic, and combined methods, there was no significant difference among the various methods used (44).

Morris, in her summary of research on kinesthetics, determined that kinesthetics reinforce other sensory impressions of words but they have certain detrimental effects such as developing arm and lip movements which result in hampering later speed and fluency (45).

In reality, there can be no single sensory approach to reading for normal children since visual perception in reading always involves a degree of auditory perception.

The research on modality is interpreted to mean that auditory and visual perception should be used with the regular reader and varying amounts of kinesthetics should be used with some remedial students.

TRANSFER OF ANALYSIS TECHNIQUES

There is very little research evidence indicating that children can transfer word analysis skills into the functional reading situation. From the research studies of Bradbury (46), Wilson (47), and Gibbons (48) one might conclude that the average reader lacks in his ability to use context in the construction of the meaning of a word.

Robinson found the following in testing fourth-grade children on words in their listening vocabularies but not in their recognition vocabularies: 1) through context clues alone the students identified about 1 percent of the test words and in only 14 percent of the cases was a meaningful synonym given: 2) through context and configuration the percentages were about the same as with just context; 3) context, configuration and beginning consonant letters, 6.4 percent; 4) context, configuration, initial and final elements, 17.8 percent; and 5) context and entire word, 35.8 percent (49). Even though questions can be raised about procedures used by Robinson in his research study, experience in the reading clinic supports his basic thesis.

BIBLIOGRAPHY

1. GRAY, WILLIAM S. *On Their Own in Reading.* Chicago: Scott, Foresman and Company, 1960, p. 10.
2. HUEY, E. B. *The Psychology and Pedagogy of Reading.* New York: Macmillan, 1912.
3. HAMILTON, FRANCIS. *The Perceptual Factors in Reading,* Columbia Univ., Contributions to Philosophy, Psychology and Education, Vol. 17, No. 1. Science Press, 1907.
4. VERNON, M. D. *The Experimental Study of Reading.* London: Cambridge Univ. Press, 1931.
5. TAYLOR, STANFORD E., *et al. Grade Level Norms for the Components of the Fundamental Reading Skill,* EDL Research and Information Bulletin No. 3. Huntington, New York: Educational Development Laboratories, Inc., 1960.
6. McKEE, PAUL. *A Primer for Parents.* Boston: Houghton Mifflin Company, 1957.
7. LeFEVRE, CARL A. *Linguistics and the Teaching of Reading.* New York: McGraw-Hill, 1964, p. 166.
8. VOGEL, M., JAYCOX, E., and WASHBURNE, C. "A Basic List of Phonetics for Grades I and II," *Elementary School Journal,* Vol. XXIII (February 1923), 436–443.
9. WASHBURNE, C., and VOGEL, M. "A Revised List of Phonics for Grade II," *Elementary School Journal,* Vol. XXVIII (June 1928), 771–777.
10. OSBURN, W. J. *Relative Value of Letter Sounds and Phonograms.* Madison, Wisconsin: Circular issued by the State Department of Instruction, 1925.
11. CORDTS, ANNA D. "An Analysis of the Sounds of English Words in a Primary Reading Vocabulary," unpublished doctoral dissertation. Iowa City: State University of Iowa, 1925. (As reported in Oaks, 604–606.)
12. ATKINS, R. E. "An Analysis of the Phonetic Elements in a Basic Reading Vocabulary," *Elementary School Journal,* Vol. XXVI (April 1926), 596–606.
13. DENNY, VELMA. "The Determination of the Phonetic Elements Most Frequently Found in Twelve Primary Word Lists," unpublished master's thesis. Minneapolis: University of Minnesota, 1937.
14. STONE, C. D. *Better Primary Reading.* St. Louis: Webster Publishing Co., 1936.
15. CATEY, W. S. "An Analytical Study of the Phonic Program Found in Basic Reading Series," unpublished master's thesis, Colorado State College of Education.
16. CORDTS, ANNA D., and McBROOM, M. "Phonics," *Classroom Teacher* (February 1928), 389–432.
17. SPACHE, GEORGE. "A Phonic Manual for Primary and Remedial Teachers," *Elementary English Review,* Vol. XVI (May 1939), 191–198.
18. BLACK, MILLARD H. "A Study of Certain Structural Elements of Words in a Primary Reading Vocabulary," unpublished master's thesis, Teachers College, Temple University, 1950, pp. 66–68.
19. OAKS, RUTH. "Vowel Situations in a Primary Reading Vocabulary," master's thesis, Teachers College, Temple University, Philadelphia, Pa.
20. CLYMER, THEODORE. "The Utility of Phonic Generalizations in the Primary Grades," *The Reading Teacher,* Vol. XVI (January 1963), 251.
21. PETTY, WALTER T., and BURNS, PAUL C. "A Summary of Investigations Relating to the English Language Arts in Elementary Education: 1963," *Elementary English* (February 1964), 124.
22. HEILMAN, ARTHUR. Statement at International Reading Association Conference, Detroit, May 1965.
23. LINEHAN, ELEANOR. "Early Instruction in Letter Names and Sounds as Related to Success in Beginning Reading," unpublished Ed. D. dissertation, Boston University, 1957.
24. HUDEK, ELIZABETH, and WENTZEL, MARGARET. "The Effect of Knowledge of Letter Names on Beginning Reading," unpublished Ed. M. thesis, Boston University, 1955.
25. SPARKS, PAUL E., and FAY, LEO C. "An Evaluation of Two Methods of Teaching Reading," *Elementary School Journal,* Vol. LVII (April 1957), 386–90.
26. HENDERSON, MARGARET G. "Progress Report on Reading Study," 1952–1955, Community Unit School District No. 4, Champaign County, Illinois, undated.
27. SAJAC, MARY H., and ALGER, NATALIE. "An Experiment to Determine the Effect of the Knowledge of Letter Names in Beginning Reading," unpublished Ed. M. thesis, Boston University, 1957.

28. BLIESMER, EMERY P., and YARBOROUGH, BETTY H. "An Evaluation on Ten Different Reading Programs," *Phi Delta Kappan,* June 1965.

29. OLSON, ARTHUR V., JR. "Growth in Word Perception as It Relates to Success in Beginning Reading," unpublished Ed. D. dissertation, Boston University, 1957.

30. ANDERSON, DOROTHY MAY. "A Study to Determine if Children Need a Mental Age of Six Years and Six Months to Learn to Identify Strange Printed Word Forms When They are Taught to Use Oral Context and the Initial Sound of the Word," unpublished Ed. D. dissertation, Colorado State College, 1960.

31. ANDERSON, I. H., and DEARBORN, W. F. *The Psychology of Teaching Reading.* New York: Ronald Press, 1952.

32. VERNON, MAGDALEN D. "The Perceptual Process in Reading," *Reading Teacher,* Vol. 13 (October 1959), 2–8.

33. MORRIS, JOYCE. "Teaching Children to Read," *Education Research,* 1959, Vol. 1, 61–75.

34. GATES, ARTHUR I., and BOND, GUY L. "Factors Determining Success and Failure in Beginning Reading" "cited by" C. W. Hunnicutt and W. J. Iverson, *Research in the Three R's.* New York: Harper & Brothers, 1958, pp. 63–70.

35. WITTY, P. A., and SIZEMORE, R. A. "Studies in Listening," *Elementary English,* 1958, Vol. 35, 538–552.

36. BERG, PAUL C. "Reading in Relation to Listening," Fourth Yearbook, Southwest Reading Conference, College and University, 1955, pp. 52–60.

37. REYNOLDS, M. C. A. "A Study of Relationships between Auditory Characteristics and specific silent reading abilities," *Journal of Educational Research,* 1953, Vol. 46, pp. 439–449.

38. POSTMAN, L., and ROSENZWEIG, M. R. "Perceptual Recognition of Words," *Journal of Speech and Hearing Disability,* 1957, Vol. 22, pp. 245–253.

39. DUGGINS, LYDIA A. "Theory and Techniques of Auditory Perception as an Approach to Reading,"in O. S. CAUSEY, ed. *The Reading Teacher's Reader.* New York: Ronald Press, 1958, pp. 35–39.

40. FEINBERG, RICHARD. "A Study of Some Aspects of Peripheral Visual Acuity," *American Journal of Optometry and Archives of American Optometry,* Vol. 62 (February-March 1959), 1–23.

41. GAGOLEWSKI, JEAN I. "Auditory Perception of Word Elements in Beginning Reading through Visual and Kinesthetic Speech Clues," unpublished Ed. D. dissertation, Boston University, 1955.

42. MILLS, ROBERT E. "An Evaluation of Techniques for Teaching Word Recognition," *Elementary School Journal,* Vol. LVI (January 1956), 221–25.

43. ROBERTS, RICHARD W., and COLEMAN, JAMES C. "An Investigation of the Role of Visual and Kinesthetic Factors in Reading Failure," *Journal of Educational Research,* Vol. LI (February 1958), 445–51.

44. RIVIKIND, HAROLD C. "The Development of a Group Technique in Word Recognition to Determine Which of Four is Most Effective with Individual Children," unpublished Ed. D. dissertation, University of Florida, 1958.

45. MORRIS, JOYCE. "Teaching Children to Read," *Education Research,* 1958, Vol. 1, pp. 38–49.

46. BRADBURY, HELEN E. "The Ability of Fourth Grade Pupils to Use Context to Construct the Meaning of a Strange Word," unpublished master's thesis, Colorado State College of Education, 1943.

47. WILSON, FRANK. "The Ability of Sixth Grade Children to Acquire the Meaning of a Strange Word from the Context," unpublished master's thesis, Colorado State College of Education, 1947.

48. GIBBONS, HELEN D. "The Ability of College Freshmen to Use Context to Construct the Meaning of Unknown Words," unpublished doctoral field study, Field Study Number Two, Colorado State College of Education, 1940.

49. ROBINSON, H. ALAN. "A Study of the Techniques of Word Identification," *The Reading Teacher,* Vol. XVI (January 1963), 238–42.

MATERIALS FOR DEVELOPING READING
VOCABULARY AND WORD-ATTACK SKILLS
Harry W. Sartain

There is no serious shortage of materials for teaching word-attack skills. The last fifteen or twenty years have seen a vigorously renewed interest in word-analysis instruction, and this trend has been given impetus by the recent loud criticisms aimed at modern education.

The publishers have hastened to meet the requests for instructional aids voiced by parents, teachers, and school administrators. The mountains of materials from which teachers may choose today can be classified roughly into eight categories:

1. Manuals and workbooks that accompany basic reader series.
2. Independent sets of graded textbooks and workbooks.
3. Miscellaneous books and workbooks.
4. Commercial duplicator sets.
5. Chart and card materials.
6. Materials to develop vocabulary through spelling.
7. Materials and experiences planned in the classroom.
8. Professional guides and references for the teacher.

Frequently these materials reflect strong differences of opinion on how word-attack skills are most effectively developed. Some are based on the limited amount of scientific

Reprinted from the *University of Pittsburgh Conference Proceedings*, No. 18 (1962), 107–120, with permission of the author and University of Pittsburgh Conference Proceedings.

research that has been done, while others ignore research and psychology in favor of Early-American myth and long-standing legend. Some materials have been planned with care and thoroughness, while others resemble a hastily tossed salad of wilted word drills and over-ripe rules camouflaged with an indigestible Flesch-phonics dressing.

Too often the teacher has been forced to use certain materials because of public pressure on the administrator rather than for the reason of having any professional conviction about the worth of these devices. Such situations confound the teacher, confuse the children, and result in eventual deterioration of the reading program.

In order to select materials for teaching reading vocabulary and word-attack skills intelligently, it is essential that a set of criteria or standards be agreed upon. The following list is offered as a guide to further discussion.

STANDARDS FOR SELECTING THE MATERIALS TO TEACH READING VOCABULARY AND WORD-ATTACK SKILLS

1. *The materials should clearly reveal that word-attack skills are tools in the process of gleaning meaning through reading rather than ends in themselves.*

All recognized reading authorities agree that reading is more than verbalizing the sounds that are symbolized in print. The child is not *reading* when he mouths sounds that convey no thought to his mind; he is only performing automatically like the well-trained parakeet. If the word-attack program emphasizes the unlocking of strange words like solving mechanical puzzles, there is grave danger that the child will fail to develop the habit of demanding meaning constantly as his eyes move over the printed page.

2. *The materials should present the skills in situations where the child is motivated to learn and practice them in order to read interesting content.*

A skill is learned more readily if the child anticipates a need for its immediate use than if its use is delayed until sometime in the distant future.

3. *The materials should provide for extensive practice of the skills in normal reading situations.*

A skill is learned only through frequent use. Materials that attempt to teach skills without providing for their functional application are likely to fail in producing good readers. Also, if children learn skills from abnormal materials, there is no guarantee that they can transfer the skills to normal reading.

4. *The materials should harmonize with, rather than conflict with, the basic reading program that is employed.*

Reading is a highly complex process and learning to read is one of the most difficult tasks that the human being ever undertakes. If the average young child is to succeed in this endeavor, he must be helped by a simple straight-forward presentation of skills. Word-attack workbooks that present the usual second-year skills while the child is still learning first-year skills in the basic materials can lead to discouragement and defeat for many children.

5. *The materials should NOT make the child overly dependent upon a single approach to word recognition, but should present several, among which are meaning clues, configuration clues, phonic clues, and structural clues.*

Written English has developed from such a varied heritage that it refuses to submit to analysis by any single, simple set of rules. Therefore the skillful reader cannot depend upon any one technique for recognizing new words. He must know several, and he must know how to try out different techniques until he finds the one that succeeds against the problem he faces at the moment.

6. *The materials should develop the ability to select the most efficient word recognition technique that can be applied in any specific situation.*

The skillful reader has learned to recognize most words immediately through configuration or context clues without stopping to analyze them. Therefore instantaneous recognition of the whole word or phrase is the final aim. If the efficient reader finds that he does not know such a word as "unforgettable," he does not begin to sound it out letter-by-letter. The analysis of a thirteen-letter word by this process would be too time-consuming. Instead he looks first for larger elements that he already knows—roots, suffixes, prefixes, and syllables. As a *last resort* he applies the letter sounding technique to any unknown syllable within the word. The materials should lead the child to apply the most efficient techniques of analysis first, to alter his approach when needed, and to test the final result by context clues.

7. *The materials should introduce the skills at the developmental levels when the children can learn them most efficiently.*

Children's hearing capability seems to develop in advance of near-point visual efficiency. Thus auditory discrimination of sounds should precede visual discrimination of word elements.

Skills development must fit the mental growth rate as well as the physiological rate. The phonetic analysis skills are too often introduced before children have the mental ability to learn them in the usual class situation. The phonics generalizations tend to be abstract and complex. The research reveals, consequently, that most children must have a mental age of six or seven years to learn phonics. Many do not attain this capacity until they are in second, third, or fourth grade. Because they stand for known concepts, whole words are more easily learned by very young children than abstract meaningless word elements. Clearly some meaning and structural clues can be learned very early, while others must be delayed until the child has adequate ability to understand them.

8. *The materials should be conductive to differentiation of instruction in accordance with individual needs.*

Since the mental age range in first-grade classes is more than four years, and the mental age range in sixth-grade classes is more than seven years, it is obvious that all of these children cannot be expected to succeed equally well in the same programs at any given chronological age.

The accounts of early reading instruction in this country tell of the frustration and despair felt by children who were drilled endlessly on word elements before they began to use them in whole words and meaningful context. Some of our critics are intent upon forcing us back into this antediluvian age of education.

9. *The materials should build inductively from known words and facts toward new skills and understandings.*

Most psychologists believe that human beings understand the separate parts of any body of knowledge better if they first see these parts together as a whole body. Therefore word analysis begins with whole words that are known and proceeds with the child's discovering each element and stating the rule for using it.

10. *The materials should provide for skills development in a logical sequence of complexity.*

One example of the application of this principle is the teaching of consonant sounds before vowel sounds. Because each vowel letter represents a number of sounds, it is easier for the small child to learn the more stable consonant sounds before the vowels.

11. *The materials should provide for the development of new skills in a meaningful context.*

The pronunciation of a word element often changes when the element appears in different words. The meaning and pronunciation of a word also depends upon the context in which it is used. Therefore the sounds of letters should not be taught separately from words, and the recognition of words should not be taught separately from the phrases in which they appear.

12. *The materials should NOT build habits which handicap a child at a later stage of development.*

Any word-attack skill that is taught should continue to function as well or better when needed in later years as it does at the time it is introduced. Also, the skills of word recognition should support rather than interfere with comprehension abilities, work study skills, speed adaptation habits, and development of literary tastes.

With these criteria in mind the study and selection of useful materials become much easier than one might think when confronted with the whole array of items that are available. Although time limitation does not permit us to review all of the materials, we can look at *a few examples* within each of the categories.

A. MANUALS AND WORKBOOKS THAT ACCOMPANY THE BASIC READER SERIES

Some of the manuals and workbooks that serve as excellent examples are those that accompany the following textbook series:

BETTS, EMMETT A., *et al. Betts Basic Readers, The Language Arts Series.* New York: American Book Company, 1958.

BOND, GUY L., *et al. Developmental Reading Series.* Chicago: Lyons and Carnahan, 1962.

GRAY, WILLIAM S., *et al. Curriculum Foundation Series.* Chicago: Scott, Foresman and Company, 1956.

O'DONNELL, MABLE, *et al. Alice and Jerry Books.* Row, Peterson and Company.

ROBINSON, HELEN M., *et al. Curriculum Foundation Series.* Chicago: Scott, Foresman and Company, 1962.

RUSSELL, DAVID H., *et al. Ginn Basic Readers.* Boston: Ginn and Company, 1957.

SHELDON, WILLIAM D., *et al. Sheldon Basic Reading Series.* Boston: Allyn and Bacon, Inc., 1957.

STAUFFER, RUSSELL G., *et al. Winston Basic Readers.* New York: Holt, Rinehart, & Winston, Inc., 1960.

Although they differ in some respects, the programs of word analysis and recognition skills developed in the teachers' manuals of these series have a number of characteristics in common. They all put word-attack skills in their proper places as *tools* for achieving *meaning* through reading; therefore they offer thought-getting reading experiences before word analysis is begun. They motivate learning and provide practice of skills through extensive reading in basic and supplementary materials. They teach most new skills inductively as needed in connection with reading the basic stories. They offer a variety of approaches to word recognition and help children learn to vary and combine techniques. They are careful not to overemphasize any skill to the point that it will prove to be a stumbling block at a later time.

Unfortunately there is a tendency in most basic series to give too little attention to the synthesis of word elements. Many lessons provide practice in analyzing words, but they fail to follow up with enough help in putting the recognized elements back together into recognizable words. Usually the teacher must provide extra practice on this essential skill.

Only two of the best known basal series make definite provision for adapting word-attack skills instruction to ability differences of children. The *Alice and Jerry Series* (Row, Peterson Company) includes in the manuals three separate forms of the lesson for each story. The *Developmental Reading Series* (Lyons and Carnahan) offers a skills program adjusted to the needs of slow learners in the workbook that accompanies the Classmate Edition.

The manuals with most of the textbook series suggest that the less capable children delay beginning book reading and then proceed at a slower pace than more capable children. When they do begin the basic program, they are usually introduced to phonetic analysis after learning only fifty to a hundred words. This is suitable for children of average ability, but the slower children do not have the mental capacity to handle phonics this soon. As a result, these skills must be re-taught at a later time if the slower children are ever going to master them.

Sometimes educators have questioned the use of basal reader workbooks at any level. Although they were used for more than thirty years without any attempt to prove their worth scientifically, two studies on this matter have been reported recently. Both revealed that basic workbooks make significant contributions to the development of reading vocabulary at certain grade levels. One found that workbooks were more necessary for teaching the slow groups of children than other groups.

Although basal reader materials usually provide a varied and rather complete program for teaching word-attack skills, they often need to be supplemented in order to meet the needs of some children. Likewise, some pupils should not be required to do all of the practice and review exercises that are offered.

B. Independent Sets of Graded Textbooks and Workbooks

The materials of this type vary greatly in philosophy and content. Consequently each example must be described separately.

1. Meighan, M., *et al. Phonics We Use*. Chicago: Lyons and Carnahan.

The series consists of a set of six workbooks to be used as needed in the primary and intermediate grades. It provides auditory and visual exercises in the recognition of consonants, vowels, syllables, meaning clues, and accent clues. The sequence of skills development is fairly similar to that of the basic reader programs. The workbooks fulfill most of the evaluation criteria, except that they do not provide extensive reading materials in which to practice the skills. Consequently they are appropriate for use along with basal programs for those children who sometimes need extra practice, or for reteaching word-attack skills to slower children who failed to master these skills because they were first introduced too early.

2. Hargrave, Rowena, and Armstrong, Leila. *Building Reading Skills*. Wichita: McCormick-Mathers, 1958.

This is another series of six workbooks to be used in primary and intermediate grades, or at higher levels when needed. It provides ear-training games, plus written lessons on consonants, vowels, syllables, prefixes, suffixes, and word meanings. The approach to word-attack is one of analyzing known words and developing understandings somewhat inductively. Included in three of the workbooks are sets of drill cards for the pupil. Although the books contain a number of

pages of story material, regular readers are needed for practicing the skills that the workbooks present. This set of materials can be used appropriately in the same way as the set described previously. The teachers' manual contains a very helpful section on supplementary materials and devices.

3. Burton, William H., *et al. Developmental Reading Text Workbooks*. Indianapolis: Bobbs-Merrill Company, 1961.

The set includes seven workbooks which vary from advanced primer to sixth grade level. The materials present word recognition clues involving context, configuration, consonants, vowels, syllabication, roots, prefixes, and suffixes. More than half of each workbook consists of selections to read for the purpose of developing many types of comprehension and work-study skills. Therefore these materials offer a reading program that is well-rounded, with proportionately less emphasis on the word-attack skills than do the sets described previously. Because the sequence of skills development is similar to that of several basic readers, these workbooks would be valuable in many situations where supplementary material is needed. A special feature contained in each workbook is a set of three tests on vocabulary, word meanings, and comprehension in sentences and paragraphs.

4. Eaton, Winifred K., and James, Bertha F. *Iroquois Phonics Series*. Syracuse: Iroquois Publishing Company, 1956.

This series consists of three primary grade work-textbooks with a separate manual for each. Unlike the three series described previously, this one approaches word-attack skills in a manner that is primarily deductive and synthetic. It begins by teaching sounds of individual letters, consonants and vowels separately from printed words. As sounds of letters and letter combinations are learned, the children put them together into words. The skills developed here are limited almost entirely to phonics. Approximately one-fourth of the content is story material that has been written to give practice in using the phonics skills. Consequently most of these stories are not of good literary quality.

5. SLOOP, CORNELIA, *et al. Phonetic Keys to Reading.* Oklahoma City: Economy Company, 1957.

This is a series of seven work-textbooks for use in the first three grades. The work begins with an eight-week period of training on letter sounds starting with vowels. Toward the end of the period the children read a few pages of pre-primer material by sounding out the new words. Thereafter the books contain a large proportion of story material, with occasional phonics exercise pages. The teacher's manuals constantly provide detailed lessons on phonics. Phonics is applied continuously in attacking the new words for every story. A few lessons on syllables, roots, prefixes, suffixes, synonyms, and homonyms are included. The purpose stated at the beginning of each lesson deal almost entirely with the mastery of eighty-two word analysis rules, or phonics keys, with a number of variations. Occasionally comprehension matters are mentioned. The authors recommend that children complete the work in these books during the first part of the year and spend the remaining weeks in reading other books.

The abstract nature of early phonics study and the introduction of sounds before they are to be used in reading could be expected to create special problems in teaching slower groups of children with this material. The bright children could learn the myriad of rules. The intense concentration on letter sounds, however, may cause serious difficulties when the child advances to higher levels. A large number of English words cannot be recognized phonetically, and a child needs other methods for attacking them independently. Also, research and experience show that children who develop the habit of seeing word parts rather than whole words and phrases tend to become slow, plodding readers who are relatively weak in certain aspects of reading comprehension. This could be disastrous in our fast-moving age. A program of this type may seem to produce wonderful results at first; however, when children reach upper grades, their slow over-analytical reading may not be acceptable.

6. JOHNSON, ELEANOR M., *et. al. New Reading Skilltext Series.* Columbus, Ohio: Charles E. Merrill Books, Inc.

This is a work-textbook series planned for grades one through six. It contains brief stories plus varied skills exercises. The comprehension and word-study skills receive considerable emphasis. The word-attack skills lessons cover picture clues, context clues, consonants, vowels, syllables, roots, prefixes, suffixes, contractions, synonyms, antonyms, homonyms, and accents. Because the materials conform to most of the selection criteria, they can be recommended for supplementary use as needed.

A couple of other well-known sets of materials are those by Selma Herr and Anna Cordts.

C. MISCELLANEOUS BOOKS AND WORKBOOKS

The examples mentioned here show that there is great variety in the types of material published.

1. HAY, JULIE, and WINGO, CHARLES E. *Reading with Phonics.* Chicago: J. B. Lippincott, 1948.

The publishers recommend that this book be used in the time ordinarily devoted to word recognition drills in the primary grades reading program. This book is typical of the extremely old-fashioned letter-by-letter phonics approach. It begins by teaching the sounds of the vowels. The colorful illustrations used with the letters can easily mislead the beginning reader to believe that "A" is the written symbol for "apple," etc. After they have learned a number of vowel and consonant sounds, the children begin to combine them into two-letter syllables and three-letter words.

The authors belong to the school of phonics enthusiasts who believe that in sounding a three-letter word the vowel should go with the first consonant instead of with the second. Thus "mat" is sounded "ma-t" instead of "m-at." The argument over which division is correct began decades ago and most authorities have concluded that dividing the word after the vowel will confuse the child when he comes to analyze words like "mate," since the sound of the letter "a" is determined by the spelling of the last part of the word, not the first part. Some persons who favor the same approach as Hay and Wingo argue that vowel sounds must be attached to any consonant sound, because a consonant cannot be voiced correctly otherwise. They also point out that in syllabication, the vowel more often joins the consonant preceding it than the one following it.

Two colors of print are used to help the child divide words according to the phonics rules of the authors. Children are asked to "climb" dozens of ladders and read lengthy lists of words in drill exercises. A few pages of sentences are provided to give the child opportunities to attack words in context. This "story" material is not only of unbelievably poor literary quality, but is sometimes inane.

The book cannot be used to supplement a basic reader program, because its approach is entirely different. A good teacher could not use it in place of the word-attack skills program with the basic reader; not only does it make reading a word-calling process, but it fails to present the context clues, the configuration clues, and the many structural clues needed in a complete vocabulary program. As a result the average or slower pupil could be expected to flounder when meeting new words that cannot be attacked phonetically.

2. DURRELL, DONALD D., *et al. Building Word Power*. Yonkers-on-Hudson: World Book Company, 1945.

Forty-eight lessons on visual perception and forty-eight lessons on auditory perception of word elements are outlined for use by primary grade teachers. A workbook is needed by the child to complete the visual exercises. The sounds are taught inductively in words. Numerous games and devices are suggested to make the exercise interesting. The authors do not claim that a complete word-attack program is presented in the book. It can be very helpful in supplementing a basic program when groups of children need the type of help that is offered.

3. FELDMAN, SHIRLEY C., and MERRILL, KATHLEEN K. *Ways to Read Words* and *More Ways to Read Words*. New York: Bureau of Publications, Teachers College, Columbia University, 1959.

These two small workbooks contain exercises on using context clues, configuration clues, word beginnings, word endings, letter sounds, and syllabication. They also contain a number of interesting games and devices which the children can cut out and use in skills development. Teachers should find the workbooks helpful as supplementary or review material.

4. ROBERTS, CLYDE. *Word Attack: A Way to Better Reading*. New York: Harcourt, Brace and Company, 1956.

The book offers 139 pages of work intended primarily for remedial groups in grades eight, nine, and ten. In its ten chapters the book provides generous quantities of exercises dealing with context clues, dictionary work, vowel sounds, consonant sounds, syllabication, prefixes, suffixes, and roots. The lists of word examples should be exceptionally helpful to all teachers of intermediate and upper grades. The book complies with most of the selection criteria if it is used for corrective or supplementary teaching along with a basic reading and literature program.

D. COMMERCIAL DUPLICATOR SETS

1. *Wordland Series (A Basic Word Analysis Program)*. Elizabethtown, Pa.: Continental Press.

The materials consist of ten 30-page sets of duplicator masters planned for grades one through five. The lessons prepared on the masters cover a wide range of skills: letter sounds and symbols, word beginnings and endings, letter substitutions, syllabication, dictionary use, and others. The quality of the lessons fluctuates from relatively poor to excellent.

Materials of this type can be of value if the teacher selects carefully and assigns to each child only those sheets that he really needs for extra practice. Unfortunately, the pages are too often duplicated in wholesale lots to be used to keep all of the children in several classes busy. Most of the children would learn more and would develop better attitudes if, instead of being required to do unnecessary busy-work, they were encouraged to read independently in an attractive, well-stocked classroom library corner.

E. CHARTS, CARD SETS, AND OTHER DEVICES

1. *Webster Word Wheels*. St. Louis: Webster Publishing Company.

Many word wheels are utilized in the set to provide practice in substituting consonants, vowels, prefixes, and suffixes in words. The wheels are especially useful as supplementary and corrective material when there is a need to concentrate on one of these skills. The manipulative aspect of the wheels makes them interesting to the children and makes possible the rapid recombining of quantities of word elements.

2. *The Phonovisual Consonant Chart. The Phonovisual Vowel Chart*. Washington: Phonovisual Products, 1960.

The two large charts present twenty-six consonant sounds with eight subspellings and seventeen vowel sounds with twenty-one subspellings along with corresponding "key-word pictures." A "method book" explains the use of the materials in kindergarten and primary grades. Two workbooks and a game book are available to accompany the charts.

The publishers state that these materials are not to be used in place of a basic program. Instead they are planned to parallel and supplement basic materials where needed. They emphasize correct enunciation of the letter sounds.

3. DURRELL, DONALD D. *Word Analysis Practice*. New York: Harcourt, Brace, and World, 1961.

The cards are packaged in Sets A, B, and C, which present 720, 1200, and 1200 words respectively. It is suggested that they be used by pairs of pupils who are reading at low fourth grade to low sixth grade levels. The activity is to sort the words on each card into three categories that are suggested by words or phrases at the bottom of the card. The paired children help each other apply known phonetic and structural clues to enable them to recognize the words that they do not know. The correct responses are given on the back of the cards to make self-checking possible. There seems to be no harm in using the cards for some supplementary purposes if the children do not find the work to be monotonous.

4. *Word-Study Charts*. Horrocks and Norwich. Boston: Ginn and Company.

The set of twenty charts offers a variety of phonetic and structural analysis illustrations. By pulling moveable strips through slots in some of the charts the teacher can demonstrate the substitutions of word elements to form new words. In most respects these charts qualify as very valuable materials to use as aids in teaching or reviewing certain phases of the basal reader word-attack program.

5. *Filmstrips.*

Both Ginn and Row, Peterson provide filmstrips to supplement the word analysis programs of their basal books. The filmstrips are helpful for review because of their relative novelty.

F. Materials to Develop Vocabulary through Spelling

Some writing programs attempt to teach children to write whatever words they need to carry out on-going communication experiences. Through this process children learn to read words that they do not already know. Although this is not one of the most common approaches to the development of reading vocabulary, it cannot be totally ignored. In addition, spelling programs frequently present many word analysis lessons that apply to reading skills growth.

1. KELLER, HELEN B., and FORSTER, MARY N. *Words for Writing: A to Z Spellers.* San Francisco: Harr Wagner Publishing Company, 1956.

The children in primary grades are given paper file boxes in which they file new words for future reference in writing. Each child has a pad of ready-printed word strips and blank strips. The teacher helps him find or write the new words that he needs. He traces it, writes it, and files it. The acts of tracing and writing are kinaesthetic approaches to word recognition, and some teachers feel that these materials help to increase the pupil's sight vocabulary.

2. RUSSELL, KARLENE E., *et al. Developing Spelling Power.* Yonkers-on-Hudson: World Book Company, 1957.

Although it is intended primarily as a remedial spelling guide for use with intermediate grade children, the lessons in this book would contribute to the development of word-attack skills. They cover consonants, vowels, blends, syllables, prefixes, suffixes, and dictionary work.

G. Materials and Experiences Planned In the Classroom

1. *Independent supplementary reading.*

The child who reads extensively has an opportunity to refine his word-attack skills and to broaden both his sight vocabulary and his understanding vocabulary. A child's reading vocabulary can never fully ripen unless he has an opportunity to read freely in hundreds of supplementary texts and library books.

2. *The picture dictionary.*

The individual picture dictionary kept by each child develops independence in word recognition, dictionary readiness skills, and ability to recall words from picture and sentence clues.

3. *Word analysis charts.*

Colorful pocket charts and picture classification charts can be utilized to enrich and extend the basic program.

H. Professional Guides and References for the Teacher

1. DURKIN, DOLORES. *Phonics and the Teaching of Reading.* New York: Bureau of Publications, Teachers College, Columbia University, 1962.

In 76 pages Dr. Durkin presents a thorough treatment of the phonics principles and methods of instruction. The book does not cover structural analysis except incidentally.

2. DEIGHTON, LEE C. *Vocabulary Development in the Classroom.* New York: Bureau of Publications, Teachers College, Columbia University, 1959.

In the first part of this 62-page book the author explains the problems encountered in teaching students to use context clues and structural clues. Then concrete suggestions are offered for an improved vocabulary development program based on invariant means of standard word parts. Another interesting section deals with vocabulary problems in reading figures of speech.

3. GRAY, WILLIAM S. *On Their Own in Reading*. Chicago: Scott, Foresman and Company, 1960.

This 248-page book is the most complete guide available on the teaching of word-attack skills. After giving a general overview of the types of word-attack skills, the author outlines detailed lessons for teaching phonetic analysis, structural analysis, and dictionary skills.

4. RUSSELL, DAVID H., and KARP, E. *Reading Aids Through the Grades*. New York: Bureau of Publications, Teachers College, Columbia University.

The booklet provides 300 suggestions for teaching a variety of reading skills.

In summary, it can be stated that the market is flooded with materials for teaching reading vocabulary and word-attack skills, but the materials vary greatly in quality and usefulness. A list of criteria can be helpful in evaluating these materials intelligently. One must be especially alert to avoid being sold a set of materials that does an excellent job of presenting one type of word-attack skills, but handicaps the child through lack of a complete well-balanced program. The "fanatic phonics" books are the ones which are most often guilty of this.

In selecting materials one must have in mind the exact purpose or purposes for which they are needed. Then there are a number of good books, workbooks, charts, and devices which can contribute to successful teaching. The basic reader materials still seem to provide the most well-rounded programs, but other good materials are readily available for supplementary and corrective teaching.

BIBLIOGRAPHY

BETTS, EMMETT A. *Foundations of Reading Instruction*. New York: American Book Company, 1957, Ch. 24.

BOND, GUY L., and FAY, LEO C. "A Report of the University of Minnesota Reading Clinic," *Journal of Educational Research*, XLIII (January 1950), 385–390.

———, and WAGNER, EVA. *Teaching the Child to Read*. New York: Macmillan Company, 1960, Chs. 9 and 10.

BLACK, MILLARD H., and WHITEHOUSE, LAVON H. "Reinforcing Reading Skills Through Workbooks," *Reading Teacher*, XV (September 1961), 19–24.

IBELING, FREDERICK W. "The Value of Supplementary Phonics Instruction," *Elementary School Journal*, LXII (December 1961), 152–156.

SARTAIN, HARRY W. "Do Reading Workbooks Increase Achievement?" *Elementary School Journal*, LXII (December 1961), 157–162.

6
Meanings and Reading

WHAT IS ADEQUATE COMPREHENSION AND WHEN IS COMPREHENSION ADEQUATE?
Russell G. Stauffer

When an attempt is made to bring the relatively articulated concept of when is comprehension adequate into the matrix of what is adequate comprehension, a concept to which surprising much attention has been given in the past, it is necessary to consider both purpose and comprehension in order to get relevant data. When man learned to translate the audible into the visible, or when he learned to record the spoken word, he instituted a dynamic process that has reshaped every aspect of thought, language, and society. When man learns similarly to translate comprehension in terms of purpose, he will have instituted a dynamic thinking process that can reshape every aspect of learning, communication, and society.

Two readily distinguishable factors are evident when these two topics are examined. They can be dealt with by considering the comparatively simple aspect first, when is reading comprehension adequate. Reading comprehension is adequate when the reader finds an answer to his purpose. Purposes may

vary from being vague, uncertain, indescribable, social-personal needs for entertainment or for emotional relief, to clearly defined, specific, singularly individual ambitions. The former may vary from a personalized interest to be entertained to an inarticulate need for mental or emotional therapy. Children may read comics daily to seek escape. Or then they may, as adults, turn to the funnies in the daily papers because they enjoy them and are entertained by them. The latter concept also varies, from a simple fact to a very complex involved theoretical consideration, such as the apogee and perigee variant of a space capsule making its 21st orbit.

What is adequate comprehension is sharply different. It serves not only as a pattern to which one aspires but also as a criterion of validity determined by those best informed in the area. This being the case it seems timely to take a look at "what is reading." The following is in my opinion the most comprehensive statement. The definition is that of Arthur S. Gates and appears in the NSSE 48th yearbook, *Reading In The Elementary Schools*. He said, "Reading is not a simple mechanical skill, nor is it a narrow

Reprinted from the *Journal of the Reading Specialist*, II (December 1962), 20–23, with permission of the publisher.

scholastic tool. Properly cultivated it is essentially a thoughtful process. If I were to say that reading is a thought getting process, is to give it too restrictive a description. It should be developed as a complex organization of patterns of higher mental processes. It can and should embrace all sorts of thinking, and problem solving. Indeed it is through reading that reading is one of the first media for cultivating many techniques of thinking and imagining." Contrast that definition with the way Gray and Rogers described comprehension in *Maturity In Reading.* "Ability to translate words into meaning, to secure a clear grasp and understanding of the ideas presented, and to sense clearly the moods and feelings intended, ability to perceive strength and weaknesses in what is read, to detect bias and propaganda, and to think critically concerning the validity and values of the ideas presented and the adequacy and thoroughness of the author's presentation, views, and conclusion. This involves an emotional apprehension either failable or unfailable as well as a penetrating intellectual grasp of what is read. Tendency to fuse the new ideas acquired by reading with previous experience does require new or clearer understanding, broadened interest, rational attitudes and proved patterns of thinking and behaving and richer and more stable personality." This is a very comprehensive statement of what is comprehension. Here are a few others.

This is what Mortimer J. Adler has to say in his book on *How To Read A Book*. "The first sense is the one in which we speak of ourselves as reading newspapers, magazines or anything else which according to our skill and talent is thoroughly intelligible to us. Such things may increase a store of information we remember but they cannot improve our understanding for understanding was equal to them before we started. The second sense is the one in which (I would say) a man has to read something that at first he does not completely understand. Here the things to be read is initially better than the reader. The writer is communicating something which can increase the reader's understanding. That communication between unequals must be possible or else one man could never learn from another, either through speech or through writing. Here by learning I mean understanding more, not remembering more information which has the same degree of intelligibility as other information you already possess." He goes on to add the following which is interesting and enlightening. Montaigne speaks of "an abecedarian ignorance that precedes knowledge, and a doctoral ignorance that comes after it." The one is the ignorance of those who, not knowing their ABC's, cannot read at all. The other is the ignorance of those who have misread many books. They are, as Pope rightly calls them, bookful blockheads, ignorantly read. There have always been literate ignoramuses who have read too widely and not well. The Greeks had a name for such mixture of learning and folly, which might be applied to the bookish but poorly read of all ages. They are all *sophomores.*

Being well read too often means the quantity, too seldom the quality of reading. It was not only the pessimistic and misanthropic Schopenhauer who inveighed against too much reading, because he found that, for the most part men read passively and glutted themselves with toxic overdoses of unassimilated information. Bacon and Hobbes made the same point. Hobbes said: "If I had read as many books as most men"—he meant 'misread'—"I should be as dull-witted as they." Bacon distinguished between "books to be tasted, others to be swallowed, and some few to be chewed and digested." The point that remains the same throughout rests on the distinction between different kinds of reading appropriate to different kinds of literature. (Adler, Mortimer J., *How To Read A Book,* pp. 39–40.)

I must burden you further with definitions of comprehension. This is a delightful one that I found a good number of years back prepared by T. S. Judd in an article entitled "The Real Purpose of A College Education." "What happens in the mind is educational, the really valuable knowledge is not that of which we can say, on such a day, in such a book, I learned this. Facts can be shoved into the mind like books into a bag and as usefully. Push in as many books as you please and the bag still has gained nothing. All that happened is that it bulges. A bag is not better for all that it is carrying. Heads can bulge from the mere mass of fact known but not assimilated into the mind substance. A phenomenon the student will have noticed at first incredulously but with growing callousness as the years pass is that very learned people are often fools. And far from this being a paradox one sees how it happens. So far from learning and foolishness being incompatible they are frequently bedfellows. There is no fool like the learned fool. A mind which merely takes in facts without assimilating them can obviously take in far more than otherwise since it can devote to learning new facts the time which better minds devote to nourishing themselves upon the old. The mind feeding upon things is education, examinations of which are mainly attempts of what remains in the memory. But the intellect which has been disciplined to the perfection of its powers, which knows and thinks while it knows, which has learned to leaven the dense mass of facts and events with the elastic force of reason, such an intellect cannot be partial, cannot be exclusive, cannot be impetuous, cannot be at a loss, cannot but be patient, collected, and majestically calm because it discerns the end in the very beginning, the origin in every end, the law in every interruption, the limit in each delay, because it ever knows where it stands and how its path flies from one point to another. The perfection of the intellect which is the result of education and its ideal to be imparted to individuals in their respective measures is the clear, calm, composition and comprehension of all things as far as finite minds can embrace them, each in its place and with its own characteristics upon it."

With these definitions in mind and this comprehensive view of comprehension, I also refer to Roger Lennon's article "What Can Be Measured?" *The Science and Philosophy of Reading and The Role Of Tests in Reading,* Vols. VIII and IX, Proceedings of the Annual Education Conferences on Reading, March 1959 and 1960, University of Delaware, Newark, Delaware. "Shall we conclude that the reading experts with their lengthy lists of objectives finely differentiated, ever more specific skills have simply been spinning a fanciful web that bears no relation to the realities of the nature of reading abilities. Or shall we charge the test makers with a lack of ingenuity in devising test exercises to provide reliability differentiable measures of salient skills with a failure to provide instruments that will match in their comprehensiveness and sensitivity the goals elaborated by the reading experts. "The truth," Lennon goes on to say, "seems to be found between the two extremes." And he goes on to say, "I offer you now my attempt to make sense of the research findings." And he said, "I am disposed to interpret the findings as suggested that we may recognize and hope to measure realiably the following components of reading ability: a general verbal factor, comprehension of explicitly stated materials, comprehension of implicit or latent meanings, and an element termed appreciation." Briefly, by the verbal factor he means in this context to connote word knowledge: breadth, depth and scope of vocabulary. Under comprehension of explicitly stated materials he includes such skills as the location of specifically stated information, comprehension of the literal meaning, comprehension of what is written, literally what is written, and the ability to follow specific directions set forth in what is read. The third component, comprehension of explicit meanings, embraces all of those outcomes that we tend to label as reasoning in reading. Included here would be the ability to draw inferences from what is read, to predict outcomes, to derive meanings from words in context, to perceive the structure of what is read, the main idea of a central thought and so on, to interpret what is read as manifested either by applying the information to the solution of a problem or by deriving some generalization or principles from it. And fourth, finally he says, we have a factor that he terms appreciation. By this he has in mind such things as sensing the intent or purpose of an author, testing the mood for a tone of the selection, perceiving the literary devices by means through which the author accomplishes his purposes. It was a very comprehensive review.

Now while I really haven't been asked to do this, I feel that I should go on and add some thoughts as to what can be done about improving comprehension. To do this I refer you to a study that was done by Chalmer L. Stacy at the University of Minn. The study is entitled *The Law of Effect in the Retained Situation with Meaningful Materials*. Stacy says this, "What do the results of this experiment mean for the direction of classroom learning by teachers?" He concludes that "application of these results would make of the classroom a place where children would actively seek or search for the answers to their problems, this process is in contrast to ones in which the answers are identified and regularly provided by the authority of a teacher or a textbook. In so far as the school deals with materials that are meaningful, structured and organized, as most would acknowledge the materials should be, the school becomes a place where learning is exploring, searching, experiencing, and interacting in an intellectual or cognitive sense as well as overtly. These results give small

comfort to the educator who would have children memorize by rote, association, or would provide answers ready made to be immediately accepted by the children."

Reading then, like thinking, is a process. It begins, goes on, and is in continual change as long as the person reads. At every step the reader has to take account of the content, its parts, its problems, its perplexities, and the portions that indicate solutions and point the way to the overcoming of intellectual obstacles. Reading and thinking always have reference to a context whether it be fiction or non-fiction and the art of reflective reading follows the same form, regardless of the context. Therefore early habits of thoughtfulness, carefulness and thoroughness should be established so that they become deep seated and persistent. Reflective reading starts with a state of doubt. Some difficulties present a perplexity and require hesitation so that thinking can foster anticipation, and imagination. Second is the act of searching, inquiring and accepting evidence that will resolve the doubt and settle the perplexity. Reading can be an obstacle to thinking, and can help extend the habit of language credulity through the spoken word or it can be a means of developing habits of reflective thinking.

In the 1933 edition of *How We Think,* Dewey lists five phases of reflective thought: suggestion, intellectualization, hypothesis, reasoning, and testing. As he develops these ideas, Dewey points out that the five steps need not follow one another in a said order. Each phase is something to perfect ideas that lead to new observations and data and help the thinker digest more accurately the relevance of the facts that he has read. Again and again he suggests that reflective thinking involves a look into the future, a forecast, a prognosis, and that of equal importance is the thinker's dependence on the wide view of his own examined experience. The first line in Hullfish and Smith's book, *Re-*

flective Thinking says, "If young people do not learn to think while in school it is fair to ask how are they to keep on learning." Can we appropriately adapt this question to reading? If young people do not learn to think while they read, how will they keep on learning? Subsequently these authors state that "reflective thinking differs from the looser kinds of thinking primarily by virtue of being directed or controlled by a purpose or the solution of a problem." They go on to say that "the quality of thinking is not to be judged by the quality of the purpose," and that "the key to effective or good thinking is the controlled views of memory and imagination in a balance that is appropriate to the particular purpose or the problem at hand." To this they then add the axiom, "the key to wisdom and good lives are ever residing in the recognition and selection of wordly problems and purposes."

It seems clear then that the art of reflective reading and thinking requires first the ability to select and to recognize worthwhile purposes; second the controlled views of sensation and feeling, perception and memory, and imagination; third, a certain artistry in judgment is needed so that value judgments become voluntary and objective. It seems clear also that to these three factors should be added Dewey's statement that all reflective thinking is a process of detecting relations. If the reader can deal with different interpretations and examine the assumptions and implications of these he will avert habits of credulity. Such habits should be started when the child first learns to read. Then as he increases in ability to recognize printed words as conveyers of ideas he will become more effective in understanding what is being said and why it is said.

Children just learning to read can be taught to sort out their experiences, to make pertinent distinctions among men, compare them with those of the author, generalize concerning the ideas presented, and do so in relation to their system of values. As they mature emotionally, intellectually, and spiritually, they can be taught how man's collective quest for wisdom is an on-going process that reflects changing attitudes and intentions and pre-occupations. They can also learn how to see things as they are and without illusion or emotional bias, and how to make choices or decisions that are sane, prudent, fair, and reasonable. Every opportunity I've had to work with children, particularly primary level children, has impressed me with their integrity, their objective sticking to the facts. They're much less apt to think off the top and they're not hemmed in by the biases and prejudices and the conformities that one begins to observe at the intermediate grades and particularly at the college and adult levels.

Such training then, as I have described, is best initiated I think in a group situation in which all of the children participating are required to deal with the same materials. Under these conditions each member of the group can act as an auditor for each other member and require a searching examination of events to determine the facts and to test their quality, validity, proof and accuracy. It becomes apparent immediately that such learning to read is a demanding task which requires a command of thinking skills as well as reading skill. Obviously, too, reading of this high calibre needs to be taught and the training should be started as it could be at the primary level by using material that can be thoroughly intelligible to the reader, or right within his experience grasp. Story material, if well structured, does lend itself to such use because again, as Adler points out, the general ground plan for reading story material resembles the rules for reading scientific or expository materials.

Gradually though, as the reading materials provided through the intermediate and secondary schools causes the reader to go beyond his immediate experiences, the training must prepare the reader to deal with scientific or expository material as a thinking reader, just as he learned to deal with the narrative variety. Then knowledge of grammar and logic becomes increasingly more valuable. This is especially so when a man reads something that at first he doesn't understand, and, as Ford points out, this is usually the case in public schools. Materials structured to be used to develop basic reading-thinking skills at the intermediate level and beyond should reflect this shift of emphasis.

As is evident, then, when the reader is trained in the way described he is given much opportunity to deal in discovery as he unravels the problems set by the story plot. In fact, in many ways this approach to reading training might be described as a problem solving approach. In so doing, the opening remarks in the preface to Polya's *How To Solve It* seem to be appropriate and I quote, "A great discovery solves a great problem, but there is great discovery in the solution of any problem. Your problem may be modest, but if it challenges your curiosity and brings into play your inventive facilities, and if you solve it by your own means you may experience the tension and enjoy the triumph of discovery." If there is one quality, then, to which every able reader must be committed, it is the ability to find and test evidence. To accomplish this high objective, pupils must become skillful in identifying the relevant and the truthful in the light of thoughtfully declared objectives.

A STUDY OF THE CORRELATION BETWEEN AWARENESS OF STRUCTURAL RELATIONSHIPS IN ENGLISH AND ABILITY IN READING COMPREHENSION*
Roy C. O'Donnell

It has often been asserted that lack of grammatical knowledge accounts for a great deal of incompetence in reading, but the various studies investigating the correlation of knowledge of grammar and ability in reading have offered no conclusive, objective evidence to support the assertion. In fact, most

Reprinted from the *Journal of Experimental Education*, **XXXI** (March 1963), 313–316, with permission of author and Dembar Educational Research Services.

* This report is based on a doctoral dissertation completed at Peabody College in January 1961.

of the studies that have been made indicate that the two are not highly correlated. It should be pointed out, however, that those who have investigated the relationship in question have not made a clear distinction between awareness of grammatical structure and knowledge of grammatical rules and terminology. They have generally based their findings on measurements of the degree of mastery of the conventional English grammar course, which, in the opinion of many modern grammarians, does not adequately represent the essentials of grammatical structure.

THE PROBLEM

The present study was designed to investigate the relationship between ability in reading comprehension and knowledge of grammatical structure. The specific question with which the study is concerned is whether there is a higher correlation between reading comprehension and awareness of structural relationships of words in sentences than there is between reading comprehension and ability to verbalize grammatical rules and terminology.

The investigation was limited to relationships that could be measured by written tests. Furthermore, it was concerned with knowledge and abilities acquired prior to the investigation, and no experimental teaching to compare relative effectiveness of different instructional approaches was involved.

The investigation of the problem necessitated the following steps: 1) basic structural relationships of words in English sentences were identified by examining textbooks based on structural linguistics; 2) a test was constructed to measure ability to recognize structural relationships; 3) the correlation of scores on the constructed test and scores on a standardized reading comprehension test was computed; 4) the correlation between scores on a standardized grammar test and reading test scores was computed; 5) the correlation of reading comprehension test scores and structure test scores was compared with the correlation of reading comprehension and grammar test scores; and 6) intelligence test scores were used to compute coefficients showing the correlation of the various tests with intelligence.

THE SUBJECTS

Arrangements were made in the spring of 1960 to give the reading test, the grammar test, and the structure test to the senior class at Bowling Green High School, Bowling Green, Kentucky.

The class was composed of 115 members—64 boys and 51 girls. The Otis Quick-Scoring Mental Ability Test had been given to 106 of the 115 members of the class near the end of the preceding semester. At the time the Otis test was administered, the ages of those taking the test ranged from 15 years, 8 months, to 19 years, five months, with a median age of 17 years, eight months. The IQ score range for the class was from 80 to 129, or from the fifth percentile to the ninety-ninth percentile, on the basis of data supplied by the test publisher. The mean IQ score was 106, corresponding to the seventieth percentile; the median IQ score was also 106.

THE PROCEDURE

Basic structural relationships of words in sentences were identified by examining four textbooks (Francis, Hill, Sledd, and Whitehall) incorporating principles of structural linguistics, and a test consisting of fifty items of the three-option multiple-response type was constructed to measure ability to recognize these relationships. In order to exclude as much lexical meaning as possible from the test items, nonsense words were used in the option sentences; however, the usual structural signals of word order, inflectional and derivational affixes, and English function words were provided.

The constructed test included six items designed to measure ability to recognize the relationship between subject and predicate, ten items to measure recognition of the relationship between verb and complement, four items to measure recognition of the relationship between coordinate elements, twenty-four items to measure recognition of relationships of the various types of modifiers and elements modified, and six items to measure recognition of the relationship between elements involved in cross-reference. The number of items of each type was decided upon after examination of the Stormzand and O'Shea study of the relative frequency of occurrence of various constructions in written English.

It was not feasible to establish validity of the test by an objective criterion, but every effort was made to construct the test so that correct responses would depend on ability to recognize the relationships involved. The reliability of the test was established by standard statistical procedures, and after preliminary testing, item analysis, and revision, the following statistical data were obtained: mean, 24.94; mode, 16; median, 24; standard deviation, 8.72; split-half reliability (Spearman-Brown formula), .88; inter-item consistency (Kuder-Richardson formula), .86.

In addition to the "Test of Recognition of Structural Relationships in English," constructed by the investigator, Test C 1: Reading Comprehension, Form Z, published by the Cooperative Test Division of the Educational Testing Service, and the Iowa Grammar Information Test, Form A, published by the University of Iowa, were administered to the subjects of the study. The number of students taking the grammar test was 113; the number taking the reading test was 108; and the number taking the structure test was 106. The number of students taking all three of the tests was 101, and Otis IQ scores were available for ninety-two of the 101 students.

The correlation coefficients of primary interest were those showing 1) the relationship between scores on the grammar test and scores on the reading test and 2) the relationship between scores on the structure test and scores on the reading test. Scores on the intelligence test were used to compute coefficients showing the relationship of the scores on the other tests to intelligence test scores; other coefficients were computed to show how the tests were related to one another.

The Pearson product-moment formula was used in computing the various correlations. Since only raw scores were obtained on the structure test, raw scores were used on the grammar test; scaled scores were used on the other tests. Correlation coefficients were computed using the separate level of comprehension and vocabulary scores on the reading tests; speed scores were considered irrelevant to the investigation. The .05 level was used in all tests of significance.

THE FINDINGS

The data showing the correlations of the various tests used in the study are presented in Table I and interpreted in the following paragraphs.

The correlation between structure test scores and Otis IQ scores was interpreted as being sufficiently low to invalidate any argument that the structure test is merely an intelligence test. The correlation of the Otis test and the grammar test was not found to be significantly higher than that of the Otis and structure tests. The correlation of the Otis and level of comprehension scores and of the Otis and vocabulary scores is in keeping with the various studies indicating a relatively high correlation between intelligence and reading ability.

The relatively high correlation of the grammar and structure test scores suggests that a common factor was being measured in both tests. The high correlation indicates that mastery of the terminology and rules of conventional grammar tends to be accompanied by ability to recognize basic structural relationships of words in sentences, but it does not necessarily imply that learning terminology and rules always results in ability to recognize structural relationships. It is possible that ability to recognize structural relationships enables the student to learn grammatical rules and terminology more easily.

The correlation of the grammar test scores and level of comprehension scores is not significantly different from the correlation of structure test scores and level of comprehension scores. This comparison does not support the hypothesis that there is a higher correlation between reading comprehension and ability to recognize structural relationships than there is between reading comprehension and knowledge of conventional grammar. In comparing the various correlations presented in Table I, however, we find that grammar test scores are more highly correlated with vocabulary scores than are structure test scores. We also find that vocabulary and level of comprehension scores are relatively highly correlated. These data suggest that knowledge of vocabulary is an important factor in both the level of comprehension and grammar test scores but is of lesser importance in the structure test scores.

To obtain statistical evidence of the extent to which knowledge of vocabulary affects the correlation of level of comprehension and grammar test scores and level of comprehension and structure test scores, the partial correlation formula was used to partial out knowledge of vocabulary. With knowledge of vocabulary held constant, the correlation of the level of comprehension and structure test scores was .15 and the correlation of the level of comprehension and grammar test

scores was —.79. Thus, with knowledge of vocabulary held constant, the correlation of the level of comprehension and grammar test scores is noticeably lower than that of level of comprehension and structure test scores.

THE CONCLUSIONS

On the basis of the findings of the study, the following conclusions were drawn:

1. Mastery of the content of the conventional English grammar course tends to be accompanied by ability to recognize basic structural relationships of words in English sentences, to the degree that these abilities are indicated by scores on the tests used.
2. With knowledge of vocabulary accounted for by a partial correlation formula, the correlation between ability to comprehend written English and ability to recognize structural relationships of words in sentences is higher than the correlation between ability to comprehend written English and ability to verbalize knowledge of grammatical terminology and rules.

TABLE I

CORRELATIONS OF TEST C 1:

READING COMPREHENSION, THE IOWA GRAMMAR INFORMATION TEST, THE "TEST OF RECOGNITION OF STRUCTURAL RELATIONSHIPS IN ENGLISH," AND THE OTIS QUICK-SCORING MENTAL ABILITY TEST WITH ONE ANOTHER

	Reading Level	Reading Vocabulary	Iowa Grammar	Structure	Otis M.A.
Reading Level	—	.76	.46	.44	.65
Reading Vocabulary	—	—	.90	.46	.75
Iowa Grammar	—	—	—	.75	.57
Structure	—	—	—	—	.48

3. The correlation between awareness of structural relationships of words in sentences and ability in reading comprehension as indicated in this study is not sufficiently high to give conclusive evidence to support the teaching of linguistic structure as a major means of developing reading comprehension. Since there are several distinct factors involved in reading, however, it does not necessarily follow that ability to recognize structural relationships is of no importance in reading comprehension.

RECOMMENDATIONS FOR FURTHER STUDY

Related problems that may merit further investigation are suggested as follows:

1. Since the present study is concerned with concepts of English structure acquired prior to the time of testing rather than the mode whereby the concepts may be acquired, it does not provide conclusive data proving that study of traditional grammar is the most effective means of forming these concepts. It would be of some value to know whether mastery of traditional grammar necessarily results in ability to recognize structural relationships or, conversely, whether a previously acquired ability to recognize structural relationships contributes to mastery of traditional grammar. If awareness of structural relationships is brought about by instruction, it would be useful to know whether instruction in structural linguistics is more, or less, effective than instruction in conventional grammar. A study of this kind might involve experimental teaching and testing on the elementary school level.

2. Since the "Test of Recognition of Structural Relationships in English" is constructed to measure ability to recognize structural relationships in English without direct application of knowledge of grammatical terminology, it appears that the test could be adapted to investigate the levels of maturity at which children develop awareness of the more complex grammatical relationships.

3. The structure test is dependent to a lesser degree than conventional grammar tests on knowledge of vocabulary, and thus it appears to more nearly isolate ability to recognize structural principles than do other tests. Therefore, it seems that the test could be used in research to discover more exactly the relative importance of the various factors in reading ability.

4. The present study is concerned only with the correlation of knowledge of grammatical structure and reading ability, but the structure test could be used to investigate the correlation of knowledge of structure and writing ability.

BIBLIOGRAPHY

CENTER, STELLA S. *The Art of Book Reading*. New York: Charles Scribner's Sons, 1952.

FRANCIS, W. NELSON. *The Structure of American English*. New York: The Ronald Press Company, 1958.

HILL, ARCHIBALD A. *Introduction to Linguistic Structures*. New York: Harcourt, Brace and Company, 1958.

SLEDD, JAMES. *A Short Introduction to English Grammar*. Chicago: Scott, Foresman and Company, 1959.

STORMZAND, MARTIN J., and O'SHEA, M. V. *How Much English Grammar?* Baltimore: Warwick and York, Inc., 1924.

WHITEHALL, HAROLD. *Structural Essentials of English*. New York: Harcourt, Brace and Company, 1958.

CONCEPTS FROM SEMANTICS AS AVENUES TO READING IMPROVEMENT
David Cooper

Since the popularization of Korzybski and Ogden and Richards in the late thirties, teachers have found in semantics a source of theories about language and language behavior which has added a vitality to the teaching of English which often seemed hopelessly buried in the rubrics of grammar and rhetoric. Although the systematic application of the principles of semantics to written and oral expression is generally widely practiced, one of the inconsistencies of the curriculum in English has been the lack of similar application to the development of reading skills. Probably for as long as any of us can remember, we have been deploring the inadequacies of reading instruction in the secondary schools. One of the more popular panaceas is "Every teacher a teacher of reading," but there is precious little evidence of ambitious school-wide programs reaching their ultimate targets, the students. The logical place to focus instruction in reading is the English class, in which all of the language skills can be integrated, and in which all students receive instruction. Such a focus does not minimize the importance of reading instruction in each of the content areas of the curriculum. But to develop an understanding of the ways in which language works in all of its facets—listening, speaking, writing, and *reading*—is a prime concern of the teacher of English. Those aspects of semantics concerned with the relation of words to objects and events in the physical world and with the techniques by which we accomplish our purposes through the use of language suggest approaches through which teachers may help develop reading skills which parallel the development of the other language skills.

The English teacher cannot limit his treatment of language to the field of literature. Most literature should not be subjected to the same kind of scientific analysis as discourse which claims to be factual, logical, and objective. We could destroy the imaginative and emotional appeal of literature if we were to apply to it the usual semantic tests of referential language. On the other hand, the student may need more insights into language than are afforded by the tools of literary criticism in order to decide about a candidate or a political issue after reading conflicting opinions, make an intelligent choice about which product to buy after reading the claims of the sellers, or make other practical decisions which might depend partly upon assessing what he has read. In developing skills in speaking and writing, students are expected to have experiences largely with expository materials dealing with all areas of knowledge, with utilitarian rather than artistic uses of language. Teaching expository reading, therefore, should be familiar ground to the English teacher.

What is needed, then, is not just the "reading specialist" to work with a limited number of remedial students, but the language spe-

Reprinted from the *English Journal*, LIII (February 1964), 85–90, with permission of the author and National Council of Teachers of English.

cialist, the English teacher, to apply his knowledge and training in a program for developing the skills of all students in the reading of non-literary as well as literary materials. The program could begin with the reinforcement of such comprehension and study skills taught in earlier grades as recognizing main ideas and significant details, reading between the lines, following cause and effect relationships, and using text and reference materials efficiently. These skills need to be applied to the increasingly complex material with which high school students are confronted. They are prerequisite to developing the reading skills which are a facet of the maturity in the use of language which the English teacher aims to develop. The "mature" reader may be defined as one who generally

—can deal skillfully with increasingly higher levels of abstraction
—suspends judgment until "all" the facts are in
—distinguishes fact from opinion
—draws inferences from and judges the validity of the ideas presented
—recognizes the author's intention(s)
—compares the views of different authors
—makes judgments concerning the quality, the effectiveness, or the completeness of what is read
—draws analogies
—goes beyond specific facts to use past experiences and relational thinking in arriving at an interpretation
—applies the ideas gained from reading to new situations
—applies the material read in the solution of problems*

* This definition, though restricted to and expanding upon aspects of reading maturity related to semantic awareness, parallels that of William S. Gray and Bernice Rogers in *Maturity in Reading* (Chicago: University of Chicago Press, 1956), pp. 54–55.

A program for developing maturity in reading might be focused around the following aspects of semantics and related language study: language and reality, the purposes of language, semantic shift, the abstraction process, metaphor, and critical reading.

LANGUAGE AND REALITY

As students progress through school, they become increasingly dependent upon printed matter divorced from direct experience. They tend to verbalize, to relate what they read only to other words and not to experience. An antidote lies in understanding of the symbolic process—of the relationship between language and reality—and in developing the habit of asking what a word represents in the physical world.

The mature reader is one who responds to words as symbols for things and not as the things themselves, who recognizes that names represent not qualities inherent in the objects, but arbitrary classifications agreed upon by the users. He is aware that a verbal map is a prediction of what is likely to occur in a relevant context, and not a fixed and complete description of reality. He is on guard against the syntactical structures which suggest that objects bearing the same name are identical, or that sense impressions are qualities of things rather than the author's reactions to them. Students need to be trained to translate the static and elementalistic structure of our language to fit the facts of a world of interrelated and orderly change which science has discovered. They need to avoid the pitfalls of an agent-action, question-answer language which places objects and events in neat, unrelated categories.

As the student deals with greater complexities, with abstract ideas further and further removed from his experience, it is essential that he develop the habits and skills needed to follow the circuitous path back from symbol to referent. He needs to develop an extensive and flexible verbal repertoire to cope with the countless nuances of emotion and thought with which symbols are imbued. He needs to recognize that an infinite variety of responses to a symbol is possible and that the accuracy of his interpretation depends upon his experience with the symbol, the possible referents for it, and upon his familiarity with the author's matrix of experience.

In the classroom, students might find and explain examples of euphemisms and word magic (reacting to a word as if it were a thing: curses, "dirty" words, patriotic labels, etc.). They can give their meanings for selected words and then compare them with those in various dictionaries in an attempt to arrive inductively at the concept of how words get meanings. They can find examples of differing newspaper reports for the same event and try to account for the differences. They can observe and describe commercial products and then compare their descriptions to those of advertisers.

THE PURPOSES OF LANGUAGE

Unless the reader has clearly defined purposes, he will read in a disorganized, unresponsive fashion. The reader is handicapped in his selection of a pace and method of reading suitable to the discourse and to his purposes unless he knows something of how language works. He has a responsibility almost as great as that of the writer in analyzing and evaluating discourse. He needs to be concerned with organizational patterns. In clear writing, the author's organization corresponds to his topics and purposes. Narration calls for time sequence, argument for analytical organization, etc. Transitions are determined by the ways in which the parts or events are related in the realities one is describing, narrating, or explaining. The English teacher needs to provide opportunities for students to practice looking for these organizational clues to the meaning of what he reads. Here is an obvious area in which the teaching of reading skills complements the teaching of composition.

Another responsibility of the reader is to fathom the ostensible purpose from the real intent of the writer. The writer may use cognitive language in persuading people to believe or do something. This may be the case in advertising or in political material which sticks to the facts. The reader needs to be aware of the situation in which a statement is made in order to judge the purpose and effect of language, since the same words in the same grammatical structures may have different functions in different situations. When the student knows how language works he can protect himself from verbal hypnosis. His reactions to the printed word should be critical and intelligent rather than automatic. He needs to recognize that no language is adequate for all time and for all purposes.

In the classroom, students can try to determine the attitudes and purposes of the users of selected words (policeman, peace officer, fuzz), phrases, and longer pieces of discourse. They might reflect on the appeal of specific passages to different readers: emotional, informative, persuasive, esthetic. They can find and analyze examples of material written for different groups of people, but for the same purpose: an election appeal or advertising addressed to farmers, intellectuals, city workers, minority groups, retired persons. They should have practice in reading various types of material for different purposes: for information, to reflect on the effect of a proposal, to understand feelings of others, to be moved, to weigh opposing opinions, etc.

SEMANTIC SHIFT

Students need to develop a flexibility in interpreting what they read which corresponds to the growing proliferation and complexity of the areas of knowledge which they explore. They need to recognize that words have no fixed meanings and that meanings shift with the contexts of time, place, and situation. In each reading situation they have to be aware of the variables of context in order to determine the writer's meaning for a word. The mature reader selects from a number of related meanings the one which best fits the circumstances, particularly when he is interpreting those high-level abstractions and statements of feeling which tend to elicit stereotyped and emotional responses. If meaning cannot be derived from context, a dictionary may help, provided that it gives a definition within the student's experience. Students need to be able to shift their viewpoints, to carry over into a new set of definitions the results gained through past experience in other frameworks.

The theoretical knowledge of the role of context and of shifts in meaning will not, of course, guarantee sound semantic reactions. Of primary importance is the overlap of experience between reader and writer. However, students can practice reading representative passages to develop awareness of multiple meanings and of the role of context, which should in turn develop an appreciation of the need for experiential background similar to an author's, in order to share his meaning. They might analyze the variations in meaning of the same word found in different contexts: Compare passages in which a contemporary American statesman, a Chinese communist, and a Periclean Greek use the word "democracy." They can find and analyze examples of similar language describing identical phenomena, but which may represent different meanings for different individuals: What makes a particular day "beautiful" for a farmer, a skier, a fisherman, a photographer? They might look for words in print which did not exist or whose meanings have changed in the past fifty years. General semanticists suggest that the device

of indexing, to differentiate one member of a class from others, and dating, to indicate that change takes place in time, may be useful reminders that a word never means the same thing twice.

THE PROCESS OF ABSTRACTION

When we abstract, we attach a label to two or more objects, events, or ideas which have some characteristic in common. Thus a table and a chair become furniture. John Smith and William Jones, who share a skin pigmentation several shades darker than that of their neighbors, are labeled Negroes. These classifications emphasize similarities and leave out differences. But every individual in a given classification differs from every other one and every individual changes over a period of time. Awareness of the process of abstraction and classification may help the reader recognize stereotyped thinking in what he reads and in his own thinking. He may realize that "William Jones, Negro, was jailed last night" makes use of an irrelevant classification, since Jones can be classified in an infinite number of ways.

In the classroom, students might check reports against experience to determine what is omitted, why different people remember different details, and what the possible referents are for the writer's abstract terms. Many high-level abstractions are not obviously reducible to expressions designating individual objects, and it would be futile to pursue every symbol back to every referent, but if students develop awareness of the omission of details in various levels of abstraction they are more likely to be aware that the inference is not the report and that people never say all there is to say about anything. Students can practice writing operational definitions for high-level abstractions, especially those with strong connotations. They might then substitute more concrete and neutral words in selected passages. They can learn to spot statements that fail to recognize that individuals in a group are different and that changes occur. They can evaluate the purpose, validity, and appropriateness of classifications in the material which they read.

METAPHOR

The recognition and evaluation of metaphor is another aspect of linguistic sophistication which becomes more important as reading tasks become more difficult. As new areas of knowledge are explored, the writer relies heavily upon metaphor to describe new experiences. The reader, as he is increasingly divorced from direct experience with the subject, must, for maximum understanding, depend upon a clear interpretation of the metaphors employed. The mature reader needs not only to recognize metaphor, but also to assess its applicability, the elements which can be applied to the new situation, and its emotive elements.

Metaphor should be taught as an integral aspect of language, the chief means by which words are given new meanings, and not merely as an ornament of poetry. Even though a metaphor is stated simply, it poses serious comprehension problems for the unsophisticated reader who may lack both the background and the insight into language to reconstruct the experience which metaphor demands of the reader. Students might begin with a recognition and analysis of the literal referent and go on to examine its relationship to what is being talked about. The sports pages are rich sources of metaphors which are easy to trace back to their literal referents: the cog of the infield; Pirates shade Giants; glass jaw; stretch run; casaba clash. In examining a metaphor they must ask themselves which elements have been selected for comparison and which have been left out. They should learn to determine the nature of the parallel relationship which is being borrowed, which elements can be ap-

plied to the new situation, and in what ways. They should not assume that relationships exist which the writer does not mean to imply do exist: What characteristics are being compared when we say someone works like a horse, treats her like a dog, or behaves like a pig, snake, rat, or fox? How has the writer employed metaphor to appeal to the emotions?

CRITICAL READING

Although "critical reading" is a shifting and amorphous term, there is unquestioned consensus that students should be trained to go beyond literal comprehension of what is read to evaluating, organizing, and inferring and drawing conclusions from their reading. The classroom can develop a concern for meaning, rather than mere fact. The student needs to be able to consider the consequences of alternate choices. In order to do this he needs not only accurate information, but freedom from the kind of communication situation in which he is restricted to automatic responses by the nature of the symbols and syntactical patterns with which he is confronted.

Understanding of the relationship between language and reality, of the purposes of language, of semantic shift, of the abstraction process, and of the nature of metaphor are all basic to mature evaluation of what is read. In teaching "critical reading," however, English teachers have customarily concentrated their efforts on training students to

—recognize underlying assumptions
—recognize common fallacies in thinking
—distinguish among fact, inference, and opinion
—distinguish between the connotation and the denotation of words
—evaluate the adequacy of general statements
—evaluate the dependability of data and the competence of authorities

All of these evaluative skills call for an awareness of how language works. Assumptions are frequently obscured by the nature of our syntactical patterns: "When did you stop beating your wife?" Perhaps the most pervasive fallacy in thinking is that based on two-valued orientation, the either-or, black-or-white way of looking at life. At least part of this elementalistic way of thinking may be ascribed to our language, or labeling habits. We tend to respond favorably to all persons or events which are classified in one way and unfavorably to all persons or events which are classified in another. The subject-predicate sentence pattern permits the reader to internalize the assumption that everything is either A or not A: "You are either for us or against us." It also fails to distinguish, syntactically, between emotive and referential language. "He is a dirty red" and "He is a member of the Communist party."

The English class can be a laboratory in which readers have opportunities to identify and evaluate assumptions, instances of two-valued orientation, statements of cause and effect, stereotypes, and unsupported generalizations. The mature reader makes evaluations on the basis of whatever characteristics he can discover, rather than on the basis of names or classifications, and he makes his evaluations tentatively. He avoids noting only characteristics which agree with his preconceptions and is on the alert for such selectivity (slanting) on the part of the writer. He interprets the writer's connotations for a word while guarding against the imposition of his own connotations.

Language study based on scholarly findings has achieved considerable recognition in the English curriculum in recent years. Curriculum guides and composition textbooks have reflected the growing concern with the relationship of language and thought. As a point of departure for the teaching of reading, the English teacher might apply much of the content of language instruction available in guides and texts. The following composite of language concepts dealt with in four recent series of secondary school composition texts suggests a possible sequence for a reading skills program based on semantics:

Grade 9
The role of context in meaning
Multiple meanings
Kinds of statements

Grade 10
The purposes of language
Distinguishing between fact and opinion
Emotive and referential language
Connotation and denotation
Shifts in meaning
The nature of questions

Grade 11
Recognizing basic errors in thinking
Loaded words
The process of symbolization (symbol and referent)
Abstract and concrete words
Pinning down the meaning of abstractions
Classification
Definition

Grade 12
Levels of abstraction (the abstraction process)
Meaning and experience
The nature of metaphor
Generalization
Recognizing assumptions

Until suitable collections of readings are developed, the teacher will have to rely upon newspapers, magazines, advertising copy, an occasional expository essay found in literature texts, and, for advanced students, such college texts as Altick's *Preface to Critical Reading* and Leary and Smith's *Thought and Statement*. If we base it upon the study and effective use of language, not only should the English teacher not shy away from teaching reading, but he should welcome the opportunity to deal with this hitherto neglected aspect of his subject.

VOCABULARY DEVELOPMENT: FACTS, FALLACIES AND PROGRAMS

Arthur S. McDonald

Teachers and researchers alike agree (with some qualifications and variations of terminology) on the importance of vocabulary knowledge to the individual at every level of schooling and development. From this point, however, the disagreements begin. Specialists differ about the nature of language, the definition and role of a word, and about the process of vocabulary building.

This article considers language as a system of processing information received in various stimuli forms into appropriate linguistic concept patterns. This linguistic processing ability is acquired and shaped by the experiences of a human born into a linguistic community. The discussion is concerned with language development at the college-adult level.

FALLACIES

Many statements, principles and procedural plans concerning the nature of vocabulary and its development embody linguistic fallacies. Some of the most important of these fallacies are:

1. A word is an entity with a fixed meaning.
2. A student either "knows" a word or he doesn't.
3. Speakers and writers have virtually complete freedom in selecting the words they use in connected speech or writing.

Reprinted from *New Concepts in College-Adult Reading, Thirteenth Yearbook of the National Reading Conference* (1964), 77–85, with permission of the author and National Reading Conference, Inc.

4. Every word in the language has an equal chance of getting into a broad enough sample of written or spoken language.
5. The frequency of a word's usage in general writing equates with the number of its meanings and with its conceptual importance in the language.
6. The reader must understand the meaning of every word he encounters.
7. Sixty per cent of English vocabulary comes from Latin and Greek.
8. A student who has had his attention called to certain common "roots" and affixes will more readily understand the meaning of unknown words containing these elements than if he had had no such training.
9. Because the most common prefixes and roots are readily distinguished and used (and on the basis of (8) above), teaching common roots and affixes is an extremely efficient way of building vocabulary.
10. Wide reading is a sure and pleasant way to build vocabulary.
11. For the college student, pronouncing an unknown word is usually helpful in ascertaining its meaning.

The above fallacies fail to take into account the nature, construction, and linguistic role of distinctive clumps of letters, each naming only one particular object or activity. Instead, words are either symbols of referent categories (classifications of acts, objects, or events occurring in the linguistic community) or they are syntactical signals. A "referent category," of course, is a *construct* signifying a rather arbitrary array of acts, objects, feeling or events.

WORDS AND MEANING

Thus, a word is *not* an entity with *a* meaning. Few, if any, words have absolute unchangeable meanings. Rather, words serve as stimuli to call up a category of meanings, the appropriate one of which must be selected by the individual in accord with the context. Often, furthermore, the recipient can construct the intended meaning *only* by considering the word together with one or two other words (e.g. "Angle on the bow," "yes men," "red cap"). Indeed, the usual response to a word form in terms of its central category attributes may be quite inappropriate for the context [e.g. "little man," "fetch" (of the wave), "fetch" (of the devil)].

A society differentiates into many cultural roles, each having special concerns and thus a special vocabulary. (As an example, consider the central attribute of "strike" for the umpire, the labor relations arbitrator, the prospector, the aviation staff officer planning an air attack.) To the degree that a group is socially homogeneous, sharing the same concerns, there will be enough overlap in vocabulary for effective communication. For instance, the labor relations arbitrator who is an enthusiastic baseball fan and who is a military reserve officer will have a broad store for overlapping central attributes for "strike."

In addition, the vocabulary of English falls into several usage levels. The most commonly differentiated of these levels are:

1. syntactical and space-time signal words. These words facilitate the smoothness of grammatical construction and function as signs of space, time, quantity and direction. Beyond an occasional shaping of

the meanings of other words, these words do not contribute to meaning. A number of studies made by language scholars and cryptographic personnel show that *100 words of this class occur 50% of the time in any sizable sample of English prose.*

2. words concerned with family and intimate friends. These involve private words, diminutives, elliptical syntax, allusions, heavy use of words in their central, concrete sense. As an example, compare the letters of a famous man (not written for publication) with his published speeches.

3. the vocabulary used in daily informal writing, informational reading (e.g. news), and recreational reading. Here, there is much use of words categorizing personal and emotional reactions, informal and customary interpersonal exchange, regular social and personal activities involved in daily living. This level accounts for a large portion of the running words in newspapers, magazines and "light" books but contributes little to the average college student's vocabulary needs.

4. words or word attributes used in formal writing and in instructional level reading (textbooks) but not ordinarily in everyday reading or writing.

5. specialized terms used by professions, trades, and special interest groups (often called "jargon").

6. words recognized when seen (either as known in some sense or as having been encountered previously) but never used by the reader himself.

7. museum pieces and archaic words, ("antidisestablishmentarianism"—dismally familiar to parents of elementary age children—and "knave"—in the sense of "serving boy"—are examples).

8. improper and taboo words. These are words considered too intense (and re-

placed by euphemisms as "passed away" for "died"); unsuitable for certain settings (as the use of the word "bomb" in an air terminal or on a commercial air liner); obscene, or of a curse nature.

9. personal inventions.

Therefore, because of these social role and usage level vocabularies, words always have the possibility of eliciting multiple responses from the reader or listener. Thus, a word can function *only in context*.

While the basic unit of context is the sentence, the word and sentence unit are affected by the paragraph, whole article and time context.

The meaning which a word arouses in a reader or listener varies in accordance with his interpretation of the situation in which that word is placed (the context) and his range of experience with the referent classification. If his interpretation is in accord with the context, he may be said to know the word.

"Know," however, is a relative term when applied to vocabulary. A student may:

1. be able to "read" in the sense of pronouncing the word acceptably.
2. have a vague understanding of the referent (a torpedo "blows things up").
3. be able to repeat a rote definition (without giving examples or rephrasing in his own words).
4. be able to use in one or more acceptable senses.
5. understand in several nuances involving central and tangential attributes.

In view of the foregoing discussion, the principal tasks confronting the teacher in the task of vocabulary development are:

1. aiding each student to increase the number of words he knows (in the sense of constructing appropriately precise meaning responses) together with extension of the range of attributes conveyed by each word;
2. making sure the student uses words in his active vocabulary accurately with proper regard for denotation and connotation.

A number of teaching approaches and programs have been devised to achieve the above goals. There are six which are currently in common use (either singly or in combination). While each method of course has some merits of its own, the following descriptions are concerned with their total impact in vocabulary development.

COMMON VOCABULARY DEVELOPMENT METHODS

1. *The language history* approach seeks to alert students to word meanings by studying word origins and the history of language development. Considerable stress is laid on the romantic or picturesque meanings words once had. (Favorites for this are "curfew," "money" and "guard.") Many students are interested in unusual word origins. Some students may be motivated to pursue a systematic word study program, noting word families and taking account of synonyms and antonyms. Those students, however, who have real need of improved vocabulary will seldom go beyond the stage of being impressed by the teacher's erudition and the acquisition of a few obsolete or "bookish" responses to words.

2. *Wide reading* is considered by many to be an efficient and pleasant way to build vocabulary. By reading many books chosen from a variety of areas of interest it would seem that students would encounter new and valuable words as well as learn new meanings for words already in their vocabularies. This method, however, has three serious weaknesses. Used alone, wide reading depends on incidental learning which cannot be

relied upon to produce systematic or transferable results. Furthermore, because of the high redundancy of English and the linear nature of the language (actor-action relationship), a tremendous number of books must be read to encounter very many words outside the lower and middle range of frequency. (In a 40,000 word book, for example, 70 to 75% of the running words will be 1000 of those in levels 1 and 3. If every remaining word could be used *only once*, the student would encounter a maximum of 12,000 words under impossible learning conditions.) Also, because of the incidental nature of the learning conditions inherent in this method, the teacher has no way of knowing whether the student has acquired the precise meaning of the word in its context, has made a vague guess, or has just skipped the unfamiliar word.

3. Another type of vocabulary building program requires the *memorization of lists of words* at periodic intervals. This approach resembles the discarded method of teaching foreign languages. Teaching words in isolation is wasteful and inadequate. Rote memory is notoriously unstable. Also, this method, in spite of adjurations to "make up sentences" and note synonyms, too often leads the student to the single word-single meaning formula. "Translation English," with its glib use of pretentious or inept diction, is a frequent outcome of reliance on the word list.

Since the same cluster of letters in English may require a number of different concept responses as the context changes, students find difficulty in using the invariant meaning approach. The resulting lack of reinforcement together with the heavy demand on rote memory makes it probable that the words "learned" (with the possible exceptions of real museum pieces) will be forgotten with almost the same rapidity as nonsense syllables.

4. Another approach to vocabulary development is *use of the dictionary*. In fact,

a number of books advise this "look it up" procedure as the first recourse when the student encounters an unfamiliar word. In using this approach, the teacher reviews proper procedures in locating words in various types of dictionaries and provides practice. Because of the multiple meanings for words and the necessity to take context into account in constructing the appropriate meaning, it is best to label the dictionary as the last resort. When other means of determining meaning have proved inadequate, the student should turn to the dictionary. Recommending the dictionary as a last, rather than first, resort lessens the arousal of guilt feeling (for not looking up the word but skipping it), prevents the fragmentation of the thought pattern and lessens the likelihood of "word pasting" (the substitution of an inappropriate synonym for the unfamiliar word).

5. Perhaps the most common method in use is *word analysis*. The student is taught meanings for the 50 to 100 Latin and Greek affixes and roots commonly occurring in English. He is trained to analyze an unfamiliar word into prefix, root and suffix (if any). From his knowledge of the "meaning" for each part, he combines the part-meanings into a meaning for the whole. From this, he infers the current meaning of the word.

Because about 40 Greek and Latin affixes and roots occur in one-fourth of the words in the Lorge 30,000 word-list and because of the large number of scientific and technical terms taken directly from or coined from Greek and Latin, this method seems to be based on the soundest rationale of all.

Unfortunately, in practice this method is highly unreliable. One student of philology observed that "if you can use it (the derivative approach), you don't need it; if you need it, you can't use it."

In Greek and Latin themselves, verbs had many variant meanings acquired during the long course of development of those languages. Consequently, a root may have from six to twenty possible meanings. Further, the force of the prefix may have been lost in Greek or Roman times, along the way from the Greco-Latin period to the present, or in English. Unfortunately, the prefix may not be a prefix at all but merely a group of letters resembling it. The following examples occurred in a vocabulary building book which uses the word analysis method.

In the lesson teaching *a, ab* as meaning "away from" with the type example being given as *ab*duct, the following words occurred, in the discussion (not, however, as part of the vocabulary to be learned): abate (ab + battuere), abet (ad + beter), abbreviate (ad + breve) and avoid (ex + vuider). (The derivations have been supplied.) It would seem that the student would be hard put to determine which words had the prefix ab "away from."

As seen above, many prefixes are disguised either by changes in Latin or by passing through French. Pseudo-prefixes mislead (*im*prove—from emprouwer). Also, some Latin prefixes were signs of completion of action and do not possess their traditional meanings at all. "Commit," "ascend," and "perfect" are notorious traps of this kind.

Even in those relatively few words in which the affixes and roots have retained their "assigned" meanings, the constructed literal meaning usually gives little help toward inferring the actual meaning of the word in context. Thus, used alone, this method is confusing and discouraging to most students.

6. The *context approach* is another program for building vocabulary. This program teaches the techniques of using contextual clues to determine appropriate word meaning. Using a variety of contextual settings, the teacher guides the student to perceive a clear connection between a word and its context. (A number of studies have shown that only about half of the college students can use contextual clues effectively.) Thus, words should be presented in several contexts requiring different meaning responses.

Although context determines word meaning, it does not necessarily (and often will not) reveal the meaning. Consequently, students must be taught to seek meaning in the wider context (paragraph, chapter) and to make use of inference from clues such as restatement, metaphor, example, contrasts, general line of thought, etc.

VOCABULARY DEVELOPMENT PROGRAMS IN PERSPECTIVE

A workable program of vocabulary development will not rely on *any one* method. Such a program will accord with the best principles of learning so that:

1. each student's vocabulary needs are ascertained.
2. interest is motivated for each student so that he develops vocabulary suited to his needs.
3. opportunity is provided for each student to proceed at his own optional learning pace.
4. the program will be in accord with good linguistic principles.
5. vocabulary is studied in a natural language setting—that of the context—appropriate for the student's ability.
6. the learning materials use words of high need for the student.
7. each student immediately knows whether his response is appropriate. (If it is not, the correct answer is at hand.)
8. diagnostic tools provide checks on progress and indicate need for corrective instruction.
9. the learning material deals with control and transferred word meanings arising from contexts built around various topics of interest, different social roles and varied usage levels.
10. opportunities are provided for further

application of learning in a new contextual setting (because it is only through usage in a multitude of contexts that the word becomes a workable asset).

Thus, a functional vocabulary program will provide each student with words he needs in such a way that he can master the conceptual categories they represent. The program will be multi-dimensional, drawing on all of the traditional methods *where appropriate* and in ways consonant with the principles of learning. As an outcome, the student will be able to guess at meanings of unfamiliar words, using one or more methods as appropriate. He will check the guess with the meaning of the whole and (where necessary) with the dictionary. He will look for familiar words used in unfamiliar ways and so gradually extend the range of referent attributes symbolized by each word.

ORGANIZATION PERCEIVED
Olive S. Niles

Because mature reading is systematic and orderly, the good reader of any age has to be aware of the thought relationships that exist in the materials he is reading. Attention to these relationships affects his reading in several ways.

THOUGHT RELATIONSHIPS

INITIAL COMPREHENSION

In the first place, accurate initial comprehension often depends on grasping the particular kind of relationship present. We may see this in the comprehension of even a single sentence. The reader who fails to grasp the contrast indicated by the *but* in this sentence has missed the main meaning:

> My father was perhaps too strict with his children, but he set an example of consistency, forthrightness, and integrity which was a legacy beyond price.

Reprinted from *Developing Study Skills in Secondary Schools*. Newark, Del.: International Reading Association (1965), 57–76, with permission of the author and International Reading Association.

EFFICIENT RECALL

Secondly, efficiency of recall depends in part upon the perceiving of some kind of order or system in the ideas to be recalled. Students sometimes need to have this basic fact of the psychology of learning made vivid for them. A simple way to do this is to put a long series of digits on the chalkboard, give the students about thirty seconds to study the series, erase the digits, and ask for recall:

$$582414924285$$

The unusual student who recognizes the pattern in the series has to learn only four digits: The date 1492 is already familiar; the last four digits are simply the first four in reverse. The student who has *not* seen the pattern has almost certainly recalled only part of the series and probably even that part inaccurately.

But perhaps the students will say that they have been asked to recall figures, not "read." The same basic fact, that awareness of pattern contributes greatly to ease of recall, can be demonstrated by presenting two passages of about equal difficulty as exercises in unaided written recall. These two passages could be chosen from a textbook the students are using. In making the first assignment, say simply this: *Read and study this passage about the Treaty of Versailles so that you can write a summary of it.* Allow an appropriate amount of time for study, depending on the length and difficulty of the piece. In giving the second assignment, say something like this: *Before you start reading this passage, notice that it consists of a list of the effects of America's failure to join the League of Nations. Be sure you keep the cause-effect pattern of writing in mind as you study and that you learn the list of effects. You will be asked to write a summary.* Allow the same amount of time for the reading and study. In each case, ask that the written summary be done without reference to the original piece. The difference in amount and quality of recall will, in most instances, be significant, if not dramatic.

CRITICAL ANALYSIS

Finally, ideas perceived in an organized form lend themselves more readily to critical analysis. One of the basic skills in critical reading is ability to weigh the significance of details. Whether or not a fact is important in a particular piece of writing depends, in part, upon the way the author has woven this fact into his organizational pattern. We may use two simple paragraphs to illustrate:

(a) Russia used rocket power to launch the first artificial satellite on October 5, 1957. Sputnik I was an aluminum ball only 23 inches in diameter and 184 pounds in weight. On November 3, Sputnik II, weighing 1120 pounds and carrying a live dog, sped into space, and Russia took the lead in a new kind of race.

(b) While the United States talked about future space travel and her scientists worked quietly, Russia startled the world twice within one month with Sputnik I on October 5, 1957 and Sputnik II on November 3.

The first was a little aluminum ball only 23 inches in diameter and 184 pounds in weight, but the second was almost ten times as heavy and carried a live dog. American admiration for a great scientific feat was mingled with a reaction of fear for the consequences of Russia's taking within so very short a time the lead in a new kind of race.

Critical reading of the two paragraphs shows that the details involved in the dates and other time references are more important to the meaning of the comparison-contrast pattern (b) than they are to the simple time-order paragraph (a).

A second basic skill in critical reading is the ability to determine the relevancy of details to the main point of a piece of writing. If the reader understands the organization pattern, he has a clue to this important matter of relevancy. In the simple listing paragraph (a) below, the reference to Charles Dickens as a critic of his society is quite irrelevant; in the comparison-contrast paragraph (b), this same detail provides an important example of the main point of the paragraph:

(a) The 19th century produced many outstanding writers and artists. Some of the world's most famous novelists lived during these years. They included Sir Walter Scott and Charles Dickens in England, Balzac in France, Dostoevski and Tolstoy in Russia. Dickens wrote several novels in which he attacked such evils in his society as the workhouses, the law courts, and child labor. The 19th century also produced great poets, among them Coleridge, Browning, and Poe. Painters and musicians who were contemporaries of these writers were Renoir, Constable, Schubert, Chopin, and Beethoven.

(b) The 19th century was a period of tremendous activity in the world of art as well as in industry. Some writers and artists were confused by contemporary life and preferred to turn to fantasy, the exotic, or the past. In England Sir Walter Scott, and in America James Fenimore Cooper, wrote fiction in which they glamorized history. Poets like Coleridge and Poe wrote of the supernatural, while architects worked to restore or copy the Gothic buildings of the Middle Ages. Other artists, however, were more concerned about the present and particularly the sociological changes the Industrial Revolution had brought. Some of the writers played an important role in bringing about reform. Charles Dickens, for example, was a severe critic of many conditions in the England of his time. The French Balzac and the Russian Tolstoy also treated life realistically and critically. Architects, too, began to turn to the present and developed the doctrine of functionalism based on the principle that buildings must suit the needs of their users. Banks, warehouses, and other buildings began to fit the needs of an industrial society.

It follows that if awareness of organizational pattern can affect accurate initial comprehension, efficient recall, and ability to read critically, it should be a major goal of reading instruction to show students how to develop this awareness. There is much to be learned; many kinds of organization appear in different kinds of writing.

ORGANIZATIONAL PATTERNS IN WRITING

All good writing has some kind of organization or structure—even though this structure may be a deliberate *lack* of structure, which, ironically, is itself a kind of structure. Some informal essayists—Charles Lamb and Cornelia Otis Skinner, for example—ramble on with what appears to be almost no sense of direction, but this is *their* structure and a basic factor in the charm of their writing.

In factual writing, a few types of organization predominate. Some years ago, the author made an informal analysis of paragraph structure in social studies, science, and language textbooks for secondary schools. The following major patterns were found in this order of frequency:

1. Enumerative order (simple listing)
2. Time order

3. Cause-effect
4. Comparison-contrast

Other persons who have done similar studies have used different names for these same patterns, and much closer distinctions have frequently been made among the various types. It is the author's opinion that elaborate classifications are not only unnecessary but actually a hazard to meaningful teaching.

Different patterns are found in imaginative writing. These include the special types of time order characteristic of fiction, the various poetic forms, and the organization present in different kinds of drama.

These basic patterns—in both factual and imaginative writing—appear in many forms and combinations, some of which may be very complex. The writer of fiction does not always proceed with his narrative: he writes descriptive paragraphs which may be enumerative in structure; he may, even, include expository paragraphs. In factual writing, the comparison-contrast paragraph or selection may contain elements of time order or of enumeration. The possibilities for combination are many.

Although this variety may confuse the researcher who is frustrated in attempts to classify and describe, it is not of great significance in the teaching process. It is not at all necessary that students be exposed to all the possible variations. The important goal is to teach the student enough so that he forms the habit of looking for order and structure in everything he reads and knows what to do with it when he finds it.

Students in secondary schools must have specific lessons in the perception of organizational patterns. The idea should not be entirely new to them. Actually, the kindergarten teacher is laying the foundation when she reads a story like "The Three Bears" and asks the children to arrange a series of pictures of events in the story in correct time order. Exercises which require that pupils follow time sequence, notice cause-effect relationships, and select "opposites" occur in all basal reading materials throughout the elementary grades. However, the serious study of organizational pattern as an aid to comprehension and recall is mainly a responsibility of the secondary school and college. Even though students are fairly mature before they give much concentrated attention to the rather advanced skills which are involved, they usually need to begin with very simple examples of basic patterns and work from there to the more complex.

PERCEIVING ORGANIZATION OF FACTUAL MATERIALS

The following excerpts from lessons are offered to illustrate a possible sequence for teaching the perception of organization of factual material. The examples are on a fairly easy secondary level. Changing the examples, not the developmental process, would lend a sophistication to the lessons which would make them suitable for more advanced high school or college classes.

Step 1—It is helpful to begin with a discussion of pattern in all phases of life. Pattern or order exists everywhere. The classroom is full of it: the face of the clock, the colors in a girl's dress, the design of the flag, the sequence of letters in words on the chalkboard. What makes *saw* different from *was*?

Outside the classroom, examples are innumerable. How does one recognize that an acquaintance is approaching except by the "pattern" of his physical features? How do the planets avoid collisions? How does a physician know that his patient has measles instead of rheumatism?

From this discussion, it is an easy step to the observation that ideas also are arranged in patterns. Students may be told what some of the common idea patterns are: time, simple listing, etc.

Step 2—With some students, particularly the younger ones (though the author has used this device with college freshmen), visual symbols representing the basic patterns may be an aid to teaching. The following may be drawn on large charts and posted in the classroom for ready reference:

> *Time order:*
> *Simple listing:*
> *Cause-effect:*
> *Comparison-contrast:*

Students need now to be shown how these patterns apply to verbal symbols. The simplest examples can be shown with lists of words or phrases. Some lists can be arranged in more than one pattern. For example, a list of names such as the following may be rearranged to show time order, simple listing, or comparison-contrast:

> Abraham Lincoln
> George Washington
> Nero
> Douglas MacArthur
> Christopher Columbus
> Adolf Hitler
> Charles Lindbergh
> John Glenn
> Al Capone

The teacher might say to the class: *Here are some names of well-known people. Tell me in what order you would arrange the list if you wanted to learn it in time order. Or, tell me in what order you would arrange the list if you wanted to bring out a contrast. Or, suppose you were simply going to learn one unusual fact about each of this group of people. In what order would you arrange the list for this purpose?* Making patterns from such unorganized lists as the one in this example is a way of showing students how facts and ideas may be manipulated to change the total effect. They may begin to understand that the author's choice of pattern does make a difference.

Step 3—Since actually making something is, perhaps, the best way to learn what order or system is used in its construction, the third step also involves the making of patterns, this time from groups of sentences. The teacher might say to the students: *Here are some groups of sentences. As they stand, they have no particular pattern. Decide how they could be rearranged so that they are put together in some orderly fashion, not just thrown together. After you have done this, see if you can tell what patterns you have made.*

Allan had developed good study habits.
School counselors found him dependable.
He was at ease in his college interview.
He was accepted at the college of his first choice.
Exams did not make him nervous.
He had two school letters to his credit.

If students can sort the effect out from the list of causes (putting it either first or last in their rearrangement), they have demonstrated that they see the cause-effect relationship of these ideas.

Step 4—The students should now be ready to identify the structure of single paragraphs and to use the pattern to help them understand the author's point. Remembering that mere classification is not the goal, the teacher should make sure at every step to show the students that recognition of pattern helps them to understand and remember. Directions to the students might be as follows: *First, skim quickly through the paragraph to see what kind of pattern it has. Then, read with the pattern in mind. Finally, answer the questions without looking back.*

During the 1830's, with Andrew Jackson in the White House, Oklahoma was made a reservation for Indians. Within fifty years, however, most of the West was settled and white men, hungry for land, wanted to move to Oklahoma. The federal government bought most of this rich territory back from the Indians and announced that set-

tlers could enter April 22, 1889. They gathered in crowds on the border. At noon a bugle blew and people dashed to claim the best lands. On that first day fifty thousand settlers moved into the territory. In one year some towns already had schools, churches, and business establishments.

1. What pattern has the author used?
2. About how long did Oklahoma remain an Indian reservation?
3. What is the main fact about the early settlement of Oklahoma by white men that the author wants to impress upon the reader?

Step 5—A great aid to the quick perception of pattern, and therefore to its maximum use, is understanding of the common words and expressions which authors use as signals to the reader. Some of these signals are obvious and clear. Students glancing through a paragraph or selection containing the following words and phrases should have no difficulty in identifying the basic patterns:

1. To begin with. . . . .
   Next. . . . .
   Not long after. . . . .
   Then. . . . .
   Finally. . . . .
2. One of the. . . . .
   however. . . . .
   In spite of. . . . .
   but. . . . .
   On the other hand. . . . .

Step 6—So far, the students have been asked to deal only with simple paragraphs and they have, hopefully, begun to examine whatever they read for some kind of structure. If they have, they are already noticing that patterns are not always simple and clear and that sometimes there seems to be no pattern at all where there should be one. It is time to discuss the fact that some writers *do* work in a muddled, disorganized way and that to recognize this fact is to begin to read critically. However, what seems muddled at first may be instead only a complex interweaving of different patterns. To develop the ability to follow these more complex patterns is a long task which probably should begin with easy examples, such as may be found in single sentences:

1. The United Kingdom is second to the United States in production of automobiles, trucks, and buses. (*comparison-contrast and simple listing*)
2. There were no horses or cattle in America before the coming of the white man; therefore, man power had to be used for many laborious and time-consuming tasks that later were performed with the help of domestic animals. (*cause-effect and time order*)

Careful analysis of the patterns in a series of sentences like this does as much, perhaps, to help students read accurately as anything the teacher could devise.

The study of mixed patterns within paragraphs is a logical next step. The following is a sample in which the basic cause-effect pattern is combined with listing (of the reasons for the high cost of production of the newspaper):

> Making a city newspaper is a costly operation. A large staff is required to collect local news, to say nothing of the effort and money which go into news reports from outside the immediate vicinity. Large newspapers support their own staffs at points around the world where news is breaking; they also subscribe to news services which give them more complete coverage. Intricate and expensive machinery and highly skilled technicians are involved in the actual printing of a great daily paper. They work at great speed when the news is hot. The price at which papers are sold to readers covers only a tiny fraction of this cost. The real revenue for the typical newspaper comes from the advertisers and is its Achilles heel. Obviously, the paper cannot often publish material which would be offensive to the men who support it. To some degree, at least, the advertisers control the policy of the paper. In this sense, we have, even in America, a press which is not completely free.

Time spent in analyzing the various thought relationships in such a paragraph is time well spent in the interests of accurate reading.

Step 7—So far, the study of pattern may not have seemed exactly practical to the student. He doesn't, in real life, make a practice of analyzing single sentences or even single paragraphs in such detail. The teacher can not begin to show him how his awareness of pattern actually "pays off." The way a student should study a piece of factual material depends on several considerations, the first and most important of which is his purpose. However, another very important factor is the way (the pattern) in which the author has presented the material. The student must learn to react somewhat as follows:

a. In this material, the author is giving me a cause and several effects of that cause. First, I must understand the cause. Then I should try to remember at least some of the effects, not necessarily in the order in which the author has presented them.

or

b. Here I have a time sequence. The easiest thing to do is to keep these facts in this time order because recalling one fact or event will trigger my recall of the next one.

or

c. This passage is based on comparison and contrast. I'll do well to concentrate on likenesses and differences.

and so on.

Most students—we hope—are familiar with some form of the SQ3R method of study. If they are young students, in junior high school, they may have met only the teacher-directed form of this study technique, the form we often call the "directed reading lesson." In any case, it is not difficult to show students how they may, as a part of the S step, learn to identify the basic pattern of what they are about to read *before* they start to read. To do this, we must give them experiences in skimming for the clues. There is no need to go outside their regular textbooks for examples. Indeed, the more often this kind of experience is related to their own texts and their daily work, the more meaningful it seems. Almost any section of material in a well-written social studies text will serve. For example, here are some of the clues from one such section:[1]

—Several conditions favored industrialization .... a number of factors combined ....
—One important factor .... supply of natural resources ....
—Another condition .... a large labor force ....
—Resources and an ample labor supply were organized by businessmen ....
—Businessmen would not have made goods unless there was a demand ....
from several sources ....

And so on. The first two words of the section (Several conditions...) alert the reader to a probable listing of these "conditions." And a small amount of skimming confirms this conclusion. The good student says to himself: *All right. I have a simple list here. Since it's just a list, it doesn't matter whether I try to remember it in the order in which the author has given it to me, but I'd better review after I finish my study to see whether I can recall all the important items in the list. As I study, I'll make note of how many important parts there are in the list.*

A second example is from another section of the same text[2] and represents a very frequent pattern in social studies material. As the student skims, he picks up these clues:

—When the new American nation came into being ....
—........... in 1796 and 1803 ......
—By 1830 ....
—During the next few decades ....
—........... in 1860.
—........... war that followed lasted from 1861 to 1865 ....

The student should conclude: *This information is in time order. I will recall the facts more easily if I note them in this order as I read and then review them in the same way.*

Step 8—Some patterns in factual writing are complex enough so that they do not yield to the analysis possible in quick skimming. The student must learn to unravel these combinations by a process of self-questioning as he proceeds through the material.

To illustrate this technique, the following section of a text[3] is reproduced in full with the insertion of the kind of "thinking question" that focuses attention on organization and on the way in which organization can contribute both to initial understanding and to recall:

> The three greatest Greek philosophers were Socrates, Plato, and Aristotle. (*What do I suspect may be the pattern of this section? If I am right, how should I study it?*) Socrates, who lived in the 5th century B.C., was known to his fellow Athenians as "the gadfly" because his persistent questioning of all ideas and actions stung his listeners into thinking. In fact, the so-called Socratic method consisted of asking questions in an attempt to arrive at truth. Socrates might begin a session by posing the question, "What is the beautiful and what the ugly?" Each response would be questioned and further questions would be posed until agreement had been reached by the participants about the precise definitions of the terms being discussed. Socrates' advice to everyone was to "know thyself."
>
> Some Athenians believed that Socrates was an immoral influence on his students be-

[1] T. Walter Wallbank and Arnold Schrier, *Living World History* (Scott, Foresman and Company, 1964).
[2] *Ibid.*, p. 513.

[3] *Ibid.*, pp. 82–86.

cause he encouraged young men to question practices of all kinds. His questioning the acts of Athenian leaders led them to place Socrates on trial, charging that he was corrupting the youth of the city. He was sentenced to death and required to drink hemlock, a poison. Socrates accepted the verdict calmly; though his friends urged him to escape, he refused because he insisted that men must obey the laws of the state. *(What other patterns are in this paragraph? What cause-effect relationships are pointed out?)*

The most notable of Socrates' pupils was Plato, who lived from 430 to 347 B.C. *(What additional time order is now apparent?)* He established the Academy in Athens, a famous school which existed for almost nine centuries. His most famous work, *The Republic*, describes an imaginary land in which each man does the work for which he is best fitted. Plato believed that there should be three classes of people: the workers to produce the necessities of life, the soldiers to guard the state, and the philosophers to rule in the interests of all. *(Stop right here! What will help me remember this?)* Private property was to be abolished and education was designed for the benefit of the rulers. Though Plato's ideas of communal life and a rigid class system seem harsh and akin to Spartan ideas, *The Republic* is an important work because it represents man's first attempt to devise a planned society.

Plato's most famous student was the 4th century philosopher, Aristotle. *(Am I sure now that the time-order pattern within the listening pattern is actually here?)* He was a brilliant thinker whose interests ranged widely. He wrote treatises in biology, astronomy, physics, ethics, and politics. His most important work consisted of studies in logic. It was Aristotle who devised the *syllogism* which consists of three propositions. If the major and minor premises are valid and related logically, the third proposition, or conclusion, inevitably follows. For example, (1) all Greeks are human; (2) Aristotle is a Greek; (3) therefore, Aristotle is human.

Like most Athenians, Aristotle believed that a person could be happy if he were mod-erate in most things. It is desirable, he felt, for all men to strike a balance between rash action and inactivity; to live between two extremes by following the Doctrine of the Mean. The best way to meet danger, for example, is through courageous action, which is the mean between foolhardiness and cowardice. In his *Politics*, Aristotle discussed the good and bad features of different kinds of governments: monarchy, aristocracy, democracy. Unlike Plato, *(Here is another clue. How should I read this next part?)* he did not describe an imaginary state nor did he find a single system ideal. *Politics* serves to point out a significant difference between the two philosophers. Where Plato often appears to deal only with abstract ideas, Aristotle seems more down-to-earth, viewing men and things in a realistic fashion.

Two important schools of Greek philosophy arose in the Hellenistic Age: Epicureanism and Stoicism. *(Does this paragraph add something which was not anticipated earlier? If so, what? If there were two "schools," they must represent two ways of thinking. What kind of pattern should I anticipate?)* The first was developed by Epicurus of Samos who maintained that a temperate life was best for reducing pain and increasing pleasure. Some of his followers misunderstood his emphasis upon pleasure, thinking he meant that one should live only to eat, drink, and be merry. Thus Epicureanism is often misinterpreted in spite of its founder's emphasis upon mental activity as a way of gaining inner peace. Zeno of Cyprus developed the system of Stoicism. Zeno taught that true happiness, or inner peace, can be achieved by man when he finds his proper place in nature. His followers were called *Stoics*, because they usually met on a *stoa*, or porch. Believing all nature to be good, the Stoics maintained that man must accept poverty, disease, or even death as the will of God. This philosophy led them to develop an indifference toward all kinds of experience, good or bad. Today the word *stoic* describes a person who does not show his feelings or emotions. *(Was I right in anticipating a contrast? If so, what were the points of contrast? Since this section of my text is basically a combination of simple listing*

*and time order, what will be the best pro-
cedure for reviewing the facts so that they
will stick in my mind?)*

Obviously, one or two experiences with
this kind of analytical reading would not produce the lasting results we want. Obviously,
also, the whole process would have its optimum effect on the students' study habits if it
were carried out, not as an exercise in a reading class, but as a part of the regular teaching
in content area classes where the material
used could be a section of the text assigned
for the next day's lesson. Students may be
bored, even resentful, of this process which,
in the beginning, is slow, perhaps even laborious. But when it is a part of work they know
they have to do anyway, and when they see
how much more completely they can recall
facts they know they have to recall, the walls
of opposition fall with a resounding crash.

The limitations of this paper do not permit
a similar analysis of the study of organization
in imaginative writing, which has many patterns of its own, patterns which occur in
almost infinite variety.

RESPONSIBILITY FOR TEACHING PATTERNS

Perhaps there is less need for teachers of
reading to be concerned about the procedures
for teaching these literary patterns since they
are generally accepted by English teachers as
their "business," whereas the patterns in factual writing are so often ignored by all teachers. Awareness of literary patterns, it should
be pointed out, has its only true value for the
student if he sees the connection between
form and meaning or sensory effect. Students
learn to analyze the flashback and to recognize it as a special kind of time order, but the
important consideration is what this variation
in a basic pattern contributes to the particular narrative involved. Many a student knows
a poem is a sonnet because it has fourteen
lines and a certain meter and rhyme scheme,
but he may never have understood the reason
why such a pattern is more effective for *this*

idea in *this* poem than, let's say, a series of
ballad stanzas.

There has been, in recent years, a trend
away from the study of literary form with
secondary school students. Collections of material organized according to structure have
tended to give way to collections organized
by theme. The pros and cons of this matter
have been fully debated elsewhere. Suffice
it to say here that students in secondary
school do need to study form in literature but
that the effectiveness of this study is dependent upon students' seeing the relationship of
form to idea and emotional impact.

Secondary school reading teachers work
under a very severe handicap in their instruction in any of the skills. No matter how hard
they try to relate what they are teaching to
the practical demands of their students' daily
study, they have great difficulty in doing so.
Unfortunately, reading teachers and content
teachers too often try to work in contiguous
rather than overlapping territories. Indeed,
there is often a high board fence between the
two. Until this fence is demolished, no completely effective teaching of any of the skills
can take place.

At present, most of us are trying to poke
any kind of hole in the fence that we can,
and we are working from both sides. We are
encouraging reading teachers to abandon, at
least part of the time, their carefully prepared
published materials for teaching reading skills
and to work more and more frequently with
the students' regular content textbooks. Only
the best of these reading teachers can do this,
for there are few guidelines and they must
devise their own lessons almost from the
start. All this takes time and a good deal of
know-how.

We are also trying to persuade teachers of
content subjects to shoulder more of the responsibility for teaching specific study skills.
This they are increasingly willing to do if
they can be shown how and if they can do
the job in connection with, not in addition to,

their teaching of the content of their courses. This, then, is the challenge and it points directly to the acute need for both pre-service and in-service education of secondary teachers in methods of teaching reading and study skills. It is completely unfair to criticize them for not doing what they have never been shown how to do.

Before the content teacher can help his students to perceive and to use organization in their study of factual materials, the teacher himself must understand its value and must be aware at least of the basic patterns. With this much background, he can be of great assistance to his students in several ways:

First, judicious questioning. He can ask the kind of questions which will encourage students to pay attention to the structure of what they have read. For example, if an author has used a cause-effect relationship, the teacher can devise questions which force the students to use this relationship in their answers. If they fail to do so, the teacher can take them back into the text to see what they have missed. Carefully planned questioning is a very effective technique for calling attention to different ways of thinking and writing. Compare, for example, the two sets of questions which relate to the following excerpt:[4]

> It has been said that the American Revolution really began when the first Englishman set foot on the soil of the New World. Certain conditions in America tended almost from the beginning to separate the colonists from their mother country.
>
> To begin with, a new national type—the American—was created. Society in the New World differed from that in Europe. Social position and wealth counted for less. The opportunities for ambitious people to better themselves were greater, since the availability of cheap land enabled almost everyone to own some property. The rough life of the frontier added another new element.

[4] *Ibid.*, pp. 400–401.

Englishmen became more self-sufficient, less inclined to follow tradition. The population differed not only because of changes among the English immigrants, but also because of the presence of other nationalities. Many hundreds of adventurous settlers emigrated from Scotland, Germany, the Netherlands, France, and Ireland.

Another factor that helped set the American colonies apart was the growth of democratic ideals. When settlers crossed the Atlantic, they carried with them the ideas of the Puritan Revolution. For example, thousands of Puritans who opposed the tyranny of Charles I moved to Massachusetts; as a result, many New Englanders were familiar with John Locke and his social contract theory.

Another important difference involved government. The American colonists enjoyed more self-government than any other colonists in the world. Every colony had a representative assembly of colonists. The first of these assemblies, the Virginia House of Burgesses, was established as early as 1619. Like their ancestors in England, colonial lawmakers soon discovered "the power of the purse." They exerted pressure on the royal governor by threatening to withhold funds. Local affairs, such as road building and repair and the enforcement of laws, were in the hands of the colonists themselves.

SET I
1. When according to this author, did the American Revolution begin?
2. Why could people in America get ahead at a fast pace?
3. How did the Puritan Revolution in England affect life in America?
4. How could early American colonists get things they wanted from their royal governors?

SET II
1. What, in general, is this section about? (This kind of question forces attention to the overall listing organization. It calls attention also to the main idea.)
2. What means does the author use to make the reader realize some of the characteristics of these early Americans? (This question requires thought about the contrasts which are brought out.)

3. How did the new Americans differ from Englishmen in the old country? (Now we are asking for details of the contrast.)
4. Why does the author say that the American Revolution began when the first Englishman set foot in the New World? (The student must recognize and use a cause-effect relationship.)

Probably Set I is fairly typical of questions most teachers would ask on this passage; it tests the students' grasp of important facts. Set II also tests knowledge of facts, but it does more than this. It gives students conscious practice in using organizational skills.

Second, survey the material. The content teacher can survey the new lesson in the textbook *with* his class, calling attention, either directly or through questions, to the organization of the material they are about to study. He can teach them to use textbook headings effectively and to realize that these headings often constitute a fairly good outline of the content. He can alert them to typical words and phrases which offer clues to different types of organization. He can ask them to anticipate from the clues "what this will probably be about": a list of . . . .; a comparison between . . . .; a story in time order of how . . . . happened, etc. At first, he should go through the lesson in his own copy of the text underlining these key words and phrases because he will have to say very often: *Notice this. To what does it alert you? What do you expect to find? If the author is giving you a cause-effect presentation, what will be the best way for you to study it?* Later, he will be able to draw more of this anticipatory response from students themselves.

Third, reading to students. The content teacher can read current materials *to* students, pausing at strategic points to ask anticipatory questions and focus attention on structure. Many teachers do not realize that reading skills and listening skills are almost identical and that through listening students can get basic ideas about pattern without having to read for themselves and also with the aid of the teacher's inflections and emphasis. This may be a particularly effective approach with groups of poor readers.

The science teacher, particularly, must depend on current materials if he is to operate anywhere near the "growing edge" of his rapidly expanding field. His textbooks are obsolescent before the ink in them is dry. Furthermore, his students are learning, or half-learning, so much from TV and other sources that they demand the new and current. Yet, there is often only one copy of this up-to-date information. The science teacher can supply this and concurrently give his class experience in thoughtful and orderly listening by reading to the class and teaching them to think as they listen.

The following[5] illustrates this process. The teacher's anticipatory questions are inserted in parenthesis:

In the stillness of a hospital room, a beam of silent sound probes deeply into a man's inner organs. Harmless ultrasonic waves can now be directed by a new medical instrument toward specific arteries supplying deep-lying organs such as the kidney, liver or brain.

Scientists have only recently begun to understand the power of this ultrasonic energy and to channel it into applied uses. *(What do you think the author will probably give us next?)* There is the dog whistle that is inaudible to human ears but brings dogs running. Underwater sonar systems and supersonic air missiles were used during World War II.

Dirt and scum can now be washed, or vibrated, clean from objects as modern as missile assemblies and engines, or as ancient as some 200 million-year-old marine fossils.

In industry, radioactive fuel elements can be tested, metals can be welded without fusion or soldered without flux, and flaws

[5] Condensed from Barbara Tufty, "*Silent Sound Works Wonders,*" *Science News Letter,* Vol. 83, No. 15, April 13, 1963, 234–235.

can be detected in solids or contaminants in liquids.

The thickness of a live hog's backfat can be measured by the echoes of ultrasonic vibrations, and insects might be controlled by raising the intensity of sound so high as to kill or repulse them.

In empty warehouses, a creeping burglar can be detected by the change he brings about in the pitch of the ultrasonic wave echoes.

When a liquid is agitated with vibrations higher than the human ear can hear, scientists have found that a remarkable cleaning effect is created that lifts dirt from all surfaces in a matter of seconds.

This is the way it works: *(In what order do you think the author will probably tell us how it works?)*

Every liquid contains thousands of bubbles ranging in size from those visible to the naked eye to those that are submicroscopic. As this liquid is agitated by mechanical vibrations, these bubbles are compressed, agitated and collapsed, generating forces of 15,000 or more pounds per square inch at the center of implosion.

This exploding force and pulsating action of bubbles act like countless tiny fingers, reaching into otherwise impenetrable crevices, blind holes, and scrubbing under the film of dirt, grease or scum to separate it from the surface.

With this method, contaminants can be lifted from surfaces of small precision parts at a rate unattainable before. *(Does this phrase "unattainable before" give us a clue as to the way the author has written the rest of her article?)* and to a degree of cleanliness that usually surpasses the most stringent industrial standard. Ball bearings, electric shaving heads, valves, tubing, wire mesh and countless other objects can be cleaned without having to take them apart or without their being touched by conventional cleaning materials.

In atomic power plants, radioactive materials and scale can be removed from fuel rods and control rods. Before the development of ultrasonic cleaners, jet-engine nozzles and oil filters had to be thrown away when dirty. The ancient art of welding met-

als has also been modernized by ultrasonic science. Without the use of heat, two metals can now be rubbed and vibrated together with such force that they exceed their natural rigidity and flow together to form a permanently welded piece.

Railroad tracks can be tested for deep flaws, as well as generators, or the wings and struts of a plane or the girders of a bridge.

By sending a vibrating ultrasonic wave through the material to be tested, scientists can spot a change of metal structure by a change in the velocity of the wave and its echo. The short ultrasonic wave lengths indicate these flaws in greater detail than formerly could be seen. *(List some of the applied uses of ultrasonic energy. What are the steps in cleaning with "sound"? Compare the older process of welding with the new method.)*

Fourth, use of visual aids. The content teacher can use modern visual devices, particularly the new projectors, to demonstrate for students the structure of what they are reading and illustrate authors' devices for making the pattern or structure clear. Imagine the science teacher, for example, projecting a page or two of his text and with overlays or other devices, perhaps in color, pointing out for students the key words and sentences which form the pattern of the material.

Imagine, also, the English teacher projecting such lines of poetry as these from Matthew Arnold's "Dover Beach" with extra spacing to show the tempo of the lines—the long caesura and the quick rush of the following phrases. In print, this is difficult to show—with a free-flow pen and a little ability to do manuscript lettering, it would be easy.

Listen!   you hear the grating roar
Of pebbles which the waves draw back,
          and fling
At their return, up the high strand,
Begin,   and cease,   and then
     again begin,
With tremulous cadence slow,   and
     bring
The eternal note of sadness in.

Imagine, also, what might be done with color to emphasize the effect of alliteration or assonance or metrical pattern. The possibilities in modern projection for dramatizing pattern and structure have yet to be explored.

Fifth, notes and outlines. The content teacher can show students how to do informal notetaking and outlining. Good notes reflect patterns and form. Again, imagine the help of the new projectors. Students are presented with material to analyze and outline. They work for a few moments on their own. The teacher turns on the projector and, before their eyes, produces informal notes or an outline based on the same material with which the students have worked. There is comment and discussion, a chance to disagree. Off goes the projector, and the students work on another short section. This kind of teaching has all the advantages of the immediate feedback in programmed instruction but retains the flexibility of class discussion.

SUMMARY

These, then, are some of the techniques that might be used to insure the transfer of basic skills taught initially, perhaps, in reading classes to the kind of situation in content classes which students recognize as "the real thing."

All except extremely handicapped students at the secondary level can grasp isolated facts in what they read. But this shotgun kind of reading is often little better than mere verbalism. It is the relationship of each fact or idea to other facts and ideas that really matters.

Once more, imagine a situation that is more typical than most English teachers would like to admit. The class is reporting on outside reading, and the teacher says: *John, it's your turn to tell about your book.*

And John begins: *Well, this book is about a fellow named Bill. He was exploring in* South America, but he got lost. But before that, he had a fight with a big snake. You see he went to South America on the spur of the moment and he didn't take the right equipment. So when the snake came for him, he was unprotected. But anyway, he was very brave. . . .

If the teacher had only said: *John, we've been talking about bravery. In the book you read, what examples of bravery did you find?*

or

Select the one most exciting incident in the story. Tell just this one incident keeping the events in the order in which they happened.

or

You read a biography, didn't you? What effects can you list of the early life of the person you read about upon his later career?

or

We have just finished reading together. . . . Compare your story with the one we all know about.

High school students need this kind of guidance in perceiving and using organization. They must learn how to discipline their thinking, how to submit their minds to the will of the author and follow his pattern of thought, and they must learn how to make their *own* patterns.

To be sure, there is more to mature reading than this, and many secondary school students are capable of reading on very advanced levels. But the "higher" reading skills, both critical and creative, will be fully achieved only when the student is capable, first, of systematic comprehension and orderly recall of what the author has said.

BIBLIOGRAPHY

CENTER, STELLA S., and PERSONS, GLADYS L. *Problems in Reading and Thinking.* New York: Macmillan, 1940.

GAINSBURG, JOSEPH C. *Advanced Skills in Reading, Books 1 and 2.* New York: Macmillan, 1962.

NILES, OLIVE S., et al. *Tactics in Reading II.* New York: Scott, Foresman, 1964.

PAUK, WALTER. *How to Study in College*. Massachusetts: Houghton Mifflin, 1962.

ROBINSON, FRANCIS P. *Effective Reading*. New York: Harper, 1962.

SCHLEICH, MIRIAM. "Improving Reading Through the Language Arts: In Grades Nine Through Fourteen," *Reading and the Language Arts*, Reading Conference Proceedings, H. A. ROBINSON, ed., Vol. XXV. Chicago: University of Chicago Press, 1963, 37–41.

SHAW, PHILLIP. "Rhetorical Guides to Reading Comprehension," *The Reading Teacher*, XI (April 1958), 239–243.

STEGNER, WALLACE E., *et al. Modern Composition, Book 3*. New York: Holt, Rinehart and Winston, 1964.

A DEFINITION OF CRITICAL THINKING
Robert H. Ennis

As a root notion, critical thinking is here taken to mean the correct assessing of statements. This basic notion was suggested by B. Othanel Smith (*3*)*: "Now if we set about to find out what . . . [a] statement means and to determine whether to accept or reject it, we would be engaged in thinking which, for lack of a better term, we shall call critical thinking." Since Smith's definition does not use any words like "correct," his notion is slightly different. Smith's concept of critical thinking, however, permits us to speak of "good critical thinking" and "poor critical thinking" without redundance or contradiction. Though this is an accepted manner of speaking, the predominant manner of speaking presumably builds the notion of correct thinking into the notion of critical thinking. Though the latter interpretation is used in this paper, it would be easy to restructure what follows and use Smith's concept. "Good critical thinking" in Smith's sense means the same as "critical thinking" as used in this paper.

Reprinted from *The Reading Teacher*, XVII (May 1964), 599–612, with permission of the author and International Reading Association.

[*Numbers in parentheses refer to Bibliography at the end of this article.]

Since there are various kinds of statements, various relations between statements and their grounds, and various stages in the process of assessment, we can expect that there will be various ways of going wrong when one attempts to think critically. In view of this fact, the aspects of critical thinking about to be presented, which may be looked upon as specific ways to avoid the pitfalls in assessment, are bound to make a rather heterogeneous list.

This list and the accompanying criteria for judging statements are based in a large part upon a study of the literature in education, philosophy, and psychology.† The list of critical thinking aspects is also based upon an analysis of a number of specimens of alleged justifications of statements, and a consequent realization of the places where these justifications can go wrong. One may look upon this list as a statement of a number of items

† References that were of help can be found in Robert H. Ennis, "A Concept of Critical Thinking," *Harvard Educational Review*, 32 (Winter, 1962), 81–111; the present article is a streamlined version of that article. The theoretical analysis of critical thinking and the proposals for needed research in that article also have been omitted here. The latter feature is expanded in an article entitled "Needed: Research in Critical Thinking," *Educational Leadership*, October 1963.

that, if taught to students, will result in a greater likelihood that they will be critical thinkers. Further refinement of this list is a continuing task, and of course much remains to be done.

MAJOR ASPECTS OF CRITICAL THINKING

A critical thinker is characterized by proficiency in judging whether:

1. A statement follows from the premises.
2. Something is an assumption.
3. An observation statement is reliable.
4. A simple generalization is warranted.
5. A hypothesis is warranted.
6. A theory is warranted.
7. An argument depends on an ambiguity.
8. A statement is overvague or overspecific.
9. An alleged authority is reliable.

Although the root notion calls for its inclusion, the judging of value statements is deliberately excluded from the above list. This exclusion admittedly weakens the attractiveness of the list, but makes the job more manageable. So long as we remember that this exclusion has occurred, we should not be confused by the truncated concept. Perhaps this gap can at some future time be at least partially filled.

The exclusion of other important kinds of thinking (creative thinking, for example) from this basic concept of critical thinking does not imply that the others are unimportant, nor does it imply that they are separable from it in practice. This exclusion is simply the result of an attempt to focus attention on one important kind of thinking.

Another aspect which has deliberately been excluded from the list is proficiency in judging whether a problem has been identified. This is excluded not because it is unimportant, but because it resolves into one or another of the items on the list (or the judging of value statements) in each of the various

meanings of "identifying a problem." This point will be developed later.

Each of the listed aspects of critical thinking will be examined and, if possible, criteria will be presented, clarified, and, when it seems necessary, at least partially justified.

1. JUDGING WHETHER A STATEMENT FOLLOWS FROM THE PREMISES

The concern of most logic books is with whether a statement follows *necessarily* from the premises. This is the judging of deduction. Reasoning in mathematics, "if-then" reasoning, and syllogistic reasoning all exemplify deduction.

The basic criterion is this: "A conclusion follows necessarily if its denial contradicts the assertion of the premises." Various rules have been developed for different types of deduction, but all see to it that this requirement is fulfilled. Well-developed sets of rules include:

1.1 The rules for handling equations and inequalities.
1.2 The rules of "if-then" reasoning:
    1.21 Denial of the "then-part" requires denial of the "if-part," but not necessarily vice versa.
    1.22 Acceptance of the "if-part" requires acceptance of the "then-part," but not necessarily vice-versa.
    1.23 Instances of an "if-then" statement are implied by the "if-then" statement.
1.3 The rules for categorical reasoning. These rules may be summarized by the following: "Whatever is a member of a general class is also a member of whatever that general class is included in, and is not a member of whatever the general class is excluded from."

A number of cases of reasoning are parallel to strict deduction, but are different in that the generalizations in use as premises do not hold universally under any conceivable circumstance; they have exceptions and limits, not all of which can be specified. To extend Waisman's term (5), they are "open-textured." Reasoning from principles and hypotheses to the world of things, men, and events is inevitably of this sort. Sometimes the exceptions and limits are so far removed that we do not have to worry about them, and in such cases we can proceed as in deduction without fear of going wrong. Sometimes the limits and exceptions are close by, in which case, still approximating the deductive model, we use words like "probable," "likely," "barring unforeseen circumstances," etc., in the conclusion.

For an example of the latter case, consider the application of that standard law of economics, "If the supply is constant and the demand for a product decreases, the price will decrease." Two of the limits of the application of this law are within the knowledge of all of us. It is intended to apply to an economy free of government control and to a sector of it that is free of monopolistic control. Mention of these limits will suffice for present purposes, although there are others.

Now let us apply this law to a situation in which there is a decrease in demand for microscopes. Applying the law deductively, we are unalterably committed to a prediction of a price decrease. But it is not wise to be unalterably committed to such a prediction. For one thing, the well-known limits of the law might be breached: the government might decide to maintain the price of microscopes and pay for the destruction of the extras; or a monopoly might be formed to maintain the price.

But secondly, other things that are not yet explicitly built into the limits might go wrong. The makers of microscopes might form a trade association and decide incorrectly that with good advertising they *can* create a demand much greater than ever before, so that they can afford to raise prices. They therefore raise prices in anticipation of a nonexistent demand.

It is because of considerations like these that qualifiers like "probable" must be included in the application of many principles. The application of that law in that situation might be, "It is probable that there will be a lowering of price." But the application would not be this at all if it can be seen that a known limit is breached or that there is some other extenuating circumstance. The point is that the application of such principles should often not be stated any more strongly than this, even though the steps in reasoning parallel those of deduction.

Thus there are two kinds of following: strict necessity and loose following. The critical thinker can do both.

2. Judging Whether Something Is an Assumption

This topic is complicated because there are various logically-different abilities that go under this title. These can be best approached through an examination of various uses of the word "assumption": the deprecatory use, the concluding use, the premise use, and the presupposition use.

2.1 *The deprecatory use and the concluding use.* The deprecatory use implies the charge that there is little or no evidence to support a given belief and that the belief is questionable. Here is an example: "You're just assuming that Frank didn't read the assignment." This deprecatory use is often found to be incorporated in the other uses, but sometimes it stands alone. As such its appearance is tantamount to a judgment that the view should perhaps be rejected, or at least be held in abeyance because of lack of support. No further discussion of the evaluation of this kind of assumption-claim is necessary here, since this is a general charge and is covered under discussion of the various other abilities.

In the concluding use, the term "assumption" is used to mark a conclusion, but the deprecatory use is involved too, since the conclusion is implied not to be fully established. Here is an example: "My assumption is that Hissarlik is at the site of Troy" (a statement made at the completion of a presentation of the evidence bearing on the location of Troy). We need not be concerned with discussing whether something is an assumption in the concluding sense; the important question is whether such an assumption is justified and that question is covered elsewhere in this paper.

The first two uses of "assumption" were specified in order to keep them out of the discussion of the next two; the following discussion does not apply to them.

2.2 *The premise use.* This kind of assumption stands anterior to a conclusion in a line of reasoning, whether the conclusion be inductive or deductive. To call something an assumption is to say that the conclusion depends upon it, and that if the conclusion is to be accepted, the alleged assumption should also be accepted. Thus the location of assumptions (in this sense) is a useful step in the evaluation of conclusions.

Here are criteria for premise-type assumptions:

2.21 Of the various possible gap-fillers, the alleged assumption should come closest to making the completed argument, proof, or explanation, a satisfactory one. (This criterion is necessary and sufficient.)

 2.211 The simplest gap-filler is ordinarily the one to choose.

 2.212 If there is a more plausible gap-filler among the more complex ones, it should be chosen. Plausibility, however, requires fitting in with existing knowledge—not being a special case.

2.22 Other conditions remaining the same, the state of affairs that is predicted could not occur (or probably would not occur) if the alleged assumption were false. (This criterion applies only to alleged empirically-necessary assumptions, but for them it is necessary and sufficient.)

2.23 The community of experts in the field would not accept the position, conclusion, or argument without first believing the assumption to be true. (This criterion is neither necessary nor sufficient, but is a good ground.)

What is a gap-filler? Consider this piece of reasoning: "Since the demand for microscopes has decreased, the price may be expected to decrease." A gap-filler here would be:

1. When the demand for a commodity decreases, the price will decrease. (It fills a gap in reasoning from the decrease in demand for microscopes to a decrease in price.)

It is not the only way to fill the gap, however. Consider these alternatives:

2. When the demand for goods and services decreases, the price decreases.

3. When the demand for optical instruments decreases, the price decreases.

4. When the demand for optical instruments (other than field glasses) decreases, the price decreases.

Since all four of these will fill the gap, it should be clear that being a gap-filler is not by itself a sufficient condition for being an assumption. The simplest gap-filler is ordinarily the one to attribute, thus ruling out No. 4. Simplicity might also be a ground for not accepting No. 2 as the assumption, since there is a conjunction of two things (goods and services) mentioned. But if the prevailing knowledge in economics admits no basis for distinguishing goods from services in the context of this principle, then simplicity is counterbalanced by the need to fit into existing knowledge. The first two gap-fillers would then be equally defensible (or indefensible) and either could be called the assumption.

Gap-filler No. 3 introduces a new twist, talking only about optical instruments. It is as simple as No. 1 but is not as general. Other things being equal, generality is to be preferred. A system of knowledge is better if it covers more cases. But if the more general gap-filler, No. 1, should be false, and the less general one, No. 3, true (or more likely to be true), the less general gap-filler is the one to choose.

Assumption-finding then is the locating of a gap-filler, the simpler the better, provided that it fits into and contributes to a system of knowledge. The assumption-finder should try to be generous to the person whose assumptions he is locating, generous in that he should try to find the best candidate for participation in a knowledge system. He should not accept a false gap-filler as the assumption until he has searched for one that fits into an acceptable body of knowledge. Put more simply in a way that covers most cases, he should search for one that is true.

While discussing gap-filling it would be well to note that there is one sometimes used criterion that is inapplicable: *logical* necessity. As exemplified by the four gap-fillers previously discussed, there is no single significant premise-type gap-filler which is logically necessary. It is always *logically* possible (though it may be extremely implausible) to complete an argument in more than one way, a point I have developed elsewhere (*2*).

Empirical necessity, 2.22, is different. To the extent that empirical statements can be necessary, there can be empirically necessary assumptions. For example, a statement which predicts that the pressure in a fixed cylinder of confined air will increase is assuming that there will be a temperature increase. Since an increase in temperature in that situation *is* necessary for there to be an increase in pressure, the assumption is empirically necessary and can be pinned on the argument with confidence.

Criterion 2.23 mentions the experts. Although their considered opinions can be wrong, they do ordinarily know what fits into their body of knowledge. And they do know what is used successfully in the field to back up arguments and conclusions. So they can ordinarily be expected to know what an argument would need in order to be a good one.

2.3 *The presupposition use.* Presuppositions are sentences which must be true for a given statement even to make sense. This is the meaning of the term "presupposition" presented by P. F. Strawson (*4*). The claim, "The governor's mistakes have caused our present plight," presupposes that the governor has made mistakes. His not having done so would make nonsense out of either the affirmation or denial of the claim. If the governor has made no mistakes, it does not even make sense to say that his mistakes have caused our plight; nor does it make sense to say that his mistakes have not caused our plight.

Presupposition-finding is useful in avoiding being swayed by false presuppositions (if the governor has made no mistakes, we should be able to react to the presupposition that he has). And presupposition-finding is useful in grasping a verbal picture, and a part or the whole of a theory.

Judging whether something is presupposed by something else is simply a matter of stating the meaning of the "something else."

3. Judging Whether an Observation Statement Is Reliable

An observation statement is a specific description. Over the years, those fields most concerned with accuracy of observation have built up a set of rules for judging the reliability of observation statements. Here is a combined list of principles from the fields of law, history, and science:

3.1 Observation statements tend to be more reliable if the *observer:*

    3.11 Was unemotional, alert, and disinterested.

    3.12 Was skilled at observing the sort of thing observed.

    3.13 Had sensory equipment that was in good condition.

    3.14 Has a reputation for veracity.

    3.15 Used precise techniques.

    3.16 Had no preconception about the way the observation would turn out.

3.2 Observation statements tend to be more reliable if the *observation conditions:*

    3.21 Were such that the observer had good access.

    3.22 Provided a satisfactory medium of observation.

3.3 Observation statements tend to be more reliable to the extent that the *statement:*

    3.31 Is close to being a statement of direct observation.

    3.32 Is corroborated.

    3.33 Is corroboratable.

    3.34 Comes from a disinterested source with a reputation for veracity.

3.4 Observation statements, if based on a record, tend to be more reliable if the *record:*

    3.41 Was made at the time of observation.

    3.42 Was made by the person making the statement.

    3.43 Is believed by the person making the statement to be correct— either because he so believed at the time the record was made, or because he believes it was the record-maker's habit to make correct records.

3.5 Observation statements tend to be more reliable than inferences made from them.

4. JUDGING WHETHER A SIMPLE GENERALIZATION IS WARRANTED

A simple generalization is a statement which covers a number of instances and holds that they share some trait. For example, that red-headed people tend to have hot tempers is a generalization. It holds that red-headed people share the trait of tending to have hot tempers. A generalization is warranted:

4.1 To the extent that there is a bulk of reliable instances of it. The greater the variability of the population, the greater the bulk needed.

4.2 To the extent that it fits into the larger structure of knowledge.

4.3 To the extent that the selecting of instances is unbiased.

    4.31 A pure random sample is unbiased.

    4.32 A systematic sample is unbiased if a careful investigation suggests that there is not a relevant cycle or trend followed by the sampling procedure.

    4.33 Stratification of a population on relevant variables and unbiased sampling within the strata, is likely to be more efficient than 4.31 or 4.32 alone.

    4.34 An unbiased sampling of clusters of the population and unbiased sampling (or complete enumeration) within the clusters is likely to be an efficient way of sampling when access to separate individual units is difficult.

4.4 To the extent that there are no counter-instances.

The generalization that red-headed people tend to have hot tempers would be warranted to the extent that there is a large number of reliable instances of red-heads with hot tempers, to the extent that we are able to account for red-heads being hot-tempered, to the extent that our instances of red-heads are picked without bias, and to the extent that there is a lack of reliable instances of red-heads with even tempers.

5. Judging Whether a Hypothesis Is Warranted

Though the word "hypothesis" is often used to refer to a simple generalization, for purposes of marking off an important kind of statement which has a different relationship to its grounds than a simple generalization I will restrict the word "hypothesis" to the job of referring to this other kind of statement. Under this usage a hypothesis is a statement which is fairly directly related to its support by virtue of its power to *explain* this support, rather than being related by virtue of the support's being composed of instances of the hypothesis, as is the case for simple generalizations.

The hypothesis can be either specific (as is the case in law and usually in history) or it can be general (as is ordinarily the case in physical sciences and the social sciences of economics, sociology, and psychology).

Here is an example of a specific hypothesis: "Hissarlik is located at the site of Troy."

Here is an example of a general hypothesis: "The pressure in a liquid varies directly as the depth, assuming the pressure at the surface to be zero."

A hypothesis is warranted to the extent that:

5.1 It explains a bulk and variety of reliable data. If a datum is explained, it can be deduced or loosely derived (in the fashion of the application of principles) from the hypothesis together with established facts or generalizations.

5.2 It is itself explained by a satisfactory system of knowledge.

5.3 It is not inconsistent with any evidence.

5.4 Its competitors are inconsistent with the evidence. This principle is the basis of controlled experiments.

5.5 It is testable. It must be, or have been, possible to make predictions from it.

For purposes of illustration let us consider the bearing of each of the criteria on each hypothesis of the above two examples of hypotheses:

Explaining a bulk and variety of reliable data, 5.1. Since Hissarlik is only an hour's walk from the sea, the Hissarlik hypothesis explains the reported (in the *Iliad*) ability of the Greeks to go back and forth from Troy several times a day. It explains why there are ruins at Hissarlik. These explained reports, it should be noted, can be derived from the Hissarlik hypotheses together with established facts or generalizations:

Hissarlik is at the site of Troy.
Hissarlik is one hour's walk from the sea.
People are able to walk back and forth several times a day between places that are one hour's walk apart.
Therefore it is probable that the Greeks were able to go back and forth from Troy to the sea several times daily (the explained fact).

Hissarlik is at the site of Troy.
A large city when abandoned tends to leave ruins.
Therefore it is probable that there are ruins at Hissarlik (the explained fact).

Of course explaining only those two pieces of evidence is not enough to establish the hypothesis. More evidence of different types must be provided.

The pressure hypothesis explains why water spurts farther from a hole near the bottom of a tank than from a hole in the middle of a tank. It also explains the proportional relationships between the following sets of readings of pressure gauges attached to the supply tank in a water system:

Distance from Top of Tank (in ft.)	Pressure Reading (in lbs./sq. in.)
0	0
5	2.1
10	4.2

These data can be derived from the hypothesis together with established facts or generalizations:

The pressure varies directly as the depth.
The greater the pressure at a hole, the farther the liquid will spurt.
The bottom hole is at a greater depth than the middle hole.
Therefore, the water spurts farther from the hole near the bottom (the explained fact).
The pressure varies directly as the depth.
The depth at 10 ft. is twice that at 5 ft.
Therefore, the pressure at 10 ft. (4.2 lbs./sq. in.) is twice that at 5 ft. (2.1 lbs./sq. in.), (the explained fact).

Again the explanation of these data alone does not establish the hypothesis. More explained data of various types are needed.

Being explained by a satisfactory system of knowledge, 5.2. If the Hissarlik hypothesis could itself be tentatively explained by established facts and generalizations, it would then be more acceptable. For example, suppose it were possible to show that the traits of the Trojans and the facts about the geography, climate, and nearby civilization at the time make it probable that the Trojan city would have developed at Hissarlik at the time that Troy was supposed to have existed. If it were possible to show that, the Hissarlik hypothesis would thereby receive support.

Similarly the pressure hypothesis is supported by showing that it can be explained, and thus derived, as follows:

Pressure in a liquid is the numerical equivalent of the weight of a regular column of liquid extending to the top of the container.
The weight of a column of liquid varies directly with its height.
Therefore, the pressure in a liquid varies directly with the depth.

Not being inconsistent with any evidence, 5.3. The Hissarlik hypothesis would be weakened if no springs could be found in the area of Hissarlik, since the *Iliad* mentions two springs in the area, one hot and one cold. The reasoning might go:

Hissarlik is at the site of Troy.
There were probably at least two springs at Troy, one hot and one cold.
Springs tend to remain in existence over the years.
Therefore, it is probable that there are at least two springs at Hissarlik, one hot and one cold.

Note that in using the absence of springs as evidence against the hypothesis, we are assuming that springs tend to remain and that the report of the *Iliad* is reliable. Either of these could be wrong. The less dependable these auxiliary assumptions are, the less dependable is our counterevidence.

The pressure hypothesis would be weakened by the discovery that water spurted out the same amounts at the middle and bottom, since the hypothesis implies otherwise. That is, it would be weakened if we did not previously have so much by way of other evidence built up in favor of the hypothesis—so much that, in this case, one would have a right to suspect such data.

Its competitors' being inconsistent with the data, 5.4. A competitor of the Hissarlik hypothesis is the hypothesis that Bunarbashi is at the site of Troy. This competing hypothesis is not consistent with the data that Bunarbashi is a three-hours' walk from the sea and that the Greeks were able to go back and forth several times daily, if we assume that the Greeks walked.

A competitor of the earlier-stated pressure hypothesis might be one to the effect that the pressure increases directly as one gets closer to the surface of the earth. This hypothesis is inconsistent with pressure gauge readings on two independent tanks, one over the other, when the top tank has the pressure gauge at its bottom, and the bottom tank has its gauge at the top. The alternative hypothesis implies that the gauge in the upper tank would give the smaller reading. The data are just the opposite.

A controlled experiment is designed to rule out competing hypotheses by producing data inconsistent with them. When we test the hypothesis that a new fertilizer will increase the growth of corn, we put the fertilizer in a corn patch, develop a companion corn patch, the control, identical in every respect possible except for fertilizer, and watch the results. If there is a difference, the fertilizer hypothesis can explain it. But it would not be explained by heavy rainfall, warm weather, sunlight, etc., since both patches supposedly received the same amount. These alternative hypotheses would justify a prediction of no difference and would thus be inconsistent with the data.

It is, of course, impossible to develop a perfectly controlled experiment, since the perfect isolation and variation of a single variable is not possible. The important thing might be a *combination* of weather and fertilizer, or the important thing might have slipped by unnoticed. But we can still see in the controlled experiment an attempt to approximate the logical goal of eliminating hypotheses by turning up data that are inconsistent with them. The controlled experiment is an efficient way of eliminating hypotheses by this method.

It should be noted that there is an implicit assumption of standard or familiar conditions in the reasoning that leads to judgments of explanation and inconsistency. For example, the inconsistency resulting from Bunarbashi's being a three-hour walk from the sea is an inconsistency only if Bunarbashi was a three-hour walk from the sea at the time of the Trojan War. In declaring the data to be inconsistent with the competing hypothesis one is gambling that the sea was not at a significantly different level at that time.

This feature of reasoning from hypotheses fits in with the notion of loose reasoning presented under Aspect No. 1. There are always possible qualifications when we apply principles to the world of things, men, and events.

Being testable, 5.5. This is a logical criterion, not a criterion of practicality or even physical possibility. The criterion requires only that it must be possible to *conceive* of what would count as evidence for, and what would count as evidence against, the hypothesis. We have already seen that this is possible for each of our hypotheses. The fact that some conceivable tests are not practically possible is not important so far as this criterion is concerned. A conceivable, though presumably physically impossible, test of the pressure hypothesis would involve swimming to the bottom of the ocean with pressure and depth gauges, recording readings at various points along the way.

An hypothesis that appears untestable is this one: "Airplane crashes are caused by gremlins," since it does not appear possible to conceive of something that would count as evidence for and to conceive of something that would count as evidence against the hypothesis. The word "appear" is used deliberately, since the conceiving of evidence for and evidence against would immediately make the hypothesis testable—and would reveal to some extent the meaning of the hypothesis.

Most hypotheses that we consider are testable in this logical sense, so this criterion does not often discredit an hypothesis. But its fulfillment is absolutely essential for hypotheses about the world of things, men, and events.

6. Judging Whether a Theory Is Warranted

The difference between a theoretic system and an hypothesis of the type we have been considering is that the former is an involved network of relations between concepts, many of which are abstract and technical, while the latter is a simple relation between two or a small number of concepts, often less abstract and technical. Examples of theoretic systems are the kinetic theory of matter, the atomic theory, Gestalt psychology, the theory of evolution, Keynesian economics, Turner's frontier theory, and classical English grammar. Obviously evaluation of theories is a demanding task. It demands more than we can ordinarily expect of elementary and secondary students. Undergraduates are sometimes better equipped, and graduate students are expected to become equipped to perform this task.

Evaluating theories is comparable to evaluating hypotheses, but much more complex. In general the same criteria apply but on a broader scale. Two modifications should be noted: the addition of the criterion of simplicity and the weakening of the effect of contrary evidence.

The criterion of simplicity calls for choosing the simpler of two competing systems, other things being equal. The classic example of the application of this criterion is the preference of the Copernican system, which considered the sun the center of the universe, to the Ptolemaic system, which looked upon the earth as the center. The Copernican system was simpler since it needed fewer cycles and epicycles to explain the movements of the planets.

Since theories have so many parts, contrary evidence does not usually result in outright rejection, but rather in adjustment to fit the contrary evidence—until the whole system becomes more complex than a competitor. The criterion of simplicity then functions.

Following are the criteria for theoretic systems. There will be brief comments, but no attempt to exemplify the operation of each will be made, because to do so would be a monumental task and would make rather laborious reading for those not versed in the fields chosen. You are invited to provide examples from a theoretic system in a field you know.

A theoretic system is warranted to the extent that:

6.31 It explains a bulk and variety of reliable data. Within the system, furthermore, the less abstract statements should be explained by the more abstract ones.

6.32 It is explained by broader theories. Some theories are so broad already that, with our present state of knowledge, to demand fulfillment of this criterion is often to demand speculation.

6.33 It is not inconsistent with any evidence. As indicated earlier, occasional inconsistency can be handled by adjusting the theory. Sometimes the inconsistency must just be accepted for lack of a better theory, and we say, "The theory does not hold for this kind of case."

6.34 Its competitors are inconsistent with the data. Again a single inconsistency does not destroy a competitor, for it too can be adjusted, but a larger number of inconsistencies damage it.

6.35 It is testable. When adjusting a theory to fit the data, people are sometimes tempted to make the theory impregnable by making it untestable. Freudian psychology is sometimes accused of being untestable.

6.36 It is simpler than its rivals. As theories are adjusted to fit new data, they may become extremely complicated, as had happened to the entire Ptolemaic system at the time of Copernicus.

7. JUDGING WHETHER AN ARGUMENT DEPENDS ON AN AMBIGUITY

The ambiguity can appear anywhere in an argument, but most frequently it appears in a shift of meaning from the sense in which the conclusion is proved to a sense in which it is applied. There is such a shift in the following line of reasoning:

There are people who sincerely believe on religious grounds that medication is wrong. They believe this because they believe that any treatment of human beings with medicine is a violation of their religious principles. "Medication" means anything intended for the prevention, cure, or alleviation of disease. Since the chlorination of water is intended for the prevention of disease, it is medication. To chlorinate water is thus to violate their religious principles.

The statement, "Chlorination is medication," is proven when the statement has one meaning: "Chlorination is something intended for the prevention, cure, or alleviation of disease." And it is applied with a different meaning: "Chlorination is treatment of human beings with medicine."

Obviously arguments that depend on ambiguities are to be rejected. No criteria can be given that will serve as guides to students in detecting ambiguities, although you can exhort them to be alert with such statements as, "Make sure that the key words are used in the same sense throughout," or "Check the argument using the key word in its ordinary sense, and if it fails, check it using the word in any technical senses that it might be employed."

8. Judging Whether a Statement Is Overvague or Overspecific

For the purposes of a given situation, a particular statement might be too vague to provide guidance. In such situations the statement should be rejected or inquired into, since in its condition its truth or falsity is irrelevant.

The statement, "Education has disappeared from the schools" (or, "There is more education in the schools than ever before") is useless in decision-making about curriculum and school finance until the terms, "education," "disappeared," and "the schools," are clarified. The statements are not specific enough to be tested and applied. They are too vague.

On the other hand, in a war-ravaged country it might be quite meaningful to say that education has disappeared from the schools (since they are now used for hospitals or housing). In this situation, "education," even loosely defined, has disappeared from the schools.

This aspect requires consideration of the purpose of the discourse and requires the judgment, "This is (or is not) specific enough for our purpose." If the purpose is to come up with curriculum and budgetary recommendations for a school system long in existence, the statement is not specific enough. If the purpose is to make a report to the leader of a war-ravaged country, it is specific enough.

It might be thought that this aspect of critical thinking is one in which people do not make mistakes. In concrete situations this tends to be true, but in abstract situations it is easy to go wrong by forgetting to put questions and answers in the context of situations with purposes. Crawshay-Williams develops this point well (1).

9. Judging Whether an Alleged Authority Is Reliable

In order to assess the statements made by an alleged authority, one must appraise his credentials. Certainly other aspects of critical thinking should also be applied, if one is able to do so. But there are times when one must make a judgment about a statement solely on the basis of the credentials of the person making the statement. An alleged authority should be accepted to the extent that:

9.1 He has a good reputation.
9.2 The statement is in his field.
9.3 He was disinterested—that is, he did

not knowingly stand to profit by the results of his statements (except that he may have stood to have his reputation affected).

9.4 His reputation could be affected by his statement and he was aware of this fact when he made his statement.

9.5 He studied the matter.

9.6 He followed the accepted procedures in coming to his conclusion (although there are legitimate exceptions to this requirement).

9.7 He was in full possession of his faculties when he made the statement.

THE REDUCTION OF PROBLEM IDENTIFICATION TO THE OTHER ASPECTS

Different kinds of judgments go under the label, "problem identification":

1. Judging that a want has been identified, as when someone says, "My problem is to learn to appreciate poetry." In this sense the judgment that the speaker has identified his problems is tantamount to the judgment that this is something the speaker, who might also be the judge, really wants to do. Problem identification here is identification of wants, either one's own, or someone else's. If they are one's own introspected wants, then critical thinking is not involved. For a person to know his wants (felt needs) is something that he cannot fail to do.

If they are someone else's wants, then identifying problems is the same as establishing explanatory hypotheses, as is the case for all subconscious wants, one's own or someone else's, for example, "Mark's problem is to get attention." Judging the identification of someone else's problem and of subconscious wants are then critical thinking of a type already discussed—judging hypotheses.

2. Judging that a valuable goal has been selected. Here is such a problem identification: "Our problem in Culver City is to increase respect for law and order." Insofar as that is a statement of an end rather than a means, the judgment that it is an adequate identification of a problem is a value judgment. For reasons indicated earlier, this type of judging, though important, is excluded from this analysis of critical thinking.

3. Judging that a means decision is adequate. For example, if the broader objective were respect for law and order, the following might be a statement of a means decision: "Our problem in Culver City is to establish a youth bureau." The judgment here that the problem has been identified does at least these two things: 1) implies endorsement of the goal of respect for law and order (this part of the judgment then is a value judgment); 2) says that the means selected will facilitate achievement of the goal and that they will be at least more likely to facilitate it than any other course of action, within the limits of existing resources and goals. These limiting goals, by the way, are another instance in which values are impressed on problem identification. To judge that the problem has been identified is to judge that no unjustified goal violation would take place if the problem were solved.

To apply the means interpretation to our example: it is there implied that establishment of a youth bureau would increase the likelihood of winning respect for law and order, and would be more likely to do so than any other course.

Judging a means decision is judging the application of a principle and judging the acceptability of the principle. To judge whether a youth bureau in Culver City would result in increased respect for law and order is to judge whether a principle about the effectiveness of youth bureaus, applied to this situation, gives us this statement with sufficient probability; and to judge whether the principle is acceptable. Judging principles comes under judging generalizations, hypotheses, or theories, depending on the principle in question.

In summary, problem identification is

many different things and often a combination of them. Elements capable of being treated under the proposed notion of critical thinking are: 1) judging the alleged identification of the wants of others and of subconscious wants (explanatory hypotheses), and 2) judging the assertion of a means of reaching a goal (judging the application of principles and judging the principles themselves). Each of these types of judging is treated elsewhere.

SUMMARY

There has been presented a root notion of critical thinking: the correct assessing of statements, and the presentation and clarification of a list of nine major aspects of critical thinking, which are based upon the root notion. These aspects get at the most important ways people can go wrong in assessing statements and can serve as a statement of elementary and intermediate goals in the teaching of critical thinking.

It has not been the purpose of this paper to suggest how to teach critical thinking, since that would vary so much from one level to another and one subject to another. Perhaps the examples will suggest teaching ideas.

BIBLIOGRAPHY

1. CRAWSHAY-WILLIAMS, RUPERT. *Methods and Criteria of Reasoning.* London: Routledge and Kegan Paul, 1957.
2. ENNIS, ROBERT H. "Assumption-Finding," in B. OTHANEL SMITH and ROBERT H. ENNIS, eds. *Language and Concepts in Education,* pp. 161–178. Chicago: Rand McNally, 1961.
3. SMITH, B. OTHANEL. "The Improvement of Critical Thinking," *Progressive Education,* 30 (March 1953), 129–134.
4. STRAWSON, P. F. *Introduction to Logical Theory.* London: Methuen, 1952.
5. WAISMAN, F. "Verifiability," in ANTONY FLEW, ed. *Logic and Language.* Oxford: Basil Blackwell & Mott, 1952.

7
The Study Skills

A CLUSTER OF SKILLS:
ESPECIALLY FOR JUNIOR HIGH SCHOOL
Alan Robinson

The junior high school is somewhat of a twilight zone as far as sequence of reading skills is concerned. There is little certainty, especially in considering study skills, about where to begin and where to go—developmentally speaking. Possibly such a predicament is valuable and healthy, for the junior high school teacher must then evaluate individual pupils in terms of specific weaknesses and strengths.

Unfortunately, though, even if the junior high school teacher is able to ascertain such weaknesses and strengths, he often does not know how to proceed to capitalize on the strengths and to overcome the weaknesses. If he is a fairly typical teacher, he has not had a single course in the teaching of reading during his days as an undergraduate. One of the recommendations growing out of the recent Harvard-Carnegie study is that "a course in basic reading instruction be required of *all* prospective secondary school teachers."[1]

Reprinted from *The Reading Teacher*, XV (September 1961), 25–28, with permission of the author and International Reading Association.

[1] Mary C. Austin and others, *The Torch Lighters* (Cambridge: Harvard University Press, 1961), p. 191.

The junior high school teacher can probably get more help, and in turn be able to give more, if study skills are considered in clusters of small units. The conventional attempts to plot full sequences of skills present too many concepts at once for the teacher and the student. For example, an "outlining cluster" might include only the following subskills in a rational sequence: reading for details, finding main ideas, changing main ideas to topics, supporting the topics with subtopics and details, labeling with outline form.

There might be individual clusters of skills necessary, however, for complete understanding of some of the subskills mentioned above. For instance, the writer of this article realized that junior high school students had difficulty in finding main ideas or key thoughts in paragraphs. At the time he was a consultant in a junior high school and, with the help of other members of the staff, a "key thought cluster" was devised. The purpose of this article is to present that cluster.

The cluster grew out of the belief that students should not be asked to find the main idea before getting a great deal of practice in learning how to read for details. It is the writer's conviction that poor and generalized comprehension is fostered by the introduction of the main idea concept too early in the learning process. The ability to recognize and formulate main ideas calls for a great deal of reading and thinking maturity. In the final analysis, in order to deal with main ideas or key thoughts, a student must be able to recognize important or key words in sentences, understand basic organizational patterns of written material, draw conclusions, and make inferences.

STEP ONE: KEY WORDS
IN A SENTENCE

Hovious' technique of sending a telegram is used to establish the concept of key words as the most important words.[2] Students quickly observe that "Arrive International Airport New York nine Wednesday evening" states the most important words in the sentence, "I shall arrive at the International Airport in New York City at nine o'clock on Wednesday evening." They also learn that, for the most part, the same essential words will be chosen by different persons, but experience may cause some people to choose fewer or more words than others. The person who knows New York City or lives there might only need "Arrive International nine Wednesday evening."

Students should then move on to underlining the key words in sentences taken from conversation. A typical sentence might be, "Please be very careful that you do not damage the brand-new desks." Essentially students will underline "do not damage" or "not damage" "new desks." Once proficiency is established at this level, and students are beginning to realize that they are finding the main ideas of sentences, much more practice should be initiated using sentences from

[2] Carol Hovious, *Flying the Printways* (Boston: D. C. Heath, 1938), p. 163.

content-area materials. Some students who find it difficult to let go of details may need the individual attention of the teacher for a while. Other students may be given more complex sentences to figure out. During this step, however, all sentences should be isolated and not presented as parts of paragraphs.

STEP TWO: KEY SENTENCE
IN A PARAGRAPH

In this step the students first learn that they need be concerned with fewer key words when sentences are treated together in paragraph form. They learn this through the experience of underlining key words in the sentences of short paragraphs. For example:

A school performs many services for the residents of a community. It offers instructional services for school-age children during the day and, often, courses for adults in the evening. It provides a meeting place for community organizations. It also serves as an active cultural center, for plays, concerts, and lectures are often scheduled.

In this paragraph the sentences are so closely linked that it is not necessary to keep repeating the subject. Students soon realize that they are primarily concerned with verbs and their objects once the subject is established.

The paragraphs presented in this step should be well structured, containing definite key sentences mainly as first and last sentences. One or two of the paragraphs may contain key sentences placed in other parts of the paragraph.

Students are asked to list the key ideas (groups of key words) they have found in the paragraph. For example, this list might have been written about the paragraph on school services:

school performs many services
offers instructional services

provides meeting place
serves as cultural center.

Students learn to *add up* the key ideas and decide whether or not one of them represents an over-all idea. It happens to be contained in the first sentence of the paragraph. Hence, in this paragraph, the over-all or main idea is contained in a key sentence at the beginning.

Here is another example. The task is a little more difficult because some of the sentences in the paragraph contain two key ideas. Students learn to treat these ideas as separate units in their search for the key sentence.

Everyone saluted as the flag was slowly raised. A smartly-dressed woman cracked a champagne bottle across the ship's prow and named it "Sea Hawk." The order was given, and the "Sea Hawk" started down the ways. A new ship was launched.

Everyone saluted + flag raised + woman cracked bottle across ship's prow + named it "Sea Hawk" + order given + started down ways = new ship launched. Obviously, the key sentence is the last sentence in the paragraph. Key idea + key idea + key idea = the over-all or main idea contained in the key sentence.

Look at this example:

Animals have interesting habits. One of the habits of some animals is to use nature's medicines when they are ill. Deer may eat twigs and the very tender bark of trees. Cats and dogs may eat grass when they are not feeling up to par. Bears often eat different kinds of roots and berries.

Deer eat twigs and tender bark + cats and dogs eat grass + bears eat roots and berries = some animals use nature's medicine when ill. The first sentence in the paragraph serves only an introductory purpose. It may be introducing a series of paragraphs which will deal with interesting habits of animals. It is not, of course, the main idea of this particular paragraph. Hence, in this case, the key sentence is the second sentence in the paragraph.

STEP THREE: THE MAIN THOUGHT IN A PARAGRAPH

After students have completed a great deal of successful practice in working with paragraphs containing key sentences in a variety of positions, they should be ready for this step. At this time they might be presented with a paragraph very much like this one:

We visited the seals frolicking in the water. Then we paid a visit to the colorful birds in the big new birdhouse. After that we stopped for a Coke and hot dog. Before going home we spent a lot of time watching the funny monkeys.

The students would again be asked to find key ideas. Visited seals + paid visit to birds + stopped for Coke and hot dog + before going home spent time watching monkeys = ? At this point numerous students will point out that there is no *stated* over-all idea.

Students must now make inferences, for the author does not state the key thought in a sentence of the paragraph. The student must look at all key ideas and determine the main idea of the paragraph himself. In this easy paragraph most students, of course, will agree that the key thought is "we visit the zoo," or something similar.

When students have mastered the basic ideas in the three-step cluster of skills using carefully structured materials, normal textbook material should provide application and reinforcement. Students soon become aware of the fact that paragraphs which are parts of chapters in books don't always stand by themselves. One main or key thought may be carried through a number of paragraphs without repetition in each paragraph. Often students will decide on the key thought by noting part of a main idea stated by the author and adding to it through their own reasoning. For instance:

It is not only radio that has given them a great deal of help. Ballistics experts can tell whether or not a bullet was fired from a particular gun by examining the bullet under a microscope. Chemists help solve crimes by analyzing blood, dust, cloth, and other materials. Photographers, also, are used in helping police solve crimes. Often photographs, especially when enlarged, reveal clues that the human eye overlooked.

Obviously, in the paragraph above, the key thought is concerned with "people and things that help police solve crimes." Clues can be found in the paragraph, but the reader can also arrive at the key thought through reasoning and the context that preceded this paragraph. Certainly a preceding paragraph, or several, dealt with "radio as it helps police solve crimes."

As students learn to look for organizational patterns in the way material is written, they will gain in ability to comprehend and retain. The teacher can best help the student by "clustering" closely related skills together in a teaching unit and by organizing the steps in a given cluster so well that the student has a series of successful experiences. *Challenge* is of tremendous importance *after* students feel that they have mastered the skill or skills to some degree. For even with the teacher's help in dealing with "clusters of skills," junior high school textbooks will present many challenges.

STUDY SKILLS FOR SUPERIOR STUDENTS IN SECONDARY SCHOOL
F. P. Robinson

Reading instruction is a regular part of most college programs (4, 8).* It deals not only with remediation of reading disabilities but also with instruction in higher levels of reading skill needed for collegiate study. This article will emphasize the value of giving instruction in higher level reading skills to superior high school students, particularly those who may be taking collegiate courses early, or those who want to learn these reading skills in preparation for later college work. It is

Reprinted from *The Reading Teacher*, XV (September 1961), 29–33, 37, with permission of the author and International Reading Association.
[*Numbers in parentheses refer to Bibliography at the end of this article.]

also obvious that these reading skills can be of value in doing high school work.

Because high schools give much emphasis to remedial work for poor readers and because superior students read so much better than their peers, it is usually difficult to interest these students in learning better reading skills. However, the fact that these higher level skills are needed in college, and are a part thereof the regular instructional program, should increase interest of superior students in maximizing their reading skills. In addition, the use of instructional materials specifically written for the college level will help indicate that higher levels of skill are being emphasized rather than remediation.

It will be necessary to show students that their reading skills are actually quite inefficient. Some data obtained from outstanding students in college will be useful here. Studies of Phi Beta Kappa and other honor roll candidates show that their rate of reading is typically little above that of other students and that they have quite inefficient study skills (6, 13). Other studies show that superior students given selections with headings in and headings omitted read the former no faster nor comprehend them any better, although evidence indicates that such headings can with training be used to increase speed and comprehension (16). A study made during World War II of superior college students referred for specialized training showed that these students had been making their A's and B's more by strength of intellect than by efficient study skills (14). When these students were asked to read and take notes their "work rate" was only ninety-three words per minute, and the quality of their notes was little better than average.

Other studies show that with a single reading the typical reader gets only about 60 percent of the ideas asked on an immediate quiz, and with immediate rereadings is able to raise his comprehension score only to about 65 percent (7). Another study of several thousand high school students showed that there is rapid forgetting after reading: within two weeks after an initial reading only 20 percent is remembered of what was known immediately after reading (17).

In brief, the average and superior student in high school and college is inefficient in his reading and study skills; he tends to excell other students in grades mostly because of differences in intellectual ability and not because of better reading and study methods.

Before turning to the nature of some of these higher level reading skills and how they may be taught, two preliminary points need to be made: (a) textbooks should be even better organized to facilitate learning and (b) when students are given better books they will not do much better unless they are taught the necessary reading skills to use the facilitative cues. While modern textbooks are written in many ways to facilitate learning, e.g., use of headings, final summaries, illustrations, etc., there is good evidence that school textbook writers and publishers are still too much bound to the typographical style of ancient papyrus times, e.g., close printed, full line paragraphs in one type size. School textbooks make little use (except in footnotes) of paragraphs printed in different type sizes to indicate degree of importance. They do not use a style (found useful in governmental and industrial publications) of indenting the whole left side of subordinate paragraphs. Academic authors seem unprepared to use pictorial material as the main form of presentation, with prose added as explanation. Few help the reader by starting chapters with summary statements or by putting their headings into question form, etc. A great deal is known that could improve textbooks, and experiments such as trying the scramble order of the recent *Tutortexts* should be encouraged and evaluated.

The second preliminary point is that superior students may not be able to read better when they are given well organized and facilitative material *unless they are given special instruction.* Earlier it was stated that inserting headings into a text does not increase reading speed or comprehension of college students. A more extensive study by Christiansen and Stordahl showed similar results and found in addition that adding such cues as underlinings, summary statements, etc., does not help uninstructed adult readers (5). Another study by Newman showed that when material is prepared which forces students to read in a manner which seems to better fit psychological knowledge of how learning takes place, the students actually do better using their own self-derived methods with which they are comfortable (*12*). Additional studies show that simple explanations of better techniques (either through reading about them or through oral explanation) are not sufficient to bring about better skill (*2, 18*). However, with supervised practice, as is necessary in learning any skill, there is a definite gain in skill to levels far beyond those attained with self-help methods (*2*). In brief, what has been discovered in developing optimum athletic and industrial skills applies to learning scholastic skills as well. Research can be used to design new higher levels of skill, and these must be taught in a coaching and practice situation.

What are some of the higher level reading and study skills? One of them is the SQ3R method—a technique devised from research findings for use in studying college textbooks (*15*). Some of the research will be summarized and the method then described. McClusky divided 118 college students into two equated groups; one group was shown how to skim over headings and summaries and the other was not shown. When these two groups were than given a selection to read, the trained group read 24 percent faster than, and just as accurately as, the control group (*11*). Holmes also set up two large equated groups of college students and had them read selections about science and history (*9*). One group was given twenty questions *before* reading. As might be expected, the group given the questions did better in answering them, but they also did as well or better on additional questions. The advantage was particularly great on tests given two weeks after reading. Still another study by Washburne indicates the best placement for such questions (*19*). In this study 1,456 high school students were divided into several groups of equal ability. Questions were given to the different groups as follows: at the beginning of reading, at the end of reading, each question just before the material answering it, each question just after the mate-rial answering it, and no questions. The test contained questions already provided as well as other questions. Of these different placements two proved most effective: all questions at the beginning of the reading and each question just before it was answered in the material.

These findings, plus the fact that textbook writers regularly use headings, numberings and summaries, provide a basis for designing the first three steps of the SQ3R methods: 1) *survey*, 2) ask a *question* before reading a section; and 3) *read* to answer that question. The reader is taught to quickly survey the headings and read the summaries before he starts to read the text. This gives him an orientation as to what the chapter will present, helps him recall what he already knows about these topics, and facilitates his subsequent readings.

We have already noted that students tend to forget much of what they learn from reading within a very short time, e.g., 80 percent within two weeks (*17*). This same study also showed that a testing-type review immediately after reading was very helpful in reducing forgetting, e.g., instead of 80 percent there was only a 20 percent loss. Other studies show that readers often do not clearly comprehend ideas as they read along, and the rapid succession of ideas in reading tends to interfere with what is comprehended because of retroactive inhibition. So there is need for a system to check on comprehension while reading and also to help in fixing ideas better in memory. Note-taking can be used for this purpose, but the manner in which most students take notes is of little help. That is, studies show that students do as well with straight reading as they do with trying to read and take notes (*1, 18*). One reason for this is that students tend to copy down phrases as soon as they find an important idea, and if the phrase is in italics they may write it down without understanding the point. Many students do not like to take notes because they write in complete sentences, which markedly slows down their reading speed.

Thus, a method must be worked out which helps the student check his comprehension as he reads, helps fix the ideas in memory, does not take too long, and is useful for later review. The fourth and fifth steps of the SQ3R method are designed to take care of these needs: 4) after completing a headed section, *recite* by writing a brief phrase from memory; and 5) immediately after reading the whole lesson *review* it by looking over the notes taken and reciting on them from memory. Notes are not taken until *after* a headed section has been read. This enables the student to read to answer his question (step 3) and then check on his comprehension and help fix the material in memory by reciting a brief answer. Waiting until the end of the section means that all of the ideas in that section can be seen in relation to each other and the most important selected; writing the note from memory means that the student has to organize his answer, and if he has trouble he can recall the material as needed; using phrases means that much time is saved in writing, and these cues will be sufficient later on for reminders in review.

The SQ3R method then consists of five steps: 1) *Survey* the headings and summaries quickly to get the general ideas which will be developed in the assignment, 2) turn the first heading into a *Question*, 3) *Read* the whole section through to answer that question, 4) at the end of the headed section stop to *Recite* from memory on the question and jot the answer down in phrases (Steps 2, 3 and 4 are repeated on each succeeding headed section), and 5) at the end of reading the assignment in this manner then immediately *Review* the lesson to organize the ideas and recite on the various points to fix them in mind. This higher-level study skill cannot be learned simply by reading about it, it must be practiced under supervision just as with learning any skill. Modifications of this skill

have also been worked out for studying collateral readings, English literature, and charts and tables (*15*).

While particular attention has been given to the explanation of one particular higher-level study skill, there are many other specialized skills which the superior secondary school student needs in college as well as in high school. Much use is made of specialized graphs, charts, maps, dictionaries, encyclopedias, resource books, etc., in college. A surprising number of college students tend to skip graphs and tables, refuse to use dictionaries and indices, or handle such material in an inefficient manner. Studies of college students' ability to use the library to find assigned books or to use easy short cuts in writing research papers show ignorance of fundamental and simple devices (*10*). Studies of the manner in which college students go about reading examination questions show that rather than use systematic skills in analysis they usually use a self-taught "jump and guess" system (*3*). In brief, superior students in high school need to learn many higher-level skills if they are to be highly effective in college work.

Since students going to college move away from their usual surroundings and conditions for study, they also need help with study habits and planning. Irregular class schedules and the need for self-planning of study time leave many students floundering. Both the home and high school usually provide study conditions with a minimum of distraction, but in college there are many places to study, and students often try to combine studying with social possibilities. Finally, many students—even superior ones—go through high school with only vaguely understood adult goals, and go on to college mostly because "everyone in school does." Such motivation is insufficient to help students direct study efforts when so many more fascinating things are possible in college. Youngsters need help in thinking about why they want to go to college so that their college efforts can be more effectively self directed.

Our points, in brief, have been: Superior students in high school are typically inefficient in study methods; they have kept ahead of others through brilliance of intellect. College work will offer them particular difficulties because of greater demands and competition and because of many distractions for poorly controlled individuals. Furthermore, superior students are interested in making outstanding records of achievement and discovery and not simply in excelling others; this demands that they learn research-designed higher-level study skills.

BIBLIOGRAPHY

1. ARNOLD, H. F. "The Comparative Efficiency of Certain Study Techniques in Fields of History," *J. Educ. Psychol.*, 33 (1942), 449–457.
2. BARTON, W. A. "Outlining as a Study Procedure," *Teach. Coll. Contri. Educ.*, No. 411, 1930.
3. BLOOM, B. S., and BRODER, L. J. *Problem Solving Processes of College Students*. Chicago: Univ. of Chicago Press, 1950.
4. CAUSEY, O. S., and ELLER, W., eds. "Starting and Improving College Reading Programs," *Eighth Yearbook of National Reading Conference*. Fort Worth: Texas Christian University Press, 1959.
5. CHRISTENSEN, C. M., and STORDAHL, K. E. "The Effect of Organizational Aids on Comprehension and Retention," *J. Educ. Psychol.*, 46 (1955), 65–74.
6. DANSKIN, D. G., and BURNETT, C. W. "Study Techniques of Those Superior Students," *Pers. & Guid. J.*, 31 (1952), 181–186.
7. ENGLISH, H. B., WELBORN, E. L., and KILLIAN, C. D. "Studies in Substance Memorization," *J. Gen. Psychol.*, 11 (1934), 233–259.
8. ENTWISLE, D. R. "Evaluations of Study-skills Courses: A Review," *J. Educ. Research*, 53 (1960), 243–251.
9. HOLMES, E. "Reading Guided by Questions versus Careful Reading and Re-reading without Questions," *School Rev.*, 39 (1931), 361–371.
10. LOUTTIT, C. M., and PATRICK, J. R. "A Study of Students' Knowledge in the Use of the Library," *J. Appl. Psychol.*, 16 (1932), 475–484.
11. McCLUSKY, H. Y. "An Experiment on the Influence of Preliminary Skimming on Reading," *J. Educ. Psychol.*, 25 (1934), 521–529.
12. NEWMAN, S. E. "Student vs. Instructor Design of Study Method," *J. Educ. Psychol.*, 48 (1957), 328–333.
13. PRESTON, R. C., and TUFTS, E. N. "The Reading Habits of Superior College Students," *J. Exper. Educ.*, 16 (1948), 196–202.
14. ROBINSON, F. P. "Study Skills of Soldiers in ASTP," *School & Soc.*, 58 (1943), 398–399.
15. ———. *Effective Study* (Revised edition). New York: Harper and Brothers, 1961.
16. ———, and HALL, PRUDENCE. "Studies of Higher Level Reading Abilities," *J. Educ. Psychol.*, 32 (1941), 241–252.
17. SPITZER, H. F. "Studies in Retention," *J. Educ. Psychol.*, 30 (1939), 641–656.
18. STORDAHL, K. E., and CHRISTENSEN, C. M. "The Effect of Study Techniques on Comprehension and Retention," *J. Educ. Research*, 46 (1956), 561–570.
19. WASHBURNE, J. N. "The Use of Questions in Social Science Material," *J. Educ. Psychol.*, 20 (1929), 321–359.

SUCCESSFUL STUDY SKILLS PROGRAMS
Jane H. Catterson

This paper will attempt to give cohesion to the papers which have been presented by describing ways in which study skills are actually being woven into the whole fabric of school programs. Each paper in this series emphasizes a different skill, and this final discussion is presented to help the readers who may find it difficult to think of skills in the context of a functioning teaching scheme. Therefore, this paper is intended to direct attention toward the use of the study skills in successful programs such as the ones described in the first article of this publication: direct teaching in reading class, direct teaching in English class, and functional-incidental teaching in content areas. It is the last category which seems to concern most of the writers and I should like to deal with this kind of teaching more completely than with the others.

DIRECT TEACHING IN
ENGLISH OR READING CLASS

An examination of the literature makes it evident that it is difficult, if not impossible, to say that some programs deal with the teaching of study skills in reading class while others deal with the teaching of study skills in English class. It seems to be true that some schools give credit for English to students who are lacking in reading and study skills

Reprinted from *Developing Study Skills in Secondary Schools.* Newark, Del.: International Reading Association (1965), 156–169, with permission of the author and International Reading Association

and who are taking a class to improve them (5).* It seems to be true just as frequently that even if a class is set up which is formally called a "reading class" or "reading lab" the time is likely to be taken from English periods and might as well be called English.

An interesting report by Berkey (4) describes just such a partial program. She writes that Centinela Valley High School District has a program in reading and study skills which starts with an 8 week introduction for all freshmen in one of the four reading labs available and continues through the year, two days a week, as part of the freshman English program. She states that skills learned in the lab are applied to regular texts "2 days a week in the regular classroom." It is not clear whether this practice in application of skills is conducted by the regular English teacher or by a reading specialist. However, the writer indicates that the whole scheme is an unqualified success and has resulted in the much wider use of libraries.

Leamnson (15) reports that in Indianapolis students are given reading training through a laboratory which all students attend once a week as part of their regular English program. Work is done with general comprehension and speed on various types of materials.

Gustafson (10), as reading coordinator for the Oakland California schools, reported that one-semester English Workshop classes

[*Numbers in parentheses refer to Bibliography at the end of this article.]

were available for pupils retarded in reading more than one year. Skills depended on the needs of the pupils and included at least some teaching in study skills for application to classroom texts.

Beacon and Gillett (3) have expressed satisfaction with the results obtained in an elective program in the high school in Eugene, Oregon. They reported that students were given help in identifying their weaknesses as reflected in the results of the *Iowa Silent Reading Test*. Practice was directed towards the skills tested by the Iowa Silent Reading Test—some of them study skills— and students were encouraged to choose their own materials and direct their own practice.

Grissom (9) does not go into detail about which skills are taught and which materials are used. However, he suggests that a well equipped reading clinic which provides plenty of materials and individualized instruction from a properly qualified reading specialist is likely to produce student, parent, and teacher satisfaction, even if the courses are non-credit.

Heavey (11) describes a special course which is offered as part of an English-reading program which is especially interesting because it is offered to gifted rather than handicapped students. The course, offered in the latter half of the tenth year, provides for systematic teaching of the skills of report writing.

Miss Heavey describes how she prepares students for work on a formal paper by teaching note-taking on 3x5 cards, using developmental reading texts as a source and discussion and comparison as a means of improving the note-taking techniques; how she directs examination of various texts for evidence that proper credit was given for sources of information and for information about current forms of annotation; how she gives practice in working with bibliographical data; and how she helps her students reduce personal notes to an outline for the final paper.

After these pre-requisite skills have been developed, the writer discusses how students are guided in finding references as they work in the library, in taking their first notes in the library, in preparing a bibliography, in stating their thesis, in preparing a preliminary draft for approval, and in writing the final draft of the paper. The writer mentions the value of following up by having the preliminary draft outline used as a springboard for class reporting and discussion.

These are examples of what can be called the "partial program." Other sources can be found in Early's (7) summary of major reports to 1957. Of the above reports, only Miss Heavey's report is directed exclusively to the development of a single major skill. Each of the others is concerned with the reading skills generally, with study skills included as part of the teaching.

Aside from the specific suggestions about skills to be taught, the reports have a general significance. They show that over the last ten years there has been an increasing recognition by school teachers and administrators of the need for specific help in reading and study skills at the high school level. A definite willingness to give that help is reflected, even if this means using time which was formerly allotted to a study of literature. Where formerly there may have been hostility towards what appeared to be a lowering of standards in English, a practical approach to the problem has resulted in the development of teaching to fit the situation.

Despite the satisfaction manifested by those who have worked very hard to develop "partial programs," a trend seems to be developing which favors study skills programs which are handled by classroom teachers in the regular content areas. Enough information has been collected about study skills and ways to teach them to make it possible for a school staff, with some specialized help, to develop a program in which study skills teaching is shared by the staff as a whole.

As every field of knowledge broadens and deepens with tremendous speed, it becomes obvious that pupils require not more "subject matter" teaching but a kind of teaching which helps them develop a better approach to learning. The authors of these papers have made it obvious that they think of study skills not as *something* to teach, but as a *way* to teach—a way of teaching which advances not only the student's knowledge of subject matter but his ability to learn other subject matter independently and at will. The aim, then, is to unify knowledge learning and the skills of acquiring knowledge.

FUNCTIONAL INCIDENTAL TEACHING BY CONTENT TEACHERS

THE INDIVIDUAL TEACHER

The fact is that some teachers of content are already aware of the values of a study skills approach to teaching. One has only to look into content teachers' publications to find that this is true. Many reports show that study skills are being taught through the work of content teachers without the direction of a special consultant.

In an article in *The Social Studies*, for example, Olcott (*18*) reports on developing an outline for the teaching of local government and suggests that one of his major objectives is "to develop the skills of using primary sources." Among the activities listed as part of his approach to the teaching subject matter is the preparation by the students of a series of maps to show how their community has grown, the preparation of a time line showing community development, and the preparation of a booklet on the organization and operation of local government. Each of these activities, obviously, is directed at improving understanding of social studies through study skills activities.

In *The English Journal*, Rast (*21*) suggests that the English teacher must not simply assign research papers but must take responsibility for seeing that the prerequisite skills are taught. He describes how he assigned a research paper and arranged to have it produced within a week by: 1) carefully choosing an area of investigation which was rich in resource material; 2) narrowing the overall topic while giving opportunity for choice within it; and 3) deliberately restricting the number of sources for each paper. He allotted class time for discussion of the various sources for each paper and where they might be found; the techniques of note-taking; and the format of the report, including its overall organization, bibliography, and footnotes. Mr. Rast suggests that the English teacher should aim at having pupils produce a number of brief reports so that they go through the steps of production a number of times with guidance, rather than require one paper, the production of which is extended over so long a period that the steps in the research process are obscured.

A report by Owen (*19*) in *The Math Teacher* shows that mathematics teachers are interested in developing their students' concepts of math through a study skills approach. She tells about work with students in a math club in which part of the activity was directed toward preparing talks from various sources on new developments in the field of mathematics and toward preparing graphs and tables based on a survey of requirements of mathematics in industry around the home school.

An article by Kuhl (*14*) is interesting because it gives evidence that teachers may collaborate on study skills projects even without pressure or guidance from administrator or specialist. Kuhl says that he taught outlining in English classes and "Near the end of the year the biology teacher and I agreed to combine on a 3 or 4 page report he required." He adds, "The students rejoiced because 'It'll be less work for us'." Kuhl and the biology teacher read the papers, each with his own purposes in mind, evidently with satisfaction for both teachers and pupils.

THE ALL SCHOOL APPROACH

If study skills can be taught through special programs and are also being taught successfully through the individual initiative of some regular content teachers, could the programs not include all of the school staff? Reports of whole school or whole system approaches to study skills programs are not numerous as yet, but such school-wide approaches are reported by Severson (22), Herber (12), Clark (5), and Shepherd (23). Their descriptions of what was actually done in their situations are worth careful examination.

A major conclusion which one draws from these reports is that *the administrator is of very great importance* in getting the program started. In some cases he may do no more than recommend the hiring of a specialist to work on a study skills program. In other cases, he may give direct guidance to the program himself. In either case, the fact that the study skills have been recognized as an area of education which requires very specific and well organized attention is of major importance in enlisting the cooperation of the school staffs.

A second conclusion which one draws from the reports is that *specialized consultant help* will be needed. Either a full time consultant must be brought in to work with the teachers of content area (12), (22) or the administrator himself must take on the task with the help of part-time consultants from universities or the community itself. Clark's report (5) suggests that he, as principal, worked with visiting consultants in the organization of his school's program.

It seems clear that a leader should *formulate some definite goals* against which to measure the program. It is very easy to start on a new approach to school subjects and forget that one may not be able to measure gains by

the same yardsticks as were used before. Barbe (2) points out that some programs appear not to work because they were not properly measured. If the purpose is teaching subject matter through study skills and study skills through subject matter, both study skills and subject matter learning should be measured. Subject matter may perhaps be tested on the old measures; but study skills learning may require the employment of a standardized test such as the *Spitzer Study Skills Test*, or an informal measure such as the preparation of a report including the presentation of some information in original graphics, or perhaps a survey of the extent and type of use of the library. All measures would, of course, be used at the beginning of the program and periodically thereafter to determine growth.

Time required for establishing the all-school program—The time involved in laying the groundwork may be quite short or reasonably long, depending on the goals set for the initial trials. Herber (12), whose plan involved the preparation by teachers of extensive study guides, worked with his own assistants and teachers of history as materials were written and put into operation within one year. He added another subject—science—and its teachers the following year.

Severson (22), on the other hand, seems not to have attempted to put any part of a program into operation until her second year. In her first year, she worked with teachers, holding discussions and workshops, both to develop understandings and teaching materials. She put the outlines of a program into operation the next year.

Clark (5) appears to have set in motion a readjustment of English classes between September and December and used the last months of the same school year to conduct in-service training courses as well as to initiate changes in each content area. As teachers completed the training, they tried the new programs in their classrooms.

Methods of working with teachers—The

all-school program is promoted and developed through individual consultations, and demonstrations. Shepherd (23) mentions the value of the "short course" type of approach and suggests an evening workshop every week for 6 weeks consecutively and two or three demonstrations a day for 3 or 4 successive days. Severson (22) indicates that work was done both with teachers of one subject area as a group and with subject representation on a centralized committee. She suggests that brief meetings "over a cup of coffee" may serve a useful purpose with small groups.

A major first step, no matter how the approach is made, is in helping content teachers become familiar with their materials in a new way. Herber (12) says, referring to the history teacher, "rather than using a skills list as a basis for his teaching he takes the materials to the list to find those skills needed to read a particular passage with understanding." Severson (22) comments that "math teachers didn't see at first how this area of teaching would relate to their subject." Early (8) suggests that a teacher may find it hard "to appraise the readability of his own textbooks because the concepts are known to him, but let him look at an unrelated field and 'concept load' begins to mean something."

Identification of skills—Reference to a skills list suggests that a *chart of skills* may be useful either as a point of departure for a program or as a goal towards which to work. The plan for such a chart is suggested by the topics discussed in this volume. The simple chart emerges if one simply lists the major areas vertically along the left hand side of the chart and below each the major facets of teaching or subskills to be introduced. If one starts a continuous line opposite each subskill at a point which suggests the relative "time of introduction" of each, some idea may be conveyed of a total teaching scheme: which skills should be considered basic and taught first; which skills should be designated as "higher level" and allowed to wait on the development of the basic skills. Strang's chart (24), although it includes more than the study skills alone, is a useful reference for suggesting suitable points to introduce various skills.

There are a number of obvious uses for this kind of flow chart. Perhaps most importantly it provides an "overview" of the skills involved in a total program. Teachers who are being introduced to a whole new set of skills and understandings are likely to become bewildered by detail unless they can be shown some graphic representation of the anatomy of this new body of knowledge. A chart of this kind can provide a stable point around which teachers can work with numbers of "subskills."

Besides assuring a better visualization of a total program, a chart of skills may be useful in clarifying the role of the individual teacher within the total framework. If a teacher can be shown what others are doing generally and at the same time check off specifically his own areas of responsibility, his goals can become steadily clearer and his teachings more pointed.

A third service which the chart may perform is to clarify the relationships of skills within each "block" and among the skills from block to block. Chapter Five on "Organization Perceived," for example, seems to suggest that teachers should work on getting main ideas of paragraphs before any attempt is made to teach the more sophisticated skills of finding the organizational pattern of a whole selection. And looking from the "Organization Perceived" to the "Organization Produced" block, one can deduce that reading for main ideas at a basic level should be practiced a good deal before formal note-taking is introduced. The chart should be useful then, in showing the relationship of the final goals to the steps involved in reaching those goals.

Limitations of skills charts—There are, of course, certain cautions which must be mentioned. The first is implied in the suggestion by both Early (8) and Artley (1) that a chart of reading skills would be best arranged in a spiral. What they seem to be suggesting is that a flat rectangular flow chart might lead teachers to introduce specific skills in a particular grade, at a level of difficulty and with materials suited to that grade, and then neglect to raise the level of complexity of the skill and the difficulty of material beyond that introductory stage. If this happened, pupils might be introduced to various study skills over their school careers but never be given the opportunity to gain real competence with these skills at a steadily rising level of complexity on increasingly difficult materials. The spiral concept suggests continuous reinforcement and increasing sophistication in the rise of a skill.

Another problem with a linear chart lies in the fact that one might deduce from its parallel lines that the teaching, learning, and application of each skill goes on independently without a background plan for integration of the skills from top to bottom of the chart. If isolated skills practice is given, students may have the ability to use particular skills one at a time, especially when directed to do so; but they may not actually do so independently if presented with a study problem which required the integrated application of several skills at once at the variety of levels dictated by the problem itself. That isolated practice is given, leaving some capable school pupils with a set of quite well developed but apparently unrelated skills, is pointed out by Perry (20) in a report to the Harvard faculty. He describes how he found that members of an incoming class at Harvard actually could do exercises on study skills but were unable to synchronize their use of such skills into the smoothly functioning attack required by a typical college study problem.

It should be noted that in the Study Skills Flow Chart no designation has been allotted to specific grade levels since it must be evident that each school system must place each stage at a grade level suitable for its students.

Materials essential to the program—Of course, a chart of skills is not a program, and most writers agree that one cannot develop a program without a variety of materials. Some materials will be required for teacher use only, to give them guidance and direction. Others will be needed in quantity for use in the student's own hands. Although there is not overall agreement about which materials would be needed first, it seems to be agreed that students should be helped as early as possible with word skills, with the use of book parts, and with the ability to get main ideas from the chapter of a book using a survey type of reading technique.

Apropos of the word skills area, Herber (12) suggests that specific vocabulary exercises are useful and recommends a "word-sorting" type of technique. Niles (17) does not mention specific vocabulary exercises but suggests that teachers need guides in teaching word pronunciation skills and the use of structure and context clues.

Although there is a quantity of commercial material available today which includes specific skills exercises of various types, each of the authors already mentioned seems to feel that no program can be operated efficiently unless some teaching guides and lesson plans are written especially for the texts which are actually in use in the classrooms. Teachers must have specific directions for teaching lessons from their texts on the use of book parts, and for the direction of a content reading lesson which employs a survey type of technique. Strang (24) suggests, as well, that teachers need guides for directing students towards the use of the library.

Actually Herber's (12) plan appears to have required the greatest quantity of special written material. He used study guides as a springboard for much of the teaching and produced each at several levels of reading

STUDY SKILLS FLOW CHART

	Stage 1	Stage 2	Stage 3	Stage 4
Using Graphic Materials				
Pictures				
Maps and Globes				
Graphs				
Tables				
Cartoons				
Using Book Parts				
Title				
Copyright				
Table of Contents				
Chapter Headings				
Index				
Glossary				
Appendix				
Introduction				
Summaries				
Using Sources				
Encyclopedias				
Atlas				
World Almanac				
Biblios				
Card Catalogue				
Reader's Guide				
Organization Perceived				
Main Ideas of Paragraph				
Details				
Organizational Pattern of Selections				
Organization Produced				
Note-taking				
Outlining				
2-step				
3-step				
Summary				
SQ 3R				
Precis				
Word Study				
Analysis				
Syllabication				
Prefix, Suffix				
Root				
Meaning				
Context				
Prefix, Suffix				
Root				

ability to meet needs within the classrooms. He suggests that these guides can be used independently, in what Durrell (6) has called "pupil teams," as the teacher moves about the room and gives help where it is needed. This problem of materials written at various levels has not been much mentioned although Karlin (13) suggests that it is likely to need attention shortly as programs gain impetus.

PROBLEMS AND CONCERNS

As early discussions explore skills, methods and materials, some need may be manifested for decisions about who should bear responsibility for each aspect of the teaching. While the goal is to see all skills applied in each class, there is some suggestion that the basic or "linking" skills may best be put into the hands of English teachers or reading specialists (22). Such skills as outlining, for example, which must eventually be applied in each classroom, might be taught initially by a small group of people working closely together and then gradually introduced into each subject field as some mastery of the skill is observed. The librarian may be useful, either as the sole teacher of the library skills or as the leader of a small group which is responsible for them.

Launching the program into the classes becomes the major concern once teachers have some grasp of goals and methods and some materials are available. Severson (22) is quite specific about this. Her teachers presented "the same topic or skills" in each class the first full day. This topic was the use of the parts of the textbook in each class, and she says that the children were taught to use the book in the most efficient manner in that particular class (22). In the second week the same dramatic kind of emphasis was given in the word study area and "each teacher in each class presented a special lesson in vocabulary." Clark's (5) report suggests that the same type of attempt was made in his school to capitalize on the effect of all teachers working on the same skills at the same time in the initial stages.

Steady revision and clarification of goals should be expected at every stage of a successful program. Shepherd (23) implies that teachers may need to be encouraged steadily in all stages of an unfamiliar program. Letson (16) says of the reading consultant, "He must have patience, tact, enthusiasm, sympathy, as well as the ability to direct the program at every turn."

ACCEPTANCE OF THE SCHOOL-WIDE STUDY SKILLS APPROACH

Although the above reports make it evident that good work is going on in the study skills field, there seem to be some major problems which stand in the way of full realization of the goal of including every subject teacher in the study skills teaching.

A major task seems to be the development of closer liaison between the people who are doing research in study skills and the potential users of the information obtained. The average secondary teacher may be unaware of what information is available about study skills. The burden of spreading this information must lie with such groups as the National Council of Teachers of English and the International Reading Association. The fact is that it is probably highly unrealistic to expect content teachers to buy a subscription to *The English Journal* or *The Reading Teacher*.

Somehow the publicity about study skills must get into the other professional journals where it will reach all teachers. Administrators, especially, should be reached. Almost every successful reading program, complete or partial, has had impetus initially from an administrator—even if that impetus involved only the suggestion to the school committee that a reading specialist be hired. Yet, we cannot be sure that information of the kind included in this publication has ever been presented at a national meeting of supervisors and administrators. In fact, any kind of national meeting of school principals and superintendents, guidance counselors, librarians and subject teachers would seem to be appropriate places to present the study skills point of view.

A second need, if we are to push study skills programs into practice in more high schools, is for provision of better programs to prepare study skills specialists for work in the schools. Most programs in reading until recently, were likely to focus on preparing the reading specialist who planned to teach reading and/or study skills himself. People with such training often feel very hesitant about attempting to give leadership to a whole staff of subject teachers. There is a distinct need for consultants, trained in supervision, who consider their major job to be working with teachers rather than with pupils.

There is, as well, a need for more experimentation in the area of study skills. Such programs as The Project English Demonstration Center at Syracuse University, in which films are being produced for use in inservice training on teaching subject related skills, warrant careful attention and wide publicity. This year a very large study of beginning reading is being financed by the United States Office of Education. Perhaps some attempt should be made to seek a similar large-scale study on the study skills.

A third point of attack on the problem of study skills teaching by all content teachers might be made through textbook publishers if these publishers can be convinced of the need for certain types of study skills practice materials, specifically study skills exercises which both spring from and lead back to the texts in actual use in the classrooms. The Science Research Associates laboratories on graph and picture reading form an excellent springboard for launching a program. However, the teacher who wishes to assure transfer of these skills to the classroom texts in use is obliged to write exercises and guides

himself for use with students. If a publisher of a content text were to produce a guide for the teaching and use of study skills with the materials of their text, and supply such a handbook free with every set of texts purchased for a school, the guide would not only give real impetus to the teaching of study skills but would constitute an important selling point for the specific text.

SUMMARY

Although an increasing number of reports suggest that partial programs of study skills teaching are becoming fairly common, there is a tendency to give serious consideration to whole school programs of study skills in which all content teachers are involved. At least a few consultants have reported success with such programs.

It is suggested that improvement of programs in the future might involve: closer liaison with reading specialists, content teachers, and administrators; better preparation of consultants; the encouragement of large scale studies of study skills teaching; and suggestions to publishers of textbooks that they consider supplying, with their texts, materials for teaching study skills.

BIBLIOGRAPHY

1. ARTLEY, STERL. "Some Must Ahead in Teaching Reading," *National Elementary Principal*, XXXV (Sept. 1955).
2. BARBE, WALTER B. "A Reading Program That Did Not Work," *Journal of Developmental Reading*, I (Oct. 1957), 17–21.
3. BEACON, R., and GILLETT, L. "The Eugene Reading Program," *High School Journal*, XXXIX (Dec. 1955), 185–188.
4. BERKEY, SALLY. "Reading and Study Skills in a High School District," *The Reading Teacher*, XVI (Nov. 1962), 102–103.
5. CLARK, ROBERT W. "Improvement in the Language Arts: A Progress Report," *The Reading Teacher*, XIV (Jan. 1961), 181–187.
6. DURRELL, DONALD D. "Challenge and Experiment in Teaching Reading," *Challenge*

and Experiment in Reading, IRA Conference Proceedings, Vol. VII. New York: Scholastic Magazines, 1962.

7. EARLY, MARGARET J. "About Successful Reading Programs," *The English Journal*, XLVI (Oct. 1957), 395–405.

8. ———. "The Meaning of Reading Instruction in Secondary Schools," *Journal of Reading*, VIII (Oct. 1964), 29.

9. GRISSOM, LOREN V. "Characteristics of Successful Reading Programs," *The English Journal*, L (Oct. 1961), 461–464, 474.

10. GUSTAFSON, MYRTLE. "A Practical Plan for Helping Retarded Readers in Secondary Schools," *California Journal of Secondary Education*, 30 (April 1955), 196–199.

11. HEAVEY, REGINA. "Teaching the Gifted to Teach Themselves," *The English Journal*, L (Jan. 1961), 39–43.

12. HERBER, HAROLD. "Teaching Secondary Students to Read History," *Reading Instruction in Secondary Schools*, Perspectives in Reading No. 2, Newark, Delaware: International Reading Association, 1964.

13. KARLIN, ROBERT. *Teaching Reading in High School*. Indianapolis: Bobbs-Merrill, 1964.

14. KUHL, FRED W. "How I Teach Outlining," *The Clearing House*, XXXV (May 1961), 547–550.

15. LEAMNSON, G. F. "Indianapolis Produces Better Readers," *School Executive*, 74 (Dec. 1954), 64–67.

16. LETSON, CHARLES. "Organizing an In-Service Program for Effective Reading Instruction in the Junior High School," *Improvement of Reading Instruction Through Classroom Practice*, IRA Conference Proceedings IX. Newark, Delaware: International Reading Association, 1964.

17. NILES, OLIVE S. "How Much Does A Content Teacher Need to Know About the Teaching of Reading?" *Improvement of Reading Through Classroom Practice*. IRA Conference Proceedings IX. Newark, Delaware: International Reading Association, 1964.

18. OLCOTT, WILLIAM. "An Outline for the Teaching of Local Government," *The Social Studies*, LI (Jan. 1960), 15.

19. OWEN, EVELYN. "What Is Going On In Your School?" *The Math Teacher*, XLV (Oct. 1952).

20. PERRY, WILLIAM O. "A Report to the Faculty," *Harvard Educational Review*, XXIX (Summer 1959), 193–200.

21. RAST, CARLISLE L. "The Beginning Research Paper," *The English Journal*, L (Oct. 1961).

22. SEVERSON, EILEEN. "A Reading Program for High School Students," *The Reading Teacher*, XVI (Nov. 1962), 103–106.

23. SHEPHERD, DAVID L. "Helping Secondary School Teachers Gain Competence In Teaching Reading," *Journal of Developmental Reading*, I (Winter 1958), 33–38.

24. STRANG, RUTH, MCCULLOUGH, CONSTANCE, and TRAXLER, ARTHUR E. *The Improvement of Reading*, Third Edition, New York: McGraw-Hill, 1961.

8

Reading for Appreciation

A PATTERN FOR TEACHING LITERATURE
Jerome Carlin

Each September before regular school days begin in our city, the typical department head greets several new members of a large English department and spends most of two days with them in informal seminars. Much of the time is devoted to methods of teaching literature.

Some day things may be different. Perhaps the chairman will usher his colleagues into a classroom for a brief, time-saving demonstration. "Let us suppose that you have reached Act Three of *Hamlet*. Instruct your students to open their textbooks to the proper page. Then in this file find the IBM card punched for *Hamlet, Act Three*. Insert it in this slot, and push this switch. Now watch." At these words the movie screen will descend before the front board. A panel in the rear wall will rise, disclosing an impressive array of hardware. One of the machines, a projector, will be activated. Moving fingers of metal will select a reel from the storage racks, slipping it without a fumble onto the spindle of the projector and allowing the automatic

Reprinted from the *English Journal*, LV (March 1966), 291–297, with permission of the author and National Council of Teachers of English.

threading device to take over. As the reel begins to spin, a master teacher will appear on screen. Looking up from his copy of *Hamlet*, he will nod pleasantly, and in his mellow voice the loudspeaker will say, "Now we are ready to deal with Act Three. . . ." Switching off the equipment after a few minutes, the chairman will comment, "So much for the teaching of literature. Now let's turn to other matters."

Or maybe that's not how it will be. Perhaps the department head will merely take the new teachers into a king-sized classroom with a lecturer's platform up front. "When you come to class here," he'll explain, "you will serve as an assistant while one of our department's master teachers lectures to the 175 students. We have four assistants on hand to keep order. Naturally we hope and expect that over the years each assistant will learn by study and by example the skills necessary to become a master teacher. . . ."

But, for the present, here are some suggestions on teaching literature that a department head might offer new teachers before they begin in September. This is just one of many possible patterns.

I

Although you will have only a limited choice of books to teach, you will still have to make some decisions on what to teach in them.

In many collections of shorter works the editors include materials ranging from simple to difficult and from adolescent-and-lowbrow to adult-and-highbrow. Start with the easy-to-read selections, those most likely to appeal to *your* students. If I were teaching a collection of short stories to a normal class, I'd begin with the one or two stories most certain to be easy, fascinating, and meaningful. Later on, I would get to the more difficult selections, those with a heavy vocabulary, subtleties of style and thought, and a depth to their philosophy.

For the literature which the class is to read in common the requirement that it be meaningful is not an idle one. The best of textbook editors sometimes fail us by including in their collections material that is heavyweight in interest but lightweight in intellectual substance. Be the textbook editor's editor. You need not teach everything in the book, and you might as well sift the material and choose the best for your purposes. (Even a novel or other longer work is sometimes taught successfully with a little judicious skipping.)

II

You will have to decide how long home-reading assignments are to be.

The more your students read, the more they will develop in reading skill. Research long ago established that extensive reading is effective. But you don't have to cite experimental evidence, and you can easily get the message across. "Play ball if you want to become a good ball player. Get out on the field, and get into the game. You can't develop skill without plenty of practice. That's true of reading, too."

Some fortunate teachers have students who can be entrusted with very indefinite or long-range assignments for home reading and who come to class each day ready for reading-in-depth discussions—but the teachers who capture such youngsters are probably the same people who win the trips to Paris in supermarket contests. If the aim is reading-in-depth and discussion-in-depth, you may do well to assign several chapters, stories, or essays for reading tonight and discussion in class tomorrow—or within a day or two.

Though healthy adolescents traditionally groan at any overnight reading task not limited enough to be completed on the homeward-bound bus, they can reasonably be expected to bear up under the rigors of a daily 40-minute assignment. In that time ninth-year students should be able to read 10,000 words, or about 25 pages of fiction when the page-length is the not uncommon one of 400 words; upper-year students can read 40 pages of the same kind.

Of course, the reading rate appropriate for encounters with such stout fellows as Stevenson's Jim Hawkins or Esther Forbes' Johnny Tremain won't do for "The Hollow Men" of T. S. Eliot. Forty pages of poetry or of philosophical essays would be too much even for a bright senior's overnight assignment. Since your students must adjust their reading rates to the nature of reading matter, you must adjust your assignments accordingly.

One difficulty in making maximum reading assignments is that a single short work—essay, short story, biographical sketch—may consist of only a few pages. Leafing through the text, then, can you find two or more related selections? That 12-page story about Albert Schweitzer and the ten-page one on Jane Addams will, together, offer more reading matter and more substance for class study. Make the two selections the reading assignment for one night and next day teach a lesson comparing these two persons who strove to serve the social good.

This program for reading-in-common and study-in-depth represents less than half of the English course. On some days when the class is working on other aspects of the language arts, homework assignments will be brief or non-existent. Those are the evenings when Joe will be pursuing his individual reading program and enjoying that book he chose on his own. Although his book won't be the subject of class study-in-depth, it ought to be the basis of a report—not a summary—serving perhaps to advertise the book to others. Early in September some teachers assign a book report for a date in October; then in October they schedule a report for November; and so on. How to make these assignments and reports interesting and challenging has been discussed often in this journal.[1]

III

You will have to make certain that the class really reads what you assign.

Like the happy battle of the sexes, the psychological warfare between teachers and pupils is conducted in a state of constant alertness to the opposition's moves. While your boys and girls are copying down your assignment, they fully intend to read those three chapters tonight. Yet the many temptations intervening between intention and fulfillment can bring quite a number to school next day, unprepared. In the ensuing lesson your thought-provoking sallies are met by a baffling silence and your clearest questions elicit confused responses. Your accusing "Have you read this story?" leads only to false swearing and starts your young charges off to a life of hypocrisy and income tax evasion. At the end of such a lesson, never send to know for whom the bell tolls. It tolls for thee.

[1] My own suggestions appear in "Your Next Book Report . . ." *English Journal*, January 1961.

Your selection of material and your approach in presenting it should tempt your youngsters to read. Sometimes, though, their choice may lie between ice cream and strawberry shortcake, the interesting short story you have assigned and the fascinating program Channel 2 is offering.

To keep each of your students faithful, nothing will be so effective as a brief quiz at the beginning of each literature lesson. Four or five simple short-answer questions can do the job. Read them aloud to the class with a brief pause for the writing of each answer. This is the place for the factual, for details of plot, for recall of the obvious—not for the thought-provoking questions which belong in an analytical discussion. "Question 1: To how many girls was Arrowsmith engaged at one time? . . . Please answer in the fewest words that you can—one word, if possible. . . . Quickly now. . . . Question 2. . . ." After collection of papers you can elicit the answers briskly, and a good student—not the same one each day, for fear of corruption—can do the marking on his own.

If you teach several classes of the same grade, however, keen tacticians in your later sections will obtain information from agents in earlier ones. The countermeasure: prepare several quizzes; or, if your lesson-planning time is too limited, give a quiz in only one or two classes each day, following a random order to maintain a surprise element.

The longer and more analytical test given at the end of your unit will be another check on whether students have done the reading. To depend solely on that, though, is like asking young Susie to put her room in order this afternoon because Cousin Jane will be her guest two weeks from today.

IV

You will have to set your own goal in each approach to a literary work.

It is not uncommon for a lesson plan to begin with an undefined aim such as this: "To study the poem, 'The Cowboy's Lament.'" Seemingly more developed is the aim: "To enable the student to understand and appreciate the poem, 'The Cowboy's Lament.'" But, partner, a man oughtn't to ride the range without any surer direction than that.

What is the student to understand and appreciate? Unless that essence has been crystallized in the teacher's thinking, the impact of his lesson is likely to be sharply reduced. The goals are clear in this example: *To study the poem "Ozymandias" for its ironic revelation of an arrogant, materialistic ruler's empty claim to immortality; to examine and appreciate Shelley's use of imagery and language in creating a myth out of a scene of ancient ruin.* As teacher-artist you may not choose to set up those particular aims for teaching Shelley's poem. Other major elements of the content or the technique may validly be central to your lesson. If you have been spending a number of weeks on a poetry unit, you might consider, for instance, that the time has come to deal more explicitly with forms and you might elect to teach the Shelley work with emphasis on its being an example of sonnet form.

Advisedly, however, the larger number of literature lesson plans should avoid making form the first consideration. Since the average person throughout his lifetime is going to be a reader, not a writer, of literary works, he should be enabled to come to grips with what a writer has to say about life and about human beings. How the author says it—structure, style, technique—will be the second consideration, but still an important one. The *art* of literature, like other arts, delights and moves the reader and—to borrow Whitman's words—invites his soul.

What you see in a work and choose as your teaching purpose will not always duplicate your colleague's aims for the same material. The peg for your lesson on a section of *Return of the Native* may be its revelation of the forces of circumstance against which the characters must struggle—and against which all of us, at times, must contend. Your colleague next door may hang his hat on a different peg; for the same chapters he may elect to examine the characters' motivation in choosing their mates. A third teacher may use the same pages to investigate the author's artistic methods: how he mixes his colors and draws his brush strokes in portraying his characters.

Had you the time, you could undoubtedly deal with all three of those aspects. Yet you cannot justifiably give class time to the study in depth of *all* the facets of a major work—or of many a minor one. Who among us could not find more than enough in *Hamlet* for an entire term's study? But we have a world enough of literary riches and so little time for our students to acquire them.

In planning, you might say to yourself, "In this literary selection what is *the* major substance, or *a* major substance, worth analyzing with my students?" Try to find in the work the author's center of concentration: a problem, a conflict, an insight into personality, a belief or an attitude held by a character or by the author himself. You won't go wrong by making this illumination of life through literature the primary aim of most of your lessons.

A snare to avoid is the distortion of the author's work by seizing upon some trivial element, some side issue, some remote implication. You may run your head into this noose if you dash along overenthusiastically on a thematic approach. True, a tidy unity can be given to the works taught during a month, two months, or the whole term, by tying them all to a theme. Yet having started with *Man against His Environment* as a theme for a literature unit, one may be reduced to teaching Poe's "Bells" as support for anti-noise legislation.

In setting your goals, you will have to rely on your own sensitivity and creativity. A department colleague or the textbook editor will often offer a helpful hint, but his personality and skills can never be entirely identical with yours. One man's magic bullet can be another man's silent spring.

V

The solid fuel to launch your lesson is motivation.

Beginning his lesson on Frost's poem about a farm chore, "Mending Wall," the master teacher draws two houses on the board and says to his suburban class: "Suppose that the back of your house faced the rear of another house, with a grassy area between the two. The families in both houses have children who play in the backyards, where they have nearly battered down the old fence on the boundary line between the two properties. The two fathers have had an estimate of $150 for the repair of this fence, and they wonder whether a better alternative wouldn't be to tear it down and to let the children from both families play in the entire unobstructed area. If you were a member of one of the families, would you favor tearing down the fence or having it repaired?"

After five minutes of discussion the class is ready to lift off. "Robert Frost has said something on a similar topic, the repair of a wall between two farms. Let's see how the circumstances and the ideas in his poem are like or unlike those in our discussion."

Another illustration of motivation is this approach to classroom discussion following an assignment to read the short story, "Load." The story deals with a young delinquent and with his parents who deeply feel their responsibility for him and for his difficulties. One lesson on this story began with brief monologues composed by the teacher and read aloud from typewritten copies by three students. The teacher made this introduction to the reading of the monologues: "Class, if you were able to get inside each character's head, you might find him thinking in the way that you are about to hear. This material is not in the story. I wrote it myself. Listen to determine what each character's attitudes are."

GIRL, *reading the mother's monologue:* Benny is only a boy. He don't mean no harm, but he just don't think what is right that he should do. I told his father, "Benny is getting in bad company." But his father don't do nothing. All he says is, "What should I do, Mama? Give him a licking?" A father should know better how to bring up a son.

BOY, *reading the father's monologue:* Ja, I gave Benny lickings when he was small—and when he got bigger, I spoke to him many, many times. I couldn't do nothing with him. Maybe I did wrong in helping the police catch him. Maybe I did wrong in how I bring him up. I guess I was a bad father.

BOY, *reading Benny's monologue:* I know I'm guilty. I killed the man, all right. But I didn't mean to do it. It was a stickup, but we didn't mean to kill anybody. . . . Besides, I'm only 18. I never had a chance. My parents never did the right thing for me. Ma loved me, but she didn't know the score—and Pa never had any feeling for me. He only hit me every time I did anything wrong—until I got too big for him to push around.

TEACHER: Let's take up the question of where these three people seem to place the blame for Benny's going wrong, and let's find the evidence in the story to confirm or deny that such ideas really were in each character's head. After that we'll analyze the story to see whether we agree with the characters in placing the blame.

Not every kind of motivation will take the form of raising a question about human relationships, and not every approach need be elaborate and dramatic. The hard-pressed planner may have too little time to create monologues with which to spark his lesson. One or two simple, straightforward questions will often be enough to establish a starting-point in the students' own experiences, attitudes, or thinking—a starting-point from which to move on in the company of the author. Here are some illustrations:

"You have heard people say, 'Things are not what they were in the good old days.' To what extent do you agree?" (*Discussion*) "Now let's look at what the author of this essay believes."

"Next week is Brotherhood Week. What is its significance to you?" . . . "Let's find out what this poet calls true brotherhood."

"Some writers have the knack of making you laugh. For instance, you have seen television stories whose scripts were written by authors specializing in humor. What are some ways by which television comedies get you to laugh?" . . . "Turning to the short story that you've read, let's examine what its humorous features are—and what techniques the author has used to create humor."

"Of all the things you eat, what tastes best to you?" . . . "What sounds do you enjoy most?" . . . "One author has made poetry out of what we've been talking about: preferences for certain things tasted, smelled, seen, touched, heard. You may or may not like his preferences or his poem—but let's find out."

Motivation is more than a frill, more than a means of getting attention. Having established a definite aim for your lesson, you seek to motivate your students' thinking from the outset. To motivate ideally is not merely to interest students in a literary work, but to swing them into position so that they can line up their sights on the target.

A note of caution is that time-devouring motivation may force you into a race with the clock during the subsequent study-in-depth of the literary work itself. What is the right time to spend on a motivating activity—three minutes, five minutes, eight minutes? If you hesitate to rely on your own intuition, you would probably be safe in apportioning no more than a fifth of the class period. At the cut-off point the enthusiasm of hand-waving, would-be contributors can be channeled into reacting toward the author's work.

VI

You will have to develop your lesson by creating a series of key questions or activities following the direction indicated by your aim and initiated by your attempt at motivation. So much is compressed, however, into even a relatively brief literary selection that a lesson pattern can readily branch out in all too many directions.

A lesson for seniors on the first five chapters of the Third Book of *The Return of the Native* may serve as illustration. This segment of the novel includes the following: a flashback to Clym Yeobright's boyhood and youth, and to his leaving the heath for a business career in London and Paris; conversations between Clym and some villagers, and between Clym and his mother, discussing his reasons for leaving Paris and returning to Egdon Heath; Mrs. Yeobright's conviction that her son is lowering himself by deserting the Parisian diamond establishment to become a "poor man's school-master"; a report that a beautiful neighbor, Eustacia Vye, has been stabbed in the arm with a knitting needle and accused by another woman of bewitching her children; Clym's first meeting with Eustacia in which he speaks of his love of his fellowmen and of the heath—and she, of her dislike for both; Mrs. Yeobright's antagonism toward Eustacia and her insistence that Clym has no insight into the girl's personality and her unsuitability as a wife for him; three months later, a rendezvous between Clym and Eustacia in which she speaks of her longing for Paris—and he, of his determination to remain on the heath; a violent argument over Eustacia and a break between Clym and his mother; Eustacia's agreeing to marry Clym with the assurance that they will move away from the heath to the livelier Budmouth.

The relationship of mother and son, superstitions about witchcraft, choice of vocation, service to society vs. materialism, customs of courtship—these and more could be discussed in relation to that part of the novel. Only thoughtful selection and willful inhibition can result in a development which will have unity and, consequently, impact.

Such a developmental pattern would grow out of this aim in one teacher's lesson: *to study Hardy's portrayal of the mismating of Clym and Eustacia through their failure to recognize their unsuitability for one another.* At the beginning of the lesson after the class had read the assigned part of the novel at home, the teacher's method of motivation was to mention the theory that "opposites attract one another" and to raise these questions: "To what extent is that true?" "To what extent is marrying one's opposite a wise thing to do?"

In his development the teacher proposed taking a close look at Clym and Eustacia in the light of the previous discussion. The rest of the lesson was based on these questions in his plan:

1. What does Mrs. Yeobright think of Eustacia and Clym as a match? (Have pupils answer after oral reading of passages on pp. 194–5, 204–6, Scribner's edition.)
2. What does Clym want in life? (Passages, 176–8)
3. What is Eustacia's attitude toward life? (Passages, 187–9, 198–202)
4. To what extent would you say that Clym and Eustacia are either opposite or alike in what they want from life?
5. Hardy, as we have said in previous lessons, makes a practice of forecasting the fate of his characters. Which sentences in these chapters hint at what the future will be for Clym and Eustacia?
6. Summary: To what extent are they a good match in marriage?
7. Application: Suppose that you knew a person like Clym in real life. What sort of wife would you consider ideal for him? What sort of husband would be ideal for Eustacia?

Getting the class to respond to the printed page is an additional asset of this lesson plan. Your average or above-average students need to sharpen their reading skills, in drawing inferences, anticipating outcomes, sensing the author's purpose, and the like. You won't give them a reading-skills text such as you would use to instruct the pupils in a remedial class. When you lead your students to answer questions by interpreting the pages of a novel open before them, you have the chance to develop their insights into reading skills—and you teach reading while you teach literature.

Finally, of this pattern for the teaching of literature can it be said that it is the right way? That chairman mentioned earlier might say to his new teachers, "The art of teaching would be much easier and much less satisfying if there were only one possible pattern. Trying other ways is part of the fun of English teaching. The first full schedule of classes will be on Wednesday. That's when the fun begins."

DEVELOPMENT OF TASTE IN LITERATURE IN THE SENIOR HIGH SCHOOL
Angela M. Broening

Reading literature as revelation, relaxation, and renewal is a rewarding habit that is accepted as a major goal of the senior high school English program (6).* Other media are competing with books for the individual's time (50). The range of nonliterary and literary materials being published necessitates that the senior high school develop taste if the student is to choose wisely (1, 6, 13, 27, 38).

To develop good taste, one must taste good books. There is a relationship between the development of literary taste and

a. the availability of a range of literature appropriate to the reader's emotional and intellectual maturity (18, 28, 38, 48)
b. teacher and librarian guidance through which the individual reader can develop criteria for choosing the right book for his purpose and mood (2, 7, 13, 18, 30, 41, 48)
c. direct teaching of interpretive reading skills (6, 10, 28)
d. satisfaction in enjoying literature as an aesthetic experience (6, 10, 18, 21, 26, 51, 52)
e. motivation for reading literature as a source of revelation, relaxation, and renewal (1, 6, 9, 11, 13, 18, 21, 28, 46).

Reprinted from the *English Journal*, LII (April 1963), 273–287, with permission of the author and National Council of Teachers of English.

[*Numbers in parentheses refer to Bibliography at the end of this article.]

There is evidence that taste has been developed among some high school students (6, 21, 48) and that taste is lacking among some high school graduates (27, 30, 51, 52). Heilman (31) claims that interest can be induced and ought to be induced and that for most youngsters the contact with what they need to be interested in will generate a workable medium of interest.

FACTORS AFFECTING TASTE

Factors affecting the development of literary appreciation include verbal intelligence, age, attitude, home background, teacher enthusiasm and literary background, methods of instruction, difficulty of meaning and reader interest in the available materials, and interpretive reading skills. Appreciation and taste require an understanding of what the selection means, involvement with the literary material, a sensitivity to the emotions engendered in the selection, an identification with the situation, response to (some say recognition of) those elements that indicate quality of expression, and the acceptance of only a high standard of writing.

The shift from listening to reading (18) may account for a temporary downgrading of taste from childhood to adolescence. As self-conscious appreciation is developed through guided reading and discussion, the reader discovers that recognition of the rightness of a word, a phrase, a metaphor, or a symbol brings richer delight than unconscious enjoyment of the total effect. At the highest stage of literary appreciation, the reader responds with delight, knows why, chooses discriminatingly, and relies on his own judgment. His reading has range and power and, in this sense, is an extension of the creative process which produced the work of literature (*18*).

Reading and Viewing—To get a similar reward from reading, as from the screens the individual watches, he must work harder for it. Reading is a highly developed skill, and the amount of reading done correlates highly with the amount of education secured by the individual. Though age, occupation, economic status, and education all influence the quantity and quality of reading, education is the greatest factor (*1*).

The effort required by the reader, involving his skill and his time, contributes heavily to the degree of availability (*14*).

Verbal Intelligence—Burton's (*9*) study of the relationship of literary appreciation to certain measurable factors reveals that verbal intelligence and silent reading ability are important factors; nonverbal intelligence has a negligible relationship. There is an important factor in appreciation of literature separate from intelligence and reading skill. There is some basis for believing that important aspects of literary appreciation can be taught even to students on lower levels of intelligence and reading skill.

Conditions Affecting Appreciation—Smith (*49*) analyzed the factors involved in learning to appreciate literature. From her thorough review of reports of experiments and of successful methods of teaching appreciation, Mrs. Smith prepared a list of factors and conditions. She submitted the list to 217 teachers and students of English, asking that they rate each of the 68 items in respect to its relative importance in acquiring the ability to appreciate literature.

Seven of the conditions she presented were rated as most important and were ranked in this order:

1. the mental set or attitude of the learner
2. clear idea of the goal or objective to be attained by the learner
3. the character of the learner's environment
4. the physical condition of the learner
5. a knowledge on the part of the learner of the things to be done in developing appreciation
6. a knowledge on the part of the learner of the difficulties to be overcome in acquiring ability to appreciate
7. statements about the material to be appreciated.

Teaching-Learning Situation—In the opinion of the teachers and students of English questioned, the teaching-learning situation must encourage the learner:

1. to read good literature
2. to respond to proper stimulation through appropriate material and its initial presentation
3. to find literature which appeals to his interests and level of experience
4. to have a receptive attitude to reading and to the kind of activity required for appreciative absorption of a literary work
5. to be pleased by the selections read and to dwell upon the satisfaction or pleasure aroused by the reading and contemplation of the selection read
6. to cultivate the power of imagery and to invent new modes of reaction in response to the thoughts expressed by the authors of the selections read
7. to comprehend what is being read and to relate to his own experiences the thoughts and feelings expressed in the selections read
8. to have mastered the mechanics of reading in order to comprehend the author's meaning.

Unnecessary Accomplishments — Mrs. Smith (*49*) also reported that, in the opinion of the persons she questioned, in order to appreciate literature the learner does NOT need:

1. a knowledge of the technicalities of literary craftsmanship
2. the acquisition of the specific meanings of unfamiliar or unusual words
3. a sense of rhythm (*31%* of the teachers thought this *was* of special importance in literary appreciation)
4. experience in literary production
5. recognition of merit (*33%* thought this important).

Principles of Aesthetic Appreciation—Mrs. Smith drew up these principles from her investigation:

1. literary art too distant in its appeal to the reader will not arouse an appreciative response
2. appreciation by "the common run of men" is essentially different in kind and quality from that of a highly sensitive or cultured person
3. appreciation of a literary selection implies grasping the work as a whole
4. the ability to appreciate literature is not inherited; it is developed through experience and training
5. consideration of the elements in a situation that should call forth an appreciative response one at a time destroys some of their aesthetic value.

Maturity in Taste—Gray (27) investigated trends in personal reading through interviews and tests and found three factors vital in the development of the mature reader:

1. cultural influence of the home
2. rewarding contacts with good literature
3. carefully planned instruction in literature.

Gray's analysis revealed that low competence in reading seriously limits the amount of reading in which adults engage. He rated maturity by interest in reading, the nature of material read, the purpose for reading, recognition and construing of meaning, and thoughtful reactions to and use of ideas acquired.

Conditions for Effective Learning—The above findings concerning the factors influencing the development of taste in literature are supported by Tyler's (*53*) analysis of the conditions for effective learning. Tyler found that learning is effective when the learner is motivated, discovers his previous ways of learning unsatisfactory, is provided with adequate and appropriate materials, has time enough to carry on the desired behavior, feels satisfaction in what is learned, has sequential practice, is encouraged to set his sights higher, and is helped to get some means of judging his own performance.

Skills and Varied Materials and Methods —Gunn (*28*) found that appreciation, satisfaction, or delight in books presupposes a grasp of reading skills and is dependent upon the teacher's use of varied reading methods and materials appropriate to the wide range of student abilities and levels of taste.

Refinement of Taste—Early (*18*) notes that "Refinement of delight requires something more than undirected and unselective reading. If the reader is to emerge from the state of reading-as-daydreaming, he needs guidance, both direct and informal, from his friends who read and talk about their reactions, from librarians, teachers, authors, and critics."

MATERIALS AFFECTING TASTE

Research on the factors affecting taste gives high priority to the availability of appropriate literary materials.

Carlsen (*11*) suggests that literary merit and content should be considered by the teacher in selecting books and in developing the literature program.

Literary Merit—Carlsen says literary merit

may be determined by asking these four questions about a piece of literature:

1. how well does the selection communicate human experience
2. how true are the assumptions made about human nature
3. how important is the experience being communicated
4. what is the quality of the language used?

Content—Carlsen believes that content should be concerned with life as it is lived in many parts of the world, in times other than the students' own, at different economic levels, and by people earning their living in different ways.

Growth in Appreciation—In evaluating a student's growth, Carlsen recommends that the teacher look at the student's cumulative reading record with these questions in mind: Has the student grown in terms of the literary merit of the materials he has selected for reading? Has he picked a variety of literary forms to read? Has the student had experiences with many kinds of people living many kinds of lives?

Simple Materials—Henry (*32*) affirms that comprehension is necessary before appreciation can take place and recommends the use of simple but artistic literary forms through which youth may experience the whole gamut of basic humanity.

Adolescent Problems—Burton (*8*) suggests novels which deal with adolescent problems similar to actual problems of today's adolescents and comments that these books can "help the student to develop a clearer outlook on the ordinary vexations that cloud his days."

Student Preferences—Davis (*15*) made a study to determine what poetry to present to students in Grades 9–12. She approached the problem by selecting 700 poems from various sources and, with the assistance of a committee of 10 English teachers and 2 principals, reduced the list to 100. Twenty other teachers, 5 from each year of secondary English, assisted in discovering which of these poems the students in Grades 9, 10, 11, and 12 liked best.

In general, these teachers followed the procedure demonstrated by Davis in these steps:

1. create a setting for the poem
2. distribute to each student a mimeographed copy of the poem
3. read aloud the poem as a whole, being careful to pronounce and enunciate each word distinctly
4. clear away any difficulties
5. assist students to see touches of beauty and to get the feel of the music of the poem
6. encourage students to associate the poem with their personal experience
7. reread the poem, recalling its pictures
8. ask for the theme of the poem
9. ascertain by a show of hands the number who liked the poem
10. distribute paper, asking each student to express his reaction to the poem in a sentence or two.

No specific information is reported on how the cooperating teachers carried out the "demonstrated method." Davis stated that no definite method of teaching was prescribed in order to allow for teacher initiative. She did, however, ask that they not teach rhetorical forms, figures of speech, rules of prosody, technical grammar, or articulation exercises.

The 53 poems which were liked by 50 percent of the pupils in any grade were "entitled to a place in the anthology," Davis concluded.

Friedman (*23*) tested college freshmen for reading range, understanding of literary techniques, and comprehension of works of literature. He concluded that even if the same literary works were taught in all high schools this would not constitute an accurate description of the *active* literary culture of the high school senior. An incidental finding of Friedman's study was that movies are not so effective as live theatre in helping students to understand a particular piece of literature.

Variety of Materials—Elledge (*19*) recommends that a wide variety of books be made available to teachers of college-bound students and that teachers themselves read more.

Williams (*55*) asserts that "spoon feeding on a rich diet of classics alone will not establish taste" and presents an effective unit for teaching judgment of prose.

METHODS AFFECTING TASTE

Research in respect to the factors affecting the development of literary taste emphasizes the importance of the methods of teaching literature and of developing comprehension and interpretive reading skills.

Reading Skills—The Curriculum Commission of the National Council of Teachers of English (*6*) states that through literature, the English teacher makes a unique contribution to the development of reading interests and tastes and that a broad program of individual reading guidance is essential in any well-rounded curriculum in literature.

Specific training in how to read fiction appreciatively includes learning (a) to evaluate the truth or falsity of the author's presentation of human experience, (b) to discover the central theme of the work and to relate the details to the theme, and (c) to follow different types of structure in the plot.

The truth or falsity of the author's presentation of human experience is determined through knowing how to read for cause and effect in events, for development or metamorphosis of character, for precision and originality in character portrayal, for authenticity of dialogue, and for validity of description.

Reading poetry appreciatively means re-

sponding to the emotional impact of rhythm, rhyme, word color, imaginative thought, and universality of human experience.

Reading drama involves identifying with characters through inferring from clues such as what the character does and says and what others say about him; noting stage directions; and, in older plays, acquiring and applying literary background of key allusions.

Skills in following various patterns of organization and in critical evaluation of the biographer's use of details to create a dominant impression contribute to the appreciative reading of biography.

Guided experience in reading essays and articles alerts the reader to inductive and deductive patterns of organization and to the use of enumeration, explanation, chronology of events, analysis, exhortation, and persuasion.

Skills and Understandings—Burton (*10*) analyzed the skills and understandings basic to high school students' growth in literary appreciation, indeed, in maturity. These are:

1. awareness of the complexity of human character
2. a firm understanding of the reality in human experience and the ability to detect oversimplification and falsity in the assumptions underlying it
3. concern with a set of values by which to regulate life.

"Though the teacher cannot guarantee emotional involvement," Burton says, "he can bring students together with selections in which the peaks of human emotion are reconstructed in the currency of adolescence."

Through machine practice for two (twenty-five minutes) periods each week, Jones (*36*) improved his students' rate and comprehension of reading. Each student selected the book of his choice and kept a record of his improvement. Because of their greater competence, the students read more and better books.

Assuming that the reading program is made up of great books, i.e., books that offer the reader a liberating experience, Bennett (4) discusses how the teacher uses private sessions with his pupils to work directly on reading speed and on mastering skills of interpretation which enhance pleasure and improve taste in reading.

Guided Reading—Handlan (30) presents evidence that *guided* rather than *free* reading more surely contributes to literary appreciation. She found that:

1. older boys and girls will not necessarily bridge the gap between adolescent and adult interests without guidance. "Freedom of opinion" about books is NOT the final step toward development of appreciation. Freedom from insincerity is the first step
2. many high school students, left to their own devices, do not grow in appreciation of the best in books, but rather remain at a relatively low level of taste
3. students given a choice of widely different books almost invariably chose the simplest books and over a 5–6 month period, none of these students gained in appreciation
4. students exposed to a collection of very good and very mediocre books will not necessarily respond to the former
5. young people are to be led subtly and carefully to books which will satisfy some of their psychological needs and at the same time provide successively more artistic fare
6. the teacher should help the student develop critical powers
7. a guided reading program is desirable in order to help students to find pleasure and profit in worthwhile books and to experience the joy and excitement that come from growth in appreciation.

Smith (48) reports that in several studies related to freshman reading in college, immature habits and interests were found. It was agreed in this body of research that habits were rather permanently formed in the secondary school.

Most of the investigators, Smith states, show extreme concern about the literary merit of the independent reading of young people. The quality of the reading is disappointing, even though the content itself is harmless.

Implications derived from research on reading interests are that high school students need:

1. a variety of good readable books and periodicals
2. acceptance by the teacher of the student on his own reading level and his present reading interests
3. guidance in reading
4. a literature program reflecting student preferences in literature as well as teacher preferences.

Caskey (13) states that it is through guided discussion and shared experiences with books that maximum development in personal growth and social understanding may occur. Whether looked at from the goalpost of reading better quality books or of achieving a higher level of personal and sound social development, it appears important for teachers to:

1. study the situations in which young people now find themselves
2. make every effort to provide suitable materials
3. give specific guidance to pupils in their reactions to situations presented in their reading.

Smiley (47) advocates a free-reading program under which students select their own books and read during class periods, with the teacher serving as adviser and consultant.

Friedrich (24), though he offers no experimental evidence on teaching poetry, suggests that the study of a poem should mean that teacher and students explore it together, relating knowledge of versification to the specific purpose or effect of a particular poem under discussion and that literary analysis should always conclude with a new synthesis.

Pierstoff (41) discusses how to challenge students through questions, etc., to understand better what they are reading and to encourage students to question each other and to exchange ideas.

Pease's (40) questions to a fan point up for teachers, as well as students, what active reading involves. "Did you scratch through the surface of the story to discover what the author had to say?" Pease asks. "Did you find the theme of each book, and then ask yourself how it applied to you? If you didn't do this, you failed to read those books."

Critical Thinking—Bens (5) states that the successful presentation of literature will result in critical thinking by the student. When interest has been aroused in one piece of literature, it is relatively easy to introduce related materials. Literature takes on new meaning and greater insight is developed if the student is asked to imagine how one author might have developed another's basic idea.

Through discussion of people's search for economic security, Dowling (17) led his students to perceptive reading and enlightened discussion. In reading his students' annotations to the same selection, he was aware of individual differences in emotional maturity and critical reading and focused his follow-up guidance in the light of this knowledge.

Convinced that pupils benefit most from their literary experiences if there is a discussion as a result of critical thinking, Raymond (43) began on the first day of school with a conversation about summer reading, movies, television, and radio programs which his students had enjoyed. He also laid plans with them for "covering the world" by having each student read a different book. Days were set aside for class discussion and guides were set up to encourage critical thinking about the content of books and emotional enjoyment of their literary elements. During this unit, Raymond reports, some 30 books were read by different individuals and shared with the class.

Individual Conferences—Burrowes (7) believes that a teacher must lead his students to the best the teacher knows in literature and must cultivate the student's judgment and discernment. To this end, he uses regular interviews with an individual student to discover his likes and dislikes in his past reading and to develop with him a short book list as a guide to personal reading. If the student does not like the books suggested, Burrowes says, the teacher and student have a basis for further discussion.

Training in reviewing books is another means Burrowes uses to develop taste in literature. He clarifies for the student what makes a good book review, checking the analysis with reviews of his own mixed in with those of professional reviewers. Mastery of this framework in understanding literature, Burrowes finds, creates readiness in the students to probe more deeply into their own reading.

Having students record their readings on a cumulative record helps to make the student's accomplishments more specific and assists the teacher in seeing the direction of the student's reading.

Burrowes encourages informal reports on reading. A student is allowed to use books, notes, and other material while he is talking freely about the books he likes. That apathy which is based on a modern mixture of innocence, television, and youth, Burrowes believes, can be rooted out by a well-organized enthusiasm.

Discussion Groups—Babb (2) shows how a high school librarian discovered the recreational needs and interests of high school boys and girls and then stimulated their reading by individualizing her comments on books, by displaying regularly "ten new books," by having students prepare and deliver book talks to English classes, and by forming reading clubs which meet with the librarian to discuss a currently popular book. These discussions are tape recorded for use by other individual students or by class groups.

Watts (*54*) explains how discussion groups with secondary-school-age boys and girls provide opportunity for free, inquiring minds to meet together in small informal groups. Those who *want to read* will make use of the book list furnished *before* the meeting. Those who don't know whether they want to read or not may use the book list *after* the meeting. Watts hopes that from discussion groups of this sort, there may be developed a cultivated minority with high critical standards which will refuse to accept the mediocre and demand the best as its right in a democracy.

Oral Reading—Reilly (*44*) undertook an experimental study to discover whether or not a silent reading method or an oral method produces greater gain in the appreciation of poetry as measured by the Abbott-Trabue "Exercises in Judging Poetry" and the Logasa-Wright "Tests for the Appreciation of Literature." The one-group method of experimentation was used. The subjects of the first experiment were twenty-three girls of the eleventh grade; those of the second numbered twenty-eight. During this experiment the methods were rotated in order to discover if the time order in the presentation had any effect on the results. Every effort was made to keep all factors except the experimental factor as nearly constant as possible.

The data indicate that the differences between the average scores of the two methods are too small to justify the conclusion that either the Oral Method or the Silent Reading Method as used in this experiment is decidedly superior. The slight positive growth found for either method may have been due to chance.

Reilly recommends that neither method be used exclusively, but that a combination of the two will produce the best results and that the "Oral" be used first for rhythm and musical effect followed by the "Silent" for supplementary and free reading.

Bartine (*3*) states that the effectiveness of certain types of literature is increased by reading them aloud. Dramatic programs organized around a personality, holiday, etc., help students to become acquainted with literature and to read it with enjoyment.

Multiple Approach—Hook (*33*) suggests a multiple approach in teaching literature in order that students may understand literature as a key to life and as an influence on life and may enjoy the artistic elements which contribute to the literary merit of a selection.

Farmer (*20*) emphasizes the desirability of creating the right climate for good reading by attractive displays of books, reading periods free from distractions, tensions relaxed, frequent discussion and conference periods in which students may share their enthusiasms and exchange ideas. Use of visual and audio aids and involvement of the students themselves in planning and directing the reading program will strengthen appreciation.

Freeman (*22*) in discussing how to teach short stories states that best results are obtained when:

1. an introduction to the story is carefully made by the teacher during a class period
2. pupils are given definite guidance for out-of-class reading
3. use is made of a variety of ways of approaching fiction in class discussions
4. an opportunity is provided for every member of the class not only to form an opinion but also to express it and to justify it.

Pooley (*42*) discusses varied patterns of approach in the teaching of literature in respect to these aims: to inculcate literary values and to provide cultural background in traditional literature; to teach selected literature for general appreciation and enjoyment, leading to standards of taste and habits of reading; and to provide experiences in wide reading and to develop independent judgment and evaluation in literature.

Jensen (35) assumes that students will more readily acquire information on types of literature and the characteristics of good writing if they have some leeway in their reading and proves his point by his account of a unit in which his students read literature by authors of their own ancestral background and books dealing with their ancestral countries. Other reading focused on changes in biography through the years, types of novels, and best sellers of the ages. The unit on best sellers, Jensen asserts, led to awareness of what constitutes literary merit, as well as to thoughtful enjoyment of good books.

Reading and Other Communication Arts —Heightened literary appreciation was achieved by Horst (34) with a class of boys in a trade-training curriculum. He read aloud short stories and brief selections from biographical essays and novels. After reading Poe's "The Tell-Tale Heart," the group saw the movie version. Some of the boys also heard Peter Lorre play the story on radio and viewed the same story on television. Comparing the written words through which the reader creates his own imagery with an actor's creative interpretation of the same story on radio and television developed in the students an awareness of how each medium gets its effects.

There are implications for improving literary taste in Yetman's (57) study of developing appreciation of motion pictures. Through showing films and then discussing them, he was able to increase his students' knowledge of how directing, acting, photography, editing, art, and music contribute to the total effectiveness of a film. These discussions of movie versions of literature, Yetman said, also deepened his students' appreciation of good books.

Dixon (16) used audio-visual materials effectively with reading materials in a unit to develop students' understanding of contemporary public affairs through a knowledge of the relevant past.

An indirect approach to literary appreciation was made by Halperin (29). He asked his students to view two famous paintings on display in the classroom. The student was to select a center of focus in one painting at a time. By projecting himself imaginatively into the thoughts and feelings of any one figure or inanimate object shown in the picture, the student wrote for fifteen minutes. The writing took the form of a short story, a monologue, an account, and an anecdote. The best writings, in the opinion of the teacher, were shared with the class and used to discuss effective communication.

Test-determined Teaching—Ziegler (58) proved that test-determined teaching in recognition of the central theme and of sense-appealing words and expressions did improve tenth-grade girls' appreciation of literary merit. The evidence was collected in four tenth-grade classes—one experimental and one control group in 10B and one experimental and one control group in 10A.

The experimental evidence of these results shows that test-determined teaching as defined in this study has produced greater growth in the two elements of literary appreciation as measured by the Ziegler Appreciation Test (ability to recognize theme and ability to select the version of a literary selection which has the greatest "verbal magic") than that made in the same period of time by pupils who were not exposed to the experimental factor and some of whom sustained a loss in appreciation.

The diagnostic practice material developed by the experimenter produced gains in both factors of appreciation—of theme and choice of a literary version.

Although the use of practice material leads to an increase of ability to choose a literary version in preference to a nonliterary one, this ability does not uniformly occur with the ability to give correct reasons for choice.

Writing Imitations—Woesner (*56*) experimented to find out whether appreciation of poetry can be increased by the writing of imitations of selected poems. The study was conducted with two classes composed of juniors and seniors in high school. The experimental group, which did the work in imitation, was compared with a control group, which followed conventional methods of study.

The results indicate that imitation used as a means of teaching appreciation of poetry is not superior to the conventional methods.

From the findings in this experiment Woesner drew these conclusions:

1. since both groups made gains regardless of the method, it seems reasonable to conclude that appreciation of poetry can be cultivated
2. imitation as a means of increasing the appreciation of poetry should be used with discrimination
3. that the conventional methods ordinarily used will produce moderately good results
4. apparently certain pupils do not respond to training in appreciation.

During the investigation, the experimenter was confronted with a number of problems. Some that would make interesting studies are the following:

1. would imitation as a means of developing appreciation in poetry be more effective if used for a longer period of time
2. what abilities can imitation develop
3. to what extent does a test measuring the component elements of appreciation test the integrated response
4. how much does teacher personality account for the lack of response on the part of pupils who seem impervious to training in appreciation?

Ineffective Teaching—Neville (*39*) claims the way poetry is taught in many schools has killed poetry as a lifelong source of enjoyment. Neville demonstrates how oral reading of poetry can enhance enjoyment, admiration, and sympathy—the study of appreciation.

Gannett (*25*), from observations based on casual contacts with a limited group of graduate students in journalism, concluded that most students enjoyed reading as children, but an impressive proportion recall that they virtually stopped reading (or at least stopped enjoying reading) in high school and not all recovered from that feeling later.

TESTS OF TASTE

Attitudes toward books are generally regarded as one valid test of the taste and values of an age. With this in view, Ford (*21*) made a study of what more than 200 senior high school students, representing 154 schools in the 49 states, said about books. Each student was represented by an impromptu essay on "What Is a Good Book?" selected at random from more than 500 compositions submitted in competition for the 1959 NCTE Achievement Awards in English, sponsored by the National Council of Teachers of English. Interestingly enough, the group was almost equally divided as to sex and ranged in age from sixteen to eighteen years.

From the analysis of what these students, who had developed literary taste, expected in a book they would call "good," Ford found these 6 qualities appearing repeatedly:

1. intellectual stimulation (⅔ of the students considered this the most important contribution of a good book)
2. moral and social insight
3. emotional satisfaction
4. opportunity for escape from overbearing tensions
5. embodiment of beauty, sensual and spiritual

6. fitting style commensurate with satisfying content.

Each student, of course, expressed in his own words how he felt and supported his statements with reference to specific pieces of literature or to his personal experiences which a specific piece of literature had illuminated for him.

There have been several attempts to develop objective tests of aspects of literary appreciation. Refuting the argument that ability to appreciate cannot be measured because the critics themselves disagree, Carroll (12) states that they have no difficulty in making gross discriminations.

It is only gross discrimination, Carroll asserts, that we may expect from most high school students. They do not possess the capacity to compare analytically one great work with another. They should be able, however, to differentiate between the creditable and the shoddy.

It is Carroll's opinion that appreciation includes (a) sensitivity to style, i.e., how words go together—rhythmical quality of prose, (b) ability to appreciate intellectually the deeper meanings of the work, and (c) emotional capacity to respond to fine shades of feeling in great works.

The basic assumption behind Carroll's Prose Appreciation Test is that fuller and deeper appreciation, e.g., of a whole book, correlates highly with ability to judge short selections of varying merits. Essentially the test measures the ability of the pupil to differentiate the less good from the bad and the less good from the good.

Burton (9) developed a short story comparison test which requires a critical comparison of two stories and a short story choice test which measures maturity of taste in the contemporary short story. Along with his two tests, Burton used Carroll's Prose Appreciation Test, the California Test of Mental Maturity, and the Iowa Silent Reading

Test to determine the factors affecting literary taste.

In an experiment in testing appreciation, Ruhlen (45) used the Abbott and Trabue Test of Ability to Judge Poetry with two eleventh-grade English classes, designated as Section A and Section B. Judgment, as measured by this test, involves recognition of emotional tone, of the imaginative quality of thought, and of rhythm. Each of these three elements is "spoiled" in one version of the poem at a time. The person taking the test selects the version he thinks best.

Following the administration of the test, Ruhlen read a poem twice to each class and then discussed with them these questions: What ideas did you get? What images or pictures were formed as you read? Did you like the poem? Why or why not?

Ruhlen reports that her students gave perceptive answers to these questions and that their scores on the second form of the test showed a significant improvement in their ability to judge poetry.

Then Ruhlen taught Section A another poem according to the method used with the first. To Section B he taught grammar. Both Section A and Section B were retested. Because Section A got higher scores on the test following the study of a second poem and because Section B got lower scores following the study of grammar, Ruhlen concluded that the changes in scores on the test were the result of the way the first poem was taught and the use of this method in the study of a second poem.

Loban (37) analyzed 14 measures of growth in literary appreciation:

1. "Plot Completion Test"—five endings are provided for the student to number in order of probability of occurrence as outcomes
2. "Guttman Technique" (reduces theme of investigation to an objective scale) can be used by building questions to

probe the student's reactions to any literature

3. "Grasp of Human Conduct" asks how the character would behave in a situation not present in the work studied

4. "Content Analysis" requests the student to write analytically about what impressed him (subsequent to the teacher's analysis of the work)

5. Adaptation of the Bogardus "Social Distance Scale"

6. Progressive Education Association (a) analyzed appreciation into seven aspects, (b) defined each aspect in terms of action and behavior, (c) prepared questions which would reveal the extent to which the students' behavior tended toward or away from literary appreciation

7. "Critical Mindedness in Reading Fiction" and "Judging the Effectiveness of Written Composition" used by the teacher to evaluate individual pupils in comparison with others in the class

8. "An Interpretation of Literature" through questions which discover the student's reaction to more definite aspects of literary appreciation

9. Evaluation of the student's cumulative reading record

10. Evaluation of maturity level, using Foster's study

11. I. A. Richards' technique providing student with poems from superior to inferior, but not so identified

12. Dora V. Smith's "Test of Contemporary Reading"

13. Mary C. Burch's "Tests of Comprehension of Literature"

14. Carroll's "Prose Appreciation Tests" measuring the ability to differentiate good from average and average from bad.

Pointing out the purposes and effectiveness of each of these measures, Loban concluded that "we cannot expect to measure literary abilities as objectively as other subjects like typing."

IMPLICATIONS OF RESEARCH

Literary taste *can* be developed and is influenced by home, school, and community stimulation to reading. Growth in literary taste is related to the emotional and intellectual status of the individual. There is a relationship between the development of literary taste and (a) direct teaching of interpretive reading skills, (b) the availability of a range of literature appropriate to the reader's emotional and intellectual maturity, (c) teacher and librarian guidance through which the individual reader can develop criteria for choosing the right book for his purpose and mood, (d) satisfaction in enjoying literature as an aesthetic experience, and (e) motivation for reading literature as a source of relaxation, revelation, and renewal.

NEEDED RESEARCH

In lieu of standardized tests, many investigators have had to prepare informal measures and to use empirical evidence in support of their claims for the effectiveness of a method or methods of developing appreciation.

Testing Devices—There is urgent need for sharper instruments for measuring the totality that is literary taste, as well as aspects of literary appreciation. New objective tests are required to diagnose the cause or causes of a student's failure to appreciate literature appropriate to his level of intellectual and emotional maturity. Objectively determined criteria should be developed to evaluate what is read, how it is read, and what lasting impressions (provocative ideas, insights into human motivation, enjoyment of verbal imagery, and appreciation of the power of language) remain with the reader.

Teaching Methods—Empirically controlled studies may well analyze how non-verbal experiences can be used along with verbal experiences in developing the literary taste of:

1. culturally deprived youth now in senior high school
2. incompetent readers
3. academically gifted students.

Studies are also needed to compare the relative effectiveness of:

1. a single-teacher approach to developing the taste of one classroom of students
2. a team-teacher approach to the development of the literary taste of the larger group of students reached by the team
3. a school-wide (interdepartmental) approach to developing literary taste.

BIBLIOGRAPHY

Abstracts of unpublished master's theses and doctoral dissertations were supplied by Dr. Nila B. Smith, Chairman of NCRE Committee on Research in Development of Taste in Literature; several additional references were supplied by David Kopel.

1. ASHEIM, LESTER. "What Do Adults Read?" in National Society for the Study of Education, *Adult Reading*, The Fifty-fifth Yearbook, Part II. Chicago: University of Chicago Press, 1956, pp. 5–28.
2. BABB, LLOYD W. "Guidance in Recreational Reading," *English Journal*, XLI (April 1952), 201–204.
3. BARTINE, NORA GEESLIN. "Literary Program," *English Journal*, XLI (October 1952), 420–423.
4. BENNETT, PAUL L. "A Reading and Writing Program for the Talented Student," *English Journal*, XLIV (September 1955), 336–337.
5. BENS, JOHN H. "Teaching Literature in the World of Mickey Spillane," *English Journal*, XLV (February 1956), 79–81.
6. BROENING, ANGELA M. *The English Language Arts in the Secondary School*, NCTE Curriculum Series, III. New York: Appleton-Century-Crofts, Inc., 1956, Ch. 5, 6. See also index under "Literature."
7. BURROWES, JOHN H. "Outside Reading," *English Journal*, XLI (April 1952), 205–206.
8. BURTON, DWIGHT L. "Books to Meet Students' Personal Needs," *English Journal*, XXXVI (November 1947), 469–473.
9. ———. "The Relationship of Literary Appreciation to Certain Measurable Factors," *Journal of Educational Psychology*, 43 (November 1952), 436–439.
10. ———. "Teaching Literature to Our Youth Today," *English Journal*, XLIV (May 1955), 274–279.
11. CARLSEN, GEORGE ROBERT. "The Dimensions of Literature," *English Journal*, XLI (April 1952), 179–186.
12. CARROLL, HERBERT A. "A Method of Measuring Prose Appreciation," *English Journal*, XXII (March 1933), 184–189.
13. CASKEY, HELEN C. "Promoting Personal and Social Growth in Grades Ten through Fourteen," *Developing Permanent Interest in Reading* (compiled and edited by HELEN M. ROBINSON), Supplementary Educational Monographs Number 84—December 1956. Chicago: University of Chicago Press, pp. 85–89.
14. CLIFT, DAVID W. "Introduction" in National Society for the Study of Education, *Adult Reading*, The Fifty-fifth Yearbook, Part II. Chicago: University of Chicago Press, 1956, p. 3.
15. DAVIS, SADA E. *Poetry Interests of Secondary School Students*, master's thesis. New Brunswick: Rutgers University.
16. DIXON, DOROTHY. "Vitalizing English Through Audio-Visual Aids," *English Journal*, XLII (September 1953), 303–307.
17. DOWLING, KATHLEEN B. "Reading To Grow," *English Journal*, XL (September 1951), 392.
18. EARLY, MARGARET J. "Stages of Growth in Literary Appreciation," *English Journal*, XLIX (March 1960), 161–167.
19. ELLEDGE, SCOTT. "What Literature Do College-Bound Students Read?" *English Journal*, XLVII (March 1958), 147–150.
20. FARMER, PAUL. "Let Literature Work Its Magic," *English Journal*, XL (April 1951), 212–218.
21. FORD, NICK AARON. "What High School Students Say About Good Books," *English Journal*, L (November 1961), 539–540, 545.
22. FREEMAN, BERNICE. "Teaching Short Stories," *English Journal*, XLIV (May 1955), 284–287.

23. FRIEDMAN, ALBERT B. "The Literary Experience of High School Seniors," *English Journal*, XLIV (December 1955), 521–554.

24. FRIEDRICH, GERHARD. "A Teaching Approach to Poetry," *English Journal*, XLIX (February 1960), 75–81.

25. GANNETT, LEWIS. "Why Do They 'Hate' the Classics?" *Child Study*, XXXIV (Spring 1957), 16–17.

26. GILL, NAOMI. "Depth Reading," *English Journal*, XLIII (September 1954), 297–303 ff.

27. GRAY, WILLIAM S. "The Challenge Faced in Promoting Desirable Reading Interests," *Education*, 79 (May 1959), 551–556.

28. GUNN, M. AGNELLA. "What Does Research in Reading Tell the Teacher of English in the Secondary School?" *English Journal*, XLVI (October 1957), 391, 393–395.

29. HALPERIN, IRVING. "Combining Art Appreciation and Imaginative Writing," *English Journal*, XL (September 1951), 396–397.

30. HANDLAN, BERTHA. "The Fallacy of Free Reading As an Approach to Appreciation," *English Journal*, XXXV (April 1946), 182–188.

31. HEILMAN, ROBERT B. "Literature and Growing Up," *English Journal*, XLV (September 1956), 303–313.

32. HENRY, GEORGE E. "Toward Vitalizing the Teaching of Literature," *English Journal*, XLIV (October 1955), 383–389.

33. HOOK, JULIUS N. "The Multiple Approach in Teaching Literature," *English Journal*, XXXVII (April 1948), 188–192.

34. HORST, J. M. "Will They Read? (An Experiment)," *English Journal*, XLII (May 1953), 260–262.

35. JENSEN, LISBETH S. "Fostering Interest in Reading," *English Journal*, XLII (October 1953), 367–370.

36. JONES, NELLIE F. "A 'Motorized' Reading Project," *English Journal*, XL (June 1951), 314, 316.

37. LOBAN, WALTER. "Evaluating Growth in the Study of Literature," *English Journal*, XXXVII (June 1948), 277–283.

38. McCULLOUGH, CONSTANCE M. "Developing Tastes and Appreciation," *English Journal*, XLVI (November 1957), 482–483.

39. NEVILLE, MARK A. "Who Killed Poetry?" *English Journal*, XLVII (March 1958), 133–138.

40. PEASE, HOWARD. "How to Read Fiction," *English Journal*, XLI (April 1952), 186–194.

41. PIERSTOFF, MARION B. "Promoting Critical Thought in the Study of Character Conduct in Literature," *English Journal*, XLVII (October 1958), 422–424.

42. POOLEY, ROBERT C. "Varied Patterns of Approach in the Teaching of Literature," *English Journal*, XXVIII (May 1939), 342–353.

43. RAYMOND, RUTH. "Free Reading in World Literature," *English Journal*, XLIV (March 1955), 160–162.

44. REILLY, SISTER MARY ROSALITA. *The Oral versus the Silent Reading Method in Developing an Appreciation of Lyric Poetry*, master's thesis. Baltimore: Johns Hopkins University.

45. RUHLEN, HELEN V. "Experiment in Testing Appreciation," *English Journal*, XV (March 1926), 202–209.

46. RUSSELL, DAVID H. "Some Research on Impact of Reading," *English Journal*, XLVII (October 1958), 398–413.

47. SMILEY, JEROME. "Children's Interests and a Free-Reading Program," *English Journal*, XLI (November 1952), 479.

48. SMITH, HELEN K. "A Survey of Current Reading Interests in Grades Ten through Fourteen," in *Developing Permanent Interest in Reading*, Supplementary Educational Monographs, No. 84, December 1956. Chicago: University of Chicago Press, 65–68.

49. SMITH, JOHNNIE RUTLAND. "An Analytical Study of the Factors Involved in Learning to Appreciate Literature," *Bulletin of the School of Education*, Indiana University, X (1933), 47–69.

50. SMITH, NILA B. "Development of Taste in Literature, I," *Elementary English*, XXXIX (November 1962), 702–709, ff.

51. SQUIRE, JAMES R. "Literacy and Literature," *English Journal*, XLIX (March 1960), 159–160.

52. ———. *The Responses of Adolescents to Literature*, doctoral dissertation. Berkeley: University of California, 1956.

53. TYLER, RALPH W. "Conditions for Effective Learning" in CROW, LESTER D. and CROW, ALICE. *Readings in Human Learning*. New York: McKay Company, Inc., 1963, p. 67.

54. WATTS, DORIS RYDER. "What's Happening to Reading?" *English Journal*, XLIII (March 1954), 127–129.

55. WILLIAMS, ELIZABETH. "Teaching Judgment of Prose Fiction," *English Journal*, XLVII (November 1958), 495–499.

56. WOESNER, INEZ ESTELLE. *A Study of the Effectiveness of Imitation as a Means of Developing Appreciation in Poetry*, master's thesis. Seattle: University of Washington, 1936.

57. YETMAN, C. DUNCAN. "Motion-Picture Appreciation and School Composition," *English Journal*, XLI (November 1952), 488–491.

58. ZIEGLER, CAROLINE LOUISE. *The Value of Test Determined Teaching in Two Elements of Literary Appreciation*, master's thesis. Baltimore: Johns Hopkins, 1931.

GATEWAY ENGLISH: TEACHING ENGLISH TO DISADVANTAGED STUDENTS
Marjorie B. Smiley

Richard, the twelve-year-old protagonist of Warren Miller's *The Cool World*, has this to say about reading:

> Once you know how to read it aint hard to learn almos any thing. Doc say, "Readin. To read Richard. That the beginnin of evry thing. You see if I not right Richard. Man." He say. "When you can read an write why you can do any thing. Do any thing. Be any thing."

This is how Richard sees it. English teachers also see reading as critical in the education of children like Richard, as the *gateway* to work or to further education. Reading is generally central in current programs for educationally disadvantaged students, but there are other important elements too. In such programs, we should consider a number of things.

First, we need to look searchingly at what we hope Richard will find on the other side of the *gateway* we would escort him through. To pose the question more explicitly: what are, what should be the aims of reading in-

Reprinted from the *English Journal*, LIV (April 1965), 265–274, with permission of the author and National Council of Teachers of English.

struction for children who are variously described as *underprivileged, deprived,* or *disadvantaged?*

English teachers cannot avoid looking at reading in the larger context of the English language arts. Even though reading may be critical, probably central, in programs designed for educationally disadvantaged children, is it sufficient? What is the place of instruction in spoken English, in listening, in written composition for these children? Is "Doc," whom Richard quotes in the brief passage above, right in his opinion that reading is "the beginning"?

And what of Richard? Who is he? Those who talk about and who design educational programs for underprivileged children often cite Richard or someone like him as a prototype. Is he?

Warren Miller's Richard is a Negro boy who has grown up in Harlem. He has lived in derelict tenements. He has never known a "real" father; his mother is harassed and thus easily angered by her son; his grandmother worries about him but is unable to help him. His well-meaning and conscientious junior high school teacher is just not with it. Alienated from the adults and institutions that might give meaning to his life, Richard searches for manhood and a sense of belonging in the pursuit of a gun and in affiliation with a gang. He tells his story as a part of putting his life in order, with the help of "Doc," from the shelter of a home for delinquent boys.

As a Negro male adolescent, Richard stands for what is the largest group among the millions of children disadvantaged by grinding poverty, by the absence of supportive adults —especially men—to whom he may look as models, and by an educational system that has frustrated and shamed him. As English teachers and as human beings we must remember Richard when we plan English programs for disadvantaged children. But to take Richard as typical of even the most grossly underprivileged adolescents is as mistaken as to forget him. Even among adolescents from the lowest income levels, from families as broken, from equally dismal segregated slums, only a very small proportion become delinquent or require intensive psychological help in residential centers. The more we learn about the difficulties which many poor families experience, the more we must be convinced of the extraordinary resilience and inner strength of those often too simply categorized as underprivileged.

As we must learn to differentiate the degrees of psychological damage, of academic and most particularly of reading retardation, while keeping in mind the latent resources of intellect and character among our most deprived students, so we must remember that most of the children even in our nation's Harlems live in intact families, in clean, and orderly homes, supported by fathers—and often mothers—who are regularly employed. These children grow up with the same kind of attention, the same parental interest in school achievement, that we sometimes seem to think are to be found only in white upper-middle-class homes. The half-truths that have coalesced into a mythology which says that all underprivileged children come from broken—and bookless—homes does incalculable damage: it lowers teachers' expectations, attenuates the curriculum, and alienates children and their parents. Low income parents, white or Negro, differ from middle class parents in their tendency to buy books and toys and to take their children to the Fair only to the extent that surpluses remaining after rent and necessities are accounted for, and may be limited, of course, to the extent that the parents' own education shapes their choices of books and experiences for their children.

MEANING OF DISADVANTAGED

Nevertheless, these children, like Richard, are disadvantaged educationally. They are disadvantaged, because segregated housing and schools cannot possibly prepare children for a full life in our democracy. They are disadvantaged, because we have not yet succeeded in making the promise of equal opportunity for freedom and for skilled and professional employment a reality, and because every limit on the promise of the future makes the tasks of learning—and of teaching—more difficult. They are disadvantaged further, because most slum schools are themselves underprivileged, though it seems obvious that if we are to look to the schools as the agent which will "allow no man's failure to prevent the success of his son," these schools, their teachers, and their programs must have unusual excellence.

But there are others besides Richard and his somewhat more fortunate Negro classmates who attend slum schools and require our special consideration. Each of our major cities now harbors a Negro ghetto; but in almost every one of these cities there is at least one other ghetto, smaller perhaps, but almost equally deteriorated and only slightly less rigidly segregated. Here most of the other educationally disadvantaged children in our nation live and attend school; today these are chiefly children of Southern rural white families and those from Spanish-speaking Puerto Rican or Mexican families. But even these, who together with Negro children constitute most of the one in three school-age, inner-city children considered educationally disadvantaged, do not complete this roster. There are, in addition, the children of migrant workers, of families marooned in the isolated "pockets of poverty" in the Appalachians, and the often forgotten children on American Indian reservations.

These are the children who are least well served by the watered-down English curriculum too often found in the substandard schools they attend. What can they be helped to achieve in English? What kind of program can contribute most to their special needs? How can English be made truly a gateway to a brighter future for them?

As to the gross effects of educational disadvantage, there are certain symptoms common to all the groups we have mentioned. Each group contributes a disproportionate number to any list of educational and social casualties: to the increasing number of adolescents and young adults who have left school at the earliest legal age, to those whose inadequacies in reading and in oral and written communication and whose poor habits of application bar them from further education, from employment, from the armed services. Since these consequences are overt and socially costly, it is not surprising that educational programs for underprivileged youth have usually been vocationally oriented. With respect to English these programs have aimed at achieving what is called "functional literacy." Their focus has been primarily remedial or corrective: major attention has been given to reading, infrequent attention has been given to speech, and almost no attention at all to anything that English teachers would consider composition.

SCOPE OF PROGRAM

Despite our almost avid interest in specific materials and methods for teaching reading to disadvantaged students, must we settle for English programs thus limited in aim and in scope? I hope we will not do this: not because I think preparation for work and a view of English as a "tool" for work—or for study in other fields—is demeaning; not because I think that reading can be taught without intensive and systematic practice of its component skills. My reservations are in part methodological. Preparation for work or for academic advancement is a motivating force only for students who already have vocational and academic aspirations. And it is with respect to these aspirations that the children we wish to reach are deprived. As the so far largely unsuccessful efforts to recruit and train young men rejected by the armed services, or older men suffering from situational unemployment, demonstrate, vocational or vocationally related skills are learned only when the job—or the chance to vote—is realistically and immediately attainable.

This kind of relationship between learning English and its direct practical consequences is not characteristic of most junior and senior high school programs. Within the setting of work study programs, of course, the relation of reading level to vocational advancement may serve to motivate students to improve their reading skills and to master the writing skills essential to secure and perform jobs. Even within the limits of vocationally oriented English programs, moreover, much more attention should be given to the teaching of spoken English than is customary. Sales and office occupations are among the few in which opportunities continue to increase in the face of growing automation. Underprivileged youth must not be passed over for employment or promotion because they speak a substandard dialect. If they are to be prepared for these opportunities in which communication skills are important, they will have to be helped to acquire a level of spoken English that is socially acceptable.

In any event, the aims and scope of programs in English for disadvantaged junior and senior high school students should rest on more than practical and methodological considerations. We are accustomed to justify the teaching of English on quite other grounds. We point to language and literature as uniquely suited to help us give order and meaning to the world we live in. We call upon literature to hold up to each new generation the models which we think will help them shape themselves. In language and literature we believe can be found those persistent strands and those variations that will serve to bind together different generations and different cultural groups. Is this view of the aims and scope of teaching English irrelevant or expendable in the education of underprivileged youth? Is it not rather especially important for those children whose difficulties with life and with learning stem from their deep feelings of alienation? What could be more "useful" than to teach English so that these alienated children may come nearer to possessing a world they now only inhabit?

The abandonment of these traditional aims in so many programs in English for disadvantaged students is almost surely on grounds of expediency rather than conviction. The reasons given, if they are made explicit, are that these students are not interested in the literature of the traditional English curriculum or that their reading level is too low to enable them to read this literature with understanding. But perhaps we should be seeking other explanations. Has the literature selected for elementary and secondary English had the effect of excluding and further alienating many of the children in our classrooms because the characters, problems, and settings are so different from their own experiences and because we have not sufficiently realized what could be done through creative teaching to bridge this gap? Unfortunately,

by the time educationally disadvantaged students reach junior or senior high school they have probably developed a strong resistance to reading and their reading skills are not adequate to the demands of much of the literature in the standard English curriculum. Nevertheless, these difficulties can be met by adaptations in materials and methods; they need not and should not limit our larger aims. It is the demands of our increasingly specialized technology that require us to help all youth to achieve the reading level that will qualify them for skilled employment. The essential values of our culture as of any culture can be orally transmitted; certainly they are not bound to a specific reading level or to particular literary works.

PROMISING PRACTICES

To agree that our central aims in teaching English should be the same for all youth does not negate the need for modifications in the methods and materials we employ. Fortunately, mounting social pressure to do something about educating underprivileged children and youth has given rise to a variety of special programs, many of them supported by the federal grants and by private foundation funds. To date the majority of the programs in English have been for elementary and pre-school children, but there are enough programs in the secondary school to provide us with a variety of constructive suggestions. Without any attempt at surveying all of these programs, I shall try to cite a number of approaches that seem to me particularly promising, examples chosen from the English programs in Cleveland, Detroit, Houston, Syracuse, New York and other systems that have given particular attention to secondary school programs for disadvantaged youth. This composite then of many ideas suggests that a good English program for disadvantaged junior and senior high school students would be something like this.

Every English program for disadvantaged junior and senior high school students should begin by introducing specific activities in listening and speaking. A fundamental reorientation of our usual teaching strategy is necessary if listening and speaking are to find their proper place in English classrooms. Instead of our customary practice of telling students, especially these students, what we expect them to learn, we must rather involve them actively in verbal inquiry. We must find ways to have our students ask the questions, make the comparisons, formulate the conclusions. The recent studies of the language of the classroom by B. Othanel Smith, Arno Bellack, and others should be of special interest to teachers of English and to teachers of disadvantaged students particularly. The development of students' skill in questioning, in inquiring which is central to curriculum experimentation based on early studies of Piaget and the more recent proposals and studies of Bruner and others are usually considered to be appropriate only to intellectually gifted and verbally advanced students. They are equally relevant, equally adaptable to methods of teaching educationally disadvantaged children and youth. We must, of course, take account of the findings of research into social class differences in language patterns that indicate that lower class children and adults make limited use of complex sentences and subordination and that these limitations restrict the ability to express complex relationships. But these findings should not lead us to the conclusion that students whose language is thus limited cannot learn to perceive and thus to formulate complex relationships. But these intellectual and language skills, which junior and senior high school teachers find already quite well developed among more privileged children, must be explicitly taught to disadvantaged children. They must be taught by making the English classroom—and hopefully every classroom—a forum for students' oral in-

quiry. They must be taught also by specific exposition and by oral practice.

Some of the difficulties underprivileged children face in learning to read is in the early stages of associating what is heard with the printed symbols for these sounds. One of the most interesting findings of recent research has been the evidence of a high degree of correlation between hearing (auding, as it is called in these studies) and reading. This is a difficulty that many such children have not yet overcome by Grade 7 or 8. These children are unlikely to have had parents with time to read aloud to them in their early years. We do not do nearly enough reading aloud to children in elementary or secondary schools. We do not make nearly enough use of the increasingly rich store of records of poetry, stories, speeches, and plays. And because as English teachers we often find it painful to listen to students who read haltingly, we give least opportunity to read aloud to those students who most need this practice. Most underprivileged children speak a substandard dialect. English teachers, unfortunately, have been taught to set quite rigid standards for spoken English. Children who have not learned these speech habits in their home environments are shamed into holding their tongues—at least in class activities. Classrooms in slum schools are typically either silent, or, more usually, frenetically noisy. It is very rare indeed to find a classroom in a slum school in which discussion is taking place. But patient teachers, alert to these children's interests, are able to involve them in discussion, in inquiry. And for children who have not yet learned to deal confidently with the printed word, oral discussion and inquiry is absolutely essential. If discussion is to take place, it is imperative that we learn to accept substandard speech; that we make the extra effort that may be required to understand. This is not to say that we have no obligation to help our students achieve socially acceptable speech patterns. But this aim and the activities necessary to realize it should not be allowed to invade and thus inhibit discussion about ideas or books.

An English program for disadvantaged students should provide systematic experiences in learning to listen with discrimination. There is at least one set of programmed materials using audio tapes already available which is designed to teach listening skills. Every English teacher can use spoken word records to give students experience in listening to increasingly longer and more complex units of oral literature.

SOCIALLY-ACCEPTABLE DIALECT

A comprehensive aural-oral program in English for disadvantaged students should include explicit pattern practice in a socially acceptable dialect. The objective of such an oral language program should, I am convinced, be concerned with the students' mastery of an approved regional colloquial speech. (Printed materials designed to provide practice in realistic spoken English situations are also beginning to be available.) Programs employing practice tapes modelled in part on the pattern practice materials developed to teach English as a second language are in experimental use at elementary, secondary, and college levels. English and speech teachers should seek the aid of linguists and dialectologists to develop programs of this kind appropriate to the requirements of specific school populations. Two cautions should be kept in mind in connection with the introduction of programs of this kind. First, it is extremely important that English and speech teachers who undertake to teach the disadvantaged student a second dialect learn to do so without censuring his native dialect. Teachers of foreign languages do not typically judge their students' native language; teachers of English and speech on the other hand are very likely to start from a correctional point of view. The student too often is taught that

his speech is "bad," and that another language, standard English in most cases, is "good." If, on the other hand, an approved dialect is taught as a "second language" teacher and learner together can escape embarrassing and hence inhibiting value judgments of native subcultural dialects.

Finally, the timing of efforts to teach disadvantaged students a second English dialect should be carefully considered. Ideally, it should be possible to develop a kind of bilingualism in two English dialects in young children. As experience and some experimentation indicate, young children may be able to learn two languages within the context of different language environments, where for example, one language is spoken at home and another at school. Some underprivileged children do by some means achieve fluency in the English of the school, even though they live in homes and neighborhoods where a socially unacceptable dialect is spoken. Those who have this mastery, however, are unlikely to be among the underprivileged students who are seriously retarded in English in the secondary school. High school students whose spoken English is restricted to a substandard dialect are usually performing below grade level in English, and probably in their other subjects as well. These students must be strongly motivated if they are to attempt a "new" English as teenagers. Successful programs in a second English dialect seem to be tied to and probably depend on students' perception of specific opportunities in employment or on their desire for further education. We would probably be wise, therefore, to place intensive speech pattern practice at these points in students' lives, that is, in the ninth or tenth or twelfth grade.

Perhaps, in the light of the overriding importance of helping underprivileged students master an approved dialect and improve their reading, the allocation of composition to a secondary place in programs for them is justified. Instruction in answering test questions, in letter writing, in precision in filling out forms is customarily included in English programs for these students. These bread-and-butter skills are important to the future of these students; English teachers need to accept the task of teaching these basic writing skills as worthwhile. But they can and should aim for more. Given opportunity for free oral expression of feelings and ideas in the English classroom, disadvantaged adolescents can be led to put these feelings and ideas on paper. Almost without exception, teachers who have given such students confidence to write about what they know have been agreeably surprised by what they have to say. Given wholehearted acceptance and genuine interest, these students, like all students, can begin to accept the always arduous task of learning to write more correctly. As their mastery of spoken English grows and as their exposure to reading increases, the writing of underprivileged students is likely to approximate that of their less disadvantaged classmates.

IMPORTANCE OF READING

But what about reading? It is reading that is popularly and professionally considered the major difficulty of disadvantaged students and thus the major responsibility of English teachers who would help these children qualify for a better future. Reading has been held to be the *gateway* to salvation, to the exercise of the franchise. At one period in our history it was the subject of legislation intended to keep the Negro in his place. Pre-Civil War laws prohibiting anyone to teach a slave to read—or to write—were not uncommon. The most recent extension of the National Defense Education Act includes provisions for preparing teacher specialists in reading as a category of teacher preparation distinctive from—though hopefully not divorced from—English. Thus, while we may disagree with "Doc" in *The Cool World*, in

thinking that speaking rather than reading is the best beginning for English programs for disadvantaged students, we cannot escape the conclusion that reading is central in such programs. Eunice Newton, in a recent article in *The Journal of Negro Education* puts it like this: "If the school cannot teach an educable child to read, there is really nothing else of importance it can teach him."

If we examine the various reading programs for disadvantaged youth that are currently offered in many junior and senior high schools, we find two basically different types, each designed to meet the needs of students with distinctive reading difficulties. One type of program, probably the most common, is that intended to teach beginning or elementary reading skills to students who have arrived at junior or even senior high school reading at first, second, or third grade, or even as "non-readers." These students are still at what Fries describes as the "transfer" stage of reading. Or using Lado's more detailed categories, these students have not yet mastered the four primary reading skills: pre-reading, or identifying the graphemes; association or "fitting" graphemes and language; the habit of reading what is spoken; and of reading aloud, or speaking what is written. These programs, typically called remedial or corrective, place major emphasis on teaching word attack skills and on vocabulary building. Through these programs, the secondary school undertakes an elementary school task. If they succeed in the initial reading task, learning to read, they have made a critical breakthrough for disadvantaged youth.

But learning to read is only a part of what must be accomplished. Young people who have made this giant and most difficult step are still not qualified either for further education or for employment in highly skilled or semi-professional levels, where employment opportunities are to be found. Certainly they are far from ready to reap the benefits of reading as a means of enlarging the self and giving order to experience. Once they have learned to read, students are at the point where they can capitalize on this achievement and begin to read to learn and to develop the skills required for those more advanced levels which Fries terms "productive" and "imaginative" stages. In Lado's more detailed breakdown the more advanced reading stages are described as follows: reading for different kinds of information; reading diversified materials and types; reading for speed and power. Most English teachers would probably agree that these reading skills are appropriate to secondary English programs. Unfortunately, very few English teachers have received explicit instruction in teaching these skills. The teaching of developmental reading is only rarely a systematic phase of junior and senior high school English. Few English courses go beyond vocabulary building and tests of the retention of specific facts. Yet it is only through intensive instruction in the full range of advanced reading skills that underprivileged students can achieve equality with their more privileged classmates. Only by mastering these skills can they qualify for any form of higher education and the kinds of employment open only to those with some education beyond high school. As secondary school English teachers we must not be satisfied to help disadvantaged students over the threshold of basic reading skills; we must turn our attention to the development of methods and materials which will enable these students to read with power.

ADAPTATIONS NOT THE ANSWER

To accept "reading with power" as an aim in teaching English to educationally disadvantaged students is to confront the question: *what* shall be read? The specially prepared reading materials prepared to teach such students elementary reading skills lack the depth, the richness and subtlety of litera-

ture. They are thus totally inadequate for teaching critical reading skills. Is *Julius Caesar* the only alternative? Some teachers of slow reading classes report that they can "get through it" in eight weeks. One must question the dramatic impact of such ordeals. Others who think or think they should think that *Julius Caesar* is part of a heritage which everyone must share compromise by using classic comics. Pressed on whether students who have read a comic book version have really read *Julius Caesar* and thus really shared the heritage, these teachers may shift their defense. Students feel better, they explain, if they think they are reading what other students are reading. Do we really believe fourteen-year-olds are thus deceived?

Adaptations of great books are sometimes defended on the ground that they provide a peg on which to hang discussion of power, loyalty, good and evil which should not be denied adolescents because they are poor readers. But cannot such discussions grow out of contemporary issues presented and discussed on television, even in tabloids? The viewers who watched, without protesting, the street corner murder of a young woman— are they not a more comprehensible and thus more powerful stimulus to a consideration of the evil of apathy than a fourth-grade rendering of Dante's *Inferno*? I think we must ask: whose feelings are wounded if standard works are not read in our classes. The disadvantaged students'? Or ours? Adaptations or cut editions of literary works should be used only when the adaptation retains the essential qualities of the original, or as with Lambs' *Tales*, has its own literary merit. And since adaptations are usually made of nineteenth-century novels and reluctant readers are more likely to be attracted to contemporary books, we should probably ask ourselves whether a modern original on the same theme would not be a wiser choice for these students.

Fortunately there are books mature enough to interest older adolescents which are within their reading range: e.g., *The Pearl* and *Lilies of the Field*. Other, more difficult books can be included in the English curriculum for slow readers by teachers who read substantial parts and select the dramatic highlights for students to read in the original. Finally, we need to exploit the rich mine of film, television, and recorded versions of novels and plays as a part of the literature program for disadvantaged students. Students who have seen and discussed the film of *Moby Dick* will be willing and able to read some excerpts from the original novel, e.g., the dramatic and ironic incident in which Queequeg rescues his tormentor.

Poetry is the literary form most likely to be omitted from the curriculum of slow and reluctant readers. Teachers who have made careful selections of poetry, however, report that it is enjoyed and understood by a wider range of readers than other literary forms. Traditional ballads and contemporary broadsides in particular can be enjoyed by junior and senior high school students reading at fourth and fifth grade. Especially when they are taught through the use of recordings by popular balladists, they enliven the English classroom and make the teaching of simple poetic elements part of the fun. (Incidentally, the use of ballads in contemporary social movements may lead some of these reluctant students to compose their own ballads without realizing that they are engaging in "creative writing.")

To argue that we include adult literature in its original form in English programs for educationally disadvantaged students, however, is not to conclude that other kinds of reading should be excluded. There is a constantly growing list of juvenile books which can serve as a bridge to adult literature for many adolescents. But until recently juvenile books have been singularly inappropriate for underprivileged minority group students in urban centers. Juveniles have presented a world so white, so orderly, so proper, so committed to happy endings in featureless settings as to provide few possibilities for disadvantaged adolescents to identify with. The exceptions, like *Hot Rod*, which portray a life more "on the wild side" serve to prove this point.

MINORITY GROUP HEROES

Gradually, however, juveniles with minority group protagonists and familiar settings have begun to appear. Some of these, like Louisa Shotwell's *Roosevelt Grady* and Dorothy Hall's *Hurricane* are good books, because, although each has a young Negro protagonist, they are not formula stories. We know that the children and adults in *Roosevelt Grady* are Negro migrant families only because the illustrations tell us so. The conflict between the young hero and a bully is within the experience of all children; the resolution is credible; the message is implied rather than expounded. Some of the juveniles with interracial casts of character, however, are as contrived as earlier middle class juveniles are. They are, nevertheless, popular with students who have never seen a book about someone like themselves in appearance.

If we seek books that will give students full rather than stereotyped images of individuals from minority groups, we will be sure to include biographies. They are important in any English curriculum, but especially important to those underprivileged students whose own life space has so few models with whom they can identify. And we can go beyond the biographies of athletes and entertainers, though these are popular and should not be ignored. Biographies of notable Negroes in all fields are available in adult and juvenile books, e.g., Charlemae Rollins' sound and readable collection of the stories of forty Negroes in *They Showed the Way*.

Unfortunately, there are relatively few biographies at a popular reading level which tell the stories of men and women from other minority groups in the United States.

In the senior high school the literature program for underprivileged students—and for all students—should include books which deal with personal and social issues directly and searchingly. Within this frame it is difficult to see how the curriculum today can fail to include books which confront the reader with the bitter and unresolved problems of racial injustice. We find *The Diary of Anne Frank* and *Hiroshima* on many English reading lists. How many include *The Fire Next Time*, the poignant and little known *A Good Man*, the almost legend-like *A Distant Drummer* by Kelley, Peter Abrahams' *Mine Boy* and *Tell Freedom* and Paton's *Cry, the Beloved Country*? Some of these are fairly difficult, but most can be read by interested adolescents reading at seventh or eighth grade. The magic of a critically important subject and of a well-known name are powerful motivators, even of reluctant readers.

The major contribution of a literature program for educationally disadvantaged students is to help them gain a sense of their own worth and their membership in the American community. It is for this reason that we need to search for books close to the lives of children who have been made to feel excluded from much of the life they see and read about. At the same time, these students also need to read books that tell of lives and times very different from their own. If books about lives like theirs can help them order and so control them, books about quite other ways of life may help them give shape to their dreams.

For many of these children, and their teachers, the most important gift of all is the dream of accomplishment. James Aggrey, a modern South African writer, shows us in this parable[1] the dream that must be learned.

Once upon a time, it seems, a man hunting in the forest caught a young eagle. He brought it home and put it among his chickens. The eagle grew in size, but contentedly shared the coop and chicken feed of his domesticated brothers.

One day a naturalist came through the forest and stopped by the forester's hut. "That bird is an eagle!" said the naturalist.

"It was," said its owner, "but I have trained it to be a chicken. It is no longer an eagle."

"No," said the naturalist, "it is an eagle still. It has the heart of an eagle. I will show you that it will fly up to the sky as eagles do."

The owner agreed to let the naturalist test his belief. They took the bird up to the roof of the hut and the naturalist said to it. "Fly! You are an eagle, stretch forth your wings and fly."

The eagle looked this way and that, and looking down, saw his brothers eating the grain on the ground. Down he jumped and joined the chickens picking at their grain.

"I told you so!" said the owner. "It is a chicken."

But the naturalist begged another chance. And once more he took the eagle to the rooftop and urged it to fly. But again the eagle jumped down to share the chicken feed in the yard.

The owner was glad to be vindicated, but he finally agreed to the naturalist's plea for just one more trial.

The next morning the naturalist rose before dawn and took the bird to the foot of a high mountain. The peaks were beginning to glitter in the rising sun. The naturalist picked up the bird and held it up facing the sun and said: "Eagle, you belong to the sky and not to the earth. Stretch forth your wings and fly!"

The bird looked around; it trembled, it looked up, and suddenly it stretched out its wings and with the scream of an eagle

[1] A paraphrase of a parable by James Aggrey in Peggy Rutherford, ed. *African Voices: An Anthology of Native African Writings* (New York: Vanguard Press, Inc., 1959).

mounted higher and higher until it disappeared in the clouds.

Reading alas, is not innate to man as flying is to eagles. But unless, like the naturalist, we are able to lift the sights of disadvantaged children to a brighter future than they now see, we are unlikely to teach them English— or anything else. Much, perhaps most of what must be done for these children must be done outside the English class and outside the school. But, in language, we do have a key to the doorway that must be opened, and in literature a universe of futures to explore.

9

Speed in Reading

OVERVIEW OF NATIONAL READING
CONFERENCE RESEARCH REVIEWS: RATE
AND COMPREHENSION, EYE MOVEMENTS,
USE OF MACHINES
Emery P. Bliesmer

The research reports read in preparation for, and cited in, the annual National Reading Conference (originally the Southwest Reading Conference) reviews have been utilized for the purpose of this paper; and this will be somewhat of an analysis or overview of trends in the indicated areas as reflected in the annual National Reading Conference (NCR) presentations. Some use has also been made of several other reviews which were rather thorough, competently done, and particularly pertinent to the areas involved. The writer has presented the NRC research reviews annually, with the exception of 1956, since he did the first one in 1952. The present overview of the research in the areas indicated is limited by the fact that the NRC reviews have been concerned mainly with college and non-college adult reading programs.

Reprinted from *Changing Concepts of Reading Instruction*, Proceedings of the International Reading Association Annual Convention, Vol. 6 (1961), 214–223, with permission of the author and International Reading Association.

RATE AND COMPREHENSION

The major concern for rate and comprehension involved in the various reports cited in the annual reviews has been the influence exerted upon these two skills by particular reading programs, procedures, or treatments. Specifically, the major concern has usually been the increase in rate and/or comprehension skill achieved as a result of some type of reading program. As has been indicated consistently in the reviews, results of the various programs have been determined in a variety of ways. Standardized reading tests have been among the evaluating instruments commonly used, although a number of unstandardized tests and other instruments have also been used frequently. Differences in test scores obtained at the beginning and at the end of programs have been the usual criteria of effectiveness. Methods of determining results have not always been clearly stated in the reports. Some results have been stated in terms of general or total reading test scores while others have been stated in terms of more specific scores (such as "rate," "comprehension," and "vocabulary"). The use of a type of "reading efficiency index" (which involves, essentially, multiplying a rate score, in terms of words per minute, and a comprehension score, in terms of "percent of comprehension") has also been noted on a number of occasions.

Studies cited in the 1952 (9),* or the first, annual review of research in college reading covered a five-year period, from 1948 through 1952. The number of studies cited as having a bearing on rate and comprehension was rather small. Somewhat higher gains in rate than in comprehension on the part of students in a University of Chicago laboratory course were reported (19); but substantial comprehension gains were reported to have been found generally to follow substantial rate gains. In reviews of succeeding years (10, 11, 12, 13, 14, 15, 16) the reports pertinent to specific programs and results obtained in such programs increased in number. Gains in rate were most often reported, with small or negligible comprehension gains usually accompanying rate gains (17, 18, 23, 26, 27, 29, 46, 56, 58, 69, 70, 72, 74, 106, 109). Reports of programs in which significant gains had been made in both rate and comprehension were also cited in several reviews (21, 35, 57, 71, 75, 78, 79). An exception was in the 1955 review (12), the fourth annual one, when approximately the same number of programs was reported to have effected significant gains in both rate and comprehension as was reported to have yielded significant increases in rate with negligible increases in comprehension. A drop in comprehension accompanying rate gains was reported on several occasions (61, 80, 105). A gain in comprehension but not in rate was indicated by one report (17).

Indications of factors influencing amount of gain in rate and/or comprehension were afforded by a single report, or by a few, in

[*Numbers in parentheses refer to Bibliography at the end of this article.]

each of several reviews. Charles (22) found greatest rate and comprehension gains, proportionately, in a University of Nebraska study improvement course made by students in the lowest quartile relative to ACE "L" scores. Burfield (19) found most gain made by readers with lowest rate scores and readers with highest comprehension scores. Kinne (49), in an analysis of gains made by various age groups, found younger groups responding better in speed and older groups responding better in comprehension. Cardwell (21) found no particular relationship between age and gain in rate; but indications of some relationship between age and comprehension gains were found. Ranson (68) found no significant differences between rate gains of students scoring high initially and those scoring low initially; but significant negative relationships were found between initial rate scores and comprehension gains. Kingston and George (48) found significant gains made during the junior year by both students who had participated in a reading improvement program as freshmen and those who had not. Significantly greater rate gains were made by the participating group, which was also the only group which made significant comprehension gains.

Indications or reminders that rate and comprehension "gains" were a function of the particular test or tests used at times were yielded in a number of reports. Traxler (100) found forty-nine types of reading ability covered in twenty-eight tests, with twenty-three being included in one test only. Cosper and Mills (27) noted a greater indication of percent of increase in speed when *Harvard Reading Tests* were used than when the *Diagnostic Reading Tests* were used, even though the former were considered more difficult. Jackson, however, reported that the *Harvard Reading Tests* yielded smaller rate gain indications than had been indicated with other tests involving more difficult material. Preston and Botel (65), finding a non-significant correlation when the *Iowa Silent Reading Tests* were given without time limits, concluded that rate and comprehension were relatively independent under any kind of timed conditions. Smith and Wood (*79*) found significant comprehension gains indicated by one test with negligible or non-significant scores indicated by another.

A number of reports of tests or testing procedures used in measuring rate and comprehension have been cited in a number of reviews, with an increase in numbers of such reports having been noted for recent years. Since this area may be treated in more detail in other papers, only citing of some of the pertinent references will be done here (*24, 31, 40, 43, 60, 67, 69*).

EYE MOVEMENTS

Many of the studies concerning machines or mechanical devices in reading programs have relevancy for the area of eye movements. However, a number of studies or reports were concerned more directly with eye movements as such. Several of Tinker's studies (*96, 97, 101*) of various factors influencing eye movements were treated in the fifth annual review presented in 1956 (*83*). Various typographical variations, type face variations, and vertical arrangements were found to influence eye movements significantly. Reading material arranged in a vertical manner was found to be slower than was reading of material arranged horizontally; but marked improvement of speed resulted from practice. Nahinsky (*62*) found a "square span" style (a second phrase appearing immediately below the first) yielding comprehension span scores significantly greater than those obtained with two other styles, conventional and spaced unit. Tillson (*94*) recorded eye movements with an "oculograph" at the beginning and at the end of a course which utilized reading films and pacers. Fewer fixations and regressions were found at the end of the program.

Two studies by Klare and his co-workers were cited in the 1957 review (*13*). In one study (*50*), "square span" presentation was found to slow readers at a first reading; but rapid improvement was found to be yielded through practice. In the second study (*51*), "easy" style, versus "hard" style, produced significantly greater words per fixation, words read per second, and recall scores. Tinker's study of the effect of various angular departures from horizontal alignment of printed lines (*98*) yielded indications that the departure should be as little as possible. In another study, Tinker (*99*) also found reading rate to be adversely affected by presentation of materials on a curved surface.

Several reports relevant to the study of eye movements were also noted in the 1958 review (*14*). Dingman (*28*) made a factorial analysis of data collected a number of years previously. He maintained that his data supported Tinker's 1946 position (*95*) that eye movements were unrelated to reading comprehension factors for normal subjects. Tinker's second extensive critical review of eye movement studies (*100*) was also cited in the 1958 review. Tinker called attention to the diminishing numbers of studies in recent years and the relatively few studies pertinent to relevant problems. He further pointed out that "some writers still adhere to the notion that training eye movements as such is an effective way to improve reading" (*100*, p. 229); and Tinker further maintained that what was needed was "less activity by dilettantes who are inadequately prepared to see the fundamental problem and unable to design suitable experiments in the field" (*100*, p. 229). Taylor (*91*) presented data with the suggestion that less than a single word is seen at a fixation by the average elementary-grade child and that college students see approximately one and one-third words at a fixation.

Westover's brief critical review of some of the research in controlled reading (*107*), presented at the 1958 IRA Conference and also cited in the 1958 review, included the conclusion that reading gains achieved through controlled reading methods were brought about through improvement of perception organization habits rather than through improvement of eye movements. He further cautioned that controlled reading to improve perceptual organization habits should be used by persons aware of the psychology of reading and of the limitations of mechanical instruments. Spache (84, 85) who was also cited, made some of these points also.

USE OF MACHINES

The use of machines or mechanical equipment for teaching reading skills has been an area for question and study for some time; and a number of the reports covered in the annual reviews have been concerned, directly or indirectly, and in entirety or in part, with this problem. A number of reports relevant to this area were cited in the first annual review (9). Although she did not regard the mechanical instruments and techniques in her program as having been the primary effecting factors, McGinnis (59) found statistically significant gains being made by the experimental groups involved in her evaluation of materials and procedures used in the reading laboratory program. Lewis (52) found that a group trained in comprehension, without instruments, made nearly three times as much gain in reading speed as did the group trained exclusively to improve eye movements (with flash-meters, metronoscopes, and mimeographed eye movement exercises). Freeburne (34) found gains made by experimental groups after three weeks of reading training (which followed three weeks of either intensive perceptual span training or intensive perceptual speed training) did not differ significantly, for either group, from gains made by a control group which had not received the perceptual span or perceptual speed training before receiving the reading training. Glock (39) failed to find evidence to show that

techniques designed especially for training eye movements were more effective generally than were other methods.

A number of studies in which machines and mechanical equipment had been used in programs was treated in each of the various reviews. Relatively few of the pertinent studies had been specific attempts to evaluate relative values or contributions of particular equipment or procedures; but a number of indications or implications was yielded. A number of studies has involved comparisons of procedures utilizing instruments and procedures which do not. Equal gains in reading ability have been reported as having been achieved by groups using rate controllers and by groups working without instruments. However, according to some reports (88, 104) instrument groups have made greater rate gains. Both Thompson (93) and Wooster (113) found higher rate gains being made by groups which had not received training on a rate controller. Rate gains of all groups in Wooster's study were significant, with no significant differences in comprehension. Barry and Smith (4) found reading levels raised by all of the eight different groups or methods involved in their study (one "method" of which consisted only of pretesting and post-testing). Glock (38) reported that a "determined effort" group, which used no mechanical method, made significantly greater increases in rate than did either a group getting tachistoscopic training or a group getting reading film training. No changes occurred in comprehension. Wilson (110) found a free reading program to develop reading skills about as well or better than other methods except for rate and vocabulary skills. Tachistoscopic training did not appear to effect noticeable rate increases; reading accelerator training did produce significant gains. Gains in reading skills continued to be accomplished in a number of programs without use of instruments or mechanical devices. (For example, see Items 6, 20, 45, 78, 89, 90, 114.)

Manolakes (53), comparing eye movement records after reading improvement training with matched groups of Marine Corps Supply School officers, found no significant differences between the group which had received tachistoscopic training and the group which had not. Significant rate increase differences were found, in favor of the group which had not received tachistoscopic training. Revisions made in a program conducted at the Fort Lee Quartermaster School (2) included reduction in the amount of time spent in tachistoscopic exercise activity and increase in the time devoted to practice of actual reading exercises.

Reported opinions of program participants as to which procedures had been most helpful have been cited in a number of the reviews. Students in Kingston's program (47) felt that accelerators and films had been most helpful and that tachistoscopic work had been least helpful. Students in a Northwestern University program (111) also felt that tachistoscopic training, one of numerous activities in the program, was not particularly helpful. Students regarded non-mechanical procedures as most helpful. Continuation of negative reactions of program participants as to effectiveness of the tachistoscope was noted in later reviews (2, 47, 104, 112); but an instance of positive reaction was also noted (80). Sommerfeld's incisive critical analysis of research involving the tachistoscope and the claims relative to basic research evidence (82) led to doubt as to the validity of reported values of the tachistoscope. The possible motivational values of the tachistoscope were noted in several reports cited (2, 47, 111); and the possible motivating values continued to be pointed out (47, 112).

Sheldon (76), in a report of a Syracuse University program, suggested that, since none of the many and varied techniques used in the program seemed to be sufficiently effective alone, the various procedures and

techniques used in combination effected the improvement. There continued to be suggestions, in reports cited in later reviews, that effectiveness was accomplished through a combination of methods and procedures (52, 76, 77, 112). Holmes (41), after an extensive analysis of the factors involved in reading disabilities, concluded that reading improvement might be brought about through various approaches in view of the possibility that reading speed and power were supported by a number of similar elements.

In reports cited in the third annual review (11), a continued use of machines and mechanical devices was noted, with rate controllers, tachistoscopes, and films seeming to be used most frequently (3). Acker's very intensive survey (1) of adult programs of military, government, and business agencies also revealed tachistoscopes, reading rate controllers, and training films as being used most frequently, in the order named. However, textbooks and workbooks were emphasized more than any single type of equipment or material. Acker's survey indicated that reading rate controllers were considered as the most valuable type of mechanical instrument used; but tachistoscopes and training films were also considered helpful. A trend toward increased use of non-mechanical materials and a decrease in time spent in using (but not in amount of) mechanical equipment was also noted; and the values of vision testing devices and the ophthalmograph were debated.

Westover (107) concluded that, while reading may be improved by controlled reading devices, there appears to be no general advantage favoring controlled reading over motivational practice. Spache (84, 85) tended to agree with Westover. Spache presented his rationale for controlled reading and also suggested the general purpose of, and the types of readers who should participate in a program of, controlled reading. He further cautioned against assuming that all persons can be taught to read more rapidly.

BIBLIOGRAPHY

1. ACKER, RALPH S. "Reading Improvement in Military, Government, and Business Agencies," *The Reading Teacher*, XIV (November 1960), 89–92.
2. ALLEN, M. ROBERT. "Adult Reading Improvement at an Army Service School," *School and Society*, LXXIV (August 4, 1951), 72–76.
3. BARBE, WALTER B. "Reading Improvement Services in Colleges and Universities," *School and Society*, LXXIV (July 7, 1951), 6–7.
4. BARRY, ROBERT F., and SMITH, PAUL E. "An Experiment in Ninth Grade Reading Improvement," *Journal of Educational Psychology*, XLV (November 1954), 407–414.
5. BEAR, ROBERT M. "Organization of College Reading Programs," *Education*, LXX (May 1950), 575–581.
6. BENNETT, A. L. "An Experiment in Reading," *Michigan Educational Journal*, XXX (January 1953), 302–303.
7. BLACK, E. L. "The Difficulties of Training College Students in Understanding What They Read," *British Journal of Educational Psychology*, XXIV (February 1954), 17–31.
8. BLAKE, WALTER S., JR. "Are Compulsory Study Skills and Reading Training Good?" *Junior College Journal*, XXV (December 1954), 231–234.
9. BLIESMER, EMERY P. "Recent Research in Reading on the College Level" in OSCAR S. CAUSEY, ed. *Improving Reading Programs for College Students and Adults*, 1952 Yearbook of Southwest Reading Conference for Colleges and Universities. Fort Worth: Texas Christian University Press, 1953, pp. 1–9.
10. ———. "Recent Research Relative to College Reading" in OSCAR S. CAUSEY, ed. *What the Colleges are Doing in Reading Improvement Programs*, Third Yearbook of the Southwest Reading Conference for Colleges and Universities. Fort Worth: Texas Christian University Press, 1954, pp. 26–43.
11. ———. "The Status of Research in College Reading" in OSCAR S. CAUSEY and ALBERT J. KINGSTON, eds. *Evaluating College Reading Programs*, Fourth Yearbook of the Southwest Reading Conference for Colleges and Universities. Forth Worth: Texas Christian University Press, 1955, pp. 28–38.
12. ———. "Recent Research in College Reading" in OSCAR S. CAUSEY, ed. *Exploring the Goals of College Reading Programs*, Fifth Yearbook of the Southwest Reading Conference for Colleges and Universities. Fort Worth: Texas Christian University Press, 1956, pp. 29–43.
13. ———. "Review of Recent Research on College and Adult Reading" in OSCAR S. CAUSEY, ed. *Significant Elements in College and Adult Reading Improvement*, Seventh Yearbook of the National Reading Conference for Colleges and Adults. Fort Worth: Texas Christian University Press, 1958, pp. 101–114.
14. ———. "Review of Recent Research on College and Adult Reading" in OSCAR S. CAUSEY and WILLIAM ELLER, eds. *Starting and Improving College Reading Programs*, Eighth Yearbook of the National Reading Conference. Fort Worth: Texas Christian University Press, 1959, pp. 171–192.
15. ———. "Review of Research on College and Non-College Adult Reading" in OSCAR S. CAUSEY and EMERY P. BLIESMER, eds. *Research and Evaluation in College Reading*, Ninth Yearbook of the National Reading Conference for Colleges and Adults. Fort Worth: Texas Christian University Press, 1960, pp. 49–62.
16. ———, and LOWE, ALVIN J. "1960 Review of Research on College and Non-College Adult Reading" in EMERY P. BLIESMER and ALBERT J. KINGSTON, eds. *Tenth Yearbook of the National Reading Conference*. (In press.)
17. BROWN, LOUISE, and LAUER, A. R. "Development of Reading Rate and Comprehension," *Journal of Developmental Reading*, III (Autumn 1959), 59–62.
18. BRYANT, N. DALE. "Reading Improvement Programs in Industry" in OSCAR S. CAUSEY, ed. *Significant Elements in College and Adult Reading Improvement*, Seventh Yearbook of the National Reading Conference for Colleges and Adults. Fort Worth: Texas Christian University Press, 1958, pp. 76–85.
19. BURFIELD, LEONE M. "Remedial Reading

in the College," *Clinical Studies in Reading I*, Chapter III, Supplementary Education Monographs, No. 68. Chicago: University of Chicago Press, June 1949.

20. BURKE, ARMAND. "Building a Remedial Reading Program," *Peabody Journal of Education*, XXXI (March 1954), 285–288.

21. CARDWELL, IRENE. "Adult Reading Improvement Without Machines," *School and Society*, LXXXII (September 3, 1955), 71, 72.

22. CHARLES, DON C. "College Reading and Study Improvement," *Journal of Higher Education*, XXII (May 1951), 265–267.

23. CLARK, EDWARD THOMAS. "A Study of the Measured and Self-Perceived Outcome of the Training Given Air Force and Other Department of Defense Personnel in a Voluntary Reading Improvement Course," *Dissertation Abstracts*, XIX (January–March 1959), 1647.

24. COOK, DESMOND L. "A Comparison of Reading Comprehension Scores Obtained Before and After a Time Announcement," *Journal of Educational Psychology*, XLVIII (November 1957), 440–446.

25. COOPER, WILLIAM HICKERSON. "Interrelationships Among General and Specialized Reading Abilities and General and Specialized Vocabularies," *Dissertation Abstracts*, XV (December 1955), 2467.

26. COSPER, RUSSELL. "Improving Reading Skill," *Journal of Communication*, III (1953), 81–84.

27. ———, and MILLS, BARRISS. "Developmental Reading at Purdue," *Journal of Higher Education*, XXIV (May 1953), 258–262.

28. DINGMAN, HARVEY F. "Factor Analysis of Eye-Movements with Reading Comprehension Scores," *Perceptual and Motor Skills*, VIII (March 1958), 37–38.

29. DUMLER, MARVIN J. "A Study of Factors Related to Gains in the Reading Rate of College Students Trained with the Tachistoscope and Accelerator," *Journal of Educational Research*, LII (September 1958), 27–30.

30. EPPLEY, MARY VINEITA (BOOTS). "The Relationship of Personal Factors and Reading Performance to Academic Achievement of Selected Oregon State College Students," *Dissertation Abstracts*, XIX (September 1958), 730.

31. FAULS, JOHN THOMAS. "Superior Readers Versus Mediocre Readers: A Comparison of Ego Organizations," *Dissertation Abstracts*, XX (February 1960), 3376–3377.

32. FINK, AUGUST ARMANDUS. "The Effects of Tachistoscopic Training in Digit Perception of Eye Movements in Reading," *Dissertation Abstracts*, XVI (July 1956), 1289.

33. FREDERICKSEN, NORMAN. "The Influence of Timing and Instructions on Cooperative Reading Test Scores," *Educational and Psychological Measurements*, XII (Winter 1952), 598–607.

34. FREEBURNE, CECIL MAX. "The Influence of Training in Perceptual Span and Perceptual Speed Upon Reading Ability," *Journal of Educational Psychology*, XL (October 1949), 321–352.

35. FRIDIAN, SISTER M., and ROSANNA, SISTER M. "A Developmental Reading Experiment in a European History Class," *Journal of Developmental Reading*, I (Winter 1958), 3–7.

36. GILBERT, L. C. "Speed of Processing Verbal Stimuli and Its Relation to Reading," *Journal of Educational Psychology*, LV (February 1959), 8–14.

37. ———. "Saccadic Eye Movements as a Factor in Visual Perception in Reading," *Journal of Educational Psychology*, LV (February 1959), 14–19.

38. GLOCK, JOHN WILLIAM. "The Relative Value of Three Methods of Improving Reading," *Dissertation Abstracts*, XV (November 1955), 2072–2073.

39. GLOCK, MARVIN D. "The Effect Upon Eye-Movements and Reading Rate at the College Level of Three Methods of Training," *Journal of Educational Psychology*, XL (February 1949), 93–106.

40. HALFTER, IRMA T., and DOUGLASS, FRANCES M. " 'Inadequate' College Readers," *Journal of Developmental Reading*, I (Summer 1958), 42–53.

41. HOLMES, JACK A. "Factors Underlying Major Reading Disabilities at the College Level," *Genetic Psychology Monographs*, XLIX (February 1954), 3–95.

42. HUMPHREY, KENNETH HARLAN. "An Investigation of Amount-Limit and Time-Limit Methods of Measuring Rate of Reading," *Journal of Developmental Reading*, I (October 1957), 41–54. See also *Dissertation Abstracts*, XV (November 1955), 2100.

43. HUNT, LYMAN C., JR. "Can We Measure

Specific Factors Associated with Reading Comprehension?" *Journal of Educational Research*, LI (November 1957), 161–172.

44. IRVINE, PAUL, JR. "An Experimental Study of the Effectiveness of Certain Methods of Teaching Reading Improvement at the College Level," *Dissertation Abstracts*, XX (December 1959), 2176.

45. JOHNSON, GRANVILLE B. "A Comparison of Two Techniques for the Improvement of Reading Skills at the College Level," *Journal of Educational Research*, XLVI (November 1952), 193–205.

46. KENWORTHY, C. W. "An Evaluation of the Results of Instruction and Practice in the Techniques of Better Reading," *Journal of Developmental Reading*, II (Summer 1959), 11–16.

47. KINGSTON, ALBERT J., JR. "Student Reaction to a College Reading Improvement Program," *Junior College Journal*, XXIII (October 1952), 98–101.

48. ———, and GEORGE, CLAY E. "The Effects of Special Reading Training Upon the Development of College Students' Reading Skills," *Journal of Educational Research*, L (February 1957), 471–476.

49. KINNE, ERNEST W. "Reading Improvement for Adults," *College English*, XV (January 1954), 222–228.

50. KLARE, G. R., NICHOLS, W. H., and SHUFORD, E. H. "The Relationship of Typographic Arrangement to the Learning of Technical Training Material," *Journal of Applied Psychology*, XLI (February 1957), 41–45.

51. KLARE, G. R., SHUFORD, E. H., and NICHOLS, W. H. "The Relationship of Style Difficulty, Practice and Ability to Efficiency of Reading and to Retention," *Journal of Applied Psychology*, XLI (August 1957), 222–226.

52. LEWIS, NORMAN. "An Investigation into Comparable Results Obtained from Two Methods of Increasing Reading Speed Among Adults," *College English*, XI (December 1949), 152–156.

53. MANOLAKES, GEORGE. "The Effects of Tachistoscopic Training in an Adult Reading Program," *Journal of Applied Psychology*, XXXVI (December 1952), 410–412.

54. MARVEL, JOHN A. *Acquisition and Retention of Reading Performance on Two Response Dimensions as Related to "Set" and Tachistoscope Training*, unpublished doc-

toral dissertation, Oklahoma University, Norman, Oklahoma, p. 99.

55. MAYHEW, JEAN B., and WEAVER, CARL H. "Four Methods of Teaching Reading Improvement at the College Level," *Journal of Developmental Reading*, III (Winter 1960), 75–83.

56. MCCONIHE, ESTHER J. "An Experimental Study of the Effects on Comprehension of Improving Readability," *American Psychologist*, XII (July 1957), 409. (Abstract.)

57. ———. "Study Skills Need Improving, Too," *Journal of Developmental Reading*, I (Autumn 1958), 40–45.

58. MCDONALD, ARTHUR S., ZOLICK, EDWIN S., and BYRNE, JAMES A. "Reading Deficiencies and Personality Factors: A Comprehensive Treatment" in OSCAR S. CAUSEY and WILLIAM ELLER, eds. *Starting and Improving College Reading Programs*, Eighth Yearbook of the National Reading Conference. Fort Worth: Texas Christian University Press, 1959, pp. 89–98.

59. MCGINNIS, DOROTHY J. "A Reading Laboratory at the College Level," *Journal of Higher Education*, XXII (February 1951), 98–101.

60. MILLER, LYLE L. "Current Use of Workbooks and Mechanical Aids" in OSCAR S. CAUSEY and WILLIAM ELLER, eds. *Starting and Improving College Reading Programs*, Eighth Yearbook of the National Reading Conference. Fort Worth: Texas Christian University Press, 1959, pp. 67–76.

61. MULLINS, CECIL J. "Reading Improvement Course Aimed to Increase Speed," *Personnel Journal*, XXXIII (October 1954), 172–174.

62. NAHINSKY, IRWIN D. "The Influence of Certain Typographical Arrangements Upon Span of Visual Comprehension," *Journal of Applied Psychology*, XL (February 1956), 36–37.

63. PATTERSON, HARRY O. "A Reading-Improvement Program in Industry" in OSCAR S. CAUSEY, ed. *Techniques and Procedures in College and Adult Reading Programs*, Sixth Yearbook of the Southwest Reading Conference for Colleges and Universities. Fort Worth: Texas Christian University Press, 1957, pp. 102–113.

64. ———. "Trends in Industry-Sponsored Reading Improvement Programs" in J. ALLEN FIGUREL, ed. *Reading for Effective*

Living, International Reading Association Conference Proceedings, III, 1958. New York: Scholastic Magazines, 1958, pp. 52–57.

65. PRESTON, RALPH C., and BOTEL, MORTON. "Reading Comprehension Tested Under Timed and Untimed Conditions," *School and Society*, LXXIV (August 4, 1951), 71.

66. ———, and TUFT, EDWIN N. "The Reading Habits of Superior College Students," *Journal of Experimental Education*, XVI (March 1948), 196–201.

67. RANKIN, EARL FREDERICK. "An Evaluation of the Cloze Procedure as a Technique for Measuring Reading Comprehension," *Dissertation Abstracts*, XIX (October 1957), 733–34.

68. RANSON, M. KATHLEEN. "An Evaluation of Certain Aspects of the Reading and Study Program at the University of Missouri," *Journal of Educational Research*, XLVIII (February 1955), 443–454.

69. REED, JAMES C. "Some Effects of Short-Term Training in Reading Under Conditions of Controlled Motivation," *Journal of Educational Psychology*, XLVII (May 1956), 257–264.

70. ROBERTSON, MALCOLM H. "An Evaluation of Reading Improvement," *Journal of Developmental Reading*, II (Autumn 1958), 60–61.

71. SANDBERG, EDWIN T. "Reading Program at Wartburg College," *Journal of Developmental Reading*, II (Winter 1959), 60–62.

72. SAYLES, DANIEL G. "The Effect of Medial Testing," *Journal of Developmental Reading*, II (Autumn 1958), 43–47.

73. SCHICK, GEORGE B. "Better-Reading Programs Show Lasting Benefits," *Personnel Journal*, XXXV (September 1956), 131–33, 141.

74. SCHWARTZ, MARVIN. "Transfer of Reading Training from Non-Technical to Technical Material," *Journal of Educational Psychology*, XLVIII (December 1957), 498–504.

75. SHAW, JAMES G. "An Evaluation of Study Skills Course," *Personnel and Guidance Journal*, XXXIII (April 1955), 465–468.

76. SHELDON, WILLIAM D. "A Course in Reading and Study Skills," *Journal of Higher Education*, XXIII (January 1952), 44–46.

77. ———. "Reading Courses in College," *NEA Journal*, XLIV (April 1955), 227–228.

78. SMITH, EDWIN H., and MARIE P. "Speed Reading in the Machine Age," *College English*, XX (February 1959), 242–244.

79. SMITH, DONALD E. P., and WOOD, ROGER L. "Reading Improvement and College Grades: A Follow-Up," *Journal of Educational Psychology*, XLVI (March 1955), 151–159.

80. SMITH, HENRY P., and TATE, THEODORE R. "Improvements of Reading Rate and Comprehension of Subjects Training with the Tachistoscope," *Journal of Educational Psychology*, XLIV (March 1953), 176–184.

81. SMUTZ, HAROLD T. "Investigation of a Reading Improvement Program in an Industrial Setting, Analyzing and Comparing the Reading Behavior with Measured Attitudes, Personality Attributes and Work Performance," *Dissertation Abstracts*, XV (August 1955), 1360–1361.

82. SOMMERFELD, ROY C. "An Evaluation of the Tachistoscope in Reading Improvement Programs" in OSCAR S. CAUSEY, ed. *What the Colleges Are Doing In Reading Improvement Programs*, Third Yearbook of the Southwest Reading Conference for Colleges and Universities. Fort Worth: Texas Christian University Press, 1954, pp. 7–25.

83. SOMMERFELD, ROY E. "Some Recent Research in College Reading" in OSCAR S. CAUSEY, ed. *Techniques and Procedures in College and Adult Reading Programs*, Sixth Yearbook of the Southwest Reading Conference for Colleges and Adults. Fort Worth: Texas Christian University Press, 1958, pp. 101–104.

84. SPACHE, GEORGE D. "A Rationale for Mechanical Methods of Improving Reading" in J. ALLEN FIGUREL, ed. *Reading for Effective Living*, International Reading Association Conference Proceedings, III (1958). New York: Scholastic Magazines, 1958, pp. 190–194.

85. ———. "A Rationale for Controlled Reading" in OSCAR S. CAUSEY, ed. *Significant Elements in College and Adult Reading Improvement*, Seventh Yearbook of the National Reading Conference for Colleges and Adults. Fort Worth: Texas Christian University Press, 1958, pp. 115–132.

86. ———, STANDLEE, LLOYD, and NEVILLE, DONALD. "Results of Three College Level Remedial Reading Procedures," *Journal of Developmental Reading*, IV (Autumn 1960), 12–16.

87. STATON, THOMAS F. "Preliminary Evidence on Permanency of Reading Rate Increases Following Intensive Training in a Reading Laboratory," *American Psychologist*, V (July 1950), 341–342.

88. ———, and MAIZE, R. C. "Voluntary Reading Improvement for Air Force Officers," *School and Society*, LXXVI (July 19, 1952), 42–44.

89. SULLIVAN, EUGENE A., JR. "Some Experiences with Reading Improvement in General Motors," *Journal of Developmental Reading*, II (Winter 1959), 12–16.

90. TANZOLA, REV. VINCENT, S. J. "Reading Training Without Mechanical Aids," *Journal of Developmental Reading*, II (Spring 1959), 12–21.

91. TAYLOR, EARL A. "The Fundamental Reading Skill," *Journal of Developmental Reading*, I (Summer 1958), 21–30.

92. TAYLOR, STANFORD E., and FRACKENPOHL, HELEN. "The Timex and Controlled Reader Teach Fundamental Reading Skills," *Audio-Visual Guide*, XXI (May 1955), 5–8.

93. THOMPSON, WARREN C. "A Book Versus Machine Experiment in Adult Reading Improvement," *College English*, XV (May 1954), 471–472.

94. TILLSON, M. W. "Changes in Eye-Movement Pattern," *Journal of Higher Education*, XXVI (November 1955), 442–445, 458.

95. TINKER, MILES A. "The Study of Eye Movements in Reading," *Psychological Bulletin*, LXIII (March 1946), 93–120.

96. ———. "Perceptual and Oculomotor Efficiency in Reading Materials in Vertical and Horizontal Arrangements," *American Journal of Psychology*, LXVIII (September 1955), 444–449.

97. ———. "Prolonged Reading Tasks in Visual Research," *Journal of Applied Psychology*, XXXIX (December 1955), 444–446.

98. ———. "Effect of Angular Alignment Upon Readability of Print," *Journal of Educational Psychology*, LXVII (October 1956), 358–363.

99. ———. "Effect of Curved Text Upon Readability of Print," *Journal of Applied Psychology*, LXI (August 1957), 218–221.

100. ———. "Recent Studies of Eye Movements in Reading," *Psychological Bulletin*, LV (July 1958), 215–231.

101. ———, and PATTERSON, DONALD G. "The Effect of Typographical Variations Upon Eye Movements in Reading," *Journal of Educational Research*, XLIX (November 1955), 171–184.

102. TRAXLER, ARTHUR E. "Critical Survey of Tests for Identifying Difficulties in Interpreting What Is Read," *Supplementary Educational Monographs*, No. 74. Chicago: University of Chicago Press, 1951, pp. 195–200.

103. VERNON, M. D. "The Improvement of Reading," *British Journal of Educational Psychology*, XXVI (June 1956), 85–93.

104. WEDEEN, SHIRLEY ULLMAN. "Mechanical Versus Non-Mechanical Reading Techniques for College Freshmen," *School and Society*, LXXIX (April 1954), 121–123.

105. WEED, EARL D., JR. "A Reading Improvement Program in Industry," *Journal of Developmental Reading*, I (Winter 1958), 27–32.

106. WEEKS, LEWIS E., JR. "Speeding Up Reading: A Self-Help Program for College Freshmen," *Journal of Developmental Reading*, III (Autumn 1959), 35–42.

107. WESTOVER, FREDERICK L. "An Evaluation of the Research on Controlled Reading" in J. ALLEN FIGUREL, ed. *Reading for Effective Living*, International Reading Association Proceedings, III. New York: Scholastic Magazines, 1958, pp. 186–190.

108. ———, and ANDERSON, WILLIAM F. "A Reading Improvement Course at the University of Alabama," *School and Society*, LXXXIII (April 28, 1956), 152–153.

109. WHEELER, D. K., and ANDERSON, A. W. "Increasing Adult Reading Speed," *Adult Education*, IX (Autumn 1958), 25–30.

110. WILSON, GRACE E., and LEAVELL, ULLIN. "An Experiment with Accelerator Training," *Peabody Journal of Education*, XXXIV (July 1956), 9–18. See also GRACE ELIZABETH WILSON, "The Comparative Value of Different Types of Developmental Reading Programs at the Tenth Grade Level," *Dissertation Abstracts*, XVI (April 1956), 194.

111. WITTY, PAUL. "Problems in the Improvement and Measurement of Growth in Reading," *School and Society*, LXXVIII (September 5, 1953), 69–73.

112. ———, STOLARZ, THEODORE, and COOPER, WILLIAM. "Some Results of a Remedial Reading Program for College Students,"

School and Society, LXXVI (December 13, 1952), 376–380.

113. WOOSTER, GEORGE F. "An Experimental Study of the Reading Rate Controller," *Journal of Educational Psychology*, XLV (November 1954), 421–426.

114. YOUNG, JAMES D. "An Experimental Comparison of Vocabulary Growth by Means of Oral Reading, Silent Reading, and Listening," *Speech Monographs*, XX (1953), 273–276.

RATE OF COMPREHENSION
Russell G. Stauffer

When an attempt is made to bring the concept of *comprehension* into the matrix of *rate of comprehension*, it is necessary to consider *purpose* and *achievement of purpose*, as well as *rate of achievement of purpose*, in order to obtain relevant data. When man learned to translate the audible into the visible—or when he learned to record the spoken word—he instituted a dynamic process that reshaped every aspect of thought, language, and society. When man learns similarly to translate comprehension in terms of purpose and rate of achievement of purpose, he will have instituted a dynamic thinking process that can reshape every aspect of learning and communication.

Of all the reading problems, that which concerns the nature and worth of comprehension is probably the one that most readily appeals to authorities. The eulogistic flavor which perceptibly tangs the word is a tribute to the respect men pay to its scope and power. Take away comprehension and what follows from it, and nothing is left. The goal of reading is apprehension to the fullest of that which is written. Should authorities be divided into opposed schools as to the nature of literal and implied understanding of ideas? Is comprehension on the one hand the approximation of meaning which is the fruit of reflective thought, or the empirical verbatim reproduction of words? Meaning obtained through reading is important, but it is intellectually significant only as a consequence of reading intentionally performed. The color of flowers viewed according to a spectral band has considerable meaning in chemistry and physics. But when flowers are admired for their beauty on a bare sensory level, the meaning of color is the same for the greenhorn and the scientist. Similarly, it is the purpose of reading that determines the significance of what is understood. As Tinker puts it: "And when comprehension itself is thought of, it must always be considered in relation to the purpose for which the reading is done." (*23*, p. 214) *

So we might ask: "When is comprehension adequate?" and "What is adequate comprehension?" On the one hand, comprehension is adequate when the reader finds an answer to his purpose. This generalization applies equally to the greenhorn and to the scientist. Purposes may vary from vague and unde-

Reprinted from *Speed Reading: Practices and Procedures*, Proceedings of the Annual Parent Conference on Reading, Vol. 10, University of Delaware, with permission of the author and Reading-Study Center, University of Delaware.

[*Numbers in parentheses refer to Bibliography at the end of this article.]

fined desires to be entertained at one end of the continuum, to clearly defined, specific, and discerning at the other end. The former may vary, too, from being a casual, occasional desire to be entertained to that of an inarticulate need for constant emotional therapy. The latter may also vary from the simple, straightforward seeking of facts or declaration of hypothesis—to complex, involved, theoretical considerations. Regardless, when the reader has found the answers sought, he has comprehended.

"What is adequate comprehension?" poses a sharply different issue. Now comprehension is not only an answer to a purpose, but also a valid answer. An adaptation of Russell's definition of critical thinking (*14*, p. 651) serves well. Adequate comprehension is a process of evaluation or categorization in terms of some previously accepted standard. This may be a criterion for validity determined by those best informed.

Reading, like thinking, is a process. It begins, goes on, and is in continual change, so long as a person reads. At every step the reader has to take account of the context— its part, its problems, its perplexities, and the portions that indicate solutions and point the way to the conclusions of the article, or the plot end of a story. Even when the reading of a plot is being done, a logical examination of the evidence may be required to avoid the fallacies of judgment resulting from an emotional basis. When the reading of informational material is done, the ability to evaluate ideas of a scientific, philosophical, or social nature is involved. Reading and thinking always occur in a context, whether fictional or nonfictional, materialistic or creative.

Reflective reading is a process that involves inference and judgment. It starts with a state of doubt. Some needs or difficulties present perplexity and require hesitation so that thinking can foster anticipations and imagination. This is followed by the act of searching for and assessing evidence that will re-solve the doubts and settle the perplexities.

Mortimer Adler says in writing about learning through reading:

> The first sense is the one in which we speak of ourselves as reading newspapers, magazines, or anything else which, according to our skill and talents, is at once thoroughly intelligible to us. Such things may increase the store of information we remember, but they cannot improve our understanding, for our understanding was equal to them before we started. Otherwise, we would have felt the shock of puzzlement and perplexity which comes from getting in over our depth —that is, if we were both alert and honest.
>
> The second sense is the one in which I would say a man has to read something that at first he does not completely understand. Here the thing to be read is initially better than the reader. The writer is communicating something which can increase the reader's understanding. Such communication between unequals must be possible, or else one man could never learn from another, either through speech or writing. Here by "learning" I mean understanding more, not remembering more information which has the same degree of intelligibility as other information you already possess. (*1*, p. 31)
>
> Montaigne speaks of "an abecedarian ignorance that precedes knowledge, and a doctoral ignorance that comes after it." The one is the ignorance of those who, not knowing their ABC's, cannot read at all. The other is the ignorance of those who have misread many books. They are, as Pope rightly calls them, bookful blockheads, ignorantly read. They have always been literate ignoramuses who have read too widely and not well. The Greeks had a name for such mixture of learning and folly, which might be applied to the bookish but poorly read of all ages. They are all *sophomores.* (*1*, p. 39)

Bacon made distinctions this way: "books to be tasted, others to be swallowed, and some few to be chewed and digested."

Gates said:

> Reading is not a simple mechanical skill, nor is it a narrow scholastic tool. Properly

cultivated, it is essentially a thoughtful process. However, to say that reading is a thought-getting process is to give it too restricted a description. It should be developed as a complex organization of patterns of higher mental processes. It can and should embrace all types of thinking, evaluating, judging, imagining, reasoning and problem-solving. (*6*, p. 3)

It seems apparent that to read is to comprehend; that the reader's purpose is the principal determiner of what is to be apprehended; that achievement of purpose is much influenced by the context—its nature and its readability—and by the reader's experience and knowledge.

WHAT CAN BE MEASURED?

A brief look at what can be measured in reading seems in order. As Roger Lennon (*10*, p. 67) put it, an unsuspecting student examining reading tests might conclude that it is possible to measure an *ad infinitum* list of skills and abilities, including speed reading. He goes on to say that it is one thing to demonstrate that these skills do exist and quite another thing to build tests which are in truth measures of these skills. Then after a selective review of research, he says:

> Shall we conclude that the reading experts, with their lengthy lists of objectives, of finely differentiated, ever more specific skills, have simply been spinning a fanciful web that bears no relation to the realities of the nature of reading ability? Or shall we charge the test-makers with a lack of ingenuity in devising test exercises to provide reliably differentiable measures of the several skills, with a failure to provide instruments that will match in their comprehensiveness and sensitivity the goals elaborated by the reading experts? The truth, it seems to me, is to be found between the two extremes. (*10*, p. 75)

Then he points out that numerous discrete reading skills are so closely related that "we must consider them virtually identical." Even

so, he does feel that we could recognize and hope to measure four components of reading ability: "1) a general verbal factor; 2) comprehension of explicitly stated material; 3) comprehension of implicit or latent meaning; and 4) an element I term 'appreciation.' " (*10*, p. 75)

Following this, Lennon turns to speed of reading and says that our assessment of rate leaves much to be desired. This conclusion he supports by noting that the relationship between speed and comprehension is complicated by the need to give attention to a reader's purposes, and the nature and difficulty of the material. He adds also that the motivational factor operating in a speed-reading test situation requires that scores obtained should always be subject to some reservations.

Tinker has said that "standardized tests . . . are of relatively little use to the teacher in appraising speed of comprehension in reading." (*23*, p. 322) And at another place Tinker says:

> They [standardized tests] are not appropriate for discovering the speed at which material is read in basic texts, supplementary books, or in the content areas. (*23*, p. 220)

Knowledge of the facts and circumstances suggests that current tests measuring comprehension have limitations that must be taken into account when test scores are interpreted. This seems to be particularly relevant when rate of reading is to be determined.

RATE AND COMPREHENSION

A recent cogent statement about rate of comprehending was made by Smith and Dechant:

> No one actually reads faster than he comprehends, but many read much more slowly than their comprehension would permit. Generally the limiting factor to rate improvement is the mind rather than the vision. (*17*, p. 222)

To separate rate from comprehension with a question such as "What is your speed of reading?" is to emphasize an unlikeness and a remoteness that makes the two concepts discrete. Actually, it might be well to drop the label *speed reading* completely.

If reading is presumed to be a means of communication—a collective product of human skill and need, a mass medium—it can be presumed to be synonymous with comprehension. Consequently, only the naïve questioner will ask "What is your rate of reading?" or indulge in a controversy about *skimming* versus *scanning* versus *reading*. To do so is to suggest that purposeful skimming or scanning, and the resultant adequate comprehension, is not reading. To do so is to reject conclusions reached by people who have done rate studies. Typical is the conclusion stated by Shores and Husbands (*16*) to the effect that the relationship between speed and comprehension is determined to a large extent by the purpose set for reading and the nature of the material.

Tinker has stated time and again that flexibility in adjusting speed is essential for proficient reading. For example:

> When this is achieved, and as occasion demands, the pupil can tear along at a very rapid rate or he can employ a moderate rate if that is appropriate, or he can read very slowly, with rereading where highly analytical reading is in order. (*23*, p. 228)

It is statements like this that seem to distort reactions to the overt act of rate adjustment and the basic philosophy of flexibility. The phrase in the above quote, "or he can read very slowly," tends to obscure the issue and to give virtue to "slowness." The result of this kind of inadvertent endorsement of "slow" reading if one wishes to do "highly analytical reading" is to develop readers who tend to read everything at the same rate (usually slow) regardless of the purpose for reading or the nature and difficulty of the material.

It is this kind of reverence for slowness that results in the mistaken notion that slowness itself produces highly analytical reading. This in turn leads to charges of irresponsibility. Typical of such charges is one made by Leichty (*9*, p. 257) when he accuses George Spache of being irresponsible. He quotes Spache as reporting that one student, after an eight-week course, "was reading 10,000 words a minute and scored 80 percent on one comprehension test and 100 percent on another." At no point does he question Spache concerning the nature and difficulty of the material of the subject read or the purpose for reading. What is more difficult to understand is that he does not challenge the test used, and apparently accepts the reported scores of 80 percent and 100 percent as valid measures. Leichty goes on to explain quite clearly the need for versatility; but he does so after saying "As English teachers, even those of us who thoughtlessly bow before the altar of speed have to spend a good share of our time teaching students to read more slowly and more thoughtfully." (*9*, p. 258) He, too, is suggesting that there is virtue in "slowness" in reading.

A re-examination of both of these rather typical quotes (Tinker, Leichty) shows that both identify practices that are essential to reflective reading. (*19*) These practices are far more relevant to highly analytical reading than the loosely interpreted symptomatic rate adjustment labeled *slowness*. Tinker spoke about rereading as an essential; and it is. The reflective reader rereads so as to interpret and evaluate. Rereading results in a rate performance that is quite different from a rate performance on a *single* reading. It seems highly inappropriate to compare performance following a single reading with a performance that involves rereading. It seems highly inappropriate to speak of "slowness" when comparisons of this kind are made. As Shores points out:

> Inasmuch as there are different relationships between rate and comprehension when rate is measured as an original reading time and when rate is measured to include rereading and question-answering time, it is important to define what is meant by rereading rate. (*15*, p. 245)

Leichty spoke about *thoughtful* reading. Then he elaborated on the need for pauses to reflect—to recall and integrate knowledge. Subsequently he discussed the limited likelihood that any reader ever understands at the 100-percent level and that no test-maker can build a test that will measure 100-percent comprehension.

All this requires us to re-examine what are considered highly acceptable reading practices—practices that reflect versatility of adjustment on the tasted, swallowed, digested levels declared by Bacon.

Repeatedly, Mortimer Adler indicates that, to accomplish the process of understanding, a reader must first approach a book or article as a whole. This he must do to grasp its unity and structure. Second, he must reapproach the book in terms of its elements. This he must do to deal adequately with a book's units of language and thought.

Thus, there are three distinct readings, which can be variously named and described as follows:

1. The first reading can be called *structural* or analytic. Here the reader proceeds from the whole to its parts.
2. The second reading can be called *interpretative* or synthetic. Here the reader proceeds from the parts to the whole.
3. The third reading can be called *critical* or evaluative. Here the reader judges the author, and decides whether he agrees or disagrees. (*1*, p. 124)

Obviously Adler is concerned with reading that is highly analytical—or with reading to learn—rather than reading purely for enjoyment. This is why he recommends reading and rereading, with stops to provide the supporting texture of thought.

Francis P. Robinson, in his book *Effective Reading,* advanced a formula for use in textbook studying on a higher-level reading-skill basis: the Survey Q3R method. The steps are clearly and sequentially stated. The student begins with a survey of the chapter or book; returns to the beginning to set up student questions; reads to answer the questions; recites the answers from memory; and, finally, reviews. When this technique is polished into an efficient method, it should result in ". . . the student reading faster, picking out the important points, and fixing them in memory." (*13*, p. 33) Of all the many proposals for improving reading efficiency, the SQ3R method seems to be the most widely used in one form or another.

The similarity between Adler's recommendation that a reader read a book in three ways and the Robinson Survey Q3R approach is readily apparent. Both are concerned with the psychology of learning—fixation, retention, and recall. Both advocate a logical, meaningful association approach as compared with a rote, memorizer approach. Both appear to be advocating what Stacey reports as a result of his experiments. He concluded that his results:

> . . . would make of the classroom a place where children would actively search for answers to their problems . . . the school becomes a place where learning is exploring, searching, experiencing, and interacting in an intellectual or cognitive sense as well as overtly. These results give small comfort to the educator who would have children memorize by rote associations or who would provide answers ready-made to be immediately accepted by children. (*18*, p. 102)

At this point, too, it seems timely to repeat Adler's admonition:

The first maxim of sound practice is an old one: the beginning of wisdom is a just appraisal of one's ignorance. So the beginning of reading as a conscious effort to understand is an accurate perception of the line between what is intelligible and what is not. (*1*, p. 32)

Only the naïve questioner will ask then "what is your rate of reading?" Those who have given thought to rate of comprehension, who have done investigations, and who have proposed methods to be used by efficient readers show clearly the need for versatility. This is especially true where reading is viewed as a means of exploring, searching, experiencing, and interacting while the reader actively searches for answers to his problems.

FLEXIBILITY OF ADJUSTMENT

In 1947 Tinker coordinated the results of the Minnesota Studies on time relations for eye movements. One of the results he reported appears to be of unusual significance: "For most reading situations, eye movements take 6 to 8% of reading time while the rest (92 to 94%) is devoted to pauses. . . ." (*22*, p. 218) In other words, it can be concluded that what goes on in the thinking center of the mind determines rate of reading, and not the movements of the eyes.

Ernest Horn, in his classic *Methods of Instruction in Social Studies,* put it this way: "The classroom teacher needs to be concerned with movements of the eyes little more than with the movements of the bones of the inner ear." (*8*, pp. 201–2)

Keeping these two ideas in mind helps one evaluate programs and devices for the improvement of rate of reading. Smith and Dechant, after making a comprehensive review, conclude that ". . . training on mechanical devices is frequently accompanied by rate improvement. It is also generally true that rate gains have an adequate degree of permanency. (*17*, p. 229) Then they add that ". . . rate gains are also obtainable without mechanical aids in programs that are book centered." In their chapter on "Speed of Reading," Tinker and McCullough say:

> In every experiment that has attempted to evaluate the use of machines, it has been found that they are no more effective in increasing rate of reading than are less complicated but sound classroom practices. (*23*, p. 227)

It seems, then, that such questions as the following are legitimate: What is your rate of reading science? or history? or fiction? or mathematics? or biology? Or, what is your rate of performance when locating a single fact or literal answer in an elementary zoology text, an advanced chemistry text, a narrative digest, an exhaustive treatise on ophthalmology? Or, what is your rate of performance when seeking a critical interpretation of an elementary text on perception, or an advanced text on astronomy, or a Caldecott Award winner?

Contrast this with a measure of a person's "speed of reading" based on a survey test in which all the items are adjusted to about a third-reader level of readability, and in which each item has about twenty-eight words and ends with a question requiring the reader to select one of four answers. (*7*) Or, consider the situation in which the reader is given an article of about 2,000 words and told to read as fast as he can with understanding. After the selection has been read the reader then finds out what it is he was supposed to have grasped as he deals with a ten-item multiple-choice test. (*11*) Then consider the situation in which the reader is given a selection of about 8,000 words and told to read to obtain an overview of the plot and its development, this to be followed by a fifty-three-item multiple-choice test. Which of these circumstances tests flexibility of adjustment, the acme of speed-reading training?

A Chinese proverb says that a picture is worth a thousand words. If this generalization is accepted only in part, how should pictures be prorated on a "words-per-minute" basis? Even if it is allowed that not all pictures are of equal value, then how are picture values determined and scaled on a "word-per-minute" basis?

If a picture of outstanding quality in terms of its value to the reader is worth a thousand words, surely maps, graphs, charts, diagrams, and other means of producing strong, clear, visual impressions must also equal a high number of words. This being the case, how does a reader adjust his pace when dealing with this kind of material? Certainly the efficient reader reads these graphic forms of presenting ideas and uses reading time.

Reading materials use various graphic techniques—some to a large degree and others to a limited degree. Their use is much dependent upon the nature of the content and the method of presentation. Periodicals like *Life, Look, National Geographic, Popular Science, Jack and Jill* make much use of graphic media. Encyclopedias, school texts, and trade books use them to varying degrees. Hence a reader is faced with an almost constant demand for reading skill in dealing with these media. And how does "reading speed" based on "words-per-minute" take all this into account? Or what test of speed reading requires a reader to deal with these kinds of media?

Words as symbols vary in length and complexity of structure. Configuration demands placed on a reader vary tremendously. No one would say that "words-per-minute" could be based on a constant, uniform configuration demand.

Many words vary in meaning from context to context and an efficient reader is prepared to deal with semantic variations. He realizes that the meaning of a word is determined largely by the context in which it is used. The semantic demands placed on a reader are not uniform from word to word and are only indirectly reflected on a "word-per-minute" measure.

In any particular context some words are of more significance than others. The quality value may vary from context to context. How, but indirectly, does a quantitative "word-per-minute" count reflect these conditions?

Readability factors put "words-per-minute" in yet another perspective. Major determinants of readability are the number of uncommon words, the number of words per sentence, the percentage of different words, the number of polysyllabic words and so on. (2) Even so, these determinants do not take into account such factors as density of facts presented, directness with which ideas are presented, organization of ideas, and so on. (12, p. 249) All of these factors obviously influence rate of reading, require versatility of adjustment, and are reflected only indirectly in a rate estimate based on a "word-per-minute" basis.

Even more unfortunate and damaging is the semantic controversy revolving about the terms *skimming, scanning,* and *reading,* as referred to earlier. It is not uncommon to hear people parry quotations about speeds of reading that exceed 1,000 words per minute by calling the act one of skimming rather than reading. This implies that skimming is not reading and rejects the concept of versatility of reading.

Skimming may be defined (20) as the ability to read swiftly and lightly to locate bits of information literally stated. If the reader's purpose is to locate answers of a literal nature, briefly stated, he should move exceedingly fast. Or he may wish to gather piecemeal facts and ideas in an entire selection or book, so he again moves along swiftly. This performance can be called superficial only if the reader fails to skim properly.

Scanning may be defined (20) as the ability to read along at a good rate on a point-by-point basis locating literal information. This performance differs from skimming in that the answer to a question may be located in different parts of the text and thus require the reader to do more than garner a single fact or a series of isolated facts. Furthermore the facts needed to answer scanning-type purposes may be of a qualifying nature and require the reader to do a certain amount of discrimination. This performance can be called superficial only if the reader fails to scan properly.

Study-type reading may be defined (20) as the ability to read carefully and reflectively, even rereading so as to pass judgment. Such reading requires more than the grasping of literal information. A reader must be able to read critically, to read between the lines, to weigh ideas against personal experience and an acceptable yardstick.

There is a belief abroad that skimming or scanning is not reading but that a study-type performance is reading. But what is far more profound is to accept the fact that each represents a practical and useful reading technique that permits a reader to adjust rate to purpose. These circumstances represent the crux of the versatility issue and must be grasped if efficient reading is to be accomplished. Where this understanding is not grasped, reading performances in terms of time are mired in the bottomless word-by-word-rate pit of inefficiency. In addition it results in naïve, sterile, pedestrian, and inane name-calling.

Words-per-minute represents a most inadequate yardstick by which to gauge an efficient reading performance. It has little, if any, value in the total scheme of flexibility of adjustment of rate to purpose, the nature and difficulty of the material, and the reader's experience and knowledge.

CONCLUSION

"One of the grave maladies of our time is the way sophistication seems to be valued above common sense. Words cease to have the plain meaning assigned to them and become wildly elastic. The manipulation of an idea seems to be more important than the integrity of an idea." (3) Let us no longer be caught up in the words-per-minute web but strive for flexibility of performance. The information explosion which is universally upon us is requiring of us a reading performance that is more in keeping with the swift coursing of ideas through the mind than reflective thought permits. Let us herald any and all procedures that will produce more efficient performances.

BIBLIOGRAPHY

1. ADLER, MORTIMER J. *How to Read a Book.* New York: Simon & Schuster, 1940.
2. CHALL, JEANNE S. *Readability: An Appraisal of Research and Applications.* Columbus, Ohio: The Ohio State University, 1958.
3. COUSINS, NORMAN. "Security and Sophistication," *Saturday Review of Literature* (June 30, 1962).
4. CUOMO, GEORGE. "How Fast Should a Person Read?" *Saturday Review* (April 21, 1962), 13–14.
5. FREEDMAN, RONALD, *et. al. Principles of Sociology*, rev. ed. New York: Holt, Rinehart & Winston, Inc., 1961.
6. GATES, ARTHUR I. "Character and Purposes of the Yearbook," *Reading in the Elementary School*, 48th Yearbook of the National Society for the Study of Education, Part II. Chicago: University of Chicago Press, 1949.
7. ———. *Gates Reading Survey Tests.* New York: Bureau of Publications, Teachers College, Columbia University, 1958.
8. HORN, ERNEST. *Methods of Instruction in the Social Studies.* New York: Charles Scribner's Sons, 1937.
9. LEICHTY, V. E. "How Slowly Do They Read?" *English Journal*, XLV (May 1956), 257–60.
10. LENNON, ROGER T. "What Can Be Measured?" *The Role of Tests in Reading*, Proceedings of the 42nd Annual Education Conference. Newark, Delaware: The Reading-Study Center, University of Delaware, 1961, pp. 67–80.
11. P. D. L. Reading Tests. St. Louis, Missouri: Perceptual Development Laboratories, Inc.
12. PETERSON, ELEANOR M. *Aspects of Readability in the Social Studies.* New York: Bu-

reau of Publications, Teachers College, Columbia University, 1954.

13. ROBINSON, FRANCIS P. *Effective Reading.* New York: Harper & Row, 1962.

14. RUSSELL, DAVID H. "Higher Mental Processes," *Encyclopedia of Educational Research,* 3d ed. New York: The Macmillan Company, 1960, pp. 645–61.

15. SHORES, J. HARLAN. "Are Fast Readers the Best Readers?—A Second Report," *Elementary English,* XXXVIII (April 1961), 236–45.

16. ———, and HUSBANDS, KENNETH L. "Are Fast Readers the Best Readers?" *Elementary English,* XXVII (January 1950), 52–57.

17. SMITH, HENRY P., and DECHANT, EMERALD. *Psychology in Teaching Reading.* Englewood Cliffs, N.J.: Prentice-Hall, Inc., 1961.

18. STACEY, CHALMERS L. "The Law of Effect in the Retained Situation with Meaningful Material," *Learning Theory in School Situations* (University of Minnesota Studies in Education No. 2). Minneapolis: The University of Minnesota Press, 1949.

19. STAUFFER, RUSSELL G. "Reflective Reading and Thinking," published in the University of Pennsylvania Schoolmen's Week Proceedings for 1961.

20. ———, BURROWS, ALVINA T., and HENDERSON, EDMUND H. *Teacher's Edition of Skillbook for Above the Clouds.* New York: Holt, Rinehart & Winston, Inc., 1962.

21. STEINBECK, JOHN. *The Pearl.* New York: Bantam Books, 1947.

22. TINKER, MILES A. "Recent Studies of Eye Movements in Reading," *Psychological Bulletin,* LV (July 1958), 215–31.

23. ———, and McCULLOUGH, CONSTANCE M. *Teaching Elementary Reading,* 2d ed. New York: Appleton-Century-Crofts, Inc., 1962.

ARE FAST READERS THE BEST READERS? —A SECOND REPORT
J. Harlan Shores

Whether fast readers are the best readers depends in large part upon what is meant by reading rate; that is, upon how rate is measured. Reading rate is ordinarily measured as an original reading time (*i.e.,* the words read per minute during a single reading and not including the time taken to answer comprehension questions), or it is measured as a total reading time including both the time for a single original reading and the time taken to answer comprehension questions. Most rate measures either do not permit rereading or discourage this practice even though some reading, such as keeping a long series of ideas in mind in proper sequence or

Reprinted from *Elementary English,* XXXVIII (April 1961), 236–245, with permission of the author and National Council of Teachers of English.

following precise directions, obviously requires rereading even by proficient readers.

It is at once apparent that a single rapid reading for superficial comprehension is a different measure from one that also includes time to answer questions. The question-answering task is often as time-consuming as is the actual reading. It is also apparent that neither of these tests is the same as a measure of the amount of time taken to read and use these materials for whatever comprehension purpose the reader has in mind.

The fact that experiments with reading speed have differed in what is measured as reading rate probably accounts in large part for the somewhat conflicting findings. Realizing that some readers go through the materials once rapidly and then reread all or part of the material for the specific purposes set by the comprehension questions, an adequate measure of reading rate must provide three scores—an original reading rate; a time for reading the questions, rereading the materials, and answering the questions; and a total time which is the sum of the previous two.

The question then, "Are fast readers the good readers?" needs to be broken down into several questions. Defining a "good reader" as one who comprehends well, we need to ask, "Are good readers those who read rapidly during an initial reading?" Do the good readers read rapidly when dealing with the study-type comprehension questions and when rereading to answer the questions? Are the good readers those who take less time in total to read, reread, and answer questions? A single answer is not adequate for these three questions and they in turn give rise to others. Are the fast readers the good readers on each of these measures regardless of the difficulty of the material and the purpose for reading? It is to these questions that this article is directed.

In the January 1950 issue of *Elementary English* this author and Kenneth L. Husbands reported an investigation concerned with the relationship between reading speed and comprehension (5).* The general conclusion of this study was that there is no relationship between reading speed and comprehension when the task is difficult. The fast reader was not the best reader when he was reading biological science material in order to solve a problem. In fact, under these conditions the efficient and able reader slowed his rate to that of the inefficient reader.

STUDENT AND ADULT POPULATIONS

The present study, like the earlier one, was conducted with sixth-grade students. However, in the current study data were also col-

[*Numbers in parentheses refer to Bibliography at the end of this article.]

lected from a group of able adult readers, and more adequate instrumentation was employed throughout.

All forty-six sixth graders of a K-12 consolidated school on the southeastern coast of the United States comprised the student population. Even though the "tourist trade" was the largest industry, each of the children included was a permanent resident of the county. It is apparent from Table 1 that the children were of average age in grade and were somewhat above average in intelligence and reading achievement. In terms of their mental ability the group may have been slightly underachieving. Table 1 also indicates that the two sixth-grade groups reading for different purposes were closely equivalent in chronological age, mental age, and measures of general reading abilities.

The adult group was taken from several advanced undergraduate and graduate university-level courses dealing with the teaching of reading. A few of these were juniors and seniors in the program preparatory to teaching in the elementary grades. The majority were experienced teachers and administrators working toward graduate degrees.

TESTS USED

With the sixth-grade students four reading rate measures provided ten rate scores, and five comprehension measures provided eleven comprehension scores. The Iowa Silent Reading Tests (2) gave one rate score based on a portion of original reading time. Three tests developed by the author, each measuring an aspect of the reading of science materials, provided three rate scores each—a measure of original reading time, a measure of rereading and question-answering time and a measure of total reading time.

Each of the rate tests provided one or more measures of comprehension and the California Achievement Tests (7) provided additional comprehension measures. Whenever sub-tests of the Iowa and California tests

TABLE 1
EQUIVALENCE OF GROUPS READING FOR MAIN IDEAS AND FOR IDEAS IN SEQUENCE
EXPRESSED IN RAW SCORES

Measure	Group A (Main Ideas)		Group B (Sequence)		Group A plus B	
	Mean	SD	Mean	SD	Mean	SD
C.A. (months)	137.48	4.28	135.83	6.51	136.65	5.41
M.A. (months)	151.57	26.88	147.61	22.92	149.59	24.78
California Reading*						
Comprehension	29.26	6.80	27.87	6.11	28.57	6.43
Total Score	104.43	14.97	103.65	15.19	104.04	14.92
Iowa Silent Reading**						
Comprehension	69.87	22.88	71.13	21.73	70.50	22.07
Rate	26.70	8.23	26.57	10.16	26.63	9.14
Total Score	122.26	35.23	124.91	36.16	123.58	35.32
Combined Scores—						
California plus Iowa						
Comprehension	99.13	28.53	99.00	26.22	99.07	27.09
Vocabulary	100.43	16.85	103.00	16.67	101.72	16.62

* *Ernest W. Tiegs and Willis W. Clark,* California Reading Test, *Los Angeles; California Test Bureau, 1950.*
** *H. A. Greene and V. H. Kelley,* Iowa Silent Reading Tests, *Yonkers-on-Hudson, N.Y.; World Book Co., 1956.*

were measuring in the same area these scores were combined for a more adequate measure. Thus the following scores were available from these two reading tests: California comprehension, Iowa comprehension, combined comprehension, combined vocabulary, combined directed reading, combined references, combined interpretation, Iowa rate (California does not provide a rate score), California total score, and Iowa total score.

Mental ages were derived from the California Test of Mental Maturity, Non-Language Section (6), and the Sequential Tests of Educational Progress (4) were used to measure achievement in science.

After the standardized tests were administered, three unpublished tests developed by the author of this study were used. One of these, called *Reading for Problem Solving in Science,* is a forty-item test measuring ability to do directed reading for the solution of problems in science. The comprehension reliability of this test with the Kuder Richard-son formula is .83. The rate reliability with the split-half method and the Spearman-Brown correction was .56 for original reading time, .43 for question answering time, and .39 for total time.

This was followed by the Directed Reading of Science Materials Tests administered in twenty successive sessions during which the 23 pupils in each sixth-grade group read a science passage of from 200 to 400 words that had been drawn from *Our Wonderful World* (8) and was at that time unfamiliar to them. Group A was instructed to read each passage for the main idea while Group B was instructed to read the same passage to keep the ideas of the passage in mind in their proper sequence. Different passages were employed for the different "tests." There was a total of twenty questions to be answered by those reading for main ideas and eighty questions for those reading for ideas in sequence. Three rate scores (original reading time, rereading and question-answering time, and total time) were taken for each of the twenty "tests." The split-half reliabilities of these tests of rate and comprehension are shown in Table 2 (*1*).

Fifty-one advanced undergraduate and graduate students read five of the same twenty selections from the *Directed Reading of Science Materials Tests* read by the sixth graders. Twenty-eight read for Purpose A (main ideas) and twenty-three read the same five selections for Purpose B (to keep ideas in mind in sequence). The adults were checked on comprehension and speed for each passage in the same manner as the sixth graders. The difference in the treatment was that the adults responded to all five passages at a single sitting whereas the children responded to only one passage at a sitting.

The adult population was deliberately chosen as a group of able readers. Most of the group were practicing elementary school teachers. A few were administrators and a few were advanced students (juniors and seniors) in a program preparatory to teaching. It may be that success in a field requiring much reading is better evidence of ability to do work-type reading than is any test now available. At any rate successful teachers and good students in teacher education programs probably can offer evidence of adequate reading skills.

As further proof of reading ability the adults scored well on the *Directed Reading of Science Materials Tests*. Their average accuracy level was 92 percent when reading for main ideas, as contrasted with 56 percent for sixth graders. When reading for the more difficult task of getting ideas in sequence the adult average accuracy level was 80 percent whereas the sixth grade level was only 42 percent. On the test of *Reading for Problem Solving in Science* the average adult accuracy level was 90 percent and the average sixth grade level was only 63 percent.

It is apparent then that the adult group used in this study are quite effective readers. It is then altogether likely that the relationships between speed and comprehension scores exhibited by this group more nearly represent the kind of relationships that are optimum than do those of sixth-grade students.

TABLE 2

RELIABILITY OF SCORES ON DIRECTED READING OF SCIENCE TESTS

Measure	Mean	Standard Deviation	Coefficient of Reliability*
Type A—			
Main Idea			
Comprehension	11.70	4.29	.80
Original Rate	443.74	126.99	.97
Question Rate	119.22	40.62	.82
Total Rate	567.35	138.48	.95
Type B—			
Ideas in Sequence			
Comprehension	36.34	10.73	.90
Original Rate	462.57	159.42	.96
Question Rate	449.87	177.68	.93
Total Rate	916.78	293.54	.98

* The split-half method and the Spearman-Brown correction were used with all scores.

TABLE 3

COEFFICIENTS OF CORRELATION BETWEEN MEASURES OF SIXTH-GRADE READING RATE AND COMPREHENSION*

| Rate Measures | Calif. Total | Iowa Total | Calif. Comprehension | Iowa Comprehension | Comprehension Measures | | | | | | | |
					Combined Comprehension	Combined Directions	Combined Interpretation	Combined References	Rdg. Problem Solving Sci.	Directed Rdg. Sci.—Main Ideas	Directed Rdg. Sci.—Sequence	Average Correlations**
Iowa Rate	.56	.82	.50	.71	.70	.54	.66	.41	.38	.46	.39	.58
Reading Problem Solving Science												
Orig. Rate	.26	.27	.09	.21	.19	.16	.29	−.09	.20	.19	.19	.18
Ques. Rate	.01	.23	.02	.28	.23	.24	.12	.23	−.28	−.22	.16	.09
Total Rate	.18	.37	.10	.37	.33	.32	.30	.16	−.09	.31	.16	.25
Directed Reading Science (Main Ideas)												
Orig. Rate	.50	.62	.31	.61	.57	.62	.49	.30	−.03	.29		.45
Ques. Rate	−.06	.20	−.10	.19	.13	.04	.17	.08	.07	.07		.08
Total Rate	.41	.57	.24	.57	.52	.52	.45	.30	−.03	.26		.39
Directed Reading Science (Sequence)												
Orig. Rate	.58	.68	.45	.55	.56	.27	.72	.19	.39	.06	.06	.47
Ques. Rate	−.02	.16	−.12	.10	.05	−.15	.23	−.09	−.13		−.46	−.05
Total Rate	.29	.47	.16	.36	.34	.07	.52	.04	.13		−.25	.22

* The signs of all correlations have been converted to a common base. No sign indicates a positive relationship between speed of reading and comprehension.
** Average correlations were calculated in terms of Z equivalents.

Early in the plans for the study serious consideration was given to the question of whether it would be appropriate to use the same measures and materials with able adult readers as are used with sixth-grade students. It is likely that literature or even "story type" material from science or the social studies that would be suitable and interesting to sixth-grade students would have little appeal for educated adults. However, the descriptive science materials used were thought to be suited to adults and of interest to them. This premise was strengthened by the fact that most of the adults indicated on an anonymous questionnaire that the materials were interesting. There is little question but that the materials made realistic adult demands upon the reading skills.

STATISTICAL METHOD

In order to substantiate that the two sixth-grade groups were not significantly different from one another in chronological age, mental age, science achievement, and general reading ability, the t test of significance of difference between means was used (1). The values of t ranged from .004 to .222 indicating that the slight differences between the two groups in these characteristics could easily be explained by chance factors.

Analysis of the data was made with product moment correlations (1) between the various rate and comprehension scores. These correlations for the sixth-grade population are set forth in Table 3. For the adult population the correlations between rate and comprehension are given in Table 4.

TABLE 4

COEFFICIENTS OF CORRELATION BETWEEN MEASURES OF ADULT READING RATE
AND COMPREHENSION*

| | Comprehension Measures | | |
Rate Measures	Directed Rdg. Sci. Main Ideas	Directed Rdg. Sci. Sequence	Reading for Problem Solving in Science
Directed Reading of Science Main Ideas**			
Orig. Rate	.03		
Ques. Rate	.10		
Total Rate	.07		
Directed Reading of Science Sequence†			
Orig. Rate		.04	
Ques. Rate		−.13	
Total Rate		−.09	
Reading for Problem Solving in Science‡			
Orig. Rate			.26
Ques. Rate			.14
Total Rate			.23

The signs of all correlations have been changed. No sign indicates a positive correlation between speed of reading and comprehension.
** N equals 28
† N equals 23
‡ N equals 19

Comparisons between sixth-grade and adult populations were based upon the rate and comprehension correlations and upon mean comprehension and rate scores.

FINDINGS—SIXTH-GRADE STUDENTS

Fast readers are the best readers when rate is measured by the Iowa Silent Reading Test. In Table 3 the correlations between Iowa rate and the various comprehensions range from .39 to .82 with an average correlation of .58, significant at the one percent level. The Iowa rate score does not correlate as strongly with the tests of science comprehension as with most of the Iowa and California tests of comprehension.

On the Reading for Problem Solving in Science Test, fast readers are not the best readers. With this type of reading there is little relationship between rate of initial reading and various measures of comprehension. The highest correlation (See Table 3) was .29 with combined interpretation and the lowest was −.09 with combined references. Although most of these show a low positive relationship between rate of reading and comprehension, all of them are low enough to be explained by chance factors.

Those who read rapidly during a single reading of the Directed Reading of Science Materials Tests also comprehend well on tests of general reading abilities. These correlations (See Table 3) were generally significant ones for both the group reading for the main idea and for the group reading for a sequence of ideas. There are, however, notable exceptions for each group. The rapid readers for main ideas are not those who comprehend well when Reading for Problem Solving in Science where a low negative correlation was found. It is also interesting to note that the correlation between speed of reading science materials and comprehension in general reading abilities as measured by the Iowa and California tests is higher than is the correlation between speed and comprehension when reading the science materials for main ideas, .29.

Exceptions to the generality that those who read rapidly during a single reading of science materials for the purpose of keeping a series of ideas in mind in proper sequence are also those who comprehend well on tests of general reading abilities are found with two of the general reading abilities. Positive correlations but low enough to be explained by chance factors are found with the factors of use of references and following directions. Thus those who read science materials rapidly for sequence are not necessarily those who use references and follow directions well. It is rather strange to find a positive correlation at all between any measure of rate of reading and these somewhat meticulous types of reading comprehension, and, at least for use of references, the correlations with rate do tend to be generally low. However, comprehension of combined directions correlates well with original rate of reading on the Iowa test and on the Directed Reading of Science Tests for main ideas.

It is also interesting to note that the fast readers are not the best readers when both speed and comprehension are measured on the Directed Reading of Science Tests for sequence of ideas. This correlation, .06, is so low that one can say that there is no relationship between rate and comprehension for this relatively difficult reading task.

For both Directed Reading of Science Tests the correlations between original reading rate and the various comprehension measures average in the upper forties (significant at the five percent level). The average correlation between original reading rate on the Reading for Problem Solving in Science Test and the various measures of comprehension was positive but low, .18, enough to be possibly explained by chance factors.

In view of the generally strong correlations

between each of the measures of initial reading time and most of the various measures of general reading comprehension, it is interesting to note that this same result is not found between comprehension scores and time taken to reread and answer questions. Invariably the correlations are low or negative between comprehension and rate of question answering, which includes rereading. In other words those who read general reading test materials rapidly on a first reading also read well, but those who reread and answer questions rapidly are not necessarily those who read well. These correlations between comprehension and rereading and question-answering time ranged from +.24 to −.28 with average correlations for the three measures (See Table 3) of +.09, +.08, and −.05.

The total rate score is a combination of the original reading rate and the question-answering rate, and it really is not as meaningful as is either of the two scores from which it was derived. However, the correlations between the various comprehension measures and the total rate scores were as high as +.57 between the Iowa comprehension test and the Purpose A (main ideas) total rate scores and as low as −.25 between comprehension and total rate on the Purpose B (sequence) test. The average correlation was not significant at the five percent level with any of the three tests deriving a total rate score.

FINDINGS—ADULTS AND CHILDREN COMPARED

The reader will recall that while the correlations between rates of original reading and comprehension of general reading abilities in the sixth-grade group were generally high, this was not true between rate and comprehension with the measures of the reading of science. While data for adults was not available regarding general reading abilities, it was possible to relate speed and comprehen-

sion measures for each of the three measures of the reading of science materials. Each of these correlations (See Table 4) was low— generally somewhat lower than it was with the children. Fast readers, even among adults, are not the best readers when reading scientific materials to solve a problem, to get the main idea, or to keep a series of ideas in mind in sequence.

A case was made earlier for regarding the fifty-one adult readers as a select group of fairly efficient readers on the basis of their professional and academic accomplishments as well as on the basis of their comprehension scores on the Directed Reading of Science and Reading for Problem Solving in Science Tests. How then do these relatively efficient readers differ from the sixth graders? It would seem that the efficient reader would adjust his rate downward, shift gears so to speak, when he was dealing with either more difficult materials or a more demanding purpose. Did the adults slow down for the more demanding tasks? Did the children?

Comparing the average comprehension score of the sixth-graders with that of the adults' (See Table 5) the children scored 8.35 to the adults' 15.91 (52 percent as well) on the Purpose B (sequence) task. On the other hand the children scored 2.78 to the adults' 4.60 (60 percent as well) on the Purpose A task, and did 70 percent as well on the RPSS (Reading for Problem Solving in Science) Test. Using these relative comprehension percentages as an index of difficulty the Purpose B task was most difficult, then Purpose A, and the RPSS Test was the least difficult.

Looking at the Original Rate—Words Per Minute column of Table 5, it is apparent that both groups slowed their rate somewhat for the more demanding tasks. The adults read the relatively easy RPSS Test at 291 words per minute. They slowed for Purpose A to 213 w.p.m., and for the more difficult Purpose B they read at only 182 w.p.m. The sixth graders also slowed somewhat as the mate-

TABLE 5

MEAN COMPREHENSION SCORES AND READING RATES FOR ADULT AND SIXTH-GRADE TESTEES*

Group	Compre-hension	Original Rate	Original Rate—WPM	Question Rate	Total Rate
Adult—Purpose A	4.60	73.28	213.15	32.25	105.53
Sixth—Purpose A	2.78	113.04	138.00	37.21	150.25
Adult—Purpose B	15.91	85.56	182.35	126.13	211.69
Sixth—Purpose B	8.35	114.17	136.62	128.30	242.47
Adult—Reading for Prob. Solv. Sci.	35.89	60.63	291.48	207.74	268.37
Sixth—Reading for Prob. Solv. Sci.	25.10	115.58	152.85	267.54	383.13

* Except for Original Rate—WPM (words per minute) the rate scores are in terms of number of five second intervals. Adult and sixth-grade scores are based upon the five passages read by both age groups.

rials became more demanding. They read the relatively easy RPSS Test at 153 w.p.m., for Purpose A at 138 w.p.m. and for the more difficult Purpose B at 137 w.p.m. But note the difference. Where the adults slowed 78 words per minute between RPSS Test materials and Purpose A and slowed another 31 words per minute between Purpose A and Purpose B, the children slowed only 14 w.p.m. between RPSS and Purpose A and only 1 w.p.m. between Purpose A and Purpose B. Even taking into account the fact that the children were reading more slowly and therefore each word per minute slower is a larger percentage of their actual rate, it is readily apparent that the adults are adjusting their rate to the difficulty of the task much more than are the children.

One way of noting this flexibility of rate on the part of the adults is that they read for Purpose A only 73 percent as rapidly as they read the RPSS Test, and they read for Purpose B only 86 percent as rapidly as they read for Purpose A. The children, on the other hand, read for Purpose A 86 percent as rapidly as they read the RPSS Test, and they read for Purpose B 99 percent as rapidly as they read for Purpose A.

Another way of noting the increased flexibility of reading rate among the adults is by comparing the average reading time for adults and sixth-graders on each of the three reading tasks. The children read the relatively easy RPSS Test materials only 52 percent as rapidly as did adults. However, they read for the more difficult Purpose A at 65 percent of the adult rate and for the most demanding Purpose B, they are reading at 75 percent of the adult rate. It is likely that this trend to read relatively more rapidly as the task becomes more demanding should be reversed for most efficient sixth-grade reading.

This pattern of less difference between child and adult rates with relatively difficult materials than with relatively easy materials is even more obvious with rereading and question answering time than it is with rate of original reading. The children answered the relatively easy RPSS Test questions 78 percent as rapidly as did the adults, but they answered the more difficult Purpose A materials at 87 percent of the adult rate and they went through the most difficult Purpose B materials at 98 percent of the adult rate. The adults are markedly adjusting their rate to the requirements of the task—slowing down and rereading when it is needed—whereas the children are making relatively minor rate adjustments as the reading demands increase.

CONCLUSIONS

1. Fast readers are the good readers when reading some kinds of materials for some purposes. When reading other kinds of materials for other purposes there is no relationship between speed of reading and ability to comprehend. In general the fast readers are the good readers on the reading tasks presented in the standardized tests of general reading ability. There is no relationship between speed of reading and comprehension for either sixth-grade children or well-educated adults when reading scientific materials for the purpose of solving a problem, getting the main idea, or for keeping a series of ideas in mind in sequence.

2. When either adults or sixth-grade children read the same materials for two different purposes and when the purpose for reading is set for the reader in advance of the reading, the purpose for reading influences the speed with which the reading is done. This finding is supported in Roossinck's study (3) of the reading of scientists and sixth-grade children.

3. There is no relationship for either adults or sixth-grade students between comprehension and rate of the work-study reading involved in responding to the comprehension questions. In other words those who work rapidly on the rereading and question answering are not necessarily the best readers.

4. Efficient adult readers are much more flexible in adjusting reading rate to the demands of the task than are sixth-grade students. In comparison to the adults, the children read relatively more rapidly as the task becomes more demanding with a consequent loss in relative comprehension. The efficient adult slows his rate and rereads as necessary in keeping with the demands of the task. Sixth-grade students need to develop this type of rate flexibility.

5. Inasmuch as there are different relationships between rate and comprehension when rate is measured as an original reading time and when rate is measured to include rereading and question-answering time, it is important to define what is meant by reading rate. This finding also suggests that authorities in the field of reading would do well to attempt to standardize a practice for measuring reading rate. Since rereading and reorganizing what is read is both necessary and time consuming when reading for some purposes, the most meaningful measure of rate would be one which offered both an original reading time and a time for rereading and answering questions. The total time, which is a sum of these two, destroys some of the specificity of the composite parts and is useful only as an indication of the total amount of time taken to complete a work-study reading task.

BIBLIOGRAPHY

1. DOWNIE, N. M., and HEATH, R. W. *Basic Statistical Methods.* New York: Harper and Brothers, 1959.
2. GREENE, H. A., and KELLEY, V. H. *Iowa Silent Reading Tests.* Yonkers-on-Hudson, N.Y.: World Book Co., 1956.
3. ROOSSINCK, ESTHER P. *Purposeful Reading of Science Materials by Scientists and Children.* Doctor's thesis. University of Illinois, 1960.
4. *Sequential Tests of Educational Progress.* Cooperative Test Division, Educational Testing Service, Princeton, N.J., 1957.
5. SHORES, J. HARLAN, and HUSBANDS, KENNETH L. "Are Fast Readers the Best Readers?" *Elementary English,* 27 (January 1950), 52–57.
6. SULLIVAN, ELIZABETH R., CLARK, WILLIS W., and TIEGS, ERNEST W. *California Test of Mental Maturity, Non-Language Section.* Los Angeles: California Test Bureau, 1951.
7. TIEGS, ERNEST W., and CLARK, WILLIS W. *California Achievement Tests.* Los Angeles: California Test Bureau, 1950.
8. ZIM, HERBERT S., Editor-in-Chief, *Our Wonderful World.* Chicago: Spencer Press, 1961.

10

A Look at the Adolescent

THE NATURE AND VALUES OF CULTURALLY DIFFERENT YOUTH
Charles J. Calitri

It is imbedded in the very heart of our American democracy that we must work at the task of improving the lives of our people who find themselves on a lower economic, social, and educational level than the great middle-class majority. There will always be classes; there will always be groups of people composing strata, even though the conditions and the characteristics of those strata may constantly change. As one group finds its way out of the prizefighting ring into professional baseball and then places some of its sons and daughters among the teachers, lawyers, doctors, engineers, and business leaders, another group forms at the lower economic level, either imported from a hungry or despotic land, or home-grown among the displaced persons of industrial towns that lose their factories and farm lands that turn into empires whose fields and orchards are harvested by itinerant laborers and pickers.

If we set aside the derelicts for whom there can be only succor and welfare, then the lowest level remains the lowest; but it is con-

stantly rising even as our entire society rises, so that the migrant workers of 1962 are no longer Steinbeck's "Joads" of the thirties. In the large cities the tenements and walkups are being leveled and replaced by large housings projects where there is grass and where ceilings do not crack and fall. Yet the bottom is still there, consisting of those people who have not had time, opportunity, or perhaps the desire to become like those of us who set the goals, form the tastes, select the art forms, and establish the values which are written into our laws and customs.

It is true that the prescription for how an American citizen shall behave, by what standards he shall live, and by what morality he shall abide are determined largely by those who have come out of schools and colleges and been brought up in middle- and upper-class families. Behind those institutions are centuries of man's learning and living, where knowledge and tradition have been brought together to make up the ways of our adjusting to one another and the world.

It is because of that history, evolved from a Judaeo-Greco-Roman-Christian-Democratic complex, that we are not content to let

Reprinted from *Improving English Skills of Culturally Different Youth* (Washington: U. S. Office of Education Bulletin, 1964), pp. 1–9.

things happen as they will. We are compelled to influence our people to adopt our basic cultural and political values, especially those embodied in our Constitution and national documents. This is as it should be. It remains only that we learn how to bring about these changes without harming others and ourselves.

One of the dangerous by-products of the attempt to raise the "cultural" and educational levels of those who are different is that, in the attempt to make them over, our teachers strip them of dignity, of individuality, and of self.

Not too many months ago a group of Puerto Rican boys were sitting at a table in a corner of a New York City high school cafeteria discussing Cuba's Castro. At other tables, nearby but somehow distantly separated, other boys of other origins looked across, some annoyed, some sneering, some hostile.

"What's the monkey talk for? Why don't they use English?"

And why not? Since they had first come to school, those Puerto Ricans had been admonished daily by their teachers to talk English, otherwise they "would never learn the language."

Somewhere else in another school a group of Negro youths were speaking in a strange kind of *bop,* that mysterious new language built upon some of the roots and forms used by Negroes more than a hundred years ago, but updated now with musical terms and common words carrying hidden meanings.

In each instance, their language was a deliberate attempt to exclude outsiders from invading their privacy. Wherever there is a congregation of people, isolated for one reason or another from the main culture, language seems to become a weapon and a wall, a bulwark for the preservation of dignity and self. It does not begin that way. Language starts with the need of men to go beyond the communion of existence, where eyes and nose and skin are sufficient to carry identifying messages to the brain so that a man knows where he is and what he feels. Language begins out of a necessity to express what is inside the self and to communicate it to someone outside the self. When there are many men living in the same time and place, who by their living together are forced to share burdens, to witness experiences in concert, to react to outer dangers as a group, language becomes the means of survival. Further developed, it becomes an art form of a people by which they reveal to one another whatever secret and irrepressible emotions and ideas have emerged out of the activity of the glands and brain.

It is here that language becomes the personal property of the individual and of groups of men and women, setting them apart as persons and as people. Because language does belong to a man, we dare not take it away. We may not demand that it be supplanted with another language, nor be suppressed, nor ridiculed. Those are destructive ways.

We may only respect the language as a part of the human being, and perhaps ask that another language be added; but such an addition can occur only if the reasons for it are understood and accepted.

The language of a minority group has the same relationship to the establishment of a sense of self as the identifying club jacket has for the teenage club or gang. When Spanish-speaking youths from Puerto Rico or Mexico defy the strictures of their teachers and the scornful glances of their non-Spanish schoolmates saying, "Why should I learn English? My language is Spanish"; and when the Puerto Rican goes further saying, "Besides I am an American citizen as much as you are," what are they saying to us? What feelings have been ruffled, what deep emotions irritated, what beliefs challenged, and what inner sense of dignity insulted?

Too often these situations have occurred. We, the teaching group, and we, the native-to-these-streets group, have somehow held ourselves higher than the newcomers. We have made them understand not that we welcome them as they are, whatever they are, but that we wish to make them over in order that they may become like us.

The Puerto Rican islands in Manhattan, the Mexican sections of California and the Southwest, the Negro Harlems of all our big cities in the North and Midwest, the three main rivers of migration running up and down the two shores and the center line of our Nation following ripening crops—these are not very different from the Delancey Street Ghettos and the Little Italys of the early 1900's. All exist because people who understand each other's ways hold themselves together against other people who would either cast them out, wall them in, absorb them, or eat them up with words like *assimilation* and *Americanization*. People do not want to be Americanized in the same way that they can be atomized, and they do not want to feel that they must develop cultural tastes and abilities to replace what they already have.

How rigid we are, we of the educated American middle class! We make Carol Kennicotts of all those who come to our main streets, or else we impose the costume and the makeup of our little stages upon all the young actors who come to play with us, pushing them into a faceless chorus line.

We tell them they must speak as we do, read as we do, follow our customs, and adopt our moral values. We attempt to impose our music and art upon them and insist that they admire our technology as if the very differences that make them what they are, individuals in their own right, make them less than we instead of only different.

The problem, then, is one not only of language and reading, but also of socialization —and beyond that, it is a problem of values and philosophy.

How far shall we go with the announced educational ideal of creating a citizenry of well-rounded men and women? How round shall we make them, turning them into marbles that can be rolled on the earth? How far shall we push to achieve the images of excellence we have before our eyes? What kind of happiness shall we insist upon their pursuing? And how profitable must their leisure time activity be? (Or do we forget that, if it is profitable and active, it is no longer leisure but work.)

On the other hand, to what extent shall we encourage difference and provide the atmosphere in which the eccentricities and the individualities of each human being may be developed for whatever purposes that impel him from the inside out? How strongly shall we adhere to the concept that a man's life belongs to him alone and he alone can determine how it shall be lived, setting up only the proviso that he not interfere with or harm any other person in the living?

I do not believe that these questions are incompatible with one another. I do not believe that we must decide for the "good citizen" over the "rugged individual," but much of our practice has been just that kind of choosing.

Perhaps it is one of the elements in the nature of man that he must feel the superiority of his way over all others, or else consider himself inferior. Perhaps it is programed into the ambivalent ego of man, which sees itself both superior and inferior at the same time, that he must hold tightly to what he is and try to change those over whom he controls, whether it be through the domination of a teacher, the weight of majority numbers, or the length of time lived in the neighborhood. In any case, these thoughts lead us to the question of what to do with those who are not all like us.

If that sense of self is in us, it is also in those who are culturally different; and this is the cause of difficulty because that very knowledge of being numerically inferior, new to a place, less affluent, or lower on a social scale inspires a battery of defenses designed to protect the ego itself. Man finds it very difficult to admit that there are those who stand above him. The poor man says the rich cannot be happy with his wealth. The illiterate says the egghead does not know which end is up when it comes to practical things. The man who has been forced by his physician and his heart attack to give up smoking says all those who smoke are idiots.

So those who are culturally different from the majority among whom they are forced to live must resent and reject efforts which they suspect are directed toward making them change, if accompanying those efforts there are indications of disapproval and denigration. Unfortunately, with intentions that are sincere and humanitarian and altruistic, we who teach or are involved in education in any of a hundred ways manage to demonstrate that we do not accept those who are different for what they are.

How do we do this? Perhaps one of the classical criticisms of Americans abroad will demonstrate it. "You think everyone must learn to speak English, so that when you come to our hotels you will be understood," an Italian said. "Why do you not bother to learn our language if you are going to travel in our country?"

"Americans think the whole world belongs to them," a French storekeeper said. "No, I cannot accept American dollars. You will have to change them into new francs."

To bring it closer to home, into the very heart of a family, let us consider the teenage child who rejects classical music as being square. It is not because he was born with a dislike for the tones and rhythms of the concerto or the symphony, but because he had been made to feel that his jazz, swing, rock 'n' roll, bop, or twist are looked down upon by his parents when they ask him "Why don't you play something decent!" We do not really intend to say that his music is indecent.

We mean only to say that we have outgrown it, that its sound is different from the sounds we have come to enjoy, that it is too loud, and that it is somehow associated in our minds with behavior systems which we cannot approve. We mean also to tell him that we find richer meanings, finer skills, and more intellectual stimulation in the more classical forms. Because we love him, we want our child to enjoy this too; but we have tried to take something away from him in the process, because a teenager's music belongs to him, is part of whatever he is, and he considers an attack upon it to be an attack upon himself.

Cultural differences mean differences in value systems, and it should be evident that I do not separate the culturally different only in terms of national, migrational, or social scale groups. Teenage children are culturally different from the adults who are their parents and teachers. The problems which attend the concept of differences are universal. Difference leads to conflict; conflict leads to offense and defense where the larger force is almost compelled by the nature of things to absorb the smaller force, and the lesser force is compelled to resist. It cannot permit itself to be assimilated out of existence.

Thus what we mean by education, the leading away from whatever is, becomes a battle joined until we are capable of seeing the process of learning and teaching as an interaction rather than the submission of one group to another.

The child has a reality which is the life he is living. He has himself and the world outside of himself which he takes in through his senses and refashions in his brain according to whatever has happened during past experiences. If we would be effective in our school communication with him, then we must admit the reality of that self in our classrooms.

But where is there a reflection of this child and of the world in which he exists? What textbook confronts him with reality? Where can he see himself? And where are those pleasant sensations which have pleased him in his own world, with which he can be motivated to enjoy this other world of school?

Our fears of exposing young people to the kind of truths their parents might find objectionable, or for which pressure groups might attack us, force us to feed a bland diet of tasteless foods, where bitter and strong flavors have already titillated young adult taste buds. We are in competition with television and motion pictures; with newspapers, magazines, and paperbacks; with crowds of friends on street corners, at beach parties, and in cellar basements. We have our pupils from homes where unhappiness is a reality, where there are unpleasant emotions which make it impossible for them to recognize a stewed prune kind of world where no child hates his father or peers. In most of our classes, then, we dare not cater to the interests of our students, even though we know that those interests will sharpen their perceptions, irritate their nerve endings, and activate their brains.

How much worse it is when the child comes to us from another language, or another segment of our society, or a traveling home with another set of values and with a much stranger concept of the world! How much more difficult when his language patterns, even in English, are built upon conceptual differences, so that a cup sits on the table because in his experience there is no need for a saucer! How much more difficult if his schooling must follow the trailer camps and the crops, or if his color pushes him into a corner apart from the clean white faces which belong to the clean white world of textbook illustrations!

So, having tried to impose our language upon young people, rejecting their mother tongue, or their peer group's meta-language, and being prevented in most places from at least dealing with truths that they will understand, we are forced out of our desire to give them something, to place before them pictures of ideals that cannot be matched. We defeat them with our assault of honesty, goodness, integrity, bravery, and courage as the qualifications of humanity, setting up for them images of excellence which are impossible of imitation. This we have managed to do for all youths, not only those who are considered culturally different.

We hold forth such values in almost uncompromising fashion, pretending that these lie behind the precepts which any fine American must follow. In doing so, we are telling them that, whatever dishonest act they may commit, whatever anger or spite they may feel against sibling or parent or neighbor, whatever fear they exhibit or act of cowardice they may perform simply because they are not superhuman, they face condemnation. We are telling them further that they are not worthy to be in the world as we see it.

This is no exaggeration. Where in the textbooks will a youth have revealed to him the weaknesses of a Washington or the inadequacies of a Lincoln? Where will he find it said that men are not always strong, that there are times which encourage cowardice because the desire to live is stronger than the desire to be heroic at a particular moment in a particular battle? Until what semester must he wait before some teacher will make an acknowledgment that our heroes were also people like Lord Jim or Fleming, and that during World War II our soldiers were capable of inhuman acts? I do not know whether we are to be forgiven or not for wanting to hide these aspects of our character which are not praiseworthy.

I have no intention of demeaning either our country's heroes or the values of our society and culture. There are characteristics of human behavior which we do admire, as a nation and a people, and there is value to our trying to emulate them. But admonition and preachment are not effective teaching methods, and the half truths of history and the fiction of shoddy fiction are both forms of exhortation. I do intend to point out that, if we are to have any success in our educational exchange with youth, then our share must be the honesty of things as they are.

Therefore, we must know how things are. Most of us who have become teachers have spent from 2 to 5 years learning about children. Where we have been fortunate, we have been taught by professors who themselves had some knowledge gained from classrooms and from facing the problems of the active teacher. In that way, if we remember what we have been taught and what we were when we were youths, then we come with some measures of competence for the teaching of youth. But how many of us have studied enough anthropology to be able to recognize the differences and accept the behavior patterns of people from another world? How many of us have been prepared by field experiences in sociology to realize what constitute the elements of a migratory population? Are we prepared to accept, without blanching, a set of values different from our own and then do no more than point out the differences, laying down no moral platitudes?

It is the failure to recognize the possibilities and the implications of cultural differences that makes for a failure with young people. We need to know, before they come to our classes, what Puerto Rican children are like and what we may expect from them. We need to know them as a cultural entity and as individuals within that culture, so that their inordinate sense of dignity not be affronted and their nationalistic yearnings not be stepped on; for their sense of already having been rejected by the new people of their new environment has made them wary of us.

We need to know that there are Negro youths who have been so buffeted by their white neighbors that they have grown a hatred for the white world, and we must learn to listen to them, trying desperately to discover what they are saying when they behave in a way that seems peculiar to us. What is the source of their defiance or their sullenness? How much do they resent the lip service some of us give to civil rights?

We need to know how to admit that there is color, not try to wipe it away as if it did not exist with a pretense that all men are the same. All men are not the same and children know it better than adults. More than that, we have to understand our own unconscious prejudices, those glances and withdrawals which communicate what we feel regarding people of different origins, even as our minds are telling us we feel nothing and our mouths are telling others that we love them.

We have to understand the fact that culturally different does not mean devoid of culture, and that children of Negro, Mexican, uneducated, bookless, and houseless families do not come to us with nothing. Let me repeat—they come with selves and with a sense of belonging to whatever group is theirs. They, too, have parents and they, too, have brothers and sisters; and in some cases they, too, have individual beds which they do not have to share with four other persons. They, too, have television and have seen motion pictures, and in these respects they are the same as any other youths.

Finally, we have to understand that many of them come to us, too often, with shattered dignity and frightened selves and that their hostility is too deep to be seen by our eyes. They have learned long ago that one can hide things from strangers who have not yet discovered how to look at other people and know what they are seeing.

These are the ones we must cultivate, must help to grow a trust in us which they justly do not have. Because until we have recognized that the values by which they have lived are often directly in contrast with the values of our society, and until we can accept their behavior, however strange and antisocial it may be from our point of view, we can never hope to help them. Perhaps we must even question ourselves and our motives once again, looking carefully at some of the concepts we have held closely in our hearts and minds.

There are other questions which we must ask ourselves. If we are convinced that one must know how to read in our society and to speak so that he can simply get along with those who do not know his language, we must remember that the language of the United States is English, not Spanish, or the Negro meta-language, or the dialects of the migratory workers. The question, then, is how much must we accomplish; where do we set the limits of our goals? Shall we try to make every child, regardless of his origin or his subgroup, an appreciator of fine literature, feeding him *Silas Marner*, or even Salinger because the books are there and he "must read for pleasure"? Must every American learn to derive his pleasure from this type of reading? Must every American learn syntax? Must they all speak with round tones and in perfect sentences? Or is there room in our world for those who will manage to communicate in less than formal ways?

The final question is for all teachers and educational administrators, for all members of the adult society who are concerned about younger people. Just what do we want to do with or to or for our children? What do we expect of them? What kind of world can we anticipate and what do we imagine will be their role in it? It is at this point, if we are wrong, that we can erect impassable walls for ourselves. When we are dealing not only with young people who are already different from us because of their age, but also with those who have differences which are a result of color, national origin, occupation, educational level, or economic status, our answers need to be clear, realistic, and as right as our intelligence can make them.

When we have found our answers and our new perspectives, or even reinforced those ideas which we already have through a new examination of this problem, then we can go about helping those youth who need our inspiration and our confidence. Then we can create images for them, not solely, out of the legendary excellences of our history, but out of ourselves—sympathetic, honest, capable, and understanding selves—with whom these young people can first of all communicate and finally, we hope, wish to emulate.

READING CONTENT THAT INTERESTS SEVENTH, EIGHTH, AND NINTH GRADE STUDENTS
Ann Jungeblut and John H. Coleman

This study reports on the interest-aversion ratings by students in grades six through ten on 155 prose selections, of 275–400 words in length. The desirability of having quantitative interest-aversion information ratings on

Reprinted from the *Journal of Educational Research*, LVIII (May-June 1965), 393–401, with permission of the authors and Dembar Educational Research Services.

the actual reading content for these students may be outlined briefly.

Reading deficiencies among far too many students with an English-speaking background have been amply documented, among others, by Gray (6),* to Bond and Tinker (1), DeBoer (2), and Smith and Dechant

[*Numbers in parentheses refer to Bibliography at the end of this article.]

(5). These young people can hardly become students in any meaningful sense of the word. They are severely handicapped for informing themselves by study of printed matter. Reading for pleasure is largely denied them for lack of facility in reading. They need help that would enable them to read comprehendingly.

When youngsters arrive at the seventh, eighth, or ninth grade with substantial deficiency in reading, the remedy needs to be applied there. The difficulty is that time for it is lacking when the need is imperative. Nevertheless, studies have shown that a substantial proportion of these students can achieve significantly improved facility in reading through efficiently planned systematic practice (3).

Using interesting content in such a reading program is highly desirable. Research tends to confirm everyday experience in this respect. Smith and Dechant take into account the effects of such factors as differences in ability, and then summarize the findings of investigations in this area thus: "The more interesting the material to the reader, the better his comprehension tends to be." (5)

This principle is generally accepted. Uncertainty has arisen as to whether a given selection which purports to interest students does appeal to them.

At best, studies of students' general interests offer inadequate guides in this respect. Evidence bearing upon how well students like each specific selection is needed. In this study, the hope was to find 32 selections for each of grades 7, 8, and 9 from 51 or 52 of those judged to be potentially interesting to students at each of the three grade levels. The length of the selection suits the requirements of an efficient developmental reading plan.

THE RATING PROCEDURE

The selection was presented on the left of a double page. Just below it was the sentence,

to be checked: Could you read the selection? Yes..... No...... Of 29,119 returns, 830 (2.85%) checked "No" to this question. The rating scale was placed next. Students were asked to read and then rate selections on a six-point response scale: Like very, very much; Like quite a lot; Like a little; Dislike a little; Dislike quite a lot; Dislike very, very much. Students placed an X in a circle next to the statement that indicated their rating. Students were not asked to give their names in order to grant the freedom of anonymity to their choices. They were asked to circle numbers giving their age and grade, and to place an X after boy or girl.

The second page, facing the selection, contained six sets of one completion and five multiple choice exercises based on the selection. These involved vocabulary, best title, main idea, facts, outline, and conclusions. On the basis of poor answers to the exercises, it was assumed that approximately another 825 students did not comprehend a particular selection well enough to give it a significant rating. Thus, nearly 27,500 ratings were analyzed.

School officers and teachers in Michigan, New York, New Jersey, Ohio, Oregon, Pennsylvania, South Carolina and Wyoming graciously agreed to assist in these studies. The investigations were conducted in February-March, 1961 and 1962. The precise number of students participating cannot be stated because ratings were anonymous and there were absentees. It is estimated that 4088 students in 146 classrooms participated as follows:

Grade	Classrooms	Average of Selections Rated
6	14	6
7	35	7
8	46	7
9	35	9
10	26	8

The selections were originally chosen for educational merit and potential interest. The Lorge Readability Index was calculated for each selection as an initial indication of best grade placement. Some selections were taken from school texts and supplementary sources. The large majority of the selections were written, however, by persons who make their living by writing.

Each selection was rated by students in three consecutive grades, 6–7–8, 7–8–9, and 8–9 and 10, except for the selections prepared for Grade 10 which were rated only by students in Grades 9 and 10. This procedure generally provided substantial ratings over a span of five years in age for both sexes. The grouping of selections was rotated so that no two classes rated the same set of selections. Teachers were asked to present units twice a week. Some further comment is needed in this connection.

Average rather than advanced or retarded classes were sought to do the rating. The assumption was that retarded readers would be likely to have interests similar to their age peers. Exigencies made it advisable to accept some known classes in remedial reading. Others were not announced, yet the answers to the exercises clearly indicated substantial reading deficiency for a considerable proportion of students. This provides added confidence that selections rated sufficiently liked would have appeal for those students in need of improving their skills in reading.

A rating of "like, very, very much" was given a value of 5: "like quite a lot," 4, and so on, to compute the medians.

RATINGS OF TWO BIOGRAPHICAL SELECTIONS

With these factors in mind, a dual purpose will be served by analyzing the ratings of two selections in detail. Interest studies have shown that students at this age range like biography. The question is whether any and every well-written biographical sketch interests them.

Both biographical selections under discussion were written by professional journalists. Each passage was taken from a longer biographical sketch that appeared in newspapers. The first one described the manner in which a well-known symphony orchestra conductor, Leonard Bernstein, set about getting his first piano lessons from an outstanding teacher. Soon his teacher, a woman, was not able to schedule any other students after his lesson because he wanted to know so much that she never knew when he would go home. The selection goes on to tell that he kept his mother up until all hours of the night playing improvisations for her. He is described as having a pleasant manner of getting his own way. The narrative moves, but it is concerned with boyhood incidents of a musician now devoted largely to classical rather than, say, music that people whistle readily. How would twelve-, thirteen-, fourteen-, or fifteen-year-old youngsters react to it?

The selection was rated by 188 pupils in grades 6, 7, and 8. The Lorge Readability Index of the passage, 5.4, suggests that its structure is reasonably uncomplicated and easy for pupils of these age levels. Nevertheless, four pupils (2.1%) indicated that they could not read the selection. Scoring the exercises also made it clear that some additional pupils were retarded in reading skills.

For the selection on Leonard Bernstein, the median interest ratings for grades 6, 7 and 8 were 4.3, 4.3, and 3.9 respectively. The median ratings of 4.3 means that more than half of the sixth and seventh graders rated this selection either "like very, very much" or "like quite a lot." In this particular case 58% of the boys and girls in these grades rated the passage this high.

Here it is interesting to note that George W. Norvell (4) has found that a particular literary selection well liked in a given grade level will usually be well liked by pupils two or three grade levels above or below that grade. The medians suggest that this biographical passage could be used for remedial reading instruction with the expectation that it would appeal to a large proportion of sixth, seventh, and eighth graders.

The second selection discusses with some brilliance the trials of a superb actor-comedian who is known, however, to a relatively limited group. The point, of course, is not his fame, but how interesting a discussion of his artistry is to fourteen-, fifteen-, and sixteen-year-olds. It is brought out in the selection that for twenty years drama critics have commended his performance over any play that he has acted in. The tenor of the passage may be sensed in the following paragraph.

> "In a certain way," he confided, "I became a comedian out of necessity"—this Menasha Skulnik not quite five feet high, who looks like a tailor in a fairy story, but who commands a stage with magnificence. "Sometimes when I played a serious part the audience used to laugh. I used to get red under my make-up. I would come out and say something like, 'No, you shall not do this,' and the audience would laugh. So I decided I was a comedian." And the world agreed with him.

This selection, too, is relatively easy for junior high-school age pupils as its Lorge Readability Index is also 5.4. A total of 194 pupils in grades 8, 9, and 10 rated it. The median interest ratings for these grade groups were 3.3, 3.6, and 3.4. More than half of the pupils, then, rated the passage with some degree of liking. However, approximately 12% of the older pupils rated it in one of the two strongest "dislike" categories.

In addition to the median ratings, the percentages of pupils who indicated one of the three "liking" ratings were computed. For the selection on Leonard Bernstein, the percentages in grades 6 through 8 were 72, 90, and 76, respectively. Chance factors may have raised the percent liking in the seventh grade. Nevertheless, more than 75 percent of the seventh and eighth graders and at least 70 percent of the sixth-grade boys and girls rated this selection with some degree of liking when they could have given an anonymous rating of dislike.

For the second selection, the percentages of liking in grades 8, 9 and 10 were 62, 70, and 68. These ratings are not seriously negative. On the other hand, this selection does not seem to evoke the degree of lively interest that many selections did. Even though the general topic is biography, and even though the passage is written in relatively uncomplicated structure, the fact is that it was not especially well-liked by students thirteen to sixteen years old. This might be due to the author's style, the incidents reported, the nature of the concepts involved, pupils' lack of experience in seeing live actors on the stage, or a variety of other factors. Be that as it may, regardless of its literary superiority, the selection does not evoke the degree of interest associated with wide appeal for youngsters at these age levels.

RATINGS BY GRADE AND TOPIC

Tables 1–4 list selections in which the total of "like" ratings equalled or exceeded 75 percent. RI, in the tables, refers to the Lorge Readability Index. Median interest ratings are also given. Differences in medians serve to indicate whether preferences tend to be stronger for boys or girls, or about equal for both. Selections are classified under general topics. Not all of the selections were well-liked, as Table 5 shows. Nevertheless, selections were found with high interest ratings. They should stimulate students in these grades to find more satisfaction in reading, when these selections are utilized in a systematic reading improvement program, than would be the case with content rated less appealing.

TABLE 1

CLASSIFICATION OF SELECTIONS INTERESTING TO STUDENTS

7th Grade

(Median number of ratings per selection, 219)

Total	RI	B	G	Both	% Like
1		Biography			
	5.4	3.9	4.5	4.3	90
2		Behavior in social situations			
	5.0	4.2	4.6	4.4	88
	6.3	3.8	4.4	4.1	91
3		Folklore			
	6.2	4.9	4.7	4.8	96
	6.3	4.1	4.6	4.4	91
	7.3	5.1	5.0	5.0	96
2		Geography			
	5.3	4.0	4.4	4.2	84
	7.3	3.7	4.0	3.8	85
6		History			
	5.0	4.0	3.9	4.0	78
	5.1	4.4	4.3	4.3	79
	5.4	4.3	4.3	4.3	91
	5.8	4.4	4.4	4.4	85
	5.9	4.6	4.3	4.4	89
	6.2	4.5	4.1	4.2	85
3		Narrative			
	4.8	4.2	4.3	4.2	79
	5.2	4.1	4.4	4.3	83
	5.9	4.1	4.7	4.3	90
4		Miscellaneous			
	5.1	3.5	3.7	3.6	76
	5.3	4.1	4.3	4.1	86
	5.7	4.3	4.1	4.3	87
	6.8	4.9	4.5	4.7	88

Total	RI	B	G	Both	% Like
		Science and Natural History			
2		Anthropology			
	5.8	4.1	3.9	4.0	85
	5.9	4.3	4.1	4.2	89
4		Biology, chemistry, physics			
	5.7	4.2	4.0	4.2	89
	5.9	3.9	3.8	3.8	80
	5.9	4.5	4.0	4.3	88
	6.5	4.1	4.1	4.1	84
5	Plants and animals in relation to agriculture and industry				
	5.1	4.2	4.0	4.0	82
	5.7	4.1	4.1	4.1	84
	6.4	3.8	4.3	4.1	80
	6.6	3.9	3.8	3.9	76
	7.1	4.3	3.9	4.1	86
3	Relation of plants and animals to growth of civilization				
	5.5	3.9	4.1	4.0	85
	5.8	3.6	3.9	3.8	78
	6.1	4.2	4.1	4.1	84

THIRTY SELECTIONS NOT WELL-LIKED

Differences in the interest-aversion ratings, Table 5, on these selections are informative. Twenty-four of the 30 selections were rated with some degree of liking by a majority of the students. Nevertheless, the proportion of pupils expressing a liking are distinctly less than those found for the 126 other selections. Consequently these 24 selections are considered less likely to stimulate retarded readers favorably than others which have been, or could be, found.

Only five of the 155 selections were given more aversive than liking ratings. The case of selection 12 in this set is interesting. It was written by a talented professional writer. It appeared in a well-known national women's magazine. The discussion was oriented solely to girls, but it detailed ways that a sense of humor could help to cope with getting disagreeable things done with a minimum of wear and tear on one's emotions and relationships with others.

This selection held the possibility of giving some troubled early teen-agers clues for handling some of their frustrations. Nevertheless, they disliked it, while four possibly equally "preachy" selections by another author and very popular singer, were rated well-liked. Neither the general topic nor the literary qualifications of an author seem to furnish an adequate guide to choosing reading selections when we wish for assurance that the selection will appeal to students.

Selections 12 and 13 of this "not well-liked" group were written by the same author. Older students may like selection 13. The percentage of students rating selection 13 as liked increases from grade 8 to 10,

as Table 5 shows. In Grade 10, 78 percent of the girls rated it liked, though 8.8 percent of the 194 raters checked that they could not read this selection with a Readability Index of 6.2.

Selections 7 (commercial geography) and 26 (termites) were rated liked by 75 percent or more raters in at least one grade. None of the ratings, however, occurred at the "like very, very much," level. These selections could be used. However, selections given more enthusiastic ratings seem more desirable. Selection 21 (sardine fishermen) meets this criterion. Ratings by 11th and 12th grade students are desirable. Selection 19 (famous writers when they were in college) also meets this criterion. It is best liked by girls, 87 percent of whom in the 9th Grade

TABLE 2

CLASSIFICATION OF SELECTIONS INTERESTING TO STUDENTS

8th Grade

(Median number of ratings per selection, 194)

Total	RI	B	G	Both	% Like	Total	RI	B	G	Both	% Like
		Topic						*Topic*			
4		Folklore						Science and Natural History			
	6.2	4.3	4.4	4.4	97	2		Biology			
	6.2	4.6	4.3	4.5	96		6.0	4.2	3.6	3.9	86
	6.7	3.9	4.7	4.4	97		6.5	4.0	3.4	3.8	78
	7.0	4.3	3.4	3.9	78	5		Economic geography and industry			
5		History—political, economic					6.4	4.0	3.8	3.9	83
	5.8	4.0	4.0	4.0	92		7.0	4.0	4.4	4.3	94
	6.0	3.8	4.1	3.9	88		7.1	4.4	4.0	4.2	89
	6.2	4.2	3.9	4.0	85		7.3	3.6	3.8	3.7	83
	6.5	4.4	4.1	4.2	88		7.4	3.8	4.2	4.0	87
	6.6	3.8	3.8	3.8	80	3		Narrative			
4		Miscellaneous					6.3	3.8	4.1	4.0	85
	5.3	3.7	4.1	3.9	85		6.4	4.2	4.1	4.2	87
	5.8	3.7	4.2	3.9	80		7.4	3.8	3.6	3.7	80
	5.8	3.8	3.7	3.8	77	4		Physical Science			
	6.5	4.0	3.8	4.0	83		5.6	4.8	4.0	4.4	91
4		Narrative					6.4	4.2	4.2	4.2	89
	6.2	3.9	4.0	3.9	79		6.6	4.3	3.8	4.1	84
	6.3	4.0	4.2	4.1	93		7.3	4.2	3.8	4.0	84
	6.5	4.4	4.6	4.5	94	1		Vocational			
	7.9	3.9	3.8	3.8	83		5.9	3.2	4.3	3.9	76

TABLE 3

CLASSIFICATION OF SELECTIONS INTERESTING TO STUDENTS

9th Grade

(Median number of ratings per selection, 177)

Total	RI	B	G	Both	% Like	Total	RI	B	G	Both	% Like
		Topic						*Topic*			
4		Biography						Science and Natural History			
	5.8	3.5	4.1	3.8	81	4		Biology			
	6.3	4.0	3.8	3.9	80		6.3	3.6	3.8	3.7	83
	6.6	4.1	3.9	4.0	84		6.3	3.9	3.8	3.8	82
	7.5	4.6	4.4	4.5	88		6.8	4.2	4.0	4.1	92
4		History and Social Problems					7.0	3.7	4.0	3.8	81
	6.4	3.7	3.7	3.7	81	2		Economic geography (historical and			
	6.8	3.8	3.8	3.8	94			contemporary)			
	7.5	3.7	3.7	3.7	90		6.4	4.1	3.8	3.9	94
	8.3	4.0	3.8	3.9	81		7.1	3.8	3.5	3.6	81
6		Miscellaneous				1		Plants, Agriculture and History			
	4.6	4.0	4.1	4.1	82		7.0	3.9	3.7	3.8	83
	4.9	3.8	4.3	4.0	86	2		Physiology			
	5.8	3.2	4.1	3.7	84		6.1	3.6	3.9	3.7	82
	6.6	3.7	4.1	3.9	82		6.7	3.9	4.0	4.0	86
	6.6	4.0	3.4	3.7	77	2		Weather			
	6.7	3.2	4.0	3.7	75		6.7	3.9	3.6	3.7	83
8		Narrative					7.2	4.3	3.9	4.1	94
	6.3	3.6	3.8	3.7	83	1		Sports			
	6.3	3.4	4.2	3.8	78		6.6	4.9	3.9	4.4	96
	6.7	3.9	3.9	3.9	88	1		Vocational			
	7.0	3.8	4.2	4.1	88		6.8	4.0	3.6	3.8	81
	7.2	3.9	4.0	3.9	87						
	7.2	3.8	4.2	4.0	78						
	7.4	4.5	3.9	4.2	89						
	7.5	3.8	4.0	3.9	88						

and 80 percent in the 10th, rated it liked as compared to a little more than 50 percent of the boys.

Two of these 30 selections, 22 (birds, insects, and animals in winter) and 24 (worries of the wheat farmer), were rated well-liked by sixth-graders, but were not rated as well-liked by older students.

Selection 8 was rated by two grades. Two school systems found it necessary at the last moment to change participating classrooms. Even so, 80 to 84 percent of the girls gave this discussion of women's rights a rating of liking. Only 3 of 228 raters said they couldn't read it. If a selection on the same topic with more appeal to boys could not be found, this one could be utilized as one that does appeal to girls.

Selection 20 (workers in a lumber camp) illustrates an interesting point. It was rated by students in grades 7, 8, and 9. Two school systems substituted two 8th grade remedial reading classes for regular classes. The respective percentages of "like" ratings are 82, 63, 80. Yet only one of 225 raters said he could not read the selection with an RI

TABLE 4

CLASSIFICATION OF SELECTIONS INTERESTING TO STUDENTS
10th Grade
(Median number of ratings per selection, 125)

Total	RI	B	G	Both	% Like	Total	RI	B	G	Both	% Like
		Topic						*Topic*			
1		Architecture				6		Narrative			
	7.2	4.2	4.4	4.3	89		5.9	3.9	4.5	4.2	95
5		Biography					6.1	4.2	4.0	4.1	85
	6.2	3.6	4.0	3.9	81		6.9	3.3	3.6	3.4	71
	6.7	3.7	3.7	3.7	75		7.1	4.6	4.2	4.3	95
	7.0	3.6	3.7	3.6	80		7.2	4.5	4.1	4.3	97
	7.2	3.2	3.7	3.5	73		7.6	3.6	3.4	3.5	67
	7.8	3.8	3.5	3.6	79	4		Science and Natural History			
1		Book Review					6.9	3.8	3.8	3.8	83
	7.6	3.9	3.4	3.6	73		7.0	3.5	3.8	3.6	79
1		History					7.2	3.4	3.8	3.5	75
	7.1	3.6	3.4	3.5	71		7.2	3.6	3.8	3.6	78
1		Miscellaneous				4		Social Problems—national and international			
	6.6	3.3	3.8	3.6	76		6.7	3.8	3.5	3.7	75
							6.8	3.5	3.6	3.5	73
							7.0	4.2	3.4	3.8	80
							7.1	3.7	4.2	3.9	81

of 6.2. Students immediately below and above the grade with the retarded readers rated it well-liked. So did the "normal" class in their grade.

SUMMARY

Student ratings indicate that the style and content of 102 selections of up to 400 words appeal differentially to 7th, 8th and 9th graders. Selections of this length meet the requirements for an efficient, systematic program for developing facility in reading at these age levels. The scope of topics is comprehensive though not all-inclusive. Nevertheless, the ratings suggest that these selections could contribute to motivating retarded readers to improve their reading skills. Then they would be better equipped, with further stimulation from school, libraries and other sources, to explore other printed materials of unique interest to them.

BIBLIOGRAPHY

1. BOND, GUY L., and TINKER, MILES A. *Reading Difficulties: Their Diagnosis and Correction.* New York: Appleton-Century-Crofts, Inc. (1957), pp. 7–8.
2. DEBOER, JOHN J. "What Does Research Reveal about Reading and the High School Student," *English Journal*, XLII (May 1958), 274–5.
3. GUILER, WALTER S., and COLEMAN, JOHN H. *Reading for Meaning*, Teacher's Manual. New York: J. B. Lippincott Co. (1955), pp. 2–3.
4. NORVELL, GEORGE W. *The Reading Interests of Young People.* New York: D. C. Heath and Company (1950), p. 262.
5. SMITH, HENRY P., and DECHANT, EMERALD V. *Psychology in Teaching Reading.* New York: Prentice-Hall, Inc. (1961), pp. 1, 2, 6.
6. *Thirty-sixth Yearbook of the National Society for the Study of Education*, Part I (1937), p. 15.

TABLE 5

SELECTIONS RATED AS NOT WELL-LIKED

(Median interest ratings of boys and girls combined by grades)

Numbers followed by % show the percent of "like" ratings

Code	RI	Grade 6		Grade 7		Grade 8		Grade 9		Grade 10	
Biography											
1	5.4					3.3	62%	3.6	70%	3.4	68%
2	5.5					3.4	65%	3.5	67%	3.5	67%
3	7.1							3.1	54%	3.2	56%
History											
4	5.0	3.6	64%	3.4	65%	3.4	68%				
5	5.5	4.4	83%	3.6	71%	3.5	71%				
6	6.0							3.3	61%	3.1	53%
7	6.1			3.1	55%	3.7	67%	3.5	79%		
8	6.5					3.4	68%	3.6	66%		
9	6.6					3.4	67%	3.3	61%	3.3	66%
10	6.8			3.4	78%	3.6	75%	3.4	74%		
11	7.6							3.0	50%	3.3	61%
Miscellaneous											
12	5.8			2.9	43%	2.6	41%	3.3	60%		
13	6.2					3.2	56%	3.5	60%	3.4	70%
14	6.4			2.9	48%	2.6	40%	3.4	61%		
15	6.8					3.2	57%	3.5	66%	3.4	72%
16	7.2							2.9	40%	2.6	39%
17	7.2							3.3	57%	3.3	64%
18	7.3					2.6	50%	3.1	52%	2.5	38%
Narrative											
19	6.5					3.2	62%	3.8	75%	3.6	71%
Occupational											
20	6.2			3.7	82%	3.3	63%	3.6	80%		
21	7.2							3.5	70%	3.6	75%
Science											
22	5.5	4.1	89%	3.9	71%	3.5	70%				
23	5.5	3.7	73%	3.6	72%	3.7	71%				
24	5.9	3.6	75%	3.7	72%	3.3	66%				
25	6.7					3.6	67%	3.4	64%	3.4	71%
26	6.9							3.5	73%	3.5	75%
27	7.0							3.1	53%	2.2	26%
28	7.2					2.9	34%	3.2	69%	3.0	50%
29	7.2							3.4	68%	3.1	52%
30	7.3							3.2	56%	3.1	44%

CONTRIBUTIONS OF READING TO PERSONAL DEVELOPMENT
David H. Russell

In his autobiography, *Safe Conduct*, Boris Pasternak says that the biography of a poet is found in what happens to those who read him. What *does* happen to a reader?

We read at four levels. At the first level we are largely concerned with the association of printed words with their sounds. In some school situations children are drilled in word-calling—"barking at words" without much attention to meaning. At the second level we read for literal meanings. We get the facts or we follow explicit directions. Such reading may have many functional values for the child finding out about India or for the suburbanite engaged in a week-end do-it-yourself project.

The other two levels of reading are more complex. At the third level we interpret what we read. That is, we go beyond the literal comprehension of the fact or the main idea to read between the lines. We draw some conclusion of our own from the passage— we envisage or predict or infer. Sometimes we reflect on the author's point of view or the relation of the material to other things we know—we evaluate or analyze critically. But we also read at a fourth level or depth. Sometimes the passage takes us beyond thoughtful analysis or critical review to a more stirring experience. We feel "the shock of recognition." We recognize a new or an important idea in the actions, characters, or values described. The impact of the material is such that we receive fresh insight into our own or others' lives. In our reading we are changed, a little, as persons.

Most reading is done at the second, literal level, and most of the writing and research in the field of reading have had to do with the first two levels. We know a lot about word perception, the teaching of phonics, and ways of developing comprehension of the printed page. Such activities make many contributions to the individual. The young child enjoys his new-found skill of working out new words, and the world's work and its week-end hobbies involve the use of much factual reading matter contributing to knowledge and skill. Reading has always been one of the individual's most important resources for gaining knowledge. Granted a modicum of reading skill in the individual, books and libraries are storehouses of information for him. Thus, reading at the second level may have many influences on personal development, as in increasing skill in making model airplanes or in preparing a traveler in Spain to get the most out of direct experiences in a foreign country. The main branch of the Berkeley Public Library has approximately 375 books whose titles begin with the words "How to ———," starting with *How to Abandon Ship* and including *How to Live with Children*. Reading at the second level can be a big help to us!

At the third level, we are not so sure of our ground as we are when concerned with

Reprinted from the *Teachers College Record*, LXI (May 1960), 435–442, with permission of Mrs. David Russell and the publisher.

word recognition or literal comprehension. A feature of recent research, however, has been considerable work on critical and creative reading abilities. In a recent study at the University of California, for example, Clark (4)* developed twenty-three lessons in reading to predict beyond the given facts and tested some ways of teaching these in the classroom. He found that tests of reading to predict were relatively independent of vocabulary and comprehension. In going from literal comprehension to personal interpretation as in prediction a reader puts more of himself into his reading. He thinks beyond the line of print. The perceptual process is the stimulus to many kinds of thinking—to drawing analogies, to checking a writer's point of view, or to beginning an attack on a personal problem. As suggested below, more work needs to be done in exploring this process of thoughtful reaction to an author's ideas.

It is at the fourth level, however, that our knowledge is slight and our needs are great, and so it is with effects of reading on individuals that this discussion is chiefly concerned. Can Pasternak or other poets influence us deeply? Do we really have *Books That Changed the World*, as the optimistic title of one publication suggests? Can a book, story, or poem change one person, much less the world? Can reading have the effect Lincoln believed it could have when he first met Harriet Beecher Stowe? On that occasion he said, "Is this the little woman whose book made such a great war?" In a world of television, radio, comic books, parents, and teachers, can a book be an experience which changes the nature of reality for the young reader? In the words of Ciardi, can it make him "quietly passionate" about an idea or a cause? Or can a book help a person to the self-insight attributed to a man who, seeing his neighbor going by in a new pink Cadillac,

[*Numbers in parentheses refer to Bibliography at the end of this article.]

said, "There, but for me, go I!" Can a book fill a boy with courage or help him find himself? Or is this too much to ask, even of great literature? Reading may be useful at all four levels, but somehow this fourth level seems the most tantalizing and important of all.

SOME POSSIBLE EFFECTS OF READING

The kind of reading that we do affects the contribution of the reading matter to our development. In the primary school grades so much of the effort goes into the first level—into the mechanics of reading, into getting the words right, toward following the sequence of the writer's thought—that the chance of added dividends is unlikely. Similarly, in the later grades, the poor reader, or the child deciphering material much too difficult for him, has little opportunity or stimulus to interpret a story or to find materials meaningful to his larger concerns or problems. Piekarz (11) has shown that when children are unable to read a passage with reasonable ease they have fewer reactions to it, with many more responses at the literal-meaning level than at the implied-meaning or evaluation level.

Accordingly, the time and effort given to the making of fluent, skillful readers at the elementary and secondary school levels may be worthwhile, not only in terms of specific aspects of reading skill but also because such reading is a basis for operation at the two higher levels of reading. Children need word-attack skills and ability to follow directions, not because they are merely going to read words or to follow directions blindly, but so that, having clearly recognized words or accurately interpreted directions, they can then go to the meanings behind the words and, if necessary, to questions about the validity of the directions.

Such an interpretation of reading is not a derogation of reading skills. Many children and adolescents work very hard to attain word recognition skills and the ability to grasp the literal meaning of a paragraph, passage, or chapter. Indeed, success in these matters may make a contribution to personal development beyond that of the facts read because of the "nothing succeeds like success" formula. The child who learns to read skillfully not only pleases his parents but contributes positively to his self-concept. The converse is even clearer. The child who has reading difficulties at the first two levels may have emotional and personality problems associated with his reading. The primary causation may not be so important as the *fact* that reading difficulties are affecting his total development adversely.

When poor readers have not achieved fluency in reading they must have help. For these pupils various types of remedial programs have been developed in schools.

For young children, one aid to fluency is to have their parents and teachers read stories to them, more complex stories than they can read for themselves. For their own first reading practice there seems no reason why children should not begin on easy, graded materials developed in light of many of the things we know about the psychology of learning. In the preschool and early primary years, children can be challenged and helped to reach higher levels of reading by the ideas in the stories read to them.

An example of such reading-listening situations affecting total development is given in a recent master's thesis by Webster (*21*). She found in a group of eighty first-graders that thirty-five expressed fear of the dark and five indicated fear of dogs. Accordingly, in groups of seven children, she read to and discussed with the children five stories dealing positively with the dark and with dogs—stories such as Margaret Wise Brown's *A Child's Good Night Book* and Ruth Dixon's *Three Little Puppies*. Three months later, an impartial judge agreed with Webster's analysis of interviews: twenty-nine out of the thirty-five children had, it seemed, reduced their fear of the dark and all five of the children had lost most of their fear of dogs. Such a study needs verification with more careful controls, but it suggests that, for young children, the "read-to" situation may affect a child's emotional development.

As a child develops the ability to read for himself some books and stories of merit, the second level of reading flourishes. He finds out not only the secret of the lost treasure but something of the lives of early Americans or something about woolgrowing in Patagonia or in Queensland. The purpose of many books, newspapers, and magazines is to inform. We live in a difficult period of man's history, and the problems which beset us demand our best knowledge and efforts. Therefore, we read for main ideas, for facts, for following a sequence of events, for seeing relationships, and for arriving at conclusions.

Teachers of English at the secondary school and college level have not always considered such reading part of their domain. Of course they must also be concerned with the third and fourth reading levels of interpretation and with the impact of great literature. The value of the information contained in a book has little or nothing to do with its value as literature. One level is concerned with getting a fact right and clear, the other is concerned with some basic human expression or need. One makes for grasp of the immediate, the other, as Bernard Berenson remarked of great pictures, makes for the enhancement of life. Most of our school texts are written and should be used at the level of accurate comprehension. I believe the problem is not "either-or" and that the teacher of English must be concerned with both kinds of reading. Skill at the first two levels seems to be basic to achievement at the third and fourth levels. But it is in the realm of imaginative literature that we usually get to the third and fourth levels of reading. It is here that writing is intrepid in its approach to problems, ingenious in its solution of difficulties, in a way that the child or adolescent cannot achieve by himself. It is at these levels that reading can operate in depth and make its greatest contribution to individual development.

Fortunately, some research evidence is beginning to be accumulated about reading at the third level of interpretation of printed materials. May I quickly suggest a variety of findings. (a) Most children do not seem to respond to some of the commoner literary devices such as metaphor or personification before they are in their teens (23). (b) Children's interpretations are influenced by their attitudes and expectancies toward what they are reading, by their previous "set" in the reading situation (5). (c) When asked to respond to short stories, adolescents give interpretational reactions as a dominant type of response; other categories of response, in order of frequency, are narrational, associational, self-involvement, literary judgment, and prescriptive judgment (19). (d) Responses to a piece of literature are largely an individual matter. Children and youth with different experiences, personalities, and needs see different things in the same character, story, or poem—and one interpretation may be just as "true" or "honest" as the other. Consequently, teachers of reading and literature should beware of looking for the one "correct" interpretation (14). (e) With adolescents, literary judgments and emotional involvements vary inversely. In other words, children and adolescents tend to suspend objectivity when emotionally involved (19). (f) The most common emotional involvements of adolescents in fiction seem to be "happiness binding" (the desire for a happy ending) and insistence upon certainty in interpretation (19). These half-dozen statements can be extended in a consideration of the process of interpretation. Perhaps the

samples are enough to show that we are beginning to accumulate some research evidence about some of the psychological factors which are involved in interpretation, whether of a good story in a third reader, a chapter or poem in a high school anthology, or an individual example of an author's work.

Unfortunately, the evidence about effects at the fourth level of reading is sparse. Perhaps it will always be shaky in the scientific sense and we shall always have to rely in part on individual testimony regarding the effects of books or literature. Down through the generations great and good men have testified to the influence of a book or books in their lives. The Greeks believed in the effect of literature on the growing boy, and Plato wrote in *The Republic*, ". . . we should do our utmost that the first stories that they hear should be so composed as to bring the fairest lessons of virtue to their ears." Much later, Stephen Vincent Benet wrote, "Books are not men and yet they are alive." Luther Burbank, the great horticulturist, testified that his whole life was changed by reading one book, *The Origin of the Species*. But the testimony of these and other men and women, interesting in itself, does not constitute evidence in the scientific sense. What about the individual's readiness for change? What about other supporting or conflicting influences in classroom, home, or community? Can a biography of sacrifice and social service influence a twelve-year-old girl for whose parents the good life consists of cocktail parties and Las Vegas week ends? If we as teachers are trying to influence the ideas and lives of young people through literature, we need to know much more about the role of the individual himself, the content of the materials, the total situation in which the reading takes place, and the overt reactions to be expected in speaking, writing and action (14).

To some teachers such analysis of the four factors influencing the impact of reading on the individual makes the whole process needlessly complex. Not every teacher of reading in the fourth grade or of literature in the tenth grade can take time to know individual children and materials in such intimate fashion, nor can they easily arrange maximum environmental conditions for reading to affect individual development. Perhaps the problem is still one for research rather than classroom practice, and yet somehow the two must be combined. All elementary and secondary teachers of literature know that some pieces are more effective than others with a group but may not have tried to discover the reason. Why does one story "hit" a group of ten-year-olds or another, a group of fifteen-year-olds "just right"? What kind of matching of material and reader can a teacher accomplish? How can this be individualized at the secondary as well as the elementary school level? What are maximal conditions when "boy meets book"?

The evidence that reading affects lives is largely confined to the subjective, individual testimony illustrated above and to some reports of bibliotherapy in individual case studies (8, 15, 17, 24). Studies by Russell (12), Smith (18), and Weingarten (22) have attempted to get at the effects of reading by requesting direct reports of them from teachers and from elementary and secondary school students. Such reports may all be too optimistic because of the desire of students to give congenial answers but they do suggest that the effects of reading may be widespread and sometimes profound. The present scattered findings can be substantiated or refuted by further research. Perhaps at the moment the teacher can only adopt the optimistic view that there are certain things that are true even if not experimentally verified. Perhaps such a faith is needed if one is to teach literature well. The possibilities are so vast that this article concludes with a few more examples of research explorations in unmapped territory.

RESEARCH ON INTERPRETATION

In addition to the investigation by Squire cited above and the studies supporting the six conclusions stated earlier, some careful investigations have been made of the interpretive process in reading. These date back at least to 1919, when Thorndike (20) published his classical study of ways children misinterpret paragraphs. One reason for flagrant errors in interpreting a factual passage he attributed to the overpotency of certain words. He said, "The mind is assailed as it were by every word in the paragraph. It must select, repress, soften, emphasize, correlate and organize, all under the influence of the right mental set or purpose or demand." This statement was explored further by Hinze (9) in a recent doctoral study at the University of California. She was interested in the cluster of associations the reader may have with certain words as explored by Jenkins, by Osgood and others. She first selected two passages, one factual (about scientific discoveries) and one emotionally charged (part of a Kafka story). Before the students saw these passages they were asked, in interview, to associate all the words they could with certain individual words from the two selections and to rate the words as positive or negative associations. Later, the students read each passage and interpreted its meaning. Hinze found clear evidence that when students had consistent emotional responses to the words in the passage, that is, all positive or all negative reactions, they tended to interpret the paragraphs objectively or "correctly," but when some of their emotional responses to the individual words were opposed to the dominant association, that is, when they had "conflict words," they had trouble giving a clear interpretation of the passage. Conflict words, in contrast to unidirectional words, caused significantly greater misinterpretation of the affective materials.

Some other investigations have given clues to the kinds of interpretation a teacher can expect. In a study (23) in England, the subject of the work was found to be most important for young children. Before they were twelve they made judgments about the ethical intention of the writer, and after twelve there emerged some feeling for "literary quality" as shown in structure and the aptness of simile or metaphor. In an American study, Harris (6) analyzed students' responses to literature into four types: translating; summarizing; inferring tone, mood, and intent; and relating technique and meaning. He devised tests of seven specific recognition skills but found on factor analysis of results that one general factor was adequate to account for the intercorrelations of the test results. This suggested that comprehension of literary materials may be a general function.

A study by Groff (5), however, emphasized the factors of individuality and attitude in interpreting paragraphs. He found that as a child reads critically, his interpretations are influenced by his attitude toward the content type of material read and his attitude toward reading as a school activity. In a factor analysis of scores on twenty-seven variables Bauer (2) found that achievement in reading was positively related to two variables, "self-expressiveness" and "drive for achievement," but negatively related to social adjustment and absence of excessive fears. Personality factors may influence reading behavior.

Another unpublished study of interpretation is that of Scribner (16), who found wide differences in the interpretation of poems by students, teachers of English, and literary critics. These differences are not great in the interpretation of relatively clear-cut poems such as Robert Frost's "The Road Not Taken." Even here, however, in a group of eighteen-year-olds, Scribner got such divergent interpretations of the main theme as

The necessity of making decisions in life.
The idea that one road may be better than the other.

The idea that it is important to think for yourself and make your own decisions.
He took the less travelled road.

These may seem varied responses from a group of eighteen-year-olds to a relatively simple poem, but Scribner found that variety in interpretation becomes much greater for the more "difficult" or ambiguous poem such as Blake's "Tiger," both in the student group itself and in terms of differences among students, teachers, and critics.

Why do students interpret a poem, story, or novel differently? We have already suggested one group of causes in the student or reader—his reading ability, his background of experience, his attitude and expectancies, his needs perhaps. The second group of causes lies in the piece of literature itself. As Hinze found, an overlap in these two occurs in the reader's associations with the individual words. It also occurs in the pupil's sensory perception of a poem or other piece of imaginative writing—his response to images in seeing, hearing, feeling, or even smelling. The piece of literature itself may affect the reader's interpretation through the arrangement or pattern; for example, the rhyme scheme or the use of onomatopoeia.

Finally, there is the symbolization in the story or poem. At the elementary level the lion is the symbol of courage, a flag of nationality, and Loki of trouble and mischief among the gods. With older children, we begin to get values attached to symbols. Some things are true and good, as motherhood, and some wrong or unworthy, as cowardice. Studies of school reading texts by Anderson (1) and by Child (3), of children's biographies by McConnell (10), and of best-selling fiction by Harvey (7) are examples of analyses of content of reading materials which may influence a reader. Thus the reader himself and the content of the material, particularly the symbolic content, may influence interpretation.

This research report is sketchy, and necessarily so. Most of it consists of spot checks instead of long-term studies of the effects of reading. We need to know much more about both cross-sectional and longitudinal aspects of each of the four factors influencing interpretation and personal development through reading. Since the days of the *New England Primer* we have had the feeling that, somehow, reading can help create a virtuous life. Almost three hundred years after the *Primer* perhaps the goal is still a good one.

BIBLIOGRAPHY

1. ANDERSON, PAUL S. "McGuffey *vs.* the Moderns in Character Training," *Phi Delta Kappan*, 38:53–58, November 1956.
2. BAUER, EDITH B. "The Interrelatedness of Personality and Achievement in Reading." Doctoral dissertation, University of California, Berkeley, 1956.
3. CHILD, IRWIN L., and others. "Children's Textbooks and Personality Development: An Exploration in the Social Psychology of Education," *Psychological Monographs*, 60, No. 3 (1946), 54.
4. CLARK, CHARLES M. "Teaching Sixth-Grade Students to Make Predictions from Reading Materials." Doctoral dissertation, University of California, Berkeley, 1958.
5. GROFF, PATRICK J. "Children's Attitudes Toward Reading and Their Critical Reading Abilities in Four Content-Type Materials." Doctoral dissertation, University of California, Berkeley, 1955.
6. HARRIS, CHESTER W. "Measurement of Comprehension of Literature," *School Review*, 56:280–89, 332–43, May-June 1948.
7. HARVEY, JOHN. "The Content Characteristics of Best-Selling Novels," *Public Opinion Quarterly*, 17:91–114, 1953.
8. HERMINGHAUS, EARL G. "The Effect of Bibliotherapy on the Attitudes and Personal and Social Adjustment of a Group of Elementary School Children." Doctoral dissertation, Washington University, 1954.
9. HINZE, HELEN A. "The Individual's Word Associations and His Interpretation of Prose Paragraphs." Doctoral dissertation, University of California, Berkeley, 1959.
10. MCCONNELL, GAITHER A. "An Analysis of Biographical Literature for Children." Doctoral dissertation, University of California, Berkeley, 1952.
11. PIEKARZ, JOSEPHINE A. "Getting Meaning from Reading," *Elementary School Journal*, 56:303–9, March 1956.
12. RUSSELL, DAVID H. "Teachers' Memories and Opinions of Children's Literature," *Elementary English*, 26:475–82, December 1949.
13. ———. "Personal Values in Reading," *The Reading Teacher*, 12:3–9, October 1958.
14. ———. "Some Research on the Impact of Reading," *English Journal*, 47:398–413, October 1958.
15. ———, and SHRODES, CAROLINE. "Contributions of Research in Bibliotherapy to the Language Arts Program," *School Review*, 58:335–42, 411–20, September-October 1950.
16. SCRIBNER, MARION. "Responses of Students, Teachers and Critics to Selected Poems," in manuscript, University of California, Berkeley.
17. SHRODES, CAROLINE. "Bibliotherapy: A Theoretical and Clinical-Experimental Study." Doctoral dissertation, University of California, Berkeley, 1949.
18. SMITH, NILA B. "Some Effects of Reading on Children," *Elementary English*, 25:271–78, May 1948.
19. SQUIRE, JAMES R. "The Responses of Adolescents to Literature Involving Selected Experiences in Personal Development." Doctoral dissertation, University of California, Berkeley, 1956.
20. THORNDIKE, EDWARD L. "Reading as Reasoning: A Study of Mistakes in Paragraph Reading," *Journal of Educational Psychology*, 8:323–32, June 1917.
21. WEBSTER, W. JANE. "Some Effects of Stories on the Reduction of Fears of First Grade Children." M.A. Seminar Study, University of California, Berkeley, 1960.
22. WEINGARTEN, SAMUEL. "Developmental Values in Voluntary Reading," *School Review*, 62:222–30, April 1954.
23. WILLIAMS, E. D., WINTER, L., and WOODS, J. K. "Tests of Literary Appreciation," *British Journal of Educational Psychology*, 8:265–84, November 1938.
24. WITTY, PAUL A. "Promoting Growth and Development Through Reading," *Elementary English*, 27:493–500, December 1950.

11

The Interest to Read

PAPERBACKS AND THE READING PROGRAM
Daniel Fishco

Paperback materials are those printed works such as pamphlets, magazines, comic books, novels, reference materials, and other sources of literature which are bound in paper rather than hard covers.

Much of the paperbound material is new. That is, it has been written especially for use as a paperbound book. A good deal of the paper-covered material is classic and successful or popular reading material originally published in hard cover form.

The paperback, it has been said by many, is a great boon to the educators of today. There is such a wealth of material available to the classroom teacher in paperback, that all educators and administrators should be made aware of the many uses and advantages of such materials.

It seems to me, that the public as well as many educators are just beginning to open their eyes to the many advantages of paperback material.

The paperback material, available today, is somewhat different from its predecessor. The paperback industry has become alerted to the needs of children, adolescents, parents, and teachers. As a result of this, much more wholesome and valuable material is available for use.

Mr. Alex Butman of Bantam Books, Inc. wrote in *Paperbacks in the Schools:*

> Books have had a tremendous impact on the progress of man.
>
> Of all the media available for the communication of our heritage and ideas, no other is so small, so portable, and so inexpensive. Books need no wires or machinery. They allow man to communicate with other men through the barriers of time. A paperback, specifically, measures 4¼ by 7½ inches and weighs only a few ounces. It is self-contained and self-sustaining. Its only basic need is for a reader.
>
> Two dynamics—the book and the teacher —have withstood replacement by technical advance in the past. It is unlikely that they will be replaced in the future. Both have the unique ability to cause the spark in the youngster that is the difference between training and educating. The paperback is the ideal book form of the present and, due to its inherent flexibility it will remain modern.
>
> The paperback offers not just a new package for an old item; it offers a new vehicle with which to enrich the learning

Reprinted from *The Wide World of Reading Instruction*, Lehigh University Conference on Reading, Vol. 5 (1966), 161–168, with permission of the author and Lehigh University.

experience and broaden it into a new education dimension.

The paperback, of course, has definite advantages in most instructional classroom programs. Children can read and own more books because they can choose and purchase them by themselves. Paperback bookstores can easily be instituted in schools thereby making available good reading material at a considerable saving over the cost of a hardbound book. The school can also use the profits from this paperback book store in order to stock the school library or for other worthwhile endeavors. The paperback books can easily be exchanged among students, thereby making availability greater. Children gain much pride and satisfaction out of seeing their own personal library "grow" larger and larger.

For some reason, students seem to associate the paperback book with pleasure reading rather than "formal school reading."

Movies and television series, which are often presented as reading material in the form of paperback books, stimulate a desire for reading and enjoyment.

The paperback materials today engulf a wide enough range of interests so that, at low cost, a classroom can have reading material pertinent to the interests of most students.

Many of the paperback publishing companies are producing more and more materials for the elementary grades. These materials are written at various levels of reading difficulty.

The unit approach to curriculum is one that invites the paperback with open arms. There are so many different titles that can be utilized in similar areas that the problem of securing a book that interests a student in a particular unit is minimized.

As more teachers become aware of the availability of paperback material, and enjoy the use of this material, the paperback will come into the school in the same manner as one sees chalk, pencils, textbooks, and paper.

An essential part of an individualized or personalized reading program is the availability of books. The problem of securing books is a great one in many classrooms. The paperback book has been coming to the rescue in this situation.

As part of the *reading* program, all books are necessary. If a child is reading for science, social studies, or literature, he is still reading. In an individualized reading program the child must read regardless of what he is reading.

We have spoken about the use of paperback books in a unit-centered curriculum and in an individualized learning situation. What about the traditional or basal oriented program?

Many classrooms still use basal texts in each of the content areas of the curriculum. The paperback book can supplement these areas quite adequately. It is up to the teacher to find out what is available and appropriate for the particular topic as well as the needs of the students. These supplementary or resource materials can be on hand so that a student has easy access to them when time permits.

There is a multitude of literature in paperback which can be used to supplement, give background to, or enrich the study and/or discussion of most stories found in our basal readers and literature anthologies.

How do we go about selecting books; finding what is available; deciding whether this material is educationally sound (or approved) for use in the classroom?

First, let us see what is available. Most publishers of paperback books publish, in addition to their general catalogues, educational book lists. The titles on those lists are approved for classroom use. All you need to do is write to the publisher and ask for the educational catalogue. Publishers are more than happy to send their brochures to you, and they will always take the time to answer any specific queries you might direct toward them.

An invaluable tool, published by the R. R. Bowker Company, is *Paperbound Books In Print*. This periodical, which is printed monthly, keeps one informed of most of the books printed in paperback form. In June of 1965, *Paperbound Books In Print* contained over 34,700 titles. The titles, authors publisher, or publishers, and the prices are some of the important lists of information contained within this great catalogue. The titles listed in the catalogue are categorized into approximately 80 areas. Of the areas listed such categories as "Juvenile and Young Adult Books," "Hobbies," "Nature," "Autobiography and Biography," "Travel and Adventure," and all of the academic and their related areas are represented.

Two other valuable resources printed by the R. R. Bowker Company are *Paperback Book Guide for High Schools*, which catalogues more than 5,000 paperbacks that are suitable for high school use and *Paperbound Book Guides For Colleges*. The latter has catalogued approximately 12,000 paperbacks for use at the college level.

The Bowker Company is presently developing a catalogue listing the available titles, in paperback, for the elementary grades. However, you should write to the Bowker Company for more information concerning the publication date of this elementary catalogue.

The Bureau of Independent Publishers and Distributors, known as BIPAD, publishes *The Paperback Goes To School*. The 1965–66 edition contains more than 3,850 titles of paperbacks recommended for the Junior and Senior High Schools.

The School Paperback Institute, Inc. publishes the *School Paperback Journal*. This journal, published nine times per academic year, is a great aid to the teacher or administrator in choosing books. The magazine also contains feature articles and many helpful suggestions.

Paperbacks In The Schools, published by Bantam Books, is a report of the "paperback explosion" written for and to teachers and parents. It also contains worthy title suggestions for classroom use.

Washington Square Press has published *Books For You*. This book contains the titles of many available paperbacks.

The next time you pick up a professional journal, *read* the advertisements. Paperback publishers *do* advertise. They advertise that which *you* need in *your* journals.

Next, we want to know whether the material is educationally sound (or approved) for use in the classroom.

In most of the material sources I have just referred to, titles are marked with asterisks, daggers, and other symbols. These markings refer to the express approval of such agencies as National Council of Teachers of English, National Education Association, American Library Association, and others. Certainly, if these groups have taken the time and energy to review, approve, and disapprove paperback selections, educational agencies must agree to the benefits gained from the utilization of such materials. In fact, the Macmillan Company has published a text titled, *Teaching The Novel In Paperback*, for use by teachers.

Until now we have spoken of a few of the many advantages of paperback use, and finding what is available.

The next question, "How do we get paperbacks for our classrooms?"

There are several ways of securing paperback books. The first, and probably most familiar to most of you, are brought to your classrooms via the Scholastic Magazines.

Another way is the establishment of a paperback book store, which was mentioned earlier. Also mentioned earlier was the book fair which can help build a paperback library.

I might mention that in a study made last year*, "It was noted that the school bookstores appealed to the adolescents . . . They like to browse and to buy paperbound books, knowing that the profits would remain in the school itself." The study also reported that 76% of the administrators involved in the study were in favor of the book fair and found that there was value in such an undertaking.

Most of you are familiar with the National Defense Education Act (N.D.E.A.). You know that this act provides for materials in reading. However, your school district must spend an amount of money and the government will match this amount.

The Elementary and Secondary Education Act of 1965, on the other hand, provides outright grants of money. Your schools are eligible, under Titles I, II, and III of this act, for money which you can use to buy reading materials. The state of Pennsylvania alone stands to receive $61,750,000.00. Let me state again. These grants are outright. All you need to do is ask about the allocation to your school district.

What success has the paperback had in the schools thus far?

In order to answer this question, let us first take a look at our neighbors in New Jersey. Last year a project which included fifty schools was undertaken in that state. Paperbacks were used extensively in grades three through twelve. However many second grades reported success using approximately seventy-five appropriate titles of paperbound books.

The results of the project were quite favorable. Some of those results reported in *Paperbound Books In New Jersey Public Schools* were:

1. There was universal agreement that the

* Reported in *Paperbound Books In New Jersey Public Schools*.

existence and use of a variety of trade paperbound books, easily accessible in the classroom, affected desirable changes in most students.

2. It was clear that these books begin to influence curricular practices in English language arts instruction from grades four through twelve.

3. . . . where such materials were used, it encouraged an overwhelmingly positive reading response from all kinds of students at all grade levels.

4. They (the students) found more time for and interest in leisure reading, and they spent more time discussing books with their friends, and making recommendations.

5. . . . reading, as a habit, was generated in the very same classes which hitherto were disinterested and passive.

6. . . . students were reading more books, borrowing more books, and talking about books more than ever before.

The recommendations of teachers and administrators who participated in the project were definitely favoring the continued and expanded use of paperbound books in the classroom as well as the school libraries.

A project emanating from Jefferson County, Colorado Public Schools reported in *The Nation's School* that:

1. Paperbacks *do* encourage student reading . . .

2. They (paperbacks) display an amazing pulling power for youngsters who have experienced reading difficulties . . .

3. Because they're cheap, paperbacks are finding their way into student-owned libraries.

4. The low cost of paperbacks has made it possible to buy multiple copies of classics and high circulation.

5. They're (paperbacks) expendable. After they were circulated about 15 times they

wore out. But 15 times fully justifies their low cost.

6. Because initial cost is so low, so is replacement.
7. Paperbound books do not lessen the use of hardbounds. We've found that the use of hardbounds has increased. It's true: Reading encourages more reading.
8. Paperbacks' low cost has enabled us to expand greatly the versatility and resources of our libraries.
9. Paperbacks have changed the thinking of a good many of our professional staff members. They no longer summarily dismiss reading of paperbacks as mostly one step above pornography.

At the conference on "The Role of Paperback Books In Education," held this past October, publishers and educators from all parts of the United States agreed to the important role the paperback is playing as an instructional tool in our classrooms.

Some of the comments I heard at the conference were:

1. Utilize paperbacks in order to reinforce the entire school curriculum.
2. Paperbacks will broaden the scope of children's reading.
3. Paperbacks can provide ready reference material for the learner.
4. The same books can be used for both recreational reading and instructional purposes.
5. The basal reader is not an answer in itself. A multitude of good reading is needed so the child can utilize what he learns.
6. Individualized reading programs can be expanded greatly.
7. Librarians need to perform only a minimum of cataloguing chores with paperbacks because they are expendable.

At this point, I would like to thank Sister May Norma Barber, S.S.N.D. of the National Catholic Education Association for this next device.

P—possession—kids can afford to own their books
A—availability—paperbacks can be purchased almost everywhere
P—program—the paperback fits the entire curricular program
E—enrichment—the paperback can and does enrich and fortify the total instructional program
R—resource material can be found in abundance in paperback form
B—bibliotherapy—reading leads to reading
A—apostolate—the reproductions of heroism and national heritage
C—curriculum development
K—knowledge which can be passed more adequately through the art of reading
S—service that the paperback affords the teacher.

One of the questions that has been asked over and over again is: "Have we been fooled by the basal reader for so many years?" Another question: "What research is available to justify entire developmental reading programs based only on a series of basal readers?"

As long as there are those teachers who do not know how to teach reading, someone or something must do it for them. The basal reader has been the educational crutch performing that service for the ineffective teacher of reading.

I could go on and on and fill you in as to that which is happening within our country's classrooms. However, you can, if you are interested, find that information in your professional journals and magazines.

Let us take a look at what some of the publishers have to offer us for *our* classrooms.

Let us look at the shelves of Washington Square Press. Here we view The Reader's Enrichment Series. This series is made up of more than forty titles. Each book contains a complete work. A teacher's edition is printed as well as a student's edition. Such additional information is provided for the reader as the life and purposes of the author, the historical background of the story, features of the author's style, and analyses of the book's characters. The teacher's edition contains the same information and has added to it an area of language arts and practical skills. The manual is designed to help teachers organize lessons, organize activities, and provide the necessary skill assistance to the student.

In addition to the Reader's Enrichment Series, Washington Square Press also publishes a new selection known as the Lantern Pocket Books. These are general reading materials for the elementary-Junior High students. There are ten titles in this series thus far. *Humorous Stories, Boy Scout Stories, Ghost Stories*, and *Science Fiction Stories* are a few of the titles offered.

On the racks of Berkley Publishing Company we see an extremely exciting selection of titles. Notice the plaid design in the upper corner of the book covers. This design is the signal that the books are approved for our use in the classroom. These books are known as the Berkley Highland Titles. These books have been approved for our use by such noted authorities as School Library Journal, American Library Association, Horn Book, and others. Just look at what the offerings are. Novels by Margaret Maze Craig, one of today's outstanding writers of young adult stories. The "Beany Malone Series," "Sherlock Holmes Stories," and science fiction novels by H. G. Wells are some of the magnetic attractions we are drawn to. What girls would not thrill to the writing of Betty Cavanna, Mary Stolz, Mildred Lawrence, Anne Emery, and Rosamund Du Jardin? For the boys, we see such titles as *Man on a Raft, War Beneath the Sea, Speedway Challenge, West Point Yearling, World Series, Young Skin Diver*, and many more exciting novels.

Now that we are in a browsing frame of mind, over there is the Grosset and Dunlap selection. Here is an entire set of books. *"The 1001 Answer to Questions About Books."* The elementary and junior high scientists could really go to town with these. What is this? Grosset and Dunlap Tempo Series. There are more than a hundred titles here for elementary, junior and senior high school readers. Adventure stories, humorous stories, romance, science fiction, sports, biography, war—there are titles for all kinds of readers with all kinds of interests.

What else is available? There is Dell Publishing Company. For the elementary school boys and girls they offer the Dell Seal Series. Presently, this series contains ten titles. Five written primarily for the girls and five of interest to the boys. However, I have read and enjoyed all ten. Then there is the Laurel Leaf Library for elementary—junior—senior high students. This series contains many of the great classics plus a wealth of fabulous and exciting reading material. If you are looking for support for the English curriculum, Dell offers us The Laurel Poetry Series, The Laurel Shakespeare Series, and the Laurel Short Stories.

You say that you want more—Look at this catalogue by Bantam. The Bantam Learning Units provide the teacher with some novel ideas. Contained here are titles of adventure, fact, fiction, novels concerning adolescent problems and experiences, animal tales, and humor. We also see the Bantam Pathfinder Editions as well as the Bantam Classics. Students of a wide variety of interests and abilities will have little difficulty finding many pleasurable hours of reading here.

How about science, math, social studies? New American Library has it. Just look through their Signet and Mentor Series.

The one thing we have not made reference to thus far is *reference itself*. Among all of those exciting titles such as *To Kill A Mocking Bird, 1001 Ways To Enjoy Your Car, The 17 Books of Young Living, Secret Service*

Chief, The Remarkable Kennedys, Lyndon B. Johnson, and so many others, Popular Library offers us some of the best in reference material. For classroom, home, or office use is the Desk Top Reference Library. This consists of a *Webster's New World Dictionary of The American Language, A Dictionary of Synonyms and Antonyms, How To Build A Better Vocabulary, Better English Made Easy,* and *A New Guide To Better Writing.* There is also a copy of *Harper's English Grammar.*

The newest, most exciting advance in paperback publishing for English teachers (and especially those directly concerned with teaching reading) is Popular Library's new Ladder Books. This is the first, low-priced "limited vocabulary" series to be made available to elementary, junior and senior high schools, in this country.

Ladder Books are, basically, "high-level interest, low-level vocabulary" books specially edited and published to meet the dire needs of the poor, slow and reluctant readers, as well as those students from the culturally deprived areas to whom English, as you and I know it, is actually a "second language."

The vocabulary levels of this new series range from 1,000 to 5,000 words. But, no effort is made to simplify the content of the Ladder Books or to "talk down" to the reader. *Simplified* English, not simple English is the goal of the series. Nothing is changed for the sake of change, nor is anything creatively re-written.

Now, what have we omitted? Art, music, foreign language, philosophy, etc., those are also available in paperback. Just contact your local distributor or write to the publishers. If it is printed, you can probably find it in a paperbound edition.

Earlier, I mentioned a paperback conference held recently. One of the keynote speakers was the well known Dr. Leland Jacobs of Columbia University. I would like to end by quoting Dr. Jacobs.

I think that one of the things that is wonderful about paperbacks is that through the use of them in the school, the individualizing of teaching practices can be facilitated economically. But classes wont get individualized just 'cause you got 'em. That isn't the making of the magic. I knew some teachers in one-room schools who used paperbacks forty years ago: Sears and Roebuck catalogs . . . The point is . . . that, as we work on the true spirit of individualizing, then economically we can have more material.

But the magic isn't in the paperback; by itself that won't make much difference. It's in the interplay of the spirit of individualizing the classrooms so that we respect the aloneness in the individual who is learning and supply the materials. And one value of the economy of the paperback is that we can still have some very beautiful hardback books, too. For I don't want children never to feel in their hands a beautifully made hardback book. But if we would save our money for really good hardback books, and use many more of the paperbacks, then we can individualize if the spirit is there, too.

And through the use of paperbacks in schools, critical thinking can be encouraged. No longer will the child have to take what one single textbook writer says about a certain thing. There are three things, it seems to me, that in critical reading we need to teach children. The first is that no writer ever says everything that there is to be said about anything. The second is that, though the author seems to be nowhere, he is everywhere in what he writes. And the third one is that it is the intent of the writer to get you to turn the page. He's going to try everything that he's got to get you to go on with him. And as long as we give children only a single source, they can't learn this very well.

One of the things that the paperback can do is to give us a chance to let kids do critical thinking by comparing one with another. I wouldn't even buy thirty of the same dictionaries for a third grade. I'd want a variety of dictionaries so that they would find that the dictionaries don't entirely agree, so that we would rear a generation who wouldn't be alarmed when the latest dictionary came out.

Through the use of paperbacks in the

schools, that wonderful et cetera of teaching can be fostered practically. A good portion of teaching is et cetera, my friends. Oh, you sit at home at night and you get the best plans that you can make, and the next day they don't work. There is always an et cetera to teaching. And you're going down a nice, great line of thinking with them, and some little scamp in that group has a better idea than you had last night. There's always an et cetera in teaching. And the paperbacks could contribute to this because we can get to a lot of stuff that was raised as the et cetera of teaching, practically and rapidly.

LISTEN, MY CHILDREN, AND YOU SHALL READ . . .
Edmund J. Farrell

I do not remember when I was first read to. Like most children of the middle class, I was subjected to pictures similar to those found in little Golden Books for pre-readers, pictures accompanied with the usual inane parental patois regarding doggies, horsies, mama cows and kitty cats. But beyond providing me with a working vocabulary which could ease me into the frivolous, antiseptic world of Dick and Jane, my parents, as I recall, did not do much. Certainly they were not people who eagerly held *Alice in Wonderland* and *Winnie the Pooh* in ready alert for their latest offspring, upon whom they could expend winter evenings reading aloud in Victorian leisure by flickering firelight.

No, I believe it was in elementary school that I first heard stories and first fell in love with literature. Though I now have only kaleidoscopic impressions of my first few years in the parochial school I attended and can no longer remember which good and gentle nun taught me what in which grade, I do recall the quiet times, the periods after sweaty recesses when, shirttails hanging and hair rumpled, we would be required to put our heads down on the desks and listen until a story or poem had performed its magic, and the savage beasts were once again soothed. It was during such periods that I first rambled with slow-witted Little Red Riding Hood to her grandmother's, that I first discovered that someone had been sleeping in our bed, that I first clambered the bean stalk with Jack and bested a giant. Enroute I learned some valuable moral lessons—that a cheap tract home can be huffed and puffed down, that one can get mighty hungry if all he touches is turned to gold, that stepmothers aren't to be trusted. But the morality was oblique, incidental, not sententious like that in the Puritan hornbook or the McGuffey Readers. What I mostly learned were the creative joys of visualizing a setting, having an empathic response to a character, feeling the heart-tingling excitement of a suspenseful plot. Too, I began to learn the sound of literature, to develop an inner ear to guide me in my attempts to discriminate between the shoddy and pretentious and the valuable and true in all writing, including my own.

Since elementary school, I have not been read to much, and the times I was read to have not always been memorable for the same reasons. Certainly I shall never forget

Reprinted from the *English Journal*, LV (Jan. 1966), 39–45, 68, with permission of the author and National Council of Teachers of English.

the woman who in the twilight of her teaching years read aloud *Tale of Two Cities* to the sophomore class in which I unfortunately sat. After six solid weeks of hearing her intone like a full-bosomed thrush whose days are numbered, I was ready to put the axe to Carton, myself. Then there was the schoolmarmish professor who, in a course in advanced Shakespearian criticism, seated over a hundred of us alphabetically and proceeded to simper and whimper his way through four tragedies and a comedy, climaxing his performance by asking on the final examination such fruitful questions as, "What are the width and depth of the outer alcove stage of the Globe Playhouse?" "What are the width and depth of the inner alcove stage of the Globe Playhouse?"

Balanced against these, though, have been favorable experiences. No one who ever heard her read in one of her courses in Dickens, Shakespeare, or Restoration Comedy shall ever forget Professor Margaret Bailey. Her chunky body thrust haphazardly into a severe gray dress that trailed near the floor, her feet shod in high-button black boots, her white hair pulled in a bun away from a face that belonged on Mt. Rushmore, Dr. Bailey simultaneously terrified and enraptured the undergraduates who flocked to her courses. Able to sever tongues with a glance and lacerate ignorance with a phrase, with her voice alone she sprang literature to life, made it grovel in the mud, prance in the sunlight, soar to the heavens. She *was* Falstaff and Uriah Heep and Hamlet and Mrs. Margery Pinchwife; she was an institution and deserved to be. After she retired, she continued to read for small groups along the San Francisco Peninsula. Before her death a couple of years ago, I took a high school class to hear her read from Nikos Kazantzakis' *The Odyssey: A Modern Sequel*, an evening, I warrant, they shall never forget.

Another indelible experience was hearing Robert Frost, in his early eighties, hold an audience for two hours as he recited from memory poem after poem in his unmistakable New England twang. And of the 60-odd conferences of teachers of English I have attended during the past decade, certainly one of the most memorable was that at which Mark Linenthal, a professor and poet at San Francisco State College, read "Tract" by William Carlos Williams, a poem which I twice readily recalled, once when Jessica Mitford's *The American Way of Death* was being widely discussed and the other when my father died two years ago.

Conditioned by many favorable memories of literature read aloud well and negatively guided by the few remembrances of it read poorly, I frequently used to read aloud to my high school classes. Sometimes I worried because I did so, assuming as many teachers do that I had no right to occupy center stage much of the time, that my reading to the students did not better prepare them to read for themselves. Had I then known what I now know, I would have spared myself whatever guilt I felt; for there is mounting evidence that the practice of reading aloud to students is pedagogically sound, particularly for culturally disadvantaged or slower students.

In the April 1965 *English Journal,* Marjorie B. Smiley, Director of the Project English Center at Hunter College, comments:

> Some of the difficulties underprivileged children face in learning to read is in the early stages of associating what is heard with the printed symbols for these sounds. One of the most interesting findings of recent research has been the evidence of a high degree of correlation between hearing (auding, as it is called in these studies) and reading. This is a difficulty that many such children have not yet overcome by Grade 7 or 8. These children are unlikely to have had parents with time to read aloud to them in their early years. We do not do nearly enough reading aloud to children in elementary or secondary schools. We do not make nearly enough use of the increasingly rich

store of records of poetry, stories, speeches, and plays. . . .

David Abercrombie, author of "Conversation and Spoken Prose" (*English Language Teaching,* October 1963), indicates that there are three broad categories of spoken language: reading aloud, monologue, and real conversation. The most obvious differences between the first two kinds of spoken language—reading aloud and monologue—which he labels "spoken prose," and conversation are these:

1. The intonation patterns of spoken prose are highly standardized; those of conversation are not.
2. Spoken prose is even in tempo; conversation is not.
3. The pauses of spoken prose are closely related to the grammatical structure of these sentences. In conversation they are frequently unpredictable.
4. Spoken prose does not make use of silences the way conversation does—silences meaningfully filled by gestures and grimaces.
5. In spoken prose stammers and errors of articulation are rare and conspicuous; in conversation they attract little attention.
6. Spoken prose has probably fewer phonetically different speech sounds than conversation has. It is important to note here that most phonemic analysis carried on through the use of informants is derived from spoken prose rather than from conversation.
7. Conversation is generally more structurally incomplete than spoken prose because part of the meaning communicated is derived from context. Sentences in conversation may lack verbs, objects, or even subjects. The sentence as traditionally defined is really a unit of prose, not of conversation.
8. Conversation has a great deal of repetition whereas spoken prose has little.
9. Conversation has many apparent meaningless words and phrases which serve to establish rapport between speakers and to act as silence fillers while a speaker thinks of what to say next.

The implications, I believe, are obvious: if youngsters are coming from backgrounds in which they never hear what Abercrombie calls spoken prose, in which even the conversation they hear is impoverished, consisting most often of commands and categorical statements lacking intellectual content and casual reasoning, then we must read to them if we ever expect them to be able to read by themselves; for the act of reading literary prose is the act of silently speaking to the printed page, or, if one prefers, of hearing the page silently speak. Such a subtle concept as tone in writing could never be taught unless one were first trained to hear and discriminate among the sounds of the written language. Here I am not speaking merely of what correspondences exist between phonemes, or basic sound units, and graphemes, the written symbols for sound units. By the sounds of the written language, I mean the total flow of the language, its rhythms, its syntactical as well as lexical clues out of which we derive speech clues—stress and pitch and juncture—and, ultimately, meaning.

Gertrude Hildreth, Professor of Education at C.C.N.Y., knows what I mean. In an article "Linguistic Factors in Early Reading Instruction" (*The Reading Teacher,* December 1964), Professor Hildreth writes:

In teaching "phonics," we have traditionally taught the speech sounds represented by letters and groups of letters. We need now to extend the study of "phonics" to include the speech melodies of phrases and sentences which in print are in part signaled by punctuation marks. That is, we need to teach larger segments of sound than we have traditionally taught. We need further to teach these larger segments of sound in association with meaning. Comprehending the meanings of phrases or sentences is the central problem for the reader. The ability to comprehend such meanings is developed by the child's experience primarily and mainly with the oral language. The more extensive the child's experience in the language of speech, therefore, the better equipped he is likely to be in getting an author's meaning.

Later in the same article she comments, "Considerable attention has been given recently to listening as a neglected aspect of oral language comprehension. Listening with acute understanding carries over to reading with understanding."

Teaching students to develop an ear for written language takes time, often years. To attune that ear, the student not only needs to hear his teachers read aloud a great deal, he needs occasional practice himself, as agonizing as it may sometimes be to an audience, in giving voice to print. Some of this practice should be conscious, that is, the student should be stopped and asked why he read a particular word, sentence, paragraph, or bit of dialogue as he did. He should be taught to locate and articulate the clues by which he interprets, and he should learn to defend reasonably his interpretation against others proffered by either the teacher or his classmates. In this process, the student should discover that there can be no absolute interpretations to written prose, though some interpretations are far sounder than others. Because the written language contains far greater ambiguity than does the spoken language, the act of composing, during which we consciously attempt to reduce the ambiguity, is dreadfully difficult for most of us. Nevertheless, we should remember and be grateful that it is this same ambiguity that enables a Shakespearean tragedy to be reinterpreted and reenacted across the centuries.

On the inadequacies of writing as a system of communication, Morton Botel, former president of International Reading Association, states at the conclusion of his article "What Linguistics Says to This Teacher of Reading and Spelling" (*The Reading Teacher,* December 1964):

> One of the most significant things for the teacher of reading to recognize is that the

interconnected systems which carry meaning are only partially represented by our system of writing. Our phonology (that is, the consonant and vowel phenomena) is represented only partially by our alphabetic system. There is no one-to-one correspondence between each phoneme and its graphic representation or grapheme. The intonational patterns, or melody of speech, are poorly represented in writing. Sentence patterns, on the other hand, are represented precisely in written sentences. Two other systems of communication, paralanguage (tone of voice) and kinesics (gestured bodily movements) interact with language to communicate meaning. Writing does not convey these structures except by such feeble devices as underlining words or exclamation points or by creative writing which represents tone and movement by words. In short, the systems of communication which convey meaning are quite imperfectly represented in writing.

Assuming that the teacher's reading aloud does eventually assist most youngsters, including the culturally disadvantaged, to read more ably by themselves, one might nonetheless wonder what value the practice has for youngsters who are truly slow, whose reading proficiency, for example, may never exceed that of third-grade.

Anyone around children or slow learners for very long soon discovers that listening comprehension far exceeds reading comprehension for many of the reasons already suggested: the speaking voice brings to interpretation *pitch, stress, pause, rhythm, tone*—audible clues to meaning which slow youngsters are unable to infer from print alone. Too often bogged down deciphering single words when left on their own, they miss both the melodies and meanings of phrases, sentences, and paragraphs. If a teacher believes, as I do, that SRA kits, *Teen-Age Tales,* and Reader's Digest Skill Builders have only limited value and seldom if ever supply students with valid literary experiences, then he will read to his class often; neither his moral nor his professional conscience will permit his letting students pass through a course in English without their realizing something about what literature is, and does. He may never bring to them *Paradise Lost* or "The Waste Land," but by sensitively reading aloud, he can at least provide them experience with reputable short stories, poems, and plays they would otherwise never know. Too, through discussing the literature he orally interprets, he may indirectly help them become more discerning critics of television and film, the media from which they will obtain most of their future vicarious experience. In fact, because they combine auditory and visual clues to meaning, I believe these media should be used far more than they are in classes for slow learners.

If one intends to do more than orally share with a class a poem or story for enjoyment alone, then he must structure his lesson carefully. At a recent conference Olive Niles, reading director for the public schools in Springfield, Massachusetts, said that reading specialists are beginning to realize that 90 percent of the reading skills we teach are taught before the youngster ever reads the selection, that the questions that follow most often only evaluate what success he has had in achieving the purposes implied by the questions. Much the same might be said for the teaching of listening skills. Unless we first motivate a student's interest in a selection and establish the purposes for his listening, we teach almost nothing and should not later wonder why our discussion questions, which again are evaluative questions, often go nowhere.

Let me give you a concrete illustration of how *not* to teach a selection.

Last semester I supervised a student teacher who was placed in a class of 18 unruly, culturally disadvantaged youngsters. On a weekly teaching schedule she indicated that on Wednesday she intended reading to the students James Baldwin's "A Fly in the Buttermilk," an essay which first appeared in *Harper's* under the title, "The Hard Kind of Courage," and was later reprinted in *Nobody Knows My Name*. Briefly, the essay concerns Baldwin's interviewing in a Southern town a Negro mother whose only child, *G.*, is the only Negro child in an all-white school. Baldwin wants to know what kind of parents can send their child day after day into a hostile environment and what kind of child can survive the hostility. After interviewing the mother (the father was at work) and ascertaining why, of 45 Negro couples who had applied to send their children to the school, only they had persisted, and after evaluating the effects upon *G.* of their decision, Baldwin interviews the principal of the school, a Caucasian, a man of good will, a man who loves children and values education, but a troubled man who has been reared in the culture of the Southern white and knows his values are in conflict. For everyone concerned, the essay is compassionate. Thinking it a splendid selection for this particular class, I arrived at the school on Wednesday, took a seat in the back of the classroom, and watched chaos and black night descend.

With no introduction to the material, the student teacher passed out the dittoed pages of the essay in reverse order—page five first, which the students immediately began to read. After she had rectified this procedure, she perched on a stool and read the daily bulletin—like all daily bulletins, no epistolary classic, but unlike most, two pages long. She then asked the students if any of them had ever heard of James Baldwin. About seven hands went up. Disregarding them, she presented a brief and desultory account of Baldwin's life to date. She then inquired whether anyone had ever read anything by James Baldwin. To my surprise, four hands went up. Disregarding these, she dropped titles plentifully upon the class. Without further ado, she then read *sotto voce*, monotonously, for four pages without stopping to interpolate a comment, ask a question, or summarize an involved passage. After page four, she quit. She had to: the students were noisier than she. She asked them how they liked the essay. Not receiving a response, she informed them they really liked it; otherwise they wouldn't have stayed quiet so long. She then asked whether they thought Baldwin was a good writer. Not receiving a response, she informed them Baldwin was a very good writer; otherwise they wouldn't have stayed quiet so long. More to spare my feelings than hers, I left.

After first reading the daily bulletin and before distributing the essay, had the student teacher provided a number of hypothetical situations which could serve to generate discussion and lead students into Baldwin's theme, the hour would have been far different. For example, she might have said to the class,

Assume that you live in the deep South, that you are the Negro parent of an intelligent boy who is attending a school for Negro children, a school which has very low standards. You want your child to have a good education. Would you be willing to send him to an all-white school if he were the only Negro child to attend?

Assume now that you are the boy. Would you be willing to attend? If you did attend, how would you behave if students started to pick on you?

Imagine that you are the principal in the school, that you believe in the value of education, that you deeply care about children, but that you have been reared as a Southern white. What might you be concerned about? How would you behave toward the boy?

Finally, assume that you are white parents in this area, that you believe strongly in school integration, but that there have been so many Southern Negroes moving into the neighborhood that your child is now one of only a handful of white children left in his school. You want him to have a good education. Would you continue to send him to the school he now attends, or would you move to a different area?

Only after such a preliminary discussion would I introduce the essay. I would give the students a chance to tell me what they know about Baldwin, I would have ready for them a sequence of questions to consider as they listened and followed along in the text, and I would read interpretively, pausing from time to time to ask a question or make a comment. After the reading, the prepared questions would be discussed. These questions would not invite personal opinion as did the preliminary discussion questions; they would focus directly on the content and style of the essay.

If I were asked what the most serious shortcoming is of the student teachers I observe, I would reply, "Their failure to motivate interest in a selection, to build bridges between students' concerns and experiences and the experiences recorded in the literature. Student teachers don't realize that assigning a selection and teaching it are not synonymous."

I can't tell any teacher, student or otherwise, what bridges to build, for what he constructs depends upon what he knows about himself, his students, and his material. I can only provide brief illustrations of what I have done:

There was the morning following the All-Star Game that I asked a group of sophomores at the University Summer Demonstration School to name the starting line-ups for me. I then asked what the opening batteries were the year before. I inquired whether anyone could remember the teams in the Rose Bowl year before last. Finally, I challenged the group to name four All-Americans from four years back. When they laughingly conceded that they couldn't name one, I pointed out that these athletes once had had considerable notoriety and asked whether it was possible, then, for one to achieve the peak of his fame when quite young and to live out the rest of his days a forgotten has-been? Under such circumstances, I inquired, wouldn't it be far better if the athlete died before he saw his fame fade? Obviously, I was leading into Housman's "To an Athlete Dying Young."

There was the class of college preparatory juniors in which I asked whether anyone had done homework for any class the night before. After the agonizing moans had ceased, I asked how many of them would have preferred watching television or cruising around. When most of the hands arose, I asked the students why, then, they bothered to do the homework, why they didn't just go enjoy themselves. I was leading into the tension all of us feel between duty and pleasure, the tension at the heart of the poem I wished to teach, Frost's "Stopping by Woods on a Snowy Evening."

There was the class of regular sophomores in which I disarmingly asked, "How many of you ever feel lonely?" After the diffident, numerous hands had been put down, I asked the students what they did when they were lonely. When many revealed that they sought the company of friends, I asked them to consider what it might be to be a king. Were kings more lonely than other people? If so, why? Eventually they were led into discussing the terrifying alienation of the regal Richard Cory.

I have purposely enraged classes to get them into a story. At the beginning of one hour in a slow class, I passed out small pieces of paper and requested each student to write his name, fold the paper, and pass it forward. I took the pieces, placed them in a recipe box, asked for a volunteer to draw three names. When the students, dutifully docile till then, wanted to know what it was all about, I told them I had finished reading their last examinations, that almost all of them had done well, but that it was my policy in a class this size to fail at least a few students. Because I wanted to be fair, I thought the best procedure was that of drawing names. Within

seconds all hell broke loose. I was shouted at, threatened with both administrative and parental power by those who were going to report me *right now*, had my sanity and I believe my parentage questioned by the toughs in the back row. I temporarily soothed ruffled tempers by saying I would reconsider my policy since it seemed so disturbing; now, though, I wanted to read them a story. I distributed the dittoed questions, and when it came, they were ready indeed for Shirley Jackson's "The Lottery."

In short, though the bridges into literature are many and varied, one must be built for nearly every selection to be taught. When I am unsure about how to build, I inevitably fall back on the one constant we have, the emotional experiences of the youngsters. No matter how slow the class, the students will have had some experience with hate, with fear, with loneliness; some bent, albeit warped at times, toward honor, toward courage, toward love. Intellectual traditions change from century to century, decade to decade, and with the explosion of knowledge in our time, often from year to year. There nevertheless remains a continuity in human experience, a continuity provided in the heritage of all men: we are born, we feel, and we die. And though we do die, our literature remains behind, reminding those who follow what it was, and is, to be human.

In concluding, allow me to summarize my two main points: First, reading literature aloud to students is not only educationally sound but for many youngsters, necessary; second, if one wishes to help students become critical listeners and if he intends *teaching* the literature he reads orally, he must plan his lessons carefully, building bridges between the youngsters' experience and that in the literature and providing sequences of questions that set the purposes for listening.

Above all, the teacher who reads to his classes should not feel he is wasting the students' time. Guilt is better saved for evaluating compositions or marking report cards.

GIVE HIM A BOOK THAT HITS HIM WHERE HE LIVES
Charles G. Spiegler

Culturally, he is bounded on the north by comic books, on the south by the pool parlor, on the east by the racing form, on the west by neighborhood small talk. Born into a home at cultural ebb tide, often raised midst turmoil and trauma, living in an intellectual ghetto, he sits in my classroom—annoyed to the point of hostility. I have asked him to read a book—any book—for a first report of the term.

The "he" I mean is no figment of my imagination. He is Barry Saltz, a 16-year-old future butcher of America (one of many such in my classroom); a present reluctant reader (one of many such in my classroom). Despite his 20/20 vision, it dismays him not an iota that he has never read a book cover-to-cover in all his 16 years, that he has never spent a rainy afternoon browsing in the library.

Scan the printed page? Not he!

I search my brain for a *book* that may appeal. "How about *Questions Boys Ask*,"[1] I recommend ever so naively, as I brandish a copy I own.

"Naaah. . . ."

I try sports, hobbies, deep-sea fishing—everything from prehistoric man of 5 million years ago to the stars millions of light years away. But I get a look that warns me—"Mister, you're wasting your time."

I am beginning to lose heart when one day it happens! I find the link I need to help move Barry Saltz from the desert island of ignorance about books he has for so long inhabited to the mainland of written words and ideas. It is a tiny link—no bigger than the cluster of warts on Barry's index finger.

Those warts really worry Barry, butcher-to-be, because as he put it, "They're gonna drive away my customers." So I ask him one day, "Why don't you get rid of them?" and learn, to my surprise, that he has an *idée fixé* about warts. They come from touching frogs, and maybe will vanish one day by magic, if you're lucky.

Sensing how deep his superstition about warts really is, I recommend a book, *Superstitious? Here's Why!*[2] urge him to read the section on warts, and agree to accept this as a report.

The result? *Mirabile dictu!* Barry Saltz practically memorizes that paragraph on warts and reads the book through cover to cover in one 4-hour sitting. Moreover, having finally gone to a library, he has now become aware of some very readable books about health and strength—a major interest. Before the semester is over, Barry Saltz can tell you all about *The Wonders Inside You*[3]

Reprinted from *Improving English Skills of Culturally Different Youth* (Washington: U. S. Office of Education Bulletin) 1964, pp. 91–99.

[1] David W. Armstrong, *Questions Boys Ask* (New York: E. P. Dutton & Co., 1955).

[2] Julie Forsyth Batchelor and Claudia De Lys, *Superstitious? Here's Why!* (New York: Harcourt, Brace & World, 1954).

[3] Margaret Cosgrove, *The Wonders Inside You* (New York: Dodd, Mead & Co., 1955).

by Cosgrove, *Magic Bullets*[4] by Sutherland, and *Boy's Book of Body Building*[5] by Pashko. True, he still refers to de Kruif's *Hunger Fighters* as "Hunger Pains"! Who cares! Barry Saltz is on his way!

Does it matter? Does it really matter that the Saltz nose now goes between the covers of a book? Is this a "summum bonum" commensurate with the effort expended? Yes, indeed! For, of all youth's divine rights during that precious period we call "The school years," I place very high the enjoyment of books. Learning how to earn a living is one thing; but in an age of steadily increasing leisure, learning how to live—joyously—is, to me, prime. And learning how to do it, among other ways, through books—is quintessential.

Perhaps no one has said it for me better than Paul Bueter, a 17-year-old senior who, after viewing *A Night to Remember*[6] on TV, was one of dozens who had remembered it vividly enough to ask for the Walter Lord original. Queried on why he wanted the book, having just seen the TV version, he gave what seems to me the classic answer to those who see TV as the substitute for reading—"Sure, it was good," he says of the TV performance, "but I don't know . . . I didn't really get the feeling of how it was on the *Titanic* on that black night. . . . How could you, with all those camera lights on the people?" In order for Paul to "really get the feeling" of that black night to remember, he needed more than brilliant camera lights. He needed the glow of his own imagination.

Yes, I'm glad I got Barry Saltz to read for other reasons. Just as we learn to write by writing, we learn to read by reading. It's not always that "Johnny doesn't read because he

can't." It's often that "Johnny can't read because he doesn't."[7]

Yes, I'm glad I got Barry Saltz to read because I know that the meat upon which our Caesar's feed is anti-intellectualism, "know nothingism." In the growing struggles between freedom and authoritarianism, it is better for us all that the Barry Saltzes be thinking, questioning, probing citizens—not vacuums or vegetables. Though there are many paths towards this end, I respect reading as one of them. I'm glad I got Barry Saltz to read.

As chairman of an academic subjects department in a New York City vocational school (from 1956 to 1961), I have had the chance to study hundreds upon hundreds of Barry Saltzes in their raw, untutored state. Coming from homes where the bedtime story at twilight had never been heard and where the television set had replaced the reading lamp, they sat in our classrooms with all the symptoms of cultural blight. Their median IQ score was 85, their reading scores were poor, and their practice of the language arts was unique. One boy who was asked at an assembly to read from Proverbs in the *Bible* prefaced his oral reading with the announcement that he would read some "proud verbs" in the *Bible*. Youngsters asked to write on the "Star-Spangled Banner," began with "Oh, say can you sing by the doors early light?" A lad, reporting on a TV show he liked insisted that the hero was "Quiet Earp." Once in a discussion, I used the term *bachelor of arts* and asked for a definition—"He's a guy who got away by staying single."

Family ties, as the ordinary middle-class youngster enjoys them, were *terra incognita* to many of my boys. Fully 20 percent lived at home with but one parent, the second having vanished, run off, or died. I had boys who had never been served a warm breakfast

[4] Louis Sutherland, *Magic Bullets* (Boston: Little, Brown & Co., 1956).

[5] Stanley Pashko, *Boy's Book of Body Building* (New York: Grosset & Dunlap).

[6] Walter Lord, *A Night to Remember* (New York: Holt, Rinehart & Winston, 1955. Bantam Paperback, 1962).

[7] Estelle H. Witzling, "Johnny Can't Read Because He Doesn't," *High Points*, 38:52–59, January 1956.

by mother since they could remember. I had boys who had never had a heart-to-heart talk with father. Yet let mother or father be called to school, on some matter disciplinary, and we were often invited to "Hit him! Whack him! I mean treat him like he was your own!"[8]

Spawned in such homes, the Barry Saltzes never go much beyond talking of "Who's gonna win the fight next week?" watching crime shows on TV, going to the movies with their dates, ogling the girlie magazines. Of the 900 boys at my city vocational school, no more than 20 ever found it worthwhile to take in a Broadway play or a concert at Carnegie Hall even though both are little more than an hour from any boy's home. "That's for eggheads," Billy Brenner, 16, tells me when I offer him a ticket. "It's too far, anyhow. You come home too late." Yet two nights a week, religiously, instead of sitting down with his homework, he marches to the bowling alley where, until midnight, he enjoys a few short beers and the thrill of crashing a 16-pound bowling ball against the varnished pins.

Small wonder, then, that when we talk to them of *Silas Marner* they hear us not. Their ears are tuned to the change-of-period bell. We may appeal to them with a lovely print of an English landscape. They see it not; their eyes are on the clock. Desperate, we bring out the great, beloved classics which are on the world's permanent best-seller lists. With pomp and ceremony, with a laying-down of red carpets, with a lighting of candelabra, we introduce children to these classics. But we leave them unmoved. So, in quiet resignation, we affix to them the label "retarded readers"; and that great cultural divide between the middle-class teacher (reared on Shakespeare and Browning and Eliot) and the sons and daughters of "blue-collar" America (so

often raised on comics, the movies, and television) becomes deeper and wider.

We've got to heal that breach, and we can! But this can be done only with understanding —the understanding that the Barry Saltzes are, as the late Elizabeth Rose of New York University put it "allergic to print"; that much of what we, his teachers, choose for him to read is not only *not* a cure for this allergy but also an *extension* of it; that only the book which "packs a wallop for him" may hope to effect a cure. The remedy? Begin with a book that hits him where he lives![9]

I learned this back in 1954 when, as a new departmental chairman, I walked into the middle of a cold war between most of the 900 students in the school and most of the English teachers. The issue at first was books, *required* books for classroom study. The battleground was the bookroom piled high with *Silas Marner* and *Giants in the Earth* (grand books for college-bound youth, but sleeping pills for vocation-bound youngsters). There was a curtain dividing pupil and teacher, which, though made only of paper and print, was no less formidable than today's Iron Curtain. You walked into classes where teachers were devoting a full term to *Silas Marner*, and you saw children with heads on desks and eyes shut. You walked into the library and rarely saw a youngster except with a prescribed booklist based on the predilections of his teacher. The long and short of it was that children were not reading, and teachers had thrown in the sponge with the excuse, "They can't!"

I believed they could, if we would but give a boy a title, a book jacket, a theme that rang true; if we could but talk to him colorfully about the world of books! Don't limit him to the confines of prescribed booklists or restrictive formulas for making book reports. Let the world and its infinite wonders be the subjects he may choose from, I begged. Let

---

[8] Charles G. Spiegler, "A Teacher's Report on a 'Tough School,'" *The New York Times Magazine*, Nov. 24, 1957.

[9] Elizabeth Rose, "Literature in the Junior High School," *English Journal*, 44:141–147.

him begin with what he likes, appeal to his interests—and he will read.

When we inaugurated a 3-day book fair, displaying 2,000 books dressed in jolly jackets and written on hundreds of lively subjects I was sure youngsters liked, there was a shaking of heads among some members of the faculty. "I'll bet you won't sell a hundred books," one asserted smugly. "All these kids want is comics and girlie books. They won't buy anything decent!"

But they did. For 3 days, while English classes were cancelled, children browsed, read at random, bought or not as fancy struck them. And when the fair was over, we knew that these were the 3 days that had shaken our smug little world. The Johnnies who would buy "only comics and girlie books" had dug into their after-school-odd-job savings to take home 1,123 good books. Granted, Bill Stern's *My Favorite Sports Stories* and *The Real Story of Lucille Ball* were best sellers, but not far behind were the *Burl Ives Song Book*, *The Red Pony*,[10] and books of science fiction. And higher than anyone dared predict were *The Cruel Sea*[11] and *Mutiny on the Bounty*.[12]

Though no teachers were panting down the students' necks to "read this!" they did guide student choice. Some, like the big, broad-shouldered lad who was about to buy *The Scarlet Letter*[13] because he thought it was a football story, needed guidance. Some, like the nature lover who was about to buy *A Tree Grows in Brooklyn*[14] because he thought it was on target for a report he was making on trees, needed guidance. Others passed by the proffered help, however, and bought many books with vocabulary loads somewhat beyond their level. It didn't matter. "Interest," George Norvell, former New York State Supervisor of English, has said, "leaps over all reading barriers, including vocabulary."[15]

Johnny wasn't sleeping through "Lit" class by now. We relegated *Silas Marner* to a basement storeroom and gave the youngsters livelier fare. Booker T. Washington in his struggles for an education became a far more genuine superman to them than the comic book man with wings. It was *Kon-Tiki*[16] on the perilous Pacific that replaced Eliot's nineteenth-century England. You could now walk into a class studying *Kon-Tiki* and see Jimmy Kolofney at the blackboard writing a letter of congratulations to Thor Heyerdahl. While he is expressing his admiration for the Skipper and "that crazy, wonderful think you done," seven boys are rehearsing in two separate corners of the room: three of them in one corner play the crewmen of the *Kon-Tiki*; the other four make up a TV panel that will ask the intrepid voyagers all about the dangers, the thrills, the uncertainties of their venture.

Before long all eyes are focused on Jimmy's letter on the blackboard, to correct it—because "You can't send junk to a big shot like that." Later the class turns to the TV panel, which raises some incisive questions on the madness, the glory, and the thrill of adventure dear to any boy's heart. It also raises a question or two that better-bred boys might not ask: "Didja ever 'chicken out'?" "Hey, didja miss girls?" The end-of-period bell rings in the nick of time.

By the end of the year, the majority of our 900 students were reading at least a book a month. Many were doing far better. Library circulation had gone from 600 to 1,500.

---

[10] John Steinbeck, *The Red Pony* (New York: Viking Press, Inc., 1959).

[11] Nicholas Monsarrat, *The Cruel Sea* (New York: Alfred A. Knopf, Inc., 1951).

[12] Charles Nordoff and James Norman Hall, *Mutiny on the Bounty* (Boston: Little, Brown & Co., 1932).

[13] Nathaniel Hawthorne, *The Scarlet Letter*.

[14] Betty Smith, *A Tree Grows in Brooklyn* (New York: Harper & Row, 1947).

[15] George W. Norvell, *The Reading Interests of Young People* (Boston: D. C. Heath & Co., 1950).

[16] Thor Heyerdahl, *Kon-Tiki* (Chicago: Rand McNally & Co., 1950).

Neither "climax" nor "denouement" cluttered up book reports now. As make-believe salesmen, kid critics, Hollywood producers, television panelists, they reported in terms they knew. "I like," "I love," "I hate," "I get mad," "It's great," "exciting," "heartwarming"—these terms indicated how books hit them. "I love that book because it suits my taste," wrote Johnny Gallardo about *Lives of a Bengal Lancer.*

Whatever the individual taste, we had given each of those 900 students a sporting chance to satisfy it. Now that the fair was over and the appetite whetted, I began to observe, ever so occasionally, especially after lunch, a paperback under the arm of a lad or two where earlier in the day there had been a lunch bag. Boys were beginning to walk off their hero sandwiches with short strolls to the neighborhood paperback gallery, sometimes bringing back a sample or two. Soon we discovered the Teen Age Book Club[17] whose titles caught the fancy of many. We were beginning to establish a rapport between children and books, helping many of our boys buy them cheaply, start their own libraries, and see for themselves how "even the smallest library is a veritable Treasure Island that takes no *Hispaniola* to reach—its buried riches no pirate's chart to locate."

This is not to boast that success was absolute and universal. We still had lots of lads like Lenny Kalter who equated the carrying of books with the role of the sissy. It wasn't until Miss Isenberg (public librarian assigned to visit our classes regularly to bestir the reluctant dragons) had introduced young Master Kalter to Henry Gregor Felsen's *Hot Rod*[18] that Lenny could identify with a character in a book—in this instance Bud Crayne, *Hot Rod*'s hero, and lover of speed. Lenny borrowed the book, devoured it, then became

so avid a reader on the subject that *Street Rod*[19] (also by Felsen), *Mexican Road Race,*[20] *Thunder Road,*[21] and *The Red Car*[22] were finished within 2 weeks. Then he began searching the stacks all over the city for "anything by Mr. Felsen." When he heard that we were planning to invite an author to visit our assembly and set the keynote for our next Book Fair, he volunteered to write the first formal letter of invitation he had ever written in his life—you guessed it—to Gregor Felsen.

Last, but hardly least, let me suggest how television far from proving a menace to reading, as is so often alleged, proved a boon. My major premise here is that culturally deprived youngsters limit their horizons to the four walls of the home, the four corners of the neighborhood, and, as with many of my boys, the six pockets of the pool table. Television is their new window to the world. Through it they find the fullest, richest array of new interests man has ever known. Where or when, for example, in all recorded history could so many Americans in the year 1962 with a flip of the dial take an hour-long journey through the White House, with its gracious First Lady as hostess and guide?

My minor premise is that interest is the key to reading. My conclusion follows naturally. Television, by creating interest, can become the road to wider reading.

I saw it strikingly one morning in April of 1956. I was sitting in my office composing my weekly bulletin when the door burst open and two of my boys came dashing in.

"Got somp'n by Ogden Nash?" came the breathless query.

Slowly I raised my head.

---

[17] Teen Age Book Club, sponsored by *Scholastic* magazine.

[18] Gregor Felsen, *Hot Rod* (New York: E. P. Dutton & Co.).

[19] Gregor Felsen, *Street Rod* (New York: Random House, 1953).

[20] Patrick O'Connor, *Mexican Road Race* (New York: Ives Washburn, 1957).

[21] William Campbell Gault, *Thunder Road* (New York: E. P. Dutton & Co., 1952).

[22] Don Stanford, *The Red Car* (New York: Funk & Wagnalls Co., 1954).

"Who?"

"Ogden Nash—you know," they exclaimed, "the guy wid dose crazy rhymes."

My pen dropped; my ears perked up. Surprised, indeed delighted, that my boys were interested in reading one of America's most literate creators of verse, I asked: "You boys doing a book report on Mr. Nash?"

"Nope!" they parried, "no book reports—we just wanna read sump'n by him. We went to the library, but the other guys beat us to it. *You* got sump'n?"

Happily I had. And happily, Tommy Gorman, a 15-year-old butcher-to-be, and Peter de Stefano, a 16-year-old baker-to-be, walked off with every copy I owned of *I'm a Stranger Here Myself*.[23] When you realize that before this day the closest Tom and Peter had come to voluntarily exposing themselves to rhythms and rhymes was the "popular song sheet," you realize what a move forward they had made.

This did not erupt full grown from the head of Zeus. It happened at a time when their English teacher found the going rough as he started a unit on poetry. So he looked for help. Since television was not a dirty word in our school, he looked to see how that week's TV programing could help. And lo, that Sunday Ed Sullivan could! For Sullivan had invited Noel Coward to read from the works of Ogden Nash to the background music of Saint Saens, as played by Andre Kostelanetz. So the homework assignment for that Sunday said, "Watch Sullivan"—not just the song, not just the dance—but *all* of it! With the results we have seen.

Teach a little "dialmanship" and TV can become an Aladdin's lamp far more wondrous than the Arabian original. Our librarian, too, recognized that and arranged a bulletin board entitled *IF YOU WATCH: WHY NOT READ*. If you watch the weather spots,

why not read *Weathercraft*[24] by Spilhaus, for example? If you watch Leonard Bernstein, why not read *Leonard Bernstein*[25] by David Ewen?

If, in fact, we really want to introduce the culturally deprived youngster to books he can read on subjects he wants to read about, we are living in an age of huge abundance. For, in truth, this is the Golden Age of Writing for Youth, with many magnificent series available to them; with real writers (Quentin Reynolds, Dorothy Canfield Fisher, John Gunther, to name but a few) writing for them.

I cannot begin to tell you of the many, many hundreds of "juveniles" I have read myself with admiration, and been privileged to review and annotate, with a very high respect for what they can mean to children, and, with genuine appreciation for what they have meant even to ancient old ME.[26]

The job of preparing the proper materials for the customer we are talking about is, however, far from complete. So formidable, indeed, is this task, with both the textbook and the trade book, I would take a leaf from the book of the Ford Foundation man who recently recommended a *Vice President-in-Charge-of-Heresy* for every school system—by proposing a *Vice President-in-Charge-of-Searching-for-and-Finding-Materials-Written-So-That-the-Children-We-Are-Concerned-With-Will-Read-Them-With-Interest*. As my first piece of advice to said VPI, I would urge: "Listen to the children you are serving." Here are their answers:

1. The subject has to be worth it to us. We like books about animals, aviation, ca-

---

[23] Ogden Nash, *I'm a Stranger Here Myself* (New York: Little, Brown, 1941).

[24] Athelstan Spilhaus, *Weathercraft* (New York: Viking Press, 1951).

[25] David Ewen, *Leonard Bernstein* (Philadelphia: Chilton Books, 1960).

[26] The reviews of the books under this category appear in the section called "Books You May Like," in Marion Monroe, Gwen Horsman, and William S. Gray, *Basic Reading Skills* (Chicago: Scott, Foresman & Co.).

reers, hobbies, sports, the sea, westerns. We love lots of adventure, plenty of excitement, slews of interesting facts about science and things.

2. Don't treat us like babies. We may not be such "hot" readers, but that doesn't mean if you give us an easy book about ducks on a farm we'll cackle over it gleefully. We had that stuff in the third grade, remember?

3. Give us lots of good pictures, good drawings, and big print. As one of the fellows said, "I can't read when the print on the pages is so small. After a while I lose my eyesight."

4. You have to know how to write. Maybe the fellow who likes to read a lot will stand for some boring parts, but not us. If you want us to read don't beat around the bush but come to the point. Give us a story that pushes us to go on to the next page and the next page—and we'll stay with it.[27]

Let us search out the books, as Robert Lawson has put it, will give these kids ". . . the chuckles . . . the gooseflesh . . . the glimpses of glory" they love. The books are here, now, asking to be discovered and enjoyed.

Books and reading are a staple in such a program not only for the well-endowed, but also for *all* the children of *all* the people. Only in the faith that there are no "second-class" citizens in our schools, a faith conceived, nurtured, and cherished in pride for nearly two centuries, can we hope to rise to the urgent tasks ahead. I am supremely confident that we shall.

[27] Charles G. Spiegler, "Reading Materials for Retarded Readers," *Materials for Reading*, Supplementary Educational Monographs, No. 6 (Chicago: University of Chicago Press, 1957).

PART 3
READING AND READING PROGRAMS

Introduction

An all-out effort to provide reading instruction wherever it is needed is preferred to fragmented attempts which reach limited numbers of students. This integrated plan is explained in Part III of this book.

Subject-matter teachers have an opportunity to help their students become better readers and at the same time master the content of their specialties. How content teachers can achieve their objectives through reading are the subjects of Chapters 12 and 13.

Davis explains how all subject-matter teachers can help students become better readers. Sochor emphasizes the importance of readiness at every instructional level. Shore's investigation demonstrates the futility of dealing with general reading ability in specific content fields. Formats in teaching science through reading are offered by the Metropolitan School Study Council. Reading and mathematics are covered by Call and Wiggins who describe how an English and mathematics teacher joined forces to promote skill in solving word problems. How teachers of vocational subjects can help their students is Levine's concern.

One of the problems with which most teachers have to deal is that of adjusting instruction to individual differences. The reading abilities of high school students vary significantly, and there are ways of coping with this condition. Parker and others describe how a multi-level program worked in an English class. Niles and Early show how classroom teachers can differentiate instruction through two-group teaching, multiple-group work, job sheets and paired practice. Noall discusses individualization through pacing, materials, and motivation. Komoski and Sohn apply techniques of programing to reading and thereby offer another approach to individualization.

The final chapter of this book explains how high school teachers and administrators can work together to establish and implement effective developmental reading programs. Artley offers a step-by-step plan that schools might follow. Carlsen analyzes the components of reading and reading programs; Campbell, Berkey and Fields, and Toops describe successful high school reading programs. Karlin concludes the section with an analysis of reading materials and admonitions for their use.

12

Developmental Reading and the Content Field

HIGH SCHOOL AND COLLEGE INSTRUCTORS CAN'T TEACH READING? NONSENSE!
Stanley E. Davis

Many competent high school and college instructors recognize that they need to be concerned with helping students at all levels of competence to improve their reading skills needed in the various subject areas. But the perennial question that plagues a conscientious instructor is "How can I cover the course content assigned by the curriculum makers and at the same time teach reading?"

This article is concerned with suggesting ways that may be helpful to the instructor in high school or college who is trying to resolve the conflict between covering assigned subject matter and helping students become better readers.

The realization that learning to read is a life-long process is not new. In recent years, however, there has been a growing uneasy awareness on the part of many workers in secondary and collegiate education that they need to be doing something about helping students to improve the reading skills that

Reprinted from *The North Central Association Quarterly*, XXXIV (April 1960), 295–299, with permission of North Central Association of Colleges and Secondary Schools.

are needed in high school, college, and later adult life. But it has not been clear just what should be done.

More and more high school and college instructors are realizing that something more constructive needs to be done than simply blaming the elementary schools for not doing a better job of teaching children to read. Elementary teachers and administrators, as a whole, are the first to realize that improvements in the teaching of reading need to be made, and they are doing an excellent job of making the needed improvements.

But regardless of the caliber of the work being done by the elementary schools in teaching children to read, it is now well known that the art of reading is so complex that no one, not even the brightest child in the best of all possible elementary schools, can learn all he needs to know about reading by the end of six or eight years of schooling.

WHY ELEMENTARY SCHOOLS CAN'T DO THE WHOLE JOB

There are at least two reasons why the elementary schools cannot be expected to do the entire job of teaching students to read, and why high schools and colleges need to take steps to insure continued growth in the reading ability of students.

1. Reading involves interpreting printed symbols and making discriminative reactions to the ideas expressed by them. The processes of interpreting and making discriminative reactions can be taught and learned only in terms of the ideas expressed by the symbols, i.e., the content of the reading material.

The elementary school cannot prepare children to read skillfully in all the different subject areas they will meet in high school, college, and adult life. Many students are able to select from their "bag" of reading skills those that are required for reading any new bit of material, without guidance from the teacher. However, even these students would be able to select appropriate reading procedures more effectively if some guidance were provided. This is certainly not a novel idea, since our whole concept of formal education is based upon the assumption that guided learning is more efficient than unguided learning.

Most students will be more successful in reading in any subject field if they are given appropriate guidance at the appropriate time. Guidance that was given five to ten years earlier may be too remote to be adequate.

2. Individual differences in reading achievement, which have been well documented and discussed in educational and psychological literature (1)*, are present at every educational level. The more effective the instruction provided at earlier levels, the greater the range of individual differences will be at the high school and college levels.

Much has been said and done about working with students who are poor readers. Many reading clinics and special reading classes have been established to provide extra help for these students. Much less thought and

[* Numbers in parentheses refer to Bibliography at the end of this article.]

energy have been given to helping students who are already average or above in reading skill. In many high school and college classrooms it is the students of better-than-average competence who are "short-changed." Too frequently the assumption is made that these students can take care of themselves.

Let's consider some ways in which subject-matter instructors in high school or college can help students become better readers without taking too much of the time needed for covering course content.

HOW SUBJECT-MATTER INSTRUCTORS CAN HELP STUDENTS BECOME BETTER READERS

There are two basic approaches to helping high school and college students to improve their reading skill. One of these involves setting up a special reading improvement program, with a reading specialist in charge. The other involves the provision of guidance in reading improvement by instructors in the various subject-matter classes.

Both of these approaches should be used, since each can accomplish things that the other cannot. The special reading improvement program in a high school or college should be set up to work with competent readers who can benefit from additional guided practice as well as with students who have reading difficulties. The personnel and facilities of this special program should also be available to subject-matter instructors who want to find ways to improve the reading skills of their students in their own classes.

In addition to referring some students for specialized help in reading, or even in the event that no specialized help is available, the subject-matter instructor can do certain things in his own classroom that will be helpful to even the best readers. An instructor does not need to be an expert in the teaching of reading in order to do these six things.

1. Give Attention to Students' Readiness for Reading the Assigned Material

There appear to be three primary factors that determine readiness for reading, or for learning via any other avenue, at any educational level, or in any particular subject field: (a) mental maturity; (b) background knowledge and skill; and (c) motivation for learning (2).

An instructor can get a reasonably good indication of the mental maturity of his students in several ways: by looking at their recent intelligence or academic aptitude test scores; by looking at their records of past achievements; and by observing the daily behavior of students in the classroom and outside.

In learning about the status of the background knowledge and skill of his students, an instructor can do several things.

1) He can look at the scores made by students on standardized reading tests;

2) He can devise two or three short reading tests of his own to supplement or replace standardized reading tests. This can be done by choosing selections from the textbook(s) to be studied, and composing several comprehension questions on the selections. These short tests can then be used to get an indication of students' rate of reading and comprehension accuracy on material of the kind that they will meet in his course. In making such tests the instructor will need to be careful not to select paragraphs containing technical terms that are not defined within those paragraphs, and that the student could not be expected to know otherwise. Since the material for these two or three tests can be selected from the content of his course, the instructor can get objective indications of his students' reading ability at the same time that he is covering subject matter. By using two or three short tests on different days, he can be better assured of the re-

liability and validity of his impressions.

3) An instructor can devise a test on the vocabulary and concepts that students will encounter in a new assignment to determine whether the students have the background knowledge required for understanding the lesson. He can then teach any concepts and terms that may be needed, as indicated by the pre-test.

If students have the mental maturity, the reading skill (and any other required skills), and the understanding of vocabulary and basic concepts required to profitably study the new material, they will be successful readers, *if they are interested*. It is well known that a strong desire to learn will compensate for many background deficiencies. In making any assignment, an instructor needs to seriously consider how he can help students to acquire the interest and drive that will help them to go ahead in spite of obstacles. The problem of motivation is, of course, an age-old one that cannot be easily solved. However, in doing the three things suggested just above, an instructor will be doing a great deal to increase the meaningfulness of reading in his subject for his students. Meaningfulness of activity is one of the major factors in motivation for that activity.

The ideas that follow also bear, at least indirectly, upon motivation.

2. Give Attention to the Readability of Assigned Textbooks and Supplementary Reading Material

Closely related to the problem of determining and increasing students' readiness for learning through reading is the question of the readability of the assigned reading matter. As early as 1923 it was recognized that much textbook material is written at an unnecessarily difficult level (6). Since that time several "readability formulae" (3, 5, 7) have been devised for estimating the difficulty of reading material. Some of these formulae can be easily applied by an instructor to reading material in his courses to give him a more objective indication of the difficulty of the material than he might otherwise have.

The desirability of providing easier reading material for some students as preparation for successful handling of the normally assigned reading, and of providing more challenging material for others, is obvious. The argument is sometimes heard that providing reading material on different levels of difficulty, particularly easier material for the less competent students, constitutes "spoon feeding" and is not compatible with the goal of maintaining high standards in education. The necessity for maintaining high standards cannot be denied. But it would seem that a good way to help the less competent students to read better and to achieve according to the high standards that we desire, is to let them read easier material on the subject as preparation for successfully handling the more difficult material that is normally assigned. Among other advantages, this would help to decrease the frustration experienced by poor readers when required to read material written in a difficult style, without adequate preparation for it.

Similarly, it seems likely that levels of achievement of the most competent students can be raised by letting them read more difficult material. This attention to readability may enable an instructor to decrease the frustration that hampers a bright student when he has to read material that is so easy as to provide no challenge for him. Even if supplementary reading material of different difficulty levels is not available, an instructor can better help students get ready to do the assigned reading if he knows something about the readability of the material.

3. Show Students How To Preview Reading Material

One of the major premises of many present-day theories of learning is that meaningful material is easier to learn and remember than is non-meaningful material. This principle is highly pertinent to learning through reading. One important way in which a reader can increase the meaningfulness of any material for himself is by previewing the material to be read before reading it in detail. This process will enable him to have some prior understanding of the content and of the major trends in the discussion. He will be less apt to let the appearance of the trees dull his perception of the forest.

Many high school and college students, even among the brightest, have not learned to preview an article, chapter, or book before reading it in detail (4). In helping students learn how to preview a selection, an instructor should first make clear why such a procedure is helpful. He can help students to realize that it is easier and more enjoyable to learn something when one can see how it is related to the whole. He can then show students how the preface, table of contents, section headings, summaries, footnotes, charts and graphs, topic sentences, index, appendices, glossary, etc., can be used to advantage in studying for this particular course.

The Survey Q3R Method of reading, involving previewing as its first step, is an excellent example of a systematic approach to reading that is based upon experimental findings in psychological studies of learning, perception, retention, motivation, etc.* (8, 9)

---

* F. P. Robinson, who originally designed the Survey Q3R Method, gives the following explanation of it (Pressey, Robinson and Horrocks, *Psychology in Education*, pp. 571–2):

Survey. The student makes a rapid survey of the headings in the assignment, to find out what major ideas are present and their sequence.

Question. The student turns the first heading into a question in order to have a seeking attitude and to know what he is reading for.

Read. The student reads the section under the heading, seeking the answer to his question.

Recite. Having read the section clear through, the student writes down brief cue phrases *from*

The few minutes required to explain and demonstrate this method of reading, using the course textbook or comparable material, will be well repaid by the increased effectiveness of students at all levels of reading skills.

4. Help Students Realize the Importance of Varying Style of Reading To Fit Material and Purpose

Many students, particularly the poorer ones, have the misconception that all reading should be done at the same rate and with the same thoroughness, regardless of material and purpose. An extreme example of this misconception may be seen in students who read everything with slow, careful deliberation. At the other extreme are the students who try to read everything rapidly. These students, and others between these extremes, do not realize that the rate and care with which a skillful reader reads a given bit of material depends upon the nature of the material and his purpose in reading it.

An instructor can emphasize two points with students in regard to varying rate and thoroughness of reading according to their purposes and the nature of the material.

1) The skillful reader asks himself, before starting to read, "What do I already know about this topic? What do I want to get from this reading—all of the major ideas and their supporting details, or just the main ideas without the details, or am I looking just for some specific items of information?
2) The skillful reader uses a systematic approach to reading, such as the Survey Q3R Method, varying its application ac-

---

memory. (No copying is done, and complete notes are not wanted.)

Steps 2, 3, and 4 are repeated for each succeeding section that has a heading.

Review. Immediately after reading the whole lesson in this way, the student tries to recall the points that have been developed in it. This is a second recitation. He glances at his notes only as needed to remind him of points not immediately recalled.

---

cording to the degree of comprehension and retention he desires.

Students who realize the importance of varying their style of reading according to their purposes and the nature of the material can achieve greater mastery of subject matter in a course. They recognize that while the course textbook requires very thorough reading, supplementary readings for additional background can frequently be read less thoroughly, hence more rapidly and in greater quantity. This, of course, presupposes that students know how to find supplementary material on the subject.

5. Help Students To Locate Supplementary Reading Material on the Subject

Wide reading in a subject helps a student to become better informed on the subject, and also helps him to read additional materials in that field more effectively. An instructor can help students to become more skillful readers as well as better informed students by helping them learn to locate reading material in his subject field. He should acquaint them with sources of bibliographies, with indices and abstracts, and with other appropriate guides to reference material.

6. Help Students Improve Their Knowledge of the Vocabulary of the Subject

Since acquaintance with the terminology of any subject is basic to reading skillfully in that subject, a major responsibility of an instructor is to help students to acquire the desire and the necessary skills for continued vocabulary improvement in the subject.

An instructor can emphasize that extensive reading constitutes one of the best bases for vocabulary improvement. In addition, he can remind students of certain skills that are useful in deciphering the meanings of strange words. While most students probably learned these skills in the elementary school, many will profit from being reminded of the applications of these skills to the vocabulary of the particular subject being studied. Among the most important of these skills are (*10*):

(a) using context clues;
(b) using phonetic clues;
(c) using structural clues—e.g., prefixes, suffixes, roots;
(d) using the dictionary.

Guidance from the instructor will help students to see how these vocabulary skills may be used in improving knowledge of vocabulary in any particular subject.

SUMMARY

Since learning to read is a lifetime process that cannot be completely mastered by the end of the elementary school, subject-matter instructors in high schools and colleges have a responsibility for helping students continue their growth in reading skill. This article has suggested ways in which a subject-matter instructor can help his students improve their reading skill at the same time that he is covering subject matter. An instructor does not need to be an expert in the teaching of reading in order to help students read better at the same time that he is covering course content.

BIBLIOGRAPHY

1. ANDERSON, IRVING H., and DEARBORN, WALTER F. *The Psychology of Teaching Reading.* New York: Ronald Press (1952), pp. 41–8.
2. CRONBACH, LEE J. *Educational Psychology.* New York: Harcourt-Brace (1954), Ch. 4–8.
3. DALE, E., and CHALL, J. S. "A Formula for Predicting Readability," *Educational Research Bulletin*, Vol. 27 (1948), 11–12, 37–54.
4. DANSKIN, D. G., and BURNETT, C. W. "Study Techniques of Those Superior Students," *Personnel and Guidance Journal*, Vol. 31, pp. 181–6.
5. FLESCH, R. F. "Marks of Readable Style," *Contributions to Education*, No. 897. Teachers College, Columbia University, 1943.
6. LIVELY, B. A., and PRESSEY, S. L. "A Method of Measuring 'Vocabularly Burden' of Textbooks," *Educational Administration and Supervision*, Vol. 9 (1923), 389–98.
7. LORGE, IRVING. "Predicting Readability," in HUNNICUTT and IVERSON, *Research in the Three R's.* New York: Harper and Brothers (1958), 184–94.
8. PRESSEY, S. L., ROBINSON, F. P., and HORROCKS, J. E. *Psychology in Education.* New York: Harper and Brothers (1959), Ch. 17.
9. ROBINSON, F. P. *Effective Study.* New York: Harper and Brothers (1946), Project II.
10. SPACHE, G., and BERG, P. *The Art of Efficient Reading.* New York: Macmillan (1955), Ch. 9–11.

READINESS AND THE DEVELOPMENT OF READING ABILITY AT ALL SCHOOL LEVELS
Elona Sochor

The concept of readiness for learning, with its implications for teaching, has long been

Reprinted from *Education*, LXXIV (May 1954), 555–560, with permission of Bobbs-Merrill Company, Inc.

recognized in education. Without a state of readiness among learners, most of what may have been developed or taught in a classroom is forfeited.

A state of readiness at any particular time

has a highly complex nature. It is a composite of a pupil's physical, social, emotional, intellectual, and language development. It reflects his past environments, his conditioning, his training, and his knowledge.

Moreover, any one of these factors cannot be isolated in reality. They are all highly interrelated in any one child, and the state of relationships may vary in different situations. In any group of children, there will be ranges in differences for each of the factors.

No pupil enters a school building devoid of any readiness. On the other hand, no two learners are alike in their states of readiness. Due to the multiplicity of factors, the ranges of differences increase as pupils grow older.

The existence of readiness for learning cannot be assumed. It must be assured, first, by appraisal and, then, by development. Being fundamental to all instruction, readiness for learning is a basic concern of all teachers at all times and at all school levels.

One important element in any instructional program is the development and use of reading ability. Since reading is a learned process, readiness is a factor which must be considered for any activity involving reading. To limit appraisal and development of readiness to beginning reading is to ignore the fact that developing reading ability is a continuous process extending in some respects into college instruction. Insuring readiness for reading must of necessity be a continuous process.

Considerations in readiness for reading then, may be classified into two categories for purposes of discussion: Those basic to any learning process; and those that apply more specifically to reading.

READINESS FOR LEARNING

Basic considerations in readiness for any kind of learning include 1) physical status, 2) mental capacity, and 3) emotional-social maturity and adjustment. In reading, "A mental, emotional, and physical readiness for sustained reading activities possesses as much significance in a modern secondary school as it does in a modern primary school." (*1*, p. 104) *

Physical Status—Much is known about the importance of physical factors. The need for recognizing physical disability is obvious. A child who is unable to see the printing on a page cannot perceive the words. The child with a hearing loss will not profit from much of the typical activity in auditory discrimination. The malnourished or ill child will be unable to put forth the sustained attention necessary in reading. Such children are not ready for the tasks demanded.

Less commonly accepted, above the "first grade," are differences in physical maturation and make-up. For example, some children do not have the visual skills necessary for reading until they reach seven years of age. Others lack the physical coordination needed for easy and fluent writing until they are nine or ten years old. Nor can all children attain the same proficiency in any one physical activity. Regardless of the level, setting up requirements which demand physical development beyond that which exists merely creates problems in attitudes and habits. Such requirements are not taking into account physical readiness.

Mental Capacity—Mental capacity is significant in learning in that it helps to determine the quality and abstractness of thinking possible. Although the reliability and validity of any intelligence quotient may be questioned, the fact remains that a range in capacity does exist. All children in the ninth grade, for example, are not capable of understanding materials designed for the "average" ninth grader. There is no method, technique, or formula to make such readiness possible. In contrast, some ninth graders will have the ability to do college-level work.

[*Numbers in parentheses refer to Bibliography at the end of this article.]

Range in intelligence has other implications for readiness. If pupils cannot grasp certain abstractions, placing them regularly in situations which demand such thinking results only in failure. If differences in capacity have not been cared for in previous teaching, those children with intelligence indices at the lower end of the scale may not have learned as much as they could have. Since those with lower capacity learn more slowly and less than those with higher, an increasingly greater range in readiness as children grow older is to be expected.

Emotional-Social Factors—Emotional maturity and social adjustment are potent factors in readiness for learning. The pupil who is overly insecure, anxious, or fearful cannot attend to learning activities without his personal problems interfering. The one who lacks self-confidence, who is too dependent on others, who cannot accept responsibility may be defeated before he enters a classroom. Inability to respond to a teacher or to classmates without hostility and resentment, to share in the normal give-and-take in a classroom frequently results in aggression or withdrawal. Ignoring such children's lack of readiness produces frustrated unachievers with unhealthy attitudes toward themselves, others, and learning.

READINESS FOR READING

Readiness for an activity involving reading has two aspects: those in the reader and those in the material to be read. Since materials are selected for children, evaluations of reading readiness begins with the child.

Among the factors which must be considered in appraising a pupil's readiness to read, regardless of the level are: *1*) a background of knowledge, *2*) oral language facility, *3*) achievement in reading, *4*) a purpose for reading, and *5*) a desire to satisfy the stated purpose by reading.

Background—A rich and varied background of information and experience is imperative for reading if a reader is to comprehend. Particularly is this true at the intermediate and secondary school levels where materials to be read are many and diversified.

A background of knowledge which includes well-organized concepts is basic to any reading, for there is no meaning inherent in printed symbols themselves. The reader attaches meaning, or concepts, to them from the background he possesses. When he has no appropriate concepts for a particular symbol the symbol remains meaningless.

If, in attempting to read a selection, the reader lacks the knowledge he should have to understand the selection, he cannot read it successfully. Moreover, encouraging him to persist with little or no comprehension merely fosters verbalism. Without information, experiences, and concepts to take to reading, a pupil is not ready to read.

On the other hand, this aspect of readiness, in helping to guarantee comprehension, results in new knowledge acquired through the reading. By using and manipulating the information and concepts he has in reconstructing an author's ideas, the reader adds to what he knows by reorganizing his concepts, generalizing, and applying what he has learned.

Insuring adequate background cannot be relegated to a particular time of the year. It is a daily process. Even when a pupil has the basis for new learning, the appropriate knowledge must be called to mind by the teacher or the pupil himself, if he knows how.

Oral Language—Reading is a language process. In the normal sequence of language development, control of the spoken symbol precedes control of the printed symbol. Thinking precedes both. Insuring oral language facility as one element in readiness for reading has two advantages.

First, the thinking process that is basic to language can best be appraised and developed through speaking. Oral expression that is precise, logical, and concise indicates the ideas have been understood and organized. The problem of interpreting and evaluating an author's ideas is far more complex than thinking about and conveying clearly one's own. If thinking does not precede speaking, it will not precede reading; and reading demands thinking.

Second, a reader must have control over the concepts, the vocabulary, and the complexity of language orally at a particular level of difficulty before he can successfully interpret printed language at the same level. He must be familiar with unusual words or expressions before he begins to read. Otherwise he may read, as one child did, "to horse" as "two horses" with resulting confusion in comprehension. Adequate oral language facility is a prerequisite to reading comprehension.

Achievement—Readiness for reading a selection assumes a particular level of achievement. "Each new learning depends upon previous learning." (*2, p. 110*) What a child has learned about the reading process in a second reader, he will need in the third reader. What a pupil has learned about these United States in the intermediate grades is basic to what he will learn in the junior high school.

Achievement at any level of difficulty in reading includes the two factors already discussed, i.e., a background of knowledge and oral language facility, plus the body of understandings, abilities, and skills necessary to reading for meaning. The latter is commonly organized into three categories: word perception, comprehension, and application. Basic to all of these categories is the realization that words stand for concrete objects, for ideas, and for feelings.

Word perception has two aspects: meaning and word form. Appropriate knowledge, previously discussed, results in the first. Ability to associate meaning to the symbol, which is basic to reading, and skills in recognizing and analyzing word forms are necessary for the second. Both aspects must exist to a suitable degree before a reader is ready to comprehend at a given level of difficulty.

The need for developing concepts has already been discussed. The ability to pronounce words correctly does not insure comprehension. Betty could say "fathoms," but she had no concept for the word. Since this was a key word, she was unable to understand the sentence. The meaning aspect of word perception is basic. Moreover, too many unknown concepts in material indicates lack of readiness for reading that material.

Ability to recognize or attack the word form itself is an index to readiness for reading a selection. Even the substitution of *a* for *the* affects meaning: "Give me a ball" is not synonymous with "Give me the ball."

Moreover, word recognition and word attack skills are developed sequentially. There is a state of readiness for the development of each one. When a child cannot hear the difference between consonant sounds, he is likely to have difficulty in 1) associating the correct sound with the visual symbol, the letter, and 2) using the consonant sound in attacking words. If he can't distinguish between long and short vowel sounds, he won't be able to apply the "final *e*" principle in reading or writing. Common is the case of the pupil who persistently omits syllables in words. Upon analysis, it becomes evident that the learner cannot identify the number of syllables heard and frequently even omits them in speech. The student who is unable to use the dictionary may lack many of the background skills that are assumed mastered before he begins to learn how to use it. In each case, the learner is not ready for the advanced skill because he lacks one or more of the basic skills.

Comprehension—Readiness to comprehend necessitates all of the factors discussed in this paper. Particularly significant are the thinking processes, the necessary concepts, and the ability to see relationships between words in context.

Thinking is basic to comprehension, and the ability to think must be established before a pupil is ready to read. Likewise, a reader must have concepts with which to think if he is to comprehend.

A student must also grasp the meaning of groups of words such as are found in phrases and sentences. He must see the relationships between sentences in a paragraph and between paragraphs in a selection.

Nor is it enough that learners be ready to grasp just the stated facts in material read. They must also be ready to draw conclusions and generalizations, to contrast and evaluate, to sense tone, mood, and intent. These comprehension skills and abilities necessitate higher levels of thinking, or critical thinking. Readers must be able to think critically before they are ready to comprehend critically.

Application—Before a pupil is ready to use or apply what he has gained from reading, he must have a great degree of understanding, he must see relationships, and he must have control over the necessary skills and abilities. For example, in outlining from several sources read, he must first understand what was stated and implied in the sources. He must see how the ideas fit together. He must be able to identify the main topics and the related, significant details. Finally, he must know how to set down these ideas in outline form. Until a pupil has the necessary understandings, abilities, and skills to do all these, he is not ready to outline from several sources independently.

Purpose—One element in readiness for reading is the identification of needs that can be satisfied through reading. These needs are the purposes for reading. Such motivation is intrinsic to the extent that the needs are actually learner needs, understood and accepted by the learner. Moreover the needs are recognized and stated prior to the reading.

Identifying a purpose for reading contributes further to readiness. It helps to insure reading for meaning in its fullest sense. It indicates whether the reading is to be a source of pleasure or of information. It dictates the depth of comprehension required and influences the rate of reading. In brief, the purpose establishes readiness by 1) identifying the "why" for the reading and 2) indicating the "how."

Interest—A desire to satisfy felt needs by reading is actually a product of all the foregoing factors. If a well-adjusted learner has a need that to him is worth solving, if he knows it can be solved by reading, and if his past experiences with reading have been successful, he will want to solve that need by reading. Needless to say, until this point is reached, he is not ready to read it.

MATERIALS

Thus far in this discussion of readiness for reading, the child has been the primary consideration. Some attention must be given to materials for reading.

Reading materials are selected in terms of the state of readiness of a learner. If a fifth-grader cannot read successfully a third level basal reader, he will be unable to read a fifth reader. If a ninth-grader is frustrated by a social studies text designed for and read well by the "average" seventh-grader, he will be more frustrated by a textbook designed for the ninth "grade" level. When a high school senior sees no need to read a physics text, he is not ready to do so.

The difficulty of materials depends largely on: 1) the number, difficulty, and strangeness of facts, 2) the vocabulary, terminology, or symbols representing those facts, and 3) the context, or language setting, of the facts.

Materials in the content fields frequently pose problems for readers. Readiness has to be present to deal with the concise, all-inclusive, expository style, and the sentences filled with unfamiliar, difficult concepts and terminology.

The fact that such readiness is assumed to be present has contributed greatly to the problem of verbalism in the schools, i.e., to the number of students who "read" with little or no comprehension.

If all materials to be read were evaluated in terms of pupil readiness before they were used with learners, the many problems that exist in reading ability today could be reduced substantially.

CONCLUSIONS

From the foregoing discussion, the following conclusions may be drawn:

1. Reading readiness functions at all levels and in all learning activities.
2. Readiness for any reading activity is complex, made up of many interrelated factors.

3. Ranges of individual differences must be recognized and considered in readiness.
4. Readiness for reading must be insured for each student 1) if learning is to take place in a healthy situation, 2) if desirable attitudes are to be created toward reading, and 3) if adequate and efficient reading ability is to be developed.

BIBLIOGRAPHY

1. BETTS, EMMETT A. *Foundations of Reading Instruction*. New York: American Book Company, Revised 1954.
2. BOND, G. L., and WAGNER, E. B. *Teaching The Child To Read*. Part II and Chapter XIII. New York: The Macmillan Company, 1950.
3. HARRISON, M. LUCILE. *Reading Readiness*. Part II. Boston: Houghton Mifflin Company, 1939.
4. MCKEE, PAUL. *The Teaching of Reading in The Elementary School*, Part I. Boston: Houghton Mifflin Company, 1948.
5. ROBINSON, HELEN M. *Why Pupils Fail in Reading*. Chicago: University of Chicago Press, 1946.
6. SAUL, LEON J. *Emotional Maturity*. Philadelphia: J. B. Lippincott Company, 1947.

SKILLS RELATED TO THE ABILITY TO READ HISTORY AND SCIENCE
J. Harlan Shores

INTRODUCTION

The statement that "every teacher should be, to a significant extent, a teacher of reading" has gained wide recognition and has led to considerable controversy.[1] The statement

Reprinted from the *Journal of Educational Research*, XXXVI (April 1943), 584–593, with permission of the author and Dembar Educational Research Services.

[1] *The Teaching of Reading: A Second Report*, Thirty-sixth Yearbook of the National Society for the Study of Education, p. 6.

assumes that reading instruction must continue beyond the reading period and beyond the elementary school. If this is true, teachers in the content fields must sacrifice time formerly spent on their content subjects to instruction on the reading abilities essential to effective reading of the materials employed in these subjects. If every teacher must teach reading, it follows that the reading requirements of the materials in a given content field are, at least in some respects, unique to that field, and that these more or less unique skills would be more effectively taught by a person well acquainted with the materials and requirements of the content field. In other words, if the teacher of science in the ninth grade must teach the ability to read science materials, there must be reading skills essential to effective reading of science that are not essential to good reading of literature, history or other content materials. If the skills all had general application it seems that they could be well-taught in a general reading period.

PROBLEM

The purpose of this study was to determine the relationships among ninth-grade pupils, between certain study and reading skills and reading comprehension of scientific and historical materials. An attempt was made to 1) study the relationship between each of the measured reading and study skills and reading comprehension of historical material; 2) to determine the relationship between each of the measured reading and study skills and reading comprehension with scientific material; 3) to better understand the relationship between both scientific and historical reading comprehension and a sampling of vocabulary from diverse fields; 4) to further explore the relationship between a vocabulary of words frequently found in historical and scientific materials and reading comprehensions in history and science. In addition, this investigation attempted 5) to determine, when relationships were discovered, the area of the population responsible for these relationships.

The aforementioned specific purposes were means to more fundamental purposes. This study attempted to contribute to a more complete understanding of the relationships involved in the developmental reading process, and thus to aid in the determination of a better reading program in the public schools.

STUDENT POPULATION AND TESTS USED

The entire first term ninth-grade population of the Central Junior High School in Kansas City, Missouri, provided the student population. A total of 380 complete cases resulted. This group seemed to be representative with respect to such factors of random sampling as socio-economic status, intelligence, reading ability, achievement, and educational experience. The nature of the statistical techniques employed in this study render unimportant possible selection with respect to relatively major factors of representativeness such as mental age and ability to read literature, science, and history.

Information was obtained with each of the tests in Table 1 for each of the 380 cases. These tests were administered under uniform testing conditions. No more than three weeks elapsed between the administration of any two tests.

METHOD

The statistical method employed in this investigation was a generalized approach to the matched-control type of research where the significance of a difference between means is found. Palmer Johnson and J. Neyman were responsible for the development of this generalized and more efficient method of analysis.[2] Good and poor groups[3]* of readers with science and history materials were compared for differences in mean ability in each

[2] Palmer O. Johnson and J. Neyman, *Tests of Certain Linear Hypotheses and Their Applications to Some Educational Problems* (London, England: Department of Statistics, University of London, University College, June 1936).

[3] Truman L. Kelley, "The Selection of Upper and Lower Groups for Validation of Test Items," *Journal of Educational Psychology*, Vol. 30 (January 1939), 17–24.

* Kelley has found that the upper and lower twenty-seven percent offers the most rigorous and efficient division. This division was closely approximated in the present study.

of the measured skills. Before each comparison the good and poor groups were rendered equivalent in mental age and ability to read literature. It was felt that with mental age uncontrolled, differences in level of mental development might account for differences between good and poor history or science readers in the various skills. Ability to read literature was controlled in order that discovered differences could not be explained by so-called factors of "general reading ability."

Since the difference in effects of the basic matching characters (mental age and ability to read literature) were determined before each comparison by the regression of the skill on the matching characters, the need for individual matching of cases disappeared. Hence, the entire populations of good and poor readers of science and history were employed without the usual loss of cases in matching. The generalized method employed in this study offered still another advantage over the usual "matched-control" approach to research. It allowed not only the determination of significant differences between the good and poor science and history readers in separate skills, but also enabled determination of the section of the population with respect to the basic matching characters where these differences were significant. Through the use of this concept known as "regions of significance," limits of mental age and ability to read literature may be set whereby it is possible to say that the discovered difference is a significant one within these limits. That is, a significant difference may be found between good and poor history readers in ability to use the index. Through the use of "regions of significance" it is found that this difference is a reliable one only for those pupils with average mental age and average to slightly superior ability to read literature.

RESULTS

The results of this investigation are summarized in Table 2. When enumerated, they are as follows:

1. In the first analysis, groups of good and poor science readers were compared for significant differences in their mean ability in each of the measured skills. The ability to read science was found significantly related

TABLE 1
INFORMATION CONCERNING TESTS USED

Name of Test	Author	Date	Reliability Coefficient*	Admin. Time	Publisher
Iowa Every-Pupil Tests of Basic Skills Test A: Silent Reading Comprehension	Horn, Ernest; McBroom, M.; Spitzer, H. F.; Greene, H. A.; Knight, F. B.	1939	.90	Approx. 85 min. (or two 45 min. periods)	Bureau of Educational Research and Service, Extension Division, University of Iowa, Iowa City, Iowa.
Part I Paragraph Comprehension			.67		
Part II Understanding of Details			.80		
Part III Organization of Ideas			.70		
Part IV Grasp of Total Meaning			.57		
Total—Parts I to IV			.90		
Part V Vocabulary			.91		

TABLE 1—continued

Name of Test	Author	Date	Reliability Coefficient*	Admin. Time	Publisher
Iowa Every-Pupil Tests of Basic Skills Test B: Basic Study Skills	Same as above	1939	.95	Approx. 90 min. (or two 45 min. periods)	Same as above.
Part I Maps			.79		
Part II Graphs, Charts			.79		
Part III References			.87		
Part IV Index			.84		
Part V Dictionary			.83		
Total			.95		
Reading Scales in Literature	Van Wagenen, M. J.	1922† (1939)	+ P. E. 3 to 8.5 C—score points	Approx. 45 min.	Educational Test Bureau, Educational Publishers, Inc. Minneapolis, Minn.
Reading Scales in Science	Van Wagenen, M. J.	1938	Same as above	Approx. 45 min.	Same as above.
Reading Scales in History	Van Wagenen, M. J.	1938	Same as above	Approx. 45 min.	Same as above.
Meaning of Words Used in Science	Swenson, E. J.	1938	.79	Approx. 20 min.	Unpublished, E. J. Swenson, College of Education, University of Minnesota, Minneapolis.
Meaning of Words Used in History	Shores, J. H.	1938	.72	Approx. 20 min.	Unpublished, J. H. Shores, College of Education, University of Minnesota, Minneapolis.
California Test of Mental Maturity— Advanced Battery (Total Score)	Sullivan, E. T.; Clark, W. W.; Tiege, E. W.	1937	.95	Two periods of approx. 45 to 50 min. each	California Test Bureau, 3636 Beverly Blvd., Los Angeles, California.

* Reliability coefficients for the Iowa tests and for the Van Wagenen tests were secured from the authors.
† Published in 1922. Published in 1939 with changes from 1922 publication only in format and scoring method. On advice of the author the 1922 tests and 1939 scoring methods were used.

to the following skills and abilities: (1) history comprehension, (2) science vocabulary knowledge, (3) general vocabulary knowledge, (4) ability to read graphs, charts, and tables, (5) understanding of details, and (6) the total score on the measured skills of silent reading comprehension. The relationship between ability to read science materials and the three following skills approached significance: (1) history vocabulary knowledge, (2) facility in the organization of ideas, and (3) ability to comprehend maps.

2. The ability to read history was found significantly related to all of the measured skills and abilities with the exception of ability to comprehend maps. Factors of mental

TABLE 2

RELATIONSHIPS BETWEEN ABILITY TO READ SCIENCE AND HISTORY AND VARIOUS READING ABILITIES*

Abilities	Science Relationships			History Relationships		
	Approximate percentiles in Region of Significance			Approximate percentiles in Region of Significance		
	Mental Age	Literature Compre-hension	Level of Signifi-cance	Mental Age	Literature Compre-hension	Level of Signifi-cance
Science Comprehension	0—100	0—100	Upper	10— 95	10— 85	Upper
History Comprehension	30—100	25—100	Upper	0—100	0—100	Upper
Science Vocabulary	10—100	10—100	Upper	0— 95	0— 85	Upper
History Vocabulary	60—100	45—100	Lower	15—100	15—100	Upper
General Vocabulary	35— 85	40— 80	Upper	15—100	5— 95	Upper
Understanding of Details	30— 90	40— 90	Upper	0— 95	0— 85	Upper
Organization of Ideas	10— 90	45—100	Lower	10— 80	10— 70	Upper
Grasp of Total Meaning			None	0— 55	0— 45	Upper
Paragraph Comprehension			None	0— 75	15— 90	Upper
Total Score: Silent Reading Comprehension	30— 65	45— 80	Upper	0— 90	0— 85	Upper
Reading Graphs, Charts, and Tables	0— 75	0— 75	Upper	0— 80	0— 75	Upper
Use of Basic References			None	10— 70	30— 90	Upper
Use of Index			None	30— 70	40— 75	Upper
Use of Dictionary			None	0—100	0—100	Upper
Comprehension of Maps	0— 60	30— 80	Lower			None
Total Score: Basic Study Skills			None	5—100	0—100	Upper

* Table 2 is as follows: The relationship between understanding of details and ability to read science is reliably established at the upper (.01) level of significance for those pupils whose coordinates in mental age and literature comprehension locate points between the thirtieth and ninetieth percentiles in mental age and also between the fortieth and ninetieth percentiles in literature comprehension. Understanding of details is related at the upper level of significance to ability to read history for all pupils except those in the upper five percent of the total mental age distribution and also in the upper fifteen percent of the total distribution in literature comprehension.

age and ability to read literature were again controlled. History reading ability was significantly related to the following skills: (1) science comprehension, (2) history vocabulary, (3) general vocabulary, (4) science vocabulary, (5) paragraph comprehension, (6) grasp of the total meaning of a reading passage, (7) organization of ideas, (8) understanding of details, (9) the total score on the measured skills of silent reading comprehension, (10) reading of graphs, charts and tables, (11) use of the index, (12) use of the dictionary, (13) use of basic references, and (14) the total score of the measured basic study skills.

3. All of the skills not found significantly related to ability to read science materials were significantly related to ability to read historical materials. These skills are: (1) paragraph comprehension, (2) grasp of the total meaning of a reading passage, (3) use of the index, (4) use of the dictionary, (5) use of basic references, (6) the total score of the measured basic study skills, (7) history vocabulary knowledge, and (8) organization of ideas. The relationship of the

latter two abilities to history comprehension is firmly established, while their relationship to science comprehension only approaches significance.

4. The only measured skill not shown to hold a significant relationship to history reading ability, comprehension of maps, approached a significant relationship to science reading ability.

5. Several of the skills and abilities were found significantly related to ability to read both scientific and historical materials. These are as follows: (1) science comprehension, (2) history comprehension, (3) science vocabulary, (4) general vocabulary, (5) reading graphs, charts, and tables, (6) understanding of details, and (7) the total score of the measured skills of silent reading comprehension.

6. In general, the areas of the student population, with respect to the basic matching criteria (mental age and literature comprehension), wherein the established relationships may be said to be significant, are larger with the history reading relationships than with the science. That is, the relationships between history reading ability and the various skills seem to be reliably established for more students than do the science relationships.

7. The location of the areas of relationship between science reading ability and the various skills shown to be related to ability to read science indicates that these relationships are generally reliable for all students with average or superior, but not very superior, mental age and ability to read literature. The significant relationships between ability to read historical materials and the various skills tend to be reliable for all students except those with very high mental age or very superior ability to read literature. Thus, with few exceptions, superiority in ability to read science must be accompanied by average or superior mental age and ability to read literature before these better science

readers are specifically and reliably better in certain related skills. On the other hand, with few exceptions, superiority in ability to read history indicates superior ability in the related skills for all students who do not have exceptionally high mental age and ability to read literature.

8. In no instance was a significant negative relationship discovered between ability to read science or history and a particular skill. That is, there was no comparison where the poorer readers of science or history were significantly superior to the better science or history readers in a particular ability. The poorer readers of science tended to be slightly superior to the better science readers in use of the index and use of references but these negative relationships fell far short of statistical significance.

CONCLUSIONS

The analysis of the data in the present study suggests the following conclusions:

1. By the time students have reached the ninth grade their reading proficiency is to a considerable extent specific to the content field in which the reading is done. To speak of "general reading ability" of ninth-grade students, without description of the content field in which the reading is done, is unwarranted in overlooking this specificity. The ability to read scientific and historical materials holds unique and different relationships to a number of reading skills. Ability to read effectively in the materials of science or history probably requires combinations of skills either not related to or not as closely related to ability to read literature as these skills are to ability to read science and history.

2. Since the results of this study offer rather conclusive evidence in refutation of the concept of a general reading ability in the ninth grade, tests devised to measure reading ability at this level should take steps to con-

trol the type of materials with which the measurement is taken. The fact that various reading abilities tend to be associated with the reading of one type of content reading material does not assure that a similar association will hold with materials of another content field. Certain reading skills are significantly related to ability to read history and science materials in a manner not explained by ability to read literature.

3. The skills measured in this study seem, in general, to be more reliably related to ability to read historical materials than to ability to read scientific materials. With a single exception, these skills are concomitants of ability to read history. The unproved implication here is that the teaching of these skills should be, at least in part, the responsibility of teachers of history. Implications such as this one are subject to change with change in the nature of the instructional program. Under different instruction the relationship between these skills and ability to read history might be altered considerably.

4. Certain of the measured reading abilities were found significantly related to ability to read history materials and not to ability to read science materials. The implication here, while needing further substantiation through additional research, is that science teachers should probably be freed from specific responsibility for development of these skills. Again, this implication might change with change in the instructional program. The only skill tending to show significant relationship to science and not history reading ability (comprehension of maps) was established at a level of doubtful significance and therefore does not warrant dependable generalizations.

5. A number of the measured abilities present significant relationships to both ability to read scientific and historical materials in a manner not explained by ability to read literature. These skills seem to be specific concomitants of both ability to read science and history. Such findings seem to imply that

since the ability to read science and history have a common close relationship to certain skills, the teaching of these skills should probably be the joint responsibility of at least the teachers of science and history. This implication needs further substantiation, and is subject to change with change in the instructional program. Such implications are also subject to practical application. For example, even though science vocabulary knowledge is significantly related to both ability to read science and history, practical considerations would tend to make the teaching of this skill largely the responsibility of the science teacher.

6. The skills and abilities measured in this study tend to divide themselves into several groups. There are those concerned with power of silent reading comprehension in the materials of several content fields, measures of specific and general vocabulary knowledges, skills concerned with the general significance or general meaning of a reading passage, skills where very exacting reading is required, and skills employed in the location of information. The skills tending to show a specific relationship to comprehension of scientific materials are those calling for power of reading comprehension, vocabulary knowledge, or a very exact type of reading. There was no established relationship between science reading ability and the skills which require facility in either location of information or ability to comprehend the general meaning of a reading passage. On the other hand each of these groups of reading abilities tended to be a concomitant of ability to read historical materials.

The good readers of science tend to be also superior in more detailed and exacting skills of reading. The good history readers tend to be also superior in all the measured types of reading responses. Neither of these trends is the resultant of ability with the type of reading required with literary materials.

7. In general, the size of the areas of rela-

tionship seems to suggest that the association between ability to read history and the various skills will be a reliable one for a larger percentage of ninth-grade students than will the established science reading relationships. The history relationships tend to be firmly established for wider ranges of values of mental age and ability to read literature.

8. The data present a noticeable trend for the relationships between history reading ability and the various skills found significantly related to history reading to be reliably established for all pupils except those with very superior mental age and ability to read literature. In contrast, the trend with science reading ability and the related skills, was for these relationships to be firmly established for pupils with average or superior, but not extremely high, values of mental age and literature comprehension.

While the analysis of the data only presents and does not explain this condition, an hypothesis as to its meaning may be offered. Assuming that the relationship between ability to read history and a particular skill is a causal one, it may be said that ability in the skill is important for good readers of history. However, it may be that ability in the skill beyond that normally achieved by pupils of high mental age and very superior ability to read literature is not necessary to efficient reading of history. Good reading ability in literature and high mental age, with their accompanying excellence in the particular skill, may be adequate for effective reading of history. Hence, additional development of the skill at this level would not be functional in discriminating good from poor readers of history.

Reasoning in like manner, a higher excellence in the particular skill is required in science than in history reading before the skill becomes a significant factor to good reading of science. It has been hypothesized that as values of mental age and ability to read literature are higher, there is an accompanying increase in the amount of the skill. Thus, it may be that only those pupils with average or superior mental age and ability to read literature have enough of the skill necessary for effective reading of science. However, ability in the skill normally achieved by pupils of extremely high mental age and very superior ability to read literature may be adequate for effective reading of science, and any additional development of the skill for these pupils would not function to discriminate good from poor readers of science.

9. The fact that ninth-grade teachers should be concerned with the teaching of reading in the content materials of science and history is plainly indicated. The data suggest some of the skills that it might be well to teach in these subjects. Further research is needed to substantiate this contention.

10. These data strengthen the viewpoint that reading in the ninth-grade is neither a simple nor general ability. Reading at this level shows varying degrees of relationship to several aspects of reading skill, depending at least in part upon the content field in which the reading is done.

PROBLEMS SUGGESTED FOR FURTHER STUDY

The results of this investigation indicate that study of the relationships between reading and study skills and reading proficiency in materials of various content fields should be a fruitful field for further research. Studies similar to the present one should be conducted in additional grades, with the reading materials of other content fields, and with additional measures of reading and study skills. It would be interesting to know the effects of reading and working rate on these relationships. The effects of varied instructional programs and methods on these relationships should also be of value.

Teachers in the content fields should conduct controlled studies to determine the effect on both achievement and reading ability in the materials of a given content field of specific instruction in the skills found related to ability to read the materials of that field. It should be valuable in studies of this nature to employ several control groups. In one group the teacher would continue in traditional manner with little specific instruction in reading. In another group an attempt would be made to teach all work-type reading skills. In a third control group, the teacher would attempt to teach those skills believed to be important to efficient reading ability and achievement in the particular subject.

Studies should be made of the effects of difficulty of materials, interest and motivation, reader's purpose, and meaning background on reading proficiency with the materials of the various content fields.

FIVE STEPS TO READING SUCCESS IN SCIENCE
Metropolitan School Study Council

SCIENCE

Many reading difficulties faced by pupils studying science arise from the introduction, all at one time, of numerous new concepts, the interpretation of mathematical formulae, and the solving of problems. To read science material successfully, pupils must master certain reading skills:

1. Locating pertinent details
2. Distinguishing between main ideas and supporting details
3. Visualizing
4. Following directions
5. Drawing inferences

To help pupils learn these reading skills, teachers will find the following sample procedures valuable as guides in developing similar lessons in their classes.

Reading skills often essential to science are included in the sample procedures in the Social Studies section of this manual. The

Reprinted from *Five Steps to Reading Success in Science, Social Studies and Mathematics* (New York: Metropolitan School Study Council, Teachers College, Columbia University, 1960), 1–7, with permission of the publisher.

teacher may wish especially to refer to the procedures for "Skimming" and "Reading Critically" in that section.

FIVE-STEP APPROACH IN SCIENCE

STEP ONE: READINESS
1. Relating the experiences and knowledge of the pupils to the new material
2. Arousing the pupils' interest in the section
   a. The challenge of solving a problem
   b. The desire to satisfy a problem
   c. The practical value of scientific knowledge

STEP TWO: CONCEPT DEVELOPMENT
1. Developing vocabulary
   a. Words and phrases new to the pupils
   b. Familiar words and phrases with new connotations
2. Clarifying ideas of measurement
   Space   Energy
   Time   Mass

STEP THREE: SILENT READING
1. Asking pupils to find answers to specific questions

2. Asking pupils to discover and follow the steps of the experiment or problem

1. Helping pupils to evaluate their answers to questions
2. Helping pupils to discover or to understand principles or theories
3. Helping pupils to see the practical application of principles or theories

STEP FIVE: REREADING (SILENT OR ORAL)
1. Checking accuracy
2. Examining critically

READING SKILL: LOCATING PERTINENT DETAILS

STEP ONE: READINESS

Pupils are aware that green vegetables are a necessary part of a balanced diet. The teacher should stimulate the pupils' curiosity about the reasons for this.

STEP TWO: CONCEPT DEVELOPMENT

The meaning of the following words and concepts should be clarified before the pupils begin the reading. These words and phrases should always be presented in written context.

green plants	*fats*
carbohydrates	*minerals*
proteins	*cellulose*

STEP THREE: SILENT READING

The pupils then should be asked to read the selection, keeping in mind the questions, "What are green plants made of?" and "What do green plants make?"

Green plants have been broken down, chemically, to find out what they are made of. They are made of certain *carbohydrates, proteins, fats, minerals*, and water. But chiefly they are made of a woody material called *cellulose* and contain large amounts of starch and sugar. . . . Sugar is made first.

Green plants make starch, cellulose, and even fat and proteins, from the sugar.[1]

STEP FOUR: DISCUSSION

The discussion should stress that green plants, broken down chemically, provide substances for building body tissue and providing energy. Pupils should be able to name the substances.

STEP FIVE: REREADING

Rereading may be necessary to check the number and kind of substances found in green plants.

READING SKILL: DISTINGUISHING BETWEEN MAIN IDEAS AND SUPPORTING DETAILS

STEP ONE: READINESS

The reading selection that follows concerns the endocrine glands. Before being asked to read this selection, students should be made generally familiar with what the endocrine glands are. The teacher should make clear to students that the purpose of reading about the endocrine glands in this instance is to discover the results of over-secretion of growth hormones in the pituitary gland. To stimulate interest, the readiness lesson might also include a discussion of the following:
1. Why individuals vary in height
2. What causes circus giants

STEP TWO: CONCEPT DEVELOPMENT

The meaning and pronunciation of the following words should be clarified before the pupils begin the reading. These words and phrases should always be presented in written context.

[1] Raymond W. Burnett, Bernard Jaffe, and Herbert S. Zim, *New World of Science* (Morristown, N. J.: Silver Burdett Co., 1953), p. 136. Quoted by permission of the publisher.

pituitary gland   *hormones*
lobes   *somotropic*
anterior   *giantism*
secretes   *acromegaly*

STEP THREE: SILENT READING

The pupils should locate details about the results of over-secretion of the growth hormone.

> The *pituitary gland* consists of two *lobes*. The *anterior* lobe *secretes* several different *hormones*. One of these, the *somotropic* (so-mo-TROP-ic) or growth hormone, regulates the growth of the skeleton. If an oversecretion of this hormone occurs during the growing years, tremendous height may be attained. This condition is called *giantism*. Circus giants over 7 feet tall, weighing 300 pounds, and wearing size 30 shoes, are examples of this disorder. If the oversecretion occurs during adult life, the bones merely thicken, as they cannot grow in length. However, the organs and soft tissues enlarge tremendously. This condition is known as *acromegaly* (ak-ro-MEG-a-lee). Victims of this disorder have greatly thickened jaw bones, enlarged noses, and greatly enlarged hands and fingers.[2]

STEP FOUR: PURPOSEFUL DISCUSSION

The following questions should be on the blackboard while the pupils are reading. Such questions aid in giving direction to the reading.

1. What condition is caused by an over-secretion of the pituitary hormone during *the growing years*? Give an example.
2. What condition is caused by an over-secretion of the pituitary gland during *adult life*? Describe the symptoms.

STEP FIVE: REREADING

The rereading may be oral or silent. Pupils may skim through text material seeking the proof of an answer they have given and then read orally to prove the point.

[2] Truman J. Moon, Paul O. Mann, and James H. Otto, *Modern Biology* (New York: Henry Holt, 1951), p. 502. Quoted by permission of the publisher.

In this particular lesson, pupils may find it necessary to reread to correct errors in spelling or pronunciation of *somotropic* or *acromegaly*. They may want to read to check on the details concerning the circus giant or the symptoms of acromegaly.

READING SKILL: VISUALIZING CONCEPTS

STEP ONE: READINESS

The teacher should arouse the interest of pupils in the atom by discussing the frequent use of *atom* or *atomic* on the radio, in the newspapers, in the movies, and on television. The pupils should be led to ask what an atom really looks like. The purpose of reading the selection will be to find the answer to that question.

STEP TWO: CONCEPT DEVELOPMENT

The pupils should become familiar with the pronunciations and definitions of the following words and phrases. These words and phrases should always be presented in written context.

atom   *positively charged*
electrons   *protons*
negatively charged   *neutrons*
  particles   *electrically neutral*
nucleus   *mass of the atom*
planetary
  electrons

STEP THREE: SILENT READING

The teacher should ask the pupils to try to picture the structure of the atom and to try to compare the size of the nucleus and its electrons.

> There is plenty of evidence to show that an *atom* consists of *electrons, negatively charged particles*, whirling about a *nucleus*. These outer electrons, usually called *planetary electrons*, are lightly scattered about the nucleus and at relatively remote distances from it. The nucleus, on the other

hand, is *positively charged* and consists of a closely packed group of *protons* and *neutrons*. A proton has a positive electrical charge, whereas a neutron is *electrically* neutral and probably results from the union of a proton and an electron. A proton is almost 2,000 times heavier than an electron so that more than 99.9 percent of the *mass of the atom* is in the nucleus.[3]

STEP FOUR: DISCUSSION

To test visualization powers, students could:

1. Draw the structure of an atom
2. Compare the structure of an atom to our solar system
3. Make a model of an atom from clay and wire

STEP FIVE: REREADING

Some rereading may be necessary to check the accuracy of the proportions of the drawing or model.

READING SKILL: FOLLOWING DIRECTIONS

STEP ONE: REREADING

In preparation for an experiment, the pupils have already discussed the use of levers as simple machines. They have learned, by observation, about levers in daily use like the crowbar, scissors, and sugar tongs. They have also learned that levers are used to do work with less effort and with more speed. They are now ready to read the directions for an experiment that will actually demonstrate the scientific principle involved.

STEP TWO: CONCEPT DEVELOPMENT

The meaning of the following words and concepts should be clarified before the pupils begin to read the experiment. These words

and phrases should always be presented in written context.

equilibrium	*unlike weights*
parallel forces	*products*
balance	*vary*
fulcrum	*sum*

STEP THREE: SILENT READING

Each pupil should be instructed to read each detail carefully and execute each step as stated.

> *Experiment 33a. Equilibrium of Parallel Forces—Balance* a meter stick in a clamp or on a *fulcrum*. Hang or stand two *unlike weights* on the stick and move them until the stick balances. Then measure the distance from each weight to the balancing point, or fulcrum. Multiply each weight by its distance to the fulcrum and compare the *products*. *Vary* the set-up as much as you like, using different weights . . . or three weights, or many weights. In every case you will find that the product of weight times distance for the left weight equals the product for the right weight (times distance from the fulcrum). When several weights are used, add the products for those on the left and check against the *sum* of products for those on the right.[4]

STEP FOUR: DISCUSSION

After each pupil has performed the experiment, he should compare the results to determine whether or not the phenomenon is consistent.

STEP FIVE: REREADING

If results indicate that there are some pupils who have not accurately followed directions, the pupils should reread to discover their errors and do the experiment again step by step.

After the lesson has been satisfactorily completed, the class is ready to discuss the

---

[3] John C. Hogg, Otis E. Alley, and Charles L. Bickel, *Chemistry, A Course for High Schools* (New York: D. Van Nostrand Co., copyright 1948), p. 274. Quoted by permission of the publisher.

[4] Robert W. Fuller, Raymond B. Brownlee, and D. Lee Baker, *Elements of Physics* (Boston: Allyn and Bacon, 1953), p. 106. Quoted by permission of the publisher.

scientific principles involved in the experiment.

READING SKILL: DRAWING INFERENCES

STEP ONE: READINESS

The teacher can prepare the class for reading the selection by discussing why many distributors of food prepackage or wrap all foods they display. Pupils will probably mention the danger of contamination from handling by customers or from flies. It should be suggested that there may be another reason why local health suggestions usually require that most perishable foods be packaged or displayed in an enclosed display case.

STEP TWO: CONCEPT DEVELOPMENT

The meanings of the following words and concepts should be clarified before the pupils begin to read. These words and phrases should always be presented in written context.

microscopic	*original formation*
germs	*carbon dioxide*
decay	*minerals*
chemical	*ptomaine poison*
compounds	

STEP THREE: SILENT READING

The pupils should be asked to figure out from the facts in the selection the answer to the following question:

What is a third reason for packaging or covering food in stores? ". . . When the *microscopic germs* that float about in the air settle on foods, they start *decay*. The materials in the goods are broken up to form new *chemical compounds*. Some of them are the same as those which entered into the *original formation* of the foods; namely, *carbon dioxide*, water, and *minerals*. When decay takes place, new compounds with bad odors are also produced, and the food changes in taste. The food may even become poisonous. *Ptomaine poison* is an example of this."[5]

STEP FOUR: DISCUSSION

In the ensuing discussion some pupils will probably say that the answer is not stated. Others who have arrived at the correct answer should then explain how they reached the conclusion that food is wrapped as a protection against contact with the air as well as with persons, animals, and insects.

STEP FIVE: REREADING

Those pupils who did not make the correct inference will reread to find the facts from which the inference was drawn.

[5] Ira C. Davis, John Burnett, and E. Wayne Gross, *Science* (New York: Henry Holt and Co., 1952), p. 514. Quoted by permission of the publisher.

READING AND MATHEMATICS
Russell J. Call and Neal A. Wiggin

The teaching of the general topic of solving word problems in mathematics is often

Reprinted from *The Mathematics Teacher*, LIX (Feb. 1966), 149–157, with permission of the authors and *The Mathematics Teacher*.

a topic of discussion at meetings of mathematics teachers. In an effort to collect data which might suggest areas for curriculum revision and improvement, the study described in this article was conducted by Dr. Russell

J. Call, Chairman of the Mathematics Department at Winnacunnet High School, Hampton, New Hampshire, and Mr. Neal A. Wiggin, House Coordinator at Hampton.

The purpose of the experiment was to determine whether there is some correlation between a student's ability to solve word problems in second year algebra and the presence or absence of special reading instruction. In particular, the experiment hoped to show that the instruction in reading would contribute to the development of skills in solving word problems.

Before any experiment is carried out, there ought to be some clear understanding of the learning theory involved, in order to discover whether or not the instructional techniques and the inferences make sense psychologically. The premises upon which this study is based are not inconsistent with Gestalt psychology.

The first step was to define the problem which we hoped to solve. We noted that students who had a high degree of proficiency in performing mathematical operations were considerably less proficient in solving word problems. There is obviously some different factor or factors at work in such situations. To state unequivocally that the problem is one of reading is risky or highly suppositious; of particular interest is the fact that students who can read all the words still have difficulty in solving the problem. Thus, the source of trouble is not entirely vocabulary, since all could identify the words and define them. What, then, is the problem? It may be that lack of reading comprehension is involved, since we know that there can be considerable discrepancy between vocabulary scores and comprehension scores on standardized reading tests.

Words are linguistic signs which call up or reactivate a memory trace; they are symbols of concepts. In and of themselves, words are nothing; they derive their meanings from the context in which they are found. The mathematical context is, or may be, quite different from some other context. Thus, mathematics reading presents some special denotations— denotations which must call into play the proper traces if inhibition is to be minimized. The technique, then, must be such that conceptualization provoked by the words must be consonant with the mathematical context. It becomes a problem akin to translation, as the sample lesson plans will show.

We settled upon the following experimental method because of its practicality within our school. First of all, one of us, Dr. Call, is a teacher of mathematics. The other, Mr. Wiggin, is a teacher of English with some specialization in the field of reading. It might, then, be possible to select two classes of comparable abilities and use one group as a control and the other as an experimental group. The next question is to consider at what level the experiment should be conducted. We decided upon a course in second-year algebra: (1) Students in second-year algebra are usually among our better students, both in mathematics and in other subject areas; thus we might reasonably expect that there would be less likelihood of widespread reading deficiency or widespread deficiency in mathematics, as there would be in general mathematics classes, for instance. (2) Since one of us, Mr. Wiggin, had never studied second-year algebra, even in high school, we concluded that this would be desirable for the reason that the instruction given in Mr. Wiggin's section would not benefit from any great familiarity with methods of teaching mathematics; thus any significant results would further emphasize the reading factor, rather than a difference in mathematical approach. (3) Lastly, as a matter of practicality, it would be easier to schedule classes on this basis, since the comparability of groups was less likely in other mathematics courses in the school.

Certain information necessary in the development of the experiment was already available in guidance files. For example, we needed to know what factors in intelligence and aptitude, as well as in previous achievement, might have a bearing on our experiment, particularly as it applied to establishing comparability between the groups. After compiling the available data, we "paired off" a student in the control group with a student in the experimental group. In this way, we could establish individual, as well as group, comparability.

The instruction in both groups lasted for ten days. During that time neither teacher consulted with the other relative to methods in use. This precaution may not have been necessary, but we had concluded that it might be possible for either of us to be influenced by what we knew was taking place in the other class.

There is one other factor which we wished to overcome as much as could be reasonably expected; that is what is known as the Hawthorne effect. In substance, what the Hawthorne effect means is that a noticeable difference is likely to occur in any experimental situation wherein the subjects are aware that they are involved in an experiment. To avoid this problem, we agreed that Dr. Call would inform the group which Mr. Wiggin was to teach that he (Dr. Call) had some important work to do in the next two weeks and that Mr. Wiggin would be standing in. Thus, neither group knew that an experiment was under way.

The instruction began, and during the period of the experiment we compiled the data. We had to be sure that we had a way to measure the results. No standardized test has been constructed which is designed to measure the results, or the kinds of instructional outcomes, which we were expecting. Thus, we had to resort to teacher-made tests. Both of us contributed items to the test, but neither was aware of what the other was including in the test. This was done to prevent any conscious, or unconscious, effort to "teach for the test."

The basic text in use was *Second Course in Algebra* by Arthur W. Weeks and Jackson B. Adkins, published by Ginn and Company in 1962. For the experiment, we taught Chapter 3, "Systems of Linear Equations, Word Problems." No new procedures were employed in the control group, and an effort was made to keep the instruction as much like that of the usual procedure as possible.

Following are two sample lesson plans from the experimental group. The principle is, in general, this: Words are just symbols with a variety of meanings until they appear in context. Thus, they derive their meaning from the whole of which they are a part. We need, then, to examine the whole first before we begin any analysis of the parts. Secondly, we should note that 5 is a symbol for a concept which may be represented by the fingers on a hand, the toes on a foot, by the tabulation sign /////, by the Roman numeral V, and by the word "five." Naturally, the same concept may be represented in other ways as well. The important factor to remember is that sounds, words, and mathematical symbols may represent the same concept. More specifically, the word "equal" and the mathematical symbol "=" are represented in problems in a variety of ways. We have to examine the whole problem, and then we have to study the parts to determine which words represent concepts that may be translated into mathematical signs. Note that in a rate-time-distance problem, "equal" is sometimes expressed as ". . . the same distance," ". . . the same speed," and so on. Also, the equal concept sometimes appears in many subtle ways. For example, we have a problem in which a man leaves his home at some given time and another man leaves his home at a later time. At some point, the second overtakes the first. Here we have to learn to observe relationships. The second man traveled less time (represented by a minus sign), but traveled the same distance (represented by an equal sign). Thus, we see that the expression "overtakes" is here equivalent to "equal," and the term "later" indicates "less" and is represented by "minus." We are not presuming in these paragraphs to present the step-by-step procedure used in the classroom. These explanations will give the reader some insight into the complex factors in reading which we believe influence the success or failure of the student attempting to solve word problems.

LESSON PLAN 1

What is a mathematics problem? When most people think of mathematics, they think of numbers or numerals; they think of computations—of addition, subtraction, multiplication, square roots, and so forth. There is no question that these are parts of mathematics. These factors are operations. They are, in fact, pure mathematical concepts, which, in and of themselves, are useless.

Mathematics, to be of use, must be capable of application, and must be applied. Now, how do we apply mathematics in life? We are confronted with some kind of situation which must be resolved by the use of mathematics. It is not enough to know how to perform the operations. We must know which operations apply to a particular situation.

Suppose that I want to lay out a baseball diamond. I must know something of the standard measurements of baseball diamonds, and I must know how to construct 90 degree angles and how to find a point 60½ feet from the vertex of an angle and equidistant from two points located on the sides of the angle 90 feet from the vertex. In other words, I need to know what the situation requires and how to perform the operations in resolving it. It does me no good at all in this situation to

know how to construct a square, if I don't know how long each baseline is and how far the pitcher's mound is located from home plate.

In any situation where mathematics is to be applied, we need first of all to acquire the data involved; it is necessary to find out such things as what the following are: 90 feet, 60½ feet, right angles, and so forth. Then we must perceive the relationships between items; then we must proceed with the operations. It is not possible for us in the classroom to set up sample situations for everyone to carry out. That is, the real application of mathematics cannot be taught in class because of physical limitations. Yet, if mathematics is to be of use, we must teach the practical application of it. If we can only perform the mathematical operations, we are a very poor substitute for a machine, because one machine can outperform many of us humans.

What I am saying, in other words, is this: If you think that the value of studying math lies in the ability to compute, you are wasting your time. Machines have already replaced you. You are training to do a job that doesn't exist. Thus, we must find a suitable substitute for practical situations in order to learn the principle involved in applying mathematics.

The best means we have at present is the word problem. Instead of confronting you with a real situation, we describe the situation to you. From our description of the problem, you must decide what computations to make; then you must make them.

My job in the next few days will be to see if I can help you learn to apply mathematics. I shall not de-emphasize accuracy in performing computations; but I shall place in the number one position the learning of "what" to do; how well you do it will take second place.

If industry can find a man who is poor at computation, but an expert at discovering what computations need to be made, he'll never be without a job. A machine can do the computation. It can't do the first job.

Any subject or field has its special vocabulary. If you are to be able to solve word problems, you must know the terminology of the field. When I say "know it," I don't mean "recognize it." I mean that you must be able to paraphrase it and give an example of it. This is the only way we can determine whether you understand the terminology you are using. Today's lesson will be partly devoted to some terminology. At the same time, we will learn to make the computations which are necessary for the kind of problems which we are about to study. *First Degree or Linear Equation:* Define "Linear" (having to do with a line). A solution is equal to a pair of values of x and y which make the statement true. The equation has an unlimited number of solutions. It is represented by a line on a graph. The conditions of a problem may be represented by two equations in two variables. Then the solution must satisfy the conditions of both equations.

$$y = 3x - 4$$
$$8x + 2y + 1 = 0$$

When they have one common solution the equations are referred to as a system. The process of finding the common solution is called "solving the system of equations." If the two equations are contradictory—if they do not have a common solution—we say the system is inconsistent. (*Illustrate*) If the two equations are equivalent, a solution of one is also a solution of the other. This kind of system is called "dependent." (*Illustrate*) At this point, let's practice a few solutions using two different methods. (*Assignment*)

LESSON PLAN 2

READING THE MATHEMATICS PROBLEM

What often happens in a problem is that students supply an answer other than the one required. Look at the problems in Exercise A-2 on page 32. What does the problem ask for in numbers 18 and 19? (The authors are asking "how many pairs of values," and not "what are the values." The less discriminating reader may supply the actual values rather than the number of pairs.) In number 19, we are asked to express x in terms of u. This is analogous to expressing a given sum of money in terms of dimes or nickels. We are really asking: "How many u's make an x?" The second part of the problem asks us to find the value of u when x is given a definite value. When we give a value to x, we are applying a condition to x. We must then find the value of u which will satisfy this condition. (Students need to learn to recognize from the words the condition or conditions which apply to the situation.)

Number 22 has a strange wording. What is asked for? What must we supply for a correct answer? (Values of x and y which will satisfy the conditions expressed by all three equations.) What do we call these systems which have a common solution? (Dependent systems.)

Do Exercise B, problem 1, page 32. Note that a solution of the equation is an answer to the problem.

Note that in problem 2, solutions to the systems of equations are not answers to the problem.

In number 4, the wording is difficult. Restate the problem in your own words so that we know that you understand what is asked for. (Possible answer: We have to find some whole number value of y. There is probably more than one value of y. The one we select will have to give us a value of x that is less than 1.) What are the conditions which apply to y? (It must be the smallest whole number which will make x have a value less than 1.) What are the conditions which apply to x? (It must be smaller than 1.)

What is asked for in number 6, on page 33? (This problem is stated in a negative fashion: "Show that no pair of values of x and y satisfies the three equations . . ." We must show that this system of equations is inconsistent.)

What is the condition applied to the equation system in number 7? ("Find the value that a must have if the three equations are to have a common solution." The condition is that they all must have a common solution.)

What is asked for in number 10? Note that we ask how many solutions, not what is the solution. Restate each part of the problem in your own words. What is the mathematical sign indicated by "the sum of"? What word represents the minus sign? (Dif-

ference) What sign is indicated by the word equal? How many different conditions apply to a? to b? to c?

What conditions apply to x in number 11?

What conditions apply to y? Note that these are simultaneous conditions.

The foregoing may be of some help in understanding the nature of the instruction in the experimental group. In all cases, the purpose was to get the meaning from the context by seeing the relationship between the parts and the whole. Mathematical signs are symbols of relationships, as well as of operations. Thus, the meaning is not readily translated from words to mathematical symbols until the relationships between the parts are clear. So much for procedure! A seven-question test was administered at the end of the experiment. The first two items were systems of equations; the last five were word problems. The first three tables indicate some of the more useful data.

Table 2 shows the initial analysis figures. Since we are dealing with reading comprehension as well as with mathematics, we have taken into account both the number of problems correctly solved and the number in which the procedure was correct but computational errors led to a wrong solution. It is reasonable to assume that if the student translated the reading into the correct mathe-

TABLE 1

ANALYSIS OF A FREQUENCY DISTRIBUTION OF WORD PROBLEM TEST SCORES OF 44 STUDENTS IN SECOND YEAR ALGEBRA CLASSES: ARITHMETIC MEAN AND STANDARD DEVIATION

Raw Score	Frequency (f)	Deviation (d)	fd	fd²
13	0	9	0	0
12	2	8	16	128
11	0	7	0	0
10	1	6	6	36
9	3	5	15	75
8	4	3	12	36
7	5	2	10	20
6	2	1	2	2
5	4	0	0	0
4	6	−1	− 6	6
3	4	−2	− 8	16
2	5	−3	−15	45
1	2	−4	− 8	32
0	6	−5	−30	150
	44		− 6	546

A.M.: 4.86
S.D.: 3.52
Median: 4

Approximate reliability coefficient of test, based on arithmetic mean, standard deviation, and number of items is .60.

The number of items used to compile these data is 18. Though there were only seven questions, there were 18 separate items which we scored.

TABLE 2

DATA ANALYSIS SHEET
(Figures based on 19-member control group and 25-member experimental group)

	Control Group	Experimental Group
Number of problems correct..	12	46
Number of procedures correct	24	69
Average number of problems correct	.63	1.8
Average number of procedures correct	1.26	2.6

TABLE 3

DIFFICULTY AND DISCRIMINATIVE POWER OF TEST ITEMS FOR
44-PUPIL DISTRIBUTION

Item Number	Number Correct			Index		
	Upper Half	Lower Half	Sum	Upper-Lower Difference	Difficulty	Discrimination
3	11	3	14	8	31	18
4	16	2	18	14	41	31
5	14	3	17	11	38	25
6	8	1	9	7	20	15
7	2	0	2	2	4	4

This table is listed for the purpose of determining whether the test items constructed by one teacher were any more difficult than those constructed by the other. There might be a possibility that the teacher of reading had made the items so that they were more readily understandable by the pupils. If this were so, both groups should have performed better on those items. The data do not seem to indicate this.

matical equation, he understood the problem. From that point on, if he made an error, we counted the procedure correct, but the answer wrong. For our purposes, it seems important to know some comparative data on what pupils did on the reading, as well as upon the computations. Thus we discover, in addition to the above data, that in the control group 63 percent were not able to solve any of the problems correctly, and 42 percent did not have any of the procedures correct; in the experimental group, however, only 20 percent got no correct solutions, and only 6 percent were unable to get any correct procedures.

The discriminative power of a test item is represented by the difference between the number of above-average and below-average pupils answering it correctly. These numbers are converted into percentages of the total group. Above-average and below-average are determined by the performance on the total test, and have nothing to do with external data. Thus, on item 3, eleven of those who scored in the upper half on the test also got item 3 correct, whereas only three of those who scored in the lower half got that item correct. According to J. Raymond Gerberich, in his book, *Measurement and Evaluation in the Modern School*, items are usually rated satisfactory individually when they have indices of discrimination of at least 10, but the average of such indices for

TABLE 4

COMPARATIVE SCORES USING READING LEVEL
AS A CONTROL

	Control Group	Experimental Group
1.	0	1
2.	2	8
3.	9	4
4.	4	2
5.	4	9
6.	8	9
7.	0	8
8.	7	7
9.	4	12
10.	0	3
11.	5	10
12.	7	5
13.	2	7
14.	3	6
15.	7	5
	$\overline{62}$	$\overline{96}$
A.M.	4.14	6.4

These scores are paired on the basis of the Co-operative Reading Test "Level" score, with not more than three points variation between scores. The actual average variation is 1.3 percentile points. Only 40 percent of the control group scored above the 4.86 mean of the two groups combined; 73.3 percent of the experimental group scored above this mean.

TABLE 5

COMPARATIVE SCORES USING VERBAL SCORE
OF DAT AS CONTROL

	Control Group	Experimental Group
1.	0	7
2.	2	4
3.	9	3
4.	0	8
5.	4	4
6.	4	2
7.	8	6
8.	0	3
9.	7	1
10.	4	9
11.	0	4
12.	5	3
13.	7	5
14.	3	9
15.	0	12
	53	80
A.M.	3.5	5.3

These scores are paired on the basis of the verbal score from the DAT, with not more than three points variation between scores. The actual average variation is 1.8 percentile points. 33.3 percent of the control group fall above the 4.86 mean; 46.6 percent of the experimental group fall above the 4.86 mean.

all items in a test should probably be above 10, preferably around 15. The average here is 18.6.

Item difficulty is usually expressed as the percentage of pupils in the above-average and below-average groups combined who answer the item correctly. Thus, the number of correct answers to each item is divided by the total number of pupils in the group to obtain the index of item difficulty. In general, items ranging from 30 to 90 percent of correct responses, with an average of 70 percent, are considered acceptable in difficulty for objective classroom tests. However, we should note that if a test is to measure effectively, there must be some items of very low discrimination power and/or difficulty in order to reach the poorest performer and the best performer. The average here is 27 percent.

There is nothing here to indicate that the items constructed by one teacher were easier than those constructed by the other.

Additional data appear in the tables that follow. In order to be as objective as possible in all conclusions, we have exerted every effort to show that the results might have come from some source other than the type of instruction used. The evidence, however, seems to be overwhelmingly in favor of the instructional techniques employed in the experimental group!

Since a number of variables are involved in this experiment, it was necessary to examine the results with the variables controlled. For example, since this was an experiment in the teaching of reading to a mathematics

TABLE 6

COMPARATIVE SCORES WHEN DAT QUANTITATIVE SCORE IS CONTROLLED

	Control Group	Experimental Group
1.	0	3
2.	2	8
3.	9	7
4.	0	4
5.	4	1
6.	4	9
7.	8	6
8.	0	8
9.	7	9
10.	4	2
11.	5	6
12.	7	7
13.	2	12
14.	3	5
15.	0	2
16.	7	5
	62	94
A.M.	3.9	5.88

These scores are paired on the basis of the Quantitative Score from the DAT, with not more than three points variation between scores. The actual average variation is .4 percentile points. 37.5 percent of the control group fall above the 4.86 mean; 66.6 percent of the experimental group fall above the 4.86 mean.

TABLE 7

COMPARATIVE SCORES WHEN I.Q. IS CONTROLLED

	Control Group	Experimental Group
1.	0	4
2.	2	4
3.	9	8
4.	0	9
5.	4	2
6.	8	12
7.	0	3
8.	0	8
9.	0	7
10.	0	8
11.	5	10
12.	7	4
13.	3	3
14.	7	5
15.	1	7
	46	94
A.M.	3.1	6.2

These scores are paired on the basis of I.Q. scores on the Otis Gamma, with not more than three points variation between scores. Actual average variation is 1.6 points. 33.3 percent of the control group and 73.3 percent of the experimental group fall above the 4.86 mean.

class, the reading ability of the subjects needed to be measured; then we paired off the subjects, one from each group, on the basis of the level of comprehension as measured by the Cooperative Reading Test. The pairs do not vary more than three percentile points; in fact, the average variation between pairs was 1.3 percentile points. Thus, for all practical purposes, it can be assumed that the reading levels were the same. Table 4 shows the results of this comparison. The two columns show the test scores on the math achievement test when the reading level is controlled. The mean score of the control group was 4.14, whereas the mean score for the experimental group was 6.4. To further solidify the significance of these results, we made a similar comparison using the verbal score of the DAT. This was done to discover whether those in one group had a greater aptitude for learning material presented in a verbal manner as opposed to a mathematical manner. If the experimental group had had a greater aptitude for verbal material, the results would have been inconclusive. Table 5 shows the comparison of the math achievement scores when this verbal factor was controlled. The mean score of the control group was 3.5; the mean score of the experimental group was 5.3. Since the pairing was done with no more than three percentile points between any two subjects (actual average variation was 1.8 points), we can assume, for all practical purposes, that there was no difference in verbal aptitude between the groups.

Another factor which had to be examined under controlled conditions was the aptitude of each group for mathematical reasoning. Obviously, if one group was better than the other in this respect, the results could not then be attributed to the difference in instructional techniques. Table 6 shows the comparison when the pairs are controlled on the basis of the quantitative score from the DAT. Pairings were so nearly identical that the mean variation on the quantitative score between each set was .4 percentile points. We were able to match sixteen pairs of students in this manner. Note that the experimental group did considerably better, with a mean score on the mathematics test of 5.88, whereas the mean score of the control group was 3.9.

Finally, we made a similar pairing on the basis of I.Q. scores from the Otis Gamma. Here we are able to match fifteen pairs, with an average variation of 1.6 points. Insofar as measurable intelligence is concerned, this is considerably closer than we had hoped to get. Thus, for all practical purposes, the groups were identical in intelligence. Again, the control group scored lower than the experimental group. In fact, the mean score is doubled by the experimental group. No matter how you slice it, the results point to a better response by the group which was taught reading.

Let us summarize the experiment and see what tentative conclusions can be drawn. Two groups were taught the same unit in second year algebra, a unit involving linear equations and word problems. The control group was taught by an experienced mathematics teacher, chairman of the mathematics department at Winnacunnet High School. The experimental group was taught by an English teacher with a limited amount of training in the teaching of reading and with no training in the teaching of mathematics. In fact, he had never had a course in Algebra II. The major difference in instructional techniques was the fact that the experimental group was taught to get the meaning from the words and translate it into mathematical symbols. This was done more in the manner of the teaching of reading than that of the teaching of mathematics. The results seem to indicate that the experimental group did better, even when reading abilities and mathematical aptitude were controlled. We make the following inferences from the data acquired:

1. There is some merit in teaching special reading skills for the solution of mathematical problems
2. Even very good readers, as measured by the Cooperative Reading Test, have difficulty in the interpretation of the kind of reading found in word problems
3. Part of the difficulty which teachers encounter in the teaching of mathematics comes from a special kind of reading disability which does not appear on standard measuring instruments
4. Part of the difficulty which teachers encounter in the teaching of mathematics is that they are not equipped to teach reading
5. If by teaching reading, instead of mathematics, we can get better results, it seems reasonable to infer that the competent mathematics teacher might get considerably better results if he were trained to teach reading of the kind encountered in mathematics problems

We also suggest that this experiment has some cogent implications for further testing. An experiment done on a much larger scale might be of significant value in making recommendations for the improvement of teacher education and in-service training. It is time we took note of the necessity for studying relationships between disciplines where no relation has seemed apparent. The experiment further points up the need for a fundamental, but good, developmental reading program in which a trained reading specialist can help to prepare materials which will improve reading skills in all subject areas. All our classes have textbooks; all our students are expected to be able to read them; yet, in the vast majority of cases, not even the high school English teacher has had any training in the teaching of reading skills. How, then, may we expect the student to come from the elementary school and continue to improve his reading skills when he is offered no instruction for that purpose? This study has shown that mathematics is one such area where reading instruction may be enormously beneficial.

SOLVING READING PROBLEMS IN VOCATIONAL SUBJECTS
Isidore N. Levine

Many teachers of trade subjects in the vocational high schools are convinced that their students can't read. The pupils show their inadequacies by being unable to cope with the texts provided for them. They indicate their limitations by their failures on the final written examinations. They are unable to read the job sheets that can be crucial in daily shop work. Every teacher would like to see some improvement in this deplorable situation.

Some shop teachers feel that reading is the job of the teacher of English. He teaches spelling, composition, vocabulary and literature—all the elements comprising the study of reading. Why doesn't the English teacher do his job well enough to solve the reading difficulties the students experience in other subjects? Perhaps the language arts teacher would assume such responsibility if he were certain he could do the work required. However, mere willingness to teach "reading" does not solve special problems to be met in instructing pupils in the art of getting meaning from a page of trade information.

SPECIALIZED VOCABULARY

What are some of those problems? Suppose we take electric wiring as a possible trade subject for teaching reading. The class in En-

Reprinted from *High Points*, XLII (April 1960), 10–27, with permission of the author and *High Points*.

glish is taught to recognize the words "splice," "junction," "tap," "tee," "knotted," "pigtail," and "Western Union." The dictionary definitions of these words are as follows:

splice—joining of ropes or timbers by overlapping

junction—joining or being joined, station

tap—(1) strike lightly (2) a stopper or plug (3) tool for cutting internal screw threads

tee—a mark from which a golf player starts, a little mound of sand and dirt

knotted—(1) joined (2) tangled. (There are eight other definitions the teacher of English could rule out as being unrelated to electrical work.)

pigtail—braid of hair hanging from the head

Western Union—a telegraph company

The final electrical wiring examination includes this typical question:

> To make a splice in a junction box where a number of wire leads are to be joined, the best splice to use is the (a) tap or tee (b) knotted tap (c) pigtail (d) Western Union.

No combination of definitions will yield a solution to the problem for the ambitious teacher of English. We can go farther and say that even accompanying illustrations for each of these splices would still leave the language arts instructor feeling that he was teaching an unfamiliar language.

Lest some teachers suppose that the electrical trades have the only occupational information the English teacher cannot read, we will take an example from the radio and television field. A recent final test in that subject carried this question:

> In a 100% modulated AM transmitter the modulator varies the carrier (a) from zero to the strength of the carrier, (b) from zero to twice the strength of the carrier, (c) from zero to half the strength of the carrier, (d) does not vary.

As an English teacher, the writer cannot help admiring any pupil who has the knowledge and understanding to read the above intelligently—not as an academic studies teacher would read it, that is, with correct pronunciation, phrasing, inflection and emphasis, but with the meaning necessary to arrive at a correct answer and to be able to explain the reason for such selection.

As a matter of fact, the above passage takes the writer back to his high school Latin study days, when he could "read" the orotund phrases of Caesar's Commentaries with little inkling as to what that ancient was trying to communicate. In the case of radio and television, there is no Latin "pony" to help understand the above question. We can go farther here and state that no application of the thousand and one skills of reading so exhaustively described in the new Board of Education Curriculum Bulletin, "Reading Grades 7–8–9. A Teacher's Guide to Curriculum Planning," can be of any help here. Reading the above properly means studying the subject.

Perhaps other examples from the trade subjects will make this situation even clearer. In the pamphlet on "Machine Shop Practice for Vocational High Schools" (Curriculum Bulletin #10—1954–1955 Series) on page 82, we find the following in part:

Unit—How to Turn Tapers by the Offset Tailstock Method

Topic—Checking Offset with Dividers

1. Set the legs of the dividers to the required offset. Adjust set-over screws until the distance between the index line on the base and the index line on the tailstock body corresponds to the setting of the dividers.

Here the teacher of English is not too puzzled since the number of technical references is limited and there is an accompanying series of illustrations with the directions. But after calling out the words and studying the drawings we are still far from a complete understanding of this first step. These directions are not meant to be read and discussed. They are useless without the equipment to which they can be applied as far as instruction is concerned.

Another illustration from still another trade will throw light on still another facet of this problem. In the course of study called "Hairdressing and Cosmetology for Vocational High Schools" (Curriculum Bulletin #8—1952–1953 Series) we note the Instruction Sheet on page 85 includes this series of steps:

FACIAL MASSAGE
Steps in Facial

1. Apply cleansing cream	6. Remove massage cream
2. Give manipulation for cleansing	7. Apply astringent
3. Remove cream	8. Apply powder base
4. Apply massage cream	9. Apply makeup
5. Give massage manipulation	

Points to Remember
Apply cream with an upward and outward movement. To remove cream dab at it lightly with tissues.

As a male teacher of English it might be a little embarrassing to study this with a class of girls, but there would be little difficulty in interpreting and understanding the words. Here at last is a trade sheet we can read. But, would it be wise to take the time in the English classroom for this? Like Shakespeare's plays, these directions are not meant to be read aloud only. They are supposed to be *acted* out and certainly not in an English room except in pantomime. And further, the trade of cosmetology has its own foreign language. Among the terms to be studied by a language-arts teacher determined to give proper reading guidance in this occupation are included:

> free edge, keratin, lunula, nippers, oil glove, pledget, French twist, effilating, sebum, bias wave, reverse roll, cuticle of hair

and hundreds of others which take years to learn properly.

VOCATIONS AND THE LANGUAGE ARTS

We have not discussed some of the implications of the English teacher's efforts to teach the reading of vocational subjects in the language-arts class. The woodworking boy who wants to know why his English teacher is taking the time to have his students read the expressions below would be compelling us to reexamine our goals in vocational education:

> Explain how to make a mortise on a leg
> List the first five steps in squaring a piece of wood to size
> Draw a marking gauge
> Name five different types of lines used in making a drawing
> Give three uses of the hack saw
> Draw a combination square

Do we want our vocational students to have a restricted curriculum involving trade experiences exclusively? Would any teacher of English accept appointment to a vocational high school knowing that he would be expected to familiarize himself sufficiently with the trades taught in that school to be able to teach the reading matter of those shops?

In desperation some shop subjects chairmen might suggest that the English teacher should interest himself in the trades of the school. They may not be impressed with the argument that the teacher of English selected his subject just as the trade teacher did, that is, because of a personal interest or talent in that field of study. Nor may it be important that the language arts instructor spent many years studying and preparing for the teaching of literature and composition. However, we may well ask such chairmen whether we have the right to deprive the vocational high student of his share of appreciation of the cultural products of writers in every field of literary expression.

The shop teacher presented with this situation might adopt one or both of the attitudes below:

1. The English teacher should teach pupils to recognize words, not teach the meaning of the words in a technical sense.
2. The English teacher should teach pupils the general skills of reading, such as selecting main ideas in a paragraph, reading for details, skimming, reading in phrases, reading with a purpose, reading to understand and follow directions, and many others; in sum, to develop those skills which some experts claim can be transferred from one type of reading matter to another.

WORD RECOGNITION IN CONTEXT

In answer to the first view, teachers of English claim that they are doing their utmost to assist students to use the various skills of word recognition when these skills are needed in the reading of literature in the language arts classes. For example, in the study of O. Henry's short story, "Gift of the Magi," the pupil meets the phrase "imputation of parsimony" in the first paragraph. The teacher will help the students analyze the parts of each difficult word (*im-pu-ta-tion*) (*par-si-mony*) where such analysis is needed. Then he will go on to discuss with the class the meaning of this phrase in the complete picture of that first paragraph. He will select as many such word groups for study as he thinks are material for the appreciation of an O. Henry story, with the hope that the student will be stimulated to look up such phrases as, "instigates the moral reflection," "with sniffles predominating," "on the lookout for the mendicancy squad," and numerous others.

If the trade instructor were to suggest that the English teacher take the opportunity to teach such word recognition skills using the technical terms of the shops, the answer would be that this learning activity would be a waste of time for teacher and student. As we have seen above, the English teacher does not merely analyze the word elements in "imputation of parsimony." What is more important is that he spends valuable class time discussing the meaning of the words as used in *that paragraph* of the story. If the teacher of English were merely to attempt analysis of the oral elements of the technical terms, he would be giving little assistance to the shop teacher anxious to have his students read for understanding. The pupils could call out the words from the examination of radio as smoothly as the teacher and still be no farther into reading the question than when they first started the analysis of words like "modulating."

TRANSFER OF TRAINING

Going on to the suggestion that the English instructor train students in the general skills of reading other than word recognition, it can be said that such practice is given in most English classes in the vocational high schools. Most schools are equipped with reading workbooks which are used to develop the general reading skills used in informational reading. However, it has yet to be determined that any such training can be carried over into the other fields of study included in the vocational school curriculum.

Let us take an example from such work-

books to reveal the possibilities of transfer of training in reading. One of the many such used in the high schools is the Scott, Foresman text called "Basic Reading Skills for High School Use" (Revised Edition, 1958). Included in this text are 18 sections, each devoted to a different reading skill such as Main Idea, Summarizing and Organizing, Word Analysis, Phrase and Sentence Meaning, etc. Suppose we turn to the section called Relationships (cause-effect, sequence). Within this section are included twelve reading selections varying in length from 150 to 1,700 words. The titles of these passages indicate that two of them are stories (A Fish Story, Old Three Toes), nine are informational essays (The Dust Storm, The Flood, The First Basketball Game, Fire-Boats to the Rescue, It's the Ham in Them, The Giants of the Galapagos, Who Is Handicapped?, and Collecting Animal Tracks) and one is a biographical sketch (Thirteen). Students are asked to read these selections and answer questions specially prepared to develop the ability to see cause and effect relationship and sequence of ideas in stories.

It is doubtful that a student who has read all these selections and scored a high percentage of correct answers is any nearer to understanding his trade text or has become more skillful in seeing cause-effect relationships in his radio work. The thinking processes to be used in these selections are not the same reasoning skills to be applied to the trade subjects. To be specific, a reading of the most technical of these essays, "It's the Ham in Them," which is concerned with amateur radio operators, is followed by such nontechnical deductions as these:

1. Why might a shut-in enjoy operating a "ham" radio outfit as a hobby?
2. Why would "ham" radio operators be valuable in any community in an emergency?
3. Why might being a "ham" be valuable to you as an individual?

Compare these questions with the following appended to chapters from the text "Elements of Radio" by Abraham and William Marcus (Prentice-Hall, 1952):

1. Why cannot the magnetic field of an electromagnet be used to send wireless messages in a practical manner?
2. Why must a reproducer be used in a radio receiver?
3. Why must a receiver have a detector?

The first set of questions can be answered without reading the text if one knows, as is explained in the first sentence of the paragraph, that a "ham" is an amateur radio operator. The latter set of questions carries no clue to the answer without the reader's having some previous knowledge and information to be obtained only in a graded course of study such as a trade subject curriculum provides.

The writer believes that most authorities who assume transfer of training in reading skills fail to take account of the cumulative knowledge of technical words and phrases needed to draw meaning from a paragraph in a textbook.

To be specific, when an English teacher uses a workbook such as "Unit Drills for Reading Comprehension" by R. Goodman (Keystone Education Press, 1955) with its 45 paragraphs and accompanying thought test questions, he is supposing that the student brings to each selection only a general knowledge of things. In fact, the pupil is expected to confine his thinking to the items in the paragraph. Thus, in the paragraph below (Paragraph 2, page 27):

If you watch a lamp which is turned very rapidly on and off, and you keep your eyes open, persistence of vision will bridge the gaps of darkness between the flashes of light, and the lamp will seem to be continuously lit. This optical afterglow explains the magic produced by the stroboscope, a new instrument which seems to freeze the swiftest motions while they are still going

on, and to stop time itself dead in its tracks. The magic is all in the eye of the beholder.

The thought questions bearing on this selection are:

The "magic" of the stroboscope is due to (1) continuous lighting, (2) intense cold, (3) slow motion, (4) behavior of the human eye, (5) a lapse of time.
"Persistence of vision" is explained by (1) darkness, (2) winking, (3) rapid flashes, (4) gaps, (5) afterimpression.

We will note two points here. First, the author has included no technical terms or phrases which he has not explained, or which could not be found in an ordinary dictionary. Second, there is no graded block of knowledge on which this paragraph depends for clarity of understanding.

Turning to a textbook in the trade, the above-mentioned text on elements of radio, let us study some typical paragraphs:

All the above methods of communication suffer from one common fault; they are useful only over comparatively short distances, a few miles at best. (p. 1)
Having mastered the theory of the crystal receiver, we are now ready to go ahead. If you have constructed the receiver described here and "listened in" on it, you must be aware that the crystal detector has shortcomings. First of all, it is difficult to manipulate. Not every spot will work. You must move the catwhisker about for some time before you touch a spot which enables you to hear radio signals in your phones. (p. 100)
The problem, therefore, is to devise a system that will build up the signal before it reaches the detector. (p. 200)
But corresponding points on each vertical arm are struck simultaneously and, therefore, the electrons are set flowing in these arms in the same direction at the same time (*up* in Fig. 199) and with equal pressure. Since the electron streams in each of the vertical arms are equal and flow toward each other, these streams cancel themselves out; hence we have no electron flow into the receiver, and, therefore, nothing can be heard. (p. 300)

You will notice in Figure 281 that in both curves the electromotive force and current reach their maximum in the same direction at the same time and are likewise at zero at the same time. When the electromotive force and current have this relationship to each other, we say that they are *in phase*. (p. 400)

On the other hand, the further up we go, the rarer the air gets—that is, there are fewer molecules in any volume. Beyond a distance of 200 miles from the earth's surface, there probably are so few molecules that ionization is virtually nil. So we see that the ionosphere is a layer or region beginning at about 60 miles beyond the surface of the earth and extending about 200 miles beyond the surface of the earth. (p. 500)

If some of the voltage from the bottom end of the coil is fed through a small variable capacitator (Cn), called a neutralizing capacitator, onto the grid of the tube, neutralization is achieved. The neutralizing capacitator controls the amount of voltage so fed to insure that it is just enough to neutralize that arising from the capacitance of the electrodes. Since this neutralizing voltage comes from the plate circuit, this method is called *plate neutralization*. (p. 600)

This continues until a whole series of bright spots, corresponding to the outline of the shore, have appeared on the screen of the tube. Since the screen of the cathode-ray tube is of the high-persistence type, the bright spots will remain for some time after the sweep has moved on to other angular positions. The result then would be a picture of the area surrounding the ship, whose position is indicated by the center of the screen. (p. 689)

Certain points should be made with respect to these paragraphs. The first paragraph is a sentence which has meaning only when read with the previous related sentences. The second paragraph notes the existence of a body of knowledge which must be brought to bear on subsequent pages for proper understanding. The third paragraph is again a sentence which states a problem developed at some length in previous paragraphs. It has little meaning in isolation, but is necessary for summation. Paragraph four refers to an illustration and demands a special type of reading rarely found in workbooks used in the English class. Here, the pupil's eyes and thoughts must shift from print to picture, a skill developed by comicbook readers but not usable for this text even by the most avid devotee of this art form. The fifth paragraph develops a technical term which may be the key to future pages in the book. Unfortunately the authors do not include this item in the index. Paragraph six leads the reader to believe that the authors are no longer discussing elements of radio. It contains a number of concepts which are clear only to a student of previous pages. The seventh paragraph would probably be double talk to most students in their third year of science. The last paragraph appears easy to understand, but it has a few terms which may or may not be keys to proper understanding of the passage: *e.g.*, "cathode ray tube," "high persistence type," "sweep" and "angular positions." The writer is not sufficiently conversant with the ideas to decide whether those technical words are the solution to the meaning of the paragraph. He is in the same position as an individual who has read a paragraph in a novel and attempts to compare his understanding of it with that of a person who has read the complete narrative. A typical example of this would be the following:

> Tom went to bed that night planning vengeance against Alfred Temple; for with shame and repentance Becky had told him all, not forgetting her own treachery; but even the longing for vengeance had to give way soon to pleasanter musings, and he fell asleep at last with Becky's latest words lingering dreamily in his ear—"Tom, how could you be so noble!"

A junior high school pupil who has read *Tom Sawyer* with understanding would be able to explain that paragraph more clearly than a college student who had never taken the opportunity to follow the adventures of that Mark Twain hero. There is little to indicate the true age, character, or motives of the individuals mentioned. The college student would not know what Becky's "treachery" encompassed, or what "planned vengeance" included.

GUIDED GROWTH IN READING

If then, we come to the conclusion that the English teacher cannot help teach reading in the trade subjects, what other solutions are there to our problem? Let us examine the conclusions of some authorities on the subject.

1. Mr. Herman Hall in his book, *Trade Training in School and Plant* (Century Company, 1930) has this to say about the problem:

> As far as the writer knows there are few if any textbooks that are likely to be of service to the trade instructor in his teaching. There are many books which may be valuable if used as reference books for occasional use in connection with some definite job.
>
> The academic instructor in the high school has all too often "gotten by" in his work with the help of a well-written textbook used as a sort of crutch to hold him up. Such instructors are prone to assign "pages so-and-so for tomorrow's lesson." If the instructor himself learns those pages, or even contrives to have them before him, he can sample his learner's ability to repeat the material contained in the pages. Such teaching will not meet the objectives of trade instruction.
>
> . . . Textbooks as such have little place in trade education . . .

2. "Guideposts in Vocational High School," a pamphlet issued by the Board of Education in 1946 states:

> Teachers of all subjects, especially English, should guide the student's growth in reading. (As we have seen above, teachers of English in most vocational high schools have taken practical steps to follow that suggestion.)

3. *Methods of Teaching Industrial Subjects* (Gerald B. Leighbody, Delmar Publishers, 1946) decries this practice:

> Some teachers follow the practice of assigning pages in text or reference books to be studied outside of regular school hours. The mere reading of material is no guarantee of comprehension or retention.

4. In the bulletin of June 1952 entitled, "Instruction in English and Speech," (page 57) it is stated that,

> It is the opinion of the committee, however, that the problem of reading cannot be solved by the teacher of English in isolation. English is to a degree a tool subject; so to a degree are other subjects. It cannot be assumed that because teachers of English teach vocabulary, pupils will know the meaning of all words, or will understand the special vocabulary and concepts of other subjects. All departments must know the factors involved in the reading process and must take direct application of the skills which are taught in the English class.

5. The authors of "Machine Shop Practice for Vocational High Schools," Board of Education Curriculum Bulletin #10, 1954–55 Series, have this to say about the problem:

> The systematic use of instruction sheets helps students learn to read and follow written directions. (page 71)
>
> Mention of references is one means of stimulating curiosity about the subject matter and of leading pupils to subject matter that will supplement instruction. However, on the instruction sheet or otherwise, the teacher should suggest only reading that is available and within the student's comprehension. (page 81)
>
> It is necessary to bear in mind that many pupils have difficulty in getting information and direction from the printed page; they prefer to depend on spoken language. However, the ability to follow written material is an important part of the equipment of the machine shop worker. . . .
>
> Show the pupils exactly how to use the various instruction sheets. For example, if you are conducting a demonstration, have a

pupil read aloud the steps of the operation while another pupil performs each step. (page 87)

The writer is of the opinion that we should reject the advice to use little or no reading in the shops. On the other hand, few trade instructors have the time or energy to become reading experts.

SHOP TEACHER AND READING

For the shop teacher, fundamental reading tasks are involved in the job sheets which guide the pupil's work from day to day. Such instruction sheets can be made the subject of reading instruction with profit to both teacher and student. As to when such instruction can take place, it seems wise for such purposes to use the shop information period when demonstrations, lectures and discussions are an important part of the procedure.

There cannot be a blueprint for every type of reading lesson in shop subjects, or academic studies, for that matter. However, it seems to the writer that a carefully thought out lesson should contain some or all of the following steps:

1. Motivation for reading
2. Study of difficult words and concepts
3. Oral reading of the selection
4. Discussion and questioning for understanding
5. Application of knowledge gained

Let us apply these steps to the teaching of the job sheet on page 82 of the Board of Education Bulletin "Machine Shop Practice for Vocational High Schools." (The first paragraph of that job was quoted previously.)

After the teacher has explained and demonstrated the required processes orally with the use of appropriate equipment, the attention of the class is turned toward the blackboard where the teacher has written the key words of the job. Among these would be included such phrases as the following:

1. required offset
2. set-over screws
3. corresponds to the setting
4. tailstock body
5. index line
6. tailstock assembly
7. toward the headstock
8. adjust set-over screws
9. amount of offset
10. inside caliper
11. caliper setting
12. secure the tool post
13. compound rest
14. extends far enough
15. lighten spindle lock

The meaning of each of these phrases may be checked by student demonstration or verbalization. Thus in teaching set-over screws, the instructor might have the pupil point to the equipment part and give its function if that is an important part of the learning. This helps concentrate attention on the appearance and spelling of key words. The teacher can take one or two of these words for study of correct spelling by erasing them and having a student write them in again. The rest of the class can be ready for corrective work if necessary.

After these are studied, the teacher reads the sheet orally, or has a capable student read it while the rest of the class follows the reading on their own sheets. Despite the emphasis on silent reading in our schools today, there are immediate values to be derived from reading the job sheets aloud. Just as in the study of a poem the English teacher dwells on the oral reading of the verses for rhythm, color and expression, similarly the trade instructor can read for pronunciation, phrasing and emphasis.

The lesson can be closed with a series of questions designed to develop various reading skills. Many job sheets have such prepared questions, but the teacher may wish to use his knowledge of the needs and capacities of his students to formulate his own tests of understanding. The teacher might thus ask his students,

1. Where would the caliper setting be taken from?
2. How far should the set-over screws be adjusted?

It is possible that neither of those questions would be of concern to an instructor. The writer cannot claim a knowledge of the subject sufficient to decide the points of emphasis on this particular job.

The results of this learning period can be tested through the use of a short quiz given perhaps before the next job is begun. The quiz might include objective questions requiring one-word or one-phrase answers, and one or two essay questions to be answered in two or three sentences if possible. Such quizzes have value in preparing students for final or midterm examinations. In most cases they can be marked by pupils who are provided with key answers.

DEVELOPMENTAL LESSON AN AID

Two things should be noted concerning this lesson. First, this training in reading skills closely parallels the developmental lesson which is the stock-in-trade of every teacher. Second, this procedure follows the steps taken in learning a language. We begin with listening and go on to speaking, reading and writing. If it is argued that the difficult words and phrases can be explained through the use of a technical dictionary, it should be understood that mere definition too often means substituting one set of unknown words for another set. For example, the definition of a set-screw as given in the glossary of W. L. Schaaf's *The Practical Outline of Mechanical Trades* reads, "A screw, usually hardened, which is used to lock a machine part in position by pressure on the point."

However, when a set-screw is actually shown to a class and its function observed, its definition can be derived by the pupils themselves. In fact, preparing a clear definition of a term may be a test of knowledge in shop subjects. Such facility with trade language may not mean the making of a good workman, but all things being equal, a worker who can handle the language of his trade in reading and writing will probably be the more efficient mechanic.

Authorities on the subject of reading list a number of skills which should receive attention in developing the ability to follow directions. Thus, in the bulletin "Reading—Grades 7–8–9" previously mentioned, such achievements as these are listed:

1. Recognizing need for preliminary reading
2. Care for complicated or confusing statements
3. Recognizing need for understanding the purpose of each step
4. Recognizing need for second reading
5. Visualizing steps during re-reading
6. Need for final review before applying directions

Most of these excellent skills will be acquired during the process of learning to read the job sheets as outlined above.

After some success with the job sheet, the instructor might attempt to use the text or periodical for reading purposes. An arrangement might be made with the school librarian to borrow appropriate trade magazines from her files to be read, studied and discussed in class.

The writer attempted to stimulate an interest in trade periodicals through the procedure mentioned above when he taught English in a vocational high school. However, the report formulated below, one of many, to be used as a basis for oral discussion, lacked vitality because there was no authority present to evaluate the relevance of the facts or their significance to the trade.

Electrical Construction and Maintenance
Vol. 55 No. 5   May 1956

Wiring for a Service Station

If a device had to be 18 inches or more above the floor level in order to comply with the Code, is it OK to install sealing fittings as close to the floor as possible?

The Code answers this question by stating that it permits the sealing fitting to be located on either side of the boundary where the Conduit run passes from a more hazardous to a less hazardous location. The answer means that you can if the pipe or other material that you are using comes out from an ordinary run and has to pass through a room of high explosives. It must be completely sealed and as tight as the sealing fitting can go.

If we were installing lights at a baseball field, could we run No. 14 wire circuits for individual light outlets which will be lamped with 1500 watt light?

We can use No. 14 wire if we limit the load on a branch circuit to 80% at 12 amps. But if you don't want to limit the load you can use No. 12 wire, which is a safer investment.

The teacher of English never did get around to asking the electrical shop teachers whether that written report made by an eighth-term student was related to the work in the shop. However, it seems that this library lesson was profitable because many boys did testify that they learned something therefrom. The English teacher did not have time in his program to include many such periods.

What is accomplished by using the assistant to teaching afforded by a job sheet, text or trade periodical? A student who uses printed sheets or textbooks in school really has two teachers: the living instructor with his foibles and sympathies, and a silent teacher who has no psychological reactions to every-day student activities. The first implements the program of learning which the curriculum envisages for the years the student will remain in school. The second will ready our student to continue to learn long after he has left school. Neither teacher can be very effective without the other. The pupil who uses no printed matter in his shop is almost at the same disadvantage as the student who takes home study courses. If we wish to train our students to take their places in the social-economic world, we cannot deny them the reading skills and habits needed to progress with the movements in industrial development.

SUMMARY

To sum up we have tried to sketch the following points in this paper.

1. Vocational students need training in reading trade subjects.
2. The English teacher is willing but unable to provide such reading instruction.
3. The vocabulary, idioms and language of the trades demand special language arts instruction to be provided only by one who is familiar with that trade.
4. Even where language is not a barrier, reading the trade subjects requires application and activity appropriate only to a shop room.
5. The tendency to compel the English teacher to solve such problems will compel us to change our objectives in vocational education.
6. The reading skills taught in the English classroom cannot be used profitably in the trade subjects.
7. A trade text or series of job sheets accumulates a host of concepts which must be mastered to make further reading possible.
8. There are solutions to this problem which are not entirely realistic.
9. Shop teachers should attempt a sample reading lesson in their trade and make

such changes in procedure as their experiences dictate.

10. Such reading lessons will have educational perquisites which will facilitate attainment of our vocational high school objectives.

James Joyce in his novel "Portrait of the Artist as a Young Man," illustrated one of the fundamental concepts of this essay in these words (Modern Library Edition—Page 221):

The language in which we are speaking is his before it is mine. How different are the words 'home,' 'Christ,' 'ale,' 'master,' on his lips and on mine! I cannot speak or write these words without unrest of spirit. His language, so familiar and so foreign, will always be for me an acquired speech. I have not made or accepted its words. My voice holds them at bay. My soul frets in the shadow of his language.

As long as students regard their trade texts with the same feeling as the person speaking above views his teacher's language, we as instructors have failed to prepare our boys and girls for vocational competency after their school days are over.

13
Individualization in Teaching Reading

MATCHING TEN READING LEVELS IN ONE CLASSROOM
Don H. Parker, Rena King, and Ruth A. Holt

"... And if you have an average class-room, let's say a ninth grade, you probably have a range of eight or ten different reading grade levels among your pupils," said the speaker.

"Eight different reading levels—in my room? And I'm using only one textbook? Oh, no! It can't be true," thought the ninth grade English teacher in the eighteenth row back. It was a warm, early fall afternoon. Around her sat some three hundred of the county's teachers. Maybe she hadn't heard correctly. She would ask the others later. But what followed was even more disconcerting.

"You ask," continued the speaker, "how well your pupils *should* read? Possibly you are one of those who would answer, 'Well enough to read the ninth grade textbook I use.' Or, possibly you'd be willing to agree with Abe Lincoln. When still a gangling, long-legged youth, he was asked by an opponent hoping to make him appear ridiculous, 'Abe, how long should a man's legs be?' After

a moment's consideration, Lincoln replied, 'Long enough to reach the ground.'

"If we accept this analogy in reading,—in all learning, for that matter—we will stop trying to pour thirty-five students into the single mold of one textbook just because they are sitting in the same classroom. Instead, we will provide each student with material that will allow his "reading legs" to reach the solid ground of comprehending what he reads—regardless of how far down or how far up that may be. Further, we will provide him with the opportunity to progress to higher reading levels, if, as, and when his 'reading legs' grow."

The room suddenly became uncomfortably warmer. The English teacher wondered why people had to think such disturbing thoughts. Couldn't we just teach school? Yes, the library and guidance and English courses had stressed individual differences and the need for meeting them, but how, *how*, HOW?

TEN READING LEVELS IDENTIFIED
The next week the supervisor dropped into the English teacher's room for a visit. "Miss

King, I know there must be some differences in reading ability among my pupils, but I don't believe it's like our speaker at the meeting said. I wonder, though, if you'd recommend a reading test I could give and see for myself?"

A few days later the phone in the supervisor's office rang. It was the English teacher. "This is Ruth Holt at Selma School." There was a note of urgency, even anxiety in her voice. "You know those reading tests? Well, it's even worse than I had dared imagine. I don't have eight reading levels—I have ten! And they range from the third grade to beyond first-year college! What do I do now?"

The supervisor smiled. There were many things she could suggest, but was this the time and place—yet? Here was that gift of Prometheus, that fire of motivation so dear to the heart of the supervisor—a brilliant, yet human flame—demanding the greatest possible care lest it die for lack of fuel or burn itself out against some stone-like barrier. Why not get additional fuel and call in more help to remove the obstacles that are bound to arise before any really on-going, creative force? After all, is it not part of a supervisor's job to know where to go for help?

"Tell you what I'll do," Miss King said. "When I go to Chapel Hill next time, I'll ask that disturbing speaker what he would suggest that we do about it."

If this were true of one school's ninth grade, how about all the other schools? Well, one thing at a time. After all, what good was a School of Education in your own State University if you couldn't sometimes dump your troubles into its lap? And Mr. Parker, their reading consultant, had stuck his neck out, so now let's see him withdraw it gracefully—or produce!

At his office in the Reading Laboratory and Clinic, Mr. Parker showed the supervisor how college students were helped in bringing their reading levels up from as low as 6th or 7th grade to that of the average college freshman.

"If so many students are coming out of our high schools four, five or even six years retarded, so that you have to have all these special facilities for them, the high schools must be doing a pretty poor job, wouldn't you say?"

"Not that exactly," said Mr. Parker. "Let's say they're doing as well as they know how at present. You see, most of the things we know in reading are relatively new and they are just beginning to find their way out of the experimental laboratories and into the hands of people who will put them to practical, everyday use."

"But how is that ever going to happen fast enough?" queried Miss King.

"That's a job for all of us and it looks like it's happening pretty fast right here and now," replied the reading consultant. He went on to explain that each student who came to the Reading Laboratory and Clinic for help was studied to determine his present reading level and his expected reading level as determined by tests of reading ability and learning capacity. Next each student was given an opportunity to place his foot on a "reading ladder" at the level at which he was now able to read and achieve reasonable understanding. He kept daily charts of his progress. As his efficiency increased, he tackled more and more difficult materials. This same idea could be extended downward and adapted to classroom work for junior and senior high school students.

"Then, as I understand it," said Miss King, "the situation in the high schools boils down to this: First, we should be teaching certain reading skills attuned to the developmental needs of the child at each stage of his growth as he progresses through school, plus the special skills involved in reading in particular subject areas. Second, since we have failed to do this beyond the early elementary grades, we must now help students go back and acquire the skills they lack so they can begin to read as well as their learning capacity allows them."

"Exactly."

"Now that Miss Holt has found the actual, present reading abilities of her students, her next step would be to find out how well each *ought* to read with some test that does not depend entirely on reading and verbal problems to measure his learning capacity, as so many intelligence tests do?"

"Right!"

"And the next step would be to prepare materials for the students that would form a 'reading ladder' on which each could climb to his own highest level at his own rate of learning and help students understand the purpose of this activity?"

"You're on the beam!"

"We might even call it a reading laboratory in our own school, mightn't we?"

"I see no reason why it wouldn't be as much a reading laboratory for your students as this one is for college students."

TESTING AND READING

In the following weeks more data was gathered. The Diagnostic Reading Tests: Survey Section had shown reading ability ranging from grade three to grade thirteen plus with a mean of 8.0. With a grade placement of 9.5, this meant an average retardation among these ninth graders of one and one-half years! Were these youngsters just not very bright? Maybe they should not be expected to read up to the level of their grade placement? Answer: They should—provided they had acquired the necessary tool skills of reading. Why? Because their actual capacity for learning to read as shown by standardized tests of intelligence comprising *both* verbal and non-verbal factors (SRA Primary Mental Abilities) showed a reading-grade-expectancy equal to their grade placement, i.e., 9.5 (mean I.Q., 103). Armed with these facts,

the supervisor arranged for a three-way conference with the principal.

"When I see people with facts and a plan for dealing with them, I'm willing to stretch our slim budget to the breaking point," said the principal. "If you're willing to put in the time to prepare the materials you've described, the least I can do is see that you get them."

The teacher and the supervisor "set to" with a will, checking from time to time on technical details with the University's reading consultant. The Charles E. Merrill *Skilltexts* formed the basis for providing ten different reading grade levels of materials, grades three through thirteen. Finally the day came to introduce these materials to the students.

"Can each of you run as fast as the others?" Miss Holt asked the class. After discussion, there were other questions. How tall *should* a ninth grader be? What is the "normal" speed of talking? Normal? Well, it began to look as though being different were normal— normal, that is, just so long as being normal is the individual's best expression of himself in the eyes of self and society. Then came the explanation of the purposes of the new miniature reading laboratory they were to have right in their own classroom; how it enabled each student to begin right now to read successfully—and to understand what he was reading. During the reading lab period which followed, each student received a folder containing an interesting story with its comprehension check, in which he could read with 80 to 90 percent understanding, whether his ability was third grade, eighth, tenth, etc. When, in subsequent periods, his Daily Progress Chart showed consistent performance on similar stories, he stepped up to the next level.

When he had finished his skill-building work for the period, the average student found fifteen or twenty minutes to indulge in free reading from a group of guidance materials. The entire Junior and Senior series of *Life Adjustment* booklets (Science Research Associates), easily accessible in their wire rack, formed the nucleus for a sort of "reading for problem solving" activity. Several copies of the Scott, Foresman *Into Your Teens* and The National Forum *Being Teen Agers* were also made available. The teacher started folders on "Classroom Manners," "Home Manners," "Boy-Girl Relationships," etc. Students eagerly added to these with clippings brought from home. Thus, in addition to materials for building specific reading skills at ten different grade levels, books discussing almost every teen-age problem were available at four or five different levels of reading difficulty. Reading for a purpose was fast becoming a reality for these ninth graders.

LEARNING NEW WORDS

Since the diagnostic reading test had shown a vocabulary deficiency in most students, possible reasons for this were talked through in class discussion. Why was a good vocabulary important? How does one learn new words? What is the best thing I can do to begin improving my vocabulary? Out of this developed a personal notebook for words encountered during literature study, or simply a word the student might hear and want for his own. Each was put on a single page. Magazine pictures or original quick sketches were used to illustrate its meanings. Underneath, the word was syllabicated, the dictionary definition given. Then came a sentence in the student's own words, forming the final link in the chain of associations binding it to the student "for keeps." Part of this was done as homework, part as classwork. In addition, students whose Daily Progress Charts began to show up unusual weaknesses in vocabulary and word attack skills found needed review and drill in special auxiliary folders with relatively high interest-level illustrations. These were created from the Scott, Foresman *Basic Skills in Reading* and the Webster *Eye and Ear Fun, Book IV*.

Activities described above were carried on twice, and sometimes three times a week in each of the three ninth grade English classes. On other days, the more traditional English course was followed. However, as this is written, six weeks since the start of the reading laboratory work, there has been a tendency for the students to want to discuss their ideas gained in free reading during reading lab periods and literature study.

Out of the total English-reading-guidance orientation, mental hygiene has emerged naturally and logically. Characters found in literature come alive when their motivations and behavior are compared with the students' own. The frustrations encountered in learning to read better, in boy-girl relationships, home problems, etc., are seen in a problem-solving context. Reading becomes both a means and an end. To synthesize their findings and bring some of the relatively abstract concepts of mental hygiene to more concrete form, the students created a series of frieze-like posters. Illustrative of these posters is one featuring a free-hand drawing of a bucking bronco with the caution: "Don't let your emotions throw you!"

EVALUATION OF THE PROJECT

What do the students think of all this? An effort to find out was made by asking five questions after the students had experienced seventeen periods of specific reading laboratory work. A brief summary of the responses of sixty students follows:

Question One: Do you like the reading laboratory? Answers: Yes, 43; some, 8; no, 9.

Question Two: Why do you like the reading lab? Answers: Improves my reading speed and comprehension, 38; interesting reading material, 24; varies classwork (to get out of English, said one!), enjoyable, improves vocabulary, etc., 18.

Question Three: What have you learned so far in the reading lab? Answers: New information from stories, 29; improved reading speed, 28; new words, 26; understand better what is read, 16; concentration, using dictionary, dividing words, keep from moving my lips, etc., 45.

Question Four: What is the most difficult thing for you in reading lab? Answers: Word study, 28; all material is easy, 11; remembering what I've read, 8; organizing ideas, 7; getting my mind on the reading, etc., 7.

Question Five: What suggestions for improving the reading lab do you have? Answers: No suggestions, 27; read the material more, 7; have reading material more interesting, 7; put reading lab in more schools, let some students write and illustrate some folders, should be graded on this work, etc., 14.

What does the teacher think?

"This year, for the first time, I have felt that I could offer my ninth graders reading materials that were on their individual reading levels," said Miss Holt. "Their own evaluation of their progress in reading and their response to the guidance activities since we've begun this program is more than enough reward for the extra time I spent preparing materials. And the materials are good for two or three more years' use!"

Said the supervisor, "We have now gained a beachhead on this business of matching reading levels *as they are* in our high schools. The way Miss Holt has combined measurable growth in reading with guidance in personal problem-solving for each student is a solid step toward what we think of as 'education' in Johnston county. Our next step is to study the relationship of a program like this to the student's total four-year high school experience. Then we'll need to help other teachers to adapt these techniques to their needs and still others to teach the specific reading skills of their subject areas."

Miss Patsy Montague, associate state educational supervisor, commented after visiting one of Miss Holt's classes, "She is doing an outstanding job of combining guidance with the reading program. It seems to me that it is very important in guidance for us to help young people to understand the reasons for their difficulties in any of their subjects and to make plans for correcting these difficulties. The boys and girls seem to be pleased with the results of their work."

While test, re-test results are not yet available, thirty-nine of the seventy-eight students were achieving satisfactory comprehension (85% or above) at a level one year or more above that at which they started, after seventeen hours' work.

"It is not unusual to see two, three and even four years' improvement in ninth grade students' comprehension level during a single year where reading laboratory procedures have continued 30 to 50 hours," said Mr. Parker, who first developed the program in Florida schools as an extension downward of college reading improvement work.

"For those whose learning capacity limits their reading to something less than grade placement," continued the reading consultant, "the reading laboratory adaptation offers a measure of personal success. The need for providing successful experiences in reading for this wider range of abilities is seen in the fact that whereas only 11 percent of our school children entered high school in 1900, this figure had risen to 73 percent by 1940. While before only the very intelligent had to learn to read, now the average and slow learners are faced with the same books. Either we make successful reading and learning experiences available to these slower learners or allow them to drop out of school to become candidates for our bulging juvenile courts. However, it will be noted that this is not a program solely for the slow learner. The rapid learner and the gifted—those reading beyond their grade placement—are challenged by skill building materials at *their* reading ability level, regardless of how far that may be above the textbook of their grade placement."

To the authors of this article, it seems that Roma Gans has succinctly summarized the benefits while stating the purposes of this frontal attack on the reading problem, in her five eminently simple yet far-reaching goals in reading instruction.

"Guide pupils," she says, "(1) to know *when* it is satisfying and to their advantage to read, both in and out of school, (2) to know how to *select* what to read, (3) to *read skillfully* what is selected, (4) to *appraise critically* the content in terms of its intended use, and (5) to know *how to use* ideas gained from reading."

ADJUSTING TO INDIVIDUAL DIFFERENCES IN ENGLISH
Olive S. Niles and Margaret J. Early

Not much more than a generation ago, high school students were more alike than different in academic ability and vocational interests. Since 1920 the high school population has multiplied two and one-half times; the number of different vocational opportunities is now estimated as high as 100,000. Preparing all kinds of pupils with all kinds and degrees of academic ability for all kinds of futures has become your job.

Because of this revolution in the population and scope of the high school, it is entirely normal for a class to have a wide range of differences in achievement. The better the teaching in the elementary school, the wider the range will be. Good teaching is not a levelling process; it capitalizes on differences and, at the same time that attempts are made to help the slow learner, the fast learner is challenged to develop at his potential speed so that the range of difference is extended, nor diminished. A ninth-grade class with a range in reading ability from third grade to college is neither unusual nor unfortunate.

Reprinted from the *Journal of Education*, CXXXVIII (Dec. 1955), 2–16, with permission of the publisher.

It does present a problem to you and to thousands of other secondary school teachers who are trying to plan for tomorrow without neglecting the job that must be done today.

If you are ready to adapt your materials and your classroom procedures to the individual differences in reading ability of your pupils, you must begin by finding the answers to three questions. The first is basically a question of philosophy of education: What goals are you and your students aiming for in the months ahead? What reading skills are necessary to reach these goals? To what degree does each student already possess these skills?

GOALS FOR THE READING PROGRAM

The answer to the first question represents flight orders for the class. Without such objectives, teacher and students both will be flying blind. It is, of course, your duty as squadron leader to chart the flight. You can find general objectives in the goals set up by the Commission on the English Curriculum of the NCTE in *The English Language Arts*, in your local course of study, and in textbooks. But the final job of defining the specific objectives for your classes still belongs to you. The standards of the community as well as the vocational and educational plans of your pupils must be taken into account. Furthermore, you must always stand ready to alter your course to fit the skills and abilities of the pupils unless you want to risk finishing the year in a magnificent solo flight.

Most English teachers would agree that the goals they aim at in the reading program are, broadly speaking, two:

—To lead pupils to find the enjoyment and profit in reading which will make their personal lives happier and their relationships to other people, to their work, and to their country richer and more rewarding.

—To teach pupils the reading skills necessary to understand their school textbooks and to read many other books with profit and zest, always within the limits of their individual abilities. Teaching the reading skills is basic, for few persons find either pleasure or profit in a book which they have not the skill to read easily.

PROVISIONS FOR INDIVIDUAL DIFFERENCES IN THE TOTAL SCHOOL PROGRAM

The need for provision for individual differences in reading skills has been recognized for a long time. Procedures, mostly administrative in nature, have been developed to relieve the most acute problems for which the traditional course of study in the language arts has had no solution. These procedures have included the following:

—the provision of special classes for slow learners

—the provision of remedial classes for average and superior pupils whose accomplishments have lagged behind their ability

—the offering of elective courses for su-

perior pupils, especially in the twelfth grade where, in some schools, pupils may elect journalism, dramatics, creative writing, and other specialized courses

—the acceleration of superior pupils who, in some schools, may complete the high school course in a shorter period of time

—the retardation of slow learners who may take a lighter program and an extra year to complete the course

—homogeneous grouping. This is the most common administrative attack on the problem of individual differences.

—curricular grouping. This type of organization tends to bring together pupils of similar vocational and educational objectives, but the range of abilities within these groups is still extensive. Only the very naive teacher believes that all the pupils in his college-preparatory groups represent the same high level of ability or that his "general" students are all drawn from the lower centiles in intelligence and achievement.

These and other administrative devices may serve to some extent to limit the range of reading abilities within class sections, but they by no means solve the problem. The classroom teacher is still face to face with a practical, every-day-in-the-week dilemma: What immediate steps can I take to provide for the individual differences in my classes? What long-range planning must I do to improve my teaching techniques and facilities?

TAKING INVENTORY

You can begin with some systematic analysis. No real progress can be made in charting a course without knowing exactly what the resources and needs of your pupils are.

Standardized survey reading tests will provide some basic information. Such a test will give you the following facts about your class:

—the range of differences

—the standing of a particular class in comparison with pupils at this grade level in other schools. If local norms have been prepared, you can see how a particular group compares with similar groups who took the same test in past years in the same school.

—a list of the individuals within the class group who are most handicapped and who need special attention

—very general clues as to the area of particular difficulty of an individual or of a class as a whole. A low vocabulary score, for example, tells you that a pupil is having trouble with words. It does *not* reveal whether his experience is so limited that he can attach no meaning to the symbols even though he can pronounce them, whether he could have understood the words if they had been pronounced for him, or what degree of power he has to "unlock" the meaning of words by observation of their parts.

Survey tests, therefore, do not provide an adequate basis for planning a skills improvement program. Much more specific information is necessary about the kinds of strengths and weaknesses pupils possess. A few standardized diagnostic reading tests are available which yield more detailed information than the survey tests. To be effective these tests must be long enough to provide reliability in their subtest scores. Some of the published tests which yield several subtest scores are diagnostically reliable only on a class basis, since the subtests are too short to yield reliable scores for individual diagnosis.

A more practical approach for many teachers, since it involves the use of materials which they already possess, is diagnosis based on informal tests with the material of these tests drawn directly from the pupils' own textbooks. This method has the added advantage of seeming more meaningful to the pupil himself. You may construct tests of this sort in either of two ways:

Type A: Start with a list of skills which you believe to be important for your work and build a series of tests covering these skills. Materials may be drawn from any convenient source, such as textbooks, magazine articles, and newspapers.

Type B: Start with a textbook which you plan to use extensively in a certain group. Analyze the book itself to determine what reading skills are most necessary for its successful use. Then build a set of tests covering these skills and using parts of the textbook itself as test material.

Each of these methods will give diagnostic information of value. The second may, and often should, lead you to conclude that the textbook needs to be supplemented strongly at both extremes: for the slow pupils and for the superior ones. Such a procedure is a test of the textbook as well as of the class. The method is applicable to textbooks in any subject matter area.

Suppose your class is a junior high school group with rather poor reading ability. You might decide to stress some of the basic skills such as the following: recognizing words by phonetic clues, reading to answer specific questions of detail, reading an index, using a dictionary, phrasing in oral reading, reading for main ideas, remembering a time sequence, reading to distinguish between fact and opinion, reading to judge characters in a story. In addition, you would probably want a test of recall, which involves several skills. The exact list of skills you select will depend on several factors, such as maturity of the pupils, material to be used by the class, and kinds of skills necessary in the assignments you plan to give. Having decided what skills to emphasize, you will construct informal tests designed to evaluate the individual pupils' abilities.

On the following pages both types of tests are illustrated. Neither sample test is intended to be complete. The first informal test, Type A, contains representative questions suitable for a junior high school group. In constructing your own test of this kind, you would want to add several more questions under each heading and perhaps select from the *Partial List of Specific Reading Skills* additional skills to test.

The second informal test, Type B, is based on a widely used high school literature anthology. It emphasizes some of the higher reading skills and was prepared for a senior high school class with fairly good general reading ability. Again, because of limitations of space, most of the material on which the test is based is not reproduced in this chapter and only sample questions are given under each part of the test. One distinct advantage of this kind of testing is that the material does not have to be mimeographed. The pupils work directly from their books.

Informal Test: Type A

I. Individual Test on Use of Word Analysis Clues.

Select a list of phonetically spelled words difficult enough to be unfamiliar to most of the pupils. Type the words with no clue to pronunciation except the accent mark. Have each pupil individually read the list of words to you while other pupils are doing written work. The pupil who can do this task easily and quickly has good mastery of word analysis skills. There will be varying degrees of slowness and inaccuracy down to the occasional secondary school pupil who has no power of word attack at all. Some typical words are *ultramundane, diopside*, and *notability*.

II. Reading to Recall Specific Detail.

Select a passage of non-fiction which contains a large amount of factual detail. Instruct pupils to read the passage and to prepare to remember it in detail. Then present them with a series of questions calling for recall of detail. Pupils answer the questions without referring to the original material. The test becomes essentially a test of skimming if the pupils are allowed to refer to the material as they answer the questions.

III. Reading an Index.

Select an index in one of the pupils' textbooks or mimeograph part of an index. Write questions to test the pupils' ability to use the alphabetical arrangement, to read subheadings, to distinguish between major and minor entries, and to use "see" and "see also" references.

IV. Using a Dictionary.

Build a test covering the main skills in using a dictionary: word meaning, syllabication, accent, use of diacritical marks, spelling, parts of speech, plurals, abbreviations, use of appendix, choosing meaning to fit context, etc.

V. Phrasing in Oral Reading.

Divide the class into groups of four or five pupils each on the basis of their standardized reading scores. Take one group at a time for oral reading. The rest of the class should be provided with a specific assignment to be done independently while the teacher is testing. Select test materials of difficulty slightly below the reading level shown by the small group in their standardized test scores. Have pupils sit to read in order to reduce to a minimum the tension which often accompanies oral reading. Let each pupil read in turn two or three connected paragraphs which he has not previously examined. As he reads, score him on phrasing. A five-point scale is usually adequate: Excellent—Good—Fair—Poor—Very Poor. The teacher experienced in informal testing can make this one oral test serve several other purposes as well, such as noting substitutions, additions, omissions, repetitions, adequacy of sight vocabulary, and phonetic attack on unfamiliar words.

PARTIAL LIST OF SPECIFIC READING SKILLS

Vocabulary Skills
Pronouncing words by use of phonetic clues
Using syllables in word pronunciation
Using context as an aid to word meaning
Using common prefixes, suffixes, and roots
    as aids to word pronunciation and
    meaning
Reading dialect

Locational Skills
Reading a table of contents
Reading an index
Using the card catalogue
Reading cross references
Using a glossary

Comprehension Skills
Reading for specific details
Reading for main ideas
Reading tables, charts, diagrams
Reading a dictionary
Organizational Reading:
    Reading to see relationship of details to
        main points
    Reading to follow directions
    Reading to follow sequence
      —plot development
      —character development
      —development of argument
    Reading to recognize patterns of orga-
        nization

      —enumerative
      —time
      —contrast, etc.
Reading to recall in pattern used by author
    Formal outlining
"Reading between the Lines" to
    Visualize
    Generalize
    Interpret figurative language
    Feel rhythm
    Make inferences
    Compare with something known before
    Distinguish between fact and opinion
    Detect bias and prejudice
    Forecast results and draw conclusions
    Evaluate
    Recognize mood
    Judge character

Speed
Skimming
Adjusting speed to nature of content
Adjusting speed to purpose in reading

Oral Reading
Phrasing
Interpreting meaning through emphasis and
    inflection
Following punctuation signals
Reading at appropriate speed

VI. Reading for Main Ideas.

Select paragraphs from any source. Informational material is most suitable. The paragraphs in the test should be of various types: paragraphs with introductory topic sentences, paragraphs with topic sentences elsewhere than at the beginning, paragraphs without topic sentences. The following is an example of the last type:

> When grand-dad was a boy, he brandished a wooden sword and toy bugle and charged up San Juan Hill with Teddy Roosevelt's Rough Riders. Not too long ago every boy spent part of his dreams as "Lindy" bumping along in the wild blue yonder in the *Spirit of St. Louis*. Within the memory of today's adolescents, the G-man reigned supreme, and cereal box tops were bartered for G-man badges, fingerprint sets, and other paraphernalia of scientific crime de-

tection. Today children sit saucer-eyed and worshipful before their television sets to watch the latest adventure of a new hero, the explorer of outer space. In a few short years, this current favorite has unseated Hopalong Cassidy as the youngsters' hero, and space helmets and ray guns have become as necessary to the children's dream world as lariats and six-shooters were a few Christmases ago.

The test may be made easy by providing the pupil with a list of main ideas which he matches with the paragraphs, or difficult by requiring that he write the main idea of each paragraph in a sentence of his own.

VII. Reading to Remember a Time Sequence.

Select several connected paragraphs, either a narrative or a description involving steps in a process. After pupils have read the material, ask them to place a jumbled series of statements in correct order without referring to the original.

A harder test is to have pupils read a similar passage and, without reference to the original, list in correct sequence the events which they consider most important.

VIII. Unaided Written Recall.

Have pupils read a passage of informative prose. Then, without referring to the material again, have them write all they remember, trying to reproduce the organization as well as the facts of the original. Papers may be scored as follows:

	Good	Fair	Poor
Recall of main ideas	✔		
Reproduction of the author's organizational pattern		✔	
Recall of detail		✔	

IX. Reading to Distinguish between Fact and Opinion.

The following sample items suggest types of tests which can be constructed.

Directions: Place an X in the space before each item which you consider a matter of opinion instead of fact.

Major leagues play a regular schedule of games which begin in April and end in September

It is fascinating to speculate on whether or not Mars is inhabited.

Directions: Find and underline at least one expression of opinion.

Franklin was the greatest American who ever lived. His influence in the politics of his day was enormous, and he was equally great in the field of science. In that field he was concerned with almost every known kind of knowledge. As an inventor he made numerous contributions. For example, he designed a new kind of stove, invented a device for lifting books to high shelves, and worked out a new kind of clock movement. He loved his city of Philadelphia. There he founded the first circulating library in America and was responsible for the founding of the University of Pennsylvania. It is a marvel to everyone how he could have done so much in one lifetime.

X. Reading to Detect Clues to Character.

Directions: Read the first chapter of Marjorie Kinnan Rawlings' *The Yearling*. Find in the story the parts which help you to know whether the following statements are true or false. On the line before each statement, write *True* or *False*. After each statement write a fact from the story which helped you to decide.

Jody was lonely.
He was a boy who noticed things around him.
He liked helping his father on the farm.
He was a strong young lad.

INFORMAL TEST: TYPE B

(The following test is based on Cook, Loban, and Baxter: *Adventures in Appreciation*, New York: Harcourt, Brace and Company, 1952.)

I. Reading Title Page and Table of Contents.

1. This book is divided into six major parts. Make a list of these six parts.
2. How many autobiographical sketches are there in the book?
3. Is the novel included in this anthology given in shortened form?

II. Using Context as an Aid to Word Meaning.

Match the words in Column A with the meanings in Column B by writing the appropriate numbers on the lines. There are three extra meanings.

A	B	C
gratify	1. wish	gratify
caprice	2. change	caprice
satiation	3. appreciate	satiation
compensation	4. reward	compensation
sustenance	5. refuse	sustenance
grudge	6. satisfy	grudge
diversion	7. necessities of life	diversion
	8. partition	
	9. give reluctantly	
	10. state of having too much	

Now turn to page 301 and read the two paragraphs which begin in the second column with the words "As for the unfortunate people . . ." All the words you have just tried to define are in these paragraphs. In Column C make a new list of meanings with the aid of the sentences in which the words appear. Do *not* make any changes in Column A.

III. Using a Glossary.

Find brief answers for the following questions in the glossary, pages 708–717.

1. Find the word *inter*. Write the word which is the key to the pronunciation of the *e* in *inter*.
2. Write any word you can think of which rhymes with the accented syllable in *epitomize*.
3. Write any word you can think of which starts with the same consonant sound as *choleric*.

IV. Reading to Recognize Mood.

A. Read the following lines and answer the questions. One-word answers may be given if the word is carefully chosen.

There was a sound of revelry by night,
And Belgium's Capital had gathered then
Her Beauty and her Chivalry, and bright
The lamps shone o'er fair women and brave
 men;
A thousand hearts beat happily; and when
Music arose with its voluptuous swell,
Soft eyes looked love to eyes which spake
 again,
And all went merry as a marriage bell;
But hush! hark! a deep sound strikes like a
 rising knell!
(From "The Eve of Waterloo," page 109)

1. What mood is suggested in the first eight lines?
2. What contrasting mood is suggested by the last line?

B. An essayist has written about things which Americans like to stand about and look at, among them street excavations. The following is one paragraph from his essay. Read it and answer the questions briefly.

Excavation watchers, as a class, are very conscientious sportsmen. You very seldom catch them watching anything else when they are on an excavation job. Fire engines may go by in the street behind their backs, old ladies may faint over their very heels, and even a man with a sidewalk stand of bouncing dolls may take up his position on the curb across the street, but the cellar-hole boys stick to their post without so much as batting an eyelash. In fact, the eyelash-batting average of some of the old-timers has gone as low as .005 in a season. (From "Sporting Life in America: Watching," page 361.)

1. Do you think the essayist is writing scientifically, humorously, or critically?
2. What are two details which made you decide on your answer to question 1?

V. Reading Figurative Language.

A. Read "Opportunity," page 200. Write one sentence in which you tell what message or idea about life the poet wanted the reader to get from this poem.

B. Read the poem at the top of page 214. With what does the poet compare the train?

VI. *Reading for Main Ideas.*

Read the first paragraph of "One Ranger: No Riot," page 276. In your own words state the main idea of this paragraph. Write just one sentence.

VII. *Reading to See the Relationship of Details to Main Points.*

A. Read the first paragraph of "Irtnog," page 366. Copy from the paragraph the words which state the main idea. You may not need to copy a whole sentence. List three of the illustrations of this main idea which the author gives in the paragraph.

B. Read the first paragraph of "One Life, One Country," page 256. Write one sentence in which you state the main point the author makes in this paragraph. List two facts which support this main idea.

VIII. *Reading to Outline.*

Read the introduction about George Eliot, pages 562–63. Note the main ideas and the details which the editor discusses. Make an outline which will include all the main points and some of the important details.

IX. *Reading for Specific Details.*

Read from "Many memories. . . .," page 300, to "To have reached . . . ," page 303. Answer the questions briefly.

1. What is the most important contribution which a hobby can make to a person's life?
2. Into what three classes does Churchill group all human beings?
3. Who are "fortune's favored children"?

X. *Reading to Visualize.*

Read the first two paragraphs of "Lead Her Like a Pigeon," page 106. Then close your book and write a description of what you saw in your imagination as you read. You may add details which the author does not give.

XI. *Reading to Make Inferences.*

Read the note before the poem "Old Christmas Morning," page 185. This is a story-poem. The characters are two women. Taulbe is a man. Now read the poem and answer these questions.

1. In what section of the country do the women live?
2. Copy the words which first show that Sally Ann Barton is suspicious and nervous.
3. What does Lomey Carter mean when she says, "I won't be stopping: Going a long ways still"?
4. Does Lomey seem nervous or calm? State a fact from the poem to prove your answer.
5. What words did Lomey's husband's ghost say to her?

ADMINISTERING INFORMAL TESTS AND INTERPRETING RESULTS

To be most effective, informal tests should be given early in the year and used as a means of long-range planning. The administration should, however, be divided among several class periods with more interesting language experiences interspersed. Several consecutive days spent entirely in testing might create poor pupil attitudes.

For ease in correcting papers and charting scores, each type of test should be answered on a separate piece of paper.

When you have the tests scored, a master chart should be made. The pupils' scores may be recorded as follows: (a) leave the space blank if, on his test, the pupil has demonstrated acceptable competence in a given skill; (b) use a single check mark if he is having some difficulty; and (c) use a double check if he is having extreme difficulty. This

SAMPLE CHART OF READING SKILLS

Pupil's Names	Vocabulary Skills				Speed	Comprehension					Locational Skills	
	Sight Vocabulary	Use of Phonetic Clues	Use of Context Clues for Meaning	Skimming	Adjusting Speed to Purpose	Reading for Specific Details	Reading for Main Ideas	Reading to Outline	Reading Figurative Language	Unaided Recall	Alphabetizing	Using Table of Contents
John B.		✔			✔							
Helen S.	✔		✔✔					✔	✔	✔✔	✔	
Robert W.			✔		✔					✔		

three-point system of checking is detailed enough for most purposes.

In the sample chart offered in this chapter only a few of the skills are indicated. Each teacher must construct a chart to fit her particular group. When read horizontally, the chart reveals the weaknesses of individual pupils. When read vertically, it indicates the competency of the class as a whole in any given skill. Thus you can see at a glance which skills need to be taught and the groupings you should make for each. If everyone in the class is weak in a given skill, whole-class instruction in that skill will be necessary.

CLASSROOM ORGANIZATION

Having taken inventory of the needs and abilities of pupils in your class, you are ready to plan instruction in such a way that the more skilled pupils may be freed from needless drill and the less skilled may be given opportunity to improve. The direction this planning takes depends partly on honest answers to some rather personal questions about you and your school. Are you ready to take a test yourself? Underline "yes" or "no."

Do you have or can you "find" at least a half hour a day which you can devote to planning *new* techniques and constructing exercises and other materials? yes no

Have *you* had any experience in sub-grouping within your classes? yes no

Have *your pupils* had any recent experience in working in an individualized or small-group program? yes no

Do you have or can you get enough printed materials of varying degrees of difficulty so that you will not have to construct too much new material yourself? yes no

Have you enough room and equipment for filing materials? yes no

Do you work under an administrator who gives you freedom of procedure in your classroom? yes no

Is your course of study flexible enough to allow modifications and innovations? yes no

A predominance of "noes" in this quiz means proceed with caution. Try your new techniques in only one class for a while. Plan brief units of instruction and return frequently to the traditional methods while you collect more equipment and more courage. When both you and your pupils have experienced the thrill of successful learning, you and they will embark on the next flight like veterans.

If new techniques are to be successful, your students must share the objectives of the program. They should see clearly the reasons for differentiation of the work. Talk over with them the results of their informal tests. Let them understand that people differ in reading skills as they do in height and weight and ability to play tennis. Be sure, too, that they see a need for applying the skills they are learning in all studies that involve reading. And all along the way they should watch their individual progress toward the objectives of the program. For smooth operation of the class, the pupils must

—know where materials are kept and who is responsible for distributing them
—understand how and where directions will be given
—be prepared to find worthwhile independent activities for themselves if they finish assigned work early

Differentiation of instruction may take a number of different forms, some of which are most appropriate in skills teaching. Other techniques, such as interest grouping and the unit method, are more appropriate in other situations.

Two-Group Teaching.

This type of grouping grows directly out of the diagnostic chart of skills. For every skill tested you can make two major pupil groupings: those pupils who have a satisfactory mastery of the skill and those who do not. While you teach the group that needs drill in a particular skill, the other group is engaged in some other worthwhile activity, perhaps under the direction of a pupil leader. Many types of activity can be devised for the group not working directly with the teacher, for example:

—library reading for pleasure
—work on projects, such as preparation for a program
—reading for a report
—creative writing
—vocabulary work

This two-group type of organization will be successful in proportion to the care with which you

—give careful directions
—train a pupil leader to distribute materials and carry out directions
—require specific evidence, usually in writing, of progress of pupils who are working independently

One more hint—when you first try the two-group organization, work with a skill that most of the class has *not* mastered. In this way your first independent work group will be small and will probably be made up of some of the brighter pupils who can best work independently. The larger group will still be under your immediate direction.

Multiple-Group Work.

The two-group plan is not a very dramatic solution to the problem of individual differences in reading skills, but it is a workable one. If you are successful with it, the temptation will be strong to move to multiple grouping. In the larger of the two groups, some pupils will master the skill more quickly than others, and you will want to split them off from the main group and give them different materials of instruction. The limitations of your materials and your energy in planning for varied groups will probably prevent you from letting this splitting process get out of hand. The organization is essentially the same as for two-group work. As the teacher, you concentrate on instructing one or two groups during each class hour. The other groups work with pupil leaders from carefully planned directions which you have prepared.

Almost completely individualized instruction in reading skills can be carried out with

---

Job Sheet

Scientists and engineers believe that within twenty years atomic energy will do the work now being done by coal, oil, and water power. But before their dream can become a reality several problems connected with the peacetime use of atomic energy must be solved. The first obstacle to be overcome is the high cost of producing atomic power. Although uranium, the basic material from which atomic energy is derived, exists in fairly large quantities, refining it is extremely difficult. Therefore, a pound lump of uranium the size of a penny matchbox costs fifty dollars, compared with steel at a few pennies a pound. Uranium in its natural state cannot produce power. But in it is a mixture of two kinds of atoms, one of which, U-235, is capable of starting a chain reaction and thus producing power. The two kinds of atoms are mixed up together, with one atom of U-235 for 140 atoms of the other type. In separating U-235 from the rest of the atoms, at least 140 one-pound blocks of uranium must be used to get one pound of U-235. The process of sifting U-235 from the rest of the atoms must be carried on in huge plants like the one at Oak Ridge. The cost of such "sifters" or nuclear reactors, as they are called, runs to twenty-five million dollars.

Even if the cost of atomic energy could be reduced, problems involved in its use would still remain. For one thing, a pound lump of

U-235 would produce nothing at all. To start a chain reaction, the neutrons flying out of the center of U-235 atoms must connect with the centers of other atoms. In a small lump, the neutrons miss connections and escape through the surface of the lump. It is estimated that the size necessary for starting a chain reaction would be nearer that of a basketball than of a penny matchbox. And the chain reaction that could be produced then would cause such intense radiation that heavy shielding would be necessary. So far, all reactors have been shielded in six-foot-thick layers of concrete to protect workers from fatal radiation.

For this reason the prospect of using atomic energy in automobiles seems pretty remote. As the size of airplanes increases, however, it is possible to think of atomically-powered aircraft. The first atomically-powered vehicle will undoubtedly be the submarine. The use of atomic energy in submarines is practical for several reasons. In the first place, a little of this fuel would go a long way. Probably a lump the size of a matchbox would not be consumed in fueling a submarine around the world. Secondly, the storage area for fuel reserves would be so small that much more space could be given to munitions and living quarters. And, of course, the speed as well as the range of the submarine would be increased dramatically.

Directions: Read this article carefully. Copy the partial outline and complete it. Do not add any items. When you have finished, check your outline with the key on the reverse of this folder.

Title . . . .

  I. Reasons for the high cost of producing atomic energy
    A. . . . .
    B. . . . .
    C. . . . .

II. . . . .
    A. Large amount needed
    B. Heavy shielding necessary

III. . . . .
    A. . . . .
    B. . . . .
    C. . . . .
      1. . . . .
      2. . . . .
      3. . . . .

---

the use of job sheets. A well-planned filing system is essential to the smooth operation of this plan. The preparatory steps are as follows:

—Collect or construct exercises in the various skills. The series of exercises for each skill should represent varying degrees of difficulty.
—Paste copies of the exercises on sheets of oak tag of uniform size. It is best to have two or three copies of each, so that more than one pupil may work on the same exercise at the same time.
—Label each sheet as to type of exercise.
—Number the sheets within each type in order of difficulty.
—Provide answer keys on the back of each oak tag sheet.
—Study each pupil's diagnostic test record.
—List by name and number the exercises which each pupil is to do.
—Give each pupil his own personal list.
—Instruct the pupils in the filing system so that they can find their own materials and return them to the proper place.
—Prepare a series of mastery tests which the student may take after he has done a given series of exercises.

As the pupil finds time in class or after school, he works individually on the skills in which he is weakest, proceeding through the various levels of difficulty and keeping a record of his own progress. When he is ready, he takes a mastery test which you administer and score.

Job sheets are particularly useful in developing the more mechanical skills, such as word analysis techniques, finding main ideas, and following the author's sequence. They are not so effective with higher reading skills, such as distinguishing between fact and opinion, where group discussion is essential to growth in skill.

PAIRED PRACTICE.

This method is especially useful for strengthening recall. Each pupil takes a partner who has about the same degree of speed and comprehension as he. One of the pair is provided with a paragraph or longer unit to read and study. His partner has a checklist of facts from the paragraph. After the pupil has finished studying, he tells his partner as much of the selection as he can remember, while the other keeps score with the help of the checklist. In a class where three levels of ability have been identified, six sets of exercises may be duplicated. Then each pair of students within a group may work on the same two exercises during one practice period. Or, a set of ten or twenty different recall cards may be prepared for each group. The cards can be rotated until the pupils have done all the exercises which are of appropriate difficulty for them. Some pupils may move up to the next level of difficulty and begin to work on this series. Clippings from newspapers, magazines, and workbooks will serve as text for recall cards, but you will have to prepare the checklists yourself since no published material of this kind is available.

THREE FINAL QUERIES

How often? Some teachers prefer to work on reading skills one or two days a week throughout the year with the rest of the time given to other aspects of the English program. Others prefer a concentrated "unit" on skills, an all-out effort for a few weeks.

How much? Will you agree that no pupil does really well in English or any other academic subject without a reasonable mastery of fundamental reading skills? If so, you may wish to consider whether you can save some time elsewhere in your program in order to give added attention to a problem as crucial as this. It is a matter of proportion, and the proportion varies from class to class. Non-college students, for example, will use reading skills much more than writing skills in out-of-school life.

How well? Evaluation of skills teaching must be continuous and systematic. Only by knowing at frequent intervals what progress is being made by individual pupils can the teacher continue to guide and motivate the program. Detailed discussion of evaluation procedures is beyond the scope of this chapter. In general, progress is measured in the following ways:

—improved pupil morale and interest because the pupil sees specific goals
—gains in scores on informal tests of the same general type as those used in the pretesting
—improvement of work in other phases of the language arts program and in other subjects
—gains in standardized tests

Recall Card

Marie Curie was perhaps the least selfish scientist who ever lived. For four years she toiled in a shed that could not be properly heated nor protected from the rain and wind. The physical labor she performed under these trying conditions would have been exhausting for the most robust workman. The shed with its crude stove and kitchen tables was donated to the Curies by the School of Medicine at the Sorbonne. All other equipment, including the pitchblende from which the Curies hoped to extract radium, they had to find for themselves. Although the Austrian government donated a ton of waste pitchblende, the Curies had to pay for shipping it from Austria to Paris. Day after day, Marie treated tons of pitchblende until in 1902, forty-five months after the experiment began, she succeeded in preparing a decigram of pure radium. Instead of patenting the process for extracting radium, the Curies gave it freely to the whole world.

Scorer's Check List

Directions to Scorer: Make a check mark beside every point made. Value of points is given in parentheses. Count up check marks and multiply by point value. Give credit when idea is similar. Do not expect exact wording.

Main Idea: Madam Curie was least selfish scientist who ever lived. (5 points)

Supporting Details: (one point each)
.... She worked like a day laborer
.... for four years
.... in a shed.
.... The shed was donated by the Faculty of Medicine
.... of the Sorbonne.
.... Its only equipment was a crude stove
.... and kitchen tables.
.... The Curies had to furnish their own equipment.
.... The Austrian government donated some used pitchblende.
.... The Curies paid the freight charges.
.... She used tons of pitchblende.
.... It took 45 months
.... to extract a decigram of radium.
.... The Curies gave the radium-extraction process freely to the world.

INDIVIDUALIZED INSTRUCTION:
MATERIALS AND TECHNIQUES
Mabel S. Noall

On the basis of what is now known about individual differences the lock-step graded system in our public schools is archaic and unrealistic. Physical development, socio-economic background, educational experience, emotional stability, interests, learning rates, work speeds, motivations, achievement levels, degree of dependence, intelligence, skills, ascendency drives, and work habits are just a few of the many ways in which students are different. Not only do students differ in all these areas, but in educational experience alone they will be different in all the various subject-matter fields, in achievement in physical, social, and intellectual skills used in the subjects, and in the mastery of content in each field.

Homogeneous grouping is little more than an euphemistic sop to the realization that these differences exist and present almost insurmountable obstacles to the traditional total classroom teaching procedures. As soon as the differences are narrowed by homogeneous grouping according to one characteristic, all the other divergencies still exist. Not only that, but any learning that takes place soon spreads the group disparities into new dimensions.

Grouping within the classroom furnishes only feeble feints at meeting the problem. Nearly all teachers seem to feel that three

Reprinted from the *Journal of Education*, CXLIII (Feb. 1961), 33–46, with permission of the publisher.

groups provide for the problems; once the groups are structured they become nearly as permanent as the assignment to classrooms. The groups travel at different speeds, toward different goals, have different experiences, and transfer from one group to another becomes the exception rather than the rule.

And what is so magic about the number three? Diversified assignments are almost always given in trinities. When more than a hundred teachers were asked to prepare lesson plans which provided for individual differences in developing reading skills, sixty-seven uniformly gave three assignments to the high, average, and low groups; seven occasionally varied this procedure; and twenty-seven ignored the problem entirely and concentrated on uniform materials and assignments.

Most secondary-school teachers still prepare a uniform lesson for the entire class. Mute evidence to this was found in the summer demonstration class experiment reported in Chapter IV. The teachers almost completely ignored good material when only fifteen copies were available for a class of twenty-two. This was true even when several levels were available in a series which could have been used on a diversified basis. When teachers used this material it was reproduced in mimeographed form to provide sufficient copies for uniform use by the entire class. A wide variety of teaching was demonstrated, much of it excellent, but in general it was on the undifferentiated basis of uniform mass teaching procedures. The teachers came from a variety of schools in several states. Although attention was not directed specifically toward diversity, the children had a wide range of ages, intellectual capacities, skills problems, social backgrounds, and motivations that were readily apparent. If the teachers taught the group on a uniform basis, it could be safely assumed that this was the typical pattern of teaching in the classrooms in the schools from which they came.

The biggest problem with any kind of grouping to meet individual differences is that grouping assumes likenesses when they may not exist. This is not to say that children should never work in groups. Group work can be very rewarding when it capitalizes on differences to bring breadth to experience. Such would be the case when five or six students read different novels of the type found in the *Scholastic Literature Unit* on courage. Discussion would highlight individual contributions, would give a wide variety of incidents to illustrate points, would sharpen and clarify the authors' divergent viewpoints. The goal of the learning and the degree to which differences would enhance or interfere with the achievement of the goal should suggest the optimum working relationship: large group, small group, entirely individual, or a combination pattern.

Because so many kinds of differences intensify the problem of a group working in unison on uniform material on reading skills, it would seem that this is one area where almost completely individualized work would give the greatest economy and the best results. Other skills, too, appear to develop best with a more individualized approach. In a study on team learning, Durrell and associates (4)* found that both spelling and arithmetic skills developed much better with pairs working at varied paces than in the

[*Numbers in parentheses refer to Bibliography at the end of this article.]

uniform classroom teaching situation. On the other hand, the English area with its emphasis on literature gave no advantage to one method over the other.

An experimental study reported in Chapter III demonstrated that over a hundred students working under direction of a single teacher could make significant improvement in reading and study skills. Chapter IV reported that a group of students working with a highly competent teacher in a unified classroom approach made no better improvement as measured by reading tests than did comparable students who worked in an individualized self-directive program. The improvement in the first study was approximately two grade levels; in the second study, nearly three grade levels for both groups. These experiments indicate that a completely individualized approach to reading skills development is possible. Were there any problems that appeared in the experimental set-up which would impede or preclude wide use of this method in high school? It was found that the program could be operated without expensive machines or equipment, but at the present time some special areas of difficulty exist. These will be discussed under the importance of pacing, adaptation of materials, and mobilizing motivation.

I. IMPORTANCE OF PACING

If a reading improvement program did nothing more than increase the speed of reading without lowering the percentage of correct responses it would have recognizable merit. As long as the percentage of correct responses remains the same a faster reader will gain more information in the same period of time than will the slower reader. Speed is important. When all other things are equal, speed in reading, in skimming, in studying, in organizing, and in all kinds of working relationships gives the advantage to the faster individual. This is true especially in our competitive culture. Some type of pacing device should be an inherent part of any skills program. An individualized program, however, needs a pacing device or technique which is highly flexible.

If every individual is going to work on a program unique to himself, a timing device would have to be adaptable to variable starting and finishing times. A student finishing the same task before others would need to know his speed immediately and be able to start without delay of any kind on something else of his own choosing. One student might be starting, another finishing, still a third or fourth at different places in different materials. All would need to be free to work under speed pressures without being impeded in any way by the pace of the others.

An optimum pacer would have to provide for variable reading rates at a variety of reading levels in material suited to developing competence in different areas of weakness. All of these flexibilities would have to be provided simultaneously to care for the differences among students. The usual way of solving this problem is to give each student an individual pacer, and sometimes different kinds of pacers to fit the needs of a particular task. This is an expensive and cumbersome solution which multiplies cost, materials and equipment accounting, and repair services.

Another problem of flexibility is presented by the changes within each student's reading pattern. Pace changes to suit the purpose and the material. Sometimes the purpose of the student shifts as he discovers new factors or unfamiliar elements in the reading situation. He uses a fluctuating speed of perception and association when unfamiliar elements multiply. Any rigid pacing device which holds the student to a rigid rate of perception will not permit the student to weigh, evaluate, and recheck while maintaining a reasonable pressure for over-all speed. The best pacing device will permit a degree of latitude for the organizing technique to operate and will en-

courage judicious and rapid skimming when appropriate.

It was found that a single intermittent timer which could be set for repeated signals at variable time intervals would supply all these needs for a large group of students at a very minimal cost. While providing for speed development, it also served a number of important correlary functions in the learning process.

Pacing, or time pressure, helps to build and sustain attention. If there is only a short time before the task must be finished, students do not waste as much time getting started. When the eyes are traveling rapidly over the printed page, the ideas in the material tend to crowd out extraneous thoughts and engage the attention. Pressure of ideas is added to the pressure of the time limits, and comprehension grows with the heightened attentiveness. Nearly all poor readers perform better on appropriated reading tests than they can be expected to perform on their own when they are under less supervision. A partial explanation lies in the time pressure. The continual refocusing of the attention through the use of short-term tasks and frequent questions probably plays a part in this rise in performance, too. A timing device that would constantly remind the person at very frequent intervals that he is working for speed, would tend to develop more sustained attention on the part of the reader. This would be true especially for the very slow reader who is unusually painfully aware of his difficulty. A timing device that gave frequent signals would also be suitable for many short-term tasks, thus adding the satisfaction that finishing a task brings to everyone. Such a device would permit frequent change of tasks with the heightened interest that change brings. Conversely, such a timing device could be used for increased speed when reading lengthy assignments if the reading were paced to specific points in the material to coincide with the time signals.

There are many subtle ways that an intermittent timer works for improved motivation. If the intervals are set at frequent intervals, such as one minute, any new work can begin at any time on the next signal. Since there is no long delay before the new work can be begun, motivation is not dissipated by an enforced waiting period. At the same time, the bell is always expected in a very brief interval, reminding the student to get ready to begin. Once ready, it is easier to go along with the timing and do the work than it would be to stop. Since each student has a limited latitude of choices as to which material he will do first and when to make changes from one type of material to another, this choice acts as motivation. The choice is never so wide that it presents a dilemma, but a choice, however limited, involves the student in the decision and is motivating. Even the fact that he can ignore the pacer when he feels a preference for a different tempo has the effect of making him inclined to work. When a student is told immediately after each question whether his answer is correct, the fact that he knows how he is doing helps him to steer his path closer to the desired goal. It is reasonable to assume that motivation develops equally well when the student is told at frequent intervals where he should be to maintain his speed. This technique of immediate reinforcement through knowledge of results is a very important characteristic of automatic teaching. When the intermittent timer is combined with scoring keys built into the materials, both rate and accuracy reinforcement of learning is provided.

Research on the Mahal Pacer—Inquiries did not reveal the existence of a low cost, intermittent timing device. A series of experimental models were used in several experimental studies and the Mahal Pacer and Pacesetters emerged from these early experiments. (*8, 9*)

Five experimental studies which tested a marked-book pacing technique have demonstrated that this technique develops better reading skills (*2, 5, 6, 7, 11*) on a wide range of reading tasks (*5*) and that these gains are retained as shown by one-year post-testing at both the junior high school (*7*) and college (*11*) levels. This method was the most favored by students of five different methods of speed development that were used in one study (*2*).

These five studies marked the evolution of a new pacing technique. The steps in this evolution were: First (*2*), all students reading copies of the same book previously marked to indicate where the student should be when the teacher called time at the end of short intervals. Second (*11*), students reading different materials marked for different reading speeds with the teacher indicating lapsed time at one-minute intervals. Third (*5, 7*), the substitution of an elapsed time indicator or intermittent timer (the Mahal Pacer) to free the teacher for more productive work. Fourth (*6*), the development of cardboard strips marked for various speeds (the Mahal Pacesetters) which could be used according to choice on any articles to replace the actual marking of books.

In 1950, Brown (*2*) conducted an experimental study at the University of Minnesota in which five methods of pacing reading were used. They were: 1) Harvard Films and Readings, 2) Tachistoscopic training, 3) Timed readings on a variety of materials, 4) Paced readings on a variety of materials, and 5) Master-Word-Vocabulary approach supplemented by a pocket-sized lexicon. Students ranked each method as to its effectiveness. In general, the paced reading was acclaimed more successful than the others. The pacing technique worked equally well with a large group or an individual. The entire text, *Efficient Reading* (*1*), had been paced and sheets with the pacing times were mimeographed and given to the individual students to permit them to work at their own speed levels. The teacher used a stop watch or a watch with a

TABLE VI

COMPARATIVE SCORES OF CONTROL AND EXPERIMENTAL GROUPS:
BEFORE AND AFTER TRAINING AND ONE YEAR LATER

Variable Group	Number	Mean	S.D.	SEM	Critical Ratio
Predicted-Grade-Point-Average					
Control	78	2.18	.67	.034	
Experimental	78	2.19	1.98	.150	.006
Cooperative Reading Test					
Control					
Before	78	55.0	5.48	.388	
One Year Later	78	57.4	6.92	.542	3.604
Experimental					
Before	78	54.9	7.55	.463	
One Year Later	78	62.4	5.83	.480	11.24
Experimental and Control Groups before the experiment					.165
Experimental and Control Groups one year later					6.906
Words-Per-Minute on *Reader's Digest* Percentage					
Control Comprehension					
One Year Later	90	328.4	47.4	7.56	
Experimental					
Before	78	228.5	30.6	6.9	
After	87	445.8	61.0	15.08	13.10
One Year Later	89	402.0	59.1	11.46	2.365
Experimental and Control Groups one year after					5.36
Experimental Group on initial and final tests					12.98
Iowa Silent Reading Test, Advanced					
Experimental Group					
Before	102	174.4	10.5	.637	
After	102	187.0	10.8	.657	13.77
One Year Later	78	184.7	10.6	1.322	1.558
Before and One Year Later					7.293

sweep second hand. At the proper time the teacher said, "next." The student adjusted his reading rate and tried to be at the proper place for each "next."

At approximately this same time another experiment using much the same pacing technique was being conducted at the University of Utah (*11*). One hundred and two students were given speed development using *Reader's Digests* with various articles marked for different word-per-minute intervals. Sampling indicated that five-eighths inch of type was equal to about 25 words, and a passage so marked every two and one-half inches would be suitable to pace 100 words-per-minute reading. For example, two and one-half inches would be equal to 100 words, and a ruler was used to compute the intervals for the markings in the *Digests*. The students were tested before the experiment, immediately after the experiment, and the seventy-eight students who were still at the university a year later were tested again at that time. As a control group, a sampling was drawn from the same entering freshman class to be measured on reading tests at the one-year post-testing. While this was not as satisfactory as a preselected sample on whom all tests had been made, it did furnish a source of comparison. Data on this experiment are reported in Table VI. The Experimental and Control Groups were alike in age, sex ratio, predicted-grade-point-average, and scores on the Co-operative Reading Test which was administered to all freshmen students. A year after the experiment the two groups were significantly different in favor of the Experimental Group on the Cooperative Reading Test and on speed in reading a fairly long *Reader's Digest* article. In comprehension on the *Reader's Digest* article there was little difference in the comparative scores. Both groups had made significant gains on *Cooperative Reading Test* scores, but the Experimental Group had a critical ratio on the before and after test scores that was more than three times as great as that of the Control Group.

The Experimental Group made statistically highly significant gains during the three-months of reading instruction on both the *Iowa Silent Reading Test* and in speed reading in the *Reader's Digest* materials. There was some loss of these gains during the following year, but the loss was not statistically significant. Enough of the gains remained to be significantly higher than the initial test scores by a wide margin. In all except percentage of comprehension on the *Digest* materials the critical ratios of the initial and final test scores for the Experimental Group greatly exceeded those of the Control Group.

This would indicate that the training resulted in improved speed and in better performance on tests, and that these gains tended to remain a year following the training.

During the two previously reported experi-ments the teachers had indicated the lapsed time interval. Since the technique was well liked and secured very good speed development, an instrument was devised to relieve the teacher for more worthwhile activity. Several models were constructed which evolved into the *Mahal Pacer*. This is an instrument designed to give an audible signal every minute, continuing to do so without resetting as long as it remains turned on. The signal is loud enough to be heard by everyone in a classroom, but short enough in duration to avoid annoyance.

In 1959, Loring (7) used the Mahal Pacer in an experiment with 200 seventh graders on a matched group basis. His groups were very carefully equated on seven variables including two intelligence tests, reading test scores, parents' occupation, spelling scores, and sex ratios. The critical ratios comparing the groups were never above .620. By using the *Reader's Digest Skill Builders* along with the regular edition of the *Digest* he was able to provide for a wide range of reading levels. One group worked with marked *Digests* and used the Mahal Pacer to build speed; the second group read the same materials without the marked-book technique. The experiment allowed for only three forty-five minute practice sessions before the post-testing. Both groups made comparable gains but not enough to be statistically significant. One year after the experiment was over both groups were retested with highly significant gains of more than three grade levels according to the test norms. The *Michigan Speed of Reading Test* (10) was used as the testing instrument. On both the post-testing and the follow-up test a year later there was a very slight trend in favor of the marked-book pacing technique, but not enough to be significant.

In 1959–60 at the University of Vermont, Goffi (5) used four comparable groups of seventy students each in a comparison of methods of building reading speed and comprehension, namely: free reading; the *Controlled Reader* (*3*) with film strip projection; the marked-book pacing; and attendance at college without any special reading program. His groups were equated on eight variables: *Cooperative Reading Test* scores, College Board Verbal Aptitude Test scores, adjusted high school graduating rank, type of high school, sex ratio, parents' occupations, parents' schooling, students' general health. By using printed text containing the same material as that presented through the *Controlled Reader* filmstrips the following variables were held uniform for all three experimental groups: (a) level of difficulty, (b) content, (c) tests on comprehension, (d) type face, (e) line length, and (f) spacing. The three experimental groups met for thirty-minute periods, twice a week, for eight weeks. Pre- and post-testing were made with alternate forms of four tests: (a) Cooperative Reading Test, (b) Diagnostic Reading Test, Survey Section, (c) Michigan Speed of Reading Test, (d) Individual eye movement photographs. Not all the data from this experimental study have been analyzed at this time. From early statistical computation it appears that the marked-book pacing group was the only one to make statistically significant gains on all four testing instruments. This would seem to indicate that it permits more adaptability to various materials read. Since this study used quite careful controls of a number of variables that affect reading and had a fairly well equated control group, the findings should yield some dependable findings.

Until the spring of 1960 the Mahal Pacer technique for building reading speeds required that the books be marked in advance according to different reading rates. To avoid this tedious job the Mahal Pacesetters were devised. The Mahal Pacesetters (*9*) are narrow cardboard strips that can be placed along the inner margin of a page in the book being read; it is marked with arrows to indicate points in the story between which there are a given number of words.

With the pacesetters, this is the way the pacing technique works: The student selects the story he wishes to read, determining the speed at which he wishes to read it. The pacesetter which corresponds to this desired speed is placed at the inner margin of the first page of the story to be read. Then the student begins reading at the first signal of the Mahal Pacer. He paces himself to be at the next arrow when the next signal is given a minute later. To read in multiples of the original speed, he passes two, three or four arrows during the interval between signals. Other pacesetters are marked for other speeds.

The pacesetter is moved by the reader so that the arrows point to the inner margin of the page being read. Both sides are marked. When reading a page on the left, the pacesetter is at the inner margin, partially covering the page on the right. Flipped over like a page, the pacesetter will then partially cover the page on the left with the arrows pointing to the inner margin of the page on the right. The pacesetter is moved from page to page as the reader proceeds with the story. If the reader begins overtaking his rate on successive signals, he shifts to a pacesetter set for a higher speed; he automatically knows that he improved his reading rate.

The Mahal Pacesetters were combined with the Mahal Pacer in an experiment conducted on Long Island in early 1960. Herber (*6*) used one hundred and eight seventh-grade students in five classes with an average I.Q. of 93. The *Courage* anthology from the Scholastic Literature Unit, designed for eighth graders, was used with the pacesetters for five daily forty-five minute reading periods. Two forms of the *Michigan Speed of Reading Test* were used for before and after testing. Data indicate that the students went from an average of 96 to 132 words-per-minute, from an average of 90 to 95 percent comprehension; this is equivalent to 1.8 grade levels of growth in one week's time. Teachers reported that "students markedly increased their reading speed; were able to recall what they had read with efficient accuracy; and that they were highly motivated by the success they experienced."

There were no control groups used in this experiment; the pre- and post-testing were only a week apart and the gains reported may be, at least in part, the result of practice on the test. Subsequent testing and further research that is more carefully controlled is needed. It may be that the skimming to mark the books contributes a valuable practice not obtained when the pacesetters are used. Most of the students in the experiments reported here have helped to prepare the books for use; this would lead to better motivation and heightened interest in the outcomes, and therefore more possibility of success.

Another experiment is in process now in Westerly, Rhode Island. Marked books, previously prepared, will be tested against copies of the same books with the Mahal Pacesetters. In a companion study, the *Courage* anthologies will be marked by the students who are going to work with the marked-book technique and the matched group will work with Mahal Pacesetters in other *Courage* books. This should give us information as to whether the Pacesetters can be substituted with good results for the markings in the books.

The marked-book technique was used in the mass differentiated skills instruction reported in Chapter III. The Mahal Pacesetters were used in the summer program reported in Chapter IV. Both groups made good gains in speed development. The self-directed individualized group used the pacesetters and made slightly more improvement on the *Michigan Speed of Reading Test* than did the teacher-taught group who did not use the technique of speed development. All seven studies involved in this experimentation, except Loring's, confirm the value of the use of this method of speed development, and Loring's brief experiment found this method as good as the free reading of the same materials. These studies were made in a wide variety of situations, in five different states, and by different individuals. They all seem to confirm the usefulness of this technique as a way of building better reading speeds.

Uses for the Mahal Pacer—The Mahal Pacer can be used in a number of ways:

1. To develop faster speeds with the *Mahal Pacesetters* or the marked book technique.
2. For paced skimming to find the answers to questions within a limited time. This is suited to any list of questions and a wide variety of materials.
3. To develop rapid perception with cross-out exercises where the student works to see how many lines he can cover in a set time, crossing out the word that is the stem word in the line.
4. For concentrated work on details. In a set time-limit the student works with short paragraphs and detailed questions to see how many he can answer correctly and to attempt to better his score on successive exercises. This is the method used with the McCall and Crabbs, *Standard Test Lessons in Reading*, Teachers College, Columbia University, 1950.
5. For speed in following directions. Stroud, Ammons and Bamman, *Improving Reading Ability*, Second Edition, Appleton-Century-Crofts, 1956, has a number of exercises of this type as well as other speeded comprehension drills.
6. For timing tests with accuracy. In such tests as the *Iowa Silent Reading Test* the subtests are short and require accurate timing. Finishing times are signaled without delay.
7. For speed tests in typing and shorthand.

8. For rapid word association work, synonym-antonym drill, work with multiple meaning words to see how many definitions or usages can be listed in a given time.
9. For more speed in applied phonics. The World Book Company *Word Analysis Cards*, developed by Durrell and associates, lend themselves well to this kind of practice.
10. For speed in writing headlines. Cut the headlines from news items clipped from the daily paper. Have the students pass and write headlines on paced, timed basis. This discourages waste of time in getting at the main idea and leads to skillful skimming.

Many more ways to use the Mahal Pacer will suggest themselves to the reader as he works with various materials.

2. MATERIALS

In examining materials suitable for mass-differentiated skills instruction, almost all that is now on the market needed some kind of adaptation. Only the *SRA Reading Laboratories*, developed by Science Research Associates, and the recently published *Word Analysis Cards* of World Book Company were ready for immediate use. A number of workbooks provide sequence and multi-level exercises, but the fact that they are in workbook form and often provide no periodic tests to permit moving on to higher level exercises when the student demonstrates competence, acts as a hindrance in their use. It was found that a number of these workbooks could be adapted to the more flexible use if two workbooks were purchased at each level, cut up, mounted on colored oaktag, and answer keys attached for ready reference. A uniform color code was used for materials in different workbooks which were all at the same level of difficulty. It is a serious handicap when the materials are not self-scoring, be-cause the reinforcement to learning that immediate knowledge of results can give is lost if the student waits for the teacher to score the exercises. Self-scoring materials involve a responsibility on the part of the student and take away some of the less fruitful drudgery from the teacher. If possible, the answers to questions should be attached to the card on which the exercise appears. This saves time and avoids confusion for the student. Of course the answers will have to be hidden during the time that the student is answering questions or working on the reading material. Periodic tests, heavily centered on the vocabulary of the particular level of difficulty, seemed to be adequate to permit the student to move on to higher level materials when the skills were the same at successive levels. In nearly all instances these tests had to be developed.

The *Reader's Digest Skill Builders* and the *Reader's Digest*, Educational Editions have the answers in the Teacher's Edition. If the answers were on a separate page as they once were, this material could be used immediately by ordering nothing but Teacher's Edition. However, this material can be adapted by mimeographing answer sheets and stapling them or Scotch-taping them to the inside cover at the back of the *Digests*. The exercises are good and varied. Guide sheets can take the children to specific series of similar exercises, but the cutting up and mounting the really valuable ones saves time and assembles materials for a specific skill into one unit.

In adapting materials, since only one copy is really needed at any specific time, any good materials in current newspapers, journals, and periodicals of all types can be utilized. Scotch tape is the best way found to mount these on the cards since thin papers and easily destroyed materials can be preserved and not smeared as they would be with pasting. If the Scotch tape is stripped around the edges of the material to overlap onto the oaktag, fairly durable materials result.

Much of the material now on the market is too carelessly structured for completely self-directed activity for the student. It needs to be more meticulously designed to meet learning problems, and it needs much more try-outs in situations with children and revisions based on these trial periods. Directions in the workbooks and texts are confusing when the material is segmented for fluidity in individual use. Very careful directions need to be given with the material, in simple vocabulary, and in as brief a form as is understandable. This requires much thought, trial with students to see that all understand immediately without any further explanation from the teacher, and revision if there is any confusion when read silently.

In constructing materials for use in areas of scarce supply, three experiments throw some light on problems of difficulty in thinking that different types of material present. Abstract materials seem about twice as difficult as concrete material when timing, syllable count, number of words, length of sentences, multiple-meaning words, and number of ideas are kept constant. Ninety-six teachers in three different classes at Boston University were given two short tests of ability to read in thought units. These tests were given on an alternating basis with half the groups taking the tests in one sequence and the other in the reverse sequence. The answers to the questions on the abstract material were only 46 percent as accurate as the answers to the questions on the concrete material. If this is confirmed by further research, it suggests a great hurdle in thinking in going from concrete to abstract reading materials.

Two studies structured on the same hypotheses are now in progress to determine the elements of difficulty and their sequence in reading maps, charts, and graphs. Dewey in North Carolina and Leach in Massachusetts, Master's candidates at Boston University in the School of Education, are conducting parallel experiments with materials constructed on the same premises. Both are using matched control groups and rather tight experimental designs. Early data seem to indicate that the sequence of difficulty of tasks in actual practice from easiest to most difficult are: (a) securing factual data from a single graphic aid, (b) securing factual data from two or more graphic aids, and of equal difficulty, securing factual data from one graphic aid when it is buried in a book and requires locational skills to find it, (c) solving a problem with material secured from more than one graphic aid in one or more books, (d) inferential thinking involving only one graphic aid, (e) inferential thinking involving more than one graphic aid.

If more detailed analysis of the results confirm these early trends, it would appear that inferential thinking is much more difficult than multiple tasks involving locational skills in securing facts. The hierarchy by which thinking functions in relationship to reading can present many pitfalls unless some of these problems are recognized and explored further.

In general, even with all the shortcomings mentioned here, the published materials will be freer of error and better in service to the children than too hastily prepared and reproduced materials that the teacher makes herself. The students can be enlisted in preparing the cut-up materials for the later individualized skill development. When the students help they become more involved in the possibilities, more responsible in an attitude of wanting to learn from the materials, and more cooperative.

The comments already given apply to materials designed for specific and orderly skills development. In an approach to meeting individual needs this is only a small part of the total picture. Multi-level materials are needed in all the content fields to meet the differences in intelligence and reading competency. No amount of teaching is going to remove these problems from the picture. Additional training in reading simply widens the spread. In fact, if the differences in reading ability have a close correlation with intelligence when analyzed on an individual basis, the teaching of reading in the school system is probably pretty good. Since variations in intelligence and reading competency will always be a disrupting force in a unified teaching approach, efforts must be made to provide many materials that cover common concepts for different levels of understanding. Rewritten and downgraded materials are not the answer because they fail to capitalize on the power that individual differences can contribute when used to widen horizons. In the literature area much is being done with paperback books to provide this variety of materials. At the recent National Council of Teachers of English Convention in Chicago (1960) the tendency to drop anthologies in favor of eight or ten complete works in paperback editions received frequent comment. If any particular choice proved unfortunate it became an easy matter to eliminate and substitute a more suitable selection. That many teachers would welcome this approach is evidenced by the heavy pre-edition orders the Scholastic Services have received for their *Scholastic Literature Units* that are now being developed. These units are organized around consideration of a common theme or problem in a wide variety of easy to difficult books. Catering to teachers who would feel insecure without a common unit which all students can read simultaneously, there are forty copies of an anthology of short selections. This moves next into six copies each of six novels, and finally provides a much wider range of titles from which the students can read. This approach can be very fruitful in the types of adaptations that it provides. With a resourceful teacher, the variety of activities that it suggests are legion.

This approach to multiple materials for content mastery would be especially appropriate in the social studies area and in all the less structured subjects. By making selection from the R. R. Bowker Company's quarterly, *Paperbound Books in Print*, a wide variety of titles can be selected in many subject areas from the 11,000 titles currently listed. A rapid exploration through this reference revealed at least 375 books that would be helpful in exploring occupational information and insights at the high school level. From this material, a much more selective choice could be made.

There are areas where the publishers are proliferating editions of the same standard books and neglecting wide and saleable factual favorites. For instance, out of eighty-two classics most recommended for junior high school and high school students, forty-one are published by several publishers, some by more than eight publishers at the present time. Sixty-nine percent of these books are paperbound at the present time; one of them cannot be bought in either a hardback or paperbound complete version. It is much more difficult to select a variety of books in the content fields outside the literary area to develop concept teaching from multiple sources. Since the factual books are in scarce supply and in growing demand this would seem to be a resourceful publisher's paradise. The simpler presentations are especially lacking, and we do have a large number of students who need them desperately. In spite of the unevenness of the offerings, much can be done in organizing available materials around concepts on the multiple book approach.

3. MOBILIZING MOTIVATION

Since so many teachers with whom this has been discussed seem to fear lack of control in a completely individualized approach to skills teaching, some suggestions on ways to organize such a program to mobilize motivation on the part of the students seem in order.

A number of teachers have had unfortunate past experience with adversely oriented and obstreperous students in the schools, and they rightly fear the chaos such a student can cause in a program of this type. A great deal can be done by proper planning and structuring of the way any program is introduced and carried on within the school. The suggestions here would apply to any academic program, and a number of them have almost universal application.

First, do very careful planning in detail before the program is introduced. Try to provide for as many contingencies as possible. Decide how you are going to involve the administrators, then the teachers, then the community, and finally the children in a dramatic exposé of the need for the program. To do this, proper ways of measuring that need must be found. In academic subjects, a wealth of tests are available from which to choose; instruments that will reveal the discrepancies between potential and performance. Plan to be able to state specifically how many children are two, three, four, or more grade levels retarded in the light of intellectual capacity. Note special grades or ability levels where the retardation seems concentrated, and be able to be specific as to particular students. This makes the presentation valid and more arresting. It is absolutely essential to disturb complacency and stir up the interest and support of the people involved. And the whole school and community should be involved in such a program. Be sure that materials, methods of appraising and recording progress, ways of advertising and displaying student gains, physical considerations of room and arrangements are all thoroughly explored and ready in advance. Dream about this a little; worry over the possibilities; above all, visualize how it will take place. Work stations placed at appropriate spots, if properly provided, can channel student traffic, cut down on congestion, save time and avoid the occasion for disorderly conduct. Small things can cause much confusion if not properly foreseen and provided for in advance. Test the materials and the organization plan with a small pilot group; this might be the teachers. It must involve actual handling of the materials and attempts to follow through on the directions.

When the program is introduced some factors will be very important to the success of the program. In the first students taken into the program be sure to include students who are socially important at the school: athletes, student-elected officers, etc. Do not permit everyone to come into the program; play up its selectivity and, thereby, its desirability. Present the goals of the program in such a way that it is readily apparent that the students will profit socially, academically, and independently. Absolutely no outward forcing of the student to take the class or enlist in the program should be tolerated, but it should be presented so attractively that there will be many compelling reasons for the student to want to be a part of all this. Change is motivating, so be sure that materials and methods of working present novelty and new ways of working. Hold back some of the more attractive materials and techniques and plan to introduce them when the program needs a shot in the arm to add new vigor. When materials are passed out to the students, preserve the element of surprise by passing them face-down to ensure curiosity to rivet attention at the time of presentation. It is very important that each student understand exactly what each exercise can do for him, how he can work to get the most personal reward from the material, and how improvement will be observed and related to his goals. The material must look as if it could give the desired improvement and the student must see the relationship if he is going to become involved in his own progress.

Competition with the students' own scores, competition with other students of equal potential, group competition for the individuals who value most the social situation, and individual rivalry for the exceptional students will all heighten motivation.

Students will work best if failures are kept as private as possible and successes are known by the group. Recognition of individual achievements of students should offer the chance for good students to fail and for poor students to succeed. Honor rolls of names of students who make most progress on specific areas are helpful. If certain students seem to be winning most of the honors, introduce new elements or change the rules.

Pace the work with briskness of presentation, time-limits, new ideas in areas where the program seems to be sagging. When a plan for checking how many synonym-antonym associations could be made in a given period of time was introduced into this material which was ordinarily merely timed, the number of students electing the material increased.

A set and preannounced time for conclusion of the program will be important to success. Progress must be appraised, summarized, and given publicity with students, parents, teachers and administration. This publicity must involve plans for the immediate future and ways to capitalize on the unfinished aspects and recently discovered new information. The plan for the future ought to have new and added aspects, unanswered questions to be explored, plans for the exploration. Motivation is always crucial to learning. Any program which fails to plan ways to disturb the status quo, mobilize the desire for change, and capitalize on human needs, deserves to fail.

BIBLIOGRAPHY

1. BROWN, JAMES I. *Efficient Reading*. Boston: D. C. Heath, 1952.
2. ———. "A Pacing Technique for Classroom Teaching of Reading," *College English* 18 (December 1956), 164–165.
3. *Controlled Reader*. Educational Development Laboratories, 75 Prospect, Huntington, New York.
4. DURRELL, DONALD D., et al. "Adapting Instruction to the Learning Needs of Children in the Intermediate Grades," *Journal of Education*, December 1959.
5. GOFFI, JOSEPH I. "A Comparison of Three Methods of Building Speed with College Freshmen." Unpublished research study, Boston University, School of Education, 1961.
6. HERBER, HAROLD L. "Using the Pacing Technique to Improve Reading Speed and Comprehension." Unpublished study, Central High School District No. 2, Alva T. Stanforth Junior High School, Elmont, New York, 1960.
7. LORING, ROBERT C., JR. "Marked Book Pacing Technique (Non-Mechanical) Versus Freed Reading." Unpublished master's thesis, Boston University, School of Education, 1960.
8. *Mahal Pacer*. Oaktron Industries, Monroe, Wisconsin.
9. *Mahal Pacesetters*. Oaktron Industries, Monroe, Wisconsin.
10. *Michigan Speed of Reading Test*. Psychological Corporation, 522 Fifth Avenue, New York 18, New York, 1957.
11. NOALL, MABEL S. "A Technique for Increasing Speed of Reading Without Machines." Unpublished study, University of Utah, 1951.

PROGRAMED INSTRUCTION
IN THE FIELD OF READING
P. Kenneth Komoski and David A. Sohn

There is a great deal of excellent teaching occurring in the field of reading and study skills in the classrooms of today. We would like to raise a question, however, about some of the learning. Let me explain. After the teacher of reading emerges from the highly theoretical environment of college, he encounters the practical world of students which presents a tangle of problems the textbooks never discussed. He soon senses, if he is a good teacher, the importance of what can be called "feedback"—the effect that his teaching has upon his students (or that he thinks it has) as observed through their responses. One authority said recently that so often we think we are teaching students wonderfully when in reality we are acting merely as clowns, amusing the students and wasting their time.[1]

The teacher, then, is reinforced by what he thinks works well with a group of students. His approach to teaching tends to become empirical. What works, works. What does not work, he discards. After a few years, the good teacher who has observed carefully and who has considered his feedback will think he can teach a group of students more effec-

Reprinted from *Challenge and Experiment in Reading*, Proceedings of the International Reading Association Annual Convention, Vol. 7 (1962), 232–236, with permission of International Reading Association.

[1] A paraphrase of a statement by discussant Marcus Konick, Dept. of Public Instruction, Harrisburg, Penna., at the Fifth Annual Meeting, College Reading Association, April 14, 1962.

tively, since he has cast out the "poor teaching" and has preserved the "best."

But the question arises, "The best for whom?" The nature of group teaching demands that he focus on the "happy median." At best he can reach only a majority of a group, and though he may try to individualize reading instruction at times, usually a subgroup of students will glean the grains of truth he scatters, while others will catch only the drift of occasional chaff in the wind.

Group feedback, therefore, usually tells the teacher what works *best* for the *most* (according to his judgment) and some of the feedback can be specious because it is easy to be fooled into believing optimistic appraisals of our own teaching. Day after day, year after year, acting as a sort of computer, the teacher adjusts according to the information that student reactions supply.

Just as a "traditional" textbook can never reach all the students it is written for, so no teacher can truly teach, using "traditional" methods, all of the students in a group. So it is that a large subgroup benefits from each year of experience the teacher records, though even students in this group will profit in varying degrees because of individual differences. There will always be some who do not learn much. Thus, as I said before, there is a great deal of excellent teaching, but unfortunately it is to some of the parts, not the whole.

Programed instruction can be a great step forward for individualized learning in the reading field. The perfect learning situation has been described as Mark Hopkins on one end of a log and a student on the other (we were amused to note that one commercial programing concern made a slip in a brochure and called it "Mark Hanna on one end of a log and a student on the other" which would no doubt be an "educational" experience but not of the type we are discussing here!). In any case, it is significant that we have the "know-how" to take much of the wisdom and teaching ability of either a Mark Hopkins or a Mark Hanna off the end of that log and put them inside a program. Excellent teachers over the years hone their skills to a fine point. These are things they *can* take with them, for too often, tragically, the skills are buried with the teacher. Even if they have written a textbook, an essay, or a monograph, they have not completely preserved their "best" because in such cases they are "telling" a student what should be done rather than arranging conditions under which each student does it. Looked at in another way, they have not experienced enough feedback from readers and then revised accordingly. In a sense their writing is an educated guess. The techniques of programing can come much nearer to preserving good teaching for posterity. A master chef may "tell" his techniques in prose, and your gourmet sauce, through following his directions, can taste like dishwater. But if this master chef programed his techniques, tested them with one student, revised according to where the student went astray, tested again, revised again, and gradually refined his program, the student's results would probably be tasty. As a matter of fact, programed cookbooks could possibly save many marriages in this country, though they might concurrently increase the incidence of obesity.

So much of the teaching of reading skills is, then, approximate. But programing allows us to be more precise because it is an applied science which refines the educational process when it is done well. Think for a moment, if you have taught reading skills, of *why* you do what you do. Are you making the students behave the way that you want them to behave (I am not speaking of discipline now)? How many of your students can talk about the SQ3R method, for instance? Yet how many of them use it consistently and efficiently? How many of your students can talk about contextual clues or the rules of grammar? How many of them use what they know about these skills to their best advantage? *Factis non verbis* is a Latin phrase meaning, "deeds, not words." You learn by doing, not by talking about doing.

Programing is an undiscovered country in many ways. Yet what we know about the science and art of programing at this point puts us in a challenging and exciting theoretical position. We can use this empirical technique in carefully controlled, experimental conditions. We can observe where the trolley jumps the track. And we can not only put the trolley back on the track but we can shape the track to fit the demands of the trolley. For varying types of students, we can shape programs which will teach them. Through testing a program *with the students*, observing *how we fail to teach by observing the students' errors*, and revising, testing, revising, testing, and revising again, time after time, we can perfect programs which *teach* students. If there are general subgroups within a class, there can be programs for each group so that minorities are not neglected and all are involved. Theoretically it is possible to have each student work according to his needs.

Up to now I have talked a lot about the programing theory. What are we doing at the Center for Programed Instruction to help the reading field? The Developmental Reading Project, with the aid of Carnegie Corporation funds, is an attempt to find a way, through programed instruction, to increase the reading ability of the retarded reader in junior high school. When we began the project, we attacked the problem from a traditional point of view. We programed discrete skills—aspects of contextual clues, phonetic analysis, and others—but we eventually became uneasy about this approach. The total picture was complex, and we got the feeling that we were trying to build an enormous intellectual house of complicated dimensions brick by brick. It began to appear that if a student went through each minute programed unit, that he should learn, he would eventually use contextual clues, phonics, and the other skills, yes, but his white beard would get in the way of the print when he read. Another important factor we considered was the fact that traditional methods had been tried time and time again with these students with little success.

At about this point we were fortunate to be able to investigate what we feel is a significant research effort in the reading field— the work of Jack A. Holmes and his colleagues on the Substrata Theory of Reading Ability. This research crystallized for us what we had thought of in a rather vague way— the enormous complexity of the reading act. It gave us some indication of why so many different roads can lead eventually to reading efficiency. The data identified important predictors of variance between good readers and poor readers for the *power* of reading and the *speed* of reading. Though criticisms may be directed at these studies, they are certainly refreshing attempts to find and describe correlates of the reading act.

We would like to pause here and state a hypothesis that remains to be proved, but, if preliminary indications are a help, has a high probability for confirmation. The nature of programing is such that when a teacher-programer programs his subject, he also teaches the reading of it. Because he does test his programs on students selected from the audience at which he aims his teaching, and because he analyzes the feedback from his audience, revising until he does his best

teaching, while he teaches his subject, he also teaches the reading of it. If he is a chemistry teacher, he teaches his students to think as chemists think and to read chemistry. If he does not do this, his program will not teach well. Therefore, our hypothesis is that *by working through a good program, a student improves his reading ability*.

It is obviously important that if this hypothesis proves to be true, the technique of programing can become a tremendously powerful tool for the teaching of reading, especially if programs are directed specifically toward those areas which separate the poor readers from the good ones.

Substrata factor analyses showed us important predictors of variance between the good reader and the poor reader in regard to reading power and speed. We are aware that the study is an analysis of a given population and that we should be cautious about making broad generalizations from it. We found, however, that it gave us indications that skills many reading experts have always felt were important proved to be important predictors in this case. Viewed in the light of programing, we began to see how aspects of these predictors might be programed. Auding ability, verbal analogies, vocabulary in context, vocabulary in isolation, phonetic association, prefixes, suffixes, Latin and Greek roots, homonymic meaning, visual verbal meaning, and dot, figure and ground have been considered important parts of the reading act in any case. These accounted for 41% of the variance in Centroid and Substrata Factors for the Power of Reading in the high school study.[2] Our problem was to include these factors in a program in a sound way.

We felt that we could not attack the entire reading population's problem at once. We set-

[2] Jack A. Holmes and Harry Singer, *The Substrata Factor Theory: Substrata Factor Differences Underlying Reading Ability in Known-Groups at the High School Level*. Mimeographed at the University of California, Berkeley, California, 1961.

tled on directing our programing at students in junior high school who were reading in grade levels 4–6, as a beginning.

Other questions arose. Should we teach the skills one by one or should we take a combined approach? What part would the negative attitude of so many retarded readers toward reading play in their performances? Many of them have heard before the story about how the teacher was going to teach them to read better, only to experience teaching that they had undergone previously, babyish materials, boredom, and failure again. It would seem that a traditional, bit-by-bit approach would work *against* us, not *for* us.

We hit upon an idea which could possibly solve this problem. Why not teach them important skills through the device of teaching them words? As each student worked through a program on vocabulary building, he would be learning more about reading words by reading. Including aspects of important predictors Holmes and his colleagues found to be important could possibly strengthen total ability over a series of units. Adding reading selections utilizing the newly learned words could encourage the students to apply skills, give them a sense of reading patterns, and lead to larger units of prose.

I would like to show a few ways in which some of these predictors can be programed. It is important to remember that these isolated frames may appear too easy, but that in a sequence, more difficult behavior would gradually be demanded from the student.

Here is a frame using *vocabulary in context:*

The *centipede* ran across the floor on its many pairs of legs. The lady almost stepped on the whole *centipede* with the toe of her shoe. It ran into a crack in the floor. A *centipede* is a ⌐chair with many legs / a large man / a tiny animal⌐.
Answer: a tiny animal.

Here is a frame involving *roots:*

The root *centum* means one hundred in Latin.
The root *pedis* means foot in Latin.
You would expect the number of feet a *centipede* has to be nearer ⌐4 / 2000 / 100⌐.
Answer: 100.

This is a frame using a *verbal analogy:*

Many legs are to *centipede* as two legs are to ⌐man / house / spider⌐.
Answer: man.

Here is a frame involving *homonymic meaning.* We feel similarities in sound, configuration (or both) can be confused by the student:

In Europe, if you want to know how long your finger is, you could measure it in ⌐centipedes / centigrades / centimeters⌐.
Answer: centimeters (you could use centipedes, but these animals are hard to hold and they bite).

This frame involves *visual verbal association* (synonoyms, antonyms):

A centipede is an ⌐insect / animal / ocean dweller⌐.
Answer: animal (insects have no more than six legs).

We have not shown all the possible types of frames, but this sampling is intended to give some indication of some types of training the retarded reader would get from the programed unit.

I would now like to show frames from a unit on the cluster of words *vacuum, drought,* and *famine.* After teaching the word *vacuum,* teaching the pronunciation of *famine,* and defining *famine,* these frames follow:

23. If there were no food in a village for two years, you would say there was (no famine / a famine).
Answer: a famine.

24. During a famine, a person would lack food. In a vacuum, a person would lack (air / food).
   Answer: air.
25. During a famine, people and animals would lack (air / food).
   Answer: food.

It is interesting to note that during the initial testing, the programer discovered that some students did not know what the phrase *lack of* meant and a short sequence on this concept had to be added to the program.

As the student proceeds through the program, the frames gradually become more difficult.

50. (1) A person cannot breathe in a
       (drought / famine / vacuum).
    (2) A person cannot eat much in a
       (drought / famine / vacuum).
    (3) A person should not waste much water in a
       (drought / famine / vacuum).
   Answer: 1. vacuum.
          2. famine (if you put vacuum, you're not wrong because you could not eat for long without air).
          3. drought.

Then, toward the end of the sequence come the terminal frames:

57. If New Jersey had no rain in 1962, there would be a (   ) which would hurt the crops.
   Answer: drought.
58. People have starved in China because a drought has caused a (   ).
   Answer: famine.
61. (1) *Vacuum* means (   ) of
       (   ) or (   ).
    (2) *Drought* means (   ) of
       (   ) for a (   )
       (   ) (   ) in a
       which usually has (   ).

(3) *Famine* means (   ) of
    (   ) for a (   )
    (   ) (   ).
Answer: 1. lack of air or gas.
       2. lack of water for a long, long time in a place which usually has enough rain.
       3. lack of food for a long, long time.

The final frames ask what each of the words mean without using any prompts. Following this unit was a reading selection of two paragraphs with questions which attempted to determine how well the student could comprehend the reading.

We ran a short experiment with two programed units of this type on retarded readers from New York City. One subjective impression of the observers was the surprisingly positive attitude many of these students had toward the reading of the units.

How much of an effect the feeling of success that a student experiences from reading such a program will have on his attitude toward reading remains to be seen, but it is a factor that we will observe closely.

The experiment indicated that the students learned the meanings of the words and that their comprehension on paragraphs which used the words improved as well. This, of course, is what we expected, if only because there was such small learning required. What effect many units and exercises over a period of time will have on students is one of the questions we are anxious to answer.

Our program is in its formative stage and it is presently experimental. We feel that we can combine much of what the Holmes' research has shown us with what we know about programed instruction, and that through this program, we may find out much about how to help the retarded reader. Our program will have research built into it. Perhaps we can measure the effect that certain variables have on the reading act. Perhaps, also, programing will allow us to refine our teaching and to know more precisely what it is that we are teaching.

One of the great problems of the reading field in the past has been that reading materials have been created that we know have improved reading. In a sense, however, their creators did not know exactly what they were doing. They did know (and the Holmes' research gives an indication as to why) that if you give students enough practice in reading, it is very likely going to bring about improvement. We all know that there are materials on the market now that primarily do just this. We do not mean to indict such reading improvement programs but merely to point out a knotty problem which is that stu-

dents have learned to read better in the past, but no one could say specifically what caused them to do so.

We feel that it is time to know more about what we are doing, and we are trying, as nearly as is possible, to investigate, through this programed technique, what works and why it works. We hope to discover not only more about how to help retarded readers, but also to open up many areas for research.

We may frequently do the wrong things, but at least we will have some indication as to why they are wrong. And we may discover some important things that are right and help to shed some light in areas where there is an abundance of darkness.

14
Organization and Administration of Reading Programs

IMPLEMENTING A DEVELOPMENTAL READING PROGRAM ON THE SECONDARY LEVEL
A. Sterl Artley

Twenty-five years ago various aspects of reading on the secondary level were being discussed in journal articles, and in a few junior and senior high schools reading programs were actually in operation. In spite of this, it has been only within the last decade, in fact within the last five years, that the importance and need for a developmental reading program in grades 7 through 12 have been fully recognized. In fact, I shall predict that when the history of reading instruction is written it will show that one of the major points of emphasis of the 1960's will be the organized extension of the developmental reading program into the secondary grades.

SURVEYS OF SECONDARY PROGRAMS

In a recent article Strang (*26*)* reports several statewide surveys indicating the extent to which reading was being taught in

Reprinted from *Reading Instruction in Secondary Schools* (Newark, Del.: International Reading Association, 1964), pp. 1–16, with permission of the author and International Reading Association.

[*Numbers in parentheses refer to Bibliography at the end of this article.]

junior high schools. For example, in 1958, 54 percent of the junior high schools of Illinois were providing reading instruction, while in 1959, 65 percent of the junior high schools of Florida were doing the same. The surveys showed, furthermore, that the majority of those programs were established within the last four or five years.

In a more recent study involving reading in the seventh and eighth grades of selected AAA Missouri schools, Smith (*24*) found some type of reading program in operation in 81 percent of the schools. When certain evaluative criteria were applied to these programs, one of which was that the program had to have been in effect prior to September 1960, only thirty-two schools remained for further study.

It is a striking fact also that the philosophy underlying the programs being developed is undergoing a change from that of the past. Whereas at one time the reading program was thought of as being remedial in nature involving a few students, now it is predicated on the belief that the program should include *all* youth rather than the few who, for one reason or another, are not reading up to expectancy. Smith found that out of 113 programs studied, 68 included all the seventh and eighth graders. Furthermore, out of 102 respondents reporting the types of program in operation, 72 stated that it was developmental in nature. Hence, insofar as this study is concerned, we are seeing an acceptance of the belief that all students can perform on increasingly higher levels in all aspects of reading as a result of a program that makes provisions for systematic and sequential growth beyond grade 6.

ESTABLISHING A READING PROGRAM

A number of issues and questions have to be faced as the need for a developmental reading program is recognized. Unlike a science program that is universally accepted as part of the curriculum and is structured and organized, a secondary school reading program is new. Administrators have no pattern to follow in organizing such a program, nor are the teachers trained to teach the courses. Anyone who works in this area is a pioneer.

Our particular concern in this paper will be a consideration of the questions and problems involved in getting a reading program established and under way—of implementing a developmental program on the secondary level. We begin by examining reports of some twenty-five reading programs that were in operation in various parts of the country. Though a program in Little Rock or St. Paul might be different from that in Norfolk or Houston, it is possible to identify a rather consistent pattern of steps leading to its implementation. Here we shall attempt to indicate these steps and show what each entails.

Assumption of leadership—The idea for a developmental reading program may have its origin in a professional course, a professional article, an educational conference, a curriculum study, an examination of the school-

wide test results, or a dissatisfaction with the existing conditions. [Campbell (*3*); Fields (*9*); Ellis (*8*); Christophe (*4*)] The idea may germinate and take form in the mind of the superintendent, the building principal, the curriculum director or coordinator, or a classroom teacher. It may represent the combined thinking of a departmental staff.

In many cases the person or group responsible for the idea has neither the time nor the training to guide it to fruition. Here the responsibility must be delegated to someone who is trained, experienced, interested, and has the time to devote to the project. Depending on the size of the school and its organizational structure this person may be someone who is already affiliated with the school system, perhaps a classroom teacher who is trained and who shows qualities of leadership. It could be the language arts supervisor or a special reading teacher. In other cases it may be necessary to employ a person with special training and experience to take over the assigned duties.

It is at this step of providing leadership that a secondary reading program frequently fails to materialize—there is no one with sufficient training and experience to take over the duties. Smith (*24*) in his study of junior high school reading programs in Missouri asked the principals of schools having no program to state their reason. The first given, 67 percent, was "lack of specialized leadership," and the second, 50 percent, was "lack of time available." The second reason is indefensible and the first indicates the absence of personnel trained for this type of activity. (Incidentally, Smith found that 21 percent of his respondents indicated that reading instruction should have been completed by the end of grade 6!)

Further evidence of this situation may be found in the Smith study to which reference has been made. In the 32 junior high schools having reading programs meeting the criteria of "comprehensiveness," 50 percent were under the direction of a person who had no training for the responsibility. Likewise, Simmons (22) in a five-state survey of certain aspects of secondary school reading programs found that the program supervisor had no formal training for the work involved in 74 percent of the small schools, 49 percent of the medium-sized schools, and 44 percent of the large schools. This condition is nearly synonymous to that of establishing a mathematics department and placing a person in charge with no training in math. In fairness to all concerned, however, the existence of many fine programs under the direction of individuals without special training attests to their willingness to take over an essential task and to learn on the job through professional reading and study.

Creating staff interest—After some person has assumed responsibility for implementing the idea of a secondary level developmental reading program, the next major task is that of arousing active staff interest, support, and participation. This step should not be considered a "selling job," but rather a process of implanting an idea and stimulating and guiding its development from within. Though the director of the program-to-be may light the fuse to an idea, it is the school staff that must develop it and furnish the driving power behind it. Each member regardless of instructional area needs to become involved in the program and come to see that he has a responsibility for its success. The program must become school-wide rather than one that belongs to a person or a single department. Granted, it might be more expeditious for the principal to mandate a program with a "let-there-be-light" edict. And quite likely, a loyal and cooperative staff would follow orders and carry on in the best way possible, but it will be the principal's or the director's program rather than one that rests on a firm foundation of staff interest and support. This is the second spot at which a good idea may have its demise.

Reports of programs in operation indicated a number of ways that the interest and support of a staff could be aroused. Christophe (4) and Miniclier (18) suggested that the staff take a critical look at the existing conditions within a school by considering the results of a school-wide testing program. Almost invariably questions will be raised, the answers to which in some way will point to a consideration of a reading program. For example, what factors lie behind failure to achieve up to grade norms? How can students be expected to achieve when they can't read the materials assigned to a given grade?

A critical examination of the results of an existing program of limited scope might point up the need for one with a broader base. For example, Johnson (14) indicated that past efforts to improve the reading situation in his school had failed because the responsibility had been vested in the English department where many of the teachers were unwilling to give sufficient time to reading. As a result of a reappraisal of the situation the need for a broader based program became obvious.

Cooper (6), in order to bring the importance of reading to the attention of his faculty, devoted several staff meetings to a discussion of recent trends affecting secondary education. These trends had to do with the increased number of students continuing into the secondary sequence with its concomitant effect on aptitude for reading, retention of youth in school, and the effect of social promotion on the junior high program. It became obvious to the faculty after discussing such questions as these that a developmental reading program should be a part of the secondary curriculum.

Several of the reports indicated that during this stage a reading specialist or authority was brought in to address the staff. This is a good suggestion provided that the speaker at this point attempts to help the faculty develop a concept of and a need for a developmental program and to help them understand that this must be a cooperative effort in which each has an opportunity and a responsibility. He should resist the temptation of telling the staff *how* to organize a program.

It would seem as though there should be at least two important results of this period of staff action that Early (7) calls "teacher readiness." The first is a series of understandings about reading itself. These would involve the concepts that reading is a process rather than a subject to be taught, and because of this, wherever reading is done an effort should be made to develop it to the highest levels of competence possible; that reading is more than pronouncing words; that regardless of the effectiveness of the elementary reading program, there is need for an extended program to promote growth for all students on the secondary level; that growth *in* reading is only a means to the end of growth *through* reading; and that individual differences among students necessitate an educational program differentiated in terms of instructional materials so that all students may successfully and honestly learn.

The second result of this step is the firm conviction that the development of a reading program is worth staff effort. Freudenreich (10) emphasizes the importance of this outcome in these words: "Unless there is a genuine interest on the part of the school staff, unless there is the realization that no other single program which the staff might plan would have as far-reaching an effect on improvement of the total teaching-learning situation in the school, then any developmental reading program, regardless of source of impetus, may not be fully effective." Interested persons, he adds, can always come up with solutions to their problems.

It should be apparent that if this second step is taken carefully, a considerable amount of time will be involved. Christophe (4) indicated that he and his staff took one semester to think through the basic issues and lay the groundwork for a program. Severson (20), Reading Consultant-Coordinator for the Nicolet High School in Milwaukee, recounts that she took one year for the initial planning stage. Better it is to move slowly and develop strong internal motivation for a new program than to move into one before the staff has accepted it and is familiar with what will be involved if one were to be undertaken.

Organizing the staff for action—Up to this point the faculty has been working as a group under the guidance of the program chairman. It is obviously difficult for a large and diversified group of staff members to make decisions and establish policies. Consequently, whenever it is felt that the staff is sufficiently committed to the development of a schoolwide reading program, it is ready for step three—organizing for action.

Reports of reading programs in progress indicated that one of the first things to be done in organizing the staff for action was to elect or appoint a representative all-school faculty committee to design a master plan for a developmental reading program and ultimately to assume responsibility for putting it into effect. This committee should be made up of representatives of the several instructional areas who will likely be key teachers or individuals who have had courses in reading or who have a special interest in designing a program. It would be advisable to add to this committee the school counselor and the librarian since these people will have important roles to play.

One of the major activities of the reading committee is that of considering such issues as the following and formulating policies regarding them:

1. Responsibility of the content area teachers
2. Special function of the English teachers
3. Special function of the school services— librarian, counselor, nurse, etc.

4. Skills and competencies to be developed in each instructional area
5. The instructional program for various groups of students—mentally accelerated, retarded, etc.
6. Grouping students for instruction
7. Differentiating instructional materials and procedures for the range of ability within the classrooms
8. Selection of appropriate instructional materials
9. Professional reading and discussion
10. Development of reading interests and tastes in all instructional areas
11. Parent instruction
12. Evaluation of the program

The reports showed that in some cases subcommittees were established to study and make recommendations to the reading committee with respect to such issues as those involving materials and equipment, skills and competencies to be developed in each area, or grouping for instruction. In considering these issues it is advisable to see that the lines of communication are kept open between the reading committee and the faculty. In the Nicolet High School in Milwaukee, for example, the members of the all-school committee relayed all information to the departments represented, and, in turn, received suggestions from them for consideration. In this manner, all staff members became acquainted with the theory, significance, and practical aspects of the reading program.

Bamman, Hogan, and Greene (*1*) give a check list of practices that would serve as an excellent guide to points to be considered by the planning committee. This is the time also at which an outside reading authority might make his best contribution to the work of the committee by acting in the capacity of a resource person or consultant. Out of his experience he can react to the thinking of the committee, help clarify issues, suggest

sources of information, and give general guidance and encouragement. The committee should not expect to be told *how* to organize a reading program, for in a sense each staff must tailor-make its own program in terms of its organization, type of student population, level of teacher competence, and quality of leadership, as well as other factors.

A special caution is offered the reading committee while it is in the midst of its planning operation. That is to avoid being lured into an easy or a seemingly painless solution to its problems. It would be so easy to conclude that self-help kits of materials in the hands of homeroom teachers would be sufficient, or that a corrective program for those reading below par would suffice, or that a reading laboratory equipped with teaching machines would be adequate.

Of all the deceptively easy solutions the one to guard against is that of turning the responsibility over to the English teachers under the assumption that since reading is one of the communications areas, "George English can do it and the rest of us won't need to get involved." This approach should be avoided for several reasons. In the first place, it negates the basic concept of developmental reading. Since reading is a process and not a subject, it is a fallacy to assume that responsibility for promoting its continued growth can be turned over to a single division, class, or teacher. All teachers, within the context of their teaching area, must develop the competencies that contribute to effective reading. In the second place, the English teachers as a group have no greater competence for teaching reading than any other group of teachers. It would be relatively difficult to find a teacher-training institution including in its curriculum a course in secondary reading procedures as part of the program for English majors. Where it is offered it is quite likely to be an elective, and academically oriented advisers are more inclined to place the student in courses in the modern novel, eighteenth century literature, or specialized courses in Byron, Shelley, and Keats than in one that deals with such mundane topics as word perception, critical reaction, or reading to ascertain idea relationships.

The above is not meant to be critical of English teachers. Traditionally, the English program on the secondary level has been concerned with grammar, literature, and composition. Reading has not been considered a part of the English curriculum, under the assumption that this area had been thoroughly covered on the elementary level. Hence, the addition of reading to the English curriculum tends to make it an extra, an adjunct, rather than an inherent part of the language arts program. There is the tendency to deal with it, as Early (7) points out, by setting up special reading classes, clinics, and workshops that continue to be appendages to the curriculum. And what started out to be an all-school program ends being little more than a program in name only, "ignored by everyone but the struggling teacher."

Eventually, the all-school committee must summarize its thinking on the issues and problems with which it has been dealing and formulate its plans and policies and submit them to the administration and faculty for approval. Severson reported that in their case after a year of planning, a report was prepared by a summer workshop in which all members of the all-school reading committee participated. It developed lesson plans, ideas, and specific suggestions for use the following fall. These ideas were put together in a *"Blue Book"* which explained the philosophy under which the program was to operate, the characteristics of good readers and symptoms of reading problems. It also included an outline of teaching plans. Regardless of the form in which it is presented, a curriculum or instructional guide very

likely will be the end product of the all-school committee's work.

PUTTING THE PROGRAM INTO OPERATION

Eventually the talking and initial planning must terminate and the gears be set in motion. Time should be included in the school schedule for the purpose of introducing the program. Severson indicated that a part of the pre-school workshop was devoted to its launching. The *"Blue Book"* was discussed and a reading specialist from a nearby university was brought in to consider problems of concern to the staff.

But setting the gears in motion is only part of the task, for in spite of the planning that has gone into the program, few, if any, of the teachers are actually prepared to teach reading. This being true, an in-service training program appears to be an essential part of those programs reported in the literature. The aim here, of course, is to help all teachers perfect their ability to promote continued growth in and through reading. A number of ways were indicated by which in-service instruction was provided. Among those mentioned were the following:

1. Demonstration lessons
2. College extension courses
3. After school, evening, or Saturday morning workshops
4. Departmental study groups
5. Reading conferences
6. Classroom visitations

Through such activities as those mentioned, understandings were developed around such topics and problems as:

1. Proper use of instructional materials
2. Methods of developing certain skills and abilities in the areas of word perception,

critical reading, propaganda analysis, etc.

3. Teaching a directed reading lesson
4. Developing a readiness for an assignment
5. Enriching the reading program for the competent reader
6. Adapting instruction to the range of reading ability in the group
7. Identifying the reading competencies to be developed in a given content area
8. Identifying particular reading needs of students and ways of meeting them
9. Making maximum use of test data
10. Grouping pupils for effective teaching
11. Classifying and grading supplementary materials
12. Developing multi-level reading lists for social studies units
13. Dividing responsibility for skill development
14. Extending the use of the school library

Loretan (16) gives a detailed explanation of the kind of in-service training program being used in certain high schools in New York City. Though this program has been developed for use in a large city, many of its features could be adapted to a smaller system. One of its interesting features is the use of reading methods demonstration teams made up of trained specialists who work primarily with beginning content area teachers. Each consultant works with a group of teachers in various subject areas, teaching demonstration lessons and conducting individual and group conferences. The value of this particular program, Loretan states, is "the psychological impact that it has in the schools in question. The whole school becomes motivated."

The question might be raised as to why such instructional helps were not given during the planning stage. The reports show that in some cases they were; yet experience seemed to indicate that in-service help was of maximum value when given at the time it was needed, when suggestions could be used immediately with a group of students. Then, too, it is difficult to pre-plan for some aspects of the program. One simply has to learn on the job. Clark (5) in discussing this point writes, "Our reading specialist planned as the project unfolded; and thus produced for us an in-service experience much nearer to our actual needs than conscious pre-planning could have produced."

EVALUATION AND MODIFICATION

After the program is well under way a period of evaluation is needed to determine its over-all effectiveness. In the journal reports where evaluation was discussed the procedures took several different forms. In some cases a reading test was given at the beginning of the year and again at the end, and the gains were measured against those of the standardization group. Unfortunately, little was done to assess reading growth in the content areas, the reason being likely that it is more difficult to find valid tests of reading performance in science, history, or mathematics. Furthermore, there was a noticeable absence of evaluative programs that measured reading in its broadest sense as construed by Gray and Rogers (11) in their *Maturity in Reading*, for example. Reading growth was strictly in terms of the areas assessed by a typical standardized test, limited usually to vocabulary and comprehension of stated meanings.

The most practical and useful evaluation comes through the day-by-day observations of those participating in the various aspects of the program—both teachers and supervisors. "How does the method, the procedure, or the technique work? How may we improve upon it?" Should be the kinds of self-evaluation questions asked. The check list of reading practices by Bamman, Hogan and

Greene referred to earlier would also be useful in evaluating the program.

A more sophisticated approach to evaluation would involve the use of experimental groups, each group employing a particular kind of approach, technique, or practice. Thornton (27), for example, described the use of this approach in the Atlanta school system. A program of reading improvement, stressing chiefly the development of rate was compared with one that emphasized vocabulary and comprehension. When it was found that the group employing the latter approach made gains greater than the one stressing rate, the program was modified accordingly.

As was just implied, the purpose of evaluation is not only to determine the growth made by the group or by individuals, but to guide subsequent development of the program. Figuratively speaking, the members of the staff are carving out the plow handles to fit their own hands. They are not superimposing upon themselves a program built by someone else but are constructing and reconstructing one that fits their own situation. Each year sees the teachers trying out new ideas as a result of the collective past experience of the entire staff.

Hill (12), after discussing the program of evaluation used in the Dubuque secondary school reading program, writes, "As the program has progressed it has been necessary to adjust the organizational plan and the instructional procedures. These changes have been the result of professional growth by the faculty and better identification of the needs of the pupils. A better understanding of the teaching problems of teachers has been gained by the administrative staff. A better understanding of the administration and its problems is being gained by the faculty." This statement of Hill's summarizes very well the idea that a dynamic program results in more effective teaching procedures as well as in professional growth and understanding

of all staff members as they become involved in a cooperative enterprise.

Possibly one of the questions that might be raised with respect to the implementation of a secondary school reading program such as that described would have to do with the amount of time required to get the program under way. True, no indication is given that this can all be done in a few weeks or even months. Severson, quoted frequently in this report, described their program as one requiring three years to get under way. Likewise, Freudenreich in his discussion of the organization of a junior high school program assumes that one year will be used for learning, one for orientation, and one for putting the program in action. Early, in her discussion of the problems to be considered by the faculty in setting up a reading program, cautions against moving before the faculty has given careful consideration to questions that "penetrate the philosophic structure on which a sound program can be erected." True, nothing should stand in the way of the teacher who wants to try out a new idea in her class before the organized program gets under way. However, if we are considering introducing an all-school program it would certainly be advisable to build it on a firm base of faculty interest, support, and competency. To do otherwise militates against the possibility of its success.

BIBLIOGRAPHY

1. BAMMAN, HENRY, HOGAN, URSULA, and GREENE, CHARLES. *Reading Instruction in the Secondary School.* New York: David McKay, 1961.
2. BLAND, PHYLLIS. "A High School Developmental Reading Program." *The Reading Teacher*, VIII (Feb. 1955), 146–152.
3. CAMPBELL, W. E. "Reading Can Be Improved," *NEA Association of Secondary School Principals Bulletin*, XL (Nov. 1956), 42–48.
4. CHRISTOPHE, LE ROY. "Want Reading Improvement? Your Principal Can Help,"

School Executive, LXXVII (Feb. 1958), 78–80.

5. CLARK, ROBERT W. "Improvement in the Language Arts: A Progress Report," *The Reading Teacher*, XIV (Jan. 1961), 181–187.

6. COOPER, JESS V. "What Should We Do About Reading in the Senior High School?" *NEA Association of Secondary School Principals Bulletin*, XLII (April 1958), 104–110.

7. EARLY, MARGARET. "A High School Faculty Considers Reading," *The Reading Teacher*, XIII (April 1960), 282–287.

8. ELLIS, U. BERKLEY. "Developmental Reading in Junior High School," *Journal of Developmental Reading*, VI (Autumn 1962), 41–49.

9. FIELDS, IRWIN. "The Centinela Valley Plan: A Mandatory Reading and Study Skills Program for Ninth Grade Students," *Journal of Developmental Reading*, IV (Summer 1961), 254–259.

10. FREUDENREICH, CARL. "How Can a Junior High School Staff Get a Schoolwide Developmental Program Underway?" in *Improving Reading in the Junior High School* (ARNO JEWETT, ed.) Bulletin 1957, No. 10. Washington: U. S. Dep't of Health, Education, and Welfare, 1957.

11. GRAY, WILLIAM S., and ROGERS, BERNICE. *Maturity in Reading*. Chicago: University of Chicago Press, 1956.

12. HILL, MARGARET KEYSER. "Organizing the Reading Improvement Program in the Secondary Schools of Dubuque," *High School Journal*, XXXIX (Nov. 1955), 106–111.

13. HORROCKS, EDNA. "Extending Reading Skills in a Large School System," in *Changing Concepts of Reading Instruction*, IRA Conference Proceedings, Vol. VI. New York: Scholastic Magazines, 1961.

14. JOHNSON, LOAZ W. "Improving Reading in Butte County High School," *Clearing House*, XXXII (Dec. 1957), 207–211.

15. LEAMNSON, GEORGE. "Indianapolis Produces Better Readers," *School Executive*, LXXIV (Dec. 1954), 64–67.

16. LORETAN, JOSEPH. "Reading Improvement in New York City Public Schools," in *Changing Concepts of Reading Instruction*.

IRA Conference Proceedings, Vol. VI. New York: Scholastic Magazines, 1961.

17. McGINNIS, DOROTHY. "Preparation and Responsibility of Secondary Teachers in the Field of Reading," *The Reading Teacher*, XIV (Nov. 1961), 92–97.

18. MINICLIER, GORDON. "Developing a Reading Program in a Secondary School," *NEA Association of Secondary School Principals Bulletin*, XLII (Feb. 1958), 127–129.

19. ROBINSON, H. ALAN, and UDALL, RICHARD. "An All-School Reading Program," *High School Journal*, XXXIX (Nov. 1955), 91–96.

20. SEVERSON, EILEEN. "A Reading Program for High School Students," *The Reading Teacher*, XVI (Nov. 1962), 103–106.

21. SHEPHERD, DAVID. "Helping Secondary School Teachers Gain Competence in Teaching Reading," *Journal of Developmental Reading*, I (Winter 1958), 33–39.

22. SIMMONS, JOHN. "Who is Responsible? The Need for Qualified Supervision of a Reading Program," *English Journal*, LII (Feb. 1963), 86–88, 93.

23. SIMPSON, ELIZABETH. "Responsibility for Secondary Level Reading Programs," in *Changing Concepts of Reading Instruction*, IRA Conference Proceedings, Vol. VI. New York: Scholastic Magazines, 1961.

24. SMITH, KENNETH. *A Survey of Seventh and Eighth Grade Reading Programs in Selected AAA Schools of Missouri*. Unpublished doctoral dissertation, University of Missouri, Columbia, Mo., 1963.

25. STRANG, RUTH, and LINDQUIST, DONALD. *The Administrator and the Improvement of Reading*. New York: Appleton-Century-Crofts, 1960.

26. STRANG, RUTH. "Progress in the Teaching of Reading in High School and College," *The Reading Teacher*, XVI (Dec. 1962), 170–177.

27. THORNTON, CECIL. "Two High School Reading Improvement Programs," *Journal of Developmental Reading*, III (Winter 1960), 115–122.

28. WILSON, ROSEMARY GREEN. "What's Happening in Reading in Philadelphia," *The Reading Teacher*, X (Feb. 1958), 185–188.

HOW TO IMPROVE THE READING SKILLS AND HABITS OF JUNIOR HIGH-SCHOOL STUDENTS?
G. Robert Carlsen

The nature of the reading problem in the junior high school is very simply stated: boys and girls coming into the schools are expected to cope with materials of instruction for which they do not have the necessary reading skills. We have been inclined to seek the answer in only one direction: how can we give instruction to youngsters so that they can read the materials of instruction. The answer undoubtedly is to be found in two directions: not only the abilities of boys and girls need to be improved, but the instructional materials and methods also need themselves to be reconsidered.

The junior high school inherits from the elementary school two kinds of students. There is a group of students who are educationally retarded in their reading ability. These students, for one or more reasons, have not profited to the limits of their ability from the reading instruction in the elementary grades. They may be the victims of the increasing enrollments in the elementary classrooms, so that they have slipped by without a teacher's catching up with certain specific blockages in their way. They may have developed reading readiness skills far later than expected of most students. So by the time they were in the third or fourth grade and were really ready to read, they had already built a defeatist attitude toward reading. They may, because of the mobility of their families, have been given reading instruction in spurts and pieces by half a dozen different school systems. They may be the victims of a sequence of poor teachers. It is possible for a system to be good, but for an individual child, quite by chance, to be assigned to a sequence of the weakest teachers in the system.

Fortunately this group of educationally retarded students is small. Estimates run between five and ten percent of the total student population.

The far larger group of students are those who, having come through a reasonably good elementary school reading program, have profited nearly to the limits of their abilities from the program. These are still a widely assorted group of students in reading ability, and they still cause the teacher a great deal of trouble. The intensive study of reading during the last fifty years has shown many of the reasons why this is true.

1. The better the reading program, the farther apart students tend to become in their reading skills. Reading does have a decided correlation with intelligence. In a good program, the child with less native endowment will progress slowly. The child with greater endowment will progress more rapidly. It is as simple as that. All are growing, but some more rapidly than others. Studies show that by the junior high-school level, the normal

Reprinted from the *National Association of Secondary School Principals Bulletin*, XLV (April 1961), 264–269, with permission of National Association of Secondary School Principals.

span will be at least eight years. Some seventh-grade pupils will be reading at third-grade level, and some at eleventh- or twelfth-grade level. This is the result of good instruction, not of poor instruction. If you continue to work on reading skills, the gap will widen so that by senior high school, it will increase to a ten- or eleven-year span. No reading program will succeed in making students alike or in raising the lower group to grade expectancy. The human brain just does not grow in a way to make such possible.

2. Reading is apparently a cluster of somewhat related skills (almost infinite in number), not a single skill as has been often assumed by teachers. A different set of skills is necessary to read a timetable from the skills used in reading a house plan. Both of these are quite different from the skills needed to read a history book. Within the school day, the skills called for vary widely. Reading literature is quite a different act from reading scientific explanations. Reading a manual of shop directions or a rule book for playing a game calls forth different skills from those used in reading mathematics. It is probable that our predilections for some subject matter areas over others are partially determined by our abilities to read the materials of those areas. It becomes obvious, then, that the elementary school cannot possibly teach students those exact skills that they need as they progress into more advanced work.

3. As a corrclary to the last statement, we are finding that developing skills in reading is a lifelong process of refinement, as are most educational undertakings. We have been inclined to assume that growth will take place automatically simply through the process of reading itself as we mature. Such does not seem to be the case. A graduate student of mine demonstrated that in a college American literature class where much reading was assigned, there was an actual regression in reading skills by the end of the semester; while in a comparable class where reading was given some attention, there was growth in reading for all levels of students. Therefore, we need, throughout the educational program, to push all students to improve their reading, although we realize we will push them farther and farther apart in the progress.

KINDS OF READING PROGRAMS

With these things in mind, I should like to describe the kinds of reading programs that I have discovered in operation in a variety of junior high schools.

THE CONTINUATION OF THE BASAL READING PROGRAM FOR ALL STUDENTS THROUGH THE SEVENTH AND EIGHTH GRADES

Such a practice makes reading a required subject for all students in the school, usually separated from the language arts classes. Many of the basal reading series now continue through at least grade eight. A number of older anthology series have recently redesigned their offerings so that selections are chosen and arranged to serve primarily for the development of reading. The programs usually contain a number of rather simple teenage tales with a high level of student interest. Many of these are arranged around some sort of topic or theme such as "Our Animal Friends." In addition, there may be a sprinkling of scientific or historical writing and some example of directions which require close reading. In such a program a good deal of attention is given to refining word attack skills, to picking out the central meaning, to using reference tools, to enhancing speed in reading, to following organizational structure, to skimming, and the like. The emphasis is away from literature as an art form helpful in understanding the nuances of living, and toward the skills of reading.

Reading Skills as a Series of Units in the Language Arts Classes

The last decades have rather steadily developed the language arts point of view in place of the older concept of English. English, in its early twentieth century meaning, was confined pretty largely to instruction in composition and written language and in literary analysis or appreciation. The language arts concept embraces at least four major areas: reading, writing, speaking, and listening with the development of literary awareness as only one part of reading. A number of junior high schools, in adopting such a point of view, have organized the program in a cycle of units in which students make a frontal attack on each of the areas for a period of a few weeks' time. Each of the years contains at least one major unit on the skills of reading for all students. An examination of recent textbooks, particularly those in composition, shows this kind of structure. The reading units, if carefully planned, usually give emphasis to two or three skills in each in a cumulative pattern. Usually they include some attention to guiding students into the world of books as well as dealing only with the skills.

Homogeneous Grouping of Students

More and more frequently junior high schools, where there are sufficient numbers of students, are grouping students in the language arts areas. Perhaps the most frequent pattern is one in which students are placed in three levels. Those who are one or more years ahead of grade placement in reading are placed in accelerated classes. Those who are one or more years below grade level, in special classes in which the major emphasis will be on the improvement of reading skills. The bulk of students then go into the middle group which, in theory, should have a reading range of not much greater than a two-year span. While many schools consider such things as I.Q., recommendation of the teachers, and maturity in grouping, I find that most rely heavily on a reading test score for placement.

Little attention is given to reading in the upper and middle groups. A great deal of attention is given in the lower group. If I may generalize from my experience of visiting many classes throughout the country where such work is going on, the top classes are a complete and absolute joy. The atmosphere is like a fast game of tennis between teacher and students and students and students. Ideas fly, work is sparkling. The middle group tends to be deadly. The feeling is that of one of teachers pulling desperately at a reluctant team of mules. The lower classes are often in the hands of a deeply dedicated and sympathetic teacher who desperately wants to produce a spark, but often with little real knowledge of what to do. She wants to help. She has usually bought some sort of canned program which she administers with imagination and sympathy, while at the same time she seriously doubts that it is really moving where she wants to go. The hope of the administration is that such an emphasis will salvage these lower boys and girls so that they can move into regular classes another year. They are helped, there is no doubt, but they are seldom salvaged. Most of them drop out of school shortly after reaching the legal withdrawal age. I come away from such visits profoundly discouraged, feeling that we have sacrificed the welfare of at least seventy-five percent of the students to that of the upper twenty-five percent. I hope that there is some other way of working.

The Clinical Program

A few schools have found a competent, highly trained individual and made it possible for him to work on a clinical basis. The clinic may isolate cases for attention through the use of a mass student testing program, or it finds its cases through teacher referrals. With present instruments, a good clinician can do an almost medical type of diagnosis of the pupil's weaknesses in reading, finding out rather specifically not only his level, but also the specific parts of the process of reading that is causing the pupil's difficulty. However a thorough diagnosis is time consuming and must be individually conducted. From such a diagnosis the clinician can then set up specific kinds of practice sessions that will really be geared to the needs of the pupil. There is no fixed schedule. The pupil may have a weekly or a bi-weekly, or even a daily appointment in the clinic. He comes during a study-hall period, or sometimes during the time he would normally be assigned to a language arts class. In a clinic that I visited recently in Clinton, Iowa, the teacher had as many as fifteen students in an ordinary classroom, each working independently on a program of remedial work that each had had set up for him.

The problem of setting up a clinic has been that of finding a trained person for the work. Schools are more apt to find a person for the job by providing a grant of money to make it possible for an individual already on the staff to take a year off and train himself for the job in a graduate school offering such a specialization.

RELATING INSTRUCTION IN READING TO THE TOTAL EDUCATIONAL PROGRAM OF THE SCHOOL

There is a somewhat elusive and yet nevertheless existing relationship between the desire, the interest, or the necessity of the individual to read and the development of his skills in reading. There is a relationship between learning to read and reading to learn, or between *skill* and *will*. The two are pretty well fused by the adolescent years and, as a result, cause major problems in trying to formalize a program. A boy, who tested with second-grade reading ability, nevertheless read with great excitement a government pamphlet on taxidermy. A girl, who seemed unable to cope with reading, was suddenly carried out of herself in the excitement of a book like *Going on Sixteen*.

How long can a pupil be held to a frontal attack on the development of a skill in and by itself before he makes use of the skill in something of value to him? How long, for example, will junior high school boys practice football before they are allowed to play a game? The more I work with adolescents, the more convinced I become that the development of a skill in and by itself has very short-lived motivational power. They enhance their skill in small doses of practice that are clearly related to something else they want to accomplish.

In the various offerings of the school, the pupil is exposed to a series of concepts geared to his interests, his maturity, and to the needs he will have in adult society. To develop these concepts, we rely heavily on reading materials. If we could take these reading assignments, analyze the particular reading skills involved in them, and conscientiously devote ten to fifteen minutes to specific problems as the assignment comes up, we might do much to develop reading ability for all students. Obviously such a program requires a level of understanding about the materials of instruction and reading on the part of all teachers. However, where it has been tried, teachers find that it pays great dividends not only in reading, but also in terms of subject matter understanding.

Such a concept might involve the use of differentiated assignments. Some in a class would be looking for different things in an assignment from others. It also involves the use of multiple materials so that different groups within the same class are tackling a concept through the use of more simplified materials than are others. Ruth Reeves reports such an experiment in the Houston Public Schools in which she demonstrated rather clearly that all students gained in reading, but, as would be expected, the better students gained more rapidly than the poor ones. This sort of program seems psychologically sound; however, there is a tendency on the part of teachers to deal with only one thing at a time. Thus in the heat of trying to get students in history to see something of the formative forces of American democracy, teachers bypass these short bits of help that might do so much.

IN CONCLUSION

In conclusion, I should like to quote from a novel by James Summers, *Operation A B C*. He says, "Reason would tell almost anyone that the ability to read was the most difficult single accomplishment ever achieved by any man. But in this day, people did not set off skyrockets and dance in the streets when their little boy tackled and subdued this Everest of culture. . . . Nor did they reward the kid's patient teacher with rubies and a crown of laurel. . . . Learning to read was taken with little more enthusiasm in the average family than the regular defrosting of the automatic refrigerator. . . . Only failure to learn causes any family comment."

We can improve the reading abilities of junior high school students, but only at a price. We must give it some sort of direct attention. In turn something now taught must give way to make the room. We must give it money. It cannot be done with a set of textbooks or the purchase of a four hundred dollar machine. It requires the constant expenditure of far greater sums for books than most schools now spend. It requires a willingness to pay teachers to develop the professional skills they do not now possess. Isn't it about time we faced the public squarely with what it takes to produce the miracles of learning?

READING CAN BE IMPROVED
W. E. Campbell

Reading can be improved in the secondary school. During the 1954–1955 school session, the faculty of Norview High School carried out a reading program that resulted in a rise of 2.3 in the median grade level of reading ability among its pupils. Let's take a look at how this result was achieved.

Although this special reading program took place last school session, it was initiated

Reprinted from the *National Association of Secondary School Principals Bulletin*, XL (November 1956), 42–48, with permission of the author and National Association of Secondary School Principals.

during the previous school year. During the annual pre-school conference prior to the initiation of the program, the faculty devoted time to study of the long-range plans of the school for improvement of its instructional program. These goals were established by the faculty in 1950. Each session the faculty singled out a primary objective for study. On this occasion it decided to give immediate attention to the objective concerned with adaptation of instruction to the wide range of abilities among the pupils.

Study relative to how this objective might be most satisfactorily achieved was continued by the faculty for several weeks. Gradually the teachers reached the conclusion that their efforts should be directed toward the improvement of the reading skills of the pupils. In reaching this decision, the teachers recognized the variance in skills possessed by the pupils and believed that reading as a fundamental skill deserved priority in attention. Furthermore, they believed that reading could be improved tremendously on the secondary-school level. The outcome of this initial faculty study of the reading problems was the selection of a committee to recommend action that should be taken.

The committee began its work by trying to learn how reading might be improved. Soon it recognized that the services of an authority in the field were needed. The committee turned for help to Dr. Ullin W. Leavell, Director of the McGuffey Reading Clinic at the University of Virginia.

During the remainder of the year, the committee studied the problem of improving reading skills in the secondary school. Under Dr. Leavell's direction, various members explored the possibilities for teaching reading and experimented with the teaching of various skills in their classes. Eventually, the committee was ready to propose a reading program for the school. This was then presented to the faculty. The proposal was accepted favorably by the group; but, since the current session was drawing to a close, final adoption was postponed until the following school year.

The program suggested to the faculty was based on the belief that the reading power of pupils can be improved through the development of specific reading skills. In order to achieve this result, the committee recommended to the faculty that the following steps should be taken to assist pupils in developing skills in reading:

1. Determination of the exact reading skills to be taught.

2. Instruction in each selected skill for ten minutes of each class period for two weeks by the teachers of four subject matter fields; namely, language arts, social studies, mathematics, and science.

3. Instruction in the selected skills by the teachers of other subjects when applicable to their particular classroom activities.

4. Use of textual materials at hand, supplemented by subject matter materials written on various grade levels.

5. Administration of the *Iowa Silent Reading Test* prior to and at the end of the program.

With regard to the specific reading skills to be taught, the faculty accepted Dr. Leavell's suggestions. The skills selected were vocabulary development, adaptive rates of reading, effective oral reading, analytical thinking in reading, synthetic thinking in reading, and reading for appreciation and pleasure. Following is an explanation of each skill in terms of suggested specific instructional activities to be undertaken by the teachers involved in the reading program.

In teaching vocabulary development, the faculty planned to help the pupils study pronunciation, synonyms, antonyms, homonyms, parts of words, clues to meanings, dictionary use, words with more than one meaning, words in the making, and suffixes for word building.

Instruction of the second skill—adaptive rates of reading—was intended to include activities involving reduction of eye pauses, phrase reading, skimming, elimination of regression, quick recognition of words, increase of eye span, checking speed in relation to comprehension, and picking up thoughts quickly. To make oral reading more effective, the teachers proposed to assist pupils in accenting syllables, recognizing vowels and consonants, checking commonly mispronounced words, interpreting character through voice, and in reading dialect.

Synthetic thinking in reading was visualized as a threefold skill: (1) getting the main idea, (2) organizing the content, and (3) reaching valid conclusions. The first part of this skill included instruction in getting the gist of the meaning, recognizing main ideas and related details, using reading guideposts, finding topic sentences as guideposts, locating key words, visualizing materials read, reading with imagination and a sense of humor, and understanding total meaning. The second part of this skill—organizing the content—involved seeing the step-by-step plan, noticing the order, learning to outline, detecting the basic plan, arranging the chronological order, and summarizing to see clearly. Reaching valid conclusions—the final aspect of synthetic thinking in reading—was concerned with reading between the lines, anticipating outcomes, solving mysteries and problems, catching the mood of the writer, judging a story, evaluating character, and seeing cause-and-effect relations.

The fifth skill—analytical thinking in reading—involved both fact finding and use of source material. The former encompassed the observing of facts as stated and implied, differentiating fact and fancy, choosing important details, finding information quickly, following directions, and reading and classifying. Use of source material was visualized as comparing sources of information, using the encyclopedia, understanding figurative language, noting how a story develops, reading travel schedules and timetables, reading charts and diagrams, and using magazine references.

Reading for appreciation and pleasure, the sixth and final skill selected by the faculty, was intended to cover such matters as seeing humor in dialect, appreciating exaggeration, appreciating words, sensing word sounds in poetry, and using imagination to get the poet's meaning.

The suggested program was presented again to the faculty during the pre-school conference prior to the next school session. After discussion, the plan was approved unanimously by the group with one reservation—that Dr. Leavell spend a day with them to demonstrate how the various reading skills might be most effectively taught. The faculty was assured that this request would be fulfilled.

Soon thereafter, Dr. Leavell came to the school and used a full day to demonstrate the teaching of the various skills. In order that all teachers might have an opportunity to see at least one demonstration, the day was organized into six parts corresponding to the six class periods of the school. Each period a group of the teachers assembled. They served as the students, with Dr. Leavell acting as the teacher. The teaching of a different skill was demonstrated each period of the day. Since all teachers did not have opportunity to be present for all demonstrations, it was planned that the teachers would provide their own interchange of experiences. Later, during the course of the reading program, the teachers exchanged freely ideas relative to the teaching of a particular skill. They found departmental meetings to be of special value for bringing out suggestions particularly applicable to the various subject matter fields.

At this point, it might be well to elaborate slightly relative to the reasoning back of the suggested program. In the first place, it can be assumed rather safely that beyond the primary grades, insufficient attention is given to actual instruction in the development of reading skills. During the upper elementary grades and in the secondary school, the pupil is taught largely along subject matter lines. Each field of study has its own body of content. The mastery of these materials becomes the primary objective. In the upper elementary grades, attention to reading may be confined to a designated period of the school day. In the secondary school, instruction in reading is generally considered the prerogative and the responsibility of the language arts teacher. The result thereof is that little attention is given to the development of the essential reading skills.

The second assumption underlying the program is that the necessary reading skills vary with the particular field of study. For example, the reading of a mathematics problem needs to be done in a way different from the rapid perusal of a work of fiction. Here, the faculty came to realize that the teaching of reading was a responsibility of each teacher, regardless of the subject matter under study.

Next, the teachers realized that the suggested program could be undertaken without loss of attention to the immediate field of content. On the other hand, the teachers developed an assurance that instruction in all fields of study should be made more effective through improvement of the reading ability of the pupils. To illustrate, the teachers discovered that the first selected skill—vocabulary development—could be taught more effectively through use of the subject matter at hand. For example, a pupil does not ordinarily learn scientific vocabulary in an English class. Even if the English teacher took time for a study of biological terms, the instruction would be less meaningful than in the biology class.

Finally, the group came to believe that the improvement of reading skills depends on actual instruction designed toward that end. In other words, the skills can be improved if effort is exerted in that direction.

What were the results achieved during this reading program? The faculty depended largely on the *Iowa Silent Reading Test* to affirm progress made. Form Advanced BM was administered in October, and form Advanced DM in April. The median standard scores are revealed in Table I. From the data presented herein, it can be ascertained that the median grade level of students in the

TABLE I

MEDIAN STANDARD SCORES IN GRADE EQUIVALENTS OF THE IOWA SILENT READING TEST FOR NORVIEW HIGH SCHOOL

Grade		No. of Pupils	Form BM October	No. of Pupils	Form DM April
Ten	Boys	165	9.58	174	11.23
	Girls	180	10.01	179	11.94
	Total	345	9.80	353	11.60
Eleven	Boys	133	10.91	144	12.58
	Girls	163	12.31	151	13.0+
	Total	296	11.41	295	13.0+
Twelve	Boys	80	11.26	105	13.0+
	Girls	121	12.35	131	13.0+
	Total	201	11.93	236	13.0+
All Grades	Boys	378	10.30	423	12.01
	Girls	464	11.21	461	13.0+
	Total	842	10.74	884	13.0+

tenth, eleventh, and twelfth grades rose from 10.7 in October, to 13.0+ in April. Whereas the sophomores increased their median from 9.8 to 11.6, the juniors advanced from 11.41 to 13.0, while the seniors progressed from 11.93 to 13.0.

However, the test results were not completely satisfying to the faculty. The teachers were curious as to how much of the improvement in reading skills might still be evident during the following school session. Consequently, form Advanced AM of the Iowa test was administered the next October. Median standard scores are presented in Table II for the eleventh and twelfth grades, the current classes involved in the reading program of the past school session.

It can be observed from Table II that retention of gained reading power was remarkably high. Grade eleven showed a median standard score of 11.60 at the end of the previous session; whereas, it now held to 11.58. Twelfth-grade pupils retained their full progress, holding to an average of 13.0+.

TABLE II

MEDIAN STANDARD SCORES IN GRADE EQUIVA-
LENTS OF THE IOWA SILENT READING TEST
FOR NORVIEW HIGH SCHOOL

Grade		No. of Pupils	Form AM October
Eleven	Boys	182	11.08
	Girls	178	13.0+
	Total	360	11.58
Twelve	Boys	142	13.0+
	Girls	148	13.0+
	Total	290	13.0+
Both Grades	Boys	324	11.75
	Girls	326	13.0+
	Total	650	13.0+

Although some variation can be noted in the separate scores for boys and girls, this does not seem unduly significant. Median scores on the Iowa test beyond the 12.5-grade level fluctuate greatly. A difference of one point on a test score results in wide differentiation of the median score.

Another aspect of the program has also been investigated—the ratio of pupils who failed classes. Although the findings in this regard cannot be considered conclusive, nevertheless, they are interesting. Plans for checking the percentage of failed pupils for each class during the coming years have already been made. Comparison of the number of failures for the two school sessions is presented in Table III, which indicates that the percentage of failed pupils for all classes decreased from 7.3 to 6.7.

The percentage of failed pupils in English classes also decreased last school session. Table IV shows that the percentage of failures for eleventh-grade English decreased from 10.5 for the first school year to 6.3 for last session. Pupils who failed twelfth-grade English declined from 3.7 to 2.9 percent. This trend was not true for freshmen and sophomores, which classes were not involved in the

TABLE III

PUPILS WHO FAILED CLASSES AT NORVIEW
HIGH SCHOOL

	First Year	Second Year
Number of failed classes	613	602
Number of pupils enrolled in school	1475	1589
Percentage of failed pupils	7.3	6.7

reading program. The percentage of failed pupils in English classes for the former group increased from 10.5 to 11.9, while the latter group rose from 10.5 to 10.8.

It cannot be proved that the improvement of reading skills was solely responsible for a lower percentage of pupils who failed classes. Probably the interest manifested by the pupils in improving their reading ability may have accounted for greater interest and effort on their part, not only in English classes but also in other classes. Truly, it can be said that their interest in the reading program was intense. This concern on the part of the pupils is largely accountable to the fact that the faculty explained to the pupils the reasons for the all-out effort to improve reading. In addi-

TABLE IV

PUPILS WHO FAILED ELEVENTH- AND
TWELFTH-GRADE ENGLISH CLASSES AT
NORVIEW HIGH SCHOOL

	First Year	Second Year
Number of pupils who failed classes in eleventh-grade English	22	22
Number of pupils enrolled	216	351
Percentage of failed pupils	10.2	6.3
Number of pupils who failed classes in twelfth-grade English	9	8
Number of pupils enrolled	244	269
Percentage of failed pupils	3.7	2.9

tion, on his first visit to the school, Dr. Leavell discussed the program with representative pupils. Therefore, it seems fairly safe to assume that the reading program provided for the pupils both motivation and improved reading skills that carried over to all subjects.

What is the present status of the reading program at Norview? Late last school session, Dr. Leavell met with the committee on reading, and plans were evolved for the current school session. These plans indicate that the faculty is determined to continue its effort to improve the reading skills of the pupils. The program now under way is based largely on a study of the results of the *Iowa Silent Reading Tests* administered last school session and during October 1955. More attention is being given to the results achieved by each pupil in the various reading skills. The plan of classroom instruction has been modified from that used last session. Following is the plan for the reading program last year:

1. Freshmen—teaching of reading skills, ten minutes daily in the English, social studies, mathematics, science, and other classes that wish to participate in the reading program.
2. Sophomores—teaching of reading skills, one period weekly in English, social studies, mathematics, and science classes.
3. Juniors—teaching of reading skills, one period weekly in English classes only.
4. Seniors—The senior English teachers will decide upon the needs of their respective classes and teach to fill those needs.

In concluding this report of how one faculty is seeking to improve the instructional program of the school through the development of the reading skills of the pupils, the writer wishes to emphasize two points. *First,* it should be kept in mind that the program started with in-service education. For several sessions the faculty had worked together toward the improvement of various aspects of the educational program; such as, guidance services, use of audio-visual materials, and the pupil activity program. Therefore, the reading program was a culmination of years of planned programs of professional growth. Actually the reading program provides an example of in-service education in operation. It is doubtful if the successes realized in the current program would have occurred if the faculty had not experienced years of working together toward advancement of the educational program of the school.

In addition, it needs to be emphasized that during the course of the study of reading, the teachers were well supplied with the materials they needed and with the consultative help they desired. These resources were made available as soon as possible after their need was apparent. Thus, little time elapsed between the statement of a need and its fulfillment. Thereby, the interest of the teachers was maintained at a high level throughout the school session.

The current plans of the school as heretofore stated indicate a determination by the faculty to carry further the efforts to improve reading skills of the pupils. It will be interesting to examine the results of the testing at the end of this session, when form Advanced CM of the Iowa test will be administered. How will progress this year compare with that achieved during the prior session? What will be the results after the program has been in operation for three or four years? What long-term possibilities does the program possess? These and other questions may be answered in time by the Norview faculty.

READING AND STUDY SKILLS PROGRAM
Sally Berkey and Irwin H. Fields

The program described in this article is the result of a concentrated effort on the part of teachers and administrators to improve the quality of reading in the four high schools of the Centinela Valley Union High School District.

Located in Southwest Los Angeles, the Centinela Valley Union High School District is made up of four high schools: Hawthorne, Lawndale, Lennox, and Leuzinger. This district began its much needed reading program in September 1959.

For several years prior to this date, Superintendent Jefferson L. Garner, along with his administrators and teachers, became increasingly concerned with the reading problem throughout the district. Since standardized achievement tests indicated that our students were not reading up to their ability, Superintendent Garner began exploring every possibility of improving reading in the four high schools. Said Dr. Garner, "The improvement of reading should be a *continuous* process. It should *not* stop when the student gets to high school. It should continue in high school, college, and throughout life. Those students who *are not* reading up to their ability should be given special help, and those students who *are* reading up to their ability should be taught to refine and polish their reading skills and techniques. Therefore, the Reading and

Study Skills Program is the answer to our problem."

The first concern of the administration in getting the program underway was to get the approval of the Board of Trustees. In June 1959, Dr. Garner met with the Board and discussed at length the need for a reading program, outlining in detail just how such a program might be incorporated into the high school curriculum. The Board, unanimously agreeing that the program be introduced, provided a budget.

The second concern was to select competent personnel. As in all worthwhile undertakings, this selection could not be made spontaneously. Careful consideration was given to the matter of choosing the *right* person for the *right* job.

Dr. Garner chose for his reading coordinators two district teachers, Mrs. Sally Berkey and Mr. Irwin Fields. Both Mrs. Berkey and Mr. Fields, having had much experience in the field of reading and special training in reading instruction, were given the responsibility of planning the reading program, developing the course of study, ordering materials and equipment, setting up the labs, training new teachers, and supervising the over-all reading program in the four high schools.

Four special reading lab teachers, one for each of the high schools, were hired to work under the supervision of the two coordinators. These lab teachers were instructed to work with and help the reading teachers in their

Reprinted from the *Journal of Secondary Education*, XXXVI (April 1961), 197–202, with permission of the publisher.

respective schools and to conduct the program according to plans.

Endeavoring to secure competent reading instructors, the district encouraged its English teachers who were to be involved in the program to take a summer course in developmental reading at the University of California, Los Angeles, with all expenses paid. Approximately twenty teachers, being fully aware that reading is one of the most important tools in the learning process, were eager to avail themselves of this opportunity. They finished the course, full of enthusiasm and confident that they were much better prepared to participate in the total reading program.

The physical layout of the Reading and Study Skills Program is a rather extensive one. In each of the four high schools there are two complete reading laboratories, which have the latest and best of equipment and materials. Set up to accommodate fifteen students at a time, each lab has four tables with sixteen chairs, ten individual reading booths, an optiglow screen, a wall clock for timed reading, a portable cabinet for projectors, magazine stands, book shelves, filing cabinets, and a teacher's desk and chair.

The reading improvement aids in each lab consist of the following: one tachistoscope, one controlled reader, one tachist-o-flasher, one S.R.A. reading accelerator, one shadowscope, and one tape recorder. Graded film and tape are available for these instruments.

There is a variety of reading materials in each lab. Carefully selected for interest as well as instructional level, these materials range from grade two through fourteen. Among the graded reading materials are the following: S.R.A. (Science Research Associates) Reading Labs, IIA, IIB, IIIA, IVA; S.R.A. Reading for Understanding Labs; *Better Reading Books*, I, II, III, by Elizabeth Simpson; *Be a Better Reader* series, I, II, III, IV, V, VI, by Nila Banton Smith; *Transfer Reading Manual*, Educational Developmental Laboratories; *Effective Reading for Adults,* by Selmer Herr; *Word Attack*, by Clyde Roberts; *Reading for Meaning*, by W. S. Guiter and J. H. Coleman; *Skill Builder* series, Reader's Digest; *How to Become a Better Reader*, by Paul Witty; and *Teen Age Tales*, by Ruth Strang and Ralph Roberts. Included also are paperback books, dictionaries, reference books, magazines and newspapers.

The warm and pleasant atmosphere of each of these fully equipped labs is conducive to reading. The attractive exhibits and the bulletin board displays of colorful book jackets serve as an incentive even to the nonreader.

Concentrated in the freshman English classes, the reading program is a *required* course. It is *mandatory* for every ninth-grade student in the district to spend eight weeks of the school year in the reading lab. (During the year 1959–1960 the lab period was only six weeks.) After all of the freshmen complete their training, the program is then offered to upper classmen for a period of four weeks, college prep students being given first preference.

Generally, the Reading and Study Skills Program was planned to help the students improve their reading habits and their study skills, two of the most important areas of the high school curriculum. Specifically, the goals of the program are to increase the reading rate, to enlarge the vocabulary, to raise the level of comprehension, and to teach the students how to study in all subject fields.

Five major tasks confront each teacher in helping his students accomplish these goals. Those tasks are as follows: (1) the development and refinement of reading techniques and skills, (2) the development of vocabulary and background concepts, (3) the development of reading interests and tastes, (4) the development of independence in reading, and (5) the development of differential attack—ability to adjust reading skills at hand.

The main emphases of the program should be noted. Reading—*always* for a *purpose*—is stressed throughout the course. Flexible reading habits to *suit* the *purpose*, skimming, rapid reading, and study reading, are given great emphasis. Among the specific exercises stressed are vocabulary building, rate building, reading for main idea, reading for details, reading to evaluate, reading to apply, reading for implications, newspaper and magazine reading, using the card catalogue, using the table of contents, indexes, etc., and using dictionaries, atlases, and encyclopedias.

Important also are the many study aids which our students are encouraged to use in all of their classes. Some of the most worthwhile ones are the following: The SQ3R Study Formula, the TQLR Listening Formula, How to Build a Vocabulary, How to Learn to Spell, How to Take Notes, How to Outline, How to Underline, How to Take a Test, How to Use the Dictionary, and How to Use the Library. From these study aids, as well as from the many reading techniques and skills, the students have a definite carry-over not only to their English classes but to all other subjects in school.

In attempting to teach those salient points outlined above, the teacher makes every effort to consider the individual needs of his students. He uses a variety of approaches and methods geared to meet those individual needs. He starts each student at his present reading level and encourages him to work up to his potential.

Before our students begin their training in the reading lab, they go through a period of motivation and orientation. During this time, the teacher constantly *talks* reading to the students and explains to them how important reading is to their success in high school and throughout life. The students visit the reading labs and become acquainted with the overall program. They also visit the library and receive instruction in its use. Here they are encouraged to check out books and to begin building up their own home libraries.

During this period the students are also made to realize the importance of general health and its relation to reading. The school nurse gives a physical check-up to all students, carefully examining their ears and eyes for every possible defect. Immediately following the examination, the nurse sends a report to the teachers and notifies the parents if corrections should be made.

This period of motivation and orientation is of paramount importance. It is during this time that the students begin to realize that reading is basic to *all* subjects and that *all* students, regardless of their reading levels, can learn to improve their reading skills and techniques.

The testing program also serves as a part of motivation. It is pointed out to the students that tests are given for *their* benefit, in order that they may know just where their strengths and weaknesses lie. The *Nelson Silent Reading Test*, Form A, is given to the students before they begin their lab training. Form B of the same test is given at the end of the lab session to see how much progress is made during the training period. Form C of the *Nelson Test* is given at the close of the school year to determine how much carry-over there is and how much achievement is made during the entire year.

When the students are thoroughly motivated and are ready to go into the reading lab for their training, the class of thirty, which is homogeneously grouped for English I, is divided in half. The regular English teacher takes fifteen of these students into one of the two reading labs, and the special reading teacher takes fifteen in the other. For a period of eight weeks these students follow a concentrated program of reading skills, techniques and study aids, as outlined above. They keep a record of their work and chart their progress in a student syllabus *specifically* developed for use in the course. At the end of the lab session, the students receive the results of the B test, and their over-all performance is discussed with them.

The follow-up phase of the reading program is perhaps one of the most important parts of the course. The students return to their regular English classes, and for the remainder of the year they spend at least one day each week in supervised classroom reading. During this time, they put into practice the reading skills and techniques which they learned in the lab. The students also continue to develop and refine their techniques. They work on vocabulary and strive to develop reading interests and tastes, as well as independence in reading. For this all important follow-up procedure, special materials and aids are available for the classroom teacher to use.

Working closely with the freshmen English teachers and the reading lab teachers in both the lab program and the follow-up procedure is the school librarian. In addition to instructing the students in the normal use of library materials, the librarian is always ready to guide the students in independent reading for both recreational and research purposes.

As was stated earlier in this article three forms of the *Nelson Silent Reading Test* are given to all ninth graders, Form A at the beginning of the lab session, Form B at the end, and Form C at the close of the school year. The improvement made by our students during the school year 1959–1960 indicates that the reading program has merit. Nine hundred and seven (907) freshmen went through three six-week sessions. The first session started in September 1959; the second in November 1959; and the third in January 1960. The average reading level of all students at the beginning of the program was seventh grade, six months (7.6). The average reading level at the end of the lab session was eighth grade, second month (8.2). This makes a total gain of six (6) months in six weeks, or one month for each week of instruction. At the end of the school year, after the students had gone through their follow-up program, the average reading level was ninth grade, five months (9.5), a gain of thirteen months (1.3) since the lab period. These figures show that an overall increase of one year and nine months (1.9) was made during the school year.

Significant also is the fact that the majority of our students made many gains which cannot be measured statistically. The strength of the total program was mirrored in the students themselves. Along with their appreciable improvement in reading, our students gained a feeling of self-confidence. They developed socially as well as educationally. Many students, for the first time, began checking books out of the classroom and school libraries. Almost all of our students seemed to have a more favorable attitude toward reading and toward school in general.

The Reading and Study Skills Program has a much broader aspect than that which is outlined above. It is the opinion of the writer that a reading program, to be complete, must be school-wide. During the school year 1959–1960, the reading coordinators endeavored to make the reading program a part of the total school system. In each school a central reading committee made up of the special lab teacher and the school librarian was set up. This committee met periodically throughout the year with each of the twelve departments in school. The purpose of these meetings was to discuss ways and means of improving reading in each subject field. The librarian offered assistance with reading materials, and the lab teacher helped with skills and techniques. This procedure proved to be very effective in that it made the majority of teachers in school realize that the teaching of reading is their responsibility.

Special counseling also became a part of the school-wide program. A special reading counselor in each high school was chosen to do individual case studies where results of the reading program were unusual. This helped to point to the kinds of changes or emphases that the reading teachers, counselors, and administrators should consider.

As a result of all of these efforts on the part of the teachers and administrators, the reading atmosphere permeated the entire school district, and the Reading and Study Skills Program was coordinated with the overall school curriculum.

During the present school year, 1960–1961, our reading program is off to a good start. Already two freshman groups have gone through the concentrated program with results comparable to those of last year. The school-wide aspect is being given even greater emphasis with the hope that *all* teachers will become teachers of reading and will feel responsible for the reading habits of their students.

Our school library is becoming more popular every day. The circulation of books is increasing, and research materials are being used more extensively. Students find it enjoyable and helpful using the reading accelerators which are placed in the libraries to stimulate the overall program. They also find a special challenge in selecting and purchasing paperback books on sale in each library. In fact, the school library is beginning to be the center of our reading program.

By no means is our reading program a perfect one. It still has much ground to cover. As the program progresses from year to year, improvements and necessary changes will have to be made. Methods and procedures will have to be adjusted; new materials and equipment will have to be added; and new teachers will have to be trained. All of these modifications, and probably many others, will be made with a sole purpose in mind—that of meeting the individual needs of our students.

THE CORE PROGRAM DOES IMPROVE READING PROFICIENCY
Myrtle Dewey Toops

The growing trend toward a richer and more challenging program of living and learning, with a practical and functional education for the early adolescent in our junior high schools, is creating much interest in the effectiveness of the 'common learnings' program, known in this paper as an adolescent-needs core curriculum, in the development of proficiency in reading. Despite the many investigations which have been made since the

Reprinted from *Educational Administration and Supervision,* XL (December 1954), 494–503, with permission of the author.

Eight-Year Study, with their favorable conclusions, there are wide differences of opinion concerning how well, and to what degree, a cooperatively planned, problem-solving type of program, which has as its chief goal the solution of the everyday problems of adolescents, can develop achievement in reading.

The first question asked by teachers in the high schools of a traditional system is, "Will these students, coming out of a core program, be able to read the social studies textbook or the American literature book in our classes?"

Laymen, parents, and the general public fear that reading is neglected in any curriculum change and ask, "Will the youth in my family or those that I wish to employ be able to read if they are educated in this new type of program?"

Research bears out that not all students in any class have ever been able to read understandingly the one textbook prescribed for all. The implications of these questions, as to the philosophical and psychological principles of modern education, are not the objectives of this paper and, therefore, they will not be pursued.

It is the belief of the author that there are far too many drop-outs in our high schools today. It is true that many students give as their reason, a failure to find little that they believe is valuable in helping them to solve their everyday problems of living. Ours is a complex society and it is our duty to gear our problems to the problems, interests, and needs of the adolescent and to use the basic skills—reading, writing, and spelling—as the tools, a means toward an end and not an end in themselves. Reading, then, is used for a definite purpose and, as a result, much improvement is made because many materials of many levels of reading achievement are made available.

It is the purpose of the writer to present the findings of a study of reading achievement in vocabulary and comprehension, conducted in two adolescent-needs core classes of thirty children each, over a period of two years in Burris Laboratory School of Ball State Teachers College in Muncie, Indiana. The sixty children spent two and one-half hours each day in the core class and were taught for two consecutive years by the same core teacher. The program was planned cooperatively by the teacher and students and the 'problems approach' was followed. Materials of many levels of reading achievement were used.

Reading was not taught as a special sub-ject at any time, except in a few extreme individual cases who needed help as the work progressed. How to locate information, how to skim, how to find central ideas, how to use indexes, charts, and graphs, how to outline, and how to take notes were taught in connection with the solving of the problems planned in the core work. A recreational reading program was a part of the planned program as well as the work type involved in problem solving.

Chronological age, hearing, and vision do not enter into the results of the study because all children ranged from eleven to thirteen years of age during the two years of study and both the hearing and vision of all children were declared normal by the school nurse and doctors.

No attempt will be made to compare the core group with a control group in the traditional type of program. The results of the study would be more reliable if several achievement tests and more than one intelligence test had been administered. No attempt will be made in the study to give reasons for the differences found in the study.

The problems, to which conclusions are sought in the study, are: Does the adolescent-needs core program develop proficiency in reading? Are there differences in the gains made by the bright, average, and below average children in mental ability? Do boys or girls make the greater gains? In which year are the gains greater?

A brief review of research related to these problems follows.

REVIEW OF RELATED RESEARCH

A significant study was made in 1944 by Wrightstone (6)* in which he compared the proficiency in reading skills of the children in one hundred classes in an activity type of program with the same number of classes in

[*Numbers in parentheses refer to Bibliography at the end of this article.]

a traditional type of program in the New York City Schools. This study showed that the mean, or average, score in reading in the activity schools excelled the mean score in the traditional schools.

In 1951 Harding (4), in a summary of investigations of a dozen studies, including the research findings of Stone, Starkey, Mitchell, Geyer, Siffered, Kilpatrick, Eaton, and Hildreth in the achievement of children in reading in formal types of schools as compared with the informal, developmental types, found the results to be skewed in every study, except the one by Eaton, toward the activity or experimental type of program. In Eaton's study, Harding found the research to show that the type of program made no difference.

Capehart, Hodges, and Berdan (1), in a study of the results of achievement in reading, found, in 1952, that core groups of students in ninth and tenth grades, paired with groups in a subject-centered program, made scores in reading achievement which were constantly higher than the matched group.

In a survey of the students in a Denver junior high school in 1945, Elklund (3) credited the method of approach, 'the problems-approach'—used in the new guidance program—as the chief reason for the significant progress which these students made in reading. Four years later Kight and Mickelson (5) found the same to be true in high-school classes, using the problems type of instruction, in the city of Los Angeles.

Cunningham, (2) in an extensive eight-month study of group behavior and group living with elementary- and junior-high-school students in the New York City Schools in 1950, found, through testing the achievement of the children, that, at all levels of intelligence, they made a gain of one year or more in reading comprehension. In comparing these scores with those gained in a more rigid program, she found that the children in the 'group living' program excelled.

In summarizing the findings in the research previously reviewed, it is pointed out that they show that the gains made in reading achievement by the children in the activity or problem type classes excelled those gains made by the children in the traditional, formal type program.

THE RESEARCH METHODS

Sixty children in Burris Laboratory School of Ball State Teachers College in Muncie, Indiana, were divided into two matched heterogeneous groups of thirty each. They were matched as evenly as it was possible to do so according to the intelligence quotients revealed by the California Test of Mental Maturity, Long Form for Grades Four to Eight. Each class had a range of IQ from 67 to 152 with an equal number of bright, average, and below average in each group. Children with IQ's of 110 to 152 were classified as bright, those from 90 to 109 as average, and those from 67 to 89 as below average. The above mentioned test was administered in the third week of September to each group of children in this sixth-grade class by the core teacher, who was well-trained in giving tests and who had established good rapport with the children. These children had no visual or auditory problems. The age ranged, for the two years, from ten years, eight months to twelve years, eight months; therefore, chronological age did not enter into the research. There were no accelerated or retarded children, from having spent less or more time in school.

In September 1948, the Standard Achievement Test for Intermediate Grades, Partial Battery, Form G, was administered to both groups and achievement was recorded in grade levels. In May 1949, after nine months in the core program, a second achievement test was given. The Stanford Test for Intermediate Grades, Form H, was administered and results were recorded in the same manner as the September test. Gains, if any, were estimated for the first year from these test results in reading.

The class was not tested at the beginning of the seventh grade but, after a period of nine months, the same teacher, who had served as core teacher for both groups for the second year, administered the Stanford Achievement Test, Advanced Form for Grades Seven to Twelve, Form M, to the group in May 1950. These test results were recorded in the form of grade level achievement and compared with both the September 1949 and the May 1949 achievement levels.

From these statistics the author has shown the results of the core program in developing proficiency in reading skills, the years wherein the greater gains were made, whether boys or girls made the greater gains, and whether the bright, average, or below average in intelligence profited most.

In pursuing this study the author was interested in making comparisons of results of the three reading achievement tests in both comprehension and vocabulary. Therefore Table 1 contains a complete tabulation of the achievement in grade level of each case in both reading areas with the average of the comprehension and vocabulary stated as 'Total Reading.'

Inasmuch as the writer wished to compare the intelligence level of each child with reading gains, the intelligence quotient of each case was included in the table, also. From this table mean gains have been computed for both the first and second years of the study. A comparison of the gains made by each sex and a comparison of mental ability and reading achievement were computed from this table.

RESULTS OF THE STUDY

The interpretations and findings reported in this research paper were based upon the data found in Table 1. This table showed that the greatest single gain in total reading for the two-year period was made by Case No. 4 and was a gain of 4.8 years. The smallest single gain was made by Case No. 60 with a gain of 0.2 years only for the same period of time. It must be pointed out that no child scored lower nor remained at the same grade level at the end of the two-year period. A comparison of single gains, made in comprehension and in vocabulary, showed comprehension slightly higher than vocabulary. The comprehension range extended from 0.1 years of gain to 5.0 years of gain. In vocabulary the range began with a low of 0.1 years and ran as high as 4.6 years. It was found that gains in comprehension were 0.4 years higher than vocabulary.

The mean gain in total reading for the entire time was 2.15 years, while the approximate median was 2.2 years. The range in gain in total reading was from 0.2 years to 4.8 years in grade levels.

The mean gain in comprehension was 2.33 years, while in vocabulary the average or mean gain was 2.05 years. It was found that gains in comprehension were 0.28 years above the gains in vocabulary.

Most cases were concentrated between gains of 2.0 years and 3.9 years. An examination of the range of gains, as shown in Table 2, revealed that thirty-six of the sixty cases lay between the range of 2.0 and 3.9 years.

The grade norm, established by the three Stanford tests, were 6.0, 7.0, and 8.0, respectively. An examination of the medians, made by these cases in total reading, showed them to be slightly above or at the standard norm. At the beginning of grade six the September test showed a median of 6.1 grade level, or 0.1 years above the norm. By the close of the sixth grade the May test produced a median of 7.0 grade level. By the close of grade seven a median of 8.3, or 0.3 years above the norm was found.

TABLE 1

READING ACHIEVEMENT AND MENTAL ABILITY SCORES IN GRADES SIX AND SEVEN
FOR THE SCHOOL YEAR OF 1948–1949 AND 1949–1950*

	Sex		I.Q.	Sept. 1948			May 1949			Gains			May 1950			Two-Year Gains		
	B	G		Par. mean.	Word mean.	Tot. read.	Par. mean.	Word mean.	Tot. read.	Par. mean.	Word mean.	Tot. mean.	Par. mean.	Word mean.	Tot. read.	Par. mean.	Word mean.	Tot. read.
1	*		152	8.1	9.3	8.7	11.3	11.3	11.3	3.2	2.0	2.6	11.3	11.3	11.3	3.2	2.0	2.6
5	*		134	7.1	8.8	7.9	11.3	10.8	11.0	4.2	2.0	3.1	11.3	11.3	11.3	4.2	2.5	3.4
10	*		123	7.7	7.9	7.8	9.6	9.3	9.4	1.9	1.4	1.6	10.5	8.8	9.6	2.8	0.9	1.8
15		*	118	7.1	8.3	7.7	11.3	9.6	10.4	3.8	1.3	1.9	10.8	11.3	11.0	3.7	3.0	2.6
20	*		116	6.6	7.5	7.0	8.6	8.8	8.7	2.0	1.3	1.7	11.1	9.3	10.2	4.5	1.8	3.2
25		*	113	5.4	4.0	4.7	6.0	5.2	5.6	0.6	1.2	0.9	7.9	6.3	7.1	2.5	2.3	2.4
30		*	110	5.6	8.3	6.9	6.5	9.0	7.7	0.9	0.7	0.8	7.5	9.0	8.2	1.9	0.7	1.3
35	*		110	4.1	6.0	5.0	6.1	6.8	6.4	2.0	0.8	1.4	8.0	8.5	8.2	3.9	2.5	3.2
40		*	108	6.0	6.3	6.1	6.3	6.3	6.3	0.3	0.0	0.2	6.6	6.5	6.5	0.6	0.2	0.4
45		*	104	7.0	7.7	7.3	7.1	8.6	7.8	0.1	0.9	0.5	7.8	10.5	9.1	0.8	2.8	1.8
50		*	99	4.3	5.8	5.0	5.6	6.8	6.2	1.3	1.0	1.2	7.1	7.3	7.2	2.8	1.5	2.2
55		*	88	4.4	4.4	4.4	4.5	5.6	5.0	0.1	1.2	0.6	5.8	5.0	5.4	1.4	0.6	1.0
60	*		67	2.5	2.9	2.7	2.5	2.7	2.6	0.0	0.2	0.1	3.0	2.8	2.9	0.5	0.1	0.2

* Every fifth case, from the original table of sixty cases is here recorded, in order to eliminate long tables. The cases are arranged from the highest IQ to the lowest IQ.

TABLE 2

RANGE OF GAINS FOR TWO YEARS WITH
FREQUENCY OF CASES IN EACH RANGE

Range of Gains	Frequency of Cases
4.0–4.8 years	1
3.0–3.9 years	12
2.0–2.9 years	24
1.0–1.9 years	17
0.0–0.9 years	6

Further study of the gains during the two-year period in total reading was carried on as shown by Table 3. This table showed that thirty-two cases scored above the grade norm in September 1948, at the beginning of grade six, and six cases below grade three. In the test given in May 1949, at the close of grade six, thirty-three cases scored above the grade norm with three cases at or below grade three. In the test given in May 1950, there were thirty-five cases above grade norm and one case below grade three. At the top bracket, 11.0–11.3, the number of cases increased from no cases in September 1948 to eleven cases in May 1950. The lower bracket remained the same with the same case staying within the bracket for the two-year period.

It must be pointed out here that those cases, which have scores of 11.3 in each of the three reading tests, were, probably, not adequately tested, because this score represents the perfect score on the test and it was not known how much greater the reading power of these cases were.

The author was interested, too, in learning which group—the above average, average, or below average—in intelligence or mental ability gained most, if any, in reading achievement. Table 4 gives this information.

The group classified as above average ranged in intelligence quotients between 111 and 152; the average group lay between 90 and 110; and the below average had intelligence quotients between 67 and 89 as determined by the California Test of Mental Ma-

turity. An examination of this table showed that fifty-four of the sixty cases had intelligence quotients ranging between 90 and 152, the average and above average groups. The above average or bright group had an 0.2 year's mean gain over the average group which showed up with a gain of 0.7 year's gain over the below average group. Thus the results showed that the cases in the above average group made the most gain. These mean gains were determined in total reading.

A third comparison, which was made, was that of gains scored by the boys and the girls. Table 5 showed a comparison in reading achievement in terms of mean gains according to sex. From this table it could be seen that the boys made an average gain of 0.17 years over the girls. Too, it was evident that the average IQ of the boys exceeded the girls by 11 points, which might be the causative factor. However, in this research it was evident that the average group in intelligence showed within 0.2 years as much gain as the above average group and the intelligence factor was evidently not significant in the development of reading proficiency in these two groups. In the below average group it appeared to be one of the causative factors. This

TABLE 3

RANGE OF GRADE ACHIEVEMENT LEVELS WITH THE FREQUENCY OF CASES WITHIN EACH LEVEL FOR THE TWO-YEAR PERIOD IN TOTAL READING

Grade Achievement Range	Frequency of Cases		
	Sept. 1948	May 1949	May 1950
11.0–11.3	0	2	11
10.0–10.9	3	8	8
9.0– 9.9	1	6	6
8.0– 8.9	9	7	10
7.0– 7.9	8	9	11
6.0– 6.9	11	10	5
5.0– 5.9	10	11	5
4.0– 4.9	12	4	3
3.0– 3.9	5	2	0
2.0– 2.9	1	1	1

TABLE 4

COMPARISON OF GAINS IN TOTAL READING
ACHIEVEMENT ACCORDING TO MENTAL
ABILITY

Range of IQ	Frequency of Cases	Mean Gains in Reading
111–152	28	2.3 years
90–110	26	2.1 years
89– 67	6	1.4 years

TABLE 5

COMPARISON OF MEAN GAINS IN READING
ACHIEVEMENT ACCORDING TO SEX

Sex	Av. IQ	No. of Cases	Mean Gains in Reading
Boys	111	29	2.24
Girls	100	31	2.07

is not proven, however. Both boys and girls averaged higher than the norms of the tests.

CONCLUSIONS

In summarizing the final results of this study, the writer believes that it was quite evident that reading was not neglected in this core program because the children showed mean gains of more than two years in grade level achievement in both comprehension and vocabulary and in total reading in the two-year period spent in the core program.

The results of the study of reading proficiency showed the following:

1. The sixty children studied made definite gains in reading comprehension and vocabulary with a mean gain of more than two years.
2. The children made a slightly greater gain the second year than they made the first year. The median for the class each year was at or above the median established by the norms of the test.

3. Children of above average intelligence scored slightly higher gains than the average intelligence group. This average group scored greater gains than the below average group. These gains were higher than the differences in the gains in the first groups mentioned.
4. In the average and above average groups intelligence did not seem to be a causative factor to any great extent, but it appeared to be a probable cause in the below average group.
5. Boys made slightly greater gains than the girls. The difference in the mean intelligence quotient of the boys exceeded the mean intelligence quotient of the girls. This may be a causative factor.
6. From all evidence presented it appeared that all children showed some gain in reading proficiency in the two-year period in the adolescent-needs core program and that reading was not neglected in the curriculum.

BIBLIOGRAPHY

1. CAPEHART, BERTIS E., HODGES, ALLEN, and BERDAN, NORMAN. "An objective evaluation of a core program," *The School Review*, 60: 84–89, February 1952.
2. CUNNINGHAM, RUTH, and Associates. *Understanding Group Behavior of Boys and Girls.* New York: Teachers College, Columbia University, 1951, pp. 446.
3. ELKLUND, JOHN M. "Reading progress through a guidance program," *The Clearing House*, 21:9–12, September 1946.
4. HARDING, LOWRY W. "How well are schools now teaching the basic skills," *Progressive Education*, 29:7–14, October 1951.
5. KIGHT, STANFORD S., and MICKELSON, JOHN M. "Problem vs. subject," *Clearing House*, 24:3–7, September 1949.
6. WRIGHTSTONE, J. WAYNE. "Evaluation of the experiment with the activity program in the New York City elementary schools," *Journal of Educational Research*, 38:252–257, December 1944.

READING MATERIALS: RATIONALE AND REVIEW
Robert Karlin

Instructional Materials are big business! Witness the association of industrial corporations with publishers and the purchase of educational publishing organizations by their cousins who had limited their activities to other areas. Although huge sums of money have been spent for instructional materials, the market has expanded as a result of new monies available to some school districts for the first time. We who have not spent much time in sections other than metropolitan will find hard to believe the fact that tens of thousands of children actually do not have enough materials from which to learn. I'm thinking of not only the economically depressed sections of the country but also so many of our rural areas where either tax money, know-how, or concern is lacking. The federal government through different titles now is making it possible for school districts to beef up their programs by providing funds for all sorts of materials. For some this means breaking new ground; for others freeing funds for other things. The net result is larger sums of money for the purchase of materials—and materials for teaching reading will not be slighted.

Competition among publishers of reading materials is keen. Each desires to corner as much of the market as possible. In order to consummate a sale amounting to several millions, one company had to demonstrate the superiority of its materials over the competition. This demonstration brings up the question of how we determine the superiority of one set of reading materials over another. Do we do this on the basis of research finds, universally-accepted criteria, judgments based upon personal prejudices—what? Perhaps a little of each—and in some instances no real judgments at all.

Although there has been some research involving the use of reading materials (such as studies in which readiness or upper level workbooks were used with one group and not another, or in which outcomes of instructional *programs* were compared), the total amount is limited. For example, one reviewer found "no major studies of the evaluation of materials or their usefulness"[1] over a three-year period. Another, three years later, summarized but two studies of the types mentioned earlier.[2] As recently as 1965 a third compiler mentioned one study that compared the use of a mechanical device "with regular methods of teaching reading."[3] We

Adapted from a paper presented at the Ninth Annual Meeting of The College Reading Association, Jersey City State College, April 2, 1966.

[1] Theodore Clymer and Helen Robinson, "Reading," in *Language Arts and Fine Arts*, Review of Educational Research, Vol. XXXI, No. 2 (April 1961), 133.

[2] Jack A. Holmes and Harry Singer, "Theoretical Models and Trends Toward More Basic Research in Reading," in *Language Arts and Fine Arts*, Review of Educational Research, Vol. XXXIV, No. 2 (April 1964), 148.

[3] Helen Robinson, "Summary of Investigations Relating to Reading, July 1, 1963 to June 30, 1964." *The Reading Teacher*, Vol. 18, No. 5 (Feb. 1965), 396.

have few if any studies which sought to determine the superiority of one set of materials over another. Perhaps from a research point of view what we are asking for cannot be done (for example, separating materials from programs). But I can envision a study in which a given skill is taught and then materials used to determine their effectiveness in strengthening its development. And self-teaching materials offer other opportunities also to ascertain superiority.

Universally-accepted criteria for reading materials? No such things. Specialists in children's literature have suggested guidelines we might follow, but what guidelines are there for choosing one set of instructional materials over another? I suppose if we were to establish any, we would be concerned about such factors as content, interest, format. Of course, the most important factor might be the extent to which our purposes are met by the materials.

I would settle for the latter, but experience tells me no such thing. Too many reading materials are chosen on the basis of what we are told about them. Publisher's promotions and claims are powerful influences in determining school sales. I would concede that selection on these bases is no worse than that emanating from ignorance.

Since we don't have much evidence about the worth of instructional materials intended to promote reading development, I will have to rely on my own experiences to assess them. Perhaps some of your own are similar to mine.

BASAL READERS

How do we rate basal readers? Let us consider the old guard first and then evaluate the newcomers.

We are all familiar with the typical basal reader with its paper-back pre-primers and one or more hardbacks for each grade level. What are their features? According to the publishers and advocates these materials deal with activities familiar to many children and based upon their common interests. The selections are graded in difficulty by controlling vocabulary load, density and difficulty of ideas, sentence length, and so on. The content includes narrative and expository selections, fiction and poetry and is presented in an attractive format to hold children's attention and promote the development of reading ability.

We are told these features are necessary and desirable. But criticisms have been leveled against these books: the content is unexciting to children (boys in particular) and does not sustain their interest; writing styles with their repetitions and limited vocabularies are of poor literary quality; the selections do not reflect the cross section of American life with its diverse peoples, values and environments; there is a limited amount of subject-matter content with which to develop reading and study skills associated with it.

There is no doubt that some of these criticisms are valid—perhaps not wholly—certainly in part—but my guess is that we apply some of our adult common sense to these materials and draw conclusions that we support strongly with the help of authority. Insofar as the unexciting content is concerned: certainly at the earliest stages, if we accept the reader's approach to word identification, there can't be much of any story, let alone exciting ones. Of course, as time goes on and children develop some basic skills, selections can contain more "meat" as well as deal with activities of a less sedentary nature. I'm all for appealing to more boys. But I'm not so sure the "action" which some critics want is the diet young children should have. Certainly it shouldn't be the sole fare.

What about poor literary quality? I don't know of anyone who would defend most basal readers on literary grounds. The first books in the series rely on limited vocabulary; such a condition can put a crimp in anyone's writing (Dr. Seuss notwithstanding). But once children have developed adequate word-attack skills, they need not be tied down to uninspired writing. With some modifications the writings of our better trade book authors could find their way into the readers. We are beginning to see some changes in this direction already occurring.

Most publishers of basal readers would plead guilty to the charge that these books reflect American middle class attitudes— white ones at that—and do not truly represent American diversity. You are all familiar with the claim that large numbers of children cannot and do not identify with the readers' characters and surroundings which are totally foreign to them; that they reject these and as a result are doomed to almost certain failure. Although I personally might prefer to include selections which more closely portray life as many people know it, I'm not so sure for example, that it is necessary to give economically and culturally disadvantaged children heavy doses of what they know all too well, or that heroes they read about have to be exclusively of their own kind. I would agree that we need diversity and balance. Here is one area which research might well explore. Some publishers, in reply to this criticism, color a face here and there. What this means to children I do not know. More about this later.

It seems to me that criticism of most readers for their failure to deal with content systematically is valid. With conditions as they are, it is unrealistic to assume that teachers will offer this instruction as children study textbooks and other materials. I would recommend the inclusion of material which is representative of the types of reading we expect our pupils to do. Surely instruction in reading content is basic.

A number of new basic series have introduced significant changes in orthography, word patterns and story settings. The materials through which a new orthography is introduced are quite similar to those with which we are familiar. One basic series that attempts to control sound patterns reads much like its counterparts of the "look, look" variety. A few others could also qualify for criticism on similar grounds. They are not literary or exciting by any stretch of the imagination. But all their worth must be assessed against standards that measure how well children learn to read and how much they desire to read.

Two sets of readers depart from the usual in that one stresses city living and the other the Negro. I would reject any set of materials which delimits a reader's perspective. Of what significance are ideas that are always comfortingly familiar? That we need some does not deny the need for others which are quite different. Do we expect the city child not to know or care about his cousins in the suburbs and rural communities? Do we assume he is a cliff dweller for all times? And a poor one at that? This brings me to the readers which are intended essentially for young Negro children. How are they different? Unlike the series which color an occasional face brown, these books deal with lives of Negro families. Although these families do not own private homes as pretentious as their white counterparts in other series, they do have their plots of grass and cars and do enjoy life in the suburbs. To the children for whom these materials are intended, this kind of life is quite foreign. How different, then, are they from the usual? In color. Will these materials help to produce better readers? My guess is that they won't, but I'm prepared to look at outcomes dispassionately.

Some of my comments have been seconded by people in the field. Undoubtedly exceptions to them will be taken by others who *feel* strongly about basal readers. Until we can devise a better mousetrap I would suggest we strive to improve them. I would take issue with those who say that basal readers have inherent weaknesses which can't be overcome. No matter how attractive they do become, the ways in which they are used will determine their effectiveness. I can foresee a time when it might be possible to dispense with basal readers—when computer retrieval systems make available to us what we want and when we want it and when teachers know what they want and what to do with it when they have it.

WORKBOOKS

Workbooks may be divided into two classes: those which are designed to be used with a reading series and others that are independent. Whether the workbooks parallel reading programs or go their own way, they contain practice exercises in one or more of the following: readiness, word identification, comprehension, study skills. Independent workbooks tend to stress individual skills (such as phonic workbooks or those intended for upper grades) than cover the wide range found in series workbooks.

One of the problems associated with workbooks is the failure of many teachers to recognize to what purposes they might be put. As I see them, workbooks contain exercises which offer *practice*: in interpreting pictures, in matching letters with sounds, in discriminating between similar words, in using context clues and recognizing word endings, in dividing words into syllables, in reading for details and main ideas, in developing vocabulary, in summarizing and outlining, in drawing conclusions, and so on. Few, if any, offer *instruction* in skill development. Pupils require practice after instruction—some more and others less—and it is possible that a discriminative teacher will find exercises in workbooks that he can use for such purposes.

Teachers as a group prefer to use workbooks rather than prepare their own materials. They argue that they provide for individual differences, save time and effort,

contain exercises superior to those which they might devise, free teachers to work with children who need extra help. The critics point to their cut-and-dried format, isolated exercises, mechanical responses, limited content. It would not be difficult to find samples to support each viewpoint.

What position do many of us take? There is nothing wrong with workbooks that we can't correct. I suspect we have been taken in by the claims some people have made for workbooks and then complain that they are not doing the job. Let's first recognize that no amount of time pupils spend with these materials will do them any good if they are unable to perform the tasks required of them. If children are weak in auditory discrimination of consonant blends and the practice exercise requires them to match these blends with pictures, what usefulness will the exercise have for them? Or if a group of children are weak in recognizing the central thought of a paragraph, will an exercise that requires them to perform this task enable them to do so? Recognize workbooks for what they are. Teach first, and assign those exercises which give practice in doing what you've taught.

This brings us to weaknesses of many workbooks. On a given page you might find a number of different components, to some of which, perhaps, your pupils are not ready to respond. Or there is an inadequate amount of practice material to which they can respond. You can overcome these weaknesses by removing the pages of different workbooks, cutting some into smaller parts and bringing together sections containing exercises covering given skills. These might be mounted and placed in envelopes for use when needed.

Another suggestion. You can obtain added mileage from some workbooks by taking ideas from their better exercises and applying them to the materials which your pupils are reading. Such practice will be of help to the busy teacher (and to one who needs ideas) as well as tie more closely skills practice to reading activity.

There is another point about workbooks I need to make. Generally, each page or exercise has a stated purpose. A careful examination of some reveals that the exercise does not fulfill the stated purpose. Once again, indiscriminate assignments will lull the user into believing pupils are engaging in and profiting from an activity when in reality no such things are happening. We must know our craft sufficiently well so that we recognize weakness wherever it occurs.

Let's take a quick look into the future: You have just taught a skills lesson to a group of children (to vary routines) who are reading on different levels. You have been working on clues for drawing conclusions. Now you need some practice material. You go to your console, push some buttons—wheels whir, and out of the units that are part of each desk come materials that are just right for each child. As soon as the child finishes the page, he inserts it into the machine which indicates the correctness of his responses. If you are seeking oral responses, the child's screen lights up, material suitable for him appears and he responds. Each correct response is confirmed; incorrect responses are noted, fresh material provided with oral explanations, followed by new practice exercises. Automatic workbooks of the future!

PACKAGED MIXES AND PROGRAMMED MATERIALS

There are a group of instructional materials which are packaged in boxes. Some contain materials intended for primary grade use; others provide materials for the middle grades, junior and senior high schools. One covers basic word identification, comprehension skills, and rate; another study skills, and so on. The features that promoters of these materials stress are their different levels of difficulty covered and minimal teacher attention required. At the higher levels they are supposed to free the teacher for other tasks.

None of these materials is truly programmed although some publishers describe them as though they were. Which does not make them self-instructional. What does this fact mean? Can you take one of these boxes, set your class loose and assume you have an on-going program? From my point of view— no. If you desire your pupils to practice what they have learned, these boxes will help you achieve this purpose. They will not assume the responsibility of providing instruction. They might make your task easier by offering ready-tailored practice materials.

There is a small number of instructional materials which use programmed techniques —more or less. Two sets of these materials have been written for beginning readers. I find them quite dull in content and design; however, they might appeal to beginners. Insofar as their work is concerned, results in producing competent readers as well as eager ones have yet to be established. We should not be prepared to accept data from vested interests until they have been verified. I do know of a tryout in which one of them was found wanting.

There are a few additional materials that follow the programmed design. It seems to me that highly creative efforts might produce instructional materials for teaching some reading skills, if not many of them. Some people feel that many of the higher-level comprehension skills require "talking out" which programming lacks. Provision for audio as well as visual treatments could fill the gaps and surround the learner with "give and take" not presently offered by successive frames of printed explanations, questions and answers. You may be familiar with the experimental program which taught a poem by helping the reader to analyze it. Perhaps more of this type of experimentation will give us insights into how we can get the job done in a meaningful and efficient way. There is still the problem of overcoming impersonal treatment with which programmers have not been concerned but learners are.

AUDIO-VISUAL AIDS

Charts, flash cards, games, word wheels, film strips, records—these and more can help you get the job done and help make learning interesting provided they are not used indiscriminately and for their own sake. You must ask yourself this question whenever you are tempted by them: Will they help my pupils learn what they don't know? If the answer is in the affirmative the second question should follow: Under what circumstances might I use them? To illustrate what I mean: here is a word game which you know children enjoy playing. What is the relationship between the words in the game and those with which a group of children has difficulty in the reading it does? If none, then that game is unsuitable. You might pattern your own game after it and substitute the troublesome words. But the game is introduced as part of a total lesson, using context, phonic and structural clues to recognize the words, developing rapid recognition of them, and dealing with them again in context. Under these circumstances playing the game is a meaningful, purposeful learning experience as well as an enjoyable one. It is not an end in itself. These comments also apply to the other kinds of instructional materials mentioned earlier.

MECHANICAL AIDS

Pacers, flashmeters, films. These are used more at the higher levels than at the lower ones since most are intended to promote rapid reading. Unlike the other materials, investigations into their validity have been conducted with elementary, secondary and college students as well as adults. The evidence we have is fairly clear: flashmeters seem to be of least value; films aren't much better; pacers, if used properly, might be helpful if only to motivate. In a summary of the research, the conclusion was reached that any gains achieved with mechanical devices might be duplicated or surpassed through natural means. Gadgets are appealing, but we tire of them if they fail to meet our expectations.

There are some new developments in gadgetry which might be promising. One is an instrument which reads words that are typed on tape. Thus a child can see words on cards at the same time that he hears them. The other is a viewing device which provides reading instruction through visual and auditory programs. Both might be useful in a skills program of a knowledgeable teacher.

SUMMARY

We have intimated, if we haven't said, that materials are no better than the teachers who use them just as our physical plants are as good as the staffs who make them. With the exception of materials that *actually* free us of teaching responsibilities, how useful instructional materials are depends on how well we understand their strengths and limitations. Some of the most simple kinds of instructional materials can be profitably employed to promote reading; on the other hand, elaborate designs, though impressive, won't help us very much. I have learned to be skeptical of claims; in a world of many marvels and much money we need more educators who say, "I'm from Missouri."

Index

Parents, *see* Home environment
Parker, Don H., 313, 358–363
Penty, Ruth C., 1, 9–12
Personality, *see* Development, personal; Emotional status
Phillips, Albert, 32, 34–35, 52, 54
Phonic skill, 129, 130–131, 137, 138, 139, 141, 143, 301–302
  measuring, 116, 117, 118, 119–120
Piaget, Jean, 235
Poetry, 79–80, 174, 177, 211, 220, 221, 222–223, 224, 226, 227, 239, 290, 297, 305, 310–311, 370
Pre-school children, 35, 82, 86
  see also Reading, beginning
Preston, Ralph C., 3, 199, 243, 250
Programed instruction, 89, 90, 91, 389–394, 429–430
Programs, reading
  administration/organization of, 9–12, 358–363, 386–387, 395–403, 414–418
  adult, 246
  all-school, 203–208, 364–375, 404–413
  content teachers and, 201–203, 204
  core, 418–424
  developmental, 9, 395–403
  free, 245
  future, 99
  poor, 57
  secondary school, 7–9, 200–209, 237–238, 358–363, 405–413
Pronunciation, word, 104, 128, 129, 137, 205
Psychotherapy, 42, 43, 44, 48, 61, 64, 105
Pupils, *see* Students

Questions, teachers', 175–176, 178, 215–216, 223, 303–304

Raymond, Dorothy M., 35, 37, 38–39, 53
Readers
  adult, 263–269
  retarded, 10, 15, 16, 31, 38, 104, 119–121, 132
Readiness, reading, 87, 89, 320–333
Reading
  beginning, 127, 130–131, 132, 137, 208, 299, 301–302
  clinics, 42, 359, 406–407
  content, 220, 234, 238–241, 276–284, 306–312
  critical, 159–160, 167–168, 253, 255, 256, 259, 324
  flexibility, 71, 122–124, 211, 255, 257–259, 268, 269, 319, 409, 416
  groups, 10, 141–142, 372–373, 376–377, 406
  guided vs. free, 222–223, 245

Reading (*cont.*)
  levels, 6, 57, 358–363
  power, 71–77
  process, 77–79, 98–99, 122, 398
  psychology of, 66–70
  specialists, 7, 16, 203, 208, 237, 303, 359, 409, 410, 417–418
  supplementary, 143
  see also Oral reading; Skills, reading
Reading improvement programs, *see* Programs, reading
Recall, *see* Memory
Remedial reading, *see* Instruction, reading; Programs, reading
Rereading, 255, 259
Retardation, reading, *see* Disability, reading
Retention, reading, *see* Memory
Reversal tendency, 34–35, 47, 120–121
Robinson, F. P., 126, 179, 195–199, 256, 260, 318*n.*, 320
Robinson, H. Alan, 126, 132–133, 134, 179, 192–195, 403
Robinson, Helen M., 26, 27, 28, 29, 32, 36, 42, 43, 53, 138, 229, 325, 425*n.*
Rogers, Bernice, 4*n.*, 5, 146, 156*n.*, 401, 403
Russell, David H., 53, 126, 138, 144, 230, 253, 260, 285–291
Rutherford, W. J., 23, 28, 53

Sartain, Harry W., 125, 135–144
Scanning, 255, 258–259
Science, reading, 6, 76, 176–177, 325–337, 413
Second grade, 43–44
Secondary schools, *see* Junior high school; Senior high school
Selzer, Charles A., 26, 32, 33, 53
Semantics, 155–160
Senior high school, 5–17, 100–105, 141–142, 270–276
  developing skills in, 195–199, 200–209, 234–241, 315–320, 326–337, 359–363, 395–403, 408–418
  literature in, 174, 210–230, 276–284, 287, 294, 298, 306–312
  vocational, 306–312, 347–357
  see also Ninth grade; Tenth grade; Twelfth grade
Seventh grade, 5–6, 240, 276–284, 405
Severson, Eileen, 203, 204, 207, 209, 398, 402, 403
Shakespeare, William, 210, 213, 238, 297, 300, 302, 308
Sheldon, William D., 15, 17, 53, 123, 138, 246, 250

Vocabulary, 8, 10, 85
  assessing, 115–121, 367
  developing, 104, 161–163, 237, 238, 245, 298, 361, 409, 416
    materials for, 135–144, 205
    methods, 163–166
    in subjects, 9, 317, 319–320, 326, 347–349, 411
Vocational schools, 306–312, 347–357
Vowels, 128, 129, 130, 131, 137

Warfel, Harry R., 19, 77–80
Weaver, Wendell W., 19, 66–70
Weisenburg, T. H., 24, 25, 30, 54
Westover, Frederick L., 244–245, 246, 251
Wiggin, Neal A., 313, 337–346

Witty, Paul A., 2, 26, 27, 34, 42–43, 54, 131, 134, 251, 291, 415
Word
  analysis, 164–165, 366
  meanings, 75, 104, 158, 162–163, 165, 258, 289–290, 368
  perception, 127–134, 323
  recognition, 98, 106, 107–108, 121, 127–128, 130, 323, 349–350
  see also Semantics; Vocabulary
Word-attack skills, 8, 10, 115–121, 128, 135–144, 237, 323
Word-blindness, 23, 30, 31
Workbooks, reading, 135, 138–142, 246, 350–353, 428–429
Writing, student, 103, 160, 198, 201, 226, 233, 236, 237